DATE DUE

GAYLORD   #3523PI   Printed in USA

Crime and Justice

Crime and Justice
A Review of Research

*Edited by Michael Tonry
and Norval Morris*
with the Support of The National Institute of Justice

VOLUME 12

The University of Chicago Press, Chicago and London

This volume was prepared under Grant Number 87-IJ-CX-0018 awarded to
the Castine Research Corporation by the National Institute of Justice, U.S.
Department of Justice, under the Omnibus Crime Control and Safe Streets
Act of 1968 as amended. Points of view or opinions expressed in this volume
are those of the editors or authors and do not necessarily represent the
official position or policies of the U.S. Department of Justice.

The University of Chicago Press, Chicago 60637
The University of Chicago Press, Ltd., London

© 1990 by The University of Chicago
All rights reserved. Published 1990
Printed in the United States of America
94 93 92 91 90 89   5 4 3 2 1

ISSN: 0192-3234
ISBN: 0-226-80808-4

LCN: 80-642217

The paper used in this publication meets the minimum requirements of American
National Standard for Information Sciences—Permanence of Paper for Printed Library
Materials, ANSI Z39.48-1984. ∞

Contents

Preface

The essays in this series are not research articles; rather, they are synthetic of research articles, surveys of research articles, drawing together studies from different scholarly disciplines bearing on a given issue of crime or its control. When this series started over a decade ago, we were of the view that that was what was lacking and was needed— some means by which the insights of the sociologist, the psychologist, the psychiatrist, the political scientist, the economist, the historian, the statistician, and the lawyer could be brought together in "state of the art" essays deepening the understanding of all. The justification for this effort lay in our belief, confirmed by our own unavailing efforts, that no one can keep up with the range of research in all these disciplines relevant to crime and its control—no desk is large enough to bear the weight of the flow of papers accumulating beyond the speed of the swiftest reader. Hence, building bridges between the islands of parochialism that characterize research in criminology remains our central purpose.

All of our essays have this purpose; some abundantly achieve it. For example, the last essay in this volume, "Toward a Developmental Criminology" by Loeber and Le Blanc is a paradigmatic example of a formidable effort to give cohesion and shape to a multidisciplinary diversity of studies of child development and delinquency. Similarly, Moffitt's essay, "The Neuropsychology of Juvenile Delinquency," addresses subjects far beyond the usual tables of contents of criminology journals. Barr and Pease's essay, "Crime Placement, Displacement, and Deflection," applies the tools of urban geography to understanding of the crime displacement effects of crime prevention efforts.

All this may sound painfully theoretical and impractical, remote from the serious mundane concerns of those victimized and threatened by crime and those in the criminal justice system who seek to serve them. We believe that would be an unfair criticism, having its origin in the popular but strange belief that knowledge of the causes of crime and of rational methods for its control are inborn and obvious, a view we do not share. And, in any event, as you will see, many of the essays in this series are of immediate practical applicability, no matter what one's opinions on crime causation and control. For example, in this volume, the practicalities of police crackdowns, of fines, of youth gangs, and of parole can hardly be doubted.

We are grateful to our authors for putting up with the often vigorous criticisms of their drafts by the reviewers and the editors, and we are grateful to the National Institute of Justice for their continued active and interested support of this series.

M. T. and N. M.

Lawrence W. Sherman

Police Crackdowns: Initial and Residual Deterrence

ABSTRACT

Police crackdowns are sudden increases in officer presence, sanctions, and threats of apprehension either for specific offenses or for all offenses in specific places. Of eighteen case studies of crackdowns, fifteen appeared to demonstrate initial deterrent effects, including two examples of long-term effects. In most long-term crackdowns with apparent initial deterrence, however, the effects began to decay after a short period, sometimes despite continued dosage of police presence or even increased dosage of police sanctions. However, five studies with postcrackdown data showed a "free bonus" of continued deterrence well after the crackdowns ended. Such "residual" deterrent effects lasted in two cases for a longer period than the crackdown itself. These findings of initial decay and residual deterrence suggest that crackdowns might be more effective if they were limited in duration and rotated across different targets. While such a policy raises certain ethical and legal questions, these should not preclude a program of experimental research to establish the residual deterrent effects of short crackdowns across a range of police tactics, offense types, and places.

One of the most widespread developments in American policing in the 1980s has been the "crackdown." Drunk driving, domestic violence,

Lawrence W. Sherman is professor of criminology, University of Maryland, and president of the Crime Control Institute, Washington, D.C. Prepared in part under Grant 85-IJ-CX-0061 from the National Institute of Justice. The help of Peter Reuter, James K. Stewart, Mark Kleiman, Joel Garner, David Bayley, Norval Morris, Michael Tonry, Ronald Clarke, George Kelling, Jan Chaiken, and Geoffrey Barnes is gratefully acknowledged.

1

public drug markets, streetwalking prostitutes, illegal parking, and even bicycle riders have all been targets for publicly announced police crackdowns. What all these target problems have in common is such a high volume of occurrence that police had previously ignored most individual transgressions. What the crackdowns had in common was a sharp increase in law enforcement resources applied to the previously underenforced laws, with a clear goal of enhancing general deterrence of the misconduct.

Police crackdowns increase enforcement resources in two basic ways that often overlap. One is an *offense-specific* policy change about how to handle specific cases, such as arresting wife beaters rather than counseling them or towing illegally parked cars rather than just ticketing them, wherever the problem is encountered. The other is a *geographically focused* increase in the dosage of police presence, which can approximate a temporary state of full enforcement of every law on the books. Both kinds of crackdowns attempt to communicate a far more powerful threat of apprehension and punishment than does "normal" policing.

Both kinds of crackdowns are highly controversial, although the geographically focused approach is probably more vulnerable to charges that police violate civil liberties. Much of the controversy centers on the effectiveness of crackdowns: Are they worth the price in tax dollars and public inconvenience? Vocal constituencies may strongly support crackdowns, but police critics often argue that crackdowns are undertaken cynically for political purposes or as an excuse for police to earn overtime pay. It is claimed that police know crackdowns are really ineffective, but cannot afford to admit that fact in public.

Similarly, academic observers have been skeptical about the effects of police crackdowns. The leading student of drunk driving enforcement has argued that such crackdowns fail to create lasting deterrence (Ross 1981), while a leading police scholar has suggested that massive, sudden increases in police patrol can deter street crimes temporarily but not over the long run (Wilson 1983, p. 64).

All of these debates fail to make important distinctions among the different kinds of deterrent effects crackdowns can produce. Among other distinctions, they fail to separate any *initial* deterrence in the immediate wake of a crackdown from the possible *residual* deterrence after the crackdown has been withdrawn and the speed with which any initial deterrence *decays* during or after the crackdown.

These distinctions suggest a new way to increase the effectiveness of police crackdowns. Rather than attempt to maintain crackdowns over long periods of time, as many departments have done, police might use their resources more effectively if crackdowns are seen as short-term efforts frequently shifted from area to area or problem to problem. *By constantly changing crackdown targets, police may reduce crime more through residual deterrence than through initial deterrence.* And by limiting the time period devoted to each target, police might also avoid wasting scarce resources on a decaying initial deterrent effect.

This essay examines the basic reasoning for this hypothesis. There is evidence that some crackdowns do create initial deterrence, or at least displacement, of some kinds of offending. However, it is hard to sustain many crackdowns over a long period, either because of decaying implementation or decaying offender perception of the crackdown as creating a high risk of apprehension. Several of the crackdowns reviewed in this essay, which were intentionally ended quite early, suggest that such risk perceptions may decay slowly, even when the actual police effort has been returned to normal. The slow decay constitutes a "free bonus" residue of deterrence. This residue fits the growing body of theory and evidence about how people make decisions under conditions of uncertainty, since intermittent, unpredictable crackdowns make risks of apprehension far more uncertain than could any system of fixed police priorities—including long-term crackdowns. But systematic empirical evidence for the residual deterrence hypothesis is still quite meager, and field experiments in police departments are needed to test it adequately.

The purpose of this essay is not to advocate crackdowns but rather to consider how they might be employed and evaluated more effectively. Section I begins with a description of the scarcity problem—a problem as old as the American police—that a rotating police crackdown policy could help to manage. Section II defines some concepts and theory for analyzing that problem and discusses its possible management by intermittent crackdowns. Section III presents a series of case studies on crackdowns on a variety of target problems that illustrate the extent and limits of our knowledge of the crackdowns. Varieties of crackdown effects are identified in Section IV. Section V proposes a research design for testing the intermittent crackdown hypothesis and includes an example of its implementation already under way in Minneapolis. It is followed by a concluding section on crackdown ethics.

I. Managing the Scarcity Problem

The basic theory of criminal justice is that crime can be deterred through certain punishment. But in modern America there is too much crime and too little law enforcement to make punishment very certain.

Despite continuing debate, there have been few recent revenue increases devoted to increasing the certainty of police apprehension per offense. After 1978, in fact, the total number of police in big cities began to decline (Bureau of Justice Statistics 1986) while reports of both serious and minor crimes increased substantially (FBI 1978–88).

A. *Triage*

There are two ways for policymakers to adapt to this dilemma of scarce police resources. One is the constant shifting of priorities suggested in this essay but rarely used in practice. The more common method is simply to set permanent "triage" priorities: some kinds of offenses are ignored and others given very little attention, so that resources can be concentrated on more serious problems.[1] In some cities, for example, police will not investigate burglaries unless the value of loss exceeds $5,000. In other cities, pot smoking and public drinking have been virtually legalized by police inattention. And until quite recently, police, prosecutors, and judges rarely took any action against minor domestic violence. These practical compromises were all seen as necessary ways to have enough personnel and prison space for armed robbers, narcotics pushers, rapists, and murderers.

One consequence of this triage approach is endless wrangling over what the priorities should be. Thus an early 1986 *New York Times* editorial took New York's police commissioner to task for failing to enforce bicycle traffic laws after three deaths and many injuries to pedestrians. The commissioner's public response was that he could not spare the personnel from dealing with the "crack" epidemic. Nonetheless, by July of that year New York police had launched an unannounced crackdown on cyclists, issuing 3,633 summonses in two weeks, and prompting Buffalo, New York, police to follow suit (Connelly, Douglas, and Mansnerus 1986).

These sporadic pressures on police are nothing new. Like the exhausted parent, police fail to crack down out of sheer poverty of resources rather than poverty of desire. The "overreach" of the criminal law (Morris and Hawkins 1970) has long made it necessary for police to ignore many, and perhaps most, violations of the criminal law (Gold-

---

[1] Triage was the system used by French doctors in World War I to divide the overwhelming number of wounded soldiers who needed medical attention into three groups: those who would die even with immediate attention, those who would live without it, and those who would live only if operated on immediately. The last group was given top priority, on a permanent basis, for the scarce attention of the doctors.

stein 1977, chap. 5). But when political pressures or the news media focus attention on some offense pattern that has been subjected to little enforcement, police resources may be temporarily diverted from normal priorities to that long-ignored problem.

The effect is almost a change in the interpretation of the criminal law, a virtual admission that the offense had previously been too low a priority to command scarce enforcement resources. The crackdown communicates to the law-breaking public a statement that, in effect, the law is back on the books. Indeed, when Milwaukee police cracked down on misdemeanor domestic violence in May 1986 with a new arrest *policy*, street officers often explained their actions to the arrestees as the result of a new *law*.

B. Historical Context

The very origins of the American police are tied to the permanent crackdown strategy. After watching public behavior patterns among recent immigrant groups become increasingly disorderly, or at least a threat to the status position of the earlier settlers (Gusfield 1963), city after city in the nineteenth century created a full-time, uniformed police force. Research on the enforcement activity of these early police departments (Levett 1975) shows that they had little impact on the level of felony arrests, which continued to be made by independent marshals and constables. Instead, the new police bureaucracies produced a drastic increase in the number of arrests for public disorder, especially drinking and fighting. Some early police officers made over ten arrests a day, a rate unheard of by modern standards—even for disorder offenses. Thus, even at their birth, a primary function of American police was to crack down on an enormous (and probably overwhelming) volume of what Reiss (1985) has labeled "soft crime."

But the widespread and persistent patterns of that behavior created inertia against sustained police enforcement, so that the first century of American policing was a saga of repeated, failed attempts to achieve a permanent crackdown on public disorder. Lincoln Steffens (1931, chap. 6) describes the 1890s efforts of New York City's protestant ministers and Police Commissioner Teddy Roosevelt to have the prostitution, gambling, and saloon-closing laws enforced, with sporadic success. William Whyte's *Street Corner Society* (1943) shows how even with systematic police corruption in Boston, in the 1930s, crackdowns on vice were a recurring political necessity but never an effective long-term policy:

While the system is organized to adjust itself to a certain quota of arrests, periodic crises of law enforcement involve serious dislocations to the racket organization. Crises arise when some spectacular event, such as an act of violence, draws public attention to conditions which have existed all the time. As an agent commented, "You remember that shooting in Maxton? After that the horse rooms and gambling places were closed up all over the county. And after that killing in Crighton, Crighton was all closed up for a few weeks." In such a time of crisis few places are actually raided, but the racketeers are told by their friends in the department that they must close their establishments, and they do—for the duration. [p. 131]

Similarly, William Westley's classic study of the Gary, Indiana, police in the late 1940s describes temporary crackdowns as a routine part of the job (1970, p. 143): "when the people of the city are aroused about some point of law enforcement such as traffic violations or vice or gambling, the police will put on a drive in those areas and the law will be enforced rigidly; for in this situation it is to the interests of the police, in line with maintenance of respect for the police in the community, to enforce the law." The periodic waves of scandal over and reform of the corruption of the police themselves in many communities (Sherman 1978) may also be seen as an instance of the crackdown phenomenon.

C. Punishment Risks Are Too Predictable

The intermittent pressures for crackdowns in different areas may temporarily disrupt the normal triage solution to the police scarcity problem. But such pressures are rare enough, or can be handled with few enough officers, so that the triage is generally kept constant. Whether the triage priorities should be permanent is a major question of police strategy.

Permanent law enforcement priorities may make the risks of punishment all too predictable for criminals. They know that the risks of being punished for killing a police officer, for example, are enormous, and they will try to avoid that offense if they are at all rational. But they also know that the risks of being caught and punished for most stranger-to-stranger crime—residential burglary, purse snatching, car theft, and lesser crimes—are very low. What is more, the risks were low yesterday and they will be low tomorrow, next year, and the year after.

This means that we need to make Reuter's (1986) important distinction between the *risk* of getting caught and the *certainty* about what that risk is for any given offense on any given day. If potential criminals were very certain of a high risk that they would be caught and punished, we might create the greatest deterrent effect. What we offer them instead is high certainty of low risk of punishment for most offenses. But for the same dollar cost, we could offer them low certainty about whether the risk of punishment is high or low at any given time and place—and perhaps reduce some kinds of crime substantially.

Risk managers in the liability insurance business would envy the highly certain risks criminals now face, especially since such insurance losses are now so highly uncertain. The rapid growth of multimillion dollar lawsuits has made insurance risks highly unpredictable: the amount of damages awarded can vary widely from case to case and from year to year within the same type of case. Insurers are understandably reluctant to bet against such uncertain odds and would greatly prefer to have the certainty that criminals enjoy in estimating the odds of punishment.

But there is no reason why criminal justice policy has to provide such easy bets for criminals. Even if scarce resources have to be rationed according to priorities, the priorities don't have to remain fixed. New York police can crack down on reckless bicyclists today and drunk drivers tomorrow or on drug dealers this week and wife beaters the next. Just as parents with many children rotate their scarce attention in succession from one child to the next, police could choose to focus briefly on one problem and then on another.

Police reluctance to rotate resources systematically among low and higher priority crime problems may be based partly on the premise that more serious problems will quickly worsen while their attention is turned away. There are both conceptual and empirical reasons for suggesting that premise may be false, and residual deterrence may help control crime while police attention is temporarily turned elsewhere.

II. Crackdown Concepts and Theory

This section defines the key concepts in police crackdowns. It then integrates them to form a theoretical argument. The hypothesis is that, given a fixed level of resources, police can create more general deterrence through rotating crackdowns than through permanent priorities.

A. Concepts

Increases in either the certainty or severity of official police reaction to a specific type of crime or all crime in a specific area are called *crackdowns*. More precisely, police crackdowns can be defined as a sudden change in activity which is usually proactive, although it can include increased likelihood of arrest during encounters initiated by citizens, and intended drastically to increase either the communicated threat or actual certainty of apprehension for a specific type or types of offense that have been highly visible or widely committed in certain identifiable places or situations.

Crackdowns must be distinguished from normal police personnel allocation decisions. The distribution of officers around a city is normally unequal per square mile since it is guided by such factors as the relative density of population, calls for service, and reported crime in each area. Simply adjusting the allocations as those factors change is not a crackdown but a fine-tuning of the permanent triage priorities. Crackdowns are focused on specific target problems (Eck and Spelman 1987), which provide the sole justification for reallocation of police resources outside the usual formula.

Police crackdowns have three possible tactical elements: presence, sanctions, and media threats. *Presence* is simply an increased ratio of police officers per potential offender, either in places or in situations. Increased presence can be accomplished either through uniformed presence (which communicates a visible threat) or plainclothes surveillance (which enhances the potential offenders' uncertainty about the risks of apprehension). *Sanctions* denote any coercive police imposition on offenders or potential offenders: stopping cars or pedestrians for identification checks, issuing warnings, mounting roadblock checkpoints, conducting breathalyzer tests, making arrests, and so on. *Media threats* are announced intentions to increase sanctioning certainty and are reported in newspapers, public service announcements on TV and radio, or even billboard campaigns.

The actual combinations of these tactical elements vary in practice. The interaction between presence and sanctions, for example, is ironically perverse: greater presence can produce more sanctions, but sanctions can reduce presence by taking police away to process arrests. In the Georgetown crackdown in 1985 (Sherman et al. 1986), Washington police avoided this dilemma by installing a booking center in a trailer parked on the street on weekend nights, saving the police a two-mile drive to the station for each arrest. Area crackdowns tend to emphasize presence, while offense-specific crackdowns emphasize sanctions. Whether a media campaign is added to the other elements of a crackdown may depend upon public interest in the problem as well as business interest in providing such advertising services free of charge.

A *backoff* is the usual sequel to a crackdown. For reasons of necessity (which may be a virtue), crackdowns rarely last forever. On rare occasions, some crackdowns may become part of the permanent triage, realigning the previous priority system. But most will eventually terminate in a backoff, which can be defined as a reduction in the visible threat or actual certainty of apprehension created by a crackdown. Backoffs occur suddenly or gradually, by policy decision or by uncorrected informal action of enforcement personnel, and by reduced presence or reduced sanctioning.

These concepts of enforcement activity and threats to take action require corresponding concepts of their effects on crime. The principal effect is some level of crime after a crackdown begins; crime either declines, remains unchanged, or increases, all to a greater or lesser degree. Any crime reduction is arguably a *general deterrent* effect, even though it fails to distinguish between the participation rate of offending in the population and the frequency rate of offending by active offenders (Blumstein et al., 1986). This distinction has never been addressed in crackdown research, although Sampson and Cohen (1988) have used it in cross-sectional deterrence analysis.

Interpreting any crime reduction as deterrence is problematic in other ways. A reduction could have been caused by incapacitation of a few active offenders early on in the crackdown. It could have been caused by other reasons, such as changing transportation patterns or declining area population (Cook and Campbell 1979). But over short-term periods with large enough numbers of offenses, it seems reasonably plausible for police to interpret a crime reduction as a deterrent effect.

The more important point is the distinction between *initial* and *residual* deterrence. If a crime reduction is achieved while the crackdown tactic—presence, sanctions, or publicity—is still in operation, then it is plausibly an initial deterrence effect. But if the crime reduction is sustained after the tactic is terminated or reduced, then it might plausibly be a residual deterrent effect. The "hangover" perceived risk of apprehension could influence decisions not to commit offenses after the risk (or the communicated threat) is actually reduced, at least until such time as other evidence shows the quasi-rational actors that the risk has returned to its prior level. *Decay*, or a gradual decline from initial changes, is therefore a central concept for crackdowns in at least three ways: crackdown decay, initial deterrence decay, and residual deterrence decay.

1. *Crackdown Decay.*   Since a crackdown requires greater police effort, the usual bureaucratic regression to the mean level of effort may cause the implementation of the crackdown itself to decay. Fewer arrests are made, fewer people are stopped, more officers are diverted to other duties, all of which could be planned by police commanders or just carried out by the lower ranks.

2. *Initial Deterrence Decay.*   With or without a decay of police effort, an initial crime reduction might decay through potential offenders learning through trial and error that they had overestimated the certainty of getting caught at the beginning of the crackdown.

3. *Residual Deterrence Decay.*   The same learning process can take place gradually after the effort is actually reduced, with the residual deterrence slowly declining as word of mouth communication and personal experience show that it is once again "safe" to offend.

B. A Drunk Driving Example

Ross (1981) concludes that, in general, the deterrent effects of a variety of crackdowns on drunk driving are only short-term effects. In a wide range of cases from different countries, Ross shows that initial reductions in auto accidents are almost always followed by gradual increases. The conceptual problem in interpreting those findings is to distinguish decay in the implementation of various crackdown tactics (such as publicity versus enforcement) and decay in deterrence, both initially (during the tactics) and residually (after they have ceased).

Ross hypothesizes that the crackdowns *initially* succeeded in deterring drunk driving by causing the potential criminals substantially to overestimate the probability of apprehension. The effects decayed when the driving public, among whom the incentives for driving after drinking are widespread, gradually realized that the absolute chances of being apprehended or punished were still minuscule (less than one in one thousand, according to an estimate Ross [1981] reports on p. 107) even though they may have doubled or more under the crackdown.

What he does not highlight is his evidence of the opposite phenomenon: the *residual deterrence* from continuing to overestimate the risks of drunk driving apprehension even after those risks have declined. For example, in discussing the enforcement blitzes in England and New Zealand, he observes (1981, p. 81–83) that "they had definite terminations, and all indexes showed that either immediately or after a short lag things looked very much as before. No permanent change was achieved." The half-empty glass for Ross is half full to me. The "short lag" after the termination of those crackdowns is the best quantitative evidence for the residual deterrence phenomenon. For if drunk driving remained reduced after the backoff began, no matter how briefly, it might be possible to obtain the same effects repeatedly. Moreover, *the "short" lag was generally for a longer period than the crackdown itself,* thus doubling or tripling the return on investment of police resources in the crackdown. What works for drunk driving may—or may not—work for other kinds of offenses.

C. Theory

Regardless of how low or high the absolute chances of punishment may be, crime control policy may be able to accomplish as much by barking as by biting or by bluffing rather than by showing its hand. If police crackdowns can create short-term deterrence by *changing* the perceived risks of apprehension, then perhaps we should not expect them to have permanent effects. What may be more effective is a continuous series of crackdowns with much publicity, and backoffs with little (or no) publicity. Such an approach would have to be careful not to exhaust the bluff through overuse, which would probably mean that intermittent and unpredictable periods between crackdowns would be necessary. This approach would also have to be careful to distinguish among different kinds of offenders in terms of the speed of their learning, since highly active criminal populations learn actual risk levels more quickly and may be less amenable to such bluffing than populations less active criminally.

The theoretical roots of this approach lie in the work of Tversky and Kahnemen (1974) on individual reactions to risk and uncertainty. The difference between the two concepts of risk and uncertainty is essential, since it may be that crackdowns affect uncertainty more than risk (Reuter 1986). If people find that their fairly certain estimates of the risk of getting caught committing a crime are suddenly disrupted by information about new police actions, their uncertainty about perceived risk may increase substantially. For example, if there is a stable 5 percent probability (risk) of getting caught throughout the year, potential offenders may be fairly certain about their own estimate. But if word goes out that the risk has doubled, even just temporarily or intermittently, then potential offenders may be so uncertain about the risk that they overestimate it in order to be safe.

Crackdowns may create residual effects, then, by raising the uncertainty about which risk level of apprehension is currently in effect, which in turn escalates the perceived level of risk beyond its normal overestimates. It takes the same number of police to create a continual apprehension risk of 5 percent as it does to vary that risk between 0 and 10 percent. It may be more cost-effective to choose the latter option, since that could keep the average perceived risk of apprehension twice as high as the average resources allocated would justify.

Expressed graphically, figure 1 shows the hypothetical difference between the perceived-risk estimates produced by stable triage and crackdown-backoff policing. It assumes that potential offenders generally overestimate the actual risk of apprehension, but that these overestimates vary proportionally in relation to information about changes in actual risk.

Compare the permanent 5 percent risk of punishment with a risk varying between 0 and 10 percent on a daily basis. The first approach offers a 100 percent certainty of a 5 percent risk, while the second offers a 50 percent certainty of a 10 percent risk. By throwing more resources at the crime problem at each crackdown "peak," we could even theoretically produce a 50 percent risk of punishment every tenth day without incurring any extra cost.

Figure 1 shows the hypothetical difference between the perceived-risk estimates produced by stable risks and intermittent crackdown risks. It assumes that potential offenders generally overestimate the actual risk of apprehension, but that these overestimates vary proportionally in relation to information about changes in actual risk. With twice the uncertainty, the perceived level of risk could, hypothetically, double (model B).

Consider your own temptation to take questionable deductions on your income tax. As an informed newspaper reader, you know that the Internal Revenue Service (IRS) has funds to audit about 5 percent of the nation's taxpayers each year, whom they select according to certain empirically generated "tipoffs" like taking a home office deduction—ongoing triage priorities. But suppose the IRS were to select all audit targets at random (much like armed robbers are caught in the act). Moreover, the random selection (with replacement) is stratified so that half of all taxpayers born on your birthday are audited (unpredictably), on average, once every ten years. And, unlike the Vietnam draft lottery—which used random selection for an even more coercive purpose—you will not be informed when your number comes up. You may find that prospect much more deterring than a low permanent chance tied to your tax cheating indicators, yet it costs the IRS no

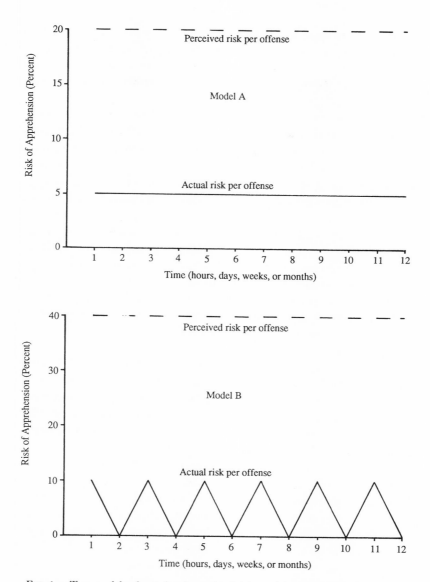

FIG. 1.—Two models of actual and perceived risk; model A: constant police resource allocations; and model B: intermittent police crackdowns.

more. Such an approach, if highly publicized through mass media and actual audit contacts, may yield less new revenue per audit, but it may increase tax revenues from those who are never audited and are currently unlikely to be audited—which is the whole point of general deterrence.

By the same logic, perhaps not as many armed robbers would hit liquor stores if, one night in ten, half the liquor stores in town had police staked out in them. Perhaps not as many people would sell drugs if they knew that on one out of every five court days convicted drug pushers would receive twenty-year sentences.[2]

The larger conceptual problem in understanding residual deterrent effects is the relationship between media messages, official actions, and potential offender perceptions about the probability of getting caught. For example, we might predict that the more intense the dosage of presence, sanctions, and media threat communication a crackdown offers, the greater the uncertainty about the actual risk level and the greater the average overestimates of risk. Consequently, the target audience will be less likely to offend (initial deterrence) and more likely to believe that message even after the actual crackdown dosage levels decline (residual deterrence).

It is also plausible to theorize that police crackdowns are particularly effective because they entail little delay. Because police crackdowns can impose punishment immediately in the form of arrest and temporary incarceration, they may produce more powerful effects than other kinds of crackdowns: imposing new legislative bans on conduct, longer prison sentences for existing offenses, or higher prosecution priorities, all of which have much less chance of immediate implementation and much greater time lag between the offense and the punishment.

Such theorizing is relatively easy. The hard part is developing, operationalizing, and testing such a theory through careful empirical research. The research reviewed below is consistent with the theory of residual deterrence from rotating crackdowns but hardly constitutes strong evidence. Field experimentation explicitly designed to test the theory, such as the Minneapolis Hot Spots Experiment described below, is required to draw any conclusions about the viability of an ongoing crackdown-backoff policy.

[2] Zimmer (1986) describes just such a system in New York, with one day in five designated as a "federal day," on which arrested drug dealers would be charged with a federal offense and run a much higher risk of a prison term than with state charges.

III. Case Studies

This section reviews the case-study evidence on the implementation of police crackdowns, with more limited evidence on their initial and residual deterrent effects. The section is organized by the target problems that recent crackdowns have addressed. It begins with a relatively detailed description of an *area-focused* crackdown in the Georgetown section of Washington, D.C., in the mid-1980s. It then considers both scholarly studies and press accounts of crackdowns on *drugs, drunk driving, prostitution, residential calls to police,* and various other targets. The drugs section includes a brief review of crackdowns by private citizens. Finally, the section interprets other police experiments in the crackdown framework.

A. *An Area Crackdown: Georgetown, 1985*

Crackdowns are often directed at a wide range of crime and disorder problems within a specific geographic area. One example of the operations and effects of area crackdowns is described in the Sherman et al. (1986) case study of the 1985 crackdown on illegal parking and disorder in the Georgetown section of Washington, D.C. The crackdown was prompted by large numbers of high-school-age youths drawn to Georgetown by the district's low minimum age (eighteen) for legal beer and wine drinking, especially after the drinking age was gradually raised in Maryland and Virginia. The crackdown was intended not only to control illegal parking and public drinking on busy weekend nights but also, as Wilson and Kelling (1982) suggest, to control street crime attracted by such disorder.

In January of 1985, the second district commander and the Georgetown area commander announced a crackdown on disorderly behavior: "The public must see that in Georgetown no breach of the law is so trivial that it can be ignored" (Roffman 1985). The police program implemented on April 5 focused on the weekend periods of large and disorderly crowds in ways designed to restore order rather than to make large numbers of arrests for violent crimes.

1. *Publicity.* The Georgetown crackdown was aided by a massive amount of publicity. The publicity, in turn, was related to the most visible element of the crackdown: a ban on weekend evening parking on certain key streets near many restaurants and bars. The Washington-area public of all ages now risked having their cars towed in Georgetown. Other elements included at least a 30 percent increase in

total weekend manpower; installing a trailer at the key intersection for booking arrestees; military police, including at least four MPs on weekend foot patrol, to deal with the large numbers of military personnel from nearby bases; increased plainclothes patrol along the residential side streets; and extra tow-trucks patrolling the area for parking enforcement. The publicity was almost instantly favorable in pronouncing the crackdown a success. The publicity kept up intermittently over the summer, in a generally favorable fashion, with continued stress on the parking enforcement. It was hard to live in the Washington area that year and not have some sense that the cops were being more vigilant in Georgetown.

2. *Parking Enforcement.* The official statistics support the impression of increased vigilance. While no comparisons to prior years were available, police told the local paper that between March and September up to eighty police and an unknown number of traffic department employees had produced 60,487 parking tickets, 9,231 moving violations, 2,062 arrests, and 6,407 vehicle tows (Barry 1985). The very high certainty of parking enforcement the crackdown created is supported by the results of a systematic poll of the street population of Georgetown done by Anne Roschelle in late 1985 (Sherman et al. 1986). Of 150 respondents interviewed at the corner of Wisconsin and M Street at different times of day or night (with sixty-seven refusals, for a 69 percent response rate in a sample of 217), 41 percent said they had gotten a parking ticket and 11 percent said they had had their cars towed since the crackdown had begun the prior spring.

3. *Disorder Enforcement.* There was a clear increase in arrests for public disorder (Sherman et al. 1986). During the first three months of the six-month crackdown, disorder arrests numbered almost twice as many as during the same period in the preceding year. By the second three-month period, the increase had dropped to 10 percent. But for the entire six-month crackdown period the average was a 40 percent increase.

Still, one is struck by how few arrests there were relative to the reported size of the crowds. Even at 500 arrests each week, that is still only some seventy per day. If even 400 arrests were made on weekends, that would be 200 per day out of 20,000 people or 1 percent of the population on the streets at peak periods. Given the descriptions of how badly behaved that population was, either police had to overlook many continued violations or their deterrent presence greatly reduced the number of disorder-arrest opportunities. There was little change in other types of arrest.

4. *The Backoff.* The police Anne Roschelle interviewed clearly indicated the backoff had begun by Halloween. Not only were there fewer officers, but, as the *Washington Post* (1986) reported, the officers who were there may have done less—a predictable example of crackdown decay. One officer said on November 15, "I haven't been looking as hard for illegally parked cars in recent months." Another said, on November 20, "I don't ticket as many cars as I did during April through August. Now that the summer is over the bulk of the crowds have gone."

5. *Effect on Crime.* What effect did the crackdown have on crime? It is hard to answer that question scientifically. This case study illustrates many of the statistical problems involved in assessing deterrent effects in natural quasi experiments (Campbell and Ross 1968), especially for very small geographic areas. Although such areas are very important for police policy, they are often too small to provide enough weekly reported crimes for an adequate statistical test. The weekly average number of street robberies in Georgetown, for example, declined by 10 percent. But because the absolute numbers dropped from only 2.6 to 2.3 per week, the reduction could easily have occurred by chance. Moreover, the Georgetown-area crime trends did not differ from the citywide trends or trends in a comparison area.

6. *Perceptions of the Crackdown.* Nonetheless, we found other evidence that the crackdown had both a short-term deterrent effect and longer-term residual deterrence. One opportunity sample of forty-nine people surveyed in local bars found that 100 percent of the respondents thought the area was less crowded, 92 percent thought it was safer, 80 percent thought there was less crime, and—a month after the crackdown ended—55 percent thought the crackdown was still in force with no backoff.

The other opportunity sample of 150 persons (at a 69 percent response rate) walking on the principal street corner (Wisconsin and M) found similar results: 87 percent were aware of the crackdown, 79 percent believed police were still enforcing the parking ban strictly (a month after the backoff), 72 percent thought the area was safer, 71 percent thought the area was less crowded, and 67 percent thought it was more orderly. Only 35 percent thought crime had gone down, but, perhaps because 11 percent of the respondents said they had been towed and 41 percent had been ticketed, 47 percent had changed their parking habits since the crackdown—something which might have made residual deterrence of illegal parking by this six-month crackdown last for many months or years.

B. Drug Crackdowns

A more common police crackdown target in the 1980s has been open-air drug markets. They have been attacked with a variety of tactics: parking a police trailer in their midst, increasing uniformed police presence, surprising drug dealers with plainclothes officers in a "jump-out" squad, and even using citizen patrols. Both the anecdotal and the statistical evidence on the effectiveness of these tactics is mixed.

1. *Police Trailer Crackdowns.*   Unlike the police trailer in Georgetown, the parking of a trailer in a drug market is not a tool for making more arrests with less booking time. It is more like sending in the fleet, rattling the saber so there will be no arrests. The Washington police employed this tactic in the most publicized drug market in the city, Hanover Place, in early 1985 (Operation Avalanche). One *Post* reporter has found the constant presence of sixty police officers per day on the block to be an effective long-term initial deterrent (Wheeler 1986; Wheeler and Horwitz 1988), at least while this presence was maintained: "For years the city's busiest cocaine market, it had become one of the deadliest blocks in town, the few residents living like prisoners in their homes. . . . Today Hanover Place remains a transformed area where children play in their yards and adults sit comfortably on front steps" (Wheeler and Horwitz 1988, p. C-5).

The effects of such massive police presence may appear obvious, as well as prohibitively expensive. (Indeed, Wheeler and Horwitz's 1988 recommendation for expanding the program is to call out the National Guard.) Yet a trailer with just two officers in it may be insufficient to deter drug dealing. An Albany, New York, alderman—whose statements may not be without political bias—reported witnessing drug deals on two separate occasions right in front of a police trailer in the Pine Hills neighborhood of that city (Kelly 1988). The alderman, who was protesting a two-year-old decision to close the local neighborhood precinct station, described the police in the trailer as vulnerable to sniper fire and unaware of what was going on outside. Meanwhile, the mayor of nearby Schenectady was persuaded to replicate the Albany two-officer trailer in a drug market (Cermak 1988).

2. *Police Presence Crackdowns.*   The evidence on police presence crackdowns is far more detailed but equally mixed. On one side stands Kleiman's (1988) generally favorable evaluations of intensified uniformed presence in drug markets in Lynn, Massachusetts, and on the Lower East Side in New York City (Operation Pressure Point). On the other stands the generally negative evaluations of such crackdowns in Lawrence, Massachusetts (Kleiman 1988; Barnett 1988), Philadelphia (Kleiman 1988), and a Washington, D.C. (Reuter et al. 1988), citywide crackdown on drug markets (Operation Clean Sweep).

3. *Lynn and Lawrence.*   Through interviews and crime statistics, Kleiman (1986, 1988) describes a crackdown, focused on a geographically small open-air heroin market in Lynn, beginning in September of 1983 and lasting at least four years. The crackdown began with six state police officers assigned for nine months (and then shifted to Lawrence) and one city officer. It was continued after nine months with four to six city officers (Kleiman 1988, p. 3). In its first ten months, the crackdown officers made 140 arrests aimed at disruption of the market. Arrests subsequently continued at a "much lower rate" (p. 4). Kleiman reports that heroin consumption apparently declined, with an 85 percent increase in local demand for drug treatment, which was unmatched statewide (p. 6). Moreover, robberies and burglaries declined substantially citywide for two years after the beginning of the crackdown, without any apparent increase in those crimes nearby (local displacement).

The experience in Lawrence with the same state police unit was less encouraging. A larger market area was harder to control, except for the most flagrant public housing project. Unlike practices in Lynn, Lawrence's police tactics emphasized search warrants more than observation-of-sale arrests. The close proximity of alternative drug markets in nearby Lowell made it difficult to restrict drug supplies to street criminals. There was no apparent decline in drug use, and there was a substantial *increase* in violent crime (Kleiman 1988).

Barnett's (1988) comments on Kleiman's analysis point out that the net increase in violent crime after the crackdown in Lawrence was greater than the reduction in Lynn. Whether this would have happened anyway, of course, no one can say. But Kleiman does suggest the classic police theory that increased drug prices (resulting from stronger drug enforcement) can foster additional robbery by addicts who accordingly need even more money to maintain their habits. Barnett finds this plausible enough to believe that the drug crackdown may have actually caused the 52 percent robbery increase in Lawrence (relative to other Massachusetts cities).

Looking solely at Lynn, Barnett also points out that the initial deterrent effect began to decay fairly soon—just like the level of drug arrest activity (but not the apparent police presence). Kleiman acknowledges that the initial deterrence could have resulted from the incapacitation of a few high-rate chronic offenders—but that could still be credited to the enforcement effort. Regardless of what mechanism produced the initial reduction, Barnett points out that robbery returned to its precrackdown levels and rose above them, despite the continuation of the police presence (fig. 2). Other offense types showed either less reduction or the same rebounding curve, with the exception of a lasting reduction in aggravated assault (an offense notorious for its vulnerability to subjective classification).

Even in one of the most apparently successful cases of a drug crackdown, then, we find two types of decay: in both implementation and initial deterrence. Yet there was no apparent decay in police *presence;* just in the level of *sanctions* (arrest activity). Because the crackdown was continued rather than shifted to another target, there was never any

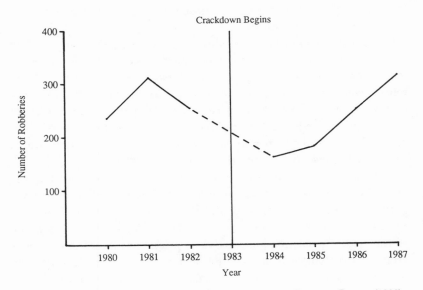

FIG. 2.—Robbery trends in Lynn, Massachusetts, 1980–87. Source.—Barnett (1988).

opportunity to observe whether a residual deterrent effect would have been produced.

4. *Lower East Side.* In early 1984, a newly appointed New York City police commissioner launched "Operation Pressure Point," a sixty-day crackdown on the Lower East Side drug markets that lasted at least two years. Prior to the crackdown, the area had offered many blatant drug bazaars, with customers attracted from all over the New York area, and where heroin buyers could be seen standing in long lines stretching around street corners. Kleiman (1988, p. 18) reports that the crackdown, at a cost of $12 million per year, used about twenty-five times as many officers as the Lynn effort, or 150 officers. (Zimmer [1986] reports it used 200–240 officers, mostly rookies and all in uniform at all times.) Like Lynn, it began with a high volume of drug arrests—sixty-five per day for the first six weeks, then dropping to twenty per day. This rate continued until at least August 1986, by which time the police had made 21,000 drug-related arrests in the target area (Kerr 1987*a*). Tactics included observation-of-sale arrests, undercover buys, raids on dealing locations, arrests for unrelated misdemeanors and violations, and tips from informers and a "hot line" phone number.

The initial deterrent effect on robbery was a 47 percent reduction in 1984 compared to 1983, and a 62 percent reduction (from thirty-four to thirteen) in homicides during the same period (Kleiman 1988). This initial effect was maintained for at least the first eight months of 1986, with a 40 percent reduction in robbery and a 69 percent reduction in homicide compared to the first eight months of 1983. There was no indication of displacement to the immediate vicinity, but there was an apparent growth in drug markets in other parts of Manhattan (Zimmer 1986).

Other observers challenge the long-term deterrence of the crackdown. While not disputing its effectiveness in suppressing street dealing, a blue-ribbon civic group concluded that the effects on robbery decayed by 43 percent in the second year of the crackdown (Citizens Crime Commission of New York City 1988). Robberies in the three-precinct target area, they report, dropped from 3,130 in 1983 to 2,073 in the first crackdown year (1984), but rose to 2,433 in the second year (1985).

Zimmer (1986) has documented how some drug dealers and users responded to the Lower East Side crackdown. She claims, apparently from interviews, that many stayed off the streets at first, waiting for law enforcement to return to "normal"; some took vacations out of the country. When the crackdown was maintained, she reports, the "drug sellers began to reemerge, developing the new [less public] marketing strategies that would decrease their risk of arrest" (1986, p. 24). Moreover, she claims that the more gentrified areas of the crackdown zone experienced no decay in the deterrence of public drug dealing, which remained suppressed. Rather, despite police concentration of more personnel on the poorer blocks, the greatest visible decay in the deterrence of street dealing was observed there.

5. *Other Manhattan Crackdowns.* Police responded to Pressure Point's apparent displacement by targeting Washington Heights, Harlem, and Washington Square Park for crackdowns. The Harlem effort reportedly failed to debilitate drug trade or reduce crime (Kerr 1987*a*), even though Kleiman reports that it made more arrests than the Lower East Side operation with only two-thirds the personnel. After 30 months, robberies were down by 30 percent in the target area (Kleiman 1986, p. 34). The Washington Square crackdown, with six arrests a day by twenty-nine officers over eight months, was hailed as a successful attack on public drug dealing; some local displacement was acknowledged, however, and there was no discussion of its effect on crime (Kerr 1987*b*).

6. *Washington.* Perhaps the most dramatic example of a citywide police-presence drug crackdown is Washington's "Operation Clean Sweep." Begun in August 1986, the crackdown allocated 100–200 officers to fifty-nine drug markets throughout the city. In its first seventeen months, it claimed 29,519 arrests, or about sixty a day. Tactics included roadblocks, observation of the open-air markets, "reverse buy" sell-and-busts by undercover officers, and the seizure of cars. The program was conducted by officers on overtime, some of whom reportedly doubled their salaries but suffered extreme exhaustion (Wheeler and Horwitz 1988). Local residents praised its efforts, but some made two key complaints: the resurgence of drug trade after police left a drug market (although with apparently some residual deterrent delay) and rapid displacement of drug markets to nearby locations (Robinson 1986). But an independent analysis found that the crackdown was "well-executed and coordinated," with high levels of prosecution, conviction, and sentencing resulting from the large numbers of arrests made (Reuter et al. 1988, p. 45).

The citywide impact of Clean Sweep on drug traffic was disappointing. While fewer drug markets operated openly (Reuter et al. 1988, p. 47), two indicators of drug use showed substantial increases from 1986 to 1987: urinalysis of arrestees and emergency room admissions (Reuter et al. 1988, chap. 2). This failure to reduce measured drug abuse may be simply a result of the late arrival of "crack" to Washington in mid-1987, a major change in the nature of the drug market. Without the operation of a strong police crackdown, the rising tide of drug abuse might even have risen much faster. The absence of any control group observations makes it impossible to tell.

What is most disturbing about this massive crackdown followed by a "crack" explosion, however, is the record increase in Washington's homicides. Homicides rose from a total of 148 in 1985 to 287 by the end of October 1988, and the percentage of homicides "attributed" to drugs rose from 17 to 68 (Molotsky 1988). Many victims were killed in crossfire between rival drug dealers exchanging shots. Some were killed on the streets, while others (including children) were killed in apartments, where more drug dealing seemed to take place after the crackdown had been in effect for a while. This pattern leads some local observers to suggest that the crackdown helped cause the increase in murders in two ways. One is that "intensified enforcement has raised the violence of the drug trades, simply because the participants feel more threatened" (Reuter et al. 1988, p. 47). Another cause is that crackdowns move drug conflicts indoors, where children and other innocent bystanders are closer at hand.

These possibilities are all the more troubling to the basic hypothesis of this essay, since the structure of Operation Clean Sweep was essentially the rotating target strategy we considered at the outset. The target rotation has been geographic rather than substantive, however, turning the local criminal justice system almost into a drug abuse control system. Perhaps rotating the substantive emphasis as well as the geographic locales of the drug markets would have produced different results; so might a greater emphasis on treatment and prevention, such as trailer-based drug treatment clinics in crackdown areas.

7. *Private Citizen Crackdowns.* The "police presence" crackdown strategy has become increasingly popular among private citizens in recent years. Citizen patrols in modern America are nothing new, dating at least from the late 1960s in Newark and Brooklyn and popularized nationally by the Guardian Angels. But the drug crackdown focus of such patrols in specific geographic areas is a recent development.

In Washington, D.C., for example, tenants of one of the worst public drug markets, Mayfair Mansions, invited members of the Black Muslims to crack down on drug dealing and gunfire in their apartment complex in April 1988. Armed only with nightsticks and walkie-talkies, the bow-tied and suited Muslim patrol started with ten members beating and stomping a man with a shotgun in front of a local television camera man; then they roughed up the camera crew, which broadcast the whole episode. But after those particular patrollers and the shotgun wielder were all charged, the patrols continued with police cooperation, restoring the courtyard to "music, basketball, volleyball, laughter, and children" (Stevens 1988a).

By midsummer, the *Washington Post* (July 12, 1988) reported that both the police and the Muslims had continued to patrol the 1,100 units, monitoring several thousand residents at Mayfair Mansions and the adjoining Paradise Manor, with striking results. By the third month, not one drug arrest or assault had occurred on the properties for thirty days. "I can't remember the last time I heard gunfire around here," said one delighted resident. By six months after it began, the drug dealing was still completely absent, although there was some argument over who deserved credit for the enormous reformation of the place (Stevens 1988b). The local police union president claimed the crime reduction was really the result of a police crackdown, with thirty to forty police officers patrolling the project nightly after the splash of initial publicity.

There was no disagreement, however, about the local displacement effects. A merchant at a small shopping center across the street from the complex claimed that the drug dealers moved to his locale. "This is the new hot spot," he claimed, reporting that the merchants' businesses and lives had been threatened by the influx from Mayfair Mansions (Stevens 1988b).

Another drug-ridden complex in the Washington area, King's Square Apartments in Maryland, hired a noncommissioned, unarmed security force of fourteen guards to provide a "jump-out" squad. The Prince George's County police put their tactics and armament under investigation and strongly disapproved of private efforts against narcotics; other local security firms say they refuse to perform antidrug enforcement. But the complex owner and local residents interviewed by a reporter claim that the force has been effective in driving drug dealers off the premises (Price 1988).

One striking feature of private drug crackdowns is a conscious lack of concern for displacement. In contrast to public police, who must deal with crime wherever it develops in the city, the landlords or tenants of specific properties suffer no costs from merely pushing drug dealing away. Displacement is almost assumed by any NIMBY (not in my back yard) effort to avoid local nuisances. This is consistent with the Barr and Pease (in this volume) analysis of displacement in general.

8. *Drug Crackdown Summary*. The study of drug crackdowns is marked by major success and failure. There are more documented crackdowns on drugs than on any other type of problem except drunk driving (see table 1). But of the two targets, the crackdowns on drugs are generally far less successful. None of the six drunk driving crackdowns appears to have backfired, but two of the six drug crackdowns may have increased crime. Moreover, there is no evidence of any residual deterrent effect from drug crackdowns. To the contrary, the market in some areas appears to be so strong that street dealing reappears almost as soon as police effort is reduced. In Queens (New York), for example, Tactical Narcotics Team (TNT) undercover officers left a target area after nine months of arresting dealers and buyers at a rate of eighty-five a week. In the first two weeks of the backoff, when regular units made thirty arrests a week, public crack dealing was reported to have revived all over the area (Pitt 1988). Finally, the apparent (but not well-documented) displacement of drug markets by crackdowns led the Citizens Crime Commission of New York (1988) to recommend against further use of the strategy against drugs (Raab 1988).

C. Drunk Driving Crackdowns

Perhaps the best studied target for police crackdowns has been drunk driving. The easily identifiable target (drivers) and relatively clear outcome measure (accidents) makes it ideal for such analysis. The major drawback of generalizing from drunk driving enforcement to other issues is the difference in the social class of the potential offenders.

Drunk drivers may include a far higher proportion of middle-class, educated offenders than do street drug dealers or robbers. This may alter the sensitivity to possible sanctions, since a drunk driving arrest can be far more devastating to a white collar worker's career than a robbery arrest is to a marginally employed person. Class differences may also make drunk driving more sensitive than other offenses to publicity about police detection efforts since better-educated persons may be more likely than others to read newspapers or follow other news media reports closely.

Whether they are typical or not, drunk drivers have been found to be highly sensitive to communicated threats of apprehension. If anything, they seem more sensitive to the threat communication than to the actual differences in police sanctioning.

The clearest evidence of this pattern comes from the New Zealand drunk driving "blitz" evaluation (Hurst and Wright [1980], as reported in Ross [1981], pp. 75–83). In two separate multiweek crackdowns aimed at intensifying police enforcement for higher certainty of apprehension per drunk-driver trip, a several-week period of public announcements preceded the actual enforcement increase. The public was told that the principal tactic would be to give breath tests at every conceivable opportunity. They were even told when the blitz would begin. Measures, both of cars parked in tavern parking lots and patients admitted to hospitals for auto crash injuries, showed substantial reductions in the weeks preceding the actual crackdown. This also occurred before the second crackdown, which was implemented six months after the first.

If one assumes New Zealanders expect a threat from their police to be carried out, then the publicity effect before and after the first blitz is not surprising. But it is striking that the residual deterrence of accidents disappeared after the end of the postblitz publicity, rising from 140-odd per week back to the preblitz level of over 190 (Ross 1981, p. 78). A publicity effect before the second blitz is perhaps more important, for it suggests that the first blitz provided a convincing demonstration of the crackdown threat and maintained its credibility. Even without publicity after the end of the second blitz, however, the residual deterrent effect lasted about as long as the blitz itself, taking as many weeks to return to the preblitz level of crashes (Ross 1981, p. 79).

The English drunk driving crackdown of 1967 also created much of its deterrent effect through publicity, with much less real increase in police alcohol tests than in New Zealand. In New Zealand, the tests were instantly quadrupled in the first blitz and doubled in the second (Ross 1981, p. 76). The English police, by contrast, only slightly more than doubled the number of tests over a four-year period (Ross 1981, p. 28). Nonetheless, England enjoyed a two-thirds reduction in nighttime/weekend traffic deaths and serious injuries (from 1,200 to 400 per month) following the passage of the law empowering police to compel blood alcohol tests from suspicious drivers and setting a .08 blood alcohol content per se definition of intoxication. Ross (1973) attributes the deterrent effect not to the implementation of the law, which faced continual obstructions from officials and magistrates, but to the ongoing publicity surrounding the controversy over the law's implementation. A comparable, if much shorter, decline occurred when a similar law was enacted in France in 1978 with even less vigorous police enforcement efforts; these effects were also attributed to publicity alone (Ross, McCleary, and Epperlein 1982).

Further evidence of the apparent need for publicity for some kinds of crackdowns to produce deterrence is found in the first Cheshire blitz on drunk driving in 1975. While the blitz increased breath tests in one week from 38 the prior year to 284 in the experiment, there was no publicity surrounding the effort. Ross (1981, p. 72) concludes that the unpublicized, fully implemented blitz produced no apparent impact on serious crashes—in sharp contrast to the dramatic crash reductions produced by a controversial and well-publicized month-long blitz two months later.

In both blitzes, the chief constable ordered his officers to "go as far as we could within the law to breathalyse all people driving between ten at night and two in the morning" generally in the course of investigating traffic accidents and violations (Ross 1981, p. 72). During the month-long, publicly debated second phase of the blitz, the number of breath tests in the county rose to six times the national average. The number of serious-injury and fatal crashes in Cheshire dropped from 115 in the prior month and 95 in the same month of the prior year to 70 during the blitz, almost a statistically significant reduction after a relatively short baseline period (twenty months). Moreover, after the publicity apparently made it clear that the one-month blitz had ended, there was a residual reduction in serious or fatal crashes for six months afterwards and a residual reduction in total crashes for three months—or substantially longer than the blitz itself.

These short-term drunk driving crackdowns provide the best measured examples of residual deterrence after a sharply defined backoff. Longer-term drunk driving crackdowns, however, show the clear pattern of initial deterrence and decay (just as in Lynn), even with increases in police sanctioning levels. The Ross (1973) evaluation of the 1967 British Road Safety Act showed that, after an initial 66 percent reduction in serious and fatal crashes in the first year of the law, the number of crashes doubled in the second year of the law and continued to rise quite steadily thereafter—despite steady increases in the number of breath tests actually administered. The Ross, McCleary, and Epperlein (1982) evaluation of the 1978 French drunk driving law showed an even shorter period of initial deterrence before crackdown decay set in, with the early 25 percent reduction in crash-related injuries entirely gone by the end of the first year.

D. Prostitution

Matthews (1986, p. 24) documents a crackdown on prostitution that dramatically transformed a London neighborhood "from a noisy and hazardous area into a relatively quiet residential one." In late 1983 a special seventeen-officer vice unit was assigned to the Finsbury Park area for a one-year period with a special mission to clean up the problem. While the baseline enforcement levels are not clear from the report, the crackdown effected a substantial increase in the number of arrests of prostitutes, pimps, and brothel keepers, and the number of cautions of their customers. Arrests and cautions combined totaled over four a day, with a good deal of other intervention making business difficult. The customer cautions appeared to be successful as a specific deterrent, since none of the same names appeared twice in police records during the period. Police also closed down several brothels in the area and convicted one major landlord of making rooms available for prostitution, acts which altered the opportunity structure for the crime.

Matthews reports that these efforts were quite successful at reducing "kerb-crawling," although no systematic data were available to support the claim. More systematic evidence (names of prostitutes arrested in nearby vice markets) supports the claim that neither the police crackdown nor the redesign of the streets that followed it led to much displacement. The apparent effect was to encourage many of the women who traveled to London from the countryside on day-trips to drop out of prostitution. There was no reported revival of prostitution after the special vice unit was withdrawn, but the street closing plan prevents us from interpreting that result as residual deterrence.

E. Residential Calls to Police

Another case of initial deterrence followed by decaying police effort and decaying effects can be found in the new police strategy of problem-oriented policing (see Goldstein 1977; Eck and Spelman 1987). In the 1987 Minneapolis Repeat Call Address Policing (RECAP) Experiment (see Sherman et al. 1989), a special unit of five police officers was assigned 125 residential addresses to which police repeatedly responded in 1986—for a total of about 10,000 calls. Their one-year assignment was to solve the problems generating those calls, thereby reducing the call volume at those addresses as well as at 125 high-volume commercial addresses. The calls included a wide range of crime and service problems, from rape and robbery to drug dealing, domestic violence and disputes, noisy parties, and vandalism to cars.

The RECAP officers used a variety of tactics, generally starting with a meeting with the landlord of the premises (except for the public housing projects). The landlords were told that they were "on the list," and were given a breakout of calls by apartment. Several landlords used the call data to support petitions for evictions, successfully obtaining the otherwise hard-to-get orders. The RECAP officers also met with resident managers, giving them both technical knowledge and inspirational messages about how to control problem tenants and tenant problems. Finally, RECAP officers left "napalm letters" on tenant doorsteps (notices requesting them to contact the RECAP unit immediately) where there had been repeated domestic disturbance calls.

The results of this crackdown, as the local news media described it, can fortunately be described with some precision (Sherman et al. 1989). Unlike any of the other research reviewed above, the RECAP experiment had a large number of units of analysis and a randomly assigned control group. This provides the most powerful research design to date showing the initial deterrence-subsequent decay pattern. After six months of RECAP efforts, the target addresses had 15 percent fewer calls than in the same period in the previous year, relative to the trends in the control group (a significant difference). But in the second six months, RECAP officers were increasingly drawn to their hardest cases, and could not apply equal attention across all addresses. Moreover, a city-wide policy of arresting domestic assailants was strictly enforced during the second half-year as a result of RECAP discoveries of noncompliance during the first half. This led to a doubling of domestic violence arrests city-wide, including in the control group. This complicates an otherwise clean interpretation of the second half results as crackdown and deterrence decay: by the fourth quarter, the target addresses had slightly more calls than the control addresses, leaving the full-year comparison with only 5 percent fewer calls at the target addresses (a nonsignificant difference).

Problem-solving tactics are hard to equate with visible police presence on a daily basis. But in the minds of landlords or targeted tenants, there may be a similar form of threat communication—perhaps more so than for the transient populations in commercial addresses, where RECAP never achieved significant reductions. There may also be a similar decay, so that by the third time police contacted the landlord about problems on the premises the landlord felt more comfortable in ignoring RECAP recommendations. Whatever the reasons, the findings suggest an operational policy of short-term targeting of active addresses, with initial assignments of three months. Long-term targeting of these addresses, given the current limitations of RECAP tactics, was clearly not a good investment. This conclusion is especially powerful in light of the hundreds of other addresses with high volumes of calls to which police could rotate their problem-solving crackdown efforts.

F. Other Crackdowns

Earlier studies of sharp increases in police personnel, often without a specific target, provide relevant findings on the effects of crackdowns. In 1966, for example, the New York City Police Department undertook a more sophisticated version of its 1954 "Operation 25" (Wilson 1975, p. 83) in which patrol personnel (mostly on foot) in the twenty-fifth precinct were doubled, followed by sharp four-month reductions in muggings, burglaries, and auto thefts. The fifty-eight-week experiment in 1966–67 increased motorized patrol by 40 percent, consisting of nine new police cars and two scooters on duty (Press 1971, p. 48). Compared to a baseline period, outdoor (but not inside) crimes of robbery, larceny, and auto theft declined significantly, although with some apparent displacement effect to nearby Central Park.

In 1977 the Nashville, Tennessee, police reported an experiment in which the amount of moving patrol under twenty miles per hour (MPH) was carefully measured and increased in four high-crime neighborhoods (Schnelle et al. 1977). Four squad cars with no duty to answer calls were assigned to supplement the one squad car normally assigned to each neighborhood. The result was a 400 percent increase in actual moving patrol, and a 4,000 percent increase in the number of hours of patrol at speeds under 20 MPH. Total daily Part I Index crime declined significantly during the two tests (one eleven-day test and one fifteen-day test) of saturation patrol in the daytime. The only crime-specific data reported were that daytime patrols failed to reduce home burglaries, but the nighttime patrols succeeded in reducing business burglaries.

Perhaps the most impressive deterrent effect of police patrol was demonstrated in the New York City subways in 1965, when a highly publicized increase in subway crime was followed by a sharp increase in subway police—from 1,200 to 3,100 officers. The new personnel resources virtually guaranteed one police officer on every train and at every station daily from 8:00 P.M. to 4:00 A.M. In the longest period of patrol work ever studied systematically, Chaiken, Lawless, and Stevenson (1975) found that over an eight-year period, subway crime during the target hours fell initially, but after two years began to rise again steadily. Like the Nashville experiment, however, the cost was very high: about $35,000 per deterred felony. And unfortunately, confidence in the study is limited by the subsequent discovery that the chief of the transit authority police was systematically undercounting and underreporting subway crimes for much of the period in question.

Chaiken (1978) reexamined the data after the charges of manipulation were made public, adjusting for the apparent reclassification of night-time crimes to daytime and analyzing misdemeanors and tollbooth robberies as crimes unlikely to have been downgraded. He again concluded that the sharp increase in police personnel had a strong initial deterrent effect, followed by a long-term increase in crime.

A final study showing deterrence from a threat communication examined the impact of a letter containing a threat of legal action sent to 62 persons known to be receiving cable television signals without paying for them (Green 1985). Two-thirds (forty) of the threat targets ceased, or at least attempted to hide, their theft by removing the visible "descrambler" device necessary for committing the theft. This study is particularly interesting because every subject was at least exposed to the same communication of the threat (although some people are known not to read their mail).

Two other field experiments suggest what happens when there is a sudden backoff eliminating a longstanding police uniformed patrol practice. One is the San Diego Field Interrogation Experiment. In 1973, field interrogations were completely eliminated from one patrol beat for nine months, while they were maintained at the same level in a matched comparison precinct. Total "suppressible" crime (mostly vandalism, petty theft, and burglary) increased by almost 40 percent in the backoff area, while it was unchanged in the comparison (Boydstun 1975, pp. 30–32). But as figure 3 reveals, the increase followed the backoff rather slowly. In the first month of no interrogations, the crime total was below the mean for the baseline period. By the second and third months crime had risen by only 20 percent above the baseline mean. Only in the fourth month did crime take off, doubling over the base mean. The data are consistent with some residual deterrent effect of the field interrogations for several months after they were stopped. Moreover, the decline in crime after the backoff was terminated by a sudden increase in field interrogations is consistent with an initial deterrence effect.

Finally, the Newark Foot Patrol Experiment (Pate 1986) showed what happened when foot patrol was suddenly and completely eliminated from four beats of less than 1,000 residents each for a period of eleven months. While there was no clear effect on crime (which is not surprising, given the low statistical power of the sample size [Sherman and Weisburd 1988]), there was strong evidence of no effect on community perceptions of crime, safety, and police service in comparison to four matched control beats. By contrast, four beats in which foot patrol was added showed substantial improvements in public perceptions. These findings lead Pate (1986, p. 155) to support the strategy of rotating police and targets: "The tactical uses of foot patrol in areas that are not accustomed to it can have clearly positive effects. In addition, it appears that such patrol can be removed, at least temporarily, without incurring negative consequences. Perhaps the best use of scarce resources, then, would be to redeploy foot patrol officers to different areas periodically."

Whatever the wisdom of rotation, the Newark evidence seems to show a longlasting residual effect on public perceptions about crime long after foot patrol is eliminated.

IV. Varieties of Crackdown Effects

Taken together, these case studies suggest several varieties of crackdown effects among at least two varieties of crackdowns themselves: short- and long-term. Other varieties of crackdowns, such as relative emphasis on presence, sanctions, and publicity, can also be distinguished. The varieties of effects concern five key questions: Was there an initial deterrent effect? Was there any crime increase? Was there apparent local displacement? Did any initial deterrence decay? Was there any residual deterrence?

Table 1 presents the answers to these questions for the eighteen case studies in which there appeared to be enough data to make a reliable judgment on most of the questions. Question marks indicate uncertainty about the findings. The definition of short-term is an observed period of less than six months. As Kleiman (1988) points out, crackdowns can be hard to stop once they are started; several of the long-term cases began with only short-term plans.

A. Initial Deterrence Successes

Perhaps the most important, if expected, conclusion from table 1 is that most of the crackdowns (fifteen of eighteen) produced initial deterrence. This evidence, even without reference to specific police dosage levels, contradicts the conclusion many have drawn from the Kansas City Preventive Patrol Experiment (Kelling et al. 1974) that variations in police presence do not affect crime. In general, increases in police

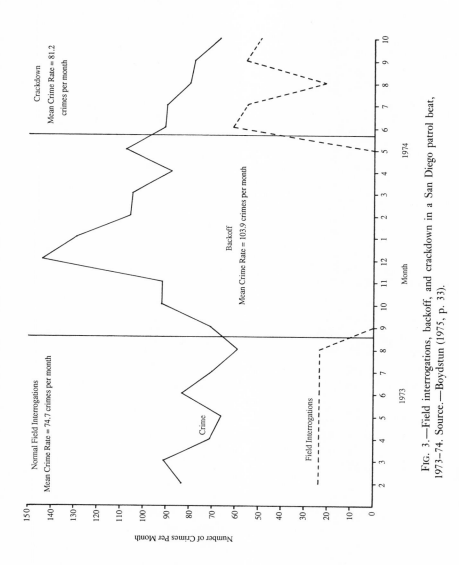

FIG. 3.—Field interrogations, backoff, and crackdown in a San Diego patrol beat, 1973–74. Source.—Boydstun (1975, p. 33).

TABLE 1
Effects of Crackdowns by Time Length

Site	Initial Deterrence	Crime Displacement	Decay	Residual Effect
A. Short-term efforts:				
New Zealand 1*	Yes	No	No	Yes
New Zealand 2*	Yes	No	No	Yes
Cheshire 1*	No	. . .	. . .	. . .
Cheshire 2*	Yes	No	No	Yes
Georgetown	(parking)	?	No?	Yes
San Diego field interrogations	Yes	?	No	Yes
B. Long-term efforts:				
Lynn, Massachusetts†	Yes	No	Yes	No
Lawrence, Massachusetts†	No	?‡	. . .	Yes
Washington, D.C. ("Clean Sweep")†	Local not city	Local‡	. . .	Yes
Washington, D.C. (Hanover Place)†	Yes	Yes	No	No
Washington, D.C. (Muslims)†	Yes	Yes	No	No
New York City (Lower East Side)†	Yes	Yes	Yes	No
New York City (Twentieth Precinct)†	Yes	Yes	Yes	No
New York City (subways)	Yes	?	Yes	No
Residential RECAP	Yes	?	Yes	No
English DWI law*	Yes	No	Yes	No
French DWI law*	Yes	No	Yes	No
London prostitution	Yes	No	No	No

NOTE.—All of these crackdowns are discussed (and sources identified) in Sec. III.
* Drunk-driving crackdown.
† Drug crackdown.
‡ Possible crime increase.

presence, sanctioning, or (as in the New Zealand preblitz publicity) media threats can be expected to produce at least brief reductions in the target crime problem. Discounting this finding (Ross 1981), because crackdowns rarely produce lasting deterrence, may miss the important point that something *can* work, predictably, to fight crime in specific ways.

B. Backfire: Crime Increases

The fifteen initial successes must be tempered not only by three failures but also by two of those cases that may have caused a crime increase (both drug crackdowns). The causal link between the crackdown and the crime increase is not strong, but it is about as strong as the causal link in the successful cases. There are plausible reasons for the Lawrence crackdown to have caused more robbery and for Washington's "Clean Sweep" to have caused more drug homicides. The point of these case studies should be that crackdowns on market-driven forces like drug markets can have complex results and that it is possible for well-intended efforts to make things worse.

C. Displacement

A more encouraging finding is that displacement was clearly indicated in only four of the crackdowns, all but one of them focused on drug markets. Drug dealing may be the most resilient and moveable crime problem to which crackdowns are applied. None of the six drunk driving crackdowns show any signs of displacement, perhaps because they affected such large geographic areas. The other cases all suffered from poor measurement of displacement, which poses a difficult task for any researcher. Some displacement will probably occur with most geographic police-presence crackdowns. But it is not yet known what proportion will be displaced and whether there will be a net reduction in offending. There are good theoretical reasons to suggest that changing the opportunity structure for crime through crackdowns can yield a net reduction in crime (Cornish and Clarke 1987; Sherman, Gartin, and Buerger 1989). Moreover, as Barr and Pease (in this volume) suggest, even total displacement can have good effects if the "deflected" crimes are less serious than they would have been otherwise.

D. Deterrence Decay

Table 1 shows two important things about decaying deterrence. One is that none of the five successful short-term crackdowns suffered deterrence decay, confirming the expectation that the decay problem may be limited to longer crackdowns. The other finding is that decay is not a universal pattern even in longer-term crackdowns. The two years of apparent continued deterrence of open drug dealing (but not robbery) in the Lower East Side, the two years of possible deterrence in New York's subways, and over six months of deterrence by Muslims and the police in Mayfair Mansions suggest that it may be possible to sustain the benefits of a crackdown under certain conditions.

Nonetheless, seven of the ten long-term crackdowns with initial deterrence saw at least some aspects of that effect decay over time. The deterrence wore off after two years in Lynn and two years in the subways, despite constant levels of police presence. It decayed after a year for England's drunk driving law, despite increases in police sanctioning levels. It decayed after nine months in residential RECAP, although with an apparent decline in police activity across all 125 locations. Across such diverse kinds of crackdowns on diverse problems in diverse cultures, these findings suggest the best prediction for the effects of a long-term crackdown will be a decay of initial deterrence.

E. Residual Deterrence Successes

Only six of the documented crackdowns measured crime during a backoff period. One of these, the unpublicized first Cheshire blitz, had no initial deterrence. All five of those that achieved initial deterrence and then backed off produced a residual effect. Three of these were for drunk driving, and one was for parking violations—distinctly middle-class offenses. Even the San Diego field interrogations were felt most strongly on minor offenses like vandalism. Whether residual deterrence can be found with more serious offenders remains an open question.

Nonetheless, the combination of the short-term residual pattern with the long-term decay suggests that much of the deterrent effect of any crackdown may result from its initial shock to the potential offenders. We cannot know how many of the decay cases would have shown residual deterrence if the crackdowns had been stopped sooner, but we can speculate that the rebounding crime rates might have looked much the same without continued expenditure of police resources. Since the major obstacle to broader police use of crackdowns is limited numbers of personnel, aiming for residual (if decaying) deterrence could make wider use of crackdowns far more feasible than trying to achieve sustained deterrence over time. The only way to be sure would be to undertake far more systematic research than we have just reviewed. The research would require varying the nature of the crackdown tactics, the target crime problems, and the length of the efforts in a series of well-controlled experiments: preferring the tortoise of such an accumulation to the hare of multivariate analysis (Zimring 1978).

V. Research Designs

A research program of this nature would have to address several problems in evaluating crackdown effects on crime. One is the small numbers of most target crimes over short time periods in specific areas, or in the entire city. Another is the difficulty of eliminating the incapacitation, displacement, and "unknown other cause" theories as rival explanations of any significant crime reductions that are observed. A final obstacle is the difficulty of creating valid control or comparison areas not receiving the crackdown, in order to eliminate the "unknown other cause" argument (Cook and Campbell 1979).

Taken one case at a time, it will always be difficult to evaluate crackdown effects. But if some way can be found to undertake large numbers of crackdowns simultaneously, then there is at least a possibility of a reliable statistical analysis by comparison to a control group. The key to such a research design is also the key to the operational policy suggested at the outset: intermittent, unpredictable, repetitive, and *brief* crackdowns on constantly shifting targets. Such a policy would allow a limited number of officers to undertake many crackdowns at once. The design has been approximated in several of the crackdowns reviewed above, such as the Operation Clean Sweep and residential RECAP. But it has never been systematically evaluated with respect to the residual deterrent effects from each brief crackdown on each specific target.

This kind of experiment has never been thought possible in the past because few cities have 100 or more patrol areas in which to vary the amount of patrol presence. Even if they do, statistical tests are quite limited. Patrol areas are quite large, and police numbers are limited. The Kansas City preventive patrol experiment (Kelling et al. 1974), in addition to other design problems (Larson 1976; Zimring 1978; Sherman 1986), ran afoul of dilution of extra patrol over too large an area with too little crime for reliable statistical tests. The density of police presence per square foot will always be extraordinarily low outside of a highly dense pedestrian area as long as the idea of covering the entire city is predominant.

But while that idea may be politically necessary, it is not necessarily the best way to conceptualize a test of the effects of police presence. Indeed, it would only make sense if crime were equally distributed around the city, a condition which no police department assumes to be true. The area boundaries for patrol cars already reflect disproportionate distribution of crime, but police are still constrained by the need to cover the city. A strong test of the crackdown theory can go beyond that constraint, at least for research purposes, while still providing some coverage to the entire city.

This is the premise of one current test of police presence as distinct from residual deterrence (Sherman and Weisburd 1988). The Minneapolis Hot Spots Patrol experiment is focused on 110 of the very small areas of the city in which disproportionately large numbers of crimes occur; fifty-five areas receive up to three hours of intermittent extra patrol presence daily for one year, and fifty-five receive only normal patrol. The selection of the 110 address clusters was suggested by an analysis of some 323,000 calls for police service in 1986 at 115,000 street addresses and intersections to which police could be dispatched (Sherman, Gartin, and Buerger 1989). This analysis found that 3 percent of all places received 50 percent of all police calls dispatched. Similarly, all robbery calls were reported at 2.2 percent of places, all rapes at 1.2 percent of places, and all auto thefts at 2.7 percent of places. These concentrations have two causes. One is that predatory crime is always rare geographically; only 3.7 percent of the city could have had a robbery, for example, even with no repeat addresses. But the concentration of crime is also significantly greater than a random (Poisson) distribution would produce, with the magnitude of concentration varying by offense type.

The Minneapolis "hot spots" experiment employed a computer mapping program (MAPINFO) to group high-crime call addresses into small clusters in which one patrol vehicle would be visible and close enough to be observed by potential offenders (Sherman and Weisburd 1988). These clusters (not individual addresses) provide large numbers of crime calls over the course of a year, an average of more than 180 each. The statistical power of the design provides an estimated 91 percent chance of finding a reduction of 15 percent in average crime calls per cluster (compared to the control clusters) as not being due to chance ($p = .05$). This reduces the bias toward the null hypothesis found in other experiments.

A similar design could be used to test for residual deterrence. In fact, the Minneapolis design almost included an additional treatment group to test the crackdown-backoff theory, but the patrol commanders involved requested a smaller number of target sites in order to provide greater dosage for a better test of continuing patrol presence. The design could have tested for residual deterrence even though the average number of calls per cluster would have been only three per week. One-day or even two-week crackdowns with perhaps multiple patrol cars per cluster would not be able to show a statistically discernible effect of each crackdown for either initial or residual deterrence. But a one-year experimental period could arguably bypass the need to look at week-to-week fluctuations.

The one-year focus on repeated, brief crackdowns follows from the theory of institutionalized, long-term uncertainty of apprehension risk. The purpose of obtaining residual deterrence is not just to show a decline in crime continuing after the extra police resources have been withdrawn. Rather, the purpose is to determine whether repeated doses of extra police effort can create enough residual and initial deterrence to lower crime more than a steady dose of the same total amount of police presence on average over the course of the year (see fig. 1).

In order to make this comparison, the original Minneapolis hot spots design had a total of 150 high crime address clusters. The 150 were to be randomly divided into three groups: 50 in the control group, 50 to receive extra police presence in an intermittent crackdown-backoff pattern, and 50 to receive about the same amount of police presence as the crackdown group spread out over the course of the year on an even, steady basis. Even without that full design, the actual test of steady presence approximates the crackdown-backoff pattern: the target address clusters will not have a police car present at all times, and when police are present they will leave to answer calls and then return unexpectedly. A better theoretical test of residual deterrence, however, might be several days of continued police presence, followed by no special policing for a week or more.

Another option for testing short-term crackdowns would be to use more active hot spot or area targets (such as drug markets) with 20 or 30 crimes per week, and one- to four-week crackdowns as the unit of analysis. Each crackdown could be followed by three to six months of observation for residual deterrence, as the New Zealand evaluation did. With enough time (two to four years), even a relatively small number of crackdown targets could provide enough units of analysis for reasonable statistical power. The basic crossover design principle suggested by Feinberg, Larntz, and Reiss (1976), in which targets alternate as control sites in random order, could control for any rival explanations including external events.

The long-term accumulation and replication of such findings for specific offenses or types of areas could produce a series of dosage-response curves to guide police policy. These curves would address the *intensity* of police presence per square foot or 1,000 people or of police sanctions per place or 1,000 people. They could also address the *length* of the crackdown periods, the length of backoff periods, and combinations of the two. Standardized measures of displacement might be used to discount the apparent deterrent effects for a net effect measure. With the predictable periods of residual deterrence such curves could provide (fig. 4), police administrators could develop relatively long-term scheduling of police personnel around crackdown target objectives. They could also make more informed choices in length of crackdowns. For example, the hypothetical in figure 4 suggests that a twelve-week crackdown could produce 33 percent more residual deterrence than a six-week one, but at 100 percent greater cost in personnel time. It also shows that there is no additional benefit of residual deterrence to be gained by extending a crackdown beyond twelve weeks. Transferring officers at that point to another location for eight weeks could yield eight weeks residual deterrence at the first site, eight weeks crackdown deterrence at the second site, and six weeks residual deterrence at the second site—a total of thirty-four weeks of deterrence from twenty weeks' work, compared to twenty-six weeks of crackdown and residual deterrence from maintaining the crackdown in one site only.

The difficulty in developing such curves is that each point requires a separately evaluated crackdown. It has taken years to develop the meager eighteen points analyzed in this review. The only way to speed the

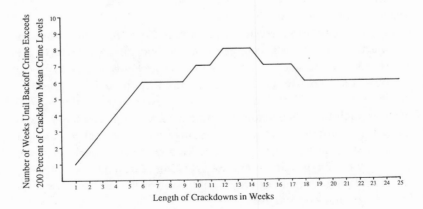

FIG. 4.—Hypothetical dosage-response curve of residual deterrence on crackdown length.

process is for a stronger partnership between police agencies and researchers to assure that more of the thousands of crackdowns undertaken annually are properly documented and incorporated into a national archive on crackdown effects.

Even in the absence of such systematic data, however, police executives can make better use of measurement to decide when to back off and to resume crackdowns. Local political pressures may complicate such flexible decisions. One way to counteract that is to make certain that the public is more generally educated about residual deterrence and promised that the extra cops will be back again soon. How soon would be determined by how quickly the residual deterrence decays. While this may conjure an image of a Dutch boy switching his thumbs from one hole to another of many in the dike (with no chance of stemming the tide), it is no different in structure from the current politically driven responses. Yet it may be far more effective.

VI. Crackdown Ethics

Regardless of the effectiveness of crackdowns on crime control, there are two key ethical questions about them. One concerns the basic concept of "getting tough." The other concerns the equity of target rotation.

A. Potential Abuses

Despite the sanitary language of science used in this essay, police language does not usually employ terms like dosage levels of police presence or increased risks of apprehension. More likely terms refer to striking various parts of the anatomy of criminal suspects. Even the term "crackdown" itself connotes striking with a club and implies an acceptable level of brutality. The term "target" connotes wartime search and destroy bombing missions. All of these associations are troubling when discussing the policing of a free society.

What is more troubling is the possibility of actual violations of civil liberties. Kleiman's (1988, p. 22) discussion of the Philadelphia "Cold Turkey" crackdown on fifty-six drug-market corners shows that such excesses have already occurred: of the 1,000 persons stopped and searched by Cold Turkey's 450 officers over four days, only 80 were arrested on narcotics charges, and 150 more for disorderly conduct. Public protest and a lawsuit brought the operation to an effective end after four days, with no measurable result except citizen hostility.

Even more concern has been raised about the Los Angeles crack-

down on gangs in early 1988, after several crossfire killings from intergang shoot-outs. Up to 1,000 officers repeatedly "swept" through gang
neighborhoods making mass arrests, up to 1,400 on a single weekend.
According to Cockburn (1988), well over two-thirds of those arrested
were released without being charged. The charges that were filed were
for such minor offenses as jaywalking, blocking a public passage, or
failing to disperse: "Police have entered apartment buildings, taken
every resident found on the premises into headquarters, arrested one
person and sent the rest home. According to [the] counsel for a group
. . . preparing a lawsuit to stop the sweeps, 'the prime basis for arrest is
being black or Hispanic.' This is a highly reasonable inference since not
a single white person has been picked up so far" (Cockburn 1988, p.
33).

The potential abuses of crackdowns are not limited to police activity.
Even volunteer citizen crackdowns have been accused of illegal
searches, harassment, and assaults such as pulling crack pipes out of
smokers' mouths (Davidson 1988). Whether done by citizens or police,
bullying people on flimsy probable cause is a highly intrusive way to
control any crime problem. "Street sweep" or loitering arrests are
highly offensive, even if they reduce older people's fear of youths, as
they apparently did in Newark (Pate et al. 1986). Moreover, the constitutional status of "sweeps" is highly questionable (Skolnick and Bayley 1986, chap. 7). Their long-term potential for building hostility to
police and undermining citizen efforts to assist crime control should
also be considered. The whole "sweep" philosophy runs counter to the
"community policing" approach fostered in many cities in recent years.

Crackdowns do not have to be done this way. The Georgetown and
drunk driving crackdowns, for example, were conducted in the bright
spotlight of middle class and media attention. Virtually no complaints
of police abuse were ever reported in those efforts. Whether the same
circumspect attention to legality is found in drug crackdowns in poor
neighborhoods is unknown.

The ethical question is whether it is proper to release a force that can
be easily abused, especially by exhausted police officers working long
hours of overtime. That question is endemic to all police activity as well
as to many other socially useful enterprises: paid child care, nuclear
power, surgery, and so on. Answering it in each case requires careful
examination of the actual risk levels and the potential for controlling
that risk through personnel screening, training, and close management.

Given the record of crackdowns to date, it appears that the risk of abuse is not unduly large. With careful management, it should be possible to operate crackdowns legally, with proper respect for the dignity and rights of all citizens.

B. Equity in Target Selection

Making apprehension risks more uncertain through crackdown targets raises several ethical issues. One is the fairness of unequal probabilities of apprehension for different offenses, or for the same offense at different places or times. This problem is hardly unique to crackdowns since it represents the status quo. Indeed, the rotating crackdown strategy would do more to equalize enforcement probabilities than continuation of the current triage system.

More troubling may be the lowering of punishment risks during backoff periods for some of the more serious offenses or higher crime locations. What effect that might have can only be determined through field tests. But if the theory is correct, rotating crackdowns should reduce crime overall more than the triage system now allows, even for those serious offenses or places. If the policy is unfair to victims of those more serious offenses during backoff periods compared to people not victimized during crackdowns, it is no more unfair than the greater resources most police give to false burglar alarms than to murder investigations.

Each city will still have to face the question of enforcement priorities. A rotating crackdown policy does not imply a mindless exhaustion of every offense type or place. Rather, it brings the enforcement priority question to the forefront of public debate, where it belongs. Such debate puts more accountability on the legislature for maintaining low priority laws such as jaywalking and blocking public passage. But it also allows discussion of such issues as whether too many people run red lights and the need for an intermittent crackdown on such conduct at many busy intersections.

The rationale for crackdowns depends heavily on the volume of violations and the distribution of that volume over time and space. There are certain places and certain offenses that may never have enough volume to merit a police crackdown. There are also offenses that, no matter how voluminous, may never be viewed as serious enough to warrant a crackdown. Finally, there are offenses that are so serious that, no matter how rare they are, police will always be expected to do their utmost to apprehend the offenders. Thus the selection of crackdown targets should depend upon a judgment that combines offense seriousness and volume.

Systematically uncertain punishment has a strong utilitarian justification for the inconsistencies it produces since it could reduce crime against all citizens, including the punished offenders. Moreover, systematic uncertainty gives every offender equal opportunity to be caught or go free, depending on the luck of the draw. If done properly, it would entail no class or race bias and be much fairer than the current decision-making patterns in many cities. A country that drafts people for war by lottery should find little wrong with apprehension risks determined by lottery.

As long as we refuse to pay for making punishment highly certain for every offense, we must continue to pick the least worst alternative. Making a low risk of punishment highly certain for most offenses is an open invitation to every rational criminal. By keeping them guessing, we may have better luck at keeping them honest.

REFERENCES

Barnett, Arnold. 1988. "Drug Crackdowns and Crime Rates: A Comment on the Kleiman Paper." In *Street-Level Drug Enforcement: Examining the Issues*, edited by Marcia R. Chaiken. Washington, D.C.: National Institute of Justice.

Barr, Robert, and Ken Pease. In this volume. "Crime Placement, Displacement, and Deflection."

Barry, Marion, Jr. 1985. "A Special Message from Mayor Marion Barry, Jr." *Georgetowner* 32(3):2.

Blumstein, Alfred, Jacqueline Cohen, Jeffrey Roth, and Christy Visher, eds. 1986. *Criminal Careers and "Career Criminals."* 2 vols. Washington, D.C.: National Academy Press.

Boydstun, John E. 1975. *San Diego Field Interrogation: Final Report*. Washington, D.C.: Police Foundation.

Bureau of Justice Statistics. 1986. *Police Employment and Expenditure Trends*. Washington, D.C.: U.S. Government Printing Office.

Campbell, Donald T., and H. Laurence Ross. 1968. "The Connecticut Crackdown on Speeding: Time-Series Data in Quasi-experimental Analysis." *Law and Society Review* 3:33–53.

Cermak, Marv. 1988. "Schnectady Mayor Wants Police Satellite Station." *Times-Union* (Albany) (August 2), sec. B, p. 4.

Chaiken, Jan M. 1978. "What Is Known about Deterrent Effects of Police Activities." In *Preventing Crime*, edited by James A. Cramer. Beverly Hills, Calif.: Sage.

Chaiken, Jan M., Michael W. Lawless, and Keith A. Stevenson. 1975. "The Impact of Police Activity on Subway Crime." *Urban Analysis* 3:173–205.

Citizens Crime Commission of New York City. 1988. *Dealing with New York City's Drug Crime Crisis: The Need for a Comprehensive Plan*. New York: Citizens Crime Commission of New York City.

Cockburn, Alexander. 1988. "Los Angeles Can't Win Drug War by Cracking the Whip." *Wall Street Journal* (May 5, eastern ed.).

Connelly, Mary, Carlyle C. Douglas, and Laura Mansnerus. 1986. "Cracking Down on City Cyclists." *New York Times* (August 24, eastern ed.).

Cook, Thomas, and Donald T. Campbell. 1979. *Quasi-Experimentation: Design and Analysis Issues for Field Settings*. Chicago: Rand-McNally.

Cornish, Derek, and Ronald V. Clarke. 1987. "Understanding Crime Displacement: An Application of Rational Choice Theory." *Criminology* 25:933–47.

Davidson, Joe. 1988. "Street Sweepers: Some Citizen Patrols Bully Drug Traffickers until They Flee Area." *Wall Street Journal* (September 26, eastern ed.).

Eck, John, and William Spelman. 1987. *Problem Solving: Problem-oriented Policing in Newport News*. Washington, D.C.: Police Executive Research Forum.

Federal Bureau of Investigation. 1978–88. *Crime in America: The Uniform Crime Reports* (annual). Washington, D.C.: Federal Bureau of Investigation.

Feinberg, Stephen, Kinley Larntz, and Albert J. Reiss, Jr. 1976. "Redesigning the Kansas City Preventive Patrol Experiment." *Evaluation* 3:124–31.

Goldstein, Herman. 1977. *Policing a Free Society*. Cambridge, Mass.: Ballinger.

Green, Gary S. 1985. "General Deterrence and Television Cable Crime: A Field Experiment in Social Control." *Criminology* 23:629–45.

Gusfield, Joseph. 1963. *Symbolic Crusade*. Urbana: University of Illinois Press.

Hurst, P., and P. Wright. 1980. "Deterrence at Last: The Ministry of Transport's Alcohol Blitzes." Paper presented at the Eighth International Conference on Alcohol, Drugs, and Traffic Safety, Stockholm.

Kelling, George L., Tony Pate, Duane Dieckman, and Charles Brown. 1974. *The Kansas City Preventive Patrol Experiment*. Washington, D.C.: Police Foundation.

Kelly, Brad. 1988. "Police Trailer Doesn't Stop Drugs, Says Alderman." *Times-Union* (Albany) (August 2), sec. B, p. 4.

Kerr, Peter. 1987a. "War on Drugs Shifting Focus to Street Deals." *New York Times* (April 13, eastern ed.).

———. 1987b. "Crushing the Drug Dealers of Washington Square." *New York Times* (November 9, eastern ed.).

Kleiman, Mark A. R. 1986. *Bringing Back Street-Level Heroin Enforcement*. Papers in Progress Series. Program in Criminal Justice Policy and Management, John F. Kennedy School of Government, Harvard University, Cambridge, Mass.

———. 1988. "Crackdowns: The Effects of Intensive Enforcement on Retail Heroin Dealing." In *Street Level Drug Enforcement: Examining the Issues*, edited by Marcia R. Chaiken. Washington, D.C.: National Institute of Justice.

Larson, Richard C., 1976. "What Happened to Patrol Operations in Kansas City?" *Evaluation* 3:117–23.

Levett, Alan. 1975. "The Centralization of City Police in the Nineteenth Century United States." Ph.D. dissertation, University of Michigan, Department of Sociology, Ann Arbor.

Matthews, Roger. 1986. *Policing Prostitution: A Multi-agency Approach.* London: Middlesex Polytechnic, Centre for Criminology.

Molotsky, Irvin. 1988. "Capital's Homicide Rate Is at a Record." *New York Times* (October 30, eastern ed.).

Morris, Norval, and Gordon Hawkins. 1970. *The Honest Politician's Guide to Crime Control.* Chicago: University of Chicago Press.

Pate, Antony M. 1986. "Experimenting with Foot Patrol: The Newark Experience." In *Community Crime Prevention: Does It Work?* edited by Dennis P. Rosenbaum. Beverly Hills, Calif.: Sage.

Pate, Antony M., Mary Ann Wycoff, Wesley Skogan, and Lawrence W. Sherman. 1986. *Reducing Fear of Crime in Houston and Newark: A Summary Report.* Washington, D.C.: Police Foundation.

Pitt, David E. 1988. "Crack Dealers Returning to Streets Narcotics Teams Had Swept Clean." *New York Times* (December 5, eastern ed.).

Press, S. James. 1971. *Some Effects of an Increase in Police Manpower in the Twentieth Precinct in New York City.* New York: New York City Rand Institute.

Price, Debbie M. 1988. "Private Antidrug Force at Pr. George's Complexes Probed." *Washington Post* (October 17).

Raab, Selwyn. 1988. "Study Faults Strategy in New York Drug Crackdown." *New York Times* (November 29, eastern ed.).

Reiss, Albert J., Jr. 1985. *Policing a City's Central District: The Oakland Story.* Washington, D.C.: National Institute of Justice.

Reuter, Peter. 1986. Personal communication with the author, May 15.

Reuter, Peter, John Haaga, Patrick Murphy, and Amy Praskac. 1988. *Drug Use and Drug Programs in the Washington Metropolitan Area.* Santa Monica, Calif.: Rand.

Robinson, Eugene. 1986. " 'Clean Sweep' Doesn't Work: Taking the Broom to Drugs Just Moves the Dirt." *Washington Post* (December 21), sec. D, p. 5.

Roffman, David. 1985. "Crimewave in Georgetown" (editorial). *Georgetowner* 31(10):2.

Ross, H. L. 1973. "Law, Science, and Accidents: The British Road Safety Act of 1967." *Journal of Legal Studies* 2:1–78.

———. 1981. *Deterring the Drinking Driver: Legal Policy and Social Control.* Lexington, Mass.: Heath.

Ross, H. L., R. McCleary, and T. Epperlein. 1982. "Deterrence of Drinking and Driving in France: An Evaluation of the Law of July 12, 1978." *Law and Society Review* 16:345–74.

Sampson, Robert J., and Jacqueline Cohen. 1988. "Deterrent Effects of the Police on Crime: A Replication and Theoretical Extension." *Law and Society Review* 22:163–89.

Schnelle, J. F., R. E. Kirchner, J. D. Casey, P. H. Uselton, and M. P. McNees. 1977. "Patrol Evaluation Research: A Multiple-Baseline Analysis of Saturation Police Patrolling during Day and Night Hours." *Journal of Applied Behavioral Research* 10:33–40.

Sherman, Lawrence W. 1978. *Scandal and Reform: Controlling Police Corruption.* Berkeley: University of California Press.

———. 1986. "Policing Communities: What Works?" In *Communities and Crime,* edited by Albert J. Reiss, Jr., and Michael Tonry. Vol. 8 of *Crime and Justice: A Review of Research,* edited by Michael Tonry and Norval Morris. Chicago: University of Chicago Press.

Sherman, Lawrence W., Michael E. Buerger, Patrick R. Gartin, Robert Dell'-Erba, and Kinley Larntz. 1989. "Beyond Dial-a-Cop: Repeat Call Address Policing." Report submitted to the National Institute of Justice, Washington, D.C., by the Crime Control Institute, Washington, D.C.

Sherman, Lawrence W., Patrick Gartin, and Michael E. Buerger. 1989. "Hot Spots of Predatory Crime: Routine Activities and the Criminology of Place." *Criminology* 27:27–55.

Sherman, Lawrence W., Anne Roschelle, Patrick R. Gartin, Deborah Linnell, and Clare Coleman. 1986. "Cracking Down and Backing Off: Residual Deterrence." Report submitted to the National Institute of Justice, Washington, D.C., by the Center for Crime Control, University of Maryland.

Sherman, Lawrence W., and David Weisburd. 1988. "Policing the Hot Spots of Crime: An Experimental Research Design." Unpublished manuscript, Crime Control Institute, Washington, D.C.

Skolnick, Jerome, and David Bayley. 1986. *The New Blue Line.* New York: Free Press.

Steffens, Lincoln. 1931. *Autobiography.* New York: Harcourt Brace.

Stevens, William K. 1988*a.* "Muslim Patrols Fight Capitol Drug Trade." *New York Times* (April 24, national ed.).

———. 1988*b.* "Muslims Keep Lid on Drugs in Capital." *New York Times* (September 26, national ed.).

Tversky, Amos, and Daniel Kahneman. 1974. "Judgment under Uncertainty: Heuristics and Biases." *Science* 185:1124–31.

Washington Post. 1986. "Crowd Control Resumed in Georgetown." *Washington Post* (May 3), sec. B, p. 4.

———. 1988. "Antidrug Patrol Restores Peace in NE Complexes." *Washington Post* (July 12), sec. B, p. 1.

Westley, William. 1970. *Violence and the Police.* Cambridge, Mass.: MIT Press.

Wheeler, Linda. 1986. "The Police Take Charge: From Drug Mart to Great Neighborhood." *American Visions* (March/April), pp. 19–23.

Wheeler, Linda, and Sari Horwitz. 1988. "Operation Clean Sweep's Future Uncertain." *Washington Post* (January 26), sec. A, p. 1.

Whyte, William F. 1943. *Street Corner Society.* Chicago: University of Chicago Press.

Wilson, James Q. 1975. *Thinking about Crime.* New York: Basic Books.

———. 1983. *Thinking about Crime* 2d ed. New York: Basic Books.

Wilson, James Q., and George L. Kelling. 1982. "Broken Windows: The Police and Neighborhood Safety." *Atlantic Monthly* 249(3):29–38.

Zimmer, Lynn. 1986. *Proactive Policing in New York and the Disruption of Street-*

Level Drug Trade. Unpublished manuscript. State University of New York College at Geneseo, Department of Sociology.

Zimring, Franklin E. 1978. "Policy Experiments in General Deterrence: 1970–75." In *Deterrence and Incapacitation: Estimating the Effects of Criminal Sanctions on Crime Rates*, edited by Alfred Blumstein, Jacqueline Cohen, and Daniel Nagin. Washington, D.C.: National Academy Press.

Sally T. Hillsman

Fines and Day Fines

ABSTRACT

Fines are often used as criminal penalties in the United States but rarely as the sole sanction for more serious cases or for repeat offenders. In Western Europe, by contrast, fines are the most often imposed sentence for most crimes, including nontrivial ones, and are sometimes by national policy the major alternative to imprisonment. In American courts, fines are used more widely and collected more frequently than has been recognized. However, patterns of use vary widely. The major difficulty American judges face is their inability to set fines that are proportionate to the severity of the offense but also equitable and fair, given differences in criminal offenders' economic circumstances. "Day fines," well developed in Western Europe, are linked to both the offender's daily income and to the gravity of the crime. Day fines have proven effective in helping courts set fine amounts that are both proportionate and just. Some American courts are now adapting day fines to the American context and are beginning to experiment with their use.

Sentencing policy in the United States has changed substantially in the last decade with the introduction of sentencing guidelines, mandatory minimum sentences, and determinate sentencing schemes. Mainstream sentencing theory and legislative activity have shifted from the concepts of individualized justice and rehabilitation toward an emphasis on incapacitation, deterrence, and retribution (or "just deserts"). These changes have contributed to the growing strain on the country's correctional resources. This is at least partly because American policymakers tend to view imprisonment not only as the primary means available for punishment of crime but also as virtually the only means.

Sally T. Hillsman is director of research at the Vera Institute of Justice, New York City. Thanks are due Barry Mahoney, Silvia S. G. Casale, and Judith A. Greene for their valuable assistance.

One result has been a policy goal of targeting scarce jail and prison space for those offenders who appear to be most deserving of it. While the movement toward sentencing guidelines and other methods of structuring sentences is beginning to achieve greater consistency in decisions involving imprisonment, policymakers are only now beginning to address the issue of how to structure sentencing decisions among noncustodial alternatives. Attention has focused on sanctions that are relatively new and undeveloped in most jurisdictions: community service, intensive probation, house arrest (with and without electronic monitoring), and restitution. There has also been renewed attention, however, to the criminal fine (Morris 1974, 1987; Carter and Cole 1979; Friedman 1983; Smith 1983–84; Hillsman 1986).

The advantages of the fine as a criminal sanction are well recognized: it is unmistakably punitive and deterrent in its aim; it is sufficiently flexible to reflect the seriousness of the offense and the level of the offender's resources; it can be coupled with other noncustodial sanctions when multiple sentencing goals are sought; it does not further undermine the offender's ties to family and community; it is relatively inexpensive to administer, relying primarily on existing agencies and procedures; and it can be financially self-sustaining and provide revenue for related social purposes such as victim compensation.

Little policy or research attention in the United States has been paid to the criminal fine. The majority of fines imposed by American courts are for traffic offenses and less serious high-volume offenses (Hillsman, Sichel, and Mahoney 1984, pp. 28–47; Cole et al. 1987, pp. 1–8). This is in sharp contrast to the sentencing practices of many Western European countries including England, West Germany, Sweden, and Austria, where fines as sole sanctions are the sentences of choice in most criminal cases, including nontrivial ones, and where the fine is, by national policy, the major alternative to imprisonment (Carter and Cole 1979; Gillespie 1980, 1981; Casale 1981; Hillsman, Sichel, and Mahoney 1984, app. C).

This essay reviews empirical research and writing on the role of criminal fines in American sentencing. The discussion also draws on European experiences that are influencing current efforts in the United States to make the fine a more useful sanction.

The essay is divided into six sections, beginning in Section I with a review of theoretical and practical arguments about the role of fines in American sentencing and the contrasting European perspectives on these issues. Recent research is then reviewed on the patterns of fine use in American and European courts (Sec. II) and on fine collection and enforcement (Sec. III). The empirical evidence suggests that fines are used more widely and for a broader range of nontrivial offenses in American trial courts than has been recognized and are, in some courts, collected and enforced more successfully and expeditiously than is commonly assumed.

Section IV discusses the day fine, a method of setting variable fine amounts that addresses issues that have troubled American policymakers—how to impose economic sanctions that are punitive but just and how to implement collection strategies that are successful but fair. Day-fine systems in West Germany and Sweden illustrate how these fining systems attempt to reconcile the potentially conflicting principles of proportionality and equity in sentencing by use of a two-stage decision process to set the amount of the fine. First, the number of day-fine units to which the offender is sentenced is determined with regard to the gravity of the offense, but without regard to the means of the offender. The monetary value of the fine unit is then determined, setting it explicitly in relation to what the offender can afford to pay, given his financial means and responsibilities. Thus the degree of punishment resulting from the day fine is in proportion to the seriousness of the offense and should cause an equivalent level of hardship for defendants of differing means; it should also be enforceable without excessive reliance on imprisonment for default. Adapting day fines to the American courts is discussed in Section V. Conclusions are presented in Section VI.

I. The Role of Fines in American Sentencing Practice

"It is not difficult to find reasons for the attractiveness of fines for sentencers. . . . Fines are unequivocally punitive, designed to deter, a significant attraction now that the treatment/rehabilitation ideal has fallen from grace. The meaning of fines is clear. Unlike community service, probation, or even custody, it is doubtful whether sentencers, defendants, victims, and public at large disagree about what a fine represents though . . . different sentencing purposes may result in considerable disagreement as to the appropriate size of a fine in any particular case" (Morgan and Bowles 1981, p. 203).

There appears to be little theoretical disagreement about the purposes, principally deterrence and retribution, served by fine sentences.

Used alone they do not incapacitate, and they are rarely thought to rehabilitate.[1] Questions about the use of fines in criminal cases tend to focus on their appropriateness in relation to other punitive sanctions, particularly incarceration, and on whether they can be set high enough, given differences in offenders' means, to accomplish these aims in a way that is also just.

Model penal codes and sentencing standards in the United States have not favored the use of fines, often rejecting them in strongly negative language: "fines are to be discouraged . . . unless some affirmative reason indicates that a fine is peculiarly appropriate" (National Commission on Reform of Federal Criminal Laws 1971, p. 296).[2] This posture has left American sentencers to rely primarily on imprisonment and probation among traditional options, to struggle with making newer intermediate punishments workable, and to fill the remaining void with "designer" sentences crafted to fit the specific circumstances of individual cases (Greene 1988; von Hirsch 1988).

This is in striking contrast to the role of fines in Western European jurisprudence. Throughout the twentieth century, criminal courts in England, West Germany, Sweden, Austria, and elsewhere in Western Europe have been renewing a long tradition of relying on fines as the basic means of punishment. Beginning with the Greeks, Romans, and ancient Germans, fines were the primary sanction in both civil and common law systems, giving way to imprisonment and probation only in the nineteenth century, primarily in America with its shift to an emphasis on rehabilitation (Rusche and Kirchheimer 1939; Beristani 1976).

The use of the fine in Western Europe as the dominant criminal penalty springs from these criminal justice systems' straightforward commitment to punishing and deterring the offender as the primary objectives of sentencing. Although the fine is viewed as less punitive than imprisonment, concern about the ill effects of custody has been voiced in Europe since the eighteenth century, and the treatment/ rehabilitation model of imprisonment never won the following that it

---

[1] Sentencing theorists occasionally view the fine as rehabilitative, insofar as paying their fines makes offenders aware of their social obligations (Miller 1956; Best and Birzon 1970), but this purpose is more commonly associated with restitution (Forer 1980).

[2] This same perspective is found in the American Law Institute's *Model Penal Code* (1962), the National Council on Crime and Delinquency *Model Sentencing Act* (1977), and the American Bar Association *Standards Relating to Sentencing Alternatives and Procedures* (1978).

enjoyed for a time in the United States.[3] In England, for example, the preference for fining is sometimes explained by assertions that, at the very least, fines are likely to be *less ineffective* in terms of subsequent behavior by offenders who are fined than are other penalties (Harris 1980, p. 10).

Fines are preferred by some because they are considered penologically effective (Morgan and Bowles 1981, p. 204). The principal bases in England for the modest assertions about the fine's deterrent value are data showing that reconviction rates for fined offenders are lower than those for offenders sentenced to probation or short-term imprisonment (McClintock 1963, p. 173; Davies 1970; Softley 1977, pp. 7–9; McCord 1985). Although such data are methodologically weak (groups of offenders sentenced to different penalties are often dissimilar in their social and criminal backgrounds), they have gained credibility because similar results have been obtained from more sophisticated research conducted in West Germany. Controlling for offense and offender characteristics (including prior record), researchers at the Max Planck Institute found that fines are *no less* effective than sentences of short-term incarceration in preventing reconviction among professional petty thieves and also among traffic offenders (who are most representative of the general population), and that fines are considerably *more* effective than either imprisonment or probation in theft, embezzlement, and fraud cases (Albrecht 1980; Albrecht and Johnson 1980).[4]

The data do not support the view that fines are criminogenic, that is, that fined offenders are given incentives to commit additional crimes to pay the fine. Indeed, research on how people pay fines suggests that money is obtained from regular sources of revenue coming into the offender's household (Softley 1973).

Why has the fine not assumed a position of greater importance in the United States? A recent national survey of judges in American trial courts reveals substantial ambivalence and confusion about the fine's role as a criminal sanction (Cole et al. 1987, pp. 16–20). Judges in both

---

[3] Rehabilitation efforts in these Western European countries have generally focused on sentences to probation that are used much less frequently and more selectively than in the United States. This is consistent with the emphasis on intensive casework in the European probation approach. The probation order in European systems, therefore, may be a less perfunctory exercise in treatment and supervision than it tends to be in the United States.

[4] Multivariate analysis of similar types of data for the Los Angeles Municipal Courts has been completed in the United States showing similar results (Glaser and Gordon 1988).

general and limited jurisdiction courts agreed that, in concept, fines can be used to sanction both the rich and the poor. However, many judges viewed fines as having little impact on the more affluent offender and believed there is no way to enforce fines effectively against the poor.

American skepticism about the value of fine sentences seems to focus on the size of the fine and questions about the fairness of using monetary penalties that flow from this. In American sentencing literature and policy discussion, it is primarily large fines in amounts fixed according to the severity of the crime that are regarded as punitive and, therefore, of deterrent value.[5] If fine amounts are high enough to achieve these aims for any but trivial offenses, however, they tend to be viewed as uncollectable, or difficult and expensive to enforce, or resulting in imprisonment for default for the typical American criminal offender. If fine amounts are sufficiently low for most offenders to pay them, the sentences are considered unfair because they advantage the more affluent offender who is perceived as being able to buy his way out of a more punitive sanction.

By contrast, European discussions of the fine's utility emphasize its variability with respect to size; because the sentence is numerical, the sentencer can adjust its amount, and therefore its punitiveness, not only in relation to the severity of the offense but also to the means of the offender. "The vast majority of indictable offenses are readily characterised in terms of the value of property or damage involved, so that fines and compensation may be readily tailored to fit both the offense and the offender" (Morgan and Bowles 1981, p. 203). In England, West Germany, Sweden, and elsewhere in Western Europe, therefore, the fine is the preeminent sentencing device, regardless of the offender's financial circumstances, precisely because its intrinsic flexibility enables the sentencer to make the amount appropriate for the full array of criminal behaviors for which deterrence or retribution are the primary sentencing aims.

In the next section I review what is known about current American fining practices to see how often fines are now imposed and for what

---

[5] This is reflected in Congress's efforts to increase fine maxima in the federal system. In 1979, the Senate Committee on the Judiciary in reporting out S 1722 commented that "It is intended by the Committee that the increased fines permitted . . . will help materially to penalize and deter white collar crime" (96–533, p. 975) and that "high fines and weekends in jail could sometimes substitute for a long prison term" (p. 973). Congress raised maximum fine amounts in 1984 to $250,000 for a felony, $25,000 for a misdemeanor, and $1,000 for an infraction (Comprehensive Crime Control Act of 1984).

types of offenses, how judges set fine amounts in courts across the country, and what success courts have collecting fines.

II. Current Patterns of Fine Use

Until quite recently, little was known about the extent to which fines are used as criminal penalties in the United States.[6] Even less was known about how they are collected and enforced or about their real or perceived effectiveness as sanctions. To fill this gap the National Institute of Justice (NIJ) supported four studies of American fining practices between 1980 and 1988 and is currently supporting a demonstration project. Combined with a few previous studies of American courts that contain some evidence about fine use, these studies provide the major source of information on American practices.

Hillsman, Sichel, and Mahoney (1984) report on the first of these NIJ-sponsored studies, which was a broad exploratory examination of American fining practice. The research was based on a telephone survey of court administrators and chief clerks in 126 limited- and general-jurisdiction courts across the United States, site visits to thirty-eight different courts, analysis of case records for a sample of 2,165 convicted defendants in five New York City courts, a review of all state and federal statutes regarding fines, examination of key appellate opinions on the fining of indigents, and a general review of relevant governmental, legal, and social science literature.

Casale and Hillsman (1986) report on the second study, an in-depth examination of fine collection and enforcement practices in four English magistrates' courts (the equivalent of American courts of limited jurisdiction), with emphasis on their relevance to American practice.

Cole et al. (1987) report on the third study; it was a national survey of 1,261 judges in general- and limited-jurisdiction trial courts inquiring about their sentencing practices, their courts' enforcement and collection activities, their attitudes toward the use of fines, and their views about the desirability and feasibility of adapting European day-fine systems to the United States. Finally, Glaser and Gordon (1988) report on the last of these studies, a multivariate analysis of sentencing and

---

[6] This is particularly troubling given the recent trend for legislatures and judges to advocate the expanded use of other financial penalties. In a National Institute of Corrections study, e.g., Mullaney (1987) found twenty-three types of service fees and five special assessments used in American courts, in addition to fines, court costs, restitution, and reparations. This proliferation of fees and financial penalties exists uneasily alongside American policymakers' deep-seated reservations about the justice of using fines as a primary criminal penalty.

recidivism among municipal court offenders punished by probation, jail, and monetary penalties in various combinations.[7]

A. *The Frequency of Fine Sentences*

Fines are used very widely as a criminal sanction (quite apart from their use in routine traffic offenses and violations of municipal ordinances) but there is enormous variability among criminal courts in the extent to which they rely on fines (Hillsman, Sichel, and Mahoney 1984, pp. 28 ff.; Cole et al. 1987, pp. 6 ff.).

In limited jurisdiction courts, for example, which handle over 90 percent of the criminal cases in the United States, fines appear to be the predominant sanction. In the 1984 report of the survey of American court administrators, 87 percent of the respondents in limited jurisdiction courts indicated that their judges use fines in all or most cases (Hillsman, Sichel, and Mahoney 1984, pp. 28 ff.). The 1987 survey of judges in lower courts confirmed this level of fine use; respondents indicated that, on average, they use fines in about 86 percent of their cases (Cole et al. 1987, pp. 6–7). Research based on actual case records supports these survey results. In New York City's misdemeanor courts, for example, the fine is the most commonly used penalty, imposed as a sole sanction in 31 percent of the cases (Zamist 1986, p. 64). It is imposed in 61 percent of the cases in New Haven's Court of Common Pleas (Feeley 1979); in 87 percent of the cases in the Columbus, Ohio, Municipal Court (Ryan 1980–81); in 53 percent of Peoria's misdemeanor cases (Gillespie 1982); and in 75–81 percent of the misdemeanor cases in the courts of Austin, Texas, Tacoma, Washington, and Mankato, Minnesota (Ragona and Ryan 1983).

General-jurisdiction trial courts that handle only felony cases use fines much less. In the 1984 court survey, 63 percent of the respondents from these courts reported that fines are used seldom or never. This is consistent with case-record analyses that indicate that fewer than 5 percent of felonies result in fines in New York City's felony courts (Zamist 1986, pp. 115–23) and in the felony courts of Detroit, Baltimore, and Chicago (Eisenstein and Jacob 1977, p. 274). There are other types of general jurisdiction courts, however, that dispose of a wide

[7] The National Institute is currently funding a demonstration project run by the Vera Institute of Justice to adapt the day-fine concept to the Criminal Court of Richmond County (Staten Island, New York) and to implement it in that court (Hillsman and Greene 1987, 1988).

variety of misdemeanor as well as felony cases; these "hybrid" courts use fines more frequently than do felony-only courts. Over half of the 1984 survey respondents from this type of upper-level trial court reported that most of their cases involve fines, and judges from general jurisdiction courts surveyed in 1987 reported using fines in about 42 percent of their cases.

It would appear, therefore, that the less frequent use of fines in American upper courts, particularly felony-only courts, which are the most visible courts and those that have been studied most often (although they handle the fewest criminal cases overall), has encouraged the prevailing belief that fines in the United States are restricted to routine traffic cases and relatively minor criminal offenses (e.g., Carter and Cole 1979; Gillespie 1981). Yet this is clearly not so. Fine use is more widespread and extensive in American sentencing than the conventional wisdom suggests.

B. The Types of Offenses Fined

The 1984 survey of court administrators and clerks suggests, and the 1987 survey of judges confirms, that fines are commonly used in sentencing a wide range of offenses. As table 1 shows, among the 126 limited- and general-jurisdiction courts surveyed, relatively serious motor vehicle crimes (primarily DWI, or driving while intoxicated, and reckless driving) are often dealt with by fines in both upper and lower courts. So also are the variety of criminal behaviors that comprise disorderly conduct and breach-of-the-peace offenses, drug-related offenses (sale and possession), some thefts, and assaults. In each of these categories (except DWI for which almost two-thirds of the courts report using fines), almost a third of all the courts report that fines are commonly used. For other categories of offenses (including criminal trespass, criminal or malicious mischief, shoplifting, bad checks, and prostitution), some courts surveyed use fines frequently, but most did not report doing so.

This variability among courts in their use of fines is as significant as the range of offenses for which fines are currently being imposed across the United States. While some of these differences undoubtedly reflect variation among jurisdictions in the type of criminal behavior falling under similar statutory offense categories, some also reflect different sentencing practices. Certain courts fine offenders; others use alternative sanctions, including incarceration. This diversity suggests that

TABLE 1

Types of Offenses for Which Fines Are Commonly Used, by Type of Court

	Frequency			
Type of Offense	Limited Jurisdiction (N = 74)	General Jurisdiction Felony, Misdemeanor, and Ordinance Violation (N = 28)	General Jurisdiction Felony Only (N = 24)	Total (N = 126)
Driving while intoxicated	54	22	2	78
Reckless driving	30	9	0	39
Violation of fish and game laws and other regulatory ordinances	24	3	0	27
Disturbing the peace/breach of the peace/disorderly conduct	32	8	1*	41
Loitering/soliciting/prostitution	15	4	0	19
Drinking in public/public drunkenness/carrying an open container	14	5	0	19

Criminal trespass	10	2	1	13
Vandalism/criminal mischief/malicious mischief/property damage	9	3	3	15
Drug-related offenses (including sale and possession)	23	10	11	44
Weapons (illegal possession, carrying concealed weapon, etc.)	6	2	1	9
Shoplifting	17	3	0	20
Bad checks	14	2	0	16
Other theft	19	9	8	36
Forgery/embezzlement	2	3	2	7
Fraud	1	4	1	6
Assault	29	14	5	48
Burglary/breaking and entering	2	6	6	14
Robbery	0	1	3	4

SOURCE.—Hillsman, Sichel, and Mahoney (1984), p. 41.

* Superior Court, Cobb County; 1% of caseload includes misdemeanors.

there is room for expanding the use of fine sentences in this country, at least in jurisdictions currently not using fines in kinds of cases for which other jurisdictions routinely impose fines.

The 1987 survey of judges also highlights the variability in fine use. As seen in table 2, 89 percent of the lower-court judges questioned about their sentencing choices for hypothetical first offenders would fine at least half the cases of assault (with minor injury to the victim), and 58 percent of the upper-court judges would do so. In residential daytime burglary cases, 46 percent of the lower-court judges report they would fine at least half the time as would 27 percent of the upper-court judges (Cole et al. 1987, p. 44).

In New York City's five misdemeanor courts, case records document this variability within and between courts in the same urban area. Fines are used with some frequency as the exclusive sentence for DWI, reckless driving, gambling, disorderly conduct, loitering, possession and

TABLE 2

Proportion of Judges Who Would Likely Impose a Fine in at Least Half the Cases Involving Selected First Offenses, by Type of Court

Offense*	General Jurisdiction		Limited Jurisdiction	
	%	N†	%	N†
Drug sale (1 ounce cocaine)	53	594	64	121
Fraud (land deal)	41	508	53	98
Burglary (daytime, residence)	27	589	46	134
Embezzlement ($10,000)	39	576	44	89
Assault (minor injury to victim)	58	610	89	501
Auto theft ($5,000 value)	36	600	54	151
Harassment	63	441	92	405
Disorderly conduct	78	444	97	488
Bad check	51	587	85	461
Shoplifting ($80 value)	69	486	91	476
Prostitution	64	375	83	276
Possession of marijuana (1 ounce)	70	573	92	433

SOURCE.—Cole et al. (1987), p. 44.

NOTE.—Question 10 (see Cole et al. 1987): "For each of the offenses below, assume that the individual is an *adult, first-time offender*, employed at a job which pays $160 per week. In general, how likely are you to impose a fine, either alone or with another sanction and what would be the typical amount of the fine?"

* Offenses are arranged in order of severity as ranked by the National Survey of Crime Severity.

† N = no. of judges who indicated that they handle the particular offense.

sale of controlled substances, prostitution, lesser degrees of assault and theft, and criminal trespass (Zamist 1986, pp. 67–77). Many of the cases fined in these New York City courts were not trivial, nor were most of the fined offenders youths or first offenders. For example, 47 percent of the misdemeanor convictions that resulted in a fine-alone sentence in the misdemeanor court located in the Bronx had entered the system on a felony complaint after screening by the district attorney's office, as had 51 percent of the cases in the Brooklyn court and 13 percent in the Manhattan court (Zamist 1986, p. 73). Furthermore, over 80 percent of the city's fined offenders were twenty years or older (p. 77), and fewer than one out of five were first offenders (pp. 77–78).

Although fining is more common in American courts than is generally believed, fine usage has not reached the levels common in Western Europe. Furthermore, the fines imposed by many American courts are often not the exclusive criminal penalty as they frequently are in Europe. In West Germany, for example, 81 percent of all adult criminal cases and 75 percent of all nontraffic criminal offenses are disposed by a fine as the sole penalty; fines are used in a third of all sexual offenses in West Germany and in 73 percent of all crimes of violence against the person (*Strafverfolgungsstatistic 1985*). In Sweden, fines are used in 83 percent of all criminal offenses and 65 percent of all nontraffic criminal offenses, including 40 percent of all offenses against persons (*Kriminalstatistik For Brott Lagforda Personer, 1987*, 1988). In England, 38 percent of persons convicted of indictable offenses (roughly equivalent to American felonies) and 89 percent of persons convicted of summary offenses (excluding traffic offenses) are sentenced to pay a fine as the sole penalty. These include 28 percent of all sexual offenses and 39 percent of all offenses of violence against the person (Home Office 1988).

C. The Forms Fine Sentences Take

Many American fine sentences appear to be composites of fines and other noncustodial sanctions, although statistical data from American courts are particularly sketchy on this issue.[8] In the 1987 judicial sur-

---

[8] National data on any aspect of sentencing are difficult to construct for the United States, particularly for lower courts. Most computerized court record systems (including offender-based transaction systems) make detailed study of sentencing patterns extremely difficult. They tend to record only the "primary" or "most severe" penalty imposed; thus it is difficult to get an accurate picture of composite sentences, particularly those involving fines that can be imposed as a condition of probation for the purposes of collection. This type of combination occurs even when the fine is the central penalty and the

vey, judges reported lower levels of fine use when asked specifically about fine-only sentences than when asked about fines generally; the proportion declines from about 86 percent of all lower-court sentences resulting in fines to about 36 percent that are fined solely, and the drop is greater for upper courts—from 42 percent to 8 percent (Cole et al. 1987, p. 6). The misdemeanor courts of New York City, therefore, in which fine sentences are typically sole penalties, reflect the practices of some, but by no means all, American lower courts.

Although many American fines are part of a composite sentence, they tend to be combined most often with other financial penalties, for example, with restitution or court costs (Cole et al. 1987, p. 8). Other fines are combined with probation, but it is not always clear whether probation is added to the fine as a collection device (as, e.g., in many Georgia courts; Sichel 1982*a*), or whether probation is the main sentence with the fine added to enhance its punitive content. All these combinations appear to be common in American courts but not in Europe. They are more common in American upper courts, where fine combinations may include a suspended jail or prison term, than in lower courts. Thus while fines are frequently used penalties in the United States, they are rarely by themselves an alternative to short terms of incarceration as fine-alone sentences are in Western Europe.

D. Fine Amounts

The common view in the United States that fines are a relatively weak punishment is related to the notion that only large fines have punitive and deterrent value but that large fines are difficult to impose because they raise issues of fairness. It is not surprising therefore to find that most fines are set at levels well below statutory limits. This is despite the fact that many state legislatures have increased statutory maxima, anticipating judicial need of higher limits in cases of better-off offenders for whom current fine levels would represent inadequate punishment (Hillsman, Sichel, and Mahoney 1984, pp. 52 ff.).

Judges have wide discretion in setting the size of a fine. Most American judges use a relatively limited range of fine amounts, primarily because they are constrained by informal "tariff" (or fixed-fine) systems that guide their decisions as to an appropriate amount. The tariff sys-

---

probation sanction is primarily a collection device (Hillsman, Sichel, and Mahoney 1984, p. 35). In such cases, computerized record systems often record only the probation sentence and not the fine (e.g., Glaser and Gordon 1988).

tems typical of American courts are based on informal understandings
that the same or similar fine amounts ("going rates") will be imposed on
all defendants convicted of a particular offense. In many courts, however, these tariffs are set with an eye to the lowest common economic
denominator of offenders coming before the court in order to ensure
that the sentences can be enforced. As a result, fixed-fine or tariff
systems generally cause fine amounts to cluster near the bottom of the
statutorily permissible range. This limits the range of offenses for
which judges consider the fine an appropriate sole penalty. Fixed-fine
systems, therefore, represent a serious restriction on the broad usefulness of fines for crimes of varying degrees of seriousness and leave
sentencing judges with few punitive but enforceable sentencing options
besides imprisonment.

This is so in New York City which is not atypical. While judges use
fines as sole sanctions in almost a third of all misdemeanor convictions,
their informal fine tariffs are set low. The modal fine amount citywide
is $50 and the median is $75; even in the city's relatively affluent and
most "suburban" community (Staten Island), fine amounts are low,
averaging around $100. In imposing such small amounts, however, the
judges are also ensuring that the courts' sentencing orders are obeyed:
despite poverty, two-thirds of all the fined offenders in New York City
(and three-quarters in Staten Island) pay in full, most within three
months of sentence (Zamist 1986, pp. 79–103).[9]

Tariff systems also cause problems for courts that routinely set high
fine amounts. Higher-fine tariffs either limit the range of offenders who
can be fined or make it difficult to enforce fines among relatively poor
offenders without resorting to imprisonment for default.

Some high-tariff systems result from informal court traditions that
encourage judges to set fine amounts in relation to factors other than the
economic circumstances of typical offenders. For example, some Georgia courts are guided by the average costs of local probation services
that collect the fines (Sichel 1982a). Other high-tariff systems occur

[9] Gillespie (1982) notes that 85 percent of misdemeanor fine sentences in Peoria are
under $150; fines in New Haven's Court of Common Pleas rarely exceed $25 (Feeley
1979); and average fine amounts in Columbus are around $100 (Ryan 1980–81). Even
assuming inflation has doubled these amounts in the years since these case records were
sampled, fine amounts are low. Indeed, in the 1986 survey of judges, they report median
fine amounts of between $75 and $150 for less serious offenses in both upper and lower
courts (Cole et al. 1986, pp. 11–12). For more serious offenses, especially convictions in
upper courts, they report somewhat higher median fine amounts, ranging from $500 to
$1,000 for drug sales, fraud, and burglary.

when court traditions or state statutes encourage (or mandate) the imposition of multiple financial penalties without regard to the total amount the offender is being required to pay. This happens because of two recent trends in American sentencing. First, judges are more frequently sentencing offenders to pay monetary restitution, often in amounts unrelated to the offender's ability to pay.[10] Second, state legislatures are requiring courts to impose an ever-broadening array of fees, costs, and reimbursements in fixed amounts on convicted offenders. These amounts are to be paid by all offenders, regardless of the severity of the offense, the sentence imposed by the judge, or the offender's ability to pay.[11]

In many American courts, individual judges struggle with the problems that arise from these systems of fine tariffs and fixed-monetary penalties. Sometimes judges try to modify the going rates for fines and the even more rigidly fixed amounts for other monetary penalties on the basis of the offender's ability to pay (Sichel 1982a; Hillsman, Sichel, and Mahoney 1984, p. 64–65, 182). Such modification efforts, however, tend to be on a case-by-case basis and may or may not conform with notions of due process or be demonstrably fair.

E. Disparity and Fairness

The diversity of fining practices in American courts and the related lack of common principles for setting fine amounts reflect American judges' "ambivalence and confusion about fining" (Cole et al. 1987, p. 19).[12] Clearly, however, this confusion does not exclude poor people in

---

[10] In England, e.g., as a matter of sentencing policy, magistrates often impose substantial fines in cases that would otherwise receive short terms of imprisonment, but they also routinely impose high restitution amounts on top of the fine (Casale and Hillsman 1986, p. 56).

[11] For example, in the Maricopa County Superior Court (Phoenix, Ariz.), virtually all felony offenders not incarcerated are subject to a mandatory probation service fee of $30 per month for a period of three years, or a total of $1,080 if probation is not terminated early. They are also required to pay at least $100 to the Victim Compensation Fund. In addition, state statutes require the court to impose the maximum amount of monetary restitution. As a result, almost half of all felony probationers are ordered by the court to pay restitution, reimbursements (primarily for public defense services), or fine sentences, and sometimes a combination of these, in addition to a probation fee and the victim compensation fund contribution (Hillsman and Greene 1988a).

[12] This confusion, according to Cole and Mahoney, can be seen in the very weak linkages between judges' attitudes toward fine sentences and their use of them. "The analysis indicates that there is a small group of judges in both general and limited jurisdiction courts who hold very positive views toward fines and are also heavy users of them in their courts. However, the more dominant pattern among the sample of trial

the United States from being fined; courts across the country are fining offenders who are far from affluent, sometimes in high amounts (Hillsman, Sichel, and Mahoney 1984, pp. 63 ff.; Cole et al. 1987, pp. 28–31). Some poor offenders are fined in lower amounts for misdemeanors such as thefts than are more affluent offenders convicted of misdemeanors such as DWI (Ryan 1980–81; Ragona and Ryan 1983). However, while most middle-class offenders are fined for these offenses, many poor offenders whom judges perceive as unlikely to be able to pay a fine are jailed instead.

Ragona, Rich, and Ryan, for example, found in each of three misdemeanor courts "a pattern of segregation of the economic sanction (fines) from other—seemingly both more and less severe—sanctions (jail and probation). It might initially seem startling to think that courts veer all the way from a jail term to a 'slap on the wrist' (probation) for cases where fines are somehow inappropriate. Yet the underlying rationale seems clear. Where defendants visibly have sufficient resources to pay, they will be fined. Where defendants lack such resources, they will be given probation, sent to jail for a (short) term, or (increasingly in recent years) sentenced to community service restitution" (1981, p. 21). Similarly, Gillespie notes that in felony cases in two Illinois counties "unemployed offenders were more likely to receive a jail sentence than employed offenders" (1982, p. 13). Glaser and Gordon (1988) report from Los Angeles that in misdemeanor convictions, a jail sentence was associated with low income or poor financial status and an unstable or low-status employment record, whereas receiving a financial penalty was associated with a good financial status and higher income. And, in the hypothetical cases judges surveyed by Cole and Mahoney were asked to sentence, a janitor (who had a prior bad check conviction and two larceny convictions) was likely to be imprisoned for the theft of a $40 pair of slacks from a department store; a middle-class accountant (who had one prior DWI conviction), however, was likely to be fined for embezzling $25,000 from his employer (Cole et al. 1987, pp. 9–10).

In summary, while fines are heavily used for a wide variety of cases in American courts, they are rarely used as broadly applicable sanctions in their own right and as alternatives to imprisonment as they are in Western Europe. Furthermore, there is evidence that fines are not

court judges is one in which usage varies extensively and attitudes do not cluster in either direction or intensity" (1987, pp. 18–19).

uniformly imposed and that jail sentences are sometimes an alternative to fines, at least for the poor.

III. Fine Collection and Enforcement

The efficacy of fines as a criminal penalty rests on the ability of courts to collect them, to do so expeditiously, and to compel payment or impose an alternative sanction if offenders fail to meet their obligations to the court. If judges cannot assume the fines will be collected, and if offenders can assume they need not pay them, the potential of this flexible and relatively inexpensive device to punish and deter is seriously eroded (Hillsman and Mahoney 1988).

Routine, systematic information on American courts' success collecting and enforcing fines, however, is lacking despite the introduction of computerized technology and the increased professionalization of court administration. Responsibility for postsentence fine administration in American courts remains fragmented, split not only among court staff but also among police, probation, prosecutors, marshals, city attorneys, and a variety of other civil agencies (Hillsman 1988). Although most courts keep adequate accounting records of individual fine payments, few have developed systems for aggregating and analyzing these data in order to monitor their own collection and enforcement performance (Hillsman, Sichel, and Mahoney 1984, pp. 91–92).[13]

A. Fine Administration

American court administrators traditionally have taken a narrow view of their responsibilities to execute this sentence. They have tended to focus on fines as court orders they must keep track of and as moneys for which they are accountable. This stance appears to stem from the fact that the heaviest volume of fines in many courts flows from traffic and minor criminal offenses, cases in which court administrators can view offenders' compliance with the sentence more from a revenue than from a law enforcement perspective (Hillsman 1988).

A broader definition of fine administration, however, is gaining ground. As courts seek to make greater use of the full range of inter-

[13] Cole and Mahoney report that many of the judges they surveyed are unfamiliar with their own courts' fine collection and enforcement procedures: "The data reported here, although far from conclusive, certainly reinforce the sense that one reason for the infrequent use of the fine as a primary alternative to incarceration and probation is the judges' lack of knowledge about (and confidence in) the process of collection and enforcement. They are only marginally involved in these processes and receive little feedback on their effectiveness" (1987, p. 28).

mediate sentences—community service, treatment orders of various types, restitution, home confinement, fines—they must confront the problem of how to ensure compliance (Hillsman 1988).[14] Without adequate enforcement, these penalties cannot attain the stature of independent, stand-alone sanctions, especially ones that can substitute for imprisonment (Smith 1983–84). Because agencies outside the court (such as law enforcement) have little organizational stake in these noncustodial cases, courts need to expand their own capacity to monitor and encourage compliance from offenders under sentence in the community and to impose more coercive means when compliance is not forthcoming.

This expanded definition of fine administration, more common in Europe, includes a quasi-correctional function. It encompasses responsibility for the enforcement as well as the collection activities that ensure fined offenders will comply with the sentence in a fair and timely fashion. Unlike newer intermediate sentences, there is already a well-established tradition in the United States that courts are the agent responsible for the collection and enforcement of fines (and other financial orders). Most American state statutes, as well as federal statutes, charge courts with this duty (Hillsman, Sichel, and Mahoney 1984, p. 86; see also Public Law 100–85, the Criminal Fine Improvement Act of 1987). While American courts have not always embraced those duties, the increased professionalization of court administration in the last decade should contribute significantly to courts' capacity to carry out this responsibility effectively.

B. Courts' Fine Collection Performance

Fines are, and have long been, big business for American courts. Of the 126 courts surveyed in 1984, 106 collected aggregate fine revenues of over $110 million in a single year. Municipal courts alone in the United States probably collect well over $700 million annually from fines (Hillsman, Sichel, and Mahoney 1984, pp. 75–79).

The fine collection rates of American courts are highly variable; but many courts are more successful than their own judges believe. New York City's lower courts, for example, collect about 75 percent of the criminal fine dollars imposed citywide within one year of sentence.

---

[14] Cole and Mahoney report that the judges they interviewed regard the low priority assigned arrest warrants for fine default by law enforcement agencies as the most common system-related problem in fine collection (1987, p. 27).

Nearly two-thirds of the criminal offenders who are fined pay in full, most within three months of sentence (Zamist, 1986, pp. 97–102).

There is no reason to assume the collection performance of New York City's courts is in any way remarkable. Indeed, there are other successful courts. Gillespie reports a collection rate for fined misdemeanants in Peoria of 80 percent (1982, p. 10), and Glaser and Gordon report that two-thirds of the fined misdemeanants in Los Angeles pay in full, and one quarter in part (1988, p. 42).

Courts in Western Europe also have high collection rates even though they serve large, heterogeneous populations and use fines extensively for serious crimes. Albrecht and Johnson report an 80 percent collection rate for the courts of Baden-Württemberg in West Germany (1980), and West German criminal justice officials indicate this result is not unusual (Greene 1987). Rates of between 70 and 80 percent are not uncommon in English magistrates' courts (Softley 1977; Casale 1981). Collection rates for repeat offenders sentenced by English magistrates to fines in lieu of imprisonment are between 55 and 75 percent despite their high amounts and offenders' unemployment and lack of financial resources (Casale and Hillsman 1986).

Fine collection statistics such as these—based on the payment performance of all (or a sample) of individual offenders fined during a specific time period and tracked over a given period (such as one year)—are rarely available because courts fail to analyze their record data adequately. The statistics we have, however, lend credibility to the rougher estimates court administrators provide about their collection performance. Four out of ten court administrators surveyed in 1984, for example, reported that half or more of fined offenders in their courts pay in full on the day of sentence. Three out of ten reported that over 80 percent of those who pay over time do so in full within the period set by the court, and another four out of ten reported full collection on schedule for between 50 and 80 percent (Hillsman, Sichel, and Mahoney 1984, p. 85). The considerable diversity in success rates in similar types of courts, however, suggests that differences in their collection techniques and enforcement strategies are important to explaining the success with which they collect fines.

C. Collection Practices[15]

Although courts are typically given the statutory duty of collecting fines, how they do so is rarely regulated by statute or administrative

---

[15] Two related, but nonetheless distinct, stages of the postsentence fine administration

rule. Courts have a limited range of methods at their disposal to encourage offenders to meet their financial obligations. Generally these involve techniques designed to set reasonable terms for payment, monitor payments closely, and encourage prompt payment. Many courts fail to use even these simple but effective tools.

1. *Installment Systems.* Setting fine payments in installments is one of the most important dimensions of a court's collection activities. Supreme Court decisions beginning with *Tate v. Short* (401 U.S. 395 [1971]) have established constitutional standards for fine collection. In *Tate*, the Court noted that "the State is not powerless to enforce judgments against those financially unable to pay a fine" but also observed that there were many alternatives to immediate imprisonment and cited with approval the state statutes providing for installment payments.

In the years following *Tate*, many states added statutory provisions authorizing installment payments in order to improve fine collections without raising constitutional issues or the specter of the debtors prison. Most courts appear to offer formal or informal installment plans to all who request time to pay because it is difficult for courts to determine who is legally "indigent" and, therefore, eligible for the special treatment required by Supreme Court decisions.

The major collection issue for courts is not whether to use installments but how to do so fairly and effectively. As Cole and Mahoney report, "installment payment arrangements seem to be widely and indiscriminately used" (1987, p. 23). This is because many courts lack general rules or standards for setting the size and frequency of payments. Even those that have such standards readily acknowledge that these tend to be administrative "rules of thumb," requiring all or most fines to be paid within a set time period, rather than rules developed from empirical analysis of offenders' behavior or from careful review of individual circumstances (Hillsman, Sichel, and Mahoney 1984, p. 90; Casale and Hillsman 1986, p. 82). As a result, courts often relax their payment rules or abandon them, with many fines either excused or written off.

---

process should be distinguished. Although the terms "collection" and "enforcement" are typically used interchangeably, they encompass different functions and methods. Some methods courts use to promote fine payment are designed to encourage or assist offenders to make payments voluntarily (e.g., reminder letters, interest charges). Still others are clearly coercive (e.g., arrest warrants, property seizures). Although all these techniques are (or should be) linked in an overall strategy to ensure compliance, methods to elicit payment that are enabling or persuasive should be viewed as part of a court's *collection* process, as distinguished from methods that are coercive and, therefore, are part of its *enforcement* effort.

Research on fine collection suggests that, to be effective, courts should first set fine amounts more closely to offenders' financial circumstances (as well as to their offenses) and then establish payment terms that are as short as possible given these conditions (Casale and Hillsman 1986, pp. 87, 117; Hillsman and Greene 1987, p. 103).

2. *Monitoring Systems.*   Virtually all courts recognize that they need to monitor fined offenders' payments in order to ensure they continue to pay, no matter how long the installment period. However, while American courts tend to do a good job keeping track of the money offenders pay, very few live up to the fine collection standard articulated by one experienced U.S. Attorney: "the key to success in collecting money owed the Government rests in prompt accounting and necessary and repeated communication with the debtor" (Sichel 1982*b*, p. 13).

Research on successful courts confirms this observation (as do the debt-collection experiences). When courts notify offenders that payments are due, closely monitor their performance, and swiftly respond to late payments, even sizable fines can be collected successfully from offenders who are not affluent (Softley and Moxon 1982; Casale and Hillsman 1986). Nevertheless, many American courts are only now beginning to introduce even the simplest monitoring systems into their fine-administration activities, and many of these are doing so primarily for traffic offenders in response to the revenue demands of local government authorities (Tait 1988; Wick 1988). Few courts in the United States have established individualized monitoring systems that maximize compliance with criminal fine sentences (see, e.g., East Court as described in Casale and Hillsman 1986, pp. 152–55, and Hillsman and Greene 1987, chap. 6), although the federal system is now moving in this direction (Hillsman 1986, pp. 6–9). While doing so might mean more court personnel, increased fine revenues and reduced reliance on incarceration for fine default are likely to cover the added expense (Millar 1984; Wick 1988).[16]

---

[16] This point has important implications for the development of an overall criminal justice policy with regard to the use of fines as criminal sanctions. While most economic models for assessing the optimal use of fines in sentencing have generally supported the notion that fines are cost effective as sentences, until recently these models have not taken collection costs or uncollected revenues directly into account. Lewis, however, has done so by applying economic models to England that reflect different sentencing and collection scenarios as applied to theft cases (1988). He concludes that "fines are an economically useful sanction and that reducing or eliminating the use of imprisonment for default, reminder letters, or means inquiries is likely to *increase the amount of theft and the net social cost of crime*" (p. 36, emphasis added).

3. *Interest and Surcharges.*   Courts can also build incentives into the collection process to encourage prompt payment. Few have done so; as a result, evidence about the effectiveness of these techniques in court' settings is lacking.

Primary among the potential incentives are interest charges on outstanding fine balances and surcharges imposed after a specified period has passed without full fine payment or when extraordinary actions must be taken to collect the fine. In 1984, the U.S. Congress enacted legislation to allow federal courts to impose interest charges to facilitate collection, and some states, such as Washington, have passed laws permitting courts to pass along some collection costs (Wick 1988).

D. Enforcement Practices

The perception that enforcement problems are insurmountable has been a drawback to the use of fines in American courts for some time (Carter and Cole 1979). Once the period for collection of the fine has passed without full payment, the court faces the necessity of compelling payment or imposing an alternative sanction. Almost half the limited-jurisdiction court judges and over 60 percent of the general-jurisdiction court judges surveyed by Cole and Mahoney perceived their courts to have moderate or major problems in the enforcement of fines (1987, p. 22). Research on fine administration suggests, however, that if the relatively simple, inexpensive, and noncoercive fine-*collection* techniques discussed above are implemented effectively, most courts will need to impose the more coercive and costly *enforcement* techniques on relatively few offenders (Softley and Moxon 1982; Casale and Hillsman 1986).

A variety of coercive methods are authorized under state and federal statutes. The most commonly used is imprisonment for default. Some courts will substitute labor for monetary payment. A few also use civil procedures, including wage garnishment and property seizure; experimentation with such techniques is more common in Western Europe (Casale and Hillsman 1986; Greene 1987).

1. *Imprisonment.*   All states provide some mechanism by which imprisonment can be used as an enforcement device (Hillsman, Sichel, and Mahoney 1984, pp. 108 ff). Practitioners in American and European courts report that the threat of immediate jailing is very effective in getting fined offenders to pay. This is confirmed by even casual observation; in most courts, the "miracle of the cells"—the dash forward, cash in hand, of family or friends after a judge threatens a

defaulter with imprisonment—is a routine occurrence (Hillsman, Sichel, and Mahoney 1984, p. 113).[17]

It is only when the fine defaulter is without funds that the threat of imprisonment becomes troubling. American judges tend to deal with this problem by asking offenders, often perfunctorily, about the reasons for their default, accepting their plea of poverty and then either extending the time to pay (which only postpones confronting the problem) or remitting the outstanding amount. However, this response is by no means universal. Over half the court administrators surveyed in 1984 reported that their judges commonly jail fine defaulters (Hillsman, Sichel, and Mahoney 1984, p. 116).

The U.S. Supreme Court has provided some, but not much, guidance on this problem (Dawson 1982; Hillsman, Sichel, and Mahoney 1984, pp. 118 ff). In three major decisions over the last two decades, the Court has addressed due process and equal protection issues arising from state courts' efforts to enforce fines by imprisonment for default (*Williams v. Illinois*, 399 U.S. 235 [1970]; *Tate v. Short*, 401 U.S. 395 [1971]; *Bearden v. Georgia*, 461 U.S. 660 [1983]). The thrust of these decisions is, as Justice White wrote in a concurring opinion in *Bearden*, that "poverty does not insulate those who break the law from punishment." However, the Court has imposed limits on the use of imprisonment and set procedural requirements when imprisonment is used.

If the offense does not carry imprisonment as an authorized penalty, for example, the Court has ruled that judges may not imprison for default unless the default is willful. If the offender is indigent, the judge must consider whether the state's interest in punishment and deterrence can be met by some noncustodial sanction before imprisoning. The Court has not ruled, however, on whether an indigent defendant in such a case can be jailed for default if he has tried but been unable to pay the fine. In *Tate* the Court explicitly left this issue open to "await the presentation of a concrete case" (p. 401), an event that is yet to occur.

In cases where the underlying offense does carry the possibility of an imprisonment sentence, judges have more leeway to enforce fines by imprisonment. If the defendant has been given time to pay and has not

---

[17] The "miracle of the cells" is also confirmed by statistical research that shows a sizable number of defaulting offenders returning to court after receiving notices that a warrant has been issued for their arrest (Zamist 1986, pp. 92–97; Casale and Hillsman 1986). Similar evidence about the effectiveness of the threat (and actual use) of jail can be found in research on the enforcement of child support orders (Chambers 1979).

done so, judges may imprison. Even under these circumstances, however, the Court's ruling in *Bearden* strongly suggests that the sentencing judge should first examine alternative measures before imprisoning. Courts in both the United States and Western Europe have begun to explore alternative enforcement approaches, particularly work programs and civil procedures (Hillsman and Mahoney 1988).

2. *Work Programs.* Work programs or community service are seldom used as a response to fine default in the United States, although the statutes of at least half the states provide a mechanism for doing so (Hillsman, Sichel, and Mahoney 1984, pp. 125 ff.). The English have not used this option because they fear that existing work programs for sentenced offenders will be overwhelmed by fine defaulters (West 1979). This is a reasonable concern largely because English courts set high fine amounts without taking systematic account of offenders' ability to pay (Casale and Hillsman 1986). By contrast, in West Germany, where fines are also designed to be punitive but are set in relation to means as well as offense severity, community service placements for fine defaulters are seldom needed but are used for those on public assistance or who are unemployed (Greene 1987).

Work programs can be expensive fine-enforcement devices, especially if they must be supervised directly by the court or by its paid agent (McDonald 1986, pp. 190–98). Nevertheless, if courts set fine amounts properly and implement collection strategies effectively, the number of fine defaulters in work programs should be kept to a minimum.

3. *Civil Procedures including Property Seizure.* The court's choice of a fine is a policy decision to punish and deter without imprisonment. Because the fine is fundamentally a noncustodial penalty, enforcement through imprisonment should generally be viewed as a failure of the fining process itself. Civil techniques to deprive the offender of his property should be tried in all but exceptional cases before depriving the offender of his liberty. In particular, as has been done successfully in Europe, American courts could develop the capacity to enforce fines through threat of property seizure (Hillsman 1988).

While the image of civil mechanisms may suggest gentle treatment of defaulters, the seizure of financial assets and the seizure and sale of personal property can result in substantial economic deprivation. Nevertheless, there appears to be relatively little use of these procedures in American courts, although most state statutes provide the legal authority to do so. European experience, however, suggests that this technique should be tried more often in routine criminal cases as well as in serious cases involving criminals with substantial assets (Casale 1981; Casale and Hillsman 1986, pp. 187–211).[18]

European experience indicates that credible threats work: it is rare that goods are actually seized and sold in payment of the fine because, as with all coercive devices, property seizure works primarily by threat. As one civilian bailiff, who serves "distress" warrants (those ordering the seizure of property) for a provincial magistrates' court in England, said: "Everyone has something he doesn't want to lose, even if no one else wants it" (Casale 1981).[19]

E. Characteristics of Successful Courts

Fining must be viewed as a process in which how the fine is imposed is inextricably linked with the success of its collection and enforcement. Setting the amount of the penalty is the key to successful fine sentencing. The amount of the fine relative to the offender's financial resources determines the potential punitive content of the sentence and its deterrent value, but it also strongly influences whether the penalty can be delivered as imposed.

Three sets of conditions characterize courts whose fine outcomes are successful (Hillsman, Sichel, and Mahoney 1984, pp. 101–4, 203–21; Casale and Hillsman 1986, pp. 99–104, 177–86). First, fines are set in relation to offenders' financial circumstances. Only then is the level of punishment appropriate to the severity of the crime meaningful to the offender and enforceable—that is, an amount the offender can be expected to pay, albeit not without incurring some financial hardship.

Second, collection procedures emphasize reasonable payment schedules, close monitoring of offenders' performance, and swift response to nonpayment.

Third, enforcement efforts to compel payment do not start with

[18] Increased emphasis on forfeiture suggests that some American courts are beginning to rely more heavily on civil procedures in at least some types of criminal cases. In addition, recent changes in federal law create a lien on an offender's property at the time a fine is imposed and permit the lien to be enforced by the efficient administrative procedures now used in federal tax cases (Comprehensive Crime Control Act of 1984 and the Fine Enforcement Act of 1984). These statutory provisions permit the federal courts, for the first time, to view the seizure of property, rather than imprisonment, as the appropriate coercive device toward which the fine enforcement process should move.

[19] In contrast to property seizure, European courts, as well as many American courts, are uneasy about the use of wage garnishments for two reasons. First, many believe that they transfer the costs of the fine default to the employer rather than to the court or to the offender; second, many are concerned that some offenders will lose their jobs because employers do not wish to process the wage attachment orders.

threats of imprisonment but are characterized by a steady progression of mounting pressure and increased threat of more coercive responses. These include civil mechanisms to deprive the offender of property and noncustodial punishments if nonwillful default appears likely; imprisonment for default is thus the last resort.

While most empirical research has focused on specific collection and enforcement devices, it is the effectiveness of courts' overall strategies that determines how successful they will be in ensuring compliance with fine sentences.

IV. The European Day Fine: Making Fines a More Useful Criminal Sanction

The experiences of several Western European countries suggest that methods are available—particularly in the form of day-fine systems— to tailor fine amounts simultaneously and with greater precision to variations in offenses and in individual circumstances. While these European countries have somewhat different social structures and welfare policies, all are characterized by an unequal distribution of wealth and a population of criminal offenders heavily drawn from the bottom ranks of that distribution (Townsend 1979; George and Lawson 1980). Thus to make broad use of economic penalties, Western European criminal justice systems have had to develop principles and practices for imposing means-based fines, and their success at doing so has attracted the attention of American judges and legal scholars for some time (Botein and Sturz 1964, p. 215; Morris 1974, pp. 7 ff., and 1987, p. 4; Gillespie 1980, 1981; Friedman 1983; Ryan 1983).

Fines are the primary alternative to imprisonment in England, West Germany, and Sweden. In West Germany, the tendency toward using the fine in lieu of short terms of imprisonment has been growing over the last hundred years (Stenner 1970; Friedman 1983). This trend became more dramatic after the country's 1969 penal code revision that directs West German courts to impose prison sentences under six months "only when special circumstances, present in the act or in the personality of the offender, make the imposition of the sentence indispensable for effecting an impression on the offender or defending the legal order" (quoted in Friedman 1983, pp. 285–86).

The more recent predominance of the fine as an alternative in the English sentencing system is less clearly attributable to a dramatic shift away from imprisonment; however, a similar pattern is discernible in England in relation to more serious offenses (Casale 1981). An analysis of convictions for offenses of violence against the person between 1938 and 1960 in England and Wales shows a shift from short-term imprisonment to the fine (McClintock 1963, p. 149).

Even in Sweden, where short-term incarceration remains a pillar of the sanctioning system, there is a clear tendency for Swedish courts to see the fine as the more appropriate sentence when the law allows either alternative (Casale 1981). Sweden has recently considered increasing its fine schedules so that fines can compete more effectively with the punitive impact of imprisonment (Greene 1987).

A. The Day-Fine Concept

Day-fine systems provide variable fine amounts that contrast directly with the fixed-fine or "going rate" systems typical of American courts.[20] All types of day fines, so-called because their amount is typically linked to an offender's daily income, have a similar underlying structure. The fundamental idea is to separate the calculation of the fine amount into two components: the first adjusts the amount for the severity of the offense and the second adjusts it for the offender's financial circumstances. While the major purpose of this approach is to give fines a more consistent impact across rich and poor, the approach also structures the sentencing process so that the outcome is more visible as well as more rational. As Friedman points out, "[The West German day-fine method] thereby offered a calculation procedure from which both an offender and a reviewing court could discern the reasons underlying the amount of the fine" (1983, p. 186).

As a practical matter, judges using a day-fine approach first set the sentence at a certain number of fine units (e.g., 20, 50, 150) reflecting the degree of punishment the judge deems appropriate for the gravity of the criminal behavior. Most day-fine systems rely on flexible but written guidelines developed by individual jurisdictions to determine the appropriate number of fine units. Offenders convicted of crimes of equivalent gravity can be assigned the number of fine units that would correspond to a sentence handed down without regard to their financial status.

The second stage is to determine the monetary value of each fine

---

[20] The idea of variable fining systems is hardly new as Friedman points out (1983, p. 281, n. 4). He calls attention to the fact that in thirteenth-century England, fine amounts were set in relation to the offender's wealth and that Jeremy Bentham advocated the variable fine in his work *The Theory of Legislation* (1931). Casale also notes the idea's long-standing tradition in Germany (1981, p. 21).

unit, basing this decision on the individual's economic circumstances. Jurisdictions using day-fine systems have developed uniform but flexible methods of calculating what is an equitable share of the offender's daily income, typically using information that is routinely available from the police, the court, the probation office, or (most often) the defendant and his or her counsel.

B. The History of Day-Fine Systems

Day-fine systems were initially proposed by Scandinavian criminologists. The first day-fine system was implemented in Finland in 1921, followed by Sweden in 1931, Cuba in 1936, Denmark in 1939, and West Germany and Austria in 1975 (Albrecht and Johnson 1980, p. 6; Casale 1981, p. 21; Friedman 1983, p. 282). The day-fine concept is also found in the penal laws of Peru (1924), Brazil (1969), Costa Rica (1972), and Bolivia (1972) (Beristani 1976, pp. 258–59, cited in Albrecht and Johnson, p. 6).[21]

The day-fine systems in Sweden and West Germany are commonly viewed as the most sophisticated (Austria's is modeled on West Germany's), and they have been the topic of most description and discussion (Thornstedt 1974, 1985; Albrecht 1980; Albrecht and Johnson 1980; Casale 1981; Friedman 1983; Hillsman, Sichel, and Mahoney 1984, app. C). The West German experience is most relevant to American policy both because it is recent and because the German legal system has greater similarity to the American system in relevant ways (e.g., with regard to legal limitations on access to information about offenders' means).

The West German day-fine system was designed as a central part of the country's first major revision of its criminal code since 1871. Its development began with the formation of a commission in 1954, resulted in passage of the first and second Criminal Law Reform Acts of 1969, and was completed when the statutory provisions mandating the day-fine system took effect in 1975 (Friedman 1983, pp. 281–87).

The use of fine sentences, particularly in lieu of short terms of imprisonment, has increased steadily in Germany since the early 1880s

---

[21] Taking account of an offender's means in determining fine amounts is also of considerable concern in England. The high court, e.g., requires a sentencing court "to consider first what type of sentence is appropriate. If it decides that the appropriate type of sentence is a fine, it is then necessary to consider what would be the appropriate amount of fine having regard to the gravity (or otherwise) of the offense. Finally . . . the court should consider whether or not to modify this amount having regard to the offender's means" (Latham 1980, pp. 85–86).

when the first official statistics became available (Albrecht and Johnson 1980, pp. 6–8). A criminal code revision introduced in 1962 allowed fines to replace short terms of imprisonment and required that they be calculated on a per diem basis (Friedman 1983, p. 284). This provision did not go far enough for some policymakers, however, who wanted all short terms eliminated because, they reasoned, such sentences could not be reconciled with any rehabilitative goal (Friedman 1983, pp. 284–85). The first Criminal Law Reform Act (1969) was a compromise, directing the West German courts to use fines as the primary sanction for crimes traditionally penalized by imprisonment, and to use short terms only when they were deemed indispensable (Friedman 1983, pp. 285–86).

The day-fine provision in the second reform act lays out the general rules for the two independent stages of fine computation to be followed by all German courts but leaves it to each jurisdiction to develop specific guidelines for determining both the exact number of day-fine units to be imposed and the precise method for valuing each unit. Courts have evolved their own guidelines and they vary by region. Observers of the West German system note, however, that in some regions the range of units for offenses gives so much latitude (e.g., ten to fifty units for theft) that it is difficult to talk of "guidelines" in any formal sense (Albrecht 1980).

In setting the number of day-fine units (*Tagessatze*)—which, by statute, can range from five to 360—West German courts must take into account the offender's culpability by examining the offender's motivation and method and the circumstances surrounding the crime. In establishing the value of each day-fine unit—which, by statute, can range from two German marks to 10,000—the courts are instructed to use some fraction of the offender's average net daily income (considering salary, pensions, welfare benefits, interest, and dividends, exclusive of taxes and business expenses for the self-employed), so long as it is not so high as to deprive the offender or his dependents of a minimal standard of living. Finally, the law calls for publication of the number of units and their value for each day-fine set by the court so that the sentence's components are known (Friedman 1983, pp. 287–88).

Sentences to short terms of imprisonment decreased dramatically after 1969 as a result of the first Criminal Law Reform Act and have continued to decline. Prior to this statutory change, over 110,000 prison sentences of less than six months were imposed each year in West Germany (20 percent of all convictions); the number declined after the code revision to just over 10,000 (1.8 percent) in 1976 (Gillespie 1980, pp. 20–21). Despite the correlative increase in fine sentencing, there has been no increase either in the rate of fine defaults or the administrative burden to the courts (Albrecht and Johnson 1980; Friedman 1983, pp. 291 ff.). The major effect of introducing the day fine appears to be an increase in the average fine amount, reflecting just punishment for the more affluent; fines for poorer offenders have remained relatively low (Albrecht and Johnson 1980, p. 10).

In assessing the policy changes that resulted in the West German day-fine system, Albrecht and Johnson (1980) observe that they centered

> on the themes of effective administration and the legitimacy of the legal system. They have tested the capacity of the criminal justice system to administer prison sentences and public willingness to forgo such sentences for relatively minor offenses. The volume of convicted offenders exceeded the capacity of prisons. . . . Political leaders and the general public are aware that the combination of fines and penal orders can be administered with relative ease, quickly, and cheaply, without undue stigmatization. . . .
> Further, greater resort to fines and probation as alternatives to imprisonment broadens the distinction between minor and "heavy" criminality as a means of taking advantage of the chance for resocializing the offender. [Pp. 7–8]

Albrecht and Johnson conclude that "Ten years after the introduction of the fine on a large scale, our data support the view that the policy has been found politically acceptable, administratively practical, and penologically sound" (p. 13).

C. Contrasts between the Swedish and West German Day-Fine Models

The Swedish and West German day-fine systems are somewhat different in operation and in what they seek to accomplish. The West German system views fines as a replacement or "ransom" for terms of incarceration and they are accordingly designed to be burdensome. Fines as "economic jail" provide a milder measure of economic deprivation in Sweden, although they can be sustained over fairly long periods (Greene 1986).

1. *The Swedish System.*   Developed in the early 1920s, Swedish day-fine sentences are based on a fairly narrow range of day-fine units, from one to 120 (180 for multiple offenses), reflecting their primary intended use for less serious offenses than is the case in West Germany. More

recent proposals would raise the day-fine unit scale to 200 units for a single offense and increase the maximum possible day-fine amount. The objectives are to encourage the imposition of day fines in lieu of imprisonment and to create provisions for the use of day fines against corporations involved in economic crimes (Greene 1987, p. 5).

Guidance as to the number of day-fine units appropriate for crimes of varying severity is provided by circulars promulgated by the regional public prosecutor's office for use in routine cases that can be resolved by prosecutor's penal orders (rather than by an appearance in court). These circulars rank offenses by their seriousness and assign a prescribed number or range of day-fine units that increases with the gravity of the offense. Swedish courts generally follow these benchmarks in routine cases and follow "unwritten rules" established by practice in more serious cases (Greene 1987, p. 7). Official statistics indicate that actual sentences in Sweden are distributed as expected from the benchmarks (*Kriminalstatistik For Brott Lagforda Personer, 1987*, 1988). Generally, no allowance is made for prior record in determining the number of day-fine units, and for some crimes (such as petty larceny), the same day fine may be given again and again with the number based entirely on the value of the property taken. For other types of crimes (drunk driving, for example), repeat offenders are unlikely to receive a series of day fines but will move up the sentencing ladder to a suspended custodial sentence (Greene 1987, p. 13).

The Swedish method for handling the second step in the day-fine process—valuing the day-fine units—is daunting in its technical complexity and is possible only because courts have legal access to income and tax records for checking the highly detailed information that is required (Thornstedt 1974, pp. 608 ff.). The method was set forth in a procedural circular issued by the state prosecutor general in 1973. The calculation is based on the individual's gross annual income, from which are subtracted business expenses, maintenance, or living expenses. There is a 20 percent reduction for persons married or living together on a regular basis, but if the other person is employed, 20 percent of the second income is added to the offender's sum. Half the basic child maintenance rate for Sweden is then subtracted for each dependent child. The day-fine value is then calculated by dividing the resulting figure by 1,000 to reduce the unit value to about one-third of the offender's daily income. This adjusted, gross day-fine value is reduced on a graduated basis to make it net of taxes and is then subject to a scale of adjustments for capital wealth and for significant debts.

The Swedish day-fine method reflects a concept of fines as providing relatively modest economic deprivation over a period of time determined by the gravity of the offense (Greene 1986, p. 9). This approach is continued in the provision in the Swedish system for converting the day fine to jail in the event of default: a sliding scale begins at ten days' imprisonment for five day-fine units but ranges to a maximum of ninety days for 180 units.

About half of all convictions for property offenses in Sweden result in fines as do half of all crimes of violence against the person; this sentencing pattern takes place in a day-fine system in which fines can range overall from about $1.50 to over $17,000. In contrast, three-quarters of all property offenses are fined in West Germany, as are two-thirds of all crimes involving violence against persons; this sentencing pattern occurs in a day-fine system in which fine amounts can range from about $5.00 to over $1.8 million. West Germany, therefore, has chosen a method for determining both the range of day-fine units and the value of each unit that results in stiffer fines than is typical in Sweden (Greene 1986, p. 9).

2. *The West German System.* The West German system provides a more severe scale of punitive impact than does the Swedish system. Although there is no direct correspondence between the number of day-fine units and terms of imprisonment imposed for similar offenses in West Germany, the 360 maximum is logically linked to the idea of a one-year prison term, an exchange that is further underscored by the statutory rule that, in cases of default, one day fine must correspond to one day of imprisonment for nonpayment (Horn 1974, p. 625).

In setting the day-fine value by statute as the net daily income (not discounted for financial responsibilities), the West German system also seems to preserve the day's-wages-for-a-jail-day exchange economy that stems from the original purpose of the reform (Greene 1986, p. 8). However, unlike Sweden (but more like the United States and England), West German courts have no formal access to the offender's income or tax records. Indeed, absolute accuracy in establishing income is not demanded by German law, which recognizes that, in some circumstances, only an approximate measure will be feasible (Friedman 1983, pp. 288–89). The West German experience indicates, therefore, that lack of formal legal recourse to means information is no barrier to the success of a day-fine system.

In practice, West German court officials have some information from the police on employment status, occupation, and living circumstances, which is supplemented by brief oral investigation by the judge. In most cases, the information can be converted, if roughly, into the net daily income. West German officials report a high degree of confidence that, in most cases, the information obtained from the offender is reliable; only with self-employed professionals and business people do they find a lack of candor and a tendency to underreport. In these cases, the judges have statutory power to assess the offender's income de facto; the judge merely announces the day-fine value based on a "best guess" as to net income. While this outcome is subject to appeal, offenders rarely do so, which suggests to one observer that "these powers are either used with judicious restraint, or tempered by the defendant's cooperation when faced with a 'generous' best guess by the judge" (Greene 1986, p. 15).

3. *Day Fines for America?*   When asked about the desirability and feasibility of experimenting with day-fine systems in the United States, over half of a national sample of trial judges said such a system could work in their courts (Mahoney and Thornton 1988). The advantages they saw from such a system are what one would expect: it would be fairer and more equitable.

The disadvantages these judges saw largely concern implementation. They feared, for example, that day fines could be difficult and expensive to administer if means information were not readily available. A potentially more difficult obstacle reported by some of the judges was their perception that a day-fine system, like other methods to structure sentencing decisions, would restrict their discretion. Such reservations, however, are not universal or necessarily lasting, particularly if judges play a central role in the process of establishing the sentencing standards. As Norval Morris has pointed out: "The experience of Minnesota and Washington [sentencing commissions] has been that, while the judges screamed and fought about the introduction of sentencing guidelines, when they got them, they adhered to them, and were pleased with them" (1987, pp. 4–5).

V. Adapting Day Fines to American Courts

In 1986, the Vera Institute of Justice in New York City began to explore possibilities for adapting the day-fine concept to courts in the United States. With planning support from the National Institute of Justice and from the German Marshall Fund of the United States, the Institute initiated the first of two planning efforts in 1986 in conjunction with the Richmond County Criminal Court (Staten Island, New York) and the Richmond County District Attorney's Office. The goal was to design a day-fine system that would replace a fixed-fine system with a method of setting variable fines, tailored specifically to the court, that would take into account offenders' means and the severity of their offenses. The day-fine system that resulted is an amalgam of the West German and the Swedish models. Judges in the Richmond court began imposing day fines in lieu of fixed fines in August 1988.

The pilot test, funded by the National Institute of Justice and the city of New York, will be completed in 1990. In addition to the use of day fines, the pilot encompasses an enhanced system of fine collection and enforcement and an evaluation to assess the overall results of the pilot (Hillsman and Greene 1987). The pilot project parallels a second effort by the Vera Institute, which is taking place in the Superior Court of Maricopa County (Phoenix, Arizona), to adapt the day-fine concept to American courts. In Phoenix, however, the emphasis is on using the day-fine's two-stage method of tailoring fine amounts to help a court rationalize not only its imposition of fines but also its use of a proliferating number of other mandatory and discretionary financial penalties.

A. Day Fines in Staten Island

The motivation behind the Richmond County Criminal Court's interest in day fines as well as for the support of the county's district attorney was expressed by one of the court's judges: "What is needed in our overall sentencing framework is an opportunity to impose a fine that is meaningfully tailored to the individual, so that the offender understands that crime does not pay, rather it is the criminal who pays" (McBrien 1988, p. 42). Similarly, the assistant district attorney in charge of the Staten Island Criminal Court, Arnold Berliner, said of the day fine: "This can make [the fine] a more viable sanction. One of the functions of criminal fines is to make it hurt a little bit. By having some idea of the economic effect, you have an idea whether it's just a slap on the wrist or for real. The way it is now, fines are basically just imposed 'off the hip.' " (Hurley 1988).[22]

Staten Island's criminal court is a fairly typical limited-jurisdiction

[22] New York statutes provide no legal barrier to introducing a day-fine system for setting fine amounts. There are, however, certain statutory limitations to experimenting with any variable fine system. Primary among these are statutory fine maxima of $1,000 for class A misdemeanors, $500 for class B misdemeanors, and $250 for violations. The second statutory limitation occurs when either fixed-fine amounts or minimum fines are mandated. In New York State, this occurs for several important vehicle and traffic law offenses routinely sentenced by judges in the Staten Island court (including, for example, DWI cases).

court, and its social and economic base makes it similar to many small American cities or moderate-sized suburban communities. Both fines and terms of imprisonment under one year are staples of the court's sentences. Fines are the single most heavily used sanction (imposed in almost half the cases, including many that are charged as felonies after screening by the prosecutor but are reduced to misdemeanors for sentencing), followed by imprisonment (imposed in almost 20 percent of the court's cases). But because the community is characterized by relative affluence, combined with a small but significant poverty population, the issue of fairness in the use of these two sentences is of concern to all.

1. *Components of the Staten Island Day-Fine Sentence.* The guidelines (or "benchmarks") for setting the number of day-fine units in use by the Staten Island court were developed by a planning group that included the judges, prosecutors, and defense lawyers as well as Vera Institute planners (Hillsman and Greene 1987, chaps. 2–4; Hillsman and Greene 1988*b*). Assuming that the West German scale of 360 day-fine units would be sufficient to cover the full range of violation, misdemeanor, and felony offenses in the New York State Penal Law, the planning group selected a partial range of five to 120 units for conviction for violations and misdemeanors in the Staten Island court. This decision brought the overall unit range closer to that of Sweden, which also uses day fines primarily for less serious offenses. A floor of five units was set to avoid trivializing fines imposed for cases at the lowest end of the scale.

To distribute the offenses sentenced in Staten Island across this 115-unit range, the planning group ranked the court's seventy most common misdemeanors and violations according to the relative degree of seriousness reflected by the criminal behaviors typically involved. This resulted in classification of six severity levels ranging from lesser offenses involving breaches of public decorum and community standards of behavior to the more serious victimizing offenses that are often charged as felonies but disposed as misdemeanors. (See table 3 for selections from this classification of penal law offenses).

Finally, each offense was assigned a specific number of day-fine units as the presumptive sentence or benchmark. However, because individual cases present judges and prosecutors with aggravating or mitigating factors not taken into account in establishing the benchmarks, the day-fine unit scales provide an upper and lower range of 15 percent on either side of the benchmark. For example, although it is assumed that judges will take prior record into account in making the initial decision whether to fine or to impose another type of sentence, a prior conviction (or an aggravating factor) might move the sentence toward the upper bound whereas no prior record (or a mitigating factor) might warrant a lower-bound fine.

Table 4 provides some examples from the full Staten Island day-fine scales. Assault third degree (Penal Law [P.L.] 120.00) is an A misdemeanor carrying a fine maximum of $1,000. However, the real-life behaviors for which offenders are convicted of this offense span a fairly wide range, according to judges, prosecutors, and defense attorneys in Staten Island. As a result, the day-fine benchmark scales distinguish four levels of assaults by the severity of the injury (minor/severe) and by the type of victim involved. Similarly, the day-fine benchmarks for petit larceny (P.L. 155.25), an A misdemeanor, also have levels, in this case reflecting the amount or value of the property taken. While many penal law offenses have only a single presumptive day-fine benchmark, set in its 15 percent plus or minus range (e.g., criminal trespass third degree, a B misdemeanor, is twenty day-fine units, with a range from seventeen to twenty-three), others have several levels to cover the behaviors subsumed under the legal or statutory categories (e.g., menacing, sexual misconduct, criminal mischief, attempted grand larceny, unauthorized use of a vehicle, criminal possession of stolen property).

The procedure for valuing the day-fine unit primarily determines how punitive the day-fine system is. The planning group in the Staten Island court decided to steer a middle course between the West German and Swedish approaches, recognizing that many of the offenses dealt with by the Staten Island court are at the less serious end (as in Sweden) but also wanting the court's day-fine system to provide an opportunity for fines to substitute for short terms of imprisonment in appropriate cases (as in West Germany).

The value of the day-fine unit in Staten Island, therefore, is based on net daily income (as in West Germany). However, this amount is adjusted downward twice, first for the offender's family responsibilities and then by a standard rate (as in Sweden) to bring the overall day-fine levels closer to the Staten Island court's current fixed-fine levels, particularly at the lower end of the severity scale.

The adjustment for dependents is based on practices commonly used in American courts for determining child support payments.[23] The

---

[23] The net daily income figure is discounted by 15 percent for the offender's self-support, 15 percent for the first dependent (including a spouse), 15 percent for the second dependent, 10 percent for the next two dependents, and five percent for each additional dependent.

TABLE 3

Broad Classification of Penal Law Offenses into Staten Island Day-Fine Benchmark Severity Levels (Partial List)

Severity Level/Penal Law Number		Behavior	Offense and Degree	Day-Fine Units	
Level 1 (95–120 Day-Fine Units):					
130.20	AM	Harm persons	Sexual misconduct	90–120	DF
120.00	AM	Harm persons	Assault 3	20–95	DF
Level 2 (65–90 Day-Fine Units):					
260.10	AM	Harm persons	Endangerment of child welfare	20–90	DF
215.50	AM	Obstruction of justice	Criminal contempt 2	75	DF
120.20	AM	Harm persons	Reckless endangerment 2	65	DF
110–155.30	AM	Property	Attempted grand larceny 4	20–65	DF
Level 3 (45–60 Day-Fine Units):					
265.01	AM	Weapons	Possession of weapon 4	35–60	DF
155.25	AM	Property	Petit larceny	5–60	DF
165.40	AM	Property	Possession of stolen property 5	5–60	DF
165.05	AM	Property	Unauthorized use of vehicle	5–60	DF
221.40	AM	Drugs	Sale of Marijuana 4	50	DF
225.05	AM	Misconduct	Promotion of gambling 2	50	DF
220.03	AM	Drugs	Possession of contraband substance 7	35–50	DF
110–120.00	BM	Harm persons	Attempted assault 3	10–45	DF

86

Level 4 (30–40 Day-Fine Units):

Code	Type	Category	Offense		Units	
170.05	AM	Theft	Forgery 3		40	DF
221.15	AM	Drugs	Possession of Marijuana 4		35	DF
110–140.15	BM	Property	Attempted criminal trespass 2		30	DF
245.00	BM	Sex crime	Public lewdness		30	DF
110–155.25	BM	Property	Attempted petit larceny		5–30	DF
110–165.40	BM	Property	Attempted possession of stolen property 5		5–30	DF

Level 5 (15–25 Day-Fine Units):

Code	Type	Category	Offense		Units	
240.37A	AM	Sex crime	Loitering/prostitution		25	DF
205.30	AM	Obstruction of justice	Resisting arrest		25	DF
110–221.40	BM	Drugs	Attempted sale of Marijuana 4		25	DF
110–265.01	BM	Weapons	Attempted possession of weapon 4		5–25	DF
110–120.20	BM	Harm persons	Attempted reckless endangerment 2		20	DF
140.10	BM	Property	Criminal trespass 3		20	DF
240.25	VIO	Misconduct	Harassment		15	DF

Level 6 (5–10 Day-Fine Units):

Code	Type	Category	Offense		Units	
165.09	AM	Property	Auto stripping 2		10	DF
221.10	BM	Drugs	Possession of Marijuana 5		5	DF
230.00	BM	Sex crime	Prostitution		5	DF
190.05	BM	Theft	Issuing bad check		5	DF
240.36	BM	Misconduct	Loitering 1		5	DF
140.05	VIO	Property	Trespass		5	DF
240.20	VIO	Misconduct	Disorderly conduct		5	DF

SOURCE.—Hillsman and Greene 1987, pp. 43–49.

NOTE.—AM = A-misdemeanor; BM = B-misdemeanor; VIO = violent.

87

TABLE 4

Two Examples of Staten Island Day-Fine Benchmarks

	Discount Number	Benchmark Number	Premium Number
Harm to person offense:			
120.00 A-misdemeanor assault 3			
(Range of 20–95 day-fine units):			
A. Substantial injury:			
Stranger to stranger; or, where victim is known to assailant, he/she is weaker, vulnerable	81	95	109
B. Minor injury:			
Stranger to stranger; or, where victim is known to assailant, he/she is weaker, vulnerable; or altercations involving use of weapon	59	70	81
C. Substantial injury:			
Altercations among acquaintances; brawls	38	45	52
D. Minor injury:			
Altercations among acquaintances; brawls	17	20	23
Property offense:			
155.25 A-misdemeanor petit larceny			
(Range of 5–60 day-fine units):			
$1,000 or more	51	60	69
$700–999	42	50	58
$500–699	34	40	46
$300–499	25	30	35
$150–299	17	20	23
$50–149	8	10	12
$1–49	4	5	6

SOURCE.—Hillsman and Greene (1987), app. B.

standard adjustment is a flat one-third for offenders with incomes above the federal poverty line, and one-half for those below it. This second adjustment has two tiers to acknowledge that a single rate would fall more heavily on lower-income offenders whose "fair share" of their net daily income could cause hardship even though it has been adjusted for their family responsibilities.

Table 5 contains portions of the table used by the Staten Island judges to calculate the day-fine unit value for each case; it is as simple and as easily used as a tax table. The judge merely locates the offender's net daily income on the left side of the table, then follows the row

TABLE 5

Dollar Value of One Day-Fine Unit by Net Daily Income and Number of Dependents

Net Daily Income ($)	Number of Dependents (Including Self)							
	1	2	3	4	5	6	7	8
3	1.28	1.05	.83	.68	.53	.45	.37	.30
4	1.70	1.40	1.10	.90	.70	.60	.50	.40
5	2.13	1.75	1.38	1.13	.88	.75	.62	.50
6	2.55	2.10	1.65	1.35	1.05	.90	.75	.60
7	2.98	2.45	1.93	1.58	1.23	1.05	.87	.70
8	3.40	2.80	2.20	1.80	1.40	1.20	1.00	.80
9	3.83	3.15	2.48	2.03	1.58	1.35	1.12	.90
10	4.25	3.50	2.75	2.25	1.75	1.50	1.25	1.00
11	4.68	3.85	3.03	2.47	1.93	1.65	1.37	1.10
12	5.10	4.20	3.30	2.70	2.10	1.80	1.50	1.20
13	5.53	4.55	3.58	2.93	2.28	1.95	1.62	1.30
14	7.85	4.90	3.85	3.15	2.45	2.10	1.75	1.40
15	8.42	5.25	4.13	3.38	2.63	2.25	1.87	1.50
16	8.98	5.60	4.40	3.60	2.80	2.40	2.00	1.60
17	9.54	5.95	4.68	3.83	2.98	2.55	2.12	1.70
18	10.10	6.30	4.95	4.05	3.15	2.70	2.25	1.80
19	10.66	8.78	5.23	4.28	3.33	2.85	2.37	1.90
20	11.22	9.24	5.50	4.50	3.50	3.00	2.50	2.00
46	25.81	21.25	16.70	13.66	10.63	9.11	7.59	4.60
47	26.37	21.71	17.06	13.96	10.86	9.31	7.75	4.70
48	26.93	22.18	17.42	14.26	11.09	9.50	7.92	6.34
49	27.49	22.64	17.79	14.55	11.32	9.70	8.08	6.47
50	28.05	23.10	18.15	14.85	11.55	9.90	8.25	6.60
51	28.61	23.56	18.51	15.15	11.78	10.10	8.41	6.73
52	29.17	24.02	18.88	15.44	12.01	10.30	8.58	6.86
53	29.73	24.49	19.24	15.74	12.24	10.49	8.74	7.00
54	30.29	24.95	19.60	16.04	12.47	10.69	8.91	7.13
55	30.86	25.41	19.97	16.34	12.71	10.89	9.07	7.26
96	53.86	44.35	34.85	28.51	22.18	19.01	15.84	12.67
97	54.42	44.81	35.21	28.81	22.41	19.21	16.00	12.80
98	54.98	45.28	35.57	29.11	22.64	19.40	16.17	12.94
99	55.54	45.74	35.94	29.40	22.87	19.60	16.33	13.07
100	56.10	46.20	36.30	29.70	23.10	19.80	16.50	13.20

across until he reaches the column reflecting the defendant's number of dependents. The figure in that cell is the dollar value of one day-fine unit appropriately discounted.

For example, a Staten Island woman with two children receiving public assistance would have a gross (and net) biweekly income of $270, or a net daily income of $19 ($270/14). Using table 5, the judge would calculate her day-fine unit value at $5.23, regardless of the crime for which she is being sentenced. A single parent with two children making $25,000 per year, say, as a clerical supervisor, grosses $962 biweekly—a net daily income of $52. Her day-fine unit value, therefore, would be $18.88 (or three and a half times more than the mother on public assistance). A single professional making an annual income of $78,000 would gross $3,000 biweekly (a net daily income of $119 which is above the range included in table 5). Her day-fine unit value would be $68 (which is thirteen times greater than the welfare mother and three and a half times greater than the clerical supervisor).

If each of these defendants were convicted of attempting to leave a local department store without paying for a $600 watch (attempted petit larceny, a twenty day-fine unit offense), their day-fine amounts, using the Staten Island method (numbers rounded), would be as follows: welfare mother, $100 ($5 × 20); clerical supervisor, $380 ($19 × 20); and professional, $1,360 ($68 × 20).

Table 6 presents a series of actual Staten Island defendants and applies the court's day-fine method to determine what the day-fine amounts would be for a series of hypothetical conviction charges that, under current sentencing policies in the court, might receive a short jail sentence. (If a Staten Island judge were to impose these day fines under current statutory caps for fines in New York State, the actual amount of the sentence could not exceed $1,000.)

2. *Collecting the Means Information.* Although some courts in the United States do not have routine methods of securing information on defendants appearing before the bench (Cole et al. 1987, pp. 13–16), others do obtain such information through the police, pretrial services agencies, or probation departments. The experience of European courts suggests that American courts can overcome most of the information obstacles to routine use of day fines.

The Staten Island court is taking this approach. The city's pretrial services agency interviews all arrested defendants in Staten Island prior to arraignment to provide the judge with information (verified when possible) relevant to the setting of release conditions, including money bail; this includes living arrangement, employment status, take-home pay, other sources of income, and dependents. The Staten Island judges, therefore, have the basic elements to value the day fine at the time of sentencing, even if this coincides with the arraignment. A brief discussion with the defendant and counsel to verify, clarify, or supplement this information when necessary has sufficed for the Staten Island judges to set day-fine amounts without difficulty.

B. Day Fines in Phoenix

The increased use of restitution and service fees, contributions, and reimbursements of many different types makes the imposition of monetary penalties far more complex in many American courts than is typical in Europe. The objective of the planning project to be carried out by the Vera Institute of Justice in conjunction with the Superior Court of Maricopa County is to apply the conceptual and practical framework developed for setting day fines in Staten Island to improving the standards and procedures used in Phoenix to impose and enforce the more complex array of monetary penalties now levied on most of its convicted felons (Hillsman and Greene 1988a).

This general-jurisdiction trial court sentences more than 8,500 felony cases annually, nearly one-quarter of which result in a term of imprisonment. Virtually all the rest are placed under the supervision of the court's probation department. These offenders are subject to mandatory probation fees, a contribution to the Victim Compensation Fund, maximum restitution, various reimbursements, and fines.

In setting these amounts, the court is provided with substantial information from its probation department. Despite the completeness of the presentence reports, however, the complexity of the monetary penalties imposed by the court raises issues that have not been fully addressed by this court (or other courts around the country). These include the extent to which severity of the offense should be factored into the amounts recommended by probation officers and set at sentencing; the manner in which indebtedness should be considered (for example, should debtors be sentenced to lower economic penalties, even when their offenses are more serious, than nondebtors convicted of less grave charges?); and how the victim's damages should be assessed.

These issues surface not only at sentencing but also in the day-to-day supervision work of field probation officers who administer the collection and enforcement process. They need more specific indicators of an offender's "ability to pay" so they can determine the appropriateness of applying increasingly coercive strategies to collect money owed the court. They need consistent and just standards that can be applied routinely to collection and enforcement decisions.

TABLE 6

Proposed Day Fines for Actual Richmond Criminal Court Defendants When A-Misdemeanor Conviction Charges Suggest a Possible Jail Sentence

Defendants*	Assault 3d Degree: Assault Resulting in a Minor Injury	Criminal Possession of Stolen Property 5th Degree: Possession of $850 Stolen Property	Criminal Possession of Controlled Substance 7th Degree: Valium	Petit Larceny: $400 Shoplift	Criminal Mischief: $130 Property Damage
Charlotte Ross: Welfare mother with six children; $446 biweekly	70 DFs × $4 unit Value = $280	50 DFs × $4 unit Value = $200	35 DFs × $4 unit Value = $140	30 DFs × $4 unit Value = $120	10 DFs × $4 unit Value = $40
William Gonzalez: Young offender living with his parents; $150 per week take-home pay	70 DFs × $12 unit Value = $840	50 DFs × $12 unit Value = $600	35 DFs × $12 unit Value = $420	30 DFs × $12 unit Value = $360	10 DFs × $12 unit Value = $120
Ramon Velasquez: Employed; supporting a wife and child; $1,200 per month take-home pay	70 DFs × $15 unit Value = $1,050	50 DFs × $15 unit Value = $750	35 DFs × $15 unit Value = $525	30 DFs × $15 unit Value = $450	10 DFs × $15 unit Value = $150
Mark Copeland: Single, employed; $600 per week take-home pay	70 DFs × $48 unit Value = $3,360	50 DFs × $48 unit Value = $2,400	35 DFs × $48 unit Value = $1,680	30 DFs × $48 unit Value = $1,440	10 DFs × $48 unit Value = $480

SOURCE.—Hillsman and Greene (1987), p. 87.

NOTE.—DFs = Day Fines.

* Defendants' names are pseudonyms.

Any means-based system of imposing variable monetary penalties should embody two fundamental principles of American jurisprudence. First, the degree of punishment imposed should be proportionate to the gravity of the crime being sanctioned. Second, the economic burden imposed by the court should be measured in relation to the means available to the offender.

Taken together, these principles provide a framework for imposing economic sanctions that encompasses essential justice and basic practicality. This is so whether the system is applied to criminal fines as a sole sanction (as in Staten Island, West Germany, or Sweden), or to the use of multiple monetary penalties as part of a sentencing package that may also include noneconomic penalties (as in Phoenix and England).

Working within Arizona's existing statutory framework, therefore, the project (which is funded by the State Justice Institute and the National Institute of Corrections) will be a collaborative effort to develop sentencing guidelines for the total package of economic sanctions imposed by the superior court. As in Staten Island, the benchmarks developed will provide a graded scale of monetary penalty units encompassing the criminal code offenses commonly handled by the court. Likewise, a simple-to-use valuation format will be devised to value the penalty units by assessing the economic means of individual offenders. The resulting product—a total dollar amount available for sanctioning—can then be used by judges to craft individual sentences that will combine any monetary penalties to be imposed within a framework that is both just and enforceable.

The project's planning group will propose a scheme for apportioning this total dollar amount among the different penalties imposed by judges. For example, by Arizona law, restitution must receive first priority. Because the value of property stolen or damaged, as well as the seriousness of physical injury involved in a given case, would already have been primary elements in determining the number of monetary penalty units imposed, restitution orders should easily fit within this broader framework. However, the relative importance and priority of other monetary penalties would also have to be weighed, and policies devised to distribute the remaining share of the maximum economic-sanction amount among them, as deemed appropriate by the court (or as required by law).

In some individual cases, this may mean that a greater economic burden than has been typical can be properly imposed as a sanction. In other cases, however, the total amount deemed appropriate for sanctioning a particular offender for a specific offense, as derived from the new day-fine procedures, may be insufficient to cover the statutorily mandated schedule of monetary penalties. While the superior court will need to impose such amounts as the law requires, it will also develop standards for their postsentence modification, based on research designed to explore how these legal rigidities affect the court's ability to enforce economic sanctions.

VI. Conclusion

The development of systematic methods for imposing variable rather than fixed fines in American courts has the potential for expanding the usefulness of the fine as an intermediate penalty, as has occurred in Western Europe, and for rationalizing the imposition of all financial penalties. That many judges from across the country believe that day fines, the most tested form of variable fining, could work in their own courts and are willing to experiment with this approach suggests that the time is ripe for such efforts. In 1973, the Task Force on Courts of the National Advisory Commission on Criminal Justice Standards and Goals found that, "properly employed, the fine is less drastic, far less costly to the public and perhaps more effective than imprisonment or community supervision" (p. 570). This observation went unheeded by the policy community for over a decade, partly because there was insufficient documentation and discussion in the United States of what constitutes the "proper" way to impose and administer fine sentences. This is changing as criminal justice systems seek ways to use imprisonment resources more wisely, to structure sentencing decisions more consistently, and to impose fines more justly whenever they are used.

REFERENCES

Albrecht, Hans-Jorg. 1980. *Strafzumessung und Vollstreckung bei Geldstrafen*. Berlin: Duncker & Humbolt.

Albrecht, Hans-Jorg, and Elmer H. Johnson. 1980. "Fines and Justice Administration: The Experience of the Federal Republic of Germany." *International Journal of Comparative and Applied Criminal Justice* 4:3–14.

American Bar Association. 1978. *Standards Relating to Sentencing Alternatives and Corrections*. Chicago: American Bar Association.

American Law Institute. 1962. *Model Penal Code and Commentaries*. Philadelphia: American Law Institute.

Bentham, Jeremy. 1931. *The Theory of Legislation*, edited by Charles Kay Ogden. New York: Harcourt Brace. (Originally published 1802.)

Beristani, Antonio. 1976. "Penal and Administrative Fines in Relation to Prison Sentences." *International Criminal Justice Review* 302:253–61 and 303:282–88.

Best, Judah, and Paul I. Birzon. 1970. "Conditions of Probation: An Analysis." In *Probation and Parole: Selected Readings*, edited by Robert M. Carter and Leslie T. Wilkins. New York: Wiley.

Botein, Bernard, and Herbert J. Sturz. 1964. "Report on Pre-trial Release Practices in Sweden, Denmark, England and Italy to the National Conference of Bail and Criminal Justice." *Journal of the International Commission of Jurists* 5(2):204–33.

Carter, James S., and George F. Cole. 1979. "The Use of Fines in England: Could the Idea Work Here?" *Judicature* 64(4):154–61.

Casale, Silvia S. G. 1981. "Fines in Europe: A Study of the Use of Fines in Selected European Countries with Empirical Research on the Problems of Fine Enforcement." Working Paper no. 10, *Fines in Sentencing*. New York: Vera Institute of Justice.

Casale, Silvia S. G., and Sally T. Hillsman. 1986. *The Enforcement of Fines as Criminal Sanctions: The English Experience and Its Relevance to American Practice.* Executive Summary. Washington, D.C.: National Institute of Justice.

Chambers, David L. 1979. *Making Fathers Pay: The Enforcement of Child Support.* Chicago: University of Chicago Press.

Cole, George F., Barry Mahoney, Marlene Thornton, and Roger A. Hansen. 1987. *The Practices and Attitudes of Trial Court Judges regarding Fines as a Criminal Sanction.* Washington, D.C.: National Institute of Justice.

Davies, Martin. 1970. *Financial Penalties and Probation.* Home Office Research Study, no. 5. London: H.M. Stationery Office.

Dawson, Alice. 1982. "Case Law and Constitutional Problems in Defaults on Fine and Costs and in the Disposition of Fine Revenues." Working Paper no. 4, *Fines in Sentencing*. New York: Vera Institute of Justice.

Eisenstein, James, and Herbert Jacob. 1977. *Felony Justice.* Boston: Little, Brown.

Feeley, Malcolm M. 1979. *The Process Is the Punishment: Handling Cases in a Lower Court.* New York: Russell Sage.

Forer, Lois G. 1980. *Criminals and Victims: A Trial Judge Reflects on Crime and Punishment.* New York: Norton.

Friedman, Gary M. 1983. "The West German Day-Fine System: A Possibility for the United States?" *University of Chicago Law Review* 50:281–304.

George, Vic, and Roger Lawson, eds. 1980. *Poverty and Inequality in Common Market Countries.* London and Boston: Routledge & Kegan Paul.

Gillespie, Robert W. 1980. "Fines as an Alternative to Incarceration: The German Experience." *Federal Probation* 44(4):20–26.

———. 1981. "Sentencing Traditional Crimes with Fines: A Comparative Analysis." *International Journal of Comparative and Applied Criminal Justice* 5(2):197–204.

———. 1982. "Economic Penalties as Criminal Sanctions: A Pilot Study of Their Use in Illinois." Paper presented at the thirty-ninth annual meeting of the American Society of Criminology, Toronto, November.

Glaser, Daniel, and Margaret A. Gordon. 1988. *Use and Effectiveness of Fines, Jail, and Probation*. Los Angeles: University of Southern California, Social Science Research Institute.

Greene, Judith A. 1986. "Suggestions for a Proposed Day Fine Plan for Richmond County." New York: Vera Institute of Justice.

———. 1987. "Report to the German Marshall Fund of the United States on Day-Fine Study Tour and Richmond Criminal Court Day-Fine Planning Conference." New York: Vera Institute of Justice.

———. 1988. "Structuring the Criminal Fine: Making an 'Intermediate Penalty' More Useful and Equitable." *Justice System Journal* 13(1):37–50.

Harris, Brian. 1980. "The Effectiveness of Sentencing." London: Justices' Clerks Society. Mimeographed.

Hillsman, Sally T. 1986. "Fines as a Criminal Sanction." New York: Vera Institute of Justice.

———. 1988. "The Growing Challenge of Fine Administration to Court Managers." *Justice System Journal* 13(1):5–16.

Hillsman, Sally T., and Judith A. Greene. 1987. *Improving the Use and Administration of Criminal Fines: A Report of the Richmond County, New York, Criminal Court Day-Fine Planning Project*. New York: Vera Institute of Justice.

———. 1988a. "Improving the Use and Administration of Monetary Penalties in Criminal Cases: An Experiment to Apply Means-based Fining Concepts and Practices to the Superior Court of Maricopa County, Arizona." New York: Vera Institute of Justice.

———. 1988b. "Tailoring Criminal Fines to the Financial Means of the Offender." *Judicature* 72(1):38–45.

Hillsman, Sally T., and Barry Mahoney. 1988. "Collecting and Enforcing Criminal Fines: A Review of Court Processes, Practices and Problems." *Justice System Journal* 13(1):17–36.

Hillsman, Sally T., Joyce L. Sichel, and Barry Mahoney. 1984. *Fines in Sentencing: A Study of the Use of the Fine as a Criminal Sanction*. Washington, D.C.: National Institute of Justice.

Home Office. 1988. *Criminal Statistics, England and Wales, 1987*. London: H.M. Stationery Office.

Horn, Erkhard. 1974. "Das Geldstrafenssystem des neuen Allgemeinen Teils des Stratgesetzbuch GB." *Neue Juristische Wochenschrift* 15:625–29.

Hurley, John E. 1988. "Island Court Refining Criminal Fine System." *Staten Island Sunday Advance* (September 11), p. A–1.

Kriminalstatistik For Brott Lagforda Personer, 1987. 1988. Stockholm: Statistiska Centralbyran.

Latham, Cecil T. 1980. "The Imposition and Enforcement of Fines." *Magistrate* 36(6):85–88.

Lewis, Donald E. 1988. "A Linear Model of Fine Enforcement with Application to England and Wales." *Journal of Quantitative Criminology* 4(1):19–37.

McBrien, Rose. 1988. "Tailoring Criminal Fines to the Financial Means of the Offender—a Richmond County Judge's View." *Judicature* 72(1):42–43.

McClintock, F. H. 1963. *Crimes of Violence*. London: Heinemann.

McCord, Joan. 1985. "Deterrence and the Light Touch of the Law." In *Reactions to Crime: The Public, the Police, Courts, and Prisons.* New York: Wiley.

McDonald, Douglas Corry. 1986. *Punishment without Walls.* New Brunswick, N.J.: Rutgers University Press.

Mahoney, Barry, and Marlene Thornton. 1988. "Means-based Fining: Views of American Trial Court Judges." *Justice System Journal* 13(1):51–63.

Millar, Ann R. 1984. *The Experimental Introduction of Fines Enforcement Officers into Two Sheriff Courts.* Edinburgh: Scottish Office, Central Research Unit.

Miller, Charles H. 1956. "The Fine: Price Tag or Rehabilitative Force?" *National Probation and Parole Association Journal* 2(October): 377–84.

Morgan, Rod, and Roger Bowles. 1981. "Fines: The Case for Review." *Criminal Law Review* (April), pp. 203–14.

Morris, Norval. 1974. *The Future of Imprisonment.* Chicago: University of Chicago Press.

————. 1987. "Alternatives to Imprisonment: Failures and Prospects." *Sam Houston State University Criminal Justice Research Bulletin* 7(3):1–6.

Mullaney, Fahy G. 1987. *Economic Sanctions in Community Corrections.* Washington, D.C.: National Institute of Corrections.

National Advisory Commission on Criminal Justice Standards and Goals. 1973. *Task Force Report: Courts.* Washington, D.C.: U. S. Government Printing Office.

National Commission on Reform of Federal Criminal Laws. 1971. *Final Report.* Washington, D.C.: U.S. Government Printing Office.

National Council on Crime and Delinquency. 1977. *Model Sentencing Act.* 2d ed. Hackensack, N.J.: National Council on Crime and Delinquency.

Ragona, Anthony J., Malcolm Rich, and John Paul Ryan. 1981. "Sentencing in Misdemeanor Courts: The Choice of Sanctions." Paper presented at the Law and Society Association annual meeting, Amherst, Mass., June.

Ragona, Anthony J., and John Paul Ryan. 1983. "Misdemeanor Courts and the Choice of Sanctions: A Comparative View." *Justice System Journal* 8(2):199–221.

Rusche, George, and Otto Kirchheimer. 1939. *Punishment and Social Structure.* New York: Russell & Russell.

Ryan, Dennis M. 1983. "Criminal Fines: A Sentencing Alternative to Short-Term Incarceration." *Iowa Law Review* 68(5):1285–1313.

Ryan, John Paul. 1980–81. "Adjudication and Sentencing in a Misdemeanor Court: The Outcome Is the Punishment." *Law and Society Review* 15(1):79–108.

Sichel, Joyce L. 1982a. "Report on Visits to Selected State and Local Courts." Working Paper no. 8, *Fines in Sentencing.* New York: Vera Institute of Justice.

————. 1982b. "U.S. District Court Fine Imposition and Collection Practices." Working Paper no. 9, *Fines in Sentencing.* New York: Vera Institute of Justice.

Smith, Michael E. 1983–84. "Will the Real Alternatives Please Stand Up." *New York University Review of Law and Social Change* 12:175–97.

Softley, Paul. 1973. *A Survey of Fine Enforcement*. Home Office Research Study no. 16. London: H.M. Stationery Office.

———. 1977. *Fines in Magistrates' Courts*. Home Office Research Study no. 43. London: H.M. Stationery Office.

Softley, Paul, and David Moxon. 1982. *Fine Enforcement: An Evaluation of Practices in Individual Courts*. Home Office Research and Planning Unit Paper no. 12. London: H.M. Stationery Office.

Stenner, Dieter. 1970. *Die kurzfristige Freiheitsstrafe und die Möglichkeiten zu ihrem Ersatz durch andere Sanktionen*. Kriminologische Schriftenreihe, Band 49.

Strafverfolgungsstatistik 1985. 1986. Wiesbaden: Statistisches Bundesamt.

Tait, Jan. 1988. "A Court-based Defendant Notification System for Traffic Defendants." *Justice System Journal* 13(1):73–79.

Thornstedt, Hans. 1974. "Skandinavische Erfahrungen mit dem Tagesbuzen-system." *Zeitschrift für die Gesamte Strafrechtswissenschaft* 86:595 ff.

———. 1985. "The Day Fine System in Sweden." *Criminal Law Review* (June), pp. 307–12.

Townsend, Peter. 1979. *Poverty in the United Kingdom: A Survey of Household Resources and Standards of Living*. Berkeley: University of California Press.

von Hirsch, Andrew. 1988. "Punishment to Fit the Criminal." *The Nation* 246(25):901–2.

West, Jenny. 1979. "Community Service for Fine Defaulters." *Justice of the Peace* 142(2):425–28.

Wick, Karen A. 1988. "Evaluating Three Notification Strategies for Collecting Delinquent Traffic Fines." *Justice System Journal* 13(1):64–72.

Zamist, Ida. 1986. *Fines in Sentencing: An Empirical Study of Fine Use, Collection and Enforcement in New York City Courts*. (Revised.) New York: Vera Institute of Justice.

Terrie E. Moffitt

The Neuropsychology of Juvenile Delinquency: A Critical Review

ABSTRACT

Research on the performance of delinquent juveniles on neuropsychological tests suggests a role for brain dysfunction in the causation of antisocial behavior. Neuropsychological tests measure constructs representative of the various mental functions of the human brain, such as language, memory, or social judgment. Poor test scores suggest compromised brain function. Because the brain is the organ we use to perceive and respond to our environment, the relations of neuropsychological factors to delinquent behavior are expressed as interactions with social and environmental influences. Most studies of the neuropsychological status of delinquents suffer from notable methodological problems. Consistent findings of delinquency-related deficits, particularly in verbal and "executive" (self-control) functions, have nonetheless been reported by many studies, including those with the strongest designs. Neuropsychological variables predict variance in delinquent behavior independent of appropriate control variables.

Neuropsychology is an applied science that relates observable abnormal behaviors to brain dysfunction or damage. The neuropsychologist uses assessment instruments to measure a subject's level of performance on tasks that sample a variety of behavioral functions, including new

Terrie E. Moffitt is associate professor of psychology at the University of Wisconsin—Madison. Preparation of this essay was supported by grants from the National Institute of Mental Health (1 R23 MH-12723-01) and the University of Wisconsin Graduate School Research Committee. Avshalom Caspi, David Farrington, Robert Hare, Karen Heimer, Richard Herrnstein, Rolf Loeber, Sarnoff Mednick, Norval Morris, Joseph Newman, Stevens Smith, and Michael Tonry are thanked for their valuable suggestions on this manuscript.

99

learning, remote memory for verbal material, receptive language, visual-motor integration, or sensory perception. When specific brain systems or processes are known to provide the foundation for normal performance of a mental function, subnormal test scores may be used to infer dysfunction of those processes or damage in those systems (Vega and Parsons 1967; Taylor 1969). Thus neuropsychological testing is a means of breaking down overall mental ability into its finer elements, quantifying those elements, and relating them to the functional status of the brain. It is generally acknowledged that most complex behaviors require the cooperation of functional systems and pathways throughout the brain rather than being conducted by single anatomical structures as nineteenth-century phrenologists imagined. Nevertheless, many cognitive and perceptual functions may be localized to areas of the brain whose integrity, while perhaps not sufficient for normal performance, is probably necessary. Increasing attention is also being given to influences upon neuropsychological test scores from nonbrain factors such as motivation, test anxiety (King et al. 1978), education (Heaton, Grant, and Matthews 1986), and social disadvantage (Moffitt 1988).

The clinical role of providing diagnostic information about brain-injured soldiers and other neurological patients brought about the advent of neuropsychological assessment following World War II (Luria 1973; Satz and Fletcher 1981; Lezak 1983). Because there were no technologies for taking images of the living brain at that time, neuropsychological testing was the best way to document the presence of a patient's brain disease or damage, and repeated testing is still the preferred way to identify trajectories of recovery or deterioration in neurological patients. More recently, neuropsychological measures have come to be used as research tools for identifying brain dysfunctions that may characterize groups who display syndromes of deviant or pathological behaviors. For example, application of neuropsychological measures as research variables is proving fruitful in the study of schizophrenia (Goldstein 1986), depression and anxiety disorders (Tucker 1981; Caine 1986), risk for alcoholism (Tarter et al. 1984), attention-deficit disorder with hyperactivity (Douglas 1983), and reading disabilities (Rourke 1983). This essay reviews studies that have assessed juvenile delinquents with neuropsychological tests.

In the original clinical and diagnostic applications of the neuropsychological method, the focus was almost entirely upon the usefulness of neuropsychological tests for detecting the presence of acquired brain damage and for identifying the anatomical location of the lesion (site of damage) within the brain (e.g., Boll 1981; Filskov and Leli 1981). By contrast, the more recent application of neuropsychological methods in the study of deviant behavioral syndromes emphasizes description of information-processing correlates of abnormal behavior (Goldstein 1987). In this view, acquired brain disease or injury is not presumed to be the sole origin of the hypothesized cognitive dysfunctions; any number of sources might be involved, including disruptions in fetal brain development, childhood exposure to neurotoxins, early environmental deprivation, fluctuating neurochemical states, and heritable individual variation in brains. Nor is the exclusive goal of this research to identify specific anatomical lesion sites in the brain that "cause" deviant behavior.[1]

The contribution that the neuropsychological method can best make to the study of pathological behavior is descriptive. It can tell us how specific deviant human behaviors relate to individual differences in the brain's capacity to perceive, process, remember, and respond to information from the environment. The concept of environment is key; the brain does not produce behavior in a vacuum. Instead, it processes information from the environment and generates responses to environmental demands. Accordingly, one of the aims of neuropsychological research on delinquency is to be able to identify individuals whose neuropsychological dysfunctions place them at risk for maladaptive behavioral responses to environmental influences. The neuropsychologist tries to understand the ways in which individuals' cognitive disabilities or vulnerabilities interact with social and environmental conditions.

Historically, many neuropsychological tests were developed to meet the practical diagnostic needs of clinicians. Because the tests gained a strong clinical reputation for "working well," many of them became widely used in research before the requisite psychometric groundwork had been established. Therefore, although a good deal is known about the ability of these tests to identify brain damage in known neurological

---

[1] One reason for this is that functional neuroanatomy is not yet well enough understood to support conclusive causal deductions. The brain's functions are staggeringly complex; a single behavior, such as a blink, can be performed independently by more than one brain structure, it may require cooperation of numerous structures, or it may be disrupted by damage far from the structure that performs it, or it could be disrupted at the biochemical level with no observable structural change at all. These complexities make functional neuroanatomy research endlessly fascinating but painstakingly slow.

cases, the meanings of test score distributions in the general population are less understood (see Moffitt and Silva 1987). In other words, although brain damage always causes poor neuropsychological test scores, we are less certain that poor neuropsychological test scores always indicate brain dysfunction. In nonclinical research samples, including delinquents, brain dysfunction is hypothesized to be present, but the levels of disability are expected to be more subtle than the gross impairment of patients with acute head injury, cerebrovascular accident, or neural tumor. In the circumstance of doing research with subjects whose brain dysfunctions are presumed to be subtle and of unknown origin, neuropsychological tests are *the* most sensitive method available for detecting subtle variation in cognitive performance. Nonetheless, to strengthen the inferences we can make from test data, corroboration should be sought from alternative neuropsychological measurement paradigms, some of which are described below in Section I. This corroborative work is just beginning.

Recent years have seen an increasing research focus on the role of central nervous system factors in antisocial behavior and delinquency, as evidenced by a number of books and reviews (Lewis and Balla 1976; Elliott 1978; Mednick and Volavka 1980; Mednick et al. 1982; Wilson and Herrnstein 1985; Werry 1986; Mednick, Moffitt, and Stack 1987; Moffitt and Mednick 1988). This essay examines published studies of the performance of delinquent juveniles on neuropsychological tests that are indicators of possible brain dysfunction. Buikhuisen (1987a) ably reviewed eleven such studies published prior to 1983. The literature has grown quickly since that time, and thirty-one reports were available for review in this essay. Neuropsychological studies of adult violent offenders and antisocial personality-disorder cases exist, and these reports are discussed where pertinent but are not examined in detail here.

In order to help readers who are not neuropsychologists understand some of the individual research reports discussed in this essay, Section I provides a primer on neuropsychological investigative methods and tests that are now in widespread use, together with some aspects of brain functioning and hypotheses relating brain functions to behavior that are useful for understanding neuropsychological theories linking cognitive abilities and behavior. Section II offers a review of various theoretical perspectives. Sections III and IV, respectively, examine methodological issues in relation to neuropsychological research on delinquent subjects and provide a substantive overview of the findings of neuropsychological research on delinquents. Section V offers some suggestions for next steps in research on the neuropsychology of antisocial behavior.

I. Neuropsychological Investigative Methods

This section describes many of the tests and test batteries that have been used as the dependent measures in the studies reviewed in Section IV. Also described are measurement tools that have not yet been used in studies of delinquency but will certainly figure prominently in future research.

A. Tests and Test Batteries

Neuropsychological tests are even more numerous and varied than the brain functions that they are designed to measure. The tests are used to gather samples of a subject's behavior on tasks whose performance characteristics have been psychometrically standardized using groups of individuals with demonstrable lesions (sites of damage, injury, or surgical cut) of the brain and individuals who are without evidence of such disease.

For illustrative purposes, let us briefly examine the neuropsychological construct of memory. There are numerous neuropsychological measures of memory function. Generally, the tests expose the subject to material to be learned[2]—perhaps a list of words (Rey Auditory Verbal Learning Test), a series of musical tones (Seashore Tonal Memory), or a configuration of geometric drawings (Benton Visual Retention Test)—and then test for retention. Measures may include the amount of material recalled after a brief single exposure ("immediate recall"); the number of practice trials required to learn the material to some criterion ("new learning"); recall of the material after performance of a similar distracting task ("interference effects"); free recall after some period of delay ("retrieval"); and ability to recognize the material when it is imbedded in an array, even when free recall is poor (thereby implying that "storage" did occur). Use of memory test data to make inferences in research depends on the truth of two premises about validity of the tests: that the tests do examine memory, and that poor test performance does result from brain dysfunction.

[2] Although some tests measure remote memory for material generally known by most members of an age cohort.

There are several approaches to understanding validity for these tests. Construct validity is demonstrated by the consistent findings that different memory tests have scores that are highly correlated with each other (Larrabee et al. 1985; Loring and Papanicolaou 1987; Crook and Larrabee 1988) and that patients with documented memory loss, such as patients with Alzheimer's dementia (Morris and Baddeley 1988), Korsakoff's syndrome (Sanders and Warrington 1971), chronic alcoholism (Oscar-Berman 1980), or amnesia following head injury (Schacter and Crovitz 1977; Levin and Goldstein 1986), score very poorly on these tests. Differential validity of the tested construct is demonstrated by showing that memory scores can vary independently of other mental function scores and from overall intelligence; that is, although general intelligence depends upon memory, it is possible for a patient to suffer specific memory impairment following a brain injury while other mental functions remain intact (e.g., the famous case of H. M., discussed in Scoville and Milner [1957]). Ecological validity is shown when performance levels on tests in the laboratory correlate positively with subjects' abilities to function in the real world (McSweeny et al. 1985; Kolonoff, Costa, and Snow 1986). For example, poor scores on tests of visuospatial memory characterize patients who become disoriented in space, wander away from their homes, and fail to recognize their relatives. Etiological validity is demonstrated when documented brain status is shown to be the source of variation in the test scores. As mentioned above, patients with dementing neurological diseases score markedly below healthy controls on memory tests, as do chronic alcoholics with documented brain involvement, patients suffering amnesia following brain surgery resection of the temporal lobes or hippocampus, or post-head-injury amnesia cases. The performance of patients with temporal lobe epilepsy has shown that poor scores on verbal memory tests are associated with lesions (injuries or damage) that produce seizure onset from the left temporal lobe of the brain, while scores on visual nonverbal tests are poor if seizures originate in the right temporal lobe (Samuels, Butters, and Fedio 1972).

It is impractical for this essay to provide evidence for validity for all the tests ever administered to delinquent samples. Lezak (1983) provides an excellent compendium of individual neuropsychological tests, with descriptions and discussions of each test and its reliability, validity, and functional interpretation. That compendium is recommended for evaluating the psychometric properties of tests mentioned in this essay.

In addition to individual tests, two preassembled test batteries are in popular clinical use, the Halstead-Reitan Neuropsychological Test Battery (for a description, see Boll [1981]) and the Luria-Nebraska Neuropsychological Battery (see Golden 1981). These batteries assemble a large number of tests, at least one to tap each major brain function. Several hours may be required to administer a full battery to a subject. The large set of scores obtained from a test battery allows comparison of a subject's strengths and weaknesses across mental functions, for example, poor visuospatial scores in the presence of other normal scores may suggest dysfunction limited to the right posterior area of the brain. Preassembled batteries are most often used in exploratory descriptive research. Many researchers prefer to tailor their test selection to their own research questions when they have specific hypotheses to test.

Neuropsychological measurements other than performance tests (e.g., using brain-imaging technology, electroencephalograms, or lateral preferences) have not often been applied to juvenile delinquents. Several of the more promising of these alternate methods are described below. Review of criminological studies using these methods is beyond the scope of this essay, but a few exemplary studies are cited here.

B. Lateral Preference

Because the motor and sensory functions of limbs are controlled by the contralateral (opposite) cerebral hemisphere, hand preference has been taken to imply cerebral dominance (relatively better function) of the contralateral hemisphere (Hecaen and Ajuriaguerra 1964). For example, if the left hemisphere is damaged in childhood, hand preference often shifts from right to left. It has been suggested that individuals characterized by left cerebral dominance exhibit more planned, rational, and verbal (and less emotional and impulsive) patterns of behavior than those who are right-hemisphere dominant (Gazzaniga 1970; Sperry 1974; Berent 1981). Gabrielli and Mednick (1980) reported that left-hand (right-hemisphere) dominance assessed at age 12 predicted delinquency at age 18; 64.7 percent of left-handers were later arrested, but only 29.5 percent of right-handers were arrested. Similarly, Fitzhugh (1973) found 32 percent of delinquents, but no controls, to be left-handed. Krynicki (1978) and Wolff et al. (1982) found not left-, but mixed-handedness to distinguish delinquents. Nachshon and Denno (1987) reported a greater incidence of left-handedness among *nonoffenders*, but some evidence of mixed lateral dominance for especially violent

offenders. Feehan et al. (1989) found no association between handedness and self-reported delinquency. Denno (1984) has reviewed the
conflicting literature on handedness and criminal behavior.

C. Dichotic Stimulus Presentation Procedures

Two research protocols have been developed that allow examination
of lateralized functions of the brain's two hemispheres. In the dichotic
listening procedure (Noffsinger 1985), differing auditory stimuli are
delivered simultaneously to the subject's two ears through headphones.
Each ear is connected by nerve pathways to both the contralateral
(opposite) hemisphere of the brain, and to the ipsilateral (same side)
cerebral hemisphere. Because the auditory pathways from a particular
ear to the contralateral hemisphere's auditory cortex are believed to be
more efficient than the ipsilateral pathways (Kimura 1967), stimuli
should be more easily recognized by the ear which is contralateral to
the hemisphere that is specialized in processing that stimulus modality.
For example, words should be best detected when delivered to the right
ear, because it projects to the left hemisphere, which is specialized for
language processing. We begin with a right-handed subject with no
hearing loss. If words delivered to the subject's right ear through headphones are detected poorly, relative to population norms, then we may
deduce that the subject's left hemisphere is probably not functioning
normally. No reports of dichotic listening studies with delinquents are
known to me, but Nachshon (1988) has discussed such studies with
antisocial-personality-disordered and violent adults.

The divided visual field (DVF) tachistoscopic method exploits the
neurophysiological organization of the visual system to allow presentation of visual stimuli directly and exclusively to each cerebral hemisphere (Zaidel 1985). The subject is instructed to focus on a central
point, and the tachistoscope apparatus flashes visual stimuli (letters or
shapes) so rapidly that the subject does not have time to move his eyes.
Two separate nerve pathways carry information from the half of each
eye's retina that is nearest the nose (nasal hemiretina) and the half of the
retina nearest the temple (temporal hemiretina) of each eye to the
brain's hemispheres. A stimulus flashed briefly in the far right visual
field will be transmitted to the left cerebral hemisphere through the
nasal hemiretina of the right eye and the temporal hemiretina of the left
eye (Beaumont 1982). Asymmetries in efficiency of processing stimuli
of different modalities (e.g., verbal or nonverbal) can be examined
using this technique, and the interpretive logic follows that described

above for dichotic listening studies. Although no DVF studies of delinquent subjects were found at this review, Hare, Williamson, and Harpur (1988) have described a series of DVF studies of cerebral organization of language in antisocial personality disorder. There are controversies (discussed below in Sec. IVA3) concerning results from neuropsychological tests that have been interpreted as representing differential deficit in verbal skills or left hemisphere dysfunction for delinquents. Application of dichotic presentation methods with delinquent subjects may shed new light on neuropsychological test findings.

D. Electrophysiological Paradigms

The ongoing rhythmic electrical activity of the brain is recorded by the electroencephalograph (EEG). One of the earliest indications of some relation between brain pathology and antisocial behavior comes from the case of a matricide without apparent motive or mental illness (Hill and Sargant 1943). The offender was found to experience abnormal brain electrical discharges under conditions of low blood sugar, and he had not eaten at the time of the murder.

The EEG is taken from electrodes placed at standard scalp sites. Recordings are described by reference to the location of the sensing electrode over the surface of the brain and by the amplitude and frequency of the sensed wave forms. Mednick et al. (1981) found excessive levels of slow alpha EEG (recorded at age eleven) to predict recidivistic offending at age eighteen, accounting for 12 percent of the variance in theft arrests. Others (e.g., Krynicki 1978; Lewis et al. 1985) have also reported abnormal EEG recordings for delinquents. Volavka (1987) and Milstein (1988) provide excellent reviews of EEG studies of criminal subjects.

In contrast to the resting EEG, evoked potentials (or event-related potentials, ERP) represent changes in the electrical activity of the brain following experimental presentation of a stimulus. The subject is attached to the EEG-recording apparatus, a recording of baseline brain electrical activity is begun, and then sounds or lights are presented, and the responding change in electrical waveforms is noted. Such change is typically too insignificant to be detected in the context of the ongoing EEG record, but ERP waveforms lasting several hundred milliseconds can be revealed by computerized averaging of the EEG over several stimulus presentations. In this way, hypotheses may be tested about the brain's orienting and information-processing capacities with respect to environmental stimulation. The ERP paradigm is proving valuable in the testing of theories about attentional mechanisms in antisocial behavior. For example, when a soft tone is typically presented just before a very loud noise, most subjects come to show a special ERP when they hear the soft tone itself, suggesting that they are vigilant to the warning meaning of the tone. When criminals show absent or delayed anticipatory ERPs in this situation, several hypotheses can be generated about why they fail to attend to warnings of punishment. Raine (1988) provides a very thorough critical review of this complex literature and an interesting theoretical perspective.

E. Neuroimaging Techniques

Within the past ten years developments have been made in noninvasive imaging of cerebral tissue. Positron Emission Tomography (PET; Maziotta and Phelps 1985) is able to provide information in visual analogue format about local cerebral blood flow and oxygen and glucose metabolism rates at differential sites in the brain following information-processing challenges. Blood, oxygen, and glucose are resources that the brain's structures require to replace energy expended during active work. By observing these measures in normal subjects we may learn which structures in the brain use resources during performance of different mental functions or motor behaviors. For example, subjects are asked to solve an item on a neuropsychological test, and then the PET scan image is observed to determine what parts of the brain used energy. By repeating the procedures on subjects with behavioral pathology, we may determine if their brains are failing to "work" in the areas and ways that normal brains work. These procedures are revolutionary because they allow us for the first time to "see" the brains of living subjects, and to see them actively processing. Nuclear Magnetic Resonance Imaging (NMRI; Bydder and Steiner 1982) scans show striking contrasts in the textures and densities of the tissues that form structures in the brain, providing clear anatomical images that may be viewed from many planes and angles, and that are not limited to the indistinct horizontal sections previously obtained with earlier techniques such as the Computed Axial Tomography (CAT) scan. These techniques are at the forefront of neuroscience research and have not yet been applied to criminal populations. They have, however, yielded fascinating findings with pathological disorders such as schizophrenia (Buchsbaum et al. 1982). At present the costs of these techniques are prohibitive. Nevertheless, given that criminal behavior is a pathology of the young, these techniques will offer our best chance to "look" at the structure and physiology of the brain noninvasively in living, antisocial subjects.

To readers who are unfamiliar with neuropsychology, the preceding brief and oversimplified descriptions of neuropsychological investigative methods and tests may seem highly technical. For purposes of this essay, however, it is less important that brain physiology and anatomy be understood in any detail than that readers be made aware that there exists a substantial body of neuropsychological knowledge that will, over time, provide richer insights into relations between brain functioning and behavior, including deviant behavior. Researchers are now beginning to apply these research methods to efforts to understand the causes of deviant behavior, and this essay attempts to pull together some of the findings of existing research with juvenile delinquents. Before describing the methodological characteristics of that research and such substantive findings as can be gleaned from it in Sections III and IV, the next section of this essay discusses existing theoretical perspectives on the relations between neuropsychology and delinquency.

II. Theoretical Perspectives

Theoretical perspectives on the question of neuropsychology and delinquency fall into two sets. Sociological delinquency theories constitute one set, which has little to say about neuropsychological status as an independent variable. The second set, neuropsychological theories, consists of theoretical formulations that attempt to explain behavior pathology from the viewpoints of developmental, personality, and neurobehavioral psychology and psychiatry. These theories are less concerned with crime in particular as the dependent variable. When sociological delinquency theories admit individual differences in cognitive abilities to consideration, their effects upon delinquency are viewed as indirect, being necessarily *mediated* through some more directly causal social variable. Neuropsychological theories, on the other hand, tend to assume that cognitive factors can produce deviant behavior patterns in a *direct* fashion.

This section consists of three parts. The first introduces the broad patterns of evidence that suggest an empirical link between central nervous system dysfunctions and delinquency; this work has been primarily descriptive and atheoretical. The second and third parts briefly summarize the contributions of sociological and neuropsychological theory to explaining the observed empirical patterns.

A. *Neuropsychological Factors and Antisocial Behavior*

The belief that neuropsychological factors are among the causes of antisocial behavior is an old one. Benjamin Rush (1812, cited in Elliott 1978, p. 147) referred to the "total perversion of the moral faculties" in individuals who displayed "innate preternatural moral depravity," proposing that "there is probably an original defective organization in those parts of the body which are occupied by the moral faculties of the mind." Three different observations or rationales have given impetus to neuropsychological study of antisocial behavior. Working primarily from neurosurgical experiments with animals, and a few human patients, Mark and Ervin (1970) and others have tried to locate the source of antisocial behavior in specific sites within the brain. Behavior as complex as human antisocial action is unlikely to be susceptible to so simple an explanation, however, and I do not discuss that body of research further in this essay. Two other sets of research findings and observations, however, do suggest some strong associations between brain functioning and antisocial behavior. It has long been observed that people suffering serious brain injuries often exhibit behaviors similar to those of some chronic repetitive offenders and that delinquents, on average, have repeatedly been shown to perform less well on intelligence tests than do nondelinquents.

Harlow (1868, cited in Macmillan 1986, p. 85) described the famous case of Phineas Gage, a railroad foreman whose frontal cranium was pierced through by an iron tamping rod propelled by a dynamite charge. Following recovery from the injury,

> The equilibrium or balance, so to speak, between his intellectual faculties and his animal propensities, seems to have been destroyed. He is fitful, irreverent, indulging at times in the grossest profanity (which was not previously his custom), manifesting but little deference for his fellows, impatient of restraint or advice when it conflicts with his desires, at times pertinaciously obstinate, yet capricious and vacillating, devising many plans of future operation, which are no sooner arranged than they are abandoned in turn for others appearing more feasible. A child in his intellectual capacity and manifestations,

he has the animal passions of a strong man. . . . In this regard his mind was radically changed, so decidedly that his friends and acquaintances said he was "no longer Gage."

Similarities are obvious between the symptoms of personality change in this patient and the descriptive criteria for antisocial personality disorder outlined by Cleckley (1976) and Hare (1985). For example, unreliability, untruthfulness, poor judgment, loss of insight, unresponsiveness in interpersonal relationships, and "failure to follow any life plan" were among the diagnostic criteria listed by Cleckley.

The syndrome of antisocial behavior caused by organic disease of the brain has frequently been described in the neurology literature. Elliott (1978) describes specific symptoms arising from damage to the frontal lobes, the limbic system, or both: lack of foresight, lack of insight (self-awareness), absence of conscience, defective affect, inability to learn from experience, diminished sense of fear, inadequate motivation for acts, poor judgment, absence of anxiety, lies and fantasies (confabulation), extreme response to alcohol, aggressive behavior, and self-defeating behavior patterns. Blumer and Benson (1975), drawing upon cases of trauma and lesions of the orbital frontal lobes, outlined the neurobehavioral diagnosis of what they termed "pseudopsychopathic syndrome," in which the major features are facetiousness, sexual and personal hedonism, disinhibition, lack of judgment, impulsivity, irritability, and absence of concern for others.

The parallels between this clinical syndrome and the personalities and behavioral histories of many chronic recidivistic criminal offenders have spawned the hypothesis that criminal behavior may arise from brain dysfunctions that are tantamount to those acquired in cases of traumatic injury to the frontal lobes of the brain. However, as Hare (1984) has pointed out, the resemblance between frontal lobe injury cases and antisocial personality disorder may be more apparent than real, and head injury produces at best an incomplete clinical presentation, lacking one or another cardinal feature. The head-injured "pseudopsychopath" may respond to stress with impulsive violence, for example, but may fail to demonstrate the full complement of repetitive property crime and fraud typical of true antisocial personality disorder. The hypothesis does have intriguing heuristic value, and studies attempting to test it are described in Section IV.

Criminologists have noticed that delinquents on average are a bit less cognitively adept than their more law-abiding peers, as indicated by their poor school attainment and relatively low scores on IQ tests. The finding of an IQ deficit of one-half standard deviation (about eight IQ points) for delinquents has become well accepted (Hirschi and Hindelang 1977; Wilson and Herrnstein 1985). The relation holds when IQ is assessed prospectively before the development of delinquency (West and Farrington 1973; Moffitt, Gabrielli, and Mednick 1981), and IQ and delinquency share variance independent of social class (Reiss and Rhodes 1961; Wolfgang, Figlio, and Sellin 1972; Moffitt, Gabrielli, and Mednick 1981), of race (Short and Strodtbeck 1965; Wolfgang, Figlio, and Sellin 1972), and of detection by police (Moffitt and Silva 1988c). Delinquent siblings have been shown to have lower IQs than nondelinquent siblings within the same families (Shulman 1929; Healy and Bronner 1936). Just *why* low IQ predicts the development of antisocial behavior patterns remains unexplained.

Neuropsychologists know that distinct patterns of impaired cognitive functions can underlie an observed general IQ deficit. That is, individuals with identical omnibus IQ scores may have very different patterns of mental strengths and weaknesses because IQ can be broken down into a set of mental abilities that are hypothetically distinguishable (although not wholly independent). A low general IQ score might result from specific and relatively isolated problems such as impaired social judgment, difficulty with language processing, poor auditory memory, or visual-motor integration failures. Each deficit type could conceivably be more differentially predictive of antisocial behavior than the overall IQ, but each would contribute to the development of antisocial behavior through different theoretical causal chains. Elucidation of a possible delinquency-specific pattern of neuropsychological deficit is needed in order to clarify the relation between delinquency and cognitive performance. In addition, delinquency is a heterogeneous entity, with legal as well as behavioral definitions, and it is likely that differently defined groups of delinquents may show different neuropsychological profiles. Neuropsychological studies can help us to describe the extent and nature of particular delinquency-related brain dysfunctions, thereby allowing us to incorporate this piece of information parsimoniously into theoretical structures concerning the etiology of delinquent behavior. Such neuropsychological studies are reviewed in Section IV.

B. Mediated Effect Formulations

Hirschi and Hindelang (1977) have discussed implications for delinquency theories from the finding that delinquents' IQ scores are significantly low. They wrote, "In the case of IQ, it would be accurate to say that theory opposes research and research ignores theory" (p. 577). They argued that, although delinquency theories ignore the intelligence variable, most may be seen to require a relation between cognitive abilities and delinquency, if we look closely enough. Strain theory (Cloward and Ohlin 1960), for example, would seem to predict a positive correlation between cognitive skills and delinquency. Boys with cognitive talents whose efforts at attaining material success are blocked because they come from socially disadvantaged origins would be predicted to be at risk for illegal behavior. Perhaps those with cognitive strengths are most able to conceptualize the discrepancy between their aspirations and achievements as unjust; to feel the strain. Similarly, Cohen's (1955) status-frustration theory views tests of cognitive ability as indices of the capacity of the child to meet middle-class achievement standards. Children at a competitive disadvantage find school aversive and turn to the delinquent subculture after rejecting middle-class values. Labeling theory also makes implicit use of neuropsychological status, according to Hirschi and Hindelang (1977). The relation between official delinquency status and low IQ is regarded as evidence that social deviance control systems discriminate against the disadvantaged, with disadvantage being indicated by low scores on mental tests (Polk and Schafer 1972). Even the rational choice models growing out of general deterrence theory (Tittle 1980; Cornish and Clarke 1986; Piliavin et al. 1986) assume an association between refraining from crime and the individual's ability to think abstractly, inhibit impulses, and consider future implications of behavior, all of which (from the perspective of neuropsychologists) are dependent upon normal functioning of the frontal lobes of the brain. A brain in good working order is prerequisite for making choices about crime rationally.

Social control theories have the least difficulty incorporating individual differences in cognitive ability. Hirschi's (1969) version of control theory predicts that intellectual capacity will have implications for how children interact with school, a crucial socializing agency. Cognitively able children will be more likely to receive rewards at school and will develop attachments to the school, but neuropsychologically handicapped children should experience school negatively and hence fail to form the attachments that prevent delinquent behavior. This formulation has received a great deal of empirical support (reviewed by Empey [1978]). One criticism of social control theory (and other criminological) accounts of cognitive deficit in delinquency is that the majority of low IQ children fail to become delinquent. The equivocal association between reading failure and delinquency (Murray 1976) illustrates that many children who experience failure at school do not become delinquent. The important question then concerns what characteristics differentiate low IQ children who do develop antisocial behavior patterns from those who do not. Control theory has assumed that IQ scores represent only a unidimensional quantity of general intellectual capacity. Such a narrow view of IQ scores precludes appreciation that distinguishable patterns of mental strengths and weaknesses can underlie identical omnibus IQ scores (Lezak 1988). It may be that some pattern of abilities is particular to children who respond antisocially to school failure.

All of these delinquency theories share two principles with regard to neuropsychological deficit. First, the effects of neuropsychological status on delinquency are conceptualized as indirect effects. Cohen (1955) and Hirschi (1969) proposed that school experience is the important mediating variable. Elliott and Voss's (1974) finding that self-report delinquency rates declined after low achievers dropped out of school seems partially to support this notion. Cloward and Ohlin (1960) might have suggested ambitions and aspirations as mediating constructs. Attraction of a deviant label mediated the relation between cognitive deficit and delinquency for Polk and Schafer (1972). If rational choice formulations considered individual differences in information-processing ability, they might come closest to admitting a direct positive effect upon deterrability, but they have not considered such differences. Second, the effects of cognitive deficits are only exerted at or after the age of school entry, when the potential delinquent encounters formal institutions of socialization (the school or the justice system). The deficits may or may not have been present at ages prior to school entry, but because the theories envisage that their effects are dependent upon mediating variables that are emergent at later ages, they make no mention of early developmental processes.

C. Direct Effect Formulations

Theoretical perspectives from psychology and child psychiatry typically assume that neuropsychological status can operate directly to produce deviant behavior. That is, because the brain is the instrument of behavior, neuropsychological factors influence development of temperament, personality, and psychopathology. Tucker (1981), for example, has emphasized the coexistence of cognitive and emotional presentations. He suggested that both poor performance on verbal neuropsychological tests and absence of anxiety reflect under-arousal of the left cerebral hemisphere, and he noted that both have been shown to characterize criminal offenders with antisocial personality disorder. In this view, dysfunction of one hemisphere of the brain contributes directly to the capacity for antisocial personality development by dampening anxiety that might otherwise prevent individuals from engaging in dangerous illicit behavior. Tucker mentioned antisocial personality only parenthetically in a lengthy treatise on hemispheric specialization and emotion, but his idea provides a clear example of a direct effect hypothesis.

Pontius (1972), Yeudall (1980), and Gorenstein (1982) have developed theories based on the observed similarity between the behavior of delinquents and "pseudopsychopathic" patients with frontal lobe brain injuries. Gorenstein and Newman (1980) also described *functional* similarities between disinhibited antisocial human behavior and experimental animal models of damage to the structures of the frontal lobes and limbic system of the brain. The normal functions of the frontal lobes of the brain include sustaining attention and concentration, abstract reasoning and concept formation, goal formulation, anticipation and planning, programming and initiation of purposive sequences of motor behavior, effective self-monitoring of behavior and self-awareness, and inhibition of unsuccessful, inappropriate, or impulsive behaviors, with adaptive shifting to alternative behaviors. These functions are commonly referred to as "executive functions," and they hold consequent implications for social judgment, self-control, responsiveness to punishment, and ethical behavior. Large numbers of clinical case studies and lesion research with human and animal subjects have fairly clearly established that executive functions are primarily subserved by the frontal lobes of the brain and by communicative connections between the frontal lobes and adjacent brain systems (see Fuster [1980]; Milner and Petrides [1984]; Kolb and Whishaw [1985]; and Stuss and Benson [1986] for reviews). The case of Phineas Gage described earlier in this section is an early classic in this literature.

Theorists working in this area tend to propose that executive dysfunctions present or latent at birth interfere with a child's ability to control his own behavior, producing an inattentive, impulsive child who is handicapped at considering the future implications of his acts. He has difficulty understanding the negative impact his behavior makes on others, fails to hold in mind abstract ideas of ethical values and future rewards, and fails to inhibit inappropriate behavior or adapt his behavior to social circumstances. Executive deficit may thus give rise to early childhood behavior problems that in turn set the stage for emerging delinquent behavior as the child grows physically older but not much more socially mature (Buikhuisen 1987*b*).

Theorists have also addressed the processes by which verbal neuropsychological deficits might contribute to antisocial behavior. The Russian neuropsychologist A. R. Luria has outlined (Luria 1961; Luria and Homskaya 1964) a comprehensive theory of the importance of speech for the self-control of behavior. Briefly, Luria ties the very young child's capacity for following verbal instructions to anatomical maturational development of the neuronal structures of the frontal lobes and left hemisphere of the brain. He also outlines the developmental process through which external parental verbal instructions and reinforcements are converted to internal verbally based self-control mechanisms. In this view, normal auditory verbal memory and verbal abstract reasoning are essential abilities in the development of self-control, and they influence socialization from the earliest parent-child interaction. Speech-based mechanisms of self-control range from virtually automatic motor programming or inhibiting of simple behaviors (e.g., No!) to "thinking things through" before embarking upon a course of complex behavior such as a robbery. Luria did not discuss delinquency in his writings, but the notion that deficient verbal mediation characterizes children with aggressive behavior problems has received some empirical support (Camp 1977; Kopp 1982). Programs designed to train verbal self-control skills have reported good results (Meichenbaum and Goodman 1971; Douglas 1972; Camp et al. 1977), but generalizability and longevity of the gains made during training remain questionable.

Other writers have also commented on how verbal deficits might influence the development of delinquency. Wilson and Herrnstein (1985) view low verbal intelligence as contributing to a present-oriented cognitive style, which in turn fosters irresponsible, exploitative behavior. Humans use language as the medium for abstract reasoning; we keep things that are "out of sight" from also becoming "out of mind" by mentally representing them with words. Therefore, language is an essential ingredient in prosocial processes such as delaying gratification or anticipating consequences. Miller (1987) integrates information about executive and verbal deficits into a formulation of antisocial personality. Miller proposes that long-standing neuropsychological impairments impede development of "a self-referential conceptual classification system for behavioral control," the absence of which predisposes to maladaptive behavioral disinhibition under interpersonal stress. Eysenck (1977), discussing his autonomic conditioning theory of antisocial personality disorder, states that stimulus generalization would be enhanced by the process of verbal labeling of misbehaviors as "naughty," "bad," or "wicked" by parents. Children with verbal-skill deficits might profit less from labeling a class of behaviors as punishment-attracting actions, thereby having to learn by trial and error. Verbally impaired children should experience more frequent punishment events than verbally adept children, but with less result in curbing their problem behavior. Savitsky and Czyzewski (1978) speculate that a deficit in verbal skills may prevent delinquents from adequately labeling their perceptions of the emotions expressed by others (victims or adversaries), and it might also limit delinquents' options, for response in threatening or ambiguous social situations, to physical reactions rather than verbal ones. If delinquents feel uncomfortable or inept with verbal communication they may be more likely to just strike out than to attempt to talk their way out of an altercation.

Tarter et al. (1984) mention the intriguing notion that children with poor communication skills may elicit less positive interaction and more physical punishment from parents, especially if the family is stressed. Consistent with Tarter's prediction, McDermott and Rourke (cited in Rourke and Fiske 1981) compared the interactions of fathers with their sons who had language deficits to the same fathers' interactions with nondeficient sibling sons and found fathers to be more negative, rejecting, and derogatory with the less verbal sons. Following from Tarter's speculation, poor verbal abilities may hinder development of the parent-child attachment bonds that forestall delinquency in Hirschi's (1969) social control theory.

Byron Rourke (1975, 1985, 1987; Rourke and Fiske 1981) has theorized that information-processing deficits present from birth are responsible for learning disabilities in sociointerpersonal as well as academic realms. Although Rourke has not discussed delinquent behavior, he has predicted specific deficits in social perceptiveness and social responsiveness following from neuropsychological dysfunction. Rourke's theory emphasizes the necessity of identifying subtypes of disability based on neuropsychological test performance, and he has extensively investigated the differential social-skills deficits and behavioral and emotional problems of children so classified. For example, he explains that children with right-hemisphere-based perceptual deficits do not receive accurate information from their visual environments.

Consequently they may fail to decipher social meaning in facial expressions, body language, and the prosodic elements of oral communication. These children are at a disadvantage in interpersonal exchanges, and hence they may behave inappropriately or tend mistakenly to attribute negative intent to relatively innocuous interpersonal exchanges. This sort of process may have implications for the development of antisocial response styles. For example, Dodge and colleagues have shown that when aggressive boys are provided with limited or ambiguous information about the motives of an actor, they often make attributions about the intentions of the actor that are biased toward malevolent intent (Dodge and Newman 1981; Dodge and Frame 1982). Habitually jumping to negative conclusions about others' intentions might predispose one toward frequent hostile behavior and could impede the development of attachment to prosocial relatives or peers.

These formulations from psychology share two principles that distinguish them from the "mediated effect" delinquency theories discussed earlier. First, they propose that neuropsychological characteristics of a child are able to influence directly the child's personality and behavioral outcomes. Mediation by formal social institutions is not perceived as a *necessary* condition for this influence, although such mediation is certainly not disallowed, and in fact an interactional perspective characterizes most of the psychological theories. Second, they specify that the child's complement of neuropsychological strengths and weaknesses is present very early in life, and that its influence upon personality and behavioral development begins with the child's earliest interactions with the environment. Antisocial behavior patterns may be perpetuated or exacerbated by school experiences, but they are established during early social learning in the family.

D. Shortcomings of Existing Theories

Neuropsychological theories were not designed to explain delinquency, and delinquency theories were constructed before the recent findings from neuropsychological research with delinquents were available. As a result, both sets of theories have gaps. There is compelling evidence that aggressive antisocial behavior is present prior to school entry, and that it is stable and predictive of delinquency and adult crime (Olweus 1979; Loeber 1982). There is also compelling evidence suggesting that early socialization within the family is important for delinquent outcomes (Loeber and Stouthamer-Loeber 1986; Snyder and Patterson 1987). Given these facts, the neuropsychological theories offer more explanatory power for early development of antisocial behavior because they assume that effects begin in early childhood. Traditional delinquency theories may have admitted neuropsychological etiological factors too late in the natural history of antisocial behavior by relegating their impact to school-age years. In addition, the predictions of delinquency theories for neuropsychological research are limited to predictions about a vague construct of insufficient general intelligence and consequent academic failure. They are not as well articulated or as precise as the predictions from the psychological theories.

Most neuropsychological theories, however, fail to articulate specific predictions for delinquent outcome. For example, are specific types of offenses more likely to follow from specific patterns of neuropsychological deficit? Are the offenses of the neuropsychologically impaired more likely to be impulsive or violent? Can neuropsychological data assist in classification of subtypes of conduct disorder? Can these data discriminate antisocial personality disorder from general criminal offending? If neuropsychological effects on the development of antisocial behavior do take place early in life, then is neuropsychological deficit most characteristic of very early onset delinquency? Neuropsychological theories suffer from not being integrated into mainstream criminology. Theorists have made no effort to account for established relations in criminology such as gender, age, or social class effects on delinquency.

There are two important shortcomings that are shared by neuropsychological and delinquency theories alike. Both fail to incorporate the positive correlation between children's and parents' cognitive abilities (Scarr and McCartney 1983). This correlation may come about because of shared genes or because low-ability parents are less likely to provide the prenatal, nutritional, or stimulating social and educational conditions necessary for optimal development of their children's cognitive capacities. The implication of the correlation is that children who are intellectually disadvantaged at learning prosocial behaviors usually have parents who are intellectually disadvantaged at teaching prosocial behaviors (Snyder and Patterson 1987). Likewise, children with difficult temperaments are likely to have parents whose own psychopathologies limit their resources for coping with a difficult child (see Rutter [1983] for a discussion of this interaction). And compromised parental intellect, parental deviance, or both, will enhance the chances that the family will be situated in a low-social-class neighborhood, exposing the child to criminogenic environmental factors outside the home. The potential interaction effects are myriad, and they have seldom been theoretically addressed.

This discussion points up the second shortcoming shared by existing theories. Most predict simple one-directional effects, with cognitive impairment (whether mediated or direct) leading to behavioral deviance and academic achievement deficits. Recursive and reciprocal effects are equally plausible (although more difficult to model statistically). For example, suppose that a child's poor verbal skills and impulsivity elicit parental rejection, rejected children may behave even more aggressively to get attention, aggressive behavior interferes with learning in school, already deficient verbal skills deteriorate further when the child fails to practice reading, the ensuing academic failure interferes with attachment to the school, the nonattached aggressive child becomes involved with delinquent peers who use drugs, delinquency-related drug use further compromises neuropsychological function, increasingly severe brain dysfunction disinhibits the youth in a violence-eliciting situation, and so on. Any number of scenarios could be envisaged, but the point is that the direction of causality may change over the developmental course.

The perspectives of sociological and neuropsychological theoretical approaches are complementary. They may be profitably combined if effects are considered as a life span reciprocal downward spiral rather than a simple one-directional effect occurring at only one age. The two sets of theories may be complementary in another way. Sociological influences may be the immediate causes of delinquent behavior, but causal sequences may begin with individual differences (Rowe and Osgood 1984). For example, associating with delinquent peers is a recognized cause of delinquent behavior, but why do children associate with delinquent peers? One probable reason behind peer affiliation is similarity of educational aspirations and achievement, and these characteristics are strongly dependent upon individual differences in verbal abilities (Moffitt and Heimer 1988). Beginning exemplary theoretical work oriented in these directions has been presented by Wilson and Herrnstein (1985), Buikhuisen (1987b), Huesmann, Eron, and Yarmel (1987), and Levine and Jordan (1987).

III. Neuropsychological Studies of Juvenile Delinquents

Published reports of the neuropsychological test scores of juvenile delinquents were identified for this essay by computerized literature search, by cross-reference checking, and by a mail survey of selected researchers working in the area. Table 1 presents the thirty-one reports identified and selected aspects of their designs. No studies were excluded because of methodological problems because one goal of this essay is to draw attention to errors to be avoided when future studies are designed. In addition to the thirty-one investigations, sixteen studies of delinquents' scores on the Porteus Maze Test (a test of impulsive problem solving) have been reviewed by Riddle and Roberts (1977). Prentice and Kelly (1963) and West and Farrington (1973) have reviewed the large literature on verbal and performance IQ discrepancies in delinquents. These related studies are too numerous for inclusion in table 1, but they are considered in the text.

Although the studies under consideration have used a wide variety of neuropsychological tests and have employed many different definitions of delinquency status, their findings have been fairly consistent. In all but one report, delinquents have scored poorly on a substantial proportion of the tests administered. Four of the studies reported findings from neurological or electroencephalographic examinations that corroborated the results from neuropsychological tests (Krynicki 1978; Lewis et al. 1979; Wolff et al. 1982; McManus et al. 1985). Across studies, the functions most consistently cited as impaired have been verbal (receptive and expressive language, oral and written) and executive functions (abstraction, planning, inhibition of inappropriate responses, mental flexibility, sequencing, attention, and concentration). Though examined less often, memory abilities have also been found to be impaired when tested. Visuospatial, sensory, and motor deficits have been found less consistently. In fact, in some studies delinquents exhibited notable strengths in one or more of the latter areas (e.g., Voorhees 1981; Karniski et al. 1982; Sobotowicz, Evans, and Laughlin 1987). Overall, the consistency of the reports has been impressive and suggests a robust relation between neuropsychological scores and delinquency. However, the findings must be viewed with caution because of several methodological shortcomings common to many of the studies.

A. Methodological Issues

The methodological problems of previous studies lie in the areas of subject selection, adequacy of controls, collection of neuropsychological data, data analysis, and failure to evaluate for specificity of effects. Each of these methodological problems is discussed in this section.

1. *Subject Selection Bias.*   In twenty-eight of the studies reviewed,

TABLE 1

Studies of Juvenile Delinquent Subjects' Performance on Neuropsychological Tests

Reference	Delinquency Definition	Tests Used	No. of Delinquents	Nondelinquent Groups	Additional Variables
Andrew (1982)	Probationers referred for psychiatric evaluation	WISC-R subtests	45 M + 23 F	None	Sex, race, violence
Appellof & Augustine (1985)	Delinquent volunteers	Frontal Lobe Battery	30 M	30 M	...
Berman & Siegal (1976)	Incarcerated in a training school	Halstead-Reitan battery and WAIS	45 M	45 M high school volunteers	Race
Brickman et al. (1984)	Incarcerated and selected for offense severity	Luria-Nebraska battery, WISC, WRAT	36 M + 26 F	None	School achievement, sex, race, violence
Denno (1989)	Police records for unselected birth cohort of black subjects	WISC, Stanford-Binet, Bender-Gestalt, WRAT, and California Achievement Test	151 M + 69 F	336 M and 431 F	Violence, socioeconomic status, sex
Fitzhugh (1973)	Court referred for psychiatric evaluation	Wechsler, Bellevue and Halstead-Reitan battery	19 M	None	...
Hinkle (1983)	Institutionalized	Bender-Gestalt and Memory for Designs	30 (sex not stated)	30 volunteers	...
Hurwitz et al. (1972) (study 1)	Adjudicated and detained	Lincoln-Oseretsky Motor Development	15 M	15 M with LD 15 M students	Learning Disability
Hurwitz et al. (1972) (study 2)	Training school residents	Tapping, Stroop, Beery VMI, Memory for Designs, Ravens Matrices, and Embedded Figures	13 M	13 M students	...
Hubble & Groff (1981)	Court referred for psychiatric evaluation	WISC-R subtests	305 M	None	...

122

Study	Sample	Tests	N	Comparison group	Control variables
Hutt & Dates (1977)	Adjudicated	Bender-Gestalt	120 M	None	...
Karniski et al. (1982)	Committed to Department of Youth Services	29 tests tapping motor, temporal-sequential, visual, and language skills	54 M	51 M volunteers	SES
Krynicki (1978)	Hospitalized assaulters	WISC-R plus 11 neuropsychological tests	15 M	6 neurological patients	Violence
Lewis et al. (1979)	Incarcerated for violence	WISC-R and Bender-Gestalt	97 M	None	Race, violence
McManus et al. (1985)	Incarcerated and selected for offense severity	Luria-Nebraska, WISC-R, and WRAT	40 M + 31 F	None	Mental disorder
Meltzer, Roditi, & Fenton (1986)	Committed to youth services	8-item battery	53 M	50 M students 26 LD youths	LD
Miller, Burdg, & Carpenter (1980)	Incarcerated in evaluation unit	WISC-R subtests	65 M + 32 F	None	Race
Moffitt & Silva (1988a)	Self-report from an unselected birth cohort	WISC-R, Pegboard, Rey Verbal Learning, Rey Complex Figure, Trail-making, Verbal Fluency, Wisconsin Card-Sorting Test, various achievement tests	71 M + 53 F	290 M + 282 F	Sex, SES, and family adversity
Moffitt & Silva (1988b)	As above, with Attention Deficit Disorder (ADD)	Battery described above	71 M + 53 F	290 M + 282 F	ADD, SES, sex, and reading achievement
Pontius & Ruttiger (1976)	Officially referred	Narratives Test	36 (sex not stated)	67 normal, 29 disturbed youths	...
Robbins et al. (1983)	Adjudicated, clinic referred for evaluation	WISC, Bender-Gestalt, Perdue Perceptual Motor, Auditory Skills Battery, WRAT	50 M	None	...
Skoff & Libon (1987)	Incarcerated	Frontal Lobe Battery	22 M	None	...

TABLE 1 (*Continued*)

Reference	Delinquency Definition	Tests Used	No. of Delinquents	Nondelinquent Groups	Additional Variables
Slavin (1978)	Under court jurisdiction	WISC, WRAT, Bender-Gestalt, motor and sensory tasks	56	None	...
Sobotowicz et al. (1987)	Incarcerated delinquents	WAIS, WRAT, Wechsler Memory Scale, plus 11 neuropsychological tests	50 M	25M LD + 25 M non-LD	Reading disability
Spellacy (1977)	Court referred residents of training school	WISC plus 10 neuropsychological tests	80 M	None	Race, violence
Tarnopol (1970)	Delinquent drop-outs in Neighborhood Youth Corps	WAIS, Bender-Gestalt, Gates Reading	102 M	None	...
Tarter et al. (1983)	Court referred for neuropsychiatric evaluation	WISC-R, Pittsburgh Initial Neuropsychological Battery and Detroit Tests of Learning Aptitude, Peabody Achievement	73 M	None	Race, violence

Study	Population	Battery	N	Comparison group	Variable
Tarter et al. (1984)	As above	Battery described above	83 M + 18 F	None	Child abuse history
Vorhees (1981)	Volunteers from a juvenile facility	Luria's Investigation, Bender-Gestalt	13 M + 15 F	5 M + 8 F high school volunteers	...
Wolff et al. (1982)	Detained in a low-security facility	IPAT IQ, Boston Naming Test, Peabody Achievement and Picture Vocabulary, Token Test, Stroop, Porteus Mazes, and Perceptual, Motor and Attention Measures	56 M	48 M high-SES / 48 M low-SES high school volunteers	SES
Yeudall, Fromm-Auch, & Davies (1982)	Severe delinquent in-patients under psychiatric treatment	WISC-R, Halstead-Reitan battery and 12 additional tests	64 M + 35 F	29 M + 18 F high school volunteers	Sex, drug history

NOTE.—WISC, WISC-R, WAIS, and WAIS-R denote Wechsler's tests of intelligence for children and adults. WRAT denotes Wide Range Achievement Test. M and F denote males and females, respectively. LD, ADD, and SES denote learning disability, attention deficit disorder, and socioeconomic status, respectively.

the subjects were a highly selected group: incarcerated volunteers, hos-
pitalized violent adolescents, adjudicated recidivistic delinquents, or
offenders referred for psychiatric evaluation. Table 1 presents the delinquency criterion for each study. Only three studies reported data
from unselected birth cohorts representative of the general population
(Moffitt and Silva 1988a and 1988b; Denno 1989). Only Moffitt and
Silva defined delinquency based on self-report data. In addition, the
subjects of most studies were well into their delinquent careers; the
modal subject age was greater than fourteen years. Samples of this type
introduce several potential sources of bias. The subjects may have been
involved in drug or alcohol abuse and in fights or motor vehicle accidents (in which they may have sustained repetitive concussions).
Lewis, Shanok, and Balla (1979) have described an elevated rate of
emergency room visits for head and facial injuries among serious delinquent offenders. A lengthy history of institutionalization and truancy
are also likely for older delinquents, leading to low educational attainment. Some of the studies reported that incarcerated subjects
evidenced reactive depressive symptoms (Yeudall and Fromm-Auch
1979; Brickman et al. 1984), or were medicated with major tranquiliz-
ers at the time of testing (Krynicki 1978; Yeudall, Fromm-Auch, and
Davies 1982). Hodgins, de Bray, and Braun (1989) have shown that
medications administered to control aggressive behavior can impair
performance on certain neuropsychological measures, and it is well
known that severe depression can produce temporary cognitive impairment (Caine 1986).

All of these factors may be expected to compromise performance on
cognitive tests, suggesting that *a delinquent lifestyle may produce neuropsychological deficit, rather than the reverse* (Shanok and Lewis 1981; Hare
1984). In addition, it is possible that the cognitively impaired delinquent is more easily apprehended by police or more likely to be referred by the courts for psychological testing. Indeed, Robbins et al.
(1983) found clinic-referred delinquents to be more neuropsychologically impaired than adjudicated delinquents who had not been referred.
On the other hand, Moffitt and Silva (1988c) found no IQ difference
between delinquents who had been arrested and those with equivalent
self-reports of delinquent behavior who had not been arrested.

Another problem is the questionable test motivation of the older
incarcerated delinquent. Tarnopol (1970, p. 205) noted that, "Testing
these subjects proved to be a most difficult task for many reasons, . . .
including factors of school-phobic fear of testing and little motivation

other than to hustle the few dollars paid them to take the tests." Finally, racial minorities are often disproportionately represented among incarcerated delinquents, and minority adolescents often perform poorly on mental tests. Poor black and Hispanic youths are often less than comfortable with mainstream English, suggesting an especial problem for interpretation of the verbal deficits most often found to characterize delinquent samples. Although nine of the reports mentioned inclusion of minority subjects, only one study (Andrew 1982) presented test scores by race; black delinquents' verbal scores were about one standard deviation below those of white delinquents. These potential sources of bias from subject selection criteria are serious. They limit generalizability of the findings and they call into question the causal direction of the relation between poor neuropsychological test scores and delinquency. Only Spreen (1981) and Denno (1989) have examined test scores collected in early childhood before the onset of delinquent behavior, yet this prospective design is essential for allowing us to rule out the possibility that the lifestyles of delinquents diminish their test scores.

2. *Comparison Groups.* Nondelinquent comparison groups were used in only half of the studies and, when used, were usually nonrandomly chosen high school volunteers, higher in social class and education than the delinquents. It is unclear whether the group differences obtained on certain education-sensitive tests were the result of true differences in cognitive function or of differing opportunities for educational enrichment. Only the Moffitt and Silva studies screened controls for nonadjudicated (self-reported or parent-reported) delinquency, thereby insuring that nondelinquent controls were actually less delinquent than the delinquent group. Because delinquent behavior is common in adolescence, if official delinquents are compared to subjects matched for age, education, and social class it is likely that the "nondelinquent" controls are not nondelinquent at all, thereby reducing the chances of detecting true group differences. The only study that found no neuropsychological deficit for delinquents was among the studies using a nondelinquent comparison group (Appellof and Augustine 1985).

3. *Data Collection and Analysis.*   In all but three cases, the choice of neuropsychological measures was apparently determined by availability of record data, based on scores that were collected during routine clinical evaluation, and collected prior to conceptualization of the research questions. As a result, the tests employed often tapped a re-

stricted range of primary cognitive functions, making the interpretation of patterns of relative strengths and weaknesses difficult. Nine of the thirty-one studies included test batteries extensive enough for detailed examination of relative deficit patterns. In only four studies (Pontius and Ruttiger 1976; Spreen 1981; Moffitt and Silva 1988*a*, 1988*b;* Denno 1989) were the neuropsychological examiners kept blind to the subjects' delinquent status in order to preclude bias. Few studies cited evidence for the reliability and validity of the tests used. The fifteen studies that failed to include nondelinquent controls compared delinquents' test scores to published norms or, worse yet, to "standards of clinical judgment." It is far from clear that the published norms for most neuropsychological tests are adequate for benchmark comparison; their appropriateness for low social class, low education, and adolescent age groups is not well established.[3]

Statistical treatment of the data was less than rigorous in most of the studies.[4] In general, little attention was paid to variables that might confound social and biological interpretations of low test scores. For example, gender and social class are known to covary with delinquency and with many neuropsychological test scores, yet only five studies statistically controlled for social class and only five studies tested for sex differences. Female subjects were included in only one-third of the reports.

The question of what factors should be controlled statistically (or by matching comparison subjects) in neuropsychological research on deviance is complex. The answer is that the choice of controls depends on the conceptual goals for the analysis. Although neuropsychological tests are designed to measure brain function, certain scores reflect multifactorial sources of variation. For example, some (but not all) neuropsychological measures covary with measures of socioeconomic status (SES). This positive correlation partially reflects SES-related influences on test scores from social factors such as lack of access to

[3] The Wechsler Intelligence Scale for Children-Revised, or WISC-R, is one exception. It is the most widely-used standardized intelligence test for seven- to sixteen-year-olds, and it includes twelve subtests, six that tap various language-based skills such as abstract reasoning, mental arithmetic and social comprehension, and five problem-solving tasks that do not require language. The former constitute the verbal IQ (VIQ) and the latter constitute the performance IQ (PIQ) scores.

[4] For example, as many as thirty individual *t*-tests of the difference between group mean scores were reported in one table, without regard for the increasing likelihood of Type 1 error when many statistical tests are performed on one set of data. Type 1 error results in the mistaken rejection of the null hypothesis that there is no difference between delinquents and controls.

quality educational experiences or cultural attitudes toward test taking. But the correlation also reflects SES-related influences upon brain integrity from biological factors such as poor prenatal health care and inadequate nutrition. In addition to this confounding of "social disadvantage" and "biological cognitive" effects from the environment, it is likely that parents' cognitive capacities are strong determinants of the SES level they are able to attain and of the social, educational, and health environments they are able to provide for their children. These same parental cognitive capacities influence the genotype of their childrens' brains through heritability. Thus, limited cognitive function may in some cases "cause" subjects to be in the lower SES categories. The causal direction of the SES-brain correlation is hypothetically bidirectional. This means that both heritable and acquired biological sources of variation in cognitive function are confounded with the purely social aspects of SES variables.

Most researchers would agree that we should control for SES before we test for associations between neuropsychological test scores and delinquency. They want to be sure that the associations can safely be interpreted as evidence that the brains of delinquents are actually dysfunctional. No one wants to be guilty of inferring brain dysfunctions if the neuropsychology/delinquency correlation is simply a spurious effect that appears solely because poor social environments incidentally produce both delinquency and low test scores. What they assume is that they know the direction of the causal relationship that is producing the correlation between test scores and SES. But, as I have argued above, SES measures are not independent of cognitive measures, and controlling for SES may camouflage real group differences in cognitive status. In our efforts to control for the purely social aspects of the neuropsychology/delinquency correlation, we will necessarily attenuate any existing real brain differences. Therefore, it is not logical to control for SES in a knee-jerk fashion (Meehl 1971). We might just as well insist that biological aspects of brain status be controlled in order to demonstrate conclusively that SES has effects on delinquency that are purely environmental (see Van Dusen, Mednick, and Gabrielli [1983], for a study of this type).

If the preceding argument is correct, it follows that those studies that have found neuropsychological variables to explain a small portion of statistical variance in delinquency despite the fact that SES was controlled (e.g., Karniski et al. 1982; Moffitt and Silva 1988*a*) provide a strong case for consideration of neuropsychology in criminological theory. As a recommendation for future analyses, we might work on breaking SES into its purely social components for research use, or we might model the hypothesized interactions between SES and brain indicators. In the short run, the results from available studies with SES controls document some independent relation between brain status and delinquency, and studies without SES controls are crucial for providing descriptive information about delinquents' deficits as they exist in nature.

4. *Specificity of Effects.*   Finally, most previous research has failed to address the specificity of the obtained neuropsychological deficits to antisocial behavior per se. Longitudinal follow-up studies of hyperactive/attention deficit disorder (ADD) children have shown them to be somewhat disproportionately represented among delinquents in adolescence (Loney et al. 1983; Weiss 1983; Satterfield 1987). Likewise, there is some evidence, although inconclusive, that reading disabled (RD) children are disproportionately represented among official delinquent populations (see Murray [1976] versus Sturge [1982]). Although there is controversy regarding the causal ordering of the association between ADD or RD and neuropsychological deficit, it is well established that ADD and RD subjects score poorly on many tests of cognitive function (for reviews see Douglas [1983], Rourke [1983], and Campbell and Werry [1986]). It is possible that much of the cognitive deficit associated with delinquency could be explained by the presence of a significant number of cases with histories of ADD or RD among delinquent samples. If so, it would be important to show that cognitive status varies with extent of delinquency within these groups.

Only one report (Moffitt and Silva 1988*b*) examined the role of ADD in the neuropsychology/delinquency relation. Four studies (Hurwitz et al. 1972; Spreen 1981; Meltzer, Roditi, and Fenton 1986; Sobotowicz, Evans, and Laughlin 1987) examined learning disabled subjects. Only the Hurwitz et al. study defined LD subjects according to currently recognized research criteria for specific reading disability, and the remainder simply used children referred for learning problems without regard to type or etiology. In three of the studies the designs did not allow discrimination of subgroup effects: either delinquent and RD groups differed in social class, or delinquent subjects were found to read as poorly as RD subjects, or over half of RD subjects were found to have arrests. Sobotowicz, Evans, and Laughlin (1987) did effectively separate learning disability and delinquency effects; their work is discussed in Section IV.

B. The New Zealand Self-Report Delinquency Project

In view of my methodological criticisms of previous work, I embarked in 1984 upon a program of research designed to offer certain design advantages for an "acid test" of the hypothesis that neuropsychological deficit is associated with delinquent behavior. Because many of the conclusions I offer in this essay rely upon agreement between the results of earlier poorly designed studies and the results of this more rigorous study, I describe the latter study here in some detail. The nature of the methodological problems of previous studies cast serious doubt on the likelihood of replicating the purported neuropsychology/delinquency relation, but the New Zealand project data have by and large been consistent with previously reported results.

The project was initiated in the context of the longitudinal Dunedin (New Zealand) Multidisciplinary Health and Development Study, in which a team of researchers, headed by Phil A. Silva, has systematically collected high-quality data for an unselected birth cohort of 1,037 children since their births in 1972. Detailed prospective data were available concerning perinatal, neurological, illness and injury, language, educational achievement, behavior disorder, family demographic, and intelligence test performance variables for six assessment waves (one every two years) prior to the first wave of neuropsychological and delinquency data collection which was undertaken at the children's thirteenth birthdays in 1985.

1. *Design Advantages.* The design avoided sampling bias by the use of this large unselected birth cohort of males and females. Delinquency was assessed by the self-report interview method, supplemented by parent and teacher reports and police contact records.[5] The subjects had voluntarily participated in comprehensive assessments semiannually since age three, and their confidence had never been violated by unit staff, yielding excellent self-report compliance. The procedure allowed for the designation of delinquent and nondelinquent comparison groups based on the agreement of reports across raters, unconfounded by the likelihood of police detection or incarceration. A research battery of neuropsychological instruments was selected

---

[5] Alternative sources of delinquency data allowed for examining adult's reports in the event that the children's ability to self-report delinquent behavior validly turned out to be limited by memory function. As it happened, the children's verbal memorization test scores were inversely correlated with both self-reports and other reports of delinquency, and the measure of visual-spatial memory was unrelated to delinquency measures, so that memory problems do not appear to invalidate the self-report method.

beforehand, in keeping with the goal of testing a broad range of cognitive and motor skills. The criteria that guided instrument selection were that each test tap theoretically important neuropsychological constructs; be widely used and commonly known; have published positive evaluations of reliability and validity; and be brief and intrinsically interesting, in order to accommodate adolescent attention spans, maximize motivation, and fit into a time-limited assessment schedule. Motivation for test taking was high; the subjects rated the neuropsychological session as "most interesting and enjoyable" among the full day of data collection exercises. The cohort was large enough to allow for calculation of its own test norms. Tests were administered blind to delinquency status, in a standardized format, within one month of the subjects' thirteenth birthdays. Delinquents were designated as subjects who earned scores above the eighty-fifth percentile for their sex for at least two of the following: subject self-report of delinquent acts (Moffitt and Silva 1989), teacher report of antisocial acts, or parent report of antisocial acts, *or* who had a police arrest record. Seventy-one boys and fifty-three girls met the criteria. New Zealand is a low-delinquency nation, with a peak age for offending somewhat later than in the United States. Thus it is unlikely that any deficits found in the subjects near their thirteenth birthdays were the result of a protracted criminal lifestyle.

2. *General Findings.* Despite the youth of the subjects and the mildness of their delinquent offense histories, the most delinquent members of the New Zealand cohort did show statistically significant impairment on test scores reflecting verbal skills, auditory verbal memory, visuospatial analysis, and visual-motor integration relative to their less delinquent peers. Corrections were made for the likelihood of Type 1 error, and results were cross-validated upon split halves of the cohort. As in previous studies, the delinquents' verbal deficits were more severe than their nonverbal deficits. Consistent with two earlier studies that tested for sex differences (Andrew 1982; Brickman et al. 1984), there was no statistically significant interaction between gender and delinquency status in relation to any neuropsychological measure; that is, the relation between neuropsychological measures and delinquency was the same for the most delinquent boys and the most delinquent girls. As a test of the strength of the neuropsychological deficit/delinquency relation, the neuropsychological variables were entered into a hierarchical regression analysis following a measure of family adversity (comprising low parental education, low parental income,

single parent status, large family size, poor maternal mental health, and a poor score on a measure of family social environment). The neuropsychological variables were found to explain a small, but significant, amount of variance in delinquency group membership beyond that accounted for by family adversity (Moffitt and Silva 1988*a*).

3. *Specificity of Effects.* Because the diagnosis of ADD was found at markedly elevated rates in the backgrounds of these delinquents, the possibility was examined that the neuropsychological deficits of delinquents might be limited to delinquents with histories of ADD. Although delinquents with past ADD (22 percent of delinquents) were much more cognitively impaired than non-ADD delinquents, both groups scored significantly below nondelinquents on verbal, visuospatial, and visual-motor integration skills. In addition, ADD delinquents scored especially poorly on auditory verbal memory; their mean memory score fell a full standard deviation below the mean memory score of controls. The ADD delinquents were found to have the poorest IQ scores at ages five, seven, nine, and eleven as well, suggesting that their age-thirteen neuropsychological test scores represented a long-standing history of cognitive dysfunction. Interestingly enough, subjects with childhood ADD who had not developed delinquent behavior (42 percent of ADD cases) were not cognitively impaired at age thirteen, nor were their IQ scores significantly below controls' at earlier ages. These findings suggest that it is the specific comorbidity (presence of two disorders in one child) of ADD and delinquency that bears further neuropsychological study (Moffitt and Silva 1988*b*). In support of this conclusion, others (Offord et al. 1979; McGee, Williams, and Silva 1984, 1985; Hinshaw 1987; Walker et al. 1987; Werry, Reeves, and Elkind 1987) have pointed to the relatively greater severity of aggressive conduct problems among children with combined ADD and antisocial behavior. In the New Zealand cohort, delinquents with ADD earned aggression ratings, from parents, teachers, and from their own self-reports, that exceeded the aggression scores of non-ADD delinquents by about two standard deviations. Prospective investigations (Farrington, Loeber, and van Kammen 1987; and see Loeber and Stouthamer-Loeber [1987] for review) have demonstrated the comorbidity of ADD and delinquency to be an excellent predictor of adult chronic criminal offending, suggesting that this subgroup, characterized by the greatest level of neuropsychological impairment, may also be at risk for developing the most lengthy and relatively serious crime careers.

In summary, the New Zealand project was designed so as to avoid

many of the problems of earlier research and to provide a more stringent test of the hypothesized association between delinquency and cognitive deficit. The findings from this project have not been dissimilar
from those previously published, and they have illustrated the
usefulness of examining subgroups of delinquents. Additional specific
findings from this research are mentioned where relevant later in this
essay. The sample is being followed up at age fifteen and beyond in
order to test the efficacy of neuropsychological variables as prospective
predictors of more serious and recidivistic offending.

IV. A Substantive Review of Neuropsychological Findings

Section III outlined major methodological criticisms of the early literature on the neuropsychology of delinquency. Nevertheless, the primary findings from this literature have been corroborated by data from
the more adequately designed New Zealand project. Because of this
replication, the results of the earlier reports are considered to be informative, if we keep in mind a healthy caution following from our initial
methodological concerns. Findings with intriguing theoretical implications have been reported, especially in the functional areas of language-
based skills and executive (or frontal lobe) functions. In addition, much
work has been done to investigate a posited specific relation between
neuropsychological deficit and violent assaultive behavior.

A. Verbal Functions and Delinquency

Since Wechsler (1944) remarked upon the diagnostic utility of a performance IQ score greater than verbal IQ score obtained when using
his intelligence scales to assess delinquents, a plethora of studies has
been published on the "PIQ>VIQ" sign in delinquency. The verbal
IQ is a composite score taken from tests of general factual knowledge,
abstract reasoning, mental arithmetic, vocabulary, social comprehension and judgment, and immediate auditory memory. The performance IQ is calculated from nonverbal tests of attention to detail,
sequential reasoning, manual design construction, visual puzzle solving, symbolic encoding and decoding, and maze completion. All of the
subtests used to calculate the VIQ score are administered orally, require an oral response, and are solved using language-based processing
skills. "Performance" subtests, on the other hand, are administered and
solved in the visuospatial mode without the necessary use of language,
and they require a manual, not an oral, response. The measures PIQ

and VIQ are probably the most well researched and reliable of those used by psychologists. Prentice and Kelly (1963) reviewed twenty-four positive reports of the PIQ>VIQ in delinquents, West and Farrington (1973) reviewed still more, and the hypothesis is still finding support (e.g., Haynes and Bensch 1981; Tarter et al. 1985). Indeed, in all neuropsychological studies reviewed here that administered the Wechsler IQ scales (WISC-R for children to age sixteen or WAIS-R for adults), delinquents' PIQs exceeded their VIQs. This is an impressively replicable finding that wants explanation.

The PIQ>VIQ effect has been taken as strongly supporting a specific deficit in language manipulation for delinquents. Because language functions are subserved by the left cerebral hemisphere in almost all individuals (see Benson and Zaidel 1985), the PIQ>VIQ findings have also been interpreted as evidence for dysfunction of the left cerebral hemisphere in the etiology of antisocial behavior. These interpretations are by no means unchallenged. Objections have been raised regarding the possible confounding of social disadvantage and reading achievement with VIQ scores and regarding the lateralized anatomical interpretation of verbal deficit. This section first reviews evidence for verbal deficit from six neuropsychological investigations. Although all studies in table 1 provide some evidence of deficit on language-based tests for delinquents, the following six studies were selected for detailed discussion because they tapped a representative sample of neuropsychological abilities, allowing comparison of verbal and nonverbal functions. They also included nondelinquent comparison groups.

1. *Description of Studies.*   Wolff et al. (1982) examined fifty-six males detained in a low-security facility (30 percent of approached inmates refused to participate). Controls were high school boys selected by high school guidance counselors (and therefore subject to unknown selection biases). Delinquents scored significantly worse than controls on tests of reading, naming, vocabulary, and receptive language. Delinquents did not differ from controls on spatial or perceptual measures in this study.

Karniski et al. (1982) tested fifty-four incarcerated boys using twenty-nine tasks that were collapsed on a rational basis into composite measures of "neuromaturation, gross motor function, temporal-sequential organization, visual processing, and auditory-language function." A comparison group consisted of fifty-one boys from schools in a predominantly blue-collar community; controls were screened for official delinquency, but 70 percent of the control families approached had declined to participate. Notable mean group differences were obtained for two of the composite measures—visual processing and auditory-language function—but differences were greatest for the auditory-language area. Only 2 percent of controls, but 29.6 percent of the delinquents, scored two or more standard deviations below the control group's mean score on language skills.

Berman and Siegal (1976) administered the Halstead-Reitan Neuropsychological Battery (including the WAIS VIQ and PIQ tests) to forty-five boys within one week of their first incarceration. The Halstead-Reitan battery contains difficult tests of abstract reasoning, rhythmic sequencing, perception of speech sounds, sensory perception, motor response inhibition, and language skills to evaluate the functional integrity of the brain as a whole. It also includes several tests of sensory and manual functions that are repeated on the body's two sides (nonvisual manual problem solving, finger tapping speed, grip strength, and sensory sensitivity to touch and sound) in order to reveal dysfunction in the brain's two hemispheres. The timing of the testing was calculated to avoid institutionalization effects upon test scores, but it is also possible that reactive depression may have been a factor in the performance of newly incarcerated subjects. The battery yielded twenty-nine scores, which were analyzed using multiple t-tests. If, in order to reduce the likelihood of Type 1 error, we consider only those t-values statistically significant beyond $p = .001$, delinquents were deficient on six of seven tests tapping verbal skills. Delinquents were more impaired than controls on only one performance test: Digit Symbol, which is similar to a "secret code" game. It requires the child to use a code system of symbols matched to an array of numbers, filling in rows of numbered boxes with the proper symbols at a rapid pace. Digit Symbol is sometimes labeled as a verbal task in other batteries.

Sobotowicz, Evans, and Laughlin (1987) compared fifty incarcerated delinquents with fifty high school controls matched for age, race, and social class. Within each group, half the subjects had learning disabilities, and half were normal learners, yielding four groups: Normal, JD (juvenile delinquents), LD (learning disabled), and JD + LD. On tests of verbal language skills, abstract verbal concept formation, and semantic and sequential memory, all three problem groups differed significantly from controls. That the non-LD delinquents differed neuropsychologically from normals was especially unexpected, because the two groups were equal on mean full-scale IQ. In this study the three problem groups actually scored better than normals on PIQ and other measures of nonverbal visuospatial skills.

As mentioned in Section III, language-based measures were also found to be more strongly associated with self-reported delinquency than were nonlanguage measures in the New Zealand project. In this project, reduction of the numerous individual test scores to five composites was accomplished by principal components analysis, and the reduction model was cross-validated using maximum-likelihood confirmatory factor analysis (Moffitt and Heimer 1988). Delinquent versus nondelinquent group differences were substantially greater for the verbal and auditory verbal memory factors than for factors representing visual-motor integration, visuospatial, and mental flexibility functions. The subgroup of delinquents with past histories of ADD showed especially poor performance on the verbal and verbal memory factors, scoring a full standard deviation below controls. Specific language-based measures on which delinquents scored poorly relative to controls were the Rey Auditory Verbal Learning Test (memorization of a word list), Verbal Fluency (rapid generation of a class of words), and the WISC-R VIQ subtests of information, similarities, arithmetic, and vocabulary.

In the New Zealand data a significant ($p = .05$) interaction effect was obtained between family adversity and verbal neuropsychological ability for self-reported aggressive delinquent acts (acts involving aggressive confrontation with a victim or adversary). The seventy-five cases characterized by both low verbal scores and adverse family environments earned a mean aggression score more than four times greater than that of any other group, suggesting that neuropsychological deficit might make children more vulnerable to the effects of a criminogenic environment. Conversely, it appeared that strong verbal neuropsychological capacity might serve as a protector against development of aggressive behavior among children reared in even the most adverse family environments.

2. *Confounding Effects from Social Disadvantage and Reading Disability.* The argument might well be made that delinquents score more poorly on tests requiring use of language skills than on nonlanguage tests because many verbal tests are more susceptible to the effects of sociocultural or educational disadvantage than are language-free tests. Delinquents, especially officially detected delinquent research samples, are predominantly from the lower social class and minority social groups who typically score at a disadvantage on verbal tasks that depend somewhat on educational attainment. We may be encouraged that the relative verbal deficit effect has proven robust in studies where

social class or family adversity effects were controlled (e.g., Moffitt, Gabrielli, and Mednick 1981; Sobotowicz, Evans, and Laughlin 1987; Moffitt and Silva 1988*b*). The delinquency-related verbal deficit has also been found within a single minority group (e.g., blacks: Tarnopol 1970; Denno 1989).

Bryant and Bradley (1985), among others, have suggested that failure to learn to read handicaps children in their efforts to learn the sorts of information and thinking skills tapped by the subtests of the verbal IQ. Children who fail to read may begin school with normal VIQ scores, but those scores might decline over time with snowballing school failure (McGee and Share 1989). In this view, the relatively low VIQ scores earned by delinquents might simply be a spurious effect of disproportionate numbers of reading disabled youngsters in officially detected delinquent research samples.[6]

A possible reading confound should cause less concern for many verbal neuropsychological tests than for subtests of the VIQ, because the latter specifically ask for information that is often gained through reading (e.g., Who invented the electric light bulb?), whereas many other verbal neuropsychological tasks do not. It is hard to imagine, for example, how reading failure might impede subjects from memorizing a list of digits. (It is easier to imagine that both reading and memory for digits depend upon the cognitive ability to form mental symbol representations.)

The possible reading confound remains, nonetheless, an important issue for interpretation of many verbal test scores. In order to evaluate this possible confound using data from the New Zealand project, delinquent and nondelinquent group differences on the neuropsychological scores were retested after entering reading achievement test scores as a covariate. Group differences remained significant at the .05 confidence level for the verbal and visuospatial factors and significant beyond the .01 level for auditory verbal memory and visual-motor integration. Also arguing against the confound are data from Sobotowicz, Evans, and Laughlin (1987), in which delinquents who were screened for the absence of learning disabilities and matched to controls for full-scale IQ scored significantly below controls on verbal neuropsychological tests.

Another way to challenge the proposed reading/VIQ confound is to

[6] Alternative views are that low scores on verbal tests represent true information-processing impairments that contribute to the development of both reading difficulty and antisocial behavior problems or that true cognitive impairment causes reading problems, which leads to school failure, which ultimately does contribute to delinquency.

search for prospective evidence of verbal skill deficits in delinquents from ages prior to learning to read. Denno (1989) reported a causal structural longitudinal model of delinquency in which reading achievement at school was a strong predictor of later delinquency, but the model also showed that physicians' ratings of subjects' speech at age four and Stanford-Binet IQ at age four were strong predictors of school-age reading ability. Preliminary analyses of age three data from the New Zealand project show that delinquents with ADD, but not all delinquents, first talked in sentences (by mother's record) a mean five months later than nondelinquents. McMichael (1979) studied 198 boys in their first two years of school, and reported that both antisocial behavior and deficits in tested skills such as visual discrimination, auditory discrimination, and vocabulary were present at school entry between ages four and one-half and five and one-half years, and preceded learning to read. These analyses suggest that the verbal deficits found for delinquents studied cross-sectionally are not spurious consequences of reading failure, but additional careful research in this area is certainly in order.

3. *Interpretations of Hemispheric Dysfunction.* A very large body of research has established that, for almost all right-handed persons and at least 60 percent of left-handers, the left hemisphere of the brain provides the anatomical substrate for receiving, processing, and expressing language. Language-based neuropsychological tests have been shown to be valid discriminators of brain damage in the left hemisphere (see Klove [1974] for review). For example, it is well known that loss of speech accompanies cerebral vascular accidents (strokes) in the left hemisphere of the brain (as revealed by neural imaging or autopsy). Drawing from this knowledge base, many researchers have reasoned that delinquents' tested language deficits must indicate that their left cerebral hemispheres are not functioning normally (e.g., Flor-Henry 1978). Although specific left hemisphere malfunction may eventually prove to be a true representation of the neuropsychological problems associated with antisocial behavior, there are two important cautions against assuming such an anatomical inference.

First, a simple verbal versus nonverbal dichotomous explanation of what the two hemispheres do has proven grossly inadequate. Rather, the two hemispheres are increasingly viewed as being individually specialized for certain *methods* of processing, in addition to specializing in processing verbal or nonverbal stimulus material. For example, research has emerged that demonstrates that the left and right hemispheres are more efficient, respectively, at sequential-analytic versus simultaneous-synthetic information processing (Dean 1984) and routinized versus novel information processing (Goldberg and Costa 1981). For example, both cerebral hemispheres can read words, but the right hemisphere only reads familiar words that can be recognized as a whole stimulus (e.g., STOP, MEN, EXIT), while the left hemisphere can read unfamiliar words by analyzing the sequence of sounds represented by the order of their letters. Functional analysis of the neuropsychological profiles of delinquent groups along these information processing dimensions may well yield new interpretations about laterality.

Second, data establishing left-hemisphere site specificity in language deficit are primarily from studies of aphasias arising from brain damage acquired in adulthood or late childhood. The developing brain has demonstrated remarkable plasticity in very early childhood, particularly in regard to lateralization of function. For example, the right hemisphere has been shown to "take over" the development of language functions in infants whose left hemispheres have been surgically removed, albeit at the cost of overall lower intellectual potential (Dennis and Whitaker 1976). Theoretical views on how neuropsychological deficit might contribute to delinquent behavior do not propose that the dysfunction results from head injury or neurological diseases that occur in adolescence.[7] On the contrary, the theories assert that the underlying deficits probably have been present since the delinquent's neonate stage, gradually influencing his personality, behavioral, and academic development. Therefore, it may prove more parsimonious to consider hypotheses of mixed or less-specialized laterality, or individual differences, in interhemispheric communication processes.

Certain data support the notion of diminished lateral specialization for language in antisocial subjects. First, although the well-known PIQ->VIQ sign has been used to support interpretations of left-hemisphere damage, it is not typically the case that only VIQ is suppressed whereas PIQ is quite normal. In all but one (Sobotowicz, Evans, and Laughlin 1987) of the studies in this review that used IQ tests, delinquents' PIQs were higher than their own VIQs, but their PIQs were also slightly lower than controls' PIQs. Such a pattern of generally compromised ability is consistent with that of children who shift lateral function following neonatal damage (Satz 1979; Satz et al. 1985). Sec-

[7] See Virkkunen, Nuutila, and Huusko (1976) for a thirty-year follow-up study showing no elevation in criminal offending rates for 507 head injury patients.

ond, using a "response competition" paradigm that assessed interference from speaking during performance of a motor finger tapping task, Wolff et al. (1982) found delinquents' *left* hands, and thus their right cerebral hemispheres, to be slowed by competition from speech. Third, Hare, Williamson, and Harpur (1988) have described results from a series of dichotic listening studies (Sec. I describes the dichotic method) with antisocial-personality-disordered prisoners, who evidenced less ear asymmetry for language than normal. The prisoners showed a combination of reduced right ear superiority and augmented left ear performance in identifying word stimuli, suggestive of less exclusory left-hemisphere dominance for language. Similar work with delinquent adolescents is needed.

These findings suggest that a hypothesis of left-hemisphere dysfunction may be too simplistic to reflect the complexity of brain bases for delinquents' observed neuropsychological deficit patterns. Nonetheless, as argued in Section I of this essay, we may benefit less from efforts at localizing the dysfunctions in the brain and more from describing how the resultant cognitive impairments might act to increase risk for delinquency.

4. *Summary.*   A profile of relatively greater weakness in verbal than visuospatial neuropsychological functions has been reported consistently in all investigations of delinquents. This verbal deficit is pervasive, affecting receptive listening and reading, problem solving, expressive speech and writing, and memory for verbal material. Possible confounds for this effect include reading failure and social disadvantage. Some data suggest that the effect is too robust to be wholly discounted by these confounding factors. A selective left-hemisphere damage interpretation may not be the best interpretation of delinquents' language deficits.

B. Delinquency-Related Deficits in Executive Functions

Section II described the resemblance between criminal behavior and the disinhibited antisocial symptoms of patients with injury to the frontal lobes of the brain as one historical rationale for neuropsychological research with delinquents. Section II also presented the theoretical positions of Pontius (1972) and others that grew out of those clinical observations. This section describes research testing the hypothesis that delinquent behavior may be associated with deficiencies in functions commonly labeled as "executive" and thought to be subserved by the frontal lobes of the brain.

1. *Developmental Lag in Executive Function.*   Pontius and Ruttiger (1976) tested Pontius's (1972) theory of frontal lobe system maturational lag by using the Narratives Test to rate stories told by school children between the ages of nine and sixteen who had been designated as "normal" or "delinquent" by their teachers. Their stories were evaluated by an examiner who was blind to group membership, using a scoring system that classifies story narratives according to four developmental stages reflecting qualities such as planning and the ability to switch the story's principle of action. Results showed that 70 percent of sixty-seven normal children, but only 47 percent of thirty-six delinquents, told stories that demonstrated their ability to switch the course of narrative action properly in response to new circumstances.

This study, although suggestive, does not represent an adequate test of executive deficit and delinquency. The definition of delinquency was not acceptable for research. No mention was made of the reliability or developmental validity of the Narratives Test scoring system. It is likely that qualitative aspects of storytelling are confounded with verbal skill level, reading experience, and gender, but these issues were not addressed. All subjects were of normal or greater IQ, implying that the delinquent group may not have been representative of delinquents at large. Group age distributions were not shown, a factor that should be important to a developmental lag hypothesis, especially as myelination (the "insulation" of nerve fibers for more efficient conduction of messages) of neural pathways is completed near puberty (Yakovlev and Lecours 1967), and the subjects ranged from nine to sixteen years old. The most important unanswered question for this study is whether inability to switch the plan of action in a story plot is indicative of a similar inability to modulate one's own *actual* behavior.

2. *Other Studies of Executive Functions.*   Pontius (1972) suggested four neuropsychological tests that should be administered to delinquents with the objective of assessing executive functions. The Wisconsin Card Sorting Test (WCST) measures abstract concept formation and the ability to inhibit a previously rewarded but now incorrect response. The WCST requires the subject to sort a deck of cards according to matching principles, such as color or the number of symbols on the cards. He must guess the principles of organization, which are frequently changed covertly by the examiner. The Stroop Color-Word Test requires inhibition of an over-learned automatic response. The subject views a list of color names, which are printed in colored inks that do not match their names. For example, where the word "red" is

printed in green ink, the subject must say the name of the ink color, thus suppressing the overlearned habit of reading the word. In the Trail-Making Test, Form B, the subject must sustain attention to two competing sequences of letters and numbers on a page, while drawing a "connect the dots" line that alternates between them and while inhibiting out-of-turn responses. Halstead's Category Test is a task in which the subject reasons inductively from categorical examples and uses this abstract information to classify new cases into categories. Clinical "frontal lobe" test batteries typically also include tests such as the Controlled Oral Word Association Test (COWAT; in which the subject generates words within a category, such as animal names, as quickly as possible without making intrusion errors), Porteus or WISC-R Mazes (requiring sustained fine motor control and planning), and other tasks requiring similar motor programming and self-control abilities. Lezak (1983) provides detailed descriptions of these tests, and cites validity studies for each.

Three studies have applied frontal lobe batteries to delinquent subjects. Skoff and Libon (1987) compared the scores of twenty-two incarcerated delinquents to published test norms for the WCST, Porteus Mazes, Trails B, Controlled Oral Word Association Test, and four additional executive tasks. One-third of their subjects scored in the impaired range on the battery as a whole. Appellof and Augustine ([1985], reported in abstract form) tested thirty male delinquents and thirty controls on the WCST, Porteus Mazes, Controlled Oral Word Association Test, and six other unnamed measures. They found no group differences. The WCST, COWAT, Trails B, Mazes, and a measure of whether the child used a planned strategy to approach the task of copying a complex drawing or copied the drawing impulsively (the Rey Osterreith Complex Figure Test) were administered to the subjects of the New Zealand study. Multiple analysis of variance demonstrated that a linear combination of these executive test scores could significantly discriminate self-reported early delinquents from non-delinquents in that cohort, even after the effects of overall IQ were statistically controlled (Moffitt and Henry 1989).

Other studies, while not focusing specifically upon executive functions, have reported data from individual measures typically included in frontal lobe batteries. These studies, taken together, provide some additional support for the association between delinquency and executive deficit. Berman and Siegal (1976) found that delinquents scored poorly on the Category Test and Trails B. Wolff et al. (1982) reported delinquency-related impairments on tests of selective attention and on the Stroop Color-Word Test. Krynicki (1978) found that delinquent subjects performed similarly to subjects with documented organic brain damage on verbal fluency and on a test of motor perseveration, which indicates difficulty inhibiting an inappropriate response on command. Four studies showed delinquents to score poorly on various tests requiring sequencing of motor behavior (Hurwitz et al. 1972; Miller, Burdg, and Carpenter 1980; Karniski et al. 1982; Brickman et al. 1984). Yeudall and Fromm-Auch (1979) concluded that the delinquent group's full-battery profile indicated frontal lobe dysfunction, but they did not report group means for specific test scores. Riddle and Roberts (1977) reviewed sixteen studies using the Porteus Maze Test Q score, which is thought to reflect psychomotor impulsiveness and poor planning. They reported that, using equal-sized groups of delinquents and controls, 70 percent of all subjects could be accurately classified using a specific cutoff point on the Q-score distribution. However, Wolff et al. (1982) included the Maze Q score in their battery and found that it was more strongly related to low social class than to delinquency. This body of studies is subject to all of the methodological criticisms noted in Section III. Their findings certainly suggest that delinquents show executive deficit, but they must be considered cautiously.

3. *Attention as an Executive Function.*   In the New Zealand cohort, delinquents with past histories of ADD were more impaired than other delinquents on certain of the executive measures (Moffitt and Henry 1989), suggesting the hypothesis that attention deficit in particular may be related to frontal lobe function. Electrophysiological and neurochemical evidence pointing to frontal lobe mediation of attentional processes has been reviewed by Stamm and Kreder (1979). Recently, using emission-computed tomography (the PET scan) to examine cerebral blood flow patterns, Lou, Henriksen, and Bruhn (1984) found focal hypoperfusion (inadequate blood flow) in the white-matter tissues connecting the frontal lobes to the rest of the brain in a series of eleven ADD patients as opposed to nine controls. The hypoperfusion was reversed by medication that controlled attentional and hyperactive symptoms.

Additional evidence that attentional mechanisms may be primary among delinquents' executive deficits comes from their especially poor performance on the WISC-R arithmetic subtest. In many studies that reported data for subtests from the WISC-R, the subtest showing the largest delinquency group differences was arithmetic (Berman and

Siegal 1976; Voorhees 1981; Brickman et al. 1984; Moffitt and Silva 1988a). The arithmetic subtest, to the uninitiated, appears to be a test of calculating skills. To the neuropsychologist, the salient aspect of this test is that it is an oral, not a written, test; the subject listens to a complex arithmetic problem, and must attend and concentrate while simultaneously recalling the problem and solving it mentally. Indeed, in factor analytic studies of the WISC-R subtests, arithmetic loads most heavily on factors taken to represent "sustained concentration" or "freedom from distraction" (Cohen [1959]; also, Hubble and Groff [1981] have shown this factor structure to hold for delinquents). Some patients with frontal lobe injuries can solve arithmetic problems with paper and pencil that they find impossible in the oral administration format because it is their attentional control that is impaired rather than their knowledge of arithmetic.

The elevated prevalence of childhood histories of attention deficit among delinquents and the close relation of attentional problems to frontal lobe dysfunction suggest that the conflicting results of previous studies of executive dysfunction may be ascribed to differential unknown rates of attention deficit symptoms among research samples. Of greater theoretical concern is an empirical question that has not been researched. Are executive dysfunctions differentially associated with the presence or absence of antisocial behavior among ADD subjects or are these functions more parsimoniously viewed as correlates of ADD but not as predictors of delinquency? And are delinquents' low scores on tests of specific executive functions (such as foresight/planning or response inhibition) epiphenomena of a more basic general deficit in attention modulation? (Perhaps ADD and "executive deficit" are simply two labels for the same construct.) The latter question is important for its treatment implications.

Although I found no research reports addressing these questions in the delinquency literature, there is work that suggests that at least the persistent, impulsive, antisocial behaviors that characterize the adult with antisocial personality disorder may be associated with executive deficits arising from problems in attention modulation. Before going further, it is important to point out that antisocial personalities are not simply older delinquents, but they are a minority distinguished from offenders in general by a syndrome of personality disorder symptoms. Nonetheless, Robins (1966, 1979) has shown that almost all antisocial personalities were delinquent as youths, so we may expect that they contribute extremes to variance on some variables in delinquent samples. Gorenstein (1982) reported that antisocial personalities showed an executive deficit in response inhibition on the Wisconsin Card Sorting Test (WCST). They perseverated with a previously rewarded response set even after contingencies changed and the response was no longer rewarded. Hare (1984), Sutker, Moan, and Allain (1983), and Sutker and Allain (1987) failed to replicate Gorenstein's finding. Newman and his colleagues have argued that the results of WCST studies may conflict because antisocial personalities' failures to inhibit inappropriate responses on tasks similar to the WCST may depend on the motivational context (or the type of feedback employed). In order to test the hypothesized effect of motivation, Newman and Kosson (1986) examined passive avoidance learning in prison inmates with and without antisocial personality disorder under conditions involving monetary rewards and punishments (high motivation) or monetary punishments only (low motivation). Despite demonstrating adequate response inhibition in the punishment-only condition, antisocial inmates committed significantly *more* punished errors than controls in the condition including reward incentives as well as punishment. In a version of the WCST involving monetary rewards and punishments delivered after every response, Newman and Howland (1989) reported that antisocial inmates committed significantly more perseverative errors than other inmates. In the absence of trial-by-trial immediate monetary feedback, inmates with antisocial personalities performed at least as well as controls. On the basis of these and other findings, Newman (1987) concluded that, once activated by the prospect of reward, individuals with antisocial personalities form a rigid attentional set that is resistant to interruption; pause and reflect less than others following punishment; and, consequently, have difficulty learning from feedback to inhibit punished behavior and to respond more appropriately on subsequent occasions. In other words, when an antisocial person's attention is fixated on the potential of obtaining a prize, they pursue it blindly, failing to be "distracted" by behavioral options that may in fact be better paths toward obtaining the reward.[8]

Raine's (1988) electrophysiological research with inmates with a diagnosis of antisocial personality disorder has also pointed to an overfocus of attentional resources as operative in that syndrome of severe antisocial behavior. Interestingly, this attentional problem bears much simi-

---

[8] This work has been duplicated by Shapiro, Quay, and Hogan (1989) with conduct-disordered boys with similar results.

larity to the conclusion reached by Douglas and Peters (1979) in a review of attention deficits in ADD children: that ADD children exhibit impairments in sustaining attention, and in shifting attention strategically when warranted, but not in selective attention if motivation is adequate. Although antisocial personality disorder and delinquency differ on very important classification dimensions, the theoretical structures linking individual differences in attentional processes to behavioral disinhibition in adult antisocials can suggest interesting hypotheses for neuropsychological research with delinquents.

4. *Summary*. Findings of delinquency-related deficits in performance on tests of executive function are mixed, and most studies have design shortcomings. Despite these cautions, there appear to be enough reports of positive results to warrant further research and theorizing in this area. The connection between attentional deficits and antisocial behavior is an especially fertile area for investigation. One important caveat is the limitation on measurement accuracy imposed by the traditionally employed tests of executive functions. Interpretation of these measures is troubled by the fact that they do not intercorrelate strongly (Hare 1984; Cox and Evans 1987), suggesting that executive function is not a unitary construct. The measures may also be less anatomically specific to the workings of the frontal lobes of the brain in the general population than has been implied by discriminative validity studies using brain-damaged patient samples (Robinson et al. 1980). Correlations of subjects' test scores with data on their frontal lobe metabolism rates obtained from neural imaging techniques would be especially enlightening. For example, Cohen and colleagues (1988) have reported a direct and differential relationship between metabolic rates in the middle frontal cortex, as determined by PET scan, and performance on tests of sustained attention. Psychometric groundwork on assessment of executive function is needed before we can confidently interpret these measures as independent variables in delinquency research.

C. Violence

The notion that brain dysfunction might relate specifically to violent behavior is an old one. The Mark and Ervin (1970) book, *Violence and the Brain*, has been influential in popularizing this idea. In addition, the well-known relation between assaultive behavior and the disinhibitory biochemical effects of alcohol on the brain (Buikhuisen, van der Plas-Korenhoff, and Bontekoe 1988) has also suggested a role for brain mechanisms in violence. The concept of a brain-based defect in impulse control is an appealing one. The connection has often been framed as a variation on the theme of neocortex-based suppression of primitive aggressive and predatory instincts that have been retained in subcortical limbic structures (often called the phylogenetically "old" or "reptilian" brain). Simply put, evolution has added brain tissue in the frontal lobes that enables primates to engage in complex prosocial behavior; the frontal lobes mind our manners. But underneath, the old structures we share with reptiles remain, and this old brain is still capable of attack behavior if it is not suppressed by the new brain. If the inhibiting processes of the frontal cortex are disrupted, or if there is damage to inhibiting neural pathways connecting the cortex and limbic system, it is posited that latent aggression is likely to be released, especially under certain aggression-eliciting circumstances. Mednick et al. (1982) have ably reviewed a large body of literature on biology and violence, and they have provided a thorough discussion of findings from neurophysiological, neuropsychological, and neurochemical research. The following section reviews studies of the neuropsychological test performance of juveniles who have engaged in violent offenses.

1. *Studies of Violence in Adults.* The peak age for violent offending in most Western nations is in the early twenties (Wilson and Herrnstein 1985; Moffitt, Mednick, and Gabrielli 1989). One natural consequence of the predominantly adult age distribution of violent offending is that there are relatively fewer neuropsychological studies of violent juveniles than of violent adults. It is beyond our scope to review the adult literature thoroughly, but certain studies' findings can be illustrative.

Convit et al. (1988), in an evaluation of predictors of assaultive behaviors in psychiatric inpatients, found that abnormality on a neurological examination was one of the four strongest predictors of inpatient assault. Similarly, Hodgins, de Bray, and Braun (1989) found poor brain functioning, reflected by low neuropsychological test scores, to be differentially associated with criminal histories of violence in a sample of mentally disordered offenders. Investigations of adults without mental disorders have also shown that neuropsychological deficits characterize violent offenders relative to property offenders (e.g., Spellacy 1978). Bryant et al. (1984) reported that 73 percent of inmates classified as brain damaged using the cut-off scores of the Luria-Nebraska Neuropsychological Test battery had committed violent offenses, compared to 28 percent of inmates not so classified. This battery consists of a large number of different neuropsychological tests, and when the number of tests on which a subject scores abnormally are counted, a sum beyond a certain cutoff has been shown to be a reliable and valid indicator that there is damage somewhere in the brain. In a fascinating analysis, Denno (1986) examined data from sixty males who had at least one initial violent offense. She entered a variety of situational parameters, victim characteristics, and offender characteristics into competing logistic regression models designed to predict subsequent offending. Low WISC full scale and verbal IQ scores (which had been collected prospectively at age seven) were found to be the strongest of all predictors of repeat aggressive offenses involving victims.

One point is made frequently in the adult studies that may have implications for the study of violence in juveniles: the distinction which should be made between the "habitual" or repeatedly assaultive violent offender and the offender with a single isolated violent incident. Nachshon (1988) noted that, in his sample, murderers scored more similarly to nonoffender controls than to assaulters on a dichotic listening test of hemispheric laterality. When he reviewed the subjects' criminal records, he found that the murderers were primarily without prior offenses, having committed a single uncharacteristic serious violent act. The assaulters, however, had lengthy records of repeated violent acts less serious than murder. Nachshon cautioned that designation of violent subjects for research should be made, not on the basis of severity of the most recent offense, but on the basis of a history of habitual violent behavior. Similarly, Williams (1969) found that EEG abnormalities were two-and-one-half times more prevalent in persistent, as opposed to one-time, violent offenders, and Hart (1987) found recidivistic violent offenders to make more errors on a dichotic listening task than subjects who had committed a single homicide, but who had no prior arrests for violence. Because juveniles will not have had as much time in which to commit repeated acts of violence, it might be difficult to distinguish one-time from recidivistic violent offenders in juvenile samples. Therefore, we might expect somewhat attenuated results from neuropsychological studies of violence in juveniles, and that is what we find.

2. *Studies of Violence in Juveniles.*   Spellacy (1977) compared forty nonviolent and forty violent adolescents, classified according to their assaultive behavior while incarcerated at a training school, on a large battery of neuropsychological tests. He reported that a discriminant function analysis using five of the test scores was able to classify 83 percent of the subjects correctly. Impairments were primarily in verbal

and memory functions. Brickman et al. (1984) also found that violence was differentially related to memory and verbal skill deficits, using the Luria-Nebraska Neuropsychological Test battery. They studied seventy-one incarcerated youths, 63 percent of whom had committed at least one act of violence.

Tarter and his colleagues have conducted a series of interesting studies using a very thorough battery of tests to evaluate boys referred from the juvenile court for neuropsychiatric evaluation. In the first study (Tarter et al. 1983), seventy-three boys were divided on the basis of their current offense into violent, nonviolent, and sexual offenders. Of forty-seven test scores, only one discriminated the groups significantly, leading the authors to conclude that there is little evidence for a relationship between delinquency and cognitive capacity. However, subjects having neurological or EEG abnormalities had been excluded from study (thereby throwing the baby out with the bath water?). It was not reported whether those exclusions were at different group rates. Also, by using only the currently charged offense for classification, it is possible that the "nonviolent" subjects had prior violent offenses or had simply not been detected in their violent acts. Finally, the sex offenders were guilty primarily of rape, which is considered a violent crime in most jurisdictions. Thus it is not clear that the distinctions made between the groups on the dimension of violence were valid. Statistically significant, though small ($r = .22–.39$), correlations were obtained between a measure of severity of the concurrent violent offense and six neuropsychological measures. Perhaps a better measure of violence for that analysis, as suggested by the adult studies, would have been the total number of violent offenses in each subject's history. The authors focused on the lack of group differences to discount any relation between delinquency and neuropsychological deficit. Nevertheless, comparison of the group means obtained against test norms suggests instead that the three combined groups would probably have differed significantly from nondelinquent controls on most of the test scores, had such controls been studied. This study was not a sound test of the relation between violence (or general delinquency) and cognitive deficit.

In a second study, Tarter et al. (1984) compared twenty-seven delinquents with histories of child abuse to seventy-four without abuse. The abused delinquents scored more poorly than the remainder on six of forty-seven tests, five of which were related to verbal and attentional skills. In addition, 44 percent of the abused group, but only 16 percent of the nonabused group, had committed assault. In this group, there-fore, some relation between assaultive behavior and cognitive deficit was seen, but its interaction with abuse history is unclear. The authors posited that verbally impaired children may be more susceptible to abuse, and then they may model their parents' abusive style of interac-tion under stress. It is also possible that abuse-incurred head injuries may impair neuropsychological function.

Lewis, Shanock, Pincus, and Glaser (1979) dichotomized ninety-seven incarcerated boys as "less violent" and "more violent." The more violent group had greater frequency of abnormal EEG readings, neurological soft signs, paranoid symptomatology, and history of abuse, but there was only one group difference obtained from fourteen tests of cognitive function (the arithmetic subtest of the WISC). Kry-nicki (1978) and Andrew (1982) also compared the test performance of violent and nonviolent juveniles, but these studies are not discussed because of their very small sample sizes and problems with confound-ing factors in the research designs.

In a longitudinal prospective study of 987 black subjects representa-tive of the population of low-income black families in Philadelphia, Denno (1989) found that no intellectual or achievement variables dis-criminated between violent offenders and recidivistic property offend-ers. Both delinquent groups scored significantly more poorly than nonarrested controls and one-time offenders on verbal IQ, the digit span test of attention and short-term auditory memory, and on several achievement measures that had been taken prospectively.

3. *Summary.* Denno's study (1989) points to three concerns we should have about the designs of the studies reviewed in this section. First, neuropsychological status should be assessed prospectively. It is entirely possible that individuals who engage in many violent alterca-tions also suffer head injuries at elevated rates when their victims hit back. This being the case, we might suspect a cross-sectional relation between neuropsychological deficits and repetitive violence in which violence caused the deficits. Studies of young boxers have indicated no long-term deficits on neuropsychological tests following repeated blows to the head (Brooks 1987; Levin et al. 1987). However, violent offend-ers are often intoxicated at the time of assault, whereas boxers are not, and intoxication is thought to exacerbate mild head injury (Levin, Ben-ton, and Grossman 1982). A prospective study such as Denno's, in

which cognitive function was assessed prior to onset of offending, is the only design capable of demonstrating temporal precedence for violence-related cognitive deficit.

Second, Denno's was the only investigation of violence to employ a nondelinquent comparison group. When this group is included, it becomes obvious that the striking differences are between delinquents and nondelinquents, and that any differences among delinquent subgroups based on offense type such as violent versus nonviolent, are relatively minimal. In addition, the Denno study was the only one to consider the offenders' complete offense histories. Most other studies made the violent/nonviolent distinction based on the present offense, a designation of questionable validity and one that ignores the point made by the adult data that repeat violent offenders differ on important dimensions from one-time violent offenders. (It is also true that repeat property offenders differ from one-time property offenders, and Denno's results imply that recidivism, regardless of offense type, may be the important correlate.) Given that most violent offending does not emerge until adulthood, division of subjects into violent and nonviolent groups at the juvenile level may be premature, contributing large amounts of classification error to the studies reviewed above.

Under these design limitations, we would expect little conclusive support for a specific association between cognitive impairment and violence to emerge from studies of juveniles. Indeed, the findings of the studies reviewed above were mixed, with about half reporting some violence-specific deficit (usually in verbal or memory functions) and half failing to detect any deficit. Even so, results from studies of *repeatedly* violent adult offenders do support the possibility of a violence-specific effect, so that such an effect should not be discounted here. Conclusions regarding violence are perhaps better drawn from the adult literature.

V. Directions for Research

This essay has examined evidence that brain dysfunction is a correlate of antisocial behavior. Neuropsychological tests validly measure constructs representative of the various cognitive, motor, and sensory functions of the human brain, and poor test scores suggest compromised brain function. Most of the studies reviewed reported consistent findings of delinquency-related deficits, particularly in verbal and "executive" (frontal lobe) functions. Neuropsychological tests were shown to predict variance statistically in delinquent behavior independently of appropriate control variables. Neuropsychological variables warrant further study as possible causal factors in delinquency. A number of issues warrant future research on the neuropsychology of delinquency.

First, among the most obvious is the need for guiding theoretical structures. We need theories that incorporate the offerings of neuropsychology and developmental psychology into the established theories of the causes of delinquency from mainstream criminology. The two bodies of theory can be complementary; as Rowe and Osgood (1984) have pointed out, individual difference variables such as cognitive ability can give greater explanatory power to sociological theory if they account for unexplained variance in delinquency within socioenvironmental conditions. Integrating the two bodies of theory can help us to understand how neuropsychological functions are related to other possible causal factors, such as family factors, peer influence, school failure, personality, poverty, and childhood behavior problems. Neuropsychological test scores are not especially strong univariate predictors of delinquent behavior. Their value for criminology lies in how they fit into the context of other known predictive factors.

Second, neuropsychological researchers should begin to adopt the sound practices of delinquency measurement that have been developed by criminologists (Klein 1987). By and large, neuropsychological researchers remain unaware of the advances in the measurement of delinquency that have been made by criminologists in the last thirty years. We should be aware of the problems inherent in studying incarcerated or clinical samples. There are important advantages to using the self-report method for assessment of delinquent behavior, to collecting delinquency data from multiple sources (police records, parents, teachers, peers), and to classifying delinquents in terms of their full offense histories and rates of recidivistic offending. These are minimal criteria for measurement quality in delinquency research.

Third, greater attention should be given to establishing the psychometric properties of many popular neuropsychological assessment instruments before we may feel confident about interpreting research results with nonpatient populations. Base rates of deficit cut-off scores, and the shapes of distributions of test scores within nonpatient populations, are not well documented (Moffitt and Silva 1987). Construct validity (Francis, Fletcher, and Rourke 1987) and discriminant validity (Robinson et al. 1980) need to be documented for many tests. Evaluation of differential deficit (Chapman and Chapman 1978) and normalization of skew (Russell 1987) are other examples of issues in need of more work if we are to apply neuropsychological tools for research outside their original clinical uses.

Fourth, more predictive strength may be attained if we can identify subgroups of delinquents among whom neuropsychological deficit seems especially prevalent. Promising candidates at present are delinquents with repeated violent offenses, with histories of attention deficit disorder, with reading disabilities, or with antisocial personality features. Then we need to examine whether the delinquent behavior of these subgroups differs from that of delinquents without neuropsychological problems (in density, age of onset, aggressiveness, etc.).

Fifth, research designs are needed that can disentangle the particular neuropsychological functions tapped by tests on which delinquents perform poorly. The process that clinical neuropsychologists call "disassociation" can possibly isolate the specific neuropsychological source of deficit performance. For example, delinquents perform very poorly on the WISC-R arithmetic subtest. Good performance on the test requires several abilities: knowledge of arithmetic, hearing and understanding the dictated problem, remembering the details of the problem, and sustaining attention and concentration while solving the problem. For theory building we should know whether delinquents' poor performance stems from a lack of knowledge of mechanical arithmetic (a failure of education or learning motivation, if ability is average), from poor auditory verbal receptive capacity (consistent with Luria's theory of internalized self-control), or from impaired ability to sustain effortful attention and concentration (focusing our research and intervention efforts upon attentional disorder).

Sixth, replication of effects across neuropsychological paradigms would strengthen inferences. For example, if delinquents show abnormalities in EEG recordings from frontal electrode sites, they should also perform poorly on tests of executive functions and should evidence frontal lobe hypoperfusion in cerebral blood flow studies. If delinquents score below controls on language-based neuropsychological tests, they might also be expected to make more right ear errors on dichotic listening tasks, have higher rates of left- or mixed-handedness, and show left-hemisphere hypometabolism of glucose on PET scans. Corroborative data from different investigation methods would provide compelling evidence of brain dysfunction in delinquents.

Seventh, investigations of possible *sources* of delinquents' neuropsychological dysfunctions would provide a valuable basis for theory construction and for intervention planning. Lewis et al. (1979) and

Tarter et al. (1984) have pointed to child abuse and neglect as possible sources of head injury in the histories of delinquents with neuropsychological impairment. Some work has begun to link two perinatal sources of cognitive deficit to the development of antisocial behavior (Moffitt, Mednick, and Gabrielli 1989). One possible source is disruption in the ontogenetic development of the fetal brain caused by maternal drug abuse or poor prenatal nutrition. Another is brain insult suffered because of complications during birth. Investigations from the field of behavior genetics are showing that some variation in neuropsychological abilities has heritable sources (e.g., Vandenberg 1969; Borecki and Ashton 1984; Martin, Jardine, and Eaves 1984; Tambs, Sundet, and Magnus 1984), but these research efforts have not been integrated into the criminology literature.

Eighth, a crucial need is for investigations that use the prospective longitudinal design (Cline 1980; Blumstein et al. 1986; Farrington, Ohlin, and Wilson 1986). Prospective designs are essential for documenting the existence of neuropsychological deficit prior to the drug abuse and violent head injuries that often accompany delinquent behavior. Longitudinal research can test presumed continuities in the relation between antisocial behavior and cognitive status over the developmental course. It can also allow testing of hypothesized chains of reciprocal causal links among cognitive status, antisocial behavior, and environmental experiences as subjects grow up.

Ninth, certain research focuses could suggest targets for preventive intervention in delinquency. If, indeed, neuropsychological risk factors are present and contributing to antisocial response styles from the earliest ages, then very early interventions might be conceived that could obviate some portion of specific deterrence or selective incapacitation efforts to curb crime later on. Research into the root sources of neuropsychological deficit may help to suggest public health interventions designed to nurture healthy brains for all infants. Research that clarifies the mediating effects of family and school factors could suggest likely points of educational intervention in early childhood. For example, many delinquents appear to have deficits in auditory-verbal learning but relative talents in visuospatial processing. Youngsters at risk could be offered intensive preschool intervention to increase their readiness for our language-based education system and more opportunities to experience academic success by using their nonverbal strengths, thereby preventing some of the erosion of self-esteem that is a hypothesized proximal cause of delinquent involvement. There is some preliminary indication from the New Zealand project that neuropsychological strengths might foster resilience to criminogenic environments, and this invulnerability potential certainly deserves further investigation.

REFERENCES

Andrew, June M. 1982. "Memory and Violent Crime among Delinquents." *Criminal Justice and Behavior* 9:364–71.

Appellof, Elaine S., and E. A. Augustine. 1985. "Prefrontal Functions in Juvenile Delinquents." *Journal of Clinical and Experimental Neuropsychology* 7:79–109.

Beaumont, J. G. 1982. *Divided Visual Field Studies in Cerebral Organization.* New York: Academic Press.

Benson, D. Frank, and Eran Zaidel. 1985. *The Dual Brain.* New York: Guilford.

Berent, Stanley. 1981. "Lateralization of Brain Function." In *Handbook of Clinical Neuropsychology*, edited by Susan B. Filskov and Thomas J. Boll. New York: Wiley.

Berman, Allan, and Andrew W. Siegal. 1976. "Adaptive and Learning Skills in Juvenile Delinquents: A Neuropsychological Analysis." *Journal of Learning Disabilities* 9:51–58.

Blumer, Dietrich, and D. Frank Benson. 1975. "Personality Changes with Frontal and Temporal Lobe Lesions." In *Psychiatric Aspects of Neurologic Disease*, edited by D. Frank Benson and Deitrich Blumer. New York: Grune & Stratton.

Blumstein, Alfred, Jacqueline Cohen, Jeffrey Roth, and Christy Visher, eds. 1986. *Criminal Careers and "Career Criminals."* Washington, D.C.: National Academy Press.

Boll, Thomas J. 1981. "The Halstead-Reitan Neuropsychology Battery." In *Handbook of Clinical Neuropsychology*, edited by Susan B. Filskov and Thomas J. Boll. New York: Wiley.

Borecki, Ingrid B., and Geoffrey C. Ashton. 1984. "Evidence for a Major Gene Influencing Performance on a Vocabulary Test." *Behavior Genetics* 14:63–80.

Brickman, Arthur S., Michael M. McManus, W. Lexington Grapentine, and Norman Alessi. 1984. "Neuropsychological Assessment of Seriously Delinquent Adolescents." *Journal of the American Academy of Child Psychiatry* 23:453–57.

Brooks, D. N. 1987. "Neurobehavioral Effects of Amateur Boxing." *Journal of Clinical and Experimental Neuropsychology* 9:259.

Bryant, Ernest T., Monte L. Scott, and Charles J. Golden. 1984. "Neuropsychological Deficits, Learning Disability, and Violent Behavior." *Journal of Consulting and Clinical Psychology* 52:323–24.

Bryant, Peter, and Lynette Bradley. 1985. *Children's Reading Problems.* Oxford: Blackwell.

Buchsbaum, Monte S., David H. Ingvar, Robert Kessler, Robert N. Waters, John Cappelletti, Daniel van Kammen, Catherine King, Jeanette L. Johnson, Ronald Manning, Richard W. Flynn, Lee S. Mann, William E. Bunney, and Louis Sokoloff. 1982. "Cerebral Glucography with Positron Tomography: Use in Normal Subjects and in Patients with Schizophrenia." *Archives of General Psychiatry* 39:251–59.

Buikhuisen, Wouter. 1987a. "Cerebral Dysfunctions and Persistent Juvenile Delinquency." In *The Causes of Crime: New Biological Approaches*, edited by Sarnoff A. Mednick, Terrie E. Moffitt, and Susan A. Stack. New York: Cambridge University Press.

———. 1987b. "Chronic Juvenile Delinquency: A Theory." In *Explaining Criminal Behavior*, edited by Wouter Buikhuisen and Sarnoff A. Mednick. Leiden: E. J. Brill.

Buikhuisen, Wouter, Corry van der Plas-Korenhoff, and Elisabeth H. M. Bontekoe. 1988. "Alcohol and Violence." In *Biological Contributions to Crime Causation*, edited by Terrie E. Moffitt and Sarnoff A. Mednick. Dordrecht: Martinus Nijhoff.

Bydder, G. M., and R. Steiner. 1982. "NMR Images of the Brain." *Neuroradiology* 23:231–40.

Caine, Eric. 1986. "The Neuropsychology of Depression: The Pseudodementia Syndrome." In *Neuropsychological Assessment of Neuropsychiatric Disorders*, edited by Igor Grant and Kenneth M. Adams. New York: Oxford University Press.

Camp, Bonnie. 1977. "Verbal Mediation in Young Aggressive Boys." *Journal of Abnormal Psychology* 86:145–53.

Camp, Bonnie W., G. E. Blom, F. Herbert, and W. J. Van Doorninck. 1977. "Think Aloud: A Program for Developing Self-Control in Young Aggressive Boys." *Journal of Abnormal Child Psychology* 5:157–69.

Campbell, Susan B., and John S. Werry. 1986. "Attention Deficit Disorder (Hyperactivity)." In *Psychopathological Disorders of Childhood*, edited by Herbert C. Quay and John S. Werry. New York: Wiley.

Chapman, Loren J., and Jean P. Chapman. 1978. "The Measurement of Differential Deficit." *Journal of Psychiatric Research* 14:303–11.

Cleckley, Hervey. 1976. *The Mask of Sanity*. St. Louis: Mosby.

Cline, Hugh F. 1980. "Criminal Behavior over the Life Span." In *Constancy and Change in Human Development*, edited by O. G. Brim and J. Kagan. Cambridge, Mass.: Harvard University Press.

Cloward, Richard E., and Lloyd E. Ohlin. 1960. *Delinquency and Opportunity*. New York: Free Press.

Cohen, Albert K. 1955. *Delinquent Boys: The Culture of the Gang*. New York: Free Press.

Cohen, J. 1959. "The Factorial Structure of the WISC at Ages 7–6, 10–6, and 13–6." *Journal of Consulting Psychology* 23:285–99.

Cohen, Robert M., William E. Semple, Michael Gross, Henry H. Holcomb, M. Susan Dowling, and Thomas E. Nordahl. 1988. "Functional Localization of Sustained Attention: Comparison to Sensory Stimulation in the Absence of Instruction." *Neuropsychiatry, Neuropsychology, and Behavioral Neurology* 1:3–20.

Convit, Antonio, Judith Jaeger, Shang Pin Lin, Morris Meisner, David Brizer, and Jan Volavka. 1988. "Prediction of Violence in Psychiatric Inpatients." In *Biological Contributions to Crime Causation*, edited by Terrie E. Moffitt and Sarnoff A. Mednick. Dordrecht: Martinus Nijhoff.

Cornish, Derek, and Ronald Clarke, eds. 1986. *The Reasoning Criminal: Rational Choice Perspectives on Offending*. New York: Springer-Verlag.

Cox, D. R., and R. W. Evans. 1987. "Measures of Frontal-Lobe Functioning in Bright Children." *Journal of Clinical and Experimental Neuropsychology* 9:28.

Crook, Thomas H., and Glen J. Larrabee. 1988. "Interrelationships among Everyday Memory Tests: Stability of Factor Structure with Age." *Neuropsychology* 2:1–12.

Dean, Raymond S. 1984. "The K-ABC: Theory and Applications for Child Neuropsychological Assessment and Research." *The Journal of Special Education* 13:239–56.

Dennis, Maureen, and H. Whitaker. 1976. "Language Acquisition following Hemidecortication: Linguistic Superiority of the Left over the Right Hemisphere." *Brain and Language* 3:404–33.

Denno, Deborah J. 1984. "Neuropsychological and Early Environmental Correlates of Sex Differences in Crime." *International Journal of Neuroscience* 23:199–214.

———. 1986. "Victim, Offender, and Situational Characteristics of Violent Crime." *Journal of Criminal Law and Criminology* 77:1142–58.

———. 1989. *Biology, Crime and Violence: New Evidence*. Cambridge: Cambridge University Press.

Dodge, Kenneth, and Cynthia Frame. 1982. "Social Cognitive Biases and Deficits in Aggressive Boys." *Child Development* 53:620–35.

Dodge, Kenneth, and Joseph Newman. 1981. "Biased Decision-Making Processes in Aggressive Boys." *Journal of Abnormal Psychology* 90:375–79.

Douglas, Virginia I. 1972. "Stop, Look, and Listen: The Problem of Sustained Attention and Impulse Control in Hyperactive and Normal Children." *Canadian Journal of Behavioral Sciences* 4:259–82.

———. 1983. "Attentional and Cognitive Problems." In *Developmental Neuropsychiatry*, edited by M. Rutter. New York: Guilford.

Douglas, Virginia I., and K. Peters. 1979. "Toward a Clearer Definition of the Attentional Deficit of Hyperactive Children." In *Attention and the Development of Cognitive Skills*, edited by G. Hale and M. Lewis. New York: Plenum.

Elliott, Delbert S., and Harwin L. Voss. 1974. *Delinquency and Dropout*. Lexington, Mass.: D.C. Heath.

Elliott, Frank A. 1978. "Neurological Aspects of Antisocial Behavior." In *The Psychopath*, edited by W. H. Reid. New York: Bruner/Mazel.

Empey, Lamar T. 1978. *American Delinquency*. Homewood, Ill.: Dorsey.

Eysenck, Hans J. 1977. *Crime and Personality*. London: Routledge & Kegan Paul.

Farrington, David P., Rolf Loeber, and Welmoet B. van Kammen. 1987. "Long-Term Criminal Outcomes of Hyperactivity-Impulsivity-Attention

Deficit and Conduct Problems in Childhood." Paper presented at the meeting of the Society for Life History Research, St. Louis, October.

Farrington, David P., Lloyd Ohlin, and James Q. Wilson. 1986. *Understanding and Controlling Crime.* New York: Springer-Verlag.

Feehan, Michael, Warren Stanton, Rob McGee, Phil Silva, and Terrie Moffitt. 1989. "Lateral Preference and Delinquent Behavior." *Journal of Abnormal Psychology* (forthcoming).

Filskov, Susan B., and Dano Leli. 1981. "Assessment of the Individual in Neuropsychological Practice." In *Handbook of Clinical Neuropsychology*, edited by Susan B. Filskov and Thomas J. Boll. New York: Wiley.

Fitzhugh, Kathleen B. 1973. "Some Neuropsychological Features of Delinquent Subjects." *Perceptual and Motor Skills* 36:494.

Flor-Henry, Pierre. 1978. "Laterality, Shifts of Cerebral Dominance, Sinistrality and Psychosis." In *Hemisphere Asymmetries of Function in Psychopathology*, edited by J. Gruzelier and Pierre Flor-Henry. Amsterdam: Elsevier.

Francis, David J., Jack M. Fletcher, and Byron P. Rourke. 1987. "Discriminant Validity of Lateral Sensorimotor Measures in Learning-disabled Children." *Journal of Clinical and Experimental Neuropsychology* 10:779–99.

Fuster, Joaquin M. 1980. *The Prefrontal Cortex.* New York: Raven.

Gabrielli, William F., and Sarnoff A. Mednick. 1980. "Sinistrality and Delinquency." *Journal of Abnormal Psychology* 89:654–61.

Gazzaniga, Michael. 1970. *The Bisected Brain.* New York: Appleton-Century-Crofts.

Goldberg, E., and L. D. Costa. 1981. "Hemisphere Differences in the Acquisition and Use of Descriptive Systems." *Brain and Language* 14:144–73.

Golden, Charles J. 1981. "A Standardized Version of Luria's Neuropsychological Tests: A Quantitative and Qualitative Approach to Neuropsychological Evaluation." In *Handbook of Clinical Neuropsychology*, edited by Susan B. Filskov and Thomas J. Boll. New York: Wiley.

Goldstein, Gerald. 1986. "The Neuropsychology of Schizophrenia." In *Neuropsychological Assessment of Neuropsychiatric Disorders*, edited by Igor Grant and Kenneth M. Adams. New York: Oxford University Press.

———. 1987. "Neuropsychiatry: Interfaces between Neuropsychology and Psychopathology." *The Clinical Neuropsychologist* 4:365–80.

Gorenstein, Eathan E. 1982. "Frontal Lobe Functions in Psychopaths." *Journal of Abnormal Psychology* 91:368–79.

Gorenstein, Eathan E., and Joseph P. Newman. 1980. "Disinhibitory Psychopathology: A New Perspective and a Model for Research." *Psychological Review* 87:301–15.

Hare, Robert D. 1984. "Performance of Psychopaths on Cognitive Tasks Related to Frontal Lobe Function." *Journal of Abnormal Psychology* 93:133–40.

———. 1985. "Comparison of Procedures for the Assessment of Psychopathy." *Journal of Consulting and Clinical Psychology* 53:7–16.

Hare, Robert D., Sherrie E. Williamson, and Timothy J. Harpur. 1988. "Psychopathy and Language." In *Biological Contributions to Crime Causation*, edited by Terrie E. Moffitt and Sarnoff A. Mednick. Dordrecht: Martinus Nijhoff.

Hart, Cedric J. 1987. "The Relevance of a Test of Speech Comprehension Deficit to Persistent Aggressiveness." *Personality and Individual Differences* 8:371–84.

Haynes, J. P., and M. Bensch. 1981. "The P>V Sign of the WISC-R and Recidivism in Delinquents." *Journal of Consulting and Clinical Psychology* 49:480–81.

Healy, W., and A. F. Bronner. 1936. *New Light on Delinquency and Its Treatment.* New Haven, Conn.: Yale University Press.

Heaton, Robert K., Igor Grant, and Charles G. Matthews. 1986. "Differences in Neuropsychological Test Performance Associated with Age, Education and Sex." In *Neuropsychological Assessment of Neuropsychiatric Disorders*, edited by Igor Grant and Kenneth M. Adams. New York: Oxford University Press.

Hecaen, H., and J. Ajuriaguerra. 1964. *Left Handedness.* New York: Grune & Stratton.

Hill, D., and W. Sargant. 1943. "A Case of Matricide." *Lancet* 244:526–27.

Hinkle, J. S. 1983. "Comparison of Reproductions of the Bender-Gestalt and Memory-for-Designs by Delinquents and Nondelinquents." *Perceptual and Motor Skills* 57:1070.

Hinshaw, Stephen P. 1987. "On the Distinction between Attentional Deficits/Hyperactivity and Conduct Problems/Aggression in Child Psychopathology." *Psychological Bulletin* 101:443–63.

Hirschi, Travis. 1969. *Causes of Delinquency.* Berkeley: University of California Press.

Hirschi, Travis, and Michael J. Hindelang. 1977. "Intelligence and Delinquency: A Revisionist Review." *American Sociological Review* 42:571–87.

Hodgins, Sheilagh, Genevieve de Bray, and Claude Braun. 1989. *Patterns of Aggression and Brain Functioning of Mentally Abnormal Offenders.* Quebec: Institut de Phillipe, Pinel de Montreal (forthcoming).

Hubble, L. M., and M. Groff. 1981. "Factor Analysis of WISC-R Scores of Male Delinquents Referred for Evaluation." *Journal of Consulting and Clinical Psychology* 49:738–39.

Huesmann, L. Rowell, Leonard D. Eron, and Patty Warnick Yarmel. 1987. "Intellectual Functioning and Aggression." *Journal of Personality and Social Psychology* 52:232–40.

Hurwitz, Irving, Roger M. A. Bibace, Peter H. Wolff, and Barbara M. Rowbotham. 1972. "Neurological Function of Normal Boys, Delinquent Boys, and Boys with Learning Problems." *Perceptual and Motor Skills* 35:387–94.

Hutt, May L., and Brian G. Dates. 1977. "Reliabilities and Inter-relationships of Two HABGT Scales in a Male Delinquency Population." *Journal of Personality Assessment* 41:353–57.

Karniski, Walt M., Melvin D. Levine, Simon Clarke, Judith S. Palfrey, and Lynn J. Meltzer. 1982. "A Study of Neurodevelopmental Findings in Early Adolescent Delinquents." *Journal of Adolescent Health Care* 3:151–59.

Kimura, Doreen. 1967. "Cerebral Dominance and the Perception of Verbal Stimuli." *Canadian Journal of Psychology* 15:166–71.

King, G. D., H. J. Hannay, B. J. Masek, and J. W. Burns. 1978. "Effects of

Anxiety and Sex on Neuropsychological Tests." *Journal of Consulting and Clinical Psychology* 46:375–76.

Klein, Malcolm W. 1987. "Watch Out for the Last Variable." In *The Causes of Crime*, edited by Sarnoff A. Mednick, Terrie E. Moffitt, and Susan A. Stack. New York: Cambridge University Press.

Klove, Hallgrim. 1974. "Validation Studies in Adult Clinical Neuropsychology." In *Clinical Neuropsychology*, edited by R. Reitan and L. Davison. Washington, D.C.: Hemisphere.

Kolb, Bryan, and Ian Q. Whishaw. 1985. *Fundamentals of Human Neuropsychology*. 2d ed. New York: Freeman.

Kolonoff, Pamela S., Louis D. Costa, and William G. Snow. 1986. "Predictors and Indicators of Quality of Life in Patients with Closed-Head Injury." *Journal of Clinical and Experimental Neuropsychology* 8:469–85.

Kopp, Claire B. 1982. "Antecedents of Self-Regulation: A Developmental Perspective." *Developmental Psychology* 18:199–214.

Krynicki, Victor E. 1978. "Cerebral Dysfunction in Repetitively Assaultive Offenders." *Journal of Nervous and Mental Disease* 166:59–67.

Larrabee, Glenn J., Robert L. Kane, John R. Schuck, and David J. Francis. 1985. "Construct Validity of Various Memory Testing Procedures." *Journal of Clinical and Experimental Neuropsychology* 7:239–50.

Levin, Harvey S., Arthur L. Benton, and Robert G. Grossman. 1982. *Neurobehavioral Consequences of Closed Head Injury*. New York: Oxford University Press.

Levin, Harvey S., and Felicia C. Goldstein. 1986. "Organization of Verbal Memory after Severe Closed-Head Injury." *Journal of Clinical and Experimental Neuropsychology* 8:634–56.

Levin, Harvey S., S. C. Lippold, A. Goldman, S. Handel, W. M. High, H. M. Eisenberg, and D. Zelitt. 1987. "Neurobehavioral Functioning and Magnetic Resonance Imaging in Young Boxers." *Journal of Clinical and Experimental Neuropsychology* 9:259.

Levine, Melvin D., and Nancy C. Jordan. 1987. "Neurodevelopmental Dysfunctions." In *The Malleability of Children*, edited by J. Gallagher and C. Ramey. Baltimore: Paul H. Brookes.

Lewis, Dorothy Otnow, and David A. Balla. 1976. *Delinquency and Psychopathology*. New York: Grune and Stratton.

Lewis, Dorothy Otnow, Ernest Moy, Lori D. Jackson, Robert Aronson, Nicholas Restifo, Susan Serra, and Alexander Simos. 1985. "Biopsychosocial Characteristics of Children Who Later Murder: A Prospective Study." *American Journal of Psychiatry* 142:1161–67.

Lewis, Dorothy Otnow, Shelly S. Shanok, and David A. Balla. 1979. "Perinatal Difficulties, Head and Face Trauma, and Child Abuse in the Medical Histories of Seriously Delinquent Children." *American Journal of Psychiatry* 136:419–23.

Lewis, Dorothy Otnow, Shelly S. Shanok, Jonathan H. Pincus, and Gilbert H. Glaser. 1979. "Violent Juvenile Delinquents: Psychiatric, Neurological, Psychological and Abuse Factors." *Journal of the American Academy of Child Psychiatry* 2:307–19.

Lezak, Muriel D. 1983. *Neuropsychological Assessment*. New York: Oxford University Press.

———. 1988. "I.Q.: R.I.P." *Journal of Clinical and Experimental Neuropsychology* 10:351–61.

Loeber, Rolf. 1982. "The Stability of Antisocial and Delinquent Child Behavior: A Review." *Child Development* 53:1431–46.

Loeber, Rolf, and Magda Stouthamer-Loeber. 1986. "Family Factors as Correlates and Predictors of Juvenile Conduct Problems and Delinquency." In *Crime and Justice: An Annual Review of Research*, vol. 7, edited by Michael Tonry and Norval Morris. Chicago: University of Chicago Press.

———. 1987. "Prediction." In *Handbook of Juvenile Delinquency*, edited by Herbert C. Quay. New York: Wiley.

Loney, Jan, Mary Anne Whaley-Klahn, Todd Kosier, and Jay Conboy. 1983. "Hyperactive Boys and Their Brothers at 21: Predictors of Aggressive and Antisocial Outcome." In *Prospective Studies of Crime and Delinquency*, edited by K. Teilmann Van Dusen and Sarnoff A. Mednick. Boston: Kluwer/Nijhoff.

Loring, David W., and Andrew C. Papanicolaou. 1987. "Memory Assessment in Neuropsychology: Theoretical Considerations and Practical Utility." *Journal of Clinical and Experimental Neuropsychology* 9:340–58.

Lou, Hans C., Leif Henriksen, and Peter Bruhn. 1984. "Focal Cerebral Hypoperfusion in Children with Dysphasia and/or Attention Deficit Disorder." *Archives of Neurology* 41:825–29.

Luria, Aleksandr R. 1961. *The Role of Speech in the Regulation of Normal and Abnormal Behavior*. New York: Basic.

———. 1973. *The Working Brain*. New York: Basic.

Luria, Aleksandr R., and E. D. Homskaya. 1964. "Disturbance in the Regulative Role of Speech with Frontal Lobe Lesions." In *The Frontal Granular Cortex and Behavior*, edited by J. M. Warren and K. Akert. New York: McGraw Hill.

McGee, Robert, and David Share. 1989. "Reading Disability and Language Deficits: Cause or Effect?" *British Journal of Disorders of Communication* (forthcoming).

McGee, Robert, Sheilah Williams, and Phil A. Silva. 1984. "Behavioral and Developmental Characteristics of Aggressive, Hyperactive, and Aggressive-Hyperactive Boys." *Journal of the American Academy of Child Psychiatry* 23:270–79.

———. 1985. "Factor Structure and Correlates of Ratings of Inattention, Hyperactivity, and Antisocial Behavior in a Large Sample of 9-Year-Old Children from the General Population." *Journal of Consulting and Clinical Psychology* 53:480–90.

McManus, Michael, Arthur Brickman, Norman E. Alessi, and W. L. Grapentine. 1985. "Neurological Dysfunction in Serious Delinquents." *Journal of the American Academy of Child Psychiatry* 24:481–85.

McMichael, Paquita. 1979. "The Hen or the Egg? Which Comes First—Antisocial Emotional Disorders or Reading Disability?" *British Journal of Educational Psychology* 49:226–38.

Macmillan, W. B. 1986. "A Wonderful Journey through Skull and Brains: The Travels of Mr. Gage's Tamping Iron." *Brain and Cognition* 5:67–107.

McSweeny, A. John, Igor Grant, Robert K. Heaton, George P. Prigatano, and Kenneth M. Adams. 1985. "Relationship of Neuropsychological Status to Everyday Functioning in Healthy and Chronically Ill Persons." *Journal of Clinical and Experimental Neuropsychology* 7:281–91.

Mark, V., and Frank R. Ervin. 1970. *Violence and the Brain*. New York: Harper & Row.

Martin, Nicholas G., R. Jardine, and L. J. Eaves. 1984. "Is There Only One Set of Genes for Different Abilities?" *Behavior Genetics* 14:355–70.

Mazziotta, John C., and Michael E. Phelps. 1985. "Metabolic Evidence of Lateralized Cerebral Function Demonstrated by Positron Emission Tomography in Patients with Neuropsychiatric Disorders and Normal Individuals." In *The Dual Brain*, edited by D. Frank Benson and Eran Zaidel. New York: Guilford.

Mednick, Sarnoff A., Michelle Harway, Birgitte Mednick, and Terrie E. Moffitt. 1981. "Longitudinal Research: North American Data Sets." In *Child Development, Information and Formation of Public Policy*, edited by Thomas E. Jordan. St. Louis: University of Missouri Press.

Mednick, Sarnoff A., Terrie E. Moffitt, and Susan A. Stack, eds. 1987. *The Causes of Crime: New Biological Approaches*. New York: Cambridge University Press.

Mednick, Sarnoff A., Vicki Pollock, Jan Volavka, and William F. Gabrielli. 1982. "Biology and Violence." In *Criminal Violence*, edited by Marvin E. Wolfgang and N. A. Weiner. Beverly Hills, Calif.: Sage.

Mednick, Sarnoff A., and Jan Volavka. 1980. "Biology and Crime." In *Crime and Justice: An Annual Review of Research*, vol. 2, edited by Norval Morris and Michael Tonry. Chicago: University of Chicago Press.

Meehl, Paul E. 1971. "High School Yearbooks: A Reply to Schwartz." *Journal of Abnormal Psychology* 77:143–48.

Meichenbaum, Donald H., and Jo Goodman. 1971. "Training Impulsive Children to Talk to Themselves: A Means of Developing Self Control." *Journal of Abnormal Psychology* 77:115–26.

Meltzer, Lynn J., Bethany N. Roditi, and Terence Fenton. 1986. "Cognitive and Learning Profiles of Delinquent and Learning-Disabled Adolescents." *Adolescence* 83:581–91.

Miller, Lamoine J., Nancy B. Burdg, and Dale Carpenter. 1980. "Application of Recategorized WISC-R Scores for Adjudicated Adolescents." *Perceptual and Motor Skills* 51:187–91.

Miller, Laurence. 1987. "Neuropsychology of the Aggressive Psychopath: An Integrative Review." *Aggressive Behavior* 13:119–40.

Milner, Brenda, and Michael Petrides. 1984. "Behavioral Effects of Frontal-Lobe Lesions in Man." *Trends in Neurosciences* (November), pp. 403–7.

Milstein, Victor. 1988. "EEG Topography in Patients with Aggressive Violent Behavior." In *Biological Contributions to Crime Causation*, edited by Terrie E. Moffitt and Sarnoff A. Mednick. Dordrecht: Martinus Nijhoff.

Moffitt, Terrie E. 1988. "Neuropsychology and Self-reported Early Delinquency in an Unselected Birth Cohort: A Preliminary Report from New Zealand." In *Biological Contributions to Crime Causation*, edited by Terrie E. Moffitt and Sarnoff A. Mednick. New York: Martinus Nijhoff.

Moffitt, Terrie E., William F. Gabrielli, and Sarnoff A. Mednick. 1981. "Socioeconomic Status, I.Q., and Delinquency." *Journal of Abnormal Psychology* 90:152–56.

Moffitt, Terrie E., and Karen Heimer. 1988. "Factor Analysis and Construct Validity of a Research Neuropsychological Test Battery." Unpublished manuscript. University of Wisconsin—Madison.

Moffitt, Terrie E., and Bill Henry. 1989. "Neuropsychological Deficits in Executive Function in Self-reported Delinquents." *Development and Psychopathology* (forthcoming).

Moffitt, Terrie E., and Sarnoff A. Mednick. 1988. *Biological Contributions to Crime Causation.* Dordrecht: Martinus Nijhoff.

Moffitt, Terrie E., Sarnoff A. Mednick, and William F. Gabrielli. 1989. "Predicting Criminal Violence: Descriptive Data and Predispositional Factors." In *Current Approaches to the Prediction of Violence*, edited by David Brizer and Martha Crowner. New York: American Psychiatric Association Press (forthcoming).

Moffitt, Terrie E., and Phil A. Silva. 1987. "WISC-R Verbal and Performance IQ Discrepancy in an Unselected Cohort: Clinical Significance and Longitudinal Stability." *Journal of Consulting and Clinical Psychology* 55:768–74.

———. 1988a. "Neuropsychological Deficit and Self-reported Delinquency in an Unselected Birth Cohort." *Journal of the American Academy of Child and Adolescent Psychiatry* 27:233–40.

———. 1988b. "Self-reported Delinquency, Neuropsychological Deficit, and History of Attention Deficit Disorder." *Journal of Abnormal Child Psychology* 16:553–69.

———. 1988c. "IQ and Delinquency: A Direct Test of the Differential Detection Hypothesis." *Journal of Abnormal Psychology* 97:330–33.

———. 1989. "Self-reported Early Delinquency: Results from an Instrument for New Zealand." *Australian and New Zealand Journal of Criminology* (forthcoming).

Morris, Robin G., and Alan D. Baddeley. 1988. "Primary and Working Memory Functioning in Alzheimer-Type Dementia." *Journal of Clinical and Experimental Neuropsychology* 10:279–96.

Murray, Charles A. 1976. *The Link between Learning Disabilities and Juvenile Delinquency: Current Theory and Knowledge.* Washington, D.C.: U.S. Department of Justice.

Nachshon, Israel. 1988. "Hemisphere Function in Violent Offenders." In *Biological Contributions to Crime Causation*, edited by Terrie E. Moffitt and Sarnoff A. Mednick. Dordrecht: Martinus Nijhoff.

Nachshon, Israel, and Deborah Denno. 1987. "Violent Behavior and Cerebral Hemisphere Function." In *The Causes of Crime*, edited by Sarnoff A. Mednick, Terrie E. Moffitt, and Susan A. Stack. New York: Cambridge University Press.

Newman, Joseph P. 1987. "Reaction to Punishment in Extroverts and Psychopaths: Implications for the Impulsive Behavior of Disinhibited Individuals." *Journal of Research in Personality* 21:464–80.

Newman, Joseph P., and Eric Howland. 1989. "The Effect of Incentives on Wisconsin Card-sorting Task Performance in Psychopaths." *Journal of Abnormal Psychology* (forthcoming).

Newman, Joseph P., and David S. Kosson. 1986. "Passive Avoidance Learning in Psychopathic and Nonpsychopathic Offenders." *Journal of Abnormal Psychology* 95:257–63.

Noffsinger, Douglas. 1985. "Dichotic-Listening Techniques in the Study of Hemispheric Asymmetries." In *The Dual Brain*, edited by D. Frank Benson and Eran Zaidel. New York: Guilford.

Offord, Dan R., K. Sullivan, N. Allen, and N. Abrams. 1979. "Delinquency and Hyperactivity." *Journal of Nervous and Mental Disease* 167:734–41.

Olweus, Dan. 1979. "Stability of Aggressive Reaction Patterns in Males: A Review." *Psychological Bulletin* 86:852–75.

Oscar-Berman, M. 1980. "Neuropsychological Consequences of Long-Term Chronic Alcoholism." *American Scientist* 68:410–49.

Piliavin, Irving, Rose Gartner, Craig Thornton, and Ross Matsueda. 1986. "Crime Deterrence and Rational Choice." *American Sociological Review* 51:101–19.

Polk, Kenneth, and W. E. Schafer. 1972. *Schools and Delinquency*. Englewood Cliffs, N.J.: Prentice Hall.

Pontius, Annelise A. 1972. "Neurological Aspects in Some Types of Delinquency, Especially among Juveniles: Toward a Neurological Model of Ethical Action." *Adolescence* 7:289–308.

Pontius, Annelise A., and K. F. Ruttiger. 1976. "Frontal Lobe System Maturational Lag in Juvenile Delinquents Shown in Narratives Test." *Adolescence* 11:509–18.

Prentice, N. M., and F. J. Kelly. 1963. "Intelligence and Delinquency: A Reconsideration." *Journal of Social Psychology* 60:327–37.

Raine, Adrian. 1988. "Evoked Potentials and Antisocial Behavior." In *Biological Contributions to Crime Causation*, edited by Terrie E. Moffitt and Sarnoff A. Mednick. Dordrecht: Martinus Nijhoff.

Reiss, Albert J., and A. L. Rhodes. 1961. "The Distribution of Juvenile Delinquency in the Social Class Structure." *American Sociological Review* 26:720–32.

Riddle, Mary, and Alan H. Roberts. 1977. "Delinquency, Delay of Gratification, Recidivism and the Porteus Maze Tests." *Psychological Bulletin* 84:417–25.

Robbins, Donna Moran, James C. Beck, Rebecca Pries, Daniel Jacobs, and Christine Smith. 1983. "Learning Disability and Neuropsychological Impairment in Adjudicated, Unincarcerated Male Delinquents." *Journal of the American Academy of Child Psychiatry* 22:40–46.

Robins, Lee N. 1966. *Deviant Children Grown Up*. Baltimore: Williams & Wilkins.

———. 1979. "Sturdy Childhood Predictors of Adult Outcomes: Replications for Longitudinal Studies." In *Stress and Mental Disorder*, edited by J. E. Barrett, R. M. Rose, and G. L. Klerman. New York: Raven.

Robinson, Amy L., Robert K. Heaton, Ralph A. W. Lehman, and Donald W. Stilson. 1980. "The Utility of the Wisconsin Card Sorting Test in Detecting and Locating Frontal Lobe Lesions." *Journal of Consulting and Clinical Psychology* 48:605–14.

Rourke, Byron P. 1975. "Brain-Behavior Relationships in Children with

Learning Disabilities: A Research Program." *American Psychologist* 30:911–20.

———. 1983. "Reading and Spelling Disabilities: A Developmental Perspective." In *Neuropsychology of Language, Reading, and Spelling*, edited by U. Kirk. New York: Academic Press.

———. 1985. "Statistical Analysis of Large Neuropsychological Data Bases: Methodological and Clinical Considerations." *Journal of Clinical and Experimental Neuropsychology* 7:631.

———. 1987. "Syndrome of Nonverbal Learning Disabilities: The Final Common Pathway of White-Matter Disease/Dysfunction?" *Clinical Psychologist* 1:209–34.

Rourke, Byron P., and John L. Fisk. 1981. "Socio-emotional Disturbances of Learning Disabled Children: The Role of Central Processing Deficits." *Bulletin of the Orton Society* 31:77–88.

Rowe, David C., and D. Wayne Osgood. 1984. "Heredity and Sociological Theories of Delinquency: A Reconsideration." *American Sociological Review* 49:526–40.

Russell, Elbert W. 1987. "A Reference Scale Method for Constructing Neuropsychological Test Batteries." *Journal of Clinical and Experimental Neuropsychology* 9:376–92.

Rutter, Michael. 1983. "Statistical and Personal Interactions: Facets and Perspectives." In *Human Development: An Interactional Perspective*, edited by David Magnusson and Vernon L. Allen. New York: Academic Press.

Samuels, I., Nelson Butters, and Paul Fedio. 1972. "Short-Term Memory Disorders Following Temporal-Lobe Removals in Humans." *Cortex* 8:283–98.

Sanders, H. I., and E. K. Warrington. 1971. "Memory for Remote Events in Amnesic Patients." *Brain* 94:661–68.

Satterfield, James H. 1987. "Childhood Diagnostic and Neurophysiological Predictors of Teenage Arrest Rates: An Eight-Year Prospective Study." In *The Causes of Crime*, edited by Sarnoff A. Mednick, Terrie E. Moffitt, and Susan A. Stack. New York: Cambridge University Press.

Satz, Paul. 1979. "A Test of Some Models of Hemispheric Speech Organization in the Left- and Right-Handed." *Science* 203:1131–33.

Satz, Paul, and Jack M. Fletcher. 1981. "Emergent Trends in Neuropsychology: An Overview." *Journal of Consulting and Clinical Psychology* 49:851–65.

Satz, Paul, Donna L. Orsini, Eric Saslow, and Rolando Henry. 1985. "Early Brain Injury and Pathological Left-Handedness: Clues to a Syndrome." In *The Dual Brain*, edited by D. Frank Benson and Eran Zaidel. New York: Guilford.

Savitsky, Jeffrey C., and Danita Czyzewski. 1978. "The Reaction of Adolescent Offenders and Nonoffenders to Nonverbal Emotion Displays." *Journal of Abnormal Child Psychology* 6:89–96.

Scarr, Sandra, and Kathleen McCartney. 1983. "How People Make Their Own Environments: A Theory of Genotype-Environment Effects." *Child Development* 54:424–35.

Schacter, D. L., and H. F. Crovitz. 1977. "Memory Function after Closed Head Injury: A Review of the Quantitative Research." *Cortex* 13:150–76.

Scoville, W. B., and Brenda Milner. 1957. "Loss of Recent Memory after Bilateral Hippocampal Lesions." *Journal of Neurology, Neurosurgery, and Psychiatry* 20:11–21.

Shanok, Shelly S., and Dorothy Otnow Lewis. 1981. "Medical Histories of Female Delinquents." *Archives of General Psychiatry* 38:211–13.

Shapiro, Steven K., Herbert C. Quay, and Anne E. Hogan. 1989. "Response Perseveration and Delayed Responding in Undersocialized Conduct Disorder." *Journal of Abnormal Psychology* (forthcoming).

Short, James F., and Fred L. Strodtbeck. 1965. *Group Process and Gang Delinquency*. Chicago: University of Chicago Press.

Shulman, H. M. 1929. *A Study of Problem Boys and Their Brothers*. Albany: New York State Crime Commission.

Skoff, B. F., and D. J. Libon. 1987. "Impaired Executive Functions in a Sample of Male Juvenile Delinquents." *Journal of Clinical and Experimental Neuro-psychology* 9:60.

Slavin, Sidney H. 1978. "Information Processing Defects in Delinquents." In *Ecologic-Biochemical Approaches to Treatment of Delinquents and Criminals*. New York: Van Nostrand Reinhold.

Snyder, James, and Gerald Patterson. 1987. "Family Interaction and Delinquent Behavior." In *Handbook of Juvenile Delinquency*, edited by Herbert C. Quay. New York: Wiley.

Sobotowicz, William, James R. Evans, and James Laughlin. 1987. "Neuropsychological Function and Social Support in Delinquency and Learning Disability." *International Journal of Clinical Neuropsychology* 9:178–86.

Spellacy, Frank. 1977. "Neuropsychological Differences between Violent and Nonviolent Adolescents." *Journal of Clinical Psychology* 33:966–69.

———. 1978. "Neuropsychological Discrimination between Violent and Nonviolent Men." *Journal of Clinical Psychology* 34:49–52.

Sperry, Roger W. 1974. "Lateral Specialization in the Surgically Separated Hemispheres." In *The Neurosciences Third Study Program*, edited by F. O. Schmitt and F. E. Worden. Cambridge, Mass.: MIT Press.

Spreen, Otfried. 1981. "The Relationship between Learning Disability, Neurological Impairment, and Delinquency." *Journal of Nervous and Mental Disease* 169:791–99.

Stamm, John S., and Sharon V. Kreder. 1979. "Minimal Brain Dysfunction: Psychological and Neuropsychological Disorders in Hyperkinetic Children." In *Handbook of Behavioral Neurology*, edited by M. Gazzaniga. New York: Plenum.

Sturge, Claire. 1982. "Reading Retardation and Antisocial Behaviour." *Journal of Child Psychology and Psychiatry* 23:21–31.

Stuss, Donald T., and D. Frank Benson. 1986. *The Frontal Lobes*. New York: Raven.

Sutker, Patricia B., and Albert Allain. 1987. "Cognitive Abstraction, Shifting, and Control: Clinical Sample Comparisons of Psychopaths and Nonpsychopaths." *Journal of Abnormal Psychology* 96:73–75.

Sutker, Patricia B., C. E. Moan, and Albert N. Allain. 1983. "Assessment of Cognitive Control in Psychopathic and Normal Prisoners." *Journal of Behavioral Assessment* 5:275–87.

Tambs, Kristin, J. M. Sundet, and P. Magnus. 1984. "Heritability Analysis of the WAIS Subtests: A Study of Twins." *Intelligence* 8:283–93.

Tarnopol, Lester. 1970. "Delinquency and Minimal Brain Dysfunction." *Journal of Learning Disabilities* 3:200–207.

Tarter, Ralph E., Andrea M. Hegedus, Arthur L. Alterman, and Lynda Katz-Garris. 1983. "Cognitive Capacities of Juvenile Violent, Nonviolent, and Sexual Offenders." *Journal of Nervous and Mental Disease* 171:564–67.

Tarter, Ralph E., Andrea M. Hegedus, G. Goldstein, C. Shelly, and Arthur L. Alterman. 1984. "Adolescent Sons of Alcoholics: Neuropsychological and Personality Characteristics." *Alcoholism: Clinical and Experimental Research* 8:330–33.

Tarter, Ralph E., Andrea M. Hegedus, Nancy E. Winsten, and Arthur L. Alterman. 1984. "Neuropsychological, Personality, and Familial Characteristics of Physically Abused Delinquents." *Journal of the American Academy of Child Psychiatry* 23:668–74.

———. 1985. "Intellectual Profiles and Violent Behavior in Juvenile Delinquents." *Journal of Psychology* 119:125–28.

Taylor, L. 1969. "Localization of Cerebral Lesions by Psychological Testing." *Clinical Neurosurgery* 16:269–87.

Tittle, Charles R. 1980. *Sanctions and Social Deviance: The Question of Deterrence.* New York: Praeger.

Tucker, Donald M. 1981. "Lateral Brain Function, Emotion, and Conceptualization." *Psychological Bulletin* 89:19–46.

Vandenberg, S. 1969. "A Twin Study of Spatial Ability." *Multivariate Behavioral Research* 4:273–94.

Van Dusen, Katherine, Sarnoff A. Mednick, and William F. Gabrielli. 1983. "Social Class and Crime in an Adoption Cohort." *Journal of Criminal Law and Criminology* 74:249–69.

Vega, Arthur, Jr., and Oscar A. Parsons. 1967. "Cross-Validation of the Halstead-Reitan Tests for Brain Damage." *Journal of Consulting and Clinical Psychology* 31:517–26.

Virkkunen, Matti, A. Nuutila, and S. Huusko. 1976. "Effect of Brain Injury on Social Adaptability." *Acta Psychiatrica Scandinavia* 53:168–72.

Volavka, Jan. 1987. "Electroencephalogram among Criminals." In *The Causes of Crime: New Biological Approaches*, edited by Sarnoff A. Mednick, Terrie E. Moffitt, and Susan A. Stack. New York: Cambridge University Press.

Voorhees, James. 1981. "Neuropsychological Differences between Juvenile Delinquents and Functional Adolescents: A Preliminary Study." *Adolescence* 16:57–66.

Walker, Jason L., Benjamin B. Lahey, George W. Hynd, and Cynthia L. Frame. 1987. "Comparison of Specific Patterns of Antisocial Behavior in Children with Conduct Disorder with or without Coexisting Hyperactivity." *Journal of Consulting and Clinical Psychology* 55:910–13.

Wechsler, David. 1944. *The Measurement of Adult Intelligence.* 3d ed. Baltimore: Williams & Wilkins.

Weiss, Gabrielle. 1983. "Long-Term Outcomes: Findings, Concepts, and Practical Implications." In *Developmental Neuropsychiatry*, edited by Michael Rutter. New York: Guilford.

Werry, John S. 1986. "Biological Factors." In *Psychopathological Disorders of Childhood*, edited by Herbert C. Quay and John S. Werry. New York: Wiley.

Werry, John S., Jan Catherine Reeves, and Gail S. Elkind. 1987. "Attention Deficit, Conduct, Oppositional, and Anxiety Disorders in Children: I. A Review of Research on Differentiating Characteristics." *Journal of the American Academy of Child and Adolescent Psychiatry* 26:133–43.

West, Donald J., and David P. Farrington. 1973. *Who Becomes Delinquent?* London: Heinemann.

Williams, D. 1969. "Neural Factors Related to Habitual Aggression." *Brain* 92:503–20.

Wilson, James Q., and Richard J. Herrnstein. 1985. *Crime and Human Nature.* New York: Simon & Schuster.

Wolff, P. H., D. Waber, M. Bauermeister, C. Cohen, and R. Ferber. 1982. "The Neuropsychological Status of Adolescent Delinquent Boys." *Journal of Child Psychology and Psychiatry* 23:267–79.

Wolfgang, Marvin E., Robert M. Figlio, and Thorsten Sellin. 1972. *Delinquency in a Birth Cohort.* Chicago: University of Chicago Press.

Yakovlev, Paul I., and Andre-Roche Lecours. 1967. "The Myelogenetic Cycles of Regional Maturation of the Brain." In *Regional Development of the Brain in Early Life*, edited by A. Minkowski. Oxford: Blackwell.

Yeudall, Lorne T. 1980. "A Neuropsychological Perspective of Persistent Juvenile Delinquency and Criminal Behavior." *Annals of the New York Academy of Science* 347:349–55.

Yeudall, Lorne T., and Delee Fromm-Auch. 1979. "Neuropsychological Impairments in Various Psychopathological Populations." In *Hemisphere Asymmetries of Function and Psychopathology*, edited by J. Gruzelier and Pierre Flor-Henry. New York: Elsevier/North Holland.

Yeudall, Lorne T., Delee Fromm-Auch, and Priscilla Davies. 1982. "Neuropsychological Impairment of Persistent Delinquency." *Journal of Nervous and Mental Disease* 170:257–65.

Zaidel, Dahlia W. 1985. "Hemifield Tachistoscopic Presentations and Hemispheric Specialization in Normal Subjects." In *The Dual Brain*, edited by D. Frank Benson and Eran Zaidel. New York: Guilford.

Irving A. Spergel

Youth Gangs: Continuity and Change

ABSTRACT

No region of the United States is without youth gangs. Gangs exist in many large and middle-size cities and are spreading to suburban and smaller communities. Youth gangs increasingly create problems in correctional and school settings. Compared with nongang offenders, gang members are responsible for a disproportionate percentage of serious and violent offenses and engage in the sale and distribution of drugs. Race or ethnicity and social isolation interact with poverty and community disorganization to account for much of the gang problem. The gang is an important social institution for low-income male youths and young adults from newcomer and residual populations because it often serves social, cultural, and economic functions no longer adequately performed by the family, the school, and the labor market. Four major policy emphases for dealing with gangs have evolved: local community mobilization, youth outreach, social opportunities, and, most recently, gang suppression. Improved policies require the integration of these approaches. Strategies of community mobilization, social support, social opportunities, and suppression should be coordinated within a framework of social control and institution building.

Youth gangs are not unique to contemporary urban America. They have existed across time and cultures. Youth gangs tend to develop during times of rapid social change and political instability. They function as a residual social institution when other institutions fail and provide a certain degree of order and solidarity for their members.

Irving A. Spergel is a professor at the School of Social Service Administration, University of Chicago. Appreciation is expressed to Malcolm Klein, Sheldon Messinger, Norval Morris, Michael Tonry, Walter Miller, Paul Tracy, David Curry, Ron Chance, Ruth Ross, and Edwina Simmons for comments on earlier drafts of this essay. Preparation of this essay was supported in part by a grant from the Office of Juvenile Justice and Delinquency Prevention, U.S. Department of Justice.

Youth gangs have existed in Western and Eastern societies for centuries. As early as the 1600s, London was "terrorized by a series of organized gangs calling themselves the Mims, Hectors, Bugles, Dead Boys . . . who found amusement in breaking windows, demolishing taverns, assaulting the watch. . . . The gangs also fought pitched battles among themselves dressed with colored ribbons to distinguish the different factions" (Pearson 1983, p. 188). In the seventeenth and eighteenth centuries, English gangs wore belts and metal pins, with designs of serpents, hearts pierced with arrows, animals, and stars.

Youth gangs in urban centers of the United States existed before the nineteenth century (Hyman 1984). A historian of gangs in New York City writes, "By 1855 it was estimated that the metropolis contained at least 30,000 men who owed allegiance to gang leaders and through them to the political leaders of Tammany Hall and the Know Nothing or Native American Party" (Asbury 1971, p. 105). The New York City Civil War Draft riots were said to have been precipitated by young Irish street gangs (Asbury 1971). Prison gangs existed in Illinois as early as the 1920s. The crimes of many of these early groups were similar to those practiced today and included "intimidation, extortion, homosexual prostitution and other illegitimate business. Riots and killings were numerous" (C. Camp and G. Camp 1988, p. 57). The gang tradition has been particularly strong in America's Southwest in recent decades. Some gangs in Los Angeles, at least in terms of name and tradition, date back sixty or more years (Pitchess 1979). Philibosian estimates that gangs are active in seventy of the eighty-four incorporated cities in Los Angeles County (1989, p. 7). One writer reports that "today a Hispanic in Los Angeles may be a fourth generation gang member" (Donovan 1988, p. 14).

Outside the United States, youth gangs and gang problems have been reported in most countries of Europe, the Soviet Union, Kenya, Tanzania, South Africa, Australia, Mexico, Brazil, Peru, Taiwan, South Korea, Hong Kong, and the People's Republic of China (Oschlies 1979; Specht 1988). Youth gangs apparently are present in both socialist and free-market societies and in both developing and developed countries.

The Japanese Yakuza (DeVos, Wagatasuma, Caudill, and Mizushima 1973), the Chinese Triads (Morgan 1960; President's Commission on Organized Crime 1985), and the Italian Mafia (Arlacchi 1986) are organized criminal adult gangs, which have youth street-gang affiliates or aspirants.

The Japanese Ministry of Justice reports that 52,275 gangsters were arrested in 1983 (excluding those arrested for relatively minor crimes; Ministry of Justice 1984*a*). The number of juveniles identified as members of gangster organizations who entered Japanese reformatory schools in 1983 was 713, or 12.3 percent of the total of 5,787 juveniles (Ministry of Justice 1984*b*).

Sir Clinton Roper observes that "ethnic gangs" are a major problem in New Zealand prisons. "They behave as a cohesive group . . . are in conflict among themselves . . . and present a real danger to prison staff"; "a predominant gang can virtually run a wing of a prison"; "they adopt stand-over tactics against non gang members, which results in many inmates seeking protective segregation where there is little available"; and "the active recruitment of new members in the institution is a strong impediment to re-integrating inmates into a law-abiding life on release" (Roper 1988).

There were and continue to be different views about the nature, scope, and severity of youth gang activities. The American boy gang was in earlier times often regarded as spirited, venturesome, and fun loving, mainly a problem of unsupervised lower-class youth from immigrant families situated in transitional inner-city areas (Puffer 1912; Thrasher 1936). Just before and after World War II certain researchers (Whyte 1943; Suttles 1968) emphasized the stable, organized, functionally constructive, protective, nonaggressive character of many youth gangs or street corner groups.

Close connections between delinquent and adult criminal groups or gangs were noted in the early research of Thrasher (1936) and Shaw and McKay (1943) and somehow disappeared in much of the theoretical speculation and research on gangs in the 1950s and early 1960s (Cohen 1955; Miller 1958; Short and Strodtbeck 1965; however, see Cloward and Ohlin 1960; Spergel 1964). These connections were reemphasized in the 1970s and 1980s (Moore 1978; Needle and Stapleton 1983; Spergel 1984; G. Camp and C. Camp 1985; Maxson, Gordon, and Klein 1985; C. Camp and G. Camp 1988).

How much youth gangs in the United States have changed over the years, especially in the last two or three decades, is unclear. According to Miller (1975, p. 75), the President's Commission on Law Enforcement and Administration of Justice (1967) and the National Advisory Committee on Criminal Justice Standards and Goals (1976) agreed that "youth gangs are not now or should not become a major object of concern. . . . Youth gang violence is not a major crime problem in the

United States . . . what gang violence does exist can fairly readily be diverted into 'constructive' channels especially through the provision of services by community agencies." Miller's study (1975, p. 75), based on a national survey, however, concluded that the youth gang problem of the mid-1970s was then of "the utmost seriousness." Tracy's study (1982), based on findings from the Philadelphia cohort studies (Wolfgang, Figlio, and Sellin 1972), demonstrates that youth gangs account for a substantial share of serious and violent crime in that city. High levels of fear of gang crime in or about schools are reported in several recent studies (Chicago Board of Education 1981; Miller 1982; Rosenbaum and Grant 1983; Dolan and Finney 1984; Kyle 1984).

In the late 1980s, gang problems received national attention, much of it stimulated by reports from California, especially Los Angeles. The executive director of the Office of Criminal Justice Planning, California, in a recent newsletter claims that "gangs and gang violence have taken on a whole new meaning. Today's gangs are a violent and insidious new form of organized crime. Heavily armed with sophisticated weapons, they are involved in drug trafficking, witness intimidation, extortion and bloody territorial wars. In some cases, they are travelling out of state to spread their violence and crime" (Howenstein 1988, p. 1).

Some recent, believable claims indicate the variability and complexity of gang problems: white power gang activities have increased somewhat in various cities (Coplon 1988); the school busing of youth from inner-city to other neighborhoods and the suburbs has brought more gang problems, at least temporarily, to some communities (Hagedorn 1988); Hispanic and some black gangs continue to be largely responsible for drive-by shootings; white gangs tend to be a major source of graffiti, vandalism, theft and burglary; undocumented Latin American youth are now present in some established gangs or are forming their own gangs; many of the recent arrivals from Latin America, the Caribbean, and Asia have become suppliers of drugs; conflicts between some black gangs over drug turf have escalated in some communities; the drug problem among black and Hispanic gangs appears to be different in terms of sale and use patterns; the Asian gang problem is spreading but is highly diverse (Duran 1987).

Youth gangs may be an endemic feature of urban culture that varies over time in its form, social meaning, and antisocial character. The late 1980s in the United States are a time and a place in which—especially in some cities—youth gangs have taken an especially disturbing form and character.

This essay has three objectives: to describe what is known about youth gangs in the United States, to explain gang phenomena, mainly within social disorganization and poverty perspectives, and to discuss the effectiveness of organized responses to the problem.

Here is how this essay is organized. Section I examines definitional issues and data sources. Section II considers the scope and seriousness of the gang problem. Sections III–V consider, respectively, the organizational character of youth gangs, membership demographics, and membership experience. Section VI discusses the social contexts of youth gang development. Section VII summarizes what is known about organized responses to gangs. The final section offers conclusions and policy recommendations.

I.   Data Sources and Definitions

The youth gang needs to be better understood. The sources of knowledge concerning youth gangs are diverse and uneven, and research and program evaluation literatures are scant. I have drawn selectively on government documents, agency and conference reports, the mass media, and practitioner or "expert" experience. Some news reports, ephemeral data, and various analyses of youth gang problems, not consistently of the best quality, are used when more reliable research sources are not yet available.

Accurate national assessments of the gang problem do not exist, except perhaps in respect to the spread of drug-gang phenomena. Fairly good general estimates can be made in some large cities for particular periods.

Various reasons exist for the lack of "good" data on gangs. The most immediate or direct data source, the gang member, is unreliable. Gang members tend to conceal and exaggerate and may not know the scope of the gang's activities (Klein 1971; Miller 1982; Spergel 1984). The news media do not consistently or regularly report gang events and often exaggerate or sensationalize the subject (Downes 1966; Cohen 1972; Patrick 1973; Gold and Mattick 1974). Miller suggests that the national media, centered in New York City, ignored the gang problem in other cities in the 1970s. For example, about 300 gang killings in 1979 and 350 in 1980 in Los Angeles went largely unreported nationally (Miller 1982; however, see Klein and Maxson 1989).

There is no national center or agency for reporting gang data. Not the U.S. Census Bureau, the U.S. Justice Department, the Federal Bureau of Investigation, the Department of Health and Human Services, the National Institute of Mental Health, or the U.S. Department of Education collect or compile national level data on youth gangs.

There has been slow progress in the development of reliable statistics on gang crime in a few large cities. However, only gross estimates are available in most cities. Some police gang units collect gang crime data, mainly on homicide and sometimes on felony assault and robbery; other index and nonindex gang crime data tend to be sporadically collected (see Needle and Stapleton 1983). Data on gang crime are often collected on an incident basis rather than on an individual offender basis. Consequently, it is difficult to target repeat offenders or to determine the extent of solo offending or nongang companionate crime committed by gang members (Reiss 1988). Considerable interest has developed recently in the creation of information systems at city, county, and state levels and in correctional institutions at different jurisdictional levels (C. Camp and G. Camp 1988).

Local values and traditions, political considerations, public pressures, organizational predispositions, news media pressures, academic influences, and statutory language all influence how law enforcement authorities establish their definitions of gangs, gang members, and gang incidents. There are striking differences between cities and states (Overend 1988).

In a recent survey, over three quarters of police departments responded that violent behavior was the key distinguishing criterion of gangs (Needle and Stapleton 1983). The Los Angeles Police Department defines "gang-related crime" as homicide, attempted murder, assault with a deadly weapon, robbery, kidnapping, shooting at an inhabited dwelling, or arson, in which the suspect or victim is identified in police files as a gang member or associate member (usually on the basis of a prior arrest or identification as a gang member). In Chicago, a wider range of crimes may be classified as gang related but only if the incident grows out of a gang function or particular circumstances. Any robbery involving a gang member is gang related in Los Angeles, but a "gang-related robbery" in Chicago must be related to the interests of gang structure. Philadelphia, Boston, New York City, and other cities (even within the state of California) have different criteria for identifying and classifying an incident as gang related (see Miller 1975, 1982).

A variety of theoretical and methodological problems have hindered the development of adequate knowledge about gangs. The approach to the study of gangs has been categorical rather than variable (Kornhauser 1978). Categories and concepts have not been clearly defined and distinguished. There has often been a failure to distinguish norms and behaviors, subcultures and gangs, gangs and delinquent groups, different ethnic gang patterns, and variability in gang problems in different cities and in gang patterns in the same city over time.

Researchers have tended to employ nonrepresentative or age-truncated samples and limited data-gathering technologies. Small non-random samples of gangs served and supplied through local youth agencies or youth projects have been studied, usually without control or comparison groups. Adolescent gangs have been almost the exclusive focus of research or program evaluation, to the exclusion of preadolescent and young adult gangs. Observational studies have been time limited—usually one to three years with no long-term systematic follow-up. Conspicuously absent have been studies of the socialization of gang youths compared with other nongang youths or of different subgroups of youths in the same gang, those who use or sell drugs and those who do not, those who are extremely violent and those who are not. Longitudinal studies that examine the stability and changing character of these structures and processes over time have not been conducted. Participant observation has been the favored mode of study, at times resulting in researcher overidentification with subjects. Insufficient use has been made of official statistics, systematic self-reports, or surveys of youths or adults in high-crime or gang-crime areas. Variations among gangs across neighborhoods, cities, and countries and across schools, prisons, and other institutional contexts have been often disregarded (however, see Spergel 1964; Downes 1966; Patrick 1973; McGahey 1986).

A. *Definitions*

The term "gang" can mean many things. Definitions in use have varied according to the perceptions and interests of the definer, academic fashions, and the changing social reality of the gang. Definitions in the 1950s and 1960s were related to issues of etiology and were based on liberal, social-reform assumptions. Definitions in the 1970s and 1980s are more descriptive, emphasize violent and criminal characteristics, and may reflect more conservative social philosophies (Klein and Maxson 1989).

Definitions evoke "intense and emotional discussions" (Miller 1977, p. 1) and can become the basis for different policies, laws, and strategies. Definitions determine whether we have a large, small, or even no problem, whether more or fewer gangs and gang members exist, and which agencies will receive funds.

Some of the more benign conceptions of the gang, used by gang members, agency personnel, and a few academics, stress the gang's residual communal or social-support function. According to one gang member, "Being in a gang means if I didn't have no family, I'll think that's where I'll be. If I didn't have no job that's where I'd be. To me it's community help without all the community. They'll understand better than my mother and father" (Hagedorn 1988, p. 131).

A former gang member, later a staff member of a local community organization, says: "A gang is what you make it. A gang is people who hang out; they don't have to be negative or positive" (Allen 1981, p. 74). Sister Falaka Fattah, director and founder of the House of Umoja, a model residential and community-based program deeply committed to social support and development of gang youth, observes: "A traditional Philadelphia black street gang was composed of friends who lived in the same neighborhood and usually had kinship links developed over generations with ties to the South. Many of these traditional gangs were founded by families, since recruitment took place at funerals where families and friends gathered in mourning" (Fattah 1988, p. 5).

The gang in this perspective may be viewed as performing significant social functions. It is an "interstitial" group, integrated or organized through conflict. While its opposition may include other baseball teams, parents, storekeepers, and gangs on the next street (Thrasher 1936), the "gang is not organized to commit delinquent acts. . . . The gang is a form of collective behavior, spontaneous and unplanned in origin" (Kornhauser 1978, p. 52). Morash observes that "gang-likeness is not a necessary condition to stimulate member's delinquency" (1983, p. 35; see also Savitz, Rosen, and Lalli 1980).

Miller observes that there are at least two ways to perceive gang activity as constructive or benign. Some community groups, agencies, and gangs may perceive gang behaviors as "normal and expectable" so long as such behavior is relatively unserious or infrequent (Miller 1977, p. 11). Gang members may be perceived as protecting their respective communities by attacking and driving out "unwanted" elements, including drug dealers or members of other races or ethnic groups (Miller 1977, pp. 13–14; see also Suttles 1968).

Some veteran gang researchers have recently changed their minds as to gang character. Earlier, Miller viewed the gang as a stable primary group, neither especially aggressive nor violent, that prepared the young male for an adult role in lower-class society (1958, 1962, 1976b). More recently, because of increased levels of violent or other illegal behavior, Miller concludes that "contemporary youth gangs pose a greater threat to public order and a greater danger to the safety of the citizenry than at any time during the past" (1975, p. 44; see also Miller 1982).

Similarly, Klein initially characterized the gang as an adolescent group perceived both by themselves and others as involved in delinquencies, but not of a serious or lethal nature (1968, 1971). In recent years, Klein and his associates report that gangs commit a large number of homicides and participate in extensive narcotics trafficking, although perhaps not as much as is commonly believed (Klein, Maxson, and Cunningham 1988; Klein 1989).

Yablonsky, by contrast, has consistently portrayed gang boys, particularly leaders and core members, as lawbreakers, trading in violence and primarily organized to carry out illegal acts (Yablonsky 1962; Haskell and Yablonsky 1982).

The principal criterion currently used to define a "gang" may be the group's participation in illegal activity. Miller suggests that the term can be applied broadly or narrowly by the key definers of the phenomena, law enforcement officers. Police departments may apply the term quite narrowly in large cities but more broadly, to cover more types of offenses, in small cities (Miller 1980). Needle and Stapleton (1983, p. 13) suggest that perception of youth gang activities as major, moderate, or minor problems varies with the number and size of youth gangs, the problems they are believed to cause, and the prevalence of youth gang activity as a proportion of total crime. The media, distressed local citizens, and outreach community agencies tend to use the term more broadly than the police to cover more categories of youth behavior.

B.   Delinquent Group versus Gang

Much juvenile crime is committed by groups of young people (Erickson and Jensen 1977; Zimring 1981). Is the "gang" equivalent simply to the concept of "delinquent group"? Shaw and McKay were interested in the companionate character of the delinquent acts for which eight out of ten youths were brought to juvenile court, but they used the terms "gang" and "delinquent group" interchangeably (Shaw and McKay 1931).

Thrasher (1936) implicitly recognized the difference between the gang and the delinquent group. Whyte's (1943) and Suttles's (1968) gangs or street-corner groups were not particularly delinquent, certainly not violent. The major theorists and researchers of gangs in the

1950s and 1960s generally viewed the delinquent gang and the delinquent group as equivalent or synonymous, although reference was made to core delinquent cliques in gangs (Cohen 1955; Cohen and Short 1958; Miller 1958, 1962; Cloward and Ohlin 1960; Short and Strodtbeck 1965; Klein 1968, 1971). Most recently, a researcher in Scandinavia conducted a series of sophisticated network analyses on the assumption that "gangs . . . simply signifies groups" (Sarnecki 1986, p. 11). However, an academic informant recently stated that Sarnecki has changed his mind. He believes that Scandinavian delinquent groups are not gangs, at least in the sense the term is used in the United States (Klein 1989). Gangs and delinquent groups are more likely to be viewed as equivalent in the study of juveniles than of older adolescents and young adults.

A number of theorists and researchers have tried to distinguish between gangs and delinquent groups (Cohen 1969a, 1969b; Kornhauser 1978; Morash 1983). Bernard Cohen insists that "gang and group delinquency are different forms of juvenile deviance and should be approached etiologically, as well as for purposes of treatment and prevention, from different starting points" (1969a, p. 108). Based on police data, he found that gang offenders were a little older and more homogeneous with respect to age, race, sex, and residence patterns than were nongang group offenders.

The more widely accepted view among academics, law enforcement, and the general populace, however, is that gangs and delinquents are closely related. The most widely used definition was developed by Klein almost twenty years ago: a gang refers "to any denotable adolescent group of youngsters who (a) are generally perceived as a distinct aggregation by others in the neighborhood, (b) recognize themselves as a denotable group (almost invariably with a group name), and (c) have been involved in a sufficient number of delinquent incidents to call forth a consistent negative response from neighborhood residents and/or law enforcement agencies" (Klein 1971, p. 111).

Miller would differentiate among twenty different categories and subcategories of law-violating youth groups, of which "turf gangs," "fighting gangs," and "gain-oriented gangs" are three subtypes (1982, chap. 1).

Curry and Spergel provide an extended definition that attempts to distinguish delinquent groups and gangs with some attention to the variability and complexity of gang structure and behavior. Group delinquency is defined as law-violating behavior committed by juveniles in relatively small groups that tend to be ephemeral, i.e., loosely organized with shifting leadership. The delinquent group is engaged in various forms of minor or serious crime. We define gang delinquency or crime as law-violating behavior committed both by juveniles and adults in or related to groups that are complexly organized although sometimes diffuse, sometimes cohesive with established leadership and rules. The gang also engages in a range of crime but significantly more violence within a framework of communal values in respect to mutual support, conflict relations with other gangs, and a tradition often of turf, colors, signs, and symbols. Subgroups of the gang may be differentially committed to various delinquent or criminal patterns, such as drug trafficking, gang fighting, or burglary. The concepts of delinquent group and youth gang are not exclusive of each other but represent distinctive social phenomena. [Curry and Spergel 1988, p. 382]

It is also possible to argue, based on recent survey data (Spergel et al. 1989), that delinquent groups in some cities can be converted or organized into youth gangs and that youth gangs in turn are changing into criminal organizations of various kinds. Much depends on population change, particularly the movement of families with gang members to nongang areas, the entrepreneurial efforts of gang drug traffickers, and the socialization of delinquent or criminal youths to gangs in prisons.

The term "youth gang" is generally used here to refer to groups and behaviors that represent an important subset of delinquent and sometimes criminal groups and their behaviors. "Delinquent group" is useful for some purposes, but my purpose here is to examine gang phenomena of contemporary interest to researchers and policymakers, and for this purpose it is "gangs," not "delinquent groups," that are the focus.

II.   Scope and Seriousness of the Gang Problem

This section summarizes the available evidence on numbers of gangs and gang members, gang members' participation in serious crime, and, particularly, gang violence and the relation between drug trafficking by gangs and violence associated with the drug trade. Although data sources are diverse, and of various reliability, some substantive information is available and provides a reasonable basis for forming conclusions about magnitudes and trends.

Youth gangs are today to be found in almost all fifty states, including

Alaska and Hawaii (and in Puerto Rico), with possible exceptions in a few northeastern and north central mountain states. Miller (1982, chap. 3) estimated that, in the late seventies, gangs were present in almost 300 cities, or 13 percent of all U.S. cities with populations of 10,000 or more. Miller (1982, chap. 2) found that five out of six, or 83 percent, of the largest cities had gang problems, as did forty-one out of 150 cities with a 100,000 or more population. Needle and Stapleton (1983) report a somewhat similar proportion: 39 percent with populations between 100,000 and 249,999 have gang problems. There are now gangs in smaller cities and suburban communities, similar in kind, but not necessarily in degree or intensity of criminality and violence; sometimes these gangs share names and loose ties with gangs in nearby large cities (Rosenbaum and Grant 1983).

Why gangs are present or are a more serious problem in certain cities and regions of the country and not in others is not clear. While no region is without youth gangs, they seem to be concentrated in certain western, midwestern, and southeastern states. A substantial number of smaller cities and communities in California, Illinois, and Florida now have gang problems. At the same time, there appear to be many more cities with delinquent youth groups than with specific gang problems (Miller 1982; Needle and Stapleton 1983). Some cities that reported gang problems in the 1970s or early 1980s apparently no longer have them in the late 1980s (Spergel et al. 1989), and some cities with current problems did not have (or recognize) them earlier. "Emerging" and "chronic" gang problem cities are now distinguished.

Gangs are present in state and federal correctional systems and in many school systems. In a 1981 study, Caltabriano calculated that 53 percent of state prisons had gangs. G. Camp and C. Camp (1985) found that thirty-two out of forty-eight, or 67 percent, of the state prison systems studied had gangs present, as did the federal system. Youth and young adult gangs were identified in state prisons on the West Coast as early as the 1950s and 1960s and in midwestern states in the 1960s and 1970s. All public high schools in Chicago and many in its suburbs report the presence of gangs or gang members and sometimes gang problems (Chicago Board of Education 1981; Spergel 1985).

A. Estimates of Numbers of Youth Gangs and Youth-Gang Membership

It is not possible to devise meaningful estimates of the number of youth gangs in the United States. Partly this is because there is no standard or national definition for the term "gang." Sometimes a number of different gangs that share the same or similar names are considered one gang; sometimes factions of a fairly small gang are reported as separate gangs. National estimates have been made primarily for rhetorical purposes. Dolan and Finney (1984, p. 12) claim that "since the close of World War II, the number of youth gangs has grown astonishingly, with a recent study revealing that there are now far more than 100,000 in the country." The estimate is sufficiently exciting that the U.S. Justice Department, Office of Juvenile Justice and Delinquency Prevention, used it in the introduction to a recent public request for proposals on gang research (*Federal Register* 1987).

It is difficult to determine the consistency or meaning of the following estimates: 760–2,700 gangs in the eight largest cities of the United States (Miller 1975, p. 18); 2,200 gangs in approximately 300 U.S. cities and towns (Miller 1982, chap. 4, pp. 30–31); 1,130 gangs in the ten largest gang-problem cities between 1970 and 1980 (Miller 1982). Furthermore, how would these estimates compare—or can be compared—to Thrasher's (1936) estimates of 1,313 gangs in Chicago in the 1920s?

Somewhat more meaningful may be estimates that law-violating delinquent youth groups, other than gangs, far exceed the number of gangs, perhaps by fifty times. Miller (1975, 1982) suggests that the number of police-recognized gangs has remained fairly constant over the past two decades in some cities. More recent observations suggest a sharp increase in some cities and a sharp decline in others (Spergel et al. 1989).

There were reports of rises in numbers of gangs, gang members, or gang incidents in the following cities in recent years. In Dade County, Florida, there are reported to have been four gangs in 1980, twenty-five in 1983, forty-seven in 1985, and eighty in 1988 (Reddick 1987; Silbert, Christiano, and Nunez-Cuenca 1988). In Los Angeles County, there were 239 gangs reported in 1985 and 400 to 650 or possibly 800 in 1988 (Los Angeles County Sheriff's Department 1985; Gott 1988; Knapp 1988; see also Philibosian 1989). In Santa Ana, Orange County, the number of cases assigned to the gang detail jumped from 286 in 1986 to 396 in 1987, including eight gang-related homicides—the highest since 1979, when there were thirteen (Schwartz 1988). In San Diego County there were three gangs and fewer than 300 street gang members in 1975, but nineteen to thirty-five gangs, if factions are included, and 2,100 street gang members in 1987 (Davidson 1987). In Phoenix, reports of numbers of gangs have seesawed, thirty-four in 1974, seventy-four in 1982, thirty-one in 1986; in the past year a surge of gang drug activity has been blamed on an influx of black young adults from Los Angeles (Frazier 1988).

In other cities over the same period, there were reports of sharp declines in gangs, membership, and gang activity. In New York City, there were 315 gangs and 20,000 members reported in 1974, 130 gangs and 10,300 members in 1982, sixty-six gangs and 1,780 gang members in 1987, and thirty-seven classified youth gangs with 1,036 members (and another fifty-three gangs with 1,020 members under investigation) in 1988 (New York State Assembly 1974a; Galea 1982, 1989; Kowski 1988). In Fort Wayne, Indiana, there were six gangs and over 2,000 members reported in 1985–86, but only three gangs and fifty members in 1988 (Hinshaw 1988). El Monte, in Los Angeles County, reported ten to twelve gangs and 1,000 gang members in the mid-1970s, but only four gangs and fifty members in 1988 (Hollopeter 1988). Louisville, Kentucky, police reported fifteen gangs and forty to fifty gang incidents per month in 1985, but only five gangs and one gang incident per month in July 1988 (Beavers 1988).

It is not clear what accounts for these shifts. We do not know if overall juvenile or young-adult crime rates or patterns of crime have changed in each of the cities. Gangs may affect the form and process of delinquent or criminal activity rather than its incidence or prevalence over time. It is possible that, if a gang or set of gangs ages in a particular community, if patterns of violent behavior are constrained, if opportunities for legitimate jobs increase, or if more rational income-producing illegal activity, such as drug trafficking, rises, then group activity may no longer be conducted through traditional turf structures.

Estimates from law enforcement or police agencies may be slightly more useful, particularly if such figures are based on arrests or focus on clearly defined "high profile" gangs. Police prevalence figures tend to be on the conservative side. Those of news reporters, academics, and community agency informants are often higher. For example, in the 1940s, the police estimated that there were sixty to 200 gangs in New York City, but a contemporary observer reported that there were then at least 250 gangs in Harlem alone (Campbell 1984b). One police commander estimates that there were 127 active gangs, with another 144 less active gangs in New York City in the 1970s (Hargrove 1981, p. 90). Another claims that there were 130 "delinquent" gangs in the early 1980s and an additional 113 gangs under investigation (Galea 1982), but an academic researcher estimates that there were 400 gangs in New

York City in 1979 (Campbell 1984*b*). Miller (1975, p. 13) states there were 1,000 gangs in Chicago in the 1960s but that the number dropped to 700 by 1974. In his 1982 report, Miller claims the number of Chicago gangs was only 250 between 1970 and 1980. Chicago Police Department estimates of the number of gangs were 110 in 1985 and 135 in 1986 and 1987.

Estimates of the number of prison gangs may also be meaningless unless characteristics of size, and the frequency and seriousness of criminal behavior, are indicated. Estimates have varied from forty-seven gangs in twenty-four prisons in a 1981 report by Caltabriano to 114 gangs in thirty-three prisons in a 1985 report (G. Camp and C. Camp 1985), which also indicates that the figure could go as high as 219 gangs if gangs with the same names in different state prisons or systems are counted. Thus a gang such as CRIPS in the California prison system is counted once in reports but exists in many different California institutions. CRIPS is made up of at least 180 street gangs whose membership is reported to be in the thousands (G. Camp and C. Camp 1985).

Questionable estimates of gangs in public schools have also been made for some of the large cities. Spergel estimated that there were fifty-three male and seven female gangs in sixty public high schools in Chicago in 1985. These were school gangs with names of high profile street gangs. The number represented 211 male factions in the sixty public high schools. Furthermore, based on police data, nineteen male and four female major youth-gang factions were also found in the city's Catholic high schools (Spergel 1985). One witness testifying before a Senate subcommittee hearing estimated that there were 207 gangs operating on public school campuses of the Los Angeles Unified School District in 1983 (Philibosian 1983, p. 4). We need to know, however, many other things, for example, how many gang-related or nongang delinquency problems were caused by gang members on school property. It is quite possible that schools with many gangs, but with small numbers in each of them, may experience fewer problems of social disorder or deviance, particularly if such schools are well run and have reasonably high academic standards, than poorly managed schools with one or two large gangs (Spergel 1985).

Membership numbers of youth gangs have also been estimated with little attention to critical factors, such as membership statuses or roles or the extent and degree of members' participation in delinquent behavior. Miller estimates that there were 96,000 gang members in 300

United States cities and towns in the 1970s, with a mean average of forty-eight members per gang. Gangs are larger on average than are other law-violating youth groups. While there are fifty times more law-violating youth groups than youth gangs, members of law-violating youth groups are only fifteen times as numerous as gang members (Miller 1982).

The proportion of a youth population estimated to be gang members ranges considerably with place and time. Thrasher (1936, p. 412) reported that "one tenth of Chicago's 350,000 boys between the ages of 10 and 20 are subject to the demoralizing influence of gangs." But Klein (1968) estimated that the census tract with the highest known number of gang members in Los Angeles in 1960 had only 6 percent of ten to seventeen year olds affiliated with gangs. A Pennsylvania civic commission report of 1969 reported that only 6.4 percent of all juvenile arrests in 1968 were known gang members (Klein 1971, p. 115). Vigil (1988) recently estimated that only 3 to 10 percent of boys in the Mexican barrios of Los Angeles are gang members.

A variety of self-report studies has been conducted. The proportion of youths declaring they are gang members does not seem to have changed radically over the past two decades, with a few exceptions. Savitz, Rosen, and Lalli (1980) determined that 12 percent of black and 14 percent of white youths in Philadelphia claimed to be gang affiliated in the mid-1970s. Only 1 percent of these self-acknowledged gang members had Philadelphia Police Department records. Another self-report study found that 10.3 percent of black youths in suburban Cook County said they were gang members (Johnstone 1981). In a self-report study in Seattle, 13 percent of youth said they belonged to gangs (Sampson 1986). In an as-yet-unpublished study of several very poor inner-city neighborhoods of Chicago, the following percentages of adult males (eighteen to forty-five years old) reported they "had belonged" to gangs: Mexican/Mexican-Americans, 3.5 percent; Puerto Ricans, 12.7 percent; whites, 10.7 percent; and blacks, 13.8 percent (Testa 1988). In another recent self-report study of four inner-city neighborhoods in three large cities across the country, one male in three reported gang membership; however, this sample may have been preselected for gang membership (Fagan, Piper, and Moore 1986).

Recent informant or "expert" estimates of the percentage of gang youth in large cities have ranged from 0.7 percent in San Antonio to 7.3 percent in New York City (Miller 1982). A California state task force report estimates that there were 50,000 gang members in Los Angeles

County (California Council on Criminal Justice 1986). However, a current estimate is 70,000 gang members in Los Angeles County (Gott 1988). A Los Angeles newspaper reports "there are 25,000 CRIPS and Blood gang members or 'associates' in Los Angeles County—an estimate based on arrests and field interrogation of persons stopped but not arrested. That represents 25 percent of the county's estimated 100,000 black men between the ages of 15 and 24" (Baker 1988a). Another estimate is that there are 70,000 CRIPS and Bloods in Los Angeles County alone (O'Connell 1988). Estimates of gang membership in Chicago have ranged from "12,000 to as many as 120,000 persons" (Bobrowski 1988, p. 40). Spergel estimates that 5 percent of students in elementary school, 10 percent in high school, 20 percent in special school programs, and 35 percent of school-age dropouts between sixteen and nineteen years old are gang members in Chicago. This produces a figure of 38,000 public school-age students who were gang members in Chicago (1985).

The estimated figures for gang members as a proportion of population necessarily are higher in criminal justice settings. They range from 0–90 percent or more. G. Camp and C. Camp (1985) estimated that 34 percent, or 5,300 of Illinois prison inmates were active gang members as of January 1984 and, not quite consistently, that 90 percent of Illinois prison inmates "are, were, or will be gang members" (p. 134). A family court worker reported that 20 percent of children going before the Queens County, New York, Family Court were involved in gang-related activities (New York State Assembly 1974b). One study of Cook County juvenile court probationers indicated that 22.7 percent were gang members (Utne and McIntyre 1982). A California Youth Authority study found that 40–45 percent of the wards could be identified as gang members in 1979, but the estimates had increased to between 70 percent and 80 percent in 1982 and 1983 (Hayes 1983). However, an official in the California Youth Authority more recently estimated that approximately a third of its 13,152 wards were "gang-identified" (Lockwood 1988).

These estimates, variable and unreliable as they may be, indicate that gangs are present in significant numbers in a variety of social contexts. Furthermore, gang membership may have reached critical proportions in certain cities, schools, and prison systems. However, the data are not clear as to the relation of numbers and proportion of gang members to problems of social disorder or criminality. Certain gangs and gang members may be only peripherally involved in delinquency or gang crime or not at all. Probably, the larger, and more concentrated the number of gang members from different gangs in a relatively small area, like a prison, the more likely serious gang-related disorder and crime are to occur (C. Camp and G. Camp 1988).

B. Youth-Gang Violence

Reasonably adequate data have begun to be available on the current nature and scope of violence committed by gang members. There is good evidence of an increase in gang-related violence and that gang members, at least those with arrest records, are responsible for a disproportionate amount of violent crime. This tends, however, to be concentrated in particular areas. The proportion of serious gang-related violence may be very high in a certain neighborhood, school, or correctional institution at a particular time. However, the proportion of serious violent crime by youth-gang members tends to be very small on a city, school system, or prison system basis. Bobrowski, who uses a definition of "gang incident" based on gang-related function or motivation rather than individual gang membership, indicates for Chicago that "Part I street gang offenses measured less than 0.8 percent of comparable city-wide gang crime [between January 1986 and July 1988]. . . . The seriousness of the problem lies not in the extent of street gang activity but in its violent character and relative concentration in certain of Chicago's community areas" (1988, p. 41). Property crime is still the major type of offense committed by gang members, often in a nongang capacity.

The classic research on types of offenses by juveniles, youths, or young adults in groups or gangs suggests that violent crime was less common for earlier periods than it is now (Thrasher 1936; Shaw and McKay 1943). Whyte (1943) stressed that street gangs in Boston did not typically engage in brawls or gang fights that resulted in serious injury. Miller (1962) and Klein (1968, 1971) insisted that gangs in the 1950s and 1960s programs that they evaluated were not particularly violent. Miller's (1962, 1976a) Boston gangs rarely used firearms, and their gang fights seldom resulted in serious injury. Klein (1971, p. 115) noted the relative rarity of the "truly violent act" among East Los Angeles Hispanic gangs in his project areas over a four-year period. Bernstein (1964) and Short and Strodtbeck (1965) reported that delinquency and violence by juvenile gangs were relatively mild. More fighting took place within the gang than against opposing gangs. The most common form of offense appeared to be "creating a disturbance," noisy rough-housing, or impeding public passage (Miller 1976*a*). Yablonsky (1962) and, to a lesser extent, Spergel (1964) were in the minority of observers when they reported that New York gangs of the 1950s frequently could be violent, with homicides occurring.

Gangs were different, however, in the 1970s and 1980s: "the weight of evidence would seem to support the conclusion that the consequences of assaultive activities by contemporary gangs are markedly more lethal than during any previous period" (Miller 1975, p. 41); "the cycles of gang homicide now seem to end with higher rates and retreat to higher plateaus before surging forward again. If homicide is any indication, gang violence has become a far more serious problem during the most recent decade" (Klein and Maxson 1989, p. 218). Miller (1975, pp. 75–76) makes stark claims: violent crime by gang members in some cities was as much as one-third of all violent crime by juveniles. Juvenile gang homicides were about 25 percent of all juvenile homicides in approximately sixty-five major cities in the United States. Block's study (1985, p. 5) more recently finds, based on police data, that gang homicide accounted for 25 percent of teenage homicides in Chicago between 1965 and 1981 and 50 percent of all Hispanic teenage homicides. In the last few years, Los Angeles probably has supplanted Chicago as the country's worst gang-violence city. There were 387 gang-related homicides in Los Angeles County in 1987, 452 in 1988, and a projected 515 for 1989 (Genelin 1989).

These statistics need not portend an inexorable upward spiral of gang violence, even though Los Angeles and Chicago may currently be recording the highest level of gang homicides in their respective histories. There are peaks and valleys in the number of gang homicides over fairly long time periods. Gang homicides averaged about seventy per year in Chicago between 1981 and 1986, sixty-three per year in the next highest period 1969–71, but only twenty-five gang homicides per year in the period between 1973 and 1978. Furthermore, gang homicides based on official statistics have sharply declined in New York City and Philadelphia in the past fifteen years. Gang homicides in Chicago as a percent of total homicides have ranged from 1.71 in 1975 to over 9 percent in 1981. Currently, gang homicides are estimated to be 10 percent of a declining base of total homicides in Chicago. During the 1981 peak year in Chicago, eighty-four gang homicides occurred.

Bob Baker, a *Los Angeles Times* reporter, adds both qualitative observation and critical meaning to the gang homicide problem. He argues that these less organized attacks, in which one or two members shoot somebody because they are trying to settle their own score, should not be called "gang killings:" "In most of Los Angeles, gang members contend that for all the publicity about killings, the gangs themselves are pretty quiet. . . . Assaults by one group of gang members on another are far less frequent than they were at the turn of the decade, when turf lines were less hardened and incursions tended to be more explosive. . . . For all the attention being paid to spectacular violence committed over soured drug deals and arguments over territory, the largest number of gang killings still occur in this haphazard chaotic way" (Baker 1988*b*).

Again, depending on how one reports and interprets these homicides, the basic youth violence situation in Los Angeles may be little different than it is in Chicago or New York. While the New York Police Department claims a very low level of gang crime, youth violence and drug violence currently "may be at an all time high" (Galea 1988). The rate of youth violence generally may be higher in Detroit than in Chicago, although Detroit police claim a very low level of youth-gang activity.

The puzzles of gang-crime statistics and what they mean are not easy to resolve. The proportion of violent crimes attributed to gang members is relatively higher than the proportion of violent crimes committed by nongang members in most social contexts. Yet we are not clear about the relationship of violent gang to nongang violent crime in seemingly similar cities. In 1987, gang homicides were 25.2 percent of the total number of homicides in Los Angeles City but 6.9 percent of the total number of homicides in Chicago. Gang felonious assaults were 11.2 percent in Los Angeles but 4.3 percent in Chicago. Gang-related robberies were 6.6 percent of the total robberies in Los Angeles, but only .8 percent of the total robberies in Chicago. These differences may reflect not only different definitions but different police practices, different local situations, and fluctuations over short-term periods.

The increase in gang violence in some cities in the past eight to ten years has been attributed to several factors. Gangs have more weapons (Miller 1975; Spergel 1983). Guns are used more often conjointly with a car. The ready availability of improved weaponry—22s, 38s, 45s, 357 magnums, A.K. 47s, Uzis, and sawed-off shotguns—is associated with the changing pattern of gang conflict. The "tradition" of intergang rumbles based on large assemblages of youth arriving for battle on foot—easily interdicted—has been supplanted by smaller mobile groups of two or three armed youths usually in a vehicle out looking for opposing gang members. While shootings are sometimes planned a day or two ahead, spur-of-the-moment decisions to attack targets of sudden opportunity are common (see also Horowitz 1983). Klein and Maxson (1989, p. 218) suggest that increased gang violence may not reflect "greater levels of violence among and between gangs [but] . . . a growth in the number of gangs or gang members . . . or an increasingly violent society [or perhaps] . . . more sophisticated gang intelligence [and law enforcement]."

The older ages of gang members may also be responsible for greater use of sophisticated weaponry and consequent violence. More and better weaponry may be available to older teenagers and young adults than to juveniles. The median gang homicide offender in Chicago has been nineteen years old and the victim twenty years old for the past ten years (Spergel 1986). Los Angeles data (Maxson, Gordon, and Klein 1985) and San Diego police statistics (San Diego Association of Governments 1982) also indicate that older adolescents and young adults are mainly involved in gang homicides.

Motorcycle and prison gangs also appear to have become more lethal. Motorcycle gangs, for example, are no longer simply "free-wheeling riders" but now engage in struggles over domination of a prison or a territory's lucrative vice or narcotics trade, prostitution, extortion, protection, and murder for hire (Davis 1982a, 1982b). These somewhat older gangs are still only partially disciplined and engage in internecine combat and brutality (G. Camp and C. Camp 1985). Half of all prison homicides are estimated to result from gang activity. Some state prisons are particularly violent. Of twenty gang killings in prisons in 1983, nine occurred in the California system. Between 1975 and 1984, there were 372 prison gang-related homicides in California, "a record unsurpassed by any other organized crime group in California" (G. Camp and C. Camp 1985, p. 2).

C. *Gang and Nongang Member Studies*

The relationship between gangs and violence is most evident when patterns of behavior by gang members and nonmembers are compared. Gang youths engage in more crime of a violent nature than do nongang but delinquent youths. Klein and Myerhoff (1967, pp. 1–2) observed that "the urban gang delinquent is different in *kind* from the urban nongang delinquent. . . . Gang members have higher police contact rates . . . and become involved in more serious delinquencies than nonmembers." Most recently a Swedish researcher found that delinquents who were group or "network" related committed more frequent and serious offenses than did nongroup or non-"network" delinquents (Sarnecki 1986).

The most consistent and impressive differences between gang and nongang offense patterns of delinquents arise from findings by different researchers in Philadelphia over a twenty-year period. Bernard Cohen (1969a, pp. 77–79), using data collected by the Philadelphia Police Department's gang unit, found evidence that "gangs engage in more violent behavior than do delinquent nongang groups": 66.4 percent of gang events but only 52.6 percent of delinquent-group events fell into violent offense categories. Only 1.4 percent of gang events but 13.7 percent of group events were property crimes. Gang members' offenses were more serious and more often involved display or use of a weapon.

Friedman, Mann, and Friedman (1975) sought to distinguish gang and nongang delinquents and nondelinquents in the early 1970s. They found that violent behavior differentiated street gang members from nongang members better than all the other legal, socioeconomic, and psychological factors studied. Gang members were also characterized by the attributes of more police arrests for nonviolent crime, more truancy, and more alcohol and drug abuse (Friedman, Mann, and Friedman 1975, pp. 599–600).

Based on a sample of the 1945 Philadelphia cohort study (Wolfgang, Figlio, and Sellin 1972), Rand (1987, pp. 155–56) found support for her hypothesis that "boys who join a gang are more delinquent than those who do not. The thirty-one boys who reported gang affiliation represented 29 percent of the total offender sample and were responsible for 50 percent of the offenses."

Tracy (1987, p. 14) is currently analyzing criminal characteristics of gang and nongang members, using the 1945 and 1958 Philadelphia birth cohort studies, based on official police records and juvenile and adult self-reports. Official offense data of the 1945 cohort show that juvenile gang membership is associated with significantly higher levels of delinquency. The offenses of gang members have higher average seriousness scores.

For nonwhites, the rate of nonviolent offenses is about 1.7 times as high for gang members as for nongang delinquents; the rate for violent offenses is almost twice as high; for aggravated assault, it is three times as high. The pattern for whites is less consistent. Analysis of the 1958 cohort, not yet completed, suggests a quite similar pattern (Tracy 1982,

1987). The self-report components of Tracy's 1945 cohort study are consistent with the official data findings.

Gang influence on criminality does not stop at the end of the juvenile period. When offense frequency and seriousness based on official and unofficial records are examined for the adult period, eighteen to twenty-six years of age, gang members equal, if not exceed, the magnitude of differences observed for the juvenile period. Thus, gang membership appears "to prolong the extent and seriousness of the criminal career" (Tracy 1987, p. 19). These conclusions are consistent with those of a Philadelphia researcher, who more than twenty years earlier noted that a "large portion of 'persistent and dangerous' juvenile gang offenders become 'even more serious' adult offenders" (Robin 1967, p. 24).

Finally, a California Department of Justice study (G. Camp and C. Camp 1985, p. 108) finds that gang members who have been released from prison commit a great many serious crimes. Two hundred and fifty gang members were randomly selected from California prison gangs (Nuestra Familia, Mexican Mafia, Black Guerrilla Family, and Aryan Brotherhood gangs), and their careers were tracked. Between 1978 and 1981, 195 of the 250 gang members were arrested, often repeatedly, for the following crimes: sixty-five misdemeanors and 350 felonies, including twenty-four arrests for murder, fifty-seven arrests for robbery, forty-six for burglary, thirty-one for narcotics offenses, forty-four for weapons offenses, and twenty-eight for assault with a deadly weapon.

D. Drugs and Violence

The relationship of gangs to drug use and drug trafficking has not been clear and received only passing attention in the classic street-gang literature (however, see Short and Strodtbeck 1965). Alcohol use and drug use usually have been addressed in tandem or not distinguished (Klein 1971). The relation between drug use and drug selling was also not systematically explored. Chein and his associates (1964) found little drug use or selling by youth gangs contacted by New York City Youth Board workers. The existence of drug using and selling gang subcultures was not clearly demonstrated in the 1950s and 1960s (Cloward and Ohlin 1960; Short and Strodtbeck 1965). Spergel (1964) found a close relationship between drug use and limited drug dealing by older youth gang members making a transition out of the gang.

The relationship between gangs, drug use, and trafficking has been found most consistently among criminal justice system populations. Of 276 documented gang members on probation in San Diego County, 207 or 75 percent had drug convictions (Davidson 1987). Moore (1978) found an integral relationship between Hispanic imprisoned gang members and drug trafficking. A close relationship between prison gangs and drug trafficking has been observed in certain state prisons over the past two decades (G. Camp and C. Camp 1985; C. Camp and G. Camp 1988). A recent study of 589 property offenders from three prison intake centers in Ohio found that drugs, unemployment, alcohol, and gangs, in that order, were the most important factors in property crime (Dinitz and Huff 1988). Most recently, a great deal of media attention has been directed to the relationship between gangs and major drug trafficking, especially rock cocaine in Los Angeles.

Earlier gang studies indicated a certain ambivalence or even negative reaction by gang members to drug use or sale in the local area. Reports of core gang members forcing drug-abusing members out of the gang, particularly those using or "shooting up" heroin, and threatening neighborhood drug dealers to stop trafficking were not uncommon (Spergel 1964; Short and Strodtbeck 1965). Many gangs, however, traditionally tolerated use of marijuana. Street workers reported that 42.5 percent of black gang members and 33.6 percent of white gang members used "pot" in the late 1950s or early 1960s. However, such drug use then had very low legitimacy among these youths (Short and Strodtbeck 1965, p. 82).

In the early 1970s, New York City officials believed that most youth gangs were not extensively involved in the sale of narcotics (Collins 1979). A New York State Assembly report (1974a, p. 5) indicated that "many gangs engage in shakedowns of area merchants and residents and others trafficking in soft drugs, such as marijuana, amphetamines, barbiturates, cocaine." By the late 1970s, however, there was evidence that gangs, particularly those containing older members with prison experience, were significantly engaged in drug dealing. The Blackstone Rangers, now the El Rukns, were a continuing target of the Chicago Police Department for drug dealing and shady property investments.

By the middle 1980s, there were reports of extensive drug use and selling by gang members in both small and large cities. Hagedorn indicates a very heavy use of drugs by gang leaders in Milwaukee. "Less than 5 percent of those interviewed said that at this time they never used drugs. . . . Sixty percent . . . admitted they used drugs (mainly marijuana) most or all of the time" (1988, p. 142). A recent Florida legislative report indicates that 92 percent of gang members admitted to experimenting with narcotics, mainly marijuana and cocaine (Reddick 1987). Fagan, Piper, and Moore (1986) report that individual prevalence rates for both drug use and delinquency were higher for gang youth in several inner-city neighborhoods than for general adolescent populations in the same area.

Drugs have become a means of making money. Nearly half of the forty-seven gang "founders" interviewed by Hagedorn said they sold drugs regularly: "over two-thirds said that members of the main group of their gang sold drugs 'regularly' and nearly all said someone in the main group sold at least 'now and then' " (1988, p. 105).

By contrast, the County of Los Angeles Probation Department insists that "gang members are now rarely addicts. Traditionally drug dealers were addicts selling to support their own habit . . . typical monthly data from probation . . . specialized drug pusher/seller intensive . . . surveillance caseload reveals that only 2 of 39 probationers had positive or "dirty" narcotic test results. Current gang drug dealers are not habitual drug users" (Los Angeles County Probation Department 1988, p. 2).

With media reports of extensive drug trafficking by gang members has come the belief that drug selling by gang members is now associated with violence. Law enforcement officials and the media, especially in the Los Angeles area, have voiced extreme alarm (*Los Angeles City News Service* 1988). All 300 black street gangs within the city are blamed for selling rock cocaine. "These gangs have a hierarchy of drug selling, with young teens at the bottom who start as lookouts or runners and later move into selling at the top of the hierarchy . . . city-wide police blame gangs for 387 homicides in 1987, almost all of it drug related" (Washington 1988). Another newspaper reporter indicates that young neighborhood males seeking to make "fast money through drugs [must] pledge at least surface loyalty to a neighborhood gang if they wanted a piece of the action" (Baker 1988*b*).

Criminal justice agencies are apparently deeply concerned. The federal Drug Enforcement Administration (1988) claims that Los Angeles street gangs, especially older former members of CRIPS, have been identified selling drugs in forty-six states. The National Council of Juvenile and Family Court Judges has recently recommended that judges take drastic action in responding to the drug-gang crisis: "Beginning in the mid-1980s some youth gangs with origins in the large urban centers of Los Angeles, Miami, Chicago, Detroit and New York, became major criminal entrepreneurs in the supply of illicit drugs. In a very short time many of the gangs have developed intrastate and interstate networks for the purpose of expanding . . . in the . . . national drug sales market. . . . Ominously these gangs are even more committed to the use of violence than the most notorious old-line criminal organizations" (Metropolitan Court Judges' Committee 1988, pp. 27, 30).

There is a range of views accounting for the gang-drug crisis. The origin of the problem is often associated with the transportation of drugs from some other city. "Los Angeles is now the main port of entry for cocaine nationwide as well as the home of 30,000 black gang members" (Donovan 1988, p. 2). Yet the explanation or blame for the current state of affairs is laid to the "1982 federal crackdown on cocaine smugglers in Miami. . . . The movers of dope decided it might be better for them to move their important drugs to another location [Los Angeles]" (Washington 1988). However, officials in Miami claim that the connection between gangs and drugs is now bigger than ever. A key problem is the trafficking of drugs by gang members traveling from cities in the Northeast to Miami.

The available research, however, suggests neither strong nor clear relations among street gang membership, drug use, drug selling, and violence. Fagan (1988) found both violent and nonviolent black and Hispanic youth gangs in inner-city communities of Chicago, Los Angeles, and San Diego; whether the gang engaged in drug trafficking was independent of whether the gang was violent. Gang involvement in violent activity is neither cause nor consequence of drug use or drug dealing: "while some incidents no doubt are precipitated by disputes over drug sales or selling territories, the majority of violent incidents do not appear to involve drug sales. Rather they continue to be part of the status, territorial, and other gang conflicts which historically have fueled gang violence" (Fagan 1988, p. 20).

Klein, Maxson, and Cunningham (1988) recently explored the relationship between gangs, drug dealing, and violence in Los Angeles. Basing their study on analysis of police records for 1984 and 1985, they found that rock cocaine dealing and its increase were principally a product of normal neighborhood drug-selling activity, often unattributable to gang activity. The occurrence of violence during cocaine sale arrest incidents was quite low; the explosion of drug homicide incidents was more characteristic of nongang than gang involvement (pp. 6, 10–11).

The diversity of views about the relation between gang membership, drug dealing, and violence at the street level can be partly attributed to such factors as city size and to drug supplies, developmental phase of gang organization and involvement in drugs, and the stability of the drug market. The traditional gang structure seems to dissolve under the impact of drug use and selling. This is particularly evident in the large northeastern cities and increasingly in midwestern large and small cities. Traditional turf-related gang violence and gang cohesion are not directly functional to drug use, selling, and associated criminal enterprise, which requires different kinds of organization, communication, and distribution.

However, the breadth or narrowness of the definition of "gang incident" and whether the unit of analysis is the gang or gang member also accounts for much of the sharp variation. A broad definition of "gang incident" is likely to find strong and frequent connections among gangs, drugs, and violence. Bobrowski (1988) states that, of sixty-two street gangs or major factions responsible for street gang crime in Chicago between January 1987 and July 1988, 90 percent, all but six, showed involvement in vice activity. Of vice offenses reported, 91 percent were drug related.

However, the relationship between arrests for drug dealing, possession, use, and violence by gang members is quite tenuous in Chicago. Bobrowski (1988, p. 25) also reports, based on Chicago Police Department statistics, that vice activity was discovered at the individual incident level in "only 2 of 82 homicides, 3 of 362 robberies, and 18 of the 4,052 street gang-related batteries and assaults" in the year-and-a-half study period. He concludes that the suggestion that "street gangs have been enmeshed in some web of violence and contentious criminality pursuant to, or in consequence of, their interests in vice appears to be unsupported by the available data" (1988, pp. 44–47). However, the Chicago Police Department definition of a gang-related incident is much narrower than that of the Los Angeles Police Department. Still, McBride (1988) of the Los Angeles County Sheriff's Department states that only 10 percent of gang homicides have been drug related.

Evidence exists in several cities at the present time for a pattern, with increasing number of exceptions, in which Hispanic gangs may be relatively more involved in traditional turf gang-related violence than are black gangs and relatively less involved in drug-related activities. In Chicago, where the total population is approximately 41 percent black and 16 percent Hispanic, there were seventy-seven Hispanic male offender suspects and sixty-six black male suspects identified by police case reports in eighty-two gang-related homicides between January 1987 and July 1988. The vast majority of black and Hispanic gang homicides, 78.7 percent, were within racial or ethnic offender-victim groups. While 45.2 percent of all serious gang-related assaults (N = 2,890) involved black suspects, 43.8 percent involved Hispanic suspects. However, 65.7 percent of vice (mainly drug) gang-related suspects (N = 4,115) were blacks, but only 27.6 percent were Hispanics. Hispanic gang members appear to be as yet less entrepreneurial when it comes to drug trafficking than black gangs (Bobrowski 1988, table 18A).

Furthermore, reports suggest that members of different ethnic or racial gangs may be differentially involved in the trafficking of different types of drugs. For example, in Los Angeles, "crack cocaine seems to be associated primarily with black youth. There seems little disagreement about the lack of involvement by Chicano youth in the crack cocaine trade" (Skolnick et al. 1988, p. 17). White motorcycle gangs "continue to produce and traffic in methamphetamine" (Philibosian 1989, p. 6). Hispanic gangs seem to be a significant problem in their use and sale of PCP and marijuana (Philibosian 1989). Chinese youth gang leaders in New York City are reported to be active in the heroin trade (Chin 1989).

However, increasing participation of gang members in drug trafficking does not mean that the relationship between drugs and gangs is interdependent and that a causal relationship necessarily exists between the development of gangs and drug dealing. Skolnick observes that the traditional turf-based Mexican-American gang in southern California has not formed for the purpose of selling drugs, but some gangs in various parts of the state have organized primarily for the purpose of distributing drugs, and the "gang" or "mob" represents a "strict 'business' operation" (1988, pp. 2–3). It is likely that black, white, and Chinese gangs are less tied to traditional gang or neighborhood norms.

Finally, the relation between drugs and gangs, as well as with violence, particularly as it bears on the socialization process, appears to be variable. There is evidence of an indirect and sequential relationship between gangs and violence and drug trafficking. Johnson et al. (1990) report, using New York City evidence, that drug-selling organizations frequently recruit persons who have previous histories of violence. Such persons, in turn, may seek out drug-selling groups. Gangs provide members with a sense of group identification and solidarity that may prove a useful qualification and may be readily transferred to a drug organization.

There is also evidence that the relation may be developing, even with the Hispanic gang. The introduction of younger boys to the drug business often serves to meet membership criteria and respect in the traditional but changing Mexican-American gang in southern California. "An individual may prove that he is worthy of respect and trust if he can show that he can sell for one of the 'homeboys' and be trusted with the merchandise" (Skolnick et al. 1988, p. 4).

III.   Gangs as Organizations

Gangs have been viewed both as loosely knit and well organized. It is possible that the loosely knit characterization refers to process, while the organized characterization refers to gang structure, form, or longevity. Thrasher (1936, p. 35) originally conceived of the ganging process "as a continuous flux and flow, and there is little permanence in most of the groups. New nuclei are constantly appearing, and the business of coalescing and recoalescing is going on everywhere in the congested area." Yablonsky (1962, p. 286) called the gang a "near-group" characterized by (1) diffuse role definition, (2) limited cohesion, (3) impermanence, (4) minimal consensus of norms, (5) shifting membership, (6) disturbed leadership, and (7) limited definitions of membership expectations. The traditional gang, according to Klein (1968), is an amorphous mass, group goals are usually minimal, membership unstable, and group norms not distinguishable from those of the surrounding neighborhood. Short and Strodtbeck noted the difficulty, if not impossibility, of drawing up lists of gangs from which probability samples could be drawn in their research, "so shifting in membership and identity are these groups" (1965, p. 10). Gold and Mattick concluded that gangs in Chicago are "loosely structured sets of companions" (1974, p. 335), less stable than other groups of adolescents (p. 37). Torres observed that Hispanic gangs in the barrios of East Los Angeles are "always in a state of flux" (1980, p. 1). By contrast, however, some of these same analysts have viewed gangs as complex organizational structures, referring to them in bureaucratic terms or even as "supergangs."

The New York City Youth Board (1960) proposed a scheme for describing the varied, purposeful structures of gangs. The *vertical gang* is

structured along age lines and comprises youngsters living on the same block or in the immediate neighborhood. There may be a younger "tots" group [eleven to thirteen years] . . . a "junior" division [thirteen to fifteen years] . . . a group of "tims" [fifteen to seventeen years] . . . the "seniors" [seventeen to twenty years and older]. The age lines are not hard and fast. This type of structure occurs where there is a long history of group existence and activity dating back ten or more years. Group morale and fighting traditions are informally handed down. This kind of group tends to be ingrown, with cousins and brothers belonging to the respective divisions. [P. 22]

A somewhat later description of the vertical gang structure in New York City in the 1970s suggested a wider spread of these age-based subunits starting with the "Baby Spades," nine to twelve years; "Young Spades," twelve to fifteen years; and "Black Spades," sixteen to thirty years (Collins 1979). More recently in Philadelphia, the police department describes three general age-related gang divisions: bottom-level midgets, twelve to fourteen years; middle-level young boys, fourteen to seventeen years; and upper-level, old-heads, eighteen to twenty-three years (Philadelphia Police Department 1987). The current fashion on the West Coast and elsewhere is to label the very young aspirants to gang membership, usually eight to twelve years, as "wannabes."

The term "clique" or "Klika" has also been used respectively for black and Mexican-American total age groups in Los Angeles (Klein 1971; Moore 1978); however, the term "set" seems to be in more current use among black gangs in Los Angeles. An entire age cohort is given a name, usually a variation of the general gang name, and remains identified with that cohort throughout its life history. Whether the clique or Klika is large or small, it represents an entire age group, rather than a small clique or subgroup of a particular gang, group, or horizontal division. These youth may be "jumped" into a gang that is the only active gang in the community. In this sense, the Klika may represent a cross between a vertical and horizontal gang structure.

Here is how the New York City Youth Board (1960) described horizontal gangs: "The *horizontally* organized group is more likely to include divisions or groupings from different blocks or neighborhoods comprising youngsters of middle or late teens with little differentiation as to age. The horizontal group may, and usually does, develop out of the vertical or self-contained group structure" (pp. 23–24).

The horizontal youth gang structure has become the most common type of structure with the spread of gangs with the same name across neighborhoods, cities, states, and countries. These structures are called coalitions, "supergangs," and nations, often originating in, or developing more sophisticated structures on the basis of, prison experience. They are particularly prevalent among black and Hispanic youth and young adults in California and Illinois. Variations of these structures, especially by ethnicity or race, are discussed below.

A. Gang Alliances

Thrasher (1936, p. 323) noted the possibility of complex affiliated gang structures decades ago: "In some cases federations of friendly gangs are formed for the promotion of common interests or protection against common enemies. These may be nothing more than loose alliances." In several cities, gangs or sets of gangs have been paired as enemies with "enmity brief, sometimes lasting" (Miller 1975). The terms "nation" and later "supergang" were coined in Chicago in the late 1960s to describe large gangs reportedly numbering in the thousands with units spread throughout the city. The term "nation" is still commonly used, particularly by gang members. Some of these gangs had hierarchies, board structures, elders, and elites (Sherman 1970). Two major multiethnic gang coalitions, as somewhat distinct from a gang nation or supergang, developed in Chicago and in Illinois prisons—the People and the Folk—in the middle 1970s. These established gang alliances contain older members, are more criminalized, and are probably more sophisticated and better organized than the gangs of the 1950s and early 1960s (Short 1976).

The origin of the People and the Folk in prison, according to Chicago Police Department information, occurred when the predominantly white Simon City Royals agreed to provide narcotics in exchange for protection by inmates belonging to the Black Disciples, a loose constellation of street gangs. Shortly thereafter and in response to the alliance, members of the Latin Kings, a constellation of gangs of mainly Hispanic (Mexican-American and Puerto Rican) composition, aligned with the Vice Lords, a constellation or nation of black gangs or factions. These alliances spread to the streets of Chicago and other midwestern and southern cities.

There are currently about thirty-one street gangs in Chicago that identify with the Folk and about twenty-seven that identify with the People. A few street gangs, about nineteen, remain independent. In addition, there are factions of gangs and gangs with unknown affiliations. Membership is about evenly divided between Folk and

People. According to a very recent report, 70 percent of the gangs identifying with the Folk are Hispanic, 19 percent are black, and 10 percent are white; 56 percent of the gangs identifying with the People are Hispanic, 22 percent are black, and 19 percent are white (Bobrowski 1988). It is not clear how many gangs or gang members outside of prison are related to these larger gang entities. Most are more closely identified with particular gangs or gang factions. There is "no centralized organization and chain of command . . . and no clear leadership has emerged. . . . In fact, local disputes, power struggles, or ignorance often result in conflict among . . . affiliates" (Bobrowski 1988, pp. 30–31).

Gang coalitions are common in the Los Angeles area and throughout California and adjoining states and in correctional institutions in several states. Black gangs are reported to be divided into two main aggregations in California: CRIPS and Bloods, with the CRIPS containing more units and members. There is some recent evidence of multiethnic or racial aggregations of these gangs with Hispanic and white gangs. CRIPS tend to be more aggressive; members of Blood sets rarely fight each other. Fights between CRIP gangs are reported to have accounted for a third to a half of all gang-versus-gang incidents in various Los Angeles jurisdictions (Baker 1988b).

The competition between the Bloods and the CRIPS has assumed almost legendary status. Members of the CRIPS—which may be a whole series of organizations, not necessarily with close relations with each other—have been arrested for a variety of crimes, mainly drug trafficking, in most states of the United States. The California Department of Corrections reportedly has acknowledged the "existence of an emerging umbrella CRIP organization known as the Consolidated CRIP Organization (C.C.O.) and a similar Blood gang organization known as United Blood Nation (U.B.N.). . . . The California Youth Authority (C.Y.A.) has an estimated black street population [comprising mainly these two gang constellations] of 5,000 inside C.Y.A. facilities and 7,000 on active parole" (Los Angeles County Sheriff's Department 1985, p. 8).

Gang typologies and organizational classifications suggest a bewildering array, complexity, and variability of structures.[1] Gangs may not

[1] A great variety of gang dimensions, as a basis for classification or typing youth gangs by academics, law-enforcement personnel, and others, has emerged in recent years. They include (1) age; (2) race/ethnicity; (3) gender composition, e.g., all male, all female, or mixed; (4) setting, e.g., street, prison, or motorcycle (G. Camp and C. Camp 1985; C.

be simply cohesive, loosely knit, or bureaucratic so much as variable small networks or parts of larger networks across neighborhoods, cities, states, and even countries (Collins 1979); these networks may be more or less cohesive or clearly structured at various periods of their development. Gang tradition and organizational networks develop independent of particular youths, leaders, cliques, and gang organizational forms (see also Sarnecki 1986; Reiss 1988).

B.   Cliques and Gang Size

The clique is the basic building block of the gang. The violent character of the gang is often determined by the membership interests of the key clique. But the size of the delinquent gang or clique has been a source of controversy among researchers over the years.

Thrasher (1936, pp. 320–21) defined the gang clique as a "spontaneous interest group usually of the conflict type which forms itself within some larger social structure such as a gang. . . . In a certain sense a well-developed clique is an embryonic gang." The idea of "delinquent group" is often congruent with that of gang clique. Shaw and McKay (1931) noted that the most frequent type of delinquent group in which juvenile offenses are committed is the small companionship group consisting of two or three boys. Downes (1966), a British researcher, observed that small cliques were responsible for the bulk of delinquency and distinguished between them and more "organized" gang behavior. Klein (1971) refers to a "specialty clique" that may be part of the larger gang structure but sometimes exists as an independent unit. It consists of three to a dozen boys. It maintains or stimulates distinctive patterned behavior, criminal, conflict, or drug use.

The clique and the gang may be viewed as parts of a network. Cliques may operate outside of gang structures and even across other

---

Camp and G. Camp 1988); (5) type of activity, e.g., social, delinquent, or violent (Yablonsky 1962; Haskell and Yablonsky 1982; Jackson and McBride 1985); (6) purpose of gang activity, e.g., defensive or aggressive (New York City Youth Board 1960; Collins 1979), turf violation, retaliation, prestige, or representing (Bobrowski 1988); (7) degree of criminality, e.g., serious, minor, or mixed (Pleines 1987); (8) level of organization, e.g., simple or corporate (Taylor 1988), vertical or horizontal; (9) stage of group formation or development, e.g., early, marginal, or well established (New York State Assembly 1974b; Collins 1979); (10) degree of activity, e.g., active, sporadic, or inactive (Philadelphia Police Department 1987); (11) nature or level of personality development or disturbance of group members (Scott 1956; Klein 1971; Jackson and McBride 1985); (12) group function, e.g., socioemotive or instrumental (Berntsen 1979; Huff 1988; Skolnick et al. 1988); (13) drug use/selling (Fagan 1988); (14) cultural development, e.g., traditional, nontraditional, or transitional (Vigil 1983; McBride 1988); (15) new types, e.g., heavy metal, punk rock, satanic, or skinheads (Baca 1988; Coplon 1988).

opposing gang structures. Theft or robbery subgroups or cliques, and, more recently, drug-trafficking cliques, may identify with the gang for socialization and conflict purposes but may recruit members from outside the gang for particular "jobs" or ally themselves with similar cliques in so-called opposition gangs. The pattern of activity of the gang may be determined by the leader or the influential clique; the particular activity—for example, intergang tension or hostility—may cause the membership of the gang to expand rapidly (Gold and Mattick 1974).

Competition between cliques may be a central dynamic leading to the gang splitting into factions or into separate gangs. The gang is seldom cohesive and at maximum strength and may be viewed as a series of loosely knit cliques, except at times of conflict (Thrasher 1936; New York City Youth Board 1960). Even this statement needs to be qualified since actual combat between gangs is usually carried out by a small group of two or three youths, although a great deal of diffuse milling and a higher rate of interaction among gang members may be observed on these occasions—more for purposes of communication and mutual excitement than directed hostility.

It is also possible to assess clique size in terms of number of arrests or participants per gang incident. The use of official data undoubtedly underestimates the number of offenders or suspects (although it overestimates the number of crimes committed by juveniles; see Zimring 1981). The co-offenders or participants may be viewed as roughly equivalent to a clique in a specific gang-related offensive event. In one Chicago study of reported violent gang incidents, Spergel (1986) found that approximately three offenders were arrested per incident. An earlier Chicago study had revealed slightly less than two offenders per gang homicide incident (Spergel 1983). In a more inclusive Los Angeles gang and nongang homicide study, Klein, Maxson, and Gordon (1987) found approximately four suspects—rather than arrested offenders—per gang homicide incident. They also found that gang homicide incidents produced about twice as many suspects as nongang homicide incidents (1987).

The size of the gang has been a source of disagreement among researchers and observers. Some have emphasized that gangs are generally small, hardly larger than a clique, ranging from four or five to twenty-five, with eight to twelve members as most common (Gold and Mattick 1974). Others have viewed the size of the gang as generally ranging from twenty-five to seventy-five members (Collins 1979), twenty-five to 200 (Philadelphia Police Department 1987), and from about thirty to 500 (Torres 1980). Since the late 1960s and until this day, some analysts believe the size of some gangs—whether as "super-gangs" or coalitions—may range into the thousands (Spergel 1972; Miller 1975, 1982; Short 1976). These numbers may include peripheral and associate as well as core members, both active and inactive, and "wannabe" members and are usually based on sightings of large groups of youth at a particular event—such as a dance or mass meeting— "declarations" by gang members that a particular school, housing project, or prison is "theirs," or estimates by law enforcement or prison officials, based on interviews, arrests, or informant observations. There is some evidence that gang size grows during periods of crisis, especially with threats of strikes or retaliations or competition for drug markets, and decreases in the absence of conflict and in the presence of "peace." Gang size may also vary for students during different school seasons or transitional periods—larger in the fall when school starts and again during school holidays, especially at the start of the spring or summer break. Recruitment efforts in the fall of the first year of high school also may produce an increase in gang ranks (see Klein 1971).

Many questions remain in respect to the relation between numbers of gang members, gang problems, and gang size. Is the number of gangs in an area or setting related to the number of gang members? Are there more gangs in newly settled communities but not necessarily more gang members compared to a settled area? We know, for example, there are more Hispanic than black gangs in Chicago but not necessarily more Hispanic gang members (Bobrowski 1988). There may be more gangs represented in a magnet or citywide high school than in a neighborhood high school. But does this mean there are more gang members or gang problems present (Spergel 1985)? Similarly gang membership and problems may or may not vary with the numbers of gangs in a particular prison (G. Camp and C. Camp 1985).

C. Types of Gang Members

The structure of the gang is based on needs for group maintenance or development. It requires that certain roles be performed and includes a variety of membership types—core members, including leaders, regulars, and sometimes associates; peripheral or fringe members; "wannabes" or recruits. The core may be regarded as an "inner clique" that is actively engaged in the everyday functioning of the gang. Core members interact frequently and relate easily to each other. They have been described as "those few who need and thrive on the totality of the gang's activity. The gang's level of violence is determined by the hard-core" (Pitchess 1979, p. 2). Core members may make key decisions, set standards, and provide support and sanction for the action of leaders. They are the key recruiters (Sarnecki 1986; Reiss 1988). Associates and peripheral members may be regular or irregular in their attendance at gang events or gatherings. Their relationships may be primarily to particular core members. They may not be seen as part of the gang by all core members or the entire group. The associates have higher status and respect than peripheral members.

"Floaters" may exist in and across gangs. They are a special kind of associate, with high status, yet are not clearly identified gang members. They are often brokers across gangs, with access to special resources, or they may exhibit special talents needed by the gang. For example, they may possess information about the activities of other gangs and serve as communication links and negotiators in times of tension or intergang conflict. They may arrange deals for weapons, drugs, or stolen property between gangs and with others outside the gang. They tend to be entrepreneurial, well respected, articulate, with many community connections.

Law-enforcement agencies have special strategic and tactical reasons for identifying different types of gang members. Most police departments want to arrest or neutralize gang leadership. But usually they also must be concerned not to exaggerate the numbers of gang members. Law-enforcement agencies distinguish among gang members, for example, as "verified" or "alleged" (New York State Assembly 1974b, p. 3), "known," "suspected," and "associated" (Baca 1988). The "hardcore" verified or known members are viewed as making up 10 to 15 percent of the gang and are the target for most law-enforcement interventions (Collins 1979).

Whether, and when, gang members maintain long-term or career roles is unclear. At one extreme, membership and gang roles are vague and shifting. Some members join for a short time—days or weeks. Gang members may "graduate" from a lower- to a higher-status gang role or even gang, particularly as they grow older. However, they may also shift from core to peripheral roles and back again. A youth may switch membership from one friendly gang to another and even to a formerly hostile gang, particularly when gang membership requires little in the way of formal identification or investment of time or energy or, more often, when the gang member's family moves or the youth must adopt membership in a dominant gang at a new school or in a correctional agency. It is not always clear to gang members who is a gang member and who is not, although the status, rank, or respect of a recognized gang member may be more readily established. Relationships among gang members may be weak and tenuous (Yablonsky 1962; Klein 1971), although not always or necessarily so (Horowitz 1983). Leadership and core-member roles, particularly in established gangs, may be viewed as long-term. Such roles assume greater stability and articulation in certain stable low-income ghetto communities and in prison (Jacobs 1977).

There appears to be general agreement, however, that core members are more involved in delinquent or criminal activities than peripheral or fringe members. Klein (1968, p. 74) reports that during the four years of the Los Angeles Group Guidance Project, "core members were charged with 70 percent more offenses than fringe members." Core members committed their first offenses at an earlier age; subsequent offenses occurred at a more rapid rate; they committed their last juvenile offenses at a later age than fringe members (1968, p. 274). Sarnecki's (1986) findings in Sweden are similar. Juveniles affiliated with the network were considerably more actively delinquent while they belonged to it and faced a greater risk of persisting in their delinquent activity, which often led to drug addiction or imprisonment. The more central the roles played by the juveniles, the greater their likelihood of continuing in a delinquent career. Those who were accomplices of the central characters in the network also ran greater risks than the average participant (1986, p. 128). Fagan (1988, p. 22), however, reports no significant differences between leaders and other kinds of members in self-reported involvement in drug and delinquent activities. However, his findings are not clearly developed and are opposed to all other research findings on this question.

Debate has also raged whether core or fringe members are more or less socially adjusted or psychologically troubled. Yablonsky (1962) claimed that core members are often psychologically disturbed or sociopathic, and fringe members more likely to be "normal." Short and Strodtbeck (1965), Klein (1971), and Gold and Mattick (1974) take an opposing position. Leadership and core members are likely to be more socially capable, perhaps more intelligent. Fringe members or "crazies" are likely to have low status or to be ostracized by the group, except for certain purposes (Horowitz 1983). The extensive set of case vignettes in the descriptive and program report of the New York City Youth Board

(1960) suggests that core and fringe members come with all sorts of personality makeups, capabilities, and disabilities and that it is extremely difficult to relate gang role to personality type.

D. Leadership

The notion of leadership is not usually clearly defined by gang members or by researchers. Some gangs have formal leadership positions such as a president or vice president. More recently, gangs in ghettoes, barrios, or prisons have referred to leaders as King, Prince, Prime Minister, General, Ambassador, Don, Chief. Some highly violent gang leaders or influentials may have no formal designation or flamboyant title and are simply called "shot callers" or "shooters" by gang members or police.

Gang researchers' disagreements center around whether leadership is a position or a function and may be only partly related to the issue of whether the gang leader is a psychopath or sociopath or relatively normal and socially capable. Klein has taken two views. He has stated that gang leadership is best defined as a "collection of *functions* that may be undertaken at various times by a number of members" (1971, p. 92). He has also stated that leadership may reside within "relatively stable, 'cool' youngsters who have earned their fighting status through a variety of abilities, fighting prowess, cool-headedness, verbal facility, athletic abilities, or inheritance from older brothers" (1969, p. 1432). Short (1963, p. 38) suggests that the "ability to get along with people is one of the basic skills associated with gang leadership."

These researchers and others have generally agreed that leaders are usually capable people and have special traits that others look up to (Thrasher 1936, pp. 345–349). Yablonsky's (1962, p. 156) view of gang leadership is at the other extreme: "Leaders are characterized by megalomania"; they are profoundly disturbed and were very insecure and unhappy as children and try to compensate through their "contemporary 'power' role of gang leader."

E. Territoriality

The notion of territoriality or turf is integral to the character of the gang. Notions of turf may vary by cultural tradition, by age, and by the changing interests of the youth gang.

Traditionally the idea of territoriality has evolved at the local community or neighborhood level. The traditional gang is organized for purposes of conflict. "Gang warfare is usually organized on a territorial basis. Each group becomes attached to a local area which it regards as peculiarly its own and through which it is dangerous for members from another group to pass" (Thrasher 1936, p. 175). The identification of gang with territory is nowhere better illustrated than in many Hispanic areas of Los Angeles where traditionally the terms "gang" and "barrio" are synonymous with the concept of neighborhood and the two terms are used interchangeably (Moore 1978) or in many Puerto Rican and Mexican-American communities of Chicago (Horowitz 1983; Spergel 1986).

Propinquity emerges as a critical factor in motivations for gang conflict. Of 188 gang incidents among 32 gangs in Philadelphia between 1966 and 1970 (homicides, stabbings, shootings, and gang fights), 60 percent occurred between gangs who shared a common boundary, and another 23 percent between gangs whose territories were two blocks or less apart. Only two incidents occurred between groups whose turfs were separated by more than ten blocks (Ley 1975, pp. 262–63). Certain inner-city groups experience not only an economic but also a social and cultural marginality. This may provide the mandate for a "territorial imperative . . . for the establishment of a small secure area where group control can be maximized against the flux and uncertainty of the . . . city" (Ley 1975, pp. 252–53). Graffiti becomes the visible manifestation of a gang's control of social space. Gang graffiti becomes denser with increasing proximity to the core of a territory. Graffiti is a clue both to the extent and intensity of "ownership" of a territory by a gang and perhaps inversely to the strength of adult community organization in the exercise of control over the particular area.

Gang territoriality is expressed in various ways. When families of gang members move from one neighborhood to another, to the suburbs, or even to other cities, branch organizations are more likely when gangs with the same names suddenly spread. Gangs more often seek to expand the perimeter of their territory into adjoining streets. A battle of gang markings and countermarkings occurs when the perimeters of two gangs' territories are unstable. Sometimes gangs expand by absorbing smaller, lower status gangs nearby (Moore, Vigil, and Garcia 1983). Conflict over gang turf may result from tensions and competition over who "owns" or controls schools, parks, jails and prison areas, illegitimate enterprises or rackets, and even political institutions of neighborhoods (Thrasher 1936; Asbury 1971; Spergel 1972; Kornblum 1974).

At the heart of the concept of territoriality or turf are two component ideas, identification and control. Control is the stronger operative or driving force for gangs. Collins (1979, pp. 68–69) observes that "street gangs have been known to actually control the activity and events of certain streets and blocks. They attempt to control playgrounds, parks, recreation centers . . . to the exclusion of all other gangsters. . . . Other gangs have been known to march in front of a witness' residence, exhibiting guns and weapons, inferring 'keep your mouth shut'."

Miller (1977, pp. 23–25) identifies three categories of turf rights: ownership rights—gangs "own" the entire area or property and control all access, departure, and activities within it; occupancy rights—gangs share or tolerate each other's use and control of a site under certain conditions, for example, deference, time, nature and amount of usage of the space; and enterprise monopoly—gangs claim exclusive right to commit certain kinds of crimes. Miller gives examples of "enterprise monopoly rights." A Boston gang claimed the exclusive rights to steal from stores in a claimed territory and forcefully excluded outsiders who attempted a store robbery in the area. Chinese gangs in a few cities, especially San Francisco, have a tradition of violence resulting from challenges to exclusive extortion rights of certain businesses.

Much of the violence among black gangs or subgroups in recent years apparently results from competition over drug markets. Gang entrepreneurs or former gang members may expand their business operations by recruiting or converting existing street groups, often in different neighborhoods or cities, to sell, store, or aid in the marketing of drugs. Conflicts develop when these new entrepreneurs enter an area controlled by another gang or criminal organization engaged in drug trafficking.

The concept of turf or territory has assumed not only varied but less rigid meaning in recent years. The physical, social, or even economic turf of a gang can shift over time and sometimes with the seasons. A particular gang may hang out or socialize in different parts of the neighborhood, city, or county. It may no longer need a specific center or building as a point of identification or control. It may engage in criminal activities in different parts of towns, cities, or states as opportunity presents itself, more often fortuitous than planned.

Miller (1977) also notes that certain cities have a less developed tradition of locality-based gangs. In the older cities with established gangs, such as New York, Philadelphia, and Chicago, as gangs become more sophisticated and criminalized there tends to be less identification with physical locations. The availability of automobiles is only one factor, and perhaps less important than criminal opportunity, in the increased mobility of certain gangs. Many turf gangs have developed traditions of retaliation or "paybacks" through "drive-by shootings." A law enforcement officer in New York City observes that criminal youth no longer hang out and now commonly move from corner to corner and neighborhood to neighborhood to join with others for a burglary, robbery, drug deal, or whatever criminal opportunity arises that day (Galea 1988). Under such circumstances, the notion of gang becomes that of delinquent or crime group; in the process, gang turf, colors, symbols, signs, name, and tradition may weaken and disappear.

The traditional or criminal sense of turf and gang identity may expand. Gangs in smaller cities or suburban areas can take on the names and symbols of large city gangs, sometimes with little or no direct contact with them. Gang turf may expand in the sense that gang coalitions and "nations" are formed, however weakly or deliberately criminally organized, across neighborhoods, cities, and states, whether for economic, status, or other reasons. It is also possible to argue that the gang is being transformed. The turf gang is being replaced by criminal organization, especially with the expansion of the street-level drug market.

IV.   Membership Demographics

This section is concerned with ecological, socioeconomic, cultural, and demographic characteristics of gang members. I examine class, culture, race or ethnicity, age, gender, and female participation as components of youth-gang structure. Interactions among gang membership, group processes, and individual personality are discussed in Section V.

A.   Class, Culture, and Race/Ethnicity

Contemporary youth gangs are located primarily in lower-class, slum, ghetto, or barrio communities; it is not clear, however, that class, culture, race, or ethnicity per se primarily account for gang problems. More likely, they interact with community characteristics like poverty, social instability, and failures of interagency organization and social isolation.

The gangs of the early part of the century in urban areas like Chicago were mainly first-generation youths born of Irish and German, and later Polish and Italian, parents who lived in areas of transition or first settlement (Thrasher 1936). To what extent they represented lower-class elements or the lowest income-sectors in their communities or in the city as a whole is not clear. We know that middle-class gangs, regardless of race or ethnicity or location, are less prevalent and certainly different in character than lower-class gangs (Myerhoff and Myerhoff 1976; see also Muehlbauer and Dodder 1983). But it is still not clear that the gang problem, at least its violent manifestation, is most severe in the poorest urban neighborhoods (Spergel 1984) or that gang members necessarily are the poorest youths or come from the poorest families in low-income communities. Delinquency and crime generally are closely associated with poverty, but the poverty relationship cannot be as strongly demonstrated for gang-related crime as for nongang crime.

The assumption that poverty, low socioeconomic status, or lower-class lifestyle is related to the prevalence of delinquent or violent youth gangs has been questioned. The communities in which black gangs flourished in the early 1960s were generally below city averages in housing standards and employment rates but not below city average unemployment rates (Cartwright and Howard 1966). Gang members often come from low median family-income census tracts in Philadelphia but not from the lowest (Cohen 1969a). The members of conflict groups in New York City were not drawn necessarily from the poorest families of the slum town areas (Spergel 1964). Many of the street gangs of New York City in the 1970s "emerged from a lower middle class lifestyle" (Collins 1979). Hispanic fighting gangs in East Los Angeles were not limited to the lowest income areas of the city (Klein 1971). The spread of gangs in Los Angeles County is reportedly due in part to the migration of upwardly mobile families with gang youth to middle-class areas (Los Angeles County Sheriff's Department 1985). Violent and criminal motorcycle gangs are reportedly composed of mainly lower-middle-class white older youth and young adults (Davis 1982a, 1982b). Recently identified white gangs in suburban communities, "Punks," "Stoners," "White Supremacists," "Satanics," and others, seem to come from lower middle-class and middle-class communities (Deukmejian 1981; Dolan and Finney 1984). The class identity of the newly developing Asian gangs is not clearly established.

Youth-gang problems in the United States continue to involve mostly blacks and Hispanics in most parts of the country, with some indications of increasing Asian gang problems and a more differentiated white youth-gang problem. The largest variety of youth-gang types occur on the West Coast, particularly in southern California, and increasingly in Texas, New Mexico, and Florida. American Indian and Asian gangs are reportedly found in Minnesota. Mixed race/ethnic membership patterns are not uncommon in many states, although black gangs tend to be all black. The relation of black American gangs to Jamaican gangs (Posses) is unclear; ethnicity may be a stronger bond than race. Hispanic gangs tend to be predominantly Mexican-American and Puerto Rican, with increasing numbers, however, of Central and South Americans. Asian youth gangs tend to be Chinese gangs of Hong Kong, Taiwan, and Vietnam; Korean; Thai; Laotian; Cambodian; Japanese; Samoan; Tongan; and Filipino. White gangs, depending on location, can be predominantly of second- and third-generation Italian, Irish, Polish, or middle-European origin in inner-city enclaves, suburban areas, or small towns. Most of the white gangs tend to have weak territorial identifications. Motorcycle gangs roam widely.

Race and ethnicity play a role in the development of the gang problem, but in more complex ways than is ordinarily conceived. Blacks and Hispanics clearly constitute the largest numbers of youths arrested for gang offenses at the present time. In his first national survey, Miller (1975) estimated that 47.6 percent of gang members in the six largest cities were blacks, 36.1 percent were Hispanics, 8.8 percent were whites, and 7.5 percent were Asians. In a more extensive survey of all gang members in nine of the largest cities, Miller (1982) found that 44.4 percent were Hispanics, 42.9 percent blacks, 9 percent whites, and 4.0 percent Asians. Miller (1982, chap. 9) speculates that illegal Hispanic immigrants, especially from Mexico, may have played a large role in the increasing numbers of gangs in California and in their spread to smaller cities and communities in that state.

Curry and Spergel (1988) report a different pattern for black and Hispanic gangs in Chicago in recent years. There was a relative and absolute increase in black gang homicides and a relative and absolute decline in Hispanic gang homicides for the 1982–85 period compared with the 1978–81 period. Black (non-Hispanic) gang homicides increased from sixty-one to 160. Hispanic gang homicides decreased from 125 to eighty-three. White (non-Hispanic) gang homicides decreased from twenty-three to twelve. The Hispanic gang homicide rate, relative to population, was the highest during the entire period (Curry and Spergel 1988). In 1986 and 1987, the black gang homicide rate began to decrease again.

By contrast, the gang homicides in the Los Angeles Sheriff's jurisdiction in recent years have been disproportionately black, although Hispanics make up a larger proportion of the population and constitute more gangs. According to law-enforcement officials, high black-gang violence is related to narcotics dealing, primarily "crack."

Some Latin street gangs in southern California have existed within particular localities for two or more generations. "Parents and in some cases even grandparents were members of the same gang. There is a sense of continuity of family identity" (Jackson and McBride 1985, p. 42). Donovan (1988, pp. 14–15) writes, "Today an Hispanic in Los Angeles may be a fourth generation gang member, and gangs comprise a distinct Hispanic subculture with their own stylized dress, language, writing, and rituals. They possess the same extended kinship structure and tight group cohesiveness found in larger Hispanic culture. . . . Their intense identification with the barrio or 'turf' translates into gang members considering themselves closer to soldiers who defend it than criminals who victimize it."

Bobrowski (1988) notes differences among Hispanic, white, and black gangs in Chicago. Symbolic property crimes are more common among Hispanic than black gang members (1988, p. 19). The ratios of personal-to-property (mainly graffiti) crime for Hispanics and whites are three to one and four to one, respectively, while for blacks it is eight to one (p. 21).

Duran (1987, p. 2) recently observed that traditional Chicano gangs in certain parts of East Los Angeles have declined in membership but that immigrant gangs from Mexico and Central and South America are on the increase. However, "traditional" Hispanic gangs that fight, kill, and risk their lives for "turf" and "respect" remain dominant.

In general, gang violence tends to be intraracial or intraethnic. Exceptions occur during periods of racial conflict (Thrasher 1936) and rapid community population change. Local gangs may be organized to defend against newcomers. However, the most serious and long-term gang conflicts arise from patterns of traditional animosity across adjacent neighborhoods with quite similar populations.

Not all low-income Hispanic or black communities necessarily or consistently produce violent gangs. Although there was a tradition of gang formation and gang violence in Philadelphia's inner-city neighborhoods in the 1970s, that did not happen in Puerto Rican enclaves. Relatively little criminal or violent gang activity occurred in Chicago's low-income black communities in the middle and late 1970s; violent gang activity at that time was particularly high in Hispanic communities.

Gang activity appears to vary by race and ethnicity, although this may be a function of acculturation, access to criminal opportunities, and community stability factors. White gangs, of a somewhat higher class level than black gangs, were reported to be more rebellious, more openly at odds with adults, more into rowdyism, drinking, drug use and sexual delinquency than black gangs in Chicago in the late 1950s and early 1960s (Short and Strodtbeck 1965). White gangs in Philadelphia in the middle 1970s were less territorially bound, less structured, and therefore more difficult to identify than black gangs (Friedman, Mann, and Adelman 1976). There were more white than black gangs in Boston in the 1950s and 1960s, and there was more violence among white gangs than among black gangs, but the level of violence among Boston gangs was and probably still is lower than in other cities (Miller 1976*b*).

White gangs, although there are relatively few of them today, come in many varieties, particularly on the West Coast: stoners, freaks, heavy-metal groups, satanic worshipers, bikers, fighting gangs. "Stoners" originally were groups made up of persistent drug or alcohol abusers; heavy-metal rock music was a common bond. One of the special traits of these original stoner groups was practice of satanism, including grave robbing and desecration of churches. Stoner groups have been known to mark off territory with graffiti. They may adopt particular dress styles (Jackson and McBride 1985, pp. 42–45). (There have been recent reports of Mexican-American stoner gangs in East Los Angeles.)

Many but not all of the Skinheads are neo-Nazi gangs who model themselves after punk rockers and Skinheads in England. They may have ties with groups such as the Ku Klux Klan, the American Nazi Party, and the National Socialist White Workers Party. The SWP (Supreme White Pride) name has recently spread from the prison to the streets. The racist and violent Skinheads have been identified in major cities on the West Coast, in the Midwest, and in the South. Their group structure and style fit the gang pattern: claiming a name, colors, tattooing, common dress, drug use, and criminal behavior. "American Skinheads are as likely to be middle class as working poor. But in other respects they are typical gang members" (Coplon 1988, p. 56; see also Jackson and McBride 1985; Anti-Defamation League 1986, 1987; and Donovan 1988).

A recent report of the Florida State legislature (Reddick 1987) noted that the Skinheads started in Jacksonville and are not uniformly found in key urban areas all over the state. They profess to "being anti-black, anti-Jew, and anti-homosexual, while promoting their pro-God, pro-white American ideology." Their activities in Florida have been "primarily harassment, violence, fighting, and provoking riots and racial incidents." Often parents of the youths are either unaware of these activities or "support" them (Reddick 1987, p. 9). Coplon (1988, p. 56) claims their ranks have swelled throughout the United States from 300 in 1986 to 3,500 in 1988.

Another type of predominantly white gang is the motorcycle gang, although Hispanic and black motorcycle gangs and groups are known to exist. Most have set eighteen or twenty-one years as minimum ages. They may have elaborate rituals, signs, symbols, tattoos, and complex organizational structures, including written constitutions, with chapters of the larger gangs in Canada and Europe as well as in many states. They consist mostly of working-class young adults, sometimes from rural areas, with limited education. They have engaged in a wide range of illegal activity, including selling and using drugs, extortion, disorderly conduct, vandalism, theft, prostitution, white slavery, and hijacking (Commission de Police du Québec 1980); ties have been reported to major criminal organizations and syndicates, particularly in transport or sale of drugs.

Increasing numbers of criminal and violent Asian youth gangs were reported in the 1970s and 1980s. Miller (1982) estimated the number of Asian youth gangs then almost equaled the number of white gangs on the West Coast. Asian gangs may now be almost twice as numerous as white gangs (Duran 1987). They have also spread from the West and East coasts to inland American cities. They tend to be more secretive than non-Asian gangs, less interested in status, honor, or reputation, but more involved in criminal gain activities, such as extortion, burglary, and narcotics selling. Asian youth gang members are sometimes used by adult criminal organizations as "enforcers" (Breen and Allen 1983). They tend to be highly mobile and are usually not closely identified with a particular turf. They are particularly difficult to detect because most police units lack Asian language facility or the confidence of Asian communities.

The different ethnic Asian gangs may be quite distinctive. There is some evidence that Japanese, Taiwanese, and Hong Kong gangs may be the best organized, perhaps the most secretive, and well disciplined. Vietnamese street gangs may be particularly mobile and have on occasion affiliated with black gangs, CRIPS and Bloods. Samoan gangs are also reported to have been assimilated into black gangs, to wear tattoos and distinctive gang dress, to use graffiti, and to have reputations for violence. Filipino gangs are apparently older, with members ranging in age from 20 to 40 years, at times adopting black or Hispanic gang characteristics, and engaging in a range of criminal activities, such as auto theft, extortion, and burglary, as well as drug trafficking (Dono-van 1988).

B. Age

In recent decades, gang activity was perceived as primarily or exclusively a teenage, if not a juvenile, phenomenon. Researchers and analysts based this perception on youth samples they examined in street work programs in the 1950s and 1960s. This perception was widespread among police and may be why mainly juvenile or youth units in many police departments deal with youth-gang problems.

The age composition of gangs undoubtedly varies by city and social setting. Nonetheless, there is growing recognition that gang membership extends at least into young adulthood, certainly to the early and perhaps mid-twenties. Thrasher's (1936) gang members ranged in age from six to fifty years but were concentrated in two groups, "earlier adolescent," eleven to seventeen years and "later adolescent," sixteen to twenty-five years. Whyte's (1943) street-gang members were in their twenties. Much of the theory and the limited research on gangs in the 1950s and 1960s, however, was based on early and middle teenage samples. While the literature of this period focused on teenage gangs, there must also have been young-adult street gangs and significant numbers of young adults even in teenage gangs. Many case histories (New York City Youth Board 1960; Yablonsky 1962; Spergel 1964; Klein 1971) provide ample evidence of the presence and influence of young adults in street gangs of that era. There may, however, have been relatively fewer older teenagers and young adults associated with gangs of the 1950s and 1960s than appears to be the case today.

However, it was already clear at least in New York City by the early 1970s that the age range of gang members was broader "at the top and the bottom than the fighting gangs of the 1950s. The age range in some gangs starts at 9 years and elevates as high as 30 years" (Collins 1979, pp. 39–40). A recent report on San Diego's gang problem indicates that the age range of gang members was twelve to thirty-one years and that the median age was nineteen years (San Diego Association of Governments 1982).

Some analysts continue to insist that the "traditional" age range of gang members is eight to twenty-one or twenty-two years, with only minor exceptions (Miller 1975, 1982). Miller (1982), using media reports, found, for example, no gang offenders or victims in Chicago who were twenty-three years of age or older ($N = 121$). Based on 1982–84 police data on 1,699 offenders and 1,557 victims, Spergel (1986) found that the age range for offenders was eight to fifty-one and for victims three to seventy-six years. Miller's mean age categories were sixteen and seventeen years; Spergel's mean age for offenders was 17.9 years and for victims 20.1 years. Bobrowski (1988) provides the most recent age data on gang offenders based on Chicago Police Department case reports for 1987 and the first half of 1988. The average age of the offender was 19.4 years and the median, eighteen years. The mode for males is seventeen years and for females, fifteen years. For victims the average age is 22.1 years, and the mode, seventeen years (Bobrowski 1988, p. 40).

Some researchers and law-enforcement officials continue to assume, without supporting data, that gang "violence appears largely in early adolescence" (Moore 1978, p. 38) or that "very young offenders commit such accomplice offenses as . . . gang fighting" (Reiss 1988). A related confusion appears to be that older gang members tend to use juveniles or younger adolescents to carry out violent attacks or "hits" against members of opposing gangs. Data on gang homicides and aggravated assaults do not support these conclusions, although juveniles may frequently be used by older gang members to commit certain property crimes, particularly drug trafficking and related activities.

The age locus of gang homicides, the most violent gang activity, is late adolescence and young adulthood. The average age of the gang homicide offender in Los Angeles in the 1980s is nineteen to twenty years (Maxson, Gordon, and Klein 1985; see also Torres 1980; and Horowitz 1983). Spergel's (1983) gang homicide offender data in Chicago for 1978–81 indicate major age categories as follows: fourteen years and under, 2.2 percent; fifteen to sixteen years, 17.6 percent; seventeen to eighteen years, 32.4 percent; nineteen to twenty years, 21.7 percent; twenty-one years and older, 25.9 percent. These percentages for the categories are approximately the same for a later 1982–85 analysis of gang homicides in Chicago (Spergel 1986).

Three interdependent factors may account for the apparently increased ages of gang youth. First, a "real" aging of the youth gang population may have occurred along with that of the general population over the last three decades. A second explanation may be the changing structure of the economy and the loss of desirable unskilled and semiskilled jobs. It has become increasingly difficult for dropout and unskilled gang youths to leave the gang and graduate to legitimate job opportunities that offer a modicum of social respect and income. Third, increased illegitimate opportunities, particularly in the drug market, may have induced older youths and younger adults to remain affiliated with gangs and to modify their structure to distribute drugs.

The age distribution of gang violence is extremely important for theory and policy. If the early or middle adolescent period accounts for most gang violence and serious gang crime, one set of theories and policy strategies may be appropriate. If it is the late adolescent and young adult period, an entirely different set of explanatory theories and policy interventions may be called for.

C.   Females and Gangs

Most gang members are males, and mainly males commit gang-related crimes, particularly violent offenses. Data on the number and distribution of females in gangs are extremely sparse. The older literature on gangs almost never refers to "gang girls" or their characteristics (Thrasher 1936). Bernard Cohen (1969a, p. 85) indicates that 6.3 percent of delinquent group members arrested in the early 1960s were females but that only 1.4 percent of juvenile gang arrests were females. Tracy (1982, pp. 10–11) found that 17 percent of violent delinquents in the 1958 Philadelphia cohort study were females but that most were arrested for nongang offenses.

Despite occasional media reports and social agency warnings, the current situation appears to be unchanged. In a study of four police districts in Chicago between 1982 and 1984 that produced 1,405 reported gang incidents, Spergel (1986) found that 95 to 98 percent of the offenders in each district were males. In a study of 345 gang homicide offenders in Chicago in the four-year period 1978–81, only one was female. Of 204 gang homicide victims for this period, six were female (Spergel 1983).

In a more recent Chicago Police study, Bobrowski (1988) reports 12,502 male offenders; females were only 2 percent of the total over a year and a half period (January 1987–July 1988). The most frequent category of index gang offenses was serious assault. Of 2,984 offenders, only 94, or 3.2 percent, were females. The pattern varies little for other gang-related offenses (Bobrowski 1988). Thus it appears that the participation of females in gang-related offenses has changed little over the past several decades.

Focusing on females as gang members rather than as gang offenders, Collins (1979, p. 51) estimated that males outnumbered females twenty to one in New York City gangs of the 1970s. He also reported that half of all street gangs in New York City had female chapters or auxiliaries. Miller (1975) reported that females made up 10 percent of gang members.

Females are most likely to be members of auxiliaries to male youth gangs, occasionally to be members of mixed-sex gangs, and least likely to be members of independent or unaffiliated female gangs. As members, Campbell (1984a) observes, females function as "partial and pale facsimiles" of male gang structures, processes, and behaviors. The female affiliate may develop a positive and distinctive solidarity or "sisterhood" on its own terms; nevertheless, female gang members still define achievement largely in male terms (Campbell 1984a). Female gang members have the same basic need for status as the males, although the criteria for its achievement are defined somewhat differently. Female gangs appear to have a higher turnover, a shorter life span, less effective organization and leadership, and a "more pervasive sense of purposelessness" than male gangs and members (Campbell 1984a).

As with males, however, it is not clear that the most delinquent and aggressive offenses are gang, rather than nongang, related. "Gang girls" are more likely to obtain police records when they are with the delinquent group or gang than when they are not. Also, the more delinquent the male gang, the more delinquent the affiliated females. Nevertheless, the larger proportion of delinquent females appears to be unaffiliated (Sarnecki 1986), and the most delinquent females are not gang affiliated.

The active gang female, like the active gang male, is part of a highly turbulent and violent social world, but violence patterns seem to be quite different. While violence occasionally occurs from being a perpetrator of a fight or in a dispute over leadership in the female auxiliary, more often it results from resistance to becoming a victim in a robbery, rape, a domestic quarrel with a male gang member, or as "defense against slights to public reputation, such as accusation of cuckolding, promiscuity" (Campbell 1984b). Much female violence results from intragroup female auxiliary tensions and disputes over affections for the same male; only rarely do females develop a reputation for use of a knife or gun or for being a vicious fighter (Brown 1977).

Females have been traditionally viewed as both the cause and the cure of much male delinquency. Evidence for these contrary assertions has not been systematically gathered. The general assumption is that females achieve status and excitement through provocation of fights between members of rival gangs, carrying messages, spying, and carrying concealed weapons. Sarnecki (1986) claims the presence of females may incite males to commit delinquent acts. Some observers, however, suggest that the female affiliate serves on its own to socialize as well as to produce or stimulate deviant behavior (Giordano 1978; Quicker 1983; Campbell 1984a). The most important approval or sanction for deviant behavior may come from interactions and norms of the auxiliary, rather than from the male gang. There is also some evidence that females may be instrumental in persuading boyfriends to leave the gang and settle down. They are instrumental in preventing males from engaging in situational gang delinquencies. Males will tend to avoid gang delinquencies in the presence of females (Klein 1971; Bowker, Gross, and Klein 1980).

A similar set of contradictory notions exists about the social and psychological character of the female as a gang member. On the one hand, female gang members are reported to have "low self-esteem," to do poorly in school, to be rebellious, and to use their affiliation with auxiliary or male gangs to shock parents or other peers (Campbell 1984a). Women in motorcycle gangs are reported to be particularly disturbed and abused. They join because of "the excitement gang life offers" but soon may be held involuntarily or stay because of fear. The motorcycle woman—often older than her street-gang equivalent—may develop strong dependency needs, plays the role of servant or prostitute, and often becomes a "battered woman" (Davis 1982a, 1982b).

Some argue that female gangs or auxiliaries are socially adaptive to life opportunities in the ghetto or barrio. Females who join the gang are often not severe deviants or misfits. They use the gang for a variety of normal typical adolescent purposes: how to get along in the harsh world of the ghetto and meet prospective mates (Bowker, Gross, and Klein 1980; Quicker 1983). They learn about grooming and keeping secrets from the adult world (Campbell 1984a).

The patterns of entry and departure from the gang or auxiliary seem to differ for girls and boys. Girls are rarely drafted. They join and leave even more casually than boys do. The age range of females entering the gang appears to be a little younger than for boys, about twelve to fourteen years. Most girls cease their membership between sixteen and eighteen years, at an earlier age than boys. Hagedorn (1988, p. 5) reports that almost all members of the four female gangs he studied in Milwaukee matured out of the female gang when they turned eighteen.

A variety of reasons have been set forth for why girls do not seem to form gangs as readily as boys, to participate extensively, or to be substantially affected by them. Thrasher (1936, p. 228) suggests that traditionally females have been less aggressive or violent than men. "The behavior of girls, powerfully backed by the great weight of . . . custom, is contrary to the gang and its activities. . . . Girls, even in urban disorganized areas, are more closely supervised and guarded than boys and are usually well incorporated in the family group or some other social structure." Brown (1977, pp. 222–23) offers these reasons why girls in Philadelphia's black ghettoes seem less attached to gangs than are boys. "First, it is common practice in the lower-class black family to assign the females the task of supervising younger siblings . . . and practicing domestic chores . . . this . . . limits the amount of exposure the female will have to street life and gang interaction. Second, lower-class black females have more exposure to mainstream ideals . . . [they] move more freely . . . between the ghetto . . . and mainstream life style than do black males. . . . Third and most important . . . females are not pressured into joining gangs [or] . . . to aid in territorial defense."

In any case, a variety of questions and issues remain in respect to who the female gang member is and why and how she participates. We know much less about the characteristics and performance of gang females than gang males.

V.   Membership Experiences

The youth gang is highly adaptive. It provides psychological, social, cultural, economic, and even political benefits when other institutions such as family, school, and employment fail. The individual grows and develops and learns to survive through his gang experience. But the gang serves the youth poorly, as a rule, in preparing him for a legitimate career and for a personally satisfying long-term life experience.

A.   Entering and Leaving the Gang

There has been little systematic research on why, how, and under what circumstances a youth joins a gang and even less research on why, how, or under what circumstances a youth leaves a gang. Most of the discussion has been at the individual or social-psychological level, with the social or economic environment as background. Beginning efforts are being made to specify risk factors for entry into a gang, for example, known association with gang members; presence of neighborhood gangs; having a relative in a gang; failure at school; prior delinquency record, particularly for aggressive acts; and drug abuse (see Nidorf 1988; Spergel and Curry 1988). Orange County, California, probation officers have developed a scheme for identifying minors "at risk of gang involvement" (Schumacher 1989).

Some recent writing attempts to account for the development of gangs, the conversion of street groups to gangs, and the break-up of gangs. The development of gangs in Los Angeles city and suburban communities has apparently occurred under various circumstances. Gang violence developed first in the city and was followed much later by drug dealing. In the suburbs, drug dealing came first, followed by gang recruitment and gang development (Valdivia 1988). In Milwaukee, one analyst recently observed that group social events can trigger gang formation: "The emergence of some of the gangs was associated with . . . youth . . . break-dancing and drill teams [that] swept the black communities. In some cases, the transition from dance groups to gangs came about as fights broke out and after dance competitions. But there were also a number of traditional corner boy groups already in existence at the time. As fighting between groups became more common, the corner boys, like the dance groups, began to define themselves as gangs" (Moore 1988, p. 12).

Gang socialization processes vary by age, context, situation, and access to alternative roles. A great many reasons for joining a gang have been identified. Some youths join a gang because of needs or wishes for recognition or status, safety or security, power, and new experiences— particularly under conditions of social deprivation (Thomas and Znaniecki 1918; Ley 1975). The youths seek identity and self-esteem they cannot find elsewhere (Cartwright, Tomson, and Schwartz 1975).

Joining a gang may be viewed as normal and respectable, particularly by the youth, even when the consequence is a series of delinquent and violent acts. Stealing, aggression, and vandalism may be secondary to the excitement of interacting with other peers of similar class, interest, need, and persuasion (Sarnecki 1986). The consequences of joining a gang and participating in delinquent acts may not be recognized by adolescents and even young adults (Deukmejian 1981; Rosenbaum and Grant 1983).

Joining a gang has been viewed by some as a desirable and expected process in certain communities. Honor, loyalty, and fellowship are viewed as the reasons youths join gangs at a certain age, particularly in lower-class ethnic communities with extended family systems and strong traditional identification of the residents with each other and the neighborhood. The gang is seen as a vehicle for "preserving the barrio and protecting its honor" (Torres 1980; see also Horowitz 1983). The gang serves as an extension of the family and the development of the clan. Older brothers, relatives, friends, and friends of friends have belonged to the gang. Multigeneration gang families identified with the same gang are not uncommon (Deukmejian 1981).

Joining a gang may also result from rational calculations to achieve personal security, particularly by males, in certain neighborhoods. The youth may be harassed or attacked on the street or in school if he is unaffiliated, belongs to the wrong gang, or comes from the wrong neighborhood. Ironically, the gang member may "feel" safer, but there is evidence to suggest that a gang member is more likely than a nongang member to be attacked by another gang member (Savitz, Rosen, and Lalli 1980).

Joining a gang may meet social and psychological developmental needs of troubled and deprived youth. It provides a way of achieving status and self-importance. The gang member can "control" turf, school, park, and even prison when he cannot perform adequately and achieve respect for himself through legitimate means in these settings (New York City Youth Board 1960; Yablonsky 1962).

Some youths indicate that they join and stay in gangs for financial reasons. The gang provides permission, contacts, and preparation for a variety of criminal gain efforts. The gang member traditionally has been able to attract the attention of adults in organized crime (Spergel 1964; Ianni 1974). In recent years, the gang has become a place to make contact with drug dealers and prepare for a career as a drug dealer or enforcer or hit man for a drug entrepreneur (Miller 1975).

Joining a gang may not be difficult. It most often occurs as the youth hangs around and comes to be accepted by certain key members: "You come to the square, you belonged to the group" (Berntsen 1979, p. 92). Forcible recruitment is not common. Intimidation is more indirect than direct. The threat of intimidation also is seldom carried out, although on occasion a youth who refuses to join can be severely beaten.

Initiation requirements have become part of the tradition of gang life (New York City Youth Board 1960; Yablonsky 1962; Jansyn 1966; Patrick 1973). These requirements, which may be in large part mythology, are said to range from drinking, using drugs, fighting other members, and running a gauntlet to stealing or shooting a member of an opposing gang.

There is little research on the process of a youth leaving a gang, but there is growing evidence that substantial numbers of gang members do not cease affiliation at the usual end of adolescence. Youths leave gangs for a great variety of reasons, including the influence of a girlfriend, interested adults, and parents. Often a kind of battle fatigue sets in. Frequent arrests and incarcerations also take a toll on the youth and his family's finances. His family may move out of the neighborhood. The gang may splinter or dissipate. As the youth reaches the end of adolescence, he may feel himself ready for a job and settling down if alternate roles are open to him (New York City Youth Board 1960; Spergel 1966).

A youth may wish to leave the gang but be unable to, particularly if he remains in close physical proximity to other gang youths in the neighborhood or prison. The threat of violence may also induce him to remain. Death for core gang members or leaders planning to leave the gang has been reported (Collins 1979, p. 35).

There is now ample evidence of the presence of young adults in gangs. Gangs composed mainly of young adults, even with middle-aged gang members, have been acknowledged. Horowitz (1983) makes the following observations in respect to Chicano gangs in Chicago.

> Only a few core members turn away from street status once they reach eighteen. Some become politically conscious, others turn to families, and a few become drug addicts. [P. 181]
>
> Once a reputation has been publicly confirmed, it does not fade away overnight. It becomes difficult for a former gang member to refrain from fighting when a breach of etiquette against him was meant as a challenge to his claim to precedence. [P. 183]
>
> Many gangs on 32nd Street have senior organizations of previous members now in their twenties, thirties and even forties. . . .
> If asked, they still identify themselves as gang members and claim other members as their best friends. [P. 184]

Hagedorn, Macon, and Moore (1986, p. 5) add, in respect to mainly black gangs in Milwaukee: "More than 70% of the 260 who founded the gangs were reported as still being involved with the gang today, more than five years after the gang was founded."

Gang members who worked in community-action programs, supported by foundation grants in the late 1960s, were typically in their twenties (Spergel et al. 1969; Poston 1971). Motorcycle gangs consist mainly of young adults. Prison gangs consist largely of young men in their twenties and thirties (Jacobs 1974, 1977; Moore 1978; G. Camp and C. Camp 1985). Street and prison gang members may graduate into extremist political groups. Some observers have come to view gang membership in recent years as "permanent and life-long" (Moore, Vigil, and Garcia 1983) and as "a way of life, a cause" (Daley 1985).

B.   Individual Status and Gang Cohesion

A need for recognition or reputation is the most common explanation for why people participate in gangs. This can be achieved through delinquent or violent activity, which involves group support or cohesion, which in turn creates a further need for status by certain members of the gang and stimulates even more delinquent and violent activity. These relationships may be nonrecursive (see fig. 1).

Status is a central concept in the explanation of the violent youth gang (see Cloward and Ohlin 1960; Spergel 1964; Short and Strodtbeck 1965; Klein 1969, 1971; Moore 1978; Horowitz 1983). The process of achieving status is sometimes interpreted by psychologically oriented analysts as a way of resolving a variety of personal and social problems.

Relationships among gang members may be viewed as a continuing struggle to manage status as defined and redefined by the gang (Thrasher 1936, pp. 275–76). Each gang member seeks status in the eyes of his peers, whether members of his gang, members of opposing gangs, peers, or adults generally in the community (Cartwright, Tomson, and Schwartz 1975).

Status can be achieved both directly and indirectly. For example, gang identification may signify power, importance, or access to illegal opportunity or markets. The drive for status can be all compelling. Indeed, arrest and imprisonment may become an important means to elevate one's status, particularly for the younger members. The gang status system thus creates special problems for traditional law enforcement.

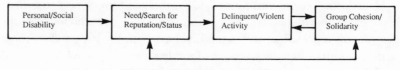

FIG. 1.—Gang-behavior paradigm

Short and Strodtbeck (1965, p. 215) observe that the "existence of the gang is crucial to an understanding of the manner in which status management is carried out by gang boys regardless of whether the threat originated from within or outside the group. The gang provides the audience for much of the acting out which occurs. . . . It's the most immediate system of rewards and punishments to which members are responsive much of the time." A situation may "arise when a gang leader acts to reduce threats to his status by instigating out-group aggression . . . leaders resort to this action because of the limited resources they have for internal control of their group—particularly when their status is attacked" (p. 185). The strong need for status comes fundamentally from the lack of resources and the weakness of controls internal and external to the group. The constant competition for honor and reputation, the precarious ranking system and hierarchical structure that "depends on continuous confirmation by others of one's placement" results in a constant state of flux, highly unstable relationships, and continual forming and reforming of the group (Horowitz 1983, p. 89; see also Patrick 1973). Nevertheless, unstable and frustrating as the gang status system is, it assumes special importance in poor or changing neighborhoods, in schools with extremely high failure rates, and increasingly in prisons.

Over time, however, a gang may stabilize. There may be less competition for positions of "honor" and less turnover among leaders and core members. Researchers disagree about the conditions under which status striving is reduced or enhanced in its contribution to delinquency and violence, particularly through the process of group cohesion.

Two sets of arguments have arisen. The first is that gangs may be more cohesive and stable than is recognized in much of the older literature. In some communities, particular gangs persist over time, members interact as friends, and mutual support develops and persists. Gang members trust and depend on each other and create strong bonds over the years. "There are few culturally accepted forms of affiliation in which they can maintain close relationships and remain tough warriors, an identity for which there are few alternatives" (Horowitz 1983, p. 179). Young adult gangs involved in a good deal of criminal activity may also require bonds of trust and mutual dependency. Jacobs emphasizes the important attitudinal dimension of gang attractiveness in prison. "By far the most important function the gangs provide their members at Stateville is psychological support . . . the organizations give to the members a sense of identification, a feeling of belonging, an air of importance. According to the Chief of the Vice-Lords, 'It's just like a religion. Once a Lord always a Lord. People would die for it. . . . The Lords allows you to feel like a man . . . it is a family with which you can identify' " (Jacobs 1977, pp. 152–53; see also Moore 1978). Jansyn (1966) observes of an Italian gang in a stable community that gangs go through periods of high and low cohesion; phases of organization and disorganization increase or decrease solidarity.

The second set of arguments is over interactions between gang cohesion or solidarity and delinquency. Jansyn (1966) argued that when gangs go through a phase of disorganization, a burst of activity—often delinquent—occurs to mobilize and cohere the group once again. Klein and Crawford (1967), by contrast, argue that group cohesion precedes delinquent behavior and that the highly cohesive gang is likelier to engage in gang activity than is the diffuse or weakly organized gang. Klein (1971) later modified this view and proposed that delinquent behavior and gang cohesiveness were interactive although the predominant direction was from cohesion to delinquent activity.

Several writers argue that delinquency and gang membership are not only important and interactive but depend on the kind of delinquency engaged in and the measures of cohesion used (Cartwright, Tomson, and Schwartz 1975; see also Morash 1983; Stafford 1984). Other researchers suggest the key element may be the need for status by persons vying for, or exercising, leadership. When a member aspires for leadership or an established leader feels threatened, gang activity—usually of a delinquent or violent character—and increased cohesion follow (Yablonsky 1962; Short and Strodtbeck 1965). The implication, therefore, is that delinquency, violence, or at least some individuals' provocative activity may occur even prior to group interaction and feelings of solidarity (see also Thrasher 1936; Kornhauser 1978).

Klein's (1971) Ladino Hills experiment in Los Angeles was an effort to test the notion that gang cohesion causes delinquency and that a reduction in group cohesion would be followed by a reduction in delinquent behavior. This first theoretically conceptualized quasi experiment in gang intervention was partly successful. Attempts at decohering the gang were successful. Gang size and the group delinquency rates were reduced. However, the rate of mutual interactions of those who remained or were part of the gang system was not reduced. Fewer delinquent gang events occurred, but individual delinquency rates did not significantly change after two years (one and a half years of program and a subsequent six-month follow-up period). Klein (1971) was most

successful in limiting the recruitment of new members and the development of a new Klika to the gang, at least over the short term.

C. Social/Personal Disability

We know little about the social and personal disabilities of gang
delinquents that distinguishes them from nongang delinquents or about
differences among types of gang youth. There has been speculation
that core members are more troubled or troublesome than fringe members (Yablonsky 1962; Klein 1971).

We have little systematic knowledge about gang members' intelligence or physical and mental health. The weight of opinion is that gang
members' intelligence may be somewhat below normal (Klein 1971)
and that they tend to be more than normally "hostile, disruptive,
defiant, aloof, distant, arrogant, and defensive" (G. Camp and C.
Camp 1985, p. 12). Yet the bases for these judgments are not clear. On
purportedly culture-free measures of arithmetic, vocabulary, memory,
and information, gang members tested lower than other lower-class
nongang boys (Short and Strodtbeck 1965). Based on performance on a
standardized intelligence test (normal is 100), Klein reports that gang
members' (N = 243) median score was 84, and only eight tested above
100. "One-third of the boys have scores that would dictate their placement in special education classes" (1971, p. 85). Farrington, Berkowitz,
and West (1982, p. 331) indicate that "frequent group fighters" tended
to have low vocabulary scores at ages ten and fourteen years. In a recent
survey of prison gangs, however, officials estimated that gang members
were of average intelligence. In fact their education level is perceived as
above average (G. Camp and C. Camp 1985). Taylor (1988) recently
reported that youths in "corporate" drug dealing gangs in Detroit did
well in school, and some came from middle-class families.

More attention has been paid to the emotional than to the intellectual
disabilities of gang members. A wide range of views exists but it tends
to emphasize the troubled and defective character of the gang member's
development. Almost all of the research is observational with few, if
any, scientific controls.

At one extreme are claims that core members tend to be pathological
and gang leaders sociopaths or megalomaniacs. The gang is a useful
channel for expression of hostility and striving for power (Yablonsky
1962; see also Cartwright, Tomson, and Schwartz 1975). Certain gang
members show a preference for aggression based on their feelings of
inferiority and their fear of being rejected or ignored by others (Gerrard

1964). Peter Scott, a British psychiatrist, concludes that the "gang proper" is an atypical form springing from pathological rather than social pressures (Scott 1956; see also Downes 1966). An observer of Glasgow gangs notes that it was not the "strongest or the fittest, the tallest or the brightest boys who became leader or lieutenants in gangs, but the most psychologically disturbed, those with lowest impulse control" (Patrick 1973, pp. 100–101).

Other analysts tend to characterize gang members as troubled, perceptually disoriented, or emotionally disturbed, but not in such fearsome terms. The gang boy is viewed as an emotionally unstable individual who has difficulty making satisfactory interpersonal relationships and "poor impulse control." The gang is an aggregate of individuals with "shared incapacities"; aggression is a "coping mechanism that receives constant reinforcement within the gang" (Klein 1971, pp. 81–85). Gang members have "worse relationships than boys who do not have a criminal record . . . those boys appeared to be anxious to be accepted by their mates" (Sarnecki 1986, p. 20). The motorcycle gang member is a "free spirit who has very little loyalty to others. His essential commitment is to himself . . . he has difficulty keeping close friends. He has no remorse about his behavior" (Davis 1982a, p. 22). Gang boys are "inferior in their general powers of concentration and in their perceptual ability to integrate meaningful wholes out of partial information" (Cartwright, Tomson, and Schwartz 1975, p. 11).

A number of writers have observed that leaders of gangs who are considerably older than the average age of members are often very personally troubled. In one gang where the average age was sixteen years, the core members were twenty-six, twenty-four, twenty-three and nineteen years, and the leader was especially violent (New York City Youth Board 1960, p. 16).

Some writers see gangs as composed of youths with social liabilities but who have certain social strengths and who find positive values in the gang. "Gang boys are less assertive. They are more reactive to false signals . . . they tend to be neurotic and anxious, less gregarious and more narcissistic." However, the gang member is not characterized by "desperation in search of stable human relationships, nurturance and security. He seems, rather, to have worked out a reasonably realistic solution to problems. The gang boy in many respects is a pragmatist" (Short and Strodtbeck 1965, pp. 231–33). Gordon (1967, p. 48) considers "gang behavior not merely an expression of individual psychological disturbances or of group norms but also as a complex of techniques through which boys in a group strive to elicit nurturant, accepting, and highly dependable responses from each other—perhaps to compensate for deprivation in their family backgrounds or other institutional contexts."

The gang member's disturbance is seen by some as functional to survival in his environment and to the gang's status system. The theme of "survival" permeates many of the explanations of why youths join gangs and do the "crazy things" they do. Few of these youths have experienced anything but severe economic deprivation. They find themselves at the brink of adulthood without education or training to compete successfully in the labor market. "Survival through 'hustling' or 'fighting' is a functional adaptation to an uncompromising social environment" (Krisberg 1974, p. 116).

Deficient homelife is often cited as an explanation of the gang member's disturbance and resort to gang membership. In one type of explanation, gang members come from "stressful family situations, especially the disproportionate female centered or transient male adult models." The identity crisis for the male adolescent Chicano is resolved by his joining the gang "which stresses male survival traits on the streets." Vigil also suggests that the gang as an institution serves the same function as male initiation rites in other cultures (Vigil 1988, pp. 5–8; see also A. Cohen 1955; Bloch and Niederhoffer 1958; Miller 1958).

A more positive view of gang-boy personality is taken by other researchers who reject the idea that most gang members are psychopathic, sociopathic, or even that they are significantly socially or personally disabled. This is implicit in Cloward and Ohlin's (1960) assumption that gang boys are not alienated from conventional institutions or middle-class values. They cannot make it in these systems or through established means and simply find alternate ways to achieve their desired objectives (see also Short and Strodtbeck 1965).

The most sanguine view of the personalities of gang members is that of Walter Miller (1958, p. 17), at least based on his earlier writings: "They are not psychopaths, nor physically or mentally 'defective'; in fact since the corner-boy supports and enforces a rigorous set of standards which demand a high degree of fitness and personal competence, the gang tends to recruit from the most able members of the community." Some gang leaders complete high school, college, or even graduate school and settle down to middle-class business or professional lives.

While there is considerable disagreement as to whether gang youths are emotionally disturbed and to what degree, there appears to be some consensus as to the dynamics of gang violence and the status and control purposes that such violence serves in the group context. For certain youths, violence in the gang context is "highly valued as a means for the achievement of reputation or 'rep' " (Yablonsky 1962, pp. 194–292). The social disabilities of gang youths "contribute to the status dilemmas of these youngsters and in this way contribute to involvement in delinquency" (Short and Strodtbeck 1965, p. 243). The need for status is pronounced among gang members and should be viewed as "compensatory over-assertion" (New York City Youth Board 1960, p. 58; see also Cartwright, Howard, and Reuterman 1970). The gang fulfills "status needs that would otherwise go unmet" (Friedman, Mann, and Friedman 1975, pp. 600–601). Gang violence, minor or major, may be viewed as an effort to establish and maintain power, whether exercised democratically or autocratically (New York City Youth Board 1960).

VI.   The Social Contexts of Gang Development

Rapid population change, social disorganization, and poverty interact to create the need for alternate social roles and career routes through residual organizations, such as youth gangs. This section examines the contexts and institutional conditions—family, school, politics, and organized crime—that encourage or support gang development.

Insight into the development of gangs has often been sought in ecological and social disorganization theories. Ecological theories attempt to relate characteristics of a population to those of space and material conditions. Social disorganization refers to the disarray of norms, values, and social and organizational relationships at system rather than subsystem levels. In other words, families, groups, and organizations may seem to function well on their own terms but not as part of a coherent formal system committed to dominant cultural norms and values.

Thrasher (1936, pp. 22–23) wrote almost sixty years ago that gangland occupies the "poverty belt," an "interstitial area" of the city characterized by "deteriorating neighborhoods, shifting populations, and the mobility and disorganization of the slum. . . . It is to a large extent isolated from the wider culture of the larger community by the processes of competition and conflict which have resulted in the selection of its population. Gangland is a phenomenon of human ecology" (see also Shaw and McKay 1943).

Urban ecologists and criminologists have speculated that different kinds or degrees of social organization may exist in low-income communities. The disorganized low-income community is characterized by more extensive deterioration and social disorder and by greater violence than are other communities (Kobrin 1951; Gold 1987). Gangs arise and develop both in more stable and less stable slum areas but assume a different character where social institutions fail to function as agencies of social control (Shaw and McKay 1931, pp. 107–8).

The growth and development of cities may be characterized by a succession of different racial, ethnic, and income groups, with "a corresponding succession of gangs, although gang names and traditions may persist in spite of changes in nationalities" (Thrasher 1936, p. 198). This process may occur in small as well as large, suburban as well as inner-city, areas where poor immigrant communities are settling, where social institutions are in the process of change, and where community organization is weak.

Short observed that two kinds of unstable or disorganized communities produced conflict subcultures or violent gangs in Chicago in the early 1960s: "Areas which have undergone very rapid transition from white to Negro, such as the West Side. . . . Here was found the fullest development of the conflict subculture . . . and areas on the fringe of expansion of the 'Black Belt' . . . in such areas, conflict most often occurred for the purpose of 'keeping the niggers' out" (Short 1963, p. 32).

The 1960s and 1970s saw the exodus of higher-status whites and nonwhites from many central city areas, a consequent increase in proportions of lower-status minorities in certain areas, and the development of segregated barrios or ghettoes, often in low-income public-housing projects. The recruitment pool from which members of youth gangs and law-violating youth groups were drawn increased (Miller 1975). The argument has been made that in the newer or changing ghetto areas, children and adolescents, clubs, pre-gangs, and established gangs teem and are in conflict with each other, as so many groups of different background and orientation come together at school, community centers, or on the streets (New York City Youth Board 1960; Breen and Allen 1983).

Gang violence may be less virulent in the stabilized low-income ghetto. Internecine conflict may subside as smaller gangs are integrated into larger better-organized gangs. Competition and conflict may be rationalized and focused on criminal gain, not simply on turf and status. This is not to deny that these relatively more stable areas with lower rates of gang conflict may have higher overall rates of delinquency and crime than do high gang-crime areas.

Systematic tests of these ideas have only begun to be carried out. Cartwright and Howard (1966) performed an ecological analysis of the prevalence of gangs in Chicago in the 1960s using community area data. They did not find support for Thrasher's (1936) notion that delinquent gangs were concentrated in Chicago's "poverty belt." Gangs in the 1960s were found in all parts of Chicago. In the 1980s, gang incidents were reported in all of the Chicago Police Department's twenty-five districts, although concentrated in certain districts. Cartwright and Howard (1966, pp. 357–58) found that high-crime-rate gang areas were coterminous with only about half of the high-crime-rate delinquency areas. In other words, high rates of gangs and gang activity were also found in lower delinquency rate areas.

Bernard Cohen (1969a, 1969b) found in the 1960s that gangs, mainly black, were located not only in relatively poor communities but in the segregated sections of the city that were culturally and socially isolated. He reasoned that certain populations, whether first-generation European immigrants in the 1920s and 1930s, blacks in the post–World War II era, and Hispanic groups most recently, may be "set apart, stereotyped and placed in a ghetto culture." The entire life experience of youth may be confined to a particular area or social context that can result in intense identification with the territory (Cohen 1969a, 1969b). Social and cultural isolation may interact with social disorganization, poverty, and low income to produce different gang problem rates.

Curry and Spergel (1988) performed an ecological analysis of the relation of gang homicide, robbery, and burglary to poverty level, unemployment rate, and mortgage investment on a community-area basis in Chicago in the 1970s and early 1980s. Gang homicide and serious delinquency rates were differentially distributed in Chicago's seventy-seven highly racially segregated community areas. The best predictors of delinquency rate were the economic variables; however, the best predictors of gang homicides were a combination of social disorganization factors that are identified with recently settled Hispanics and income variations.

The interaction of social disorganization and lack of legitimate resources probably largely accounts for the development of deviant group and subcultural phenomena in a variety of contexts. The family, the school, politics, organized crime, and the prison may contribute in special ways to the formation and development of gang patterns and individual gang-member behavior. Very limited direct attention has been paid to the relation of gangs to these institutional contexts. What we know is usually a product of studies designed for other purposes, such as the relations between family and delinquency; school and delinquent peer groups; assessment of safe schools; the nature of participation in grass-roots or "machine" politics; patterns of recruitment to organized crime; or organizational change. Some exceptions exist: Thrasher's (1936) chapter on "The Gang in Politics," Cloward and Ohlin's (1960) formulation of the "criminal subculture," and Spergel's (1964) discussions of "Racketville" and "Haulburg."

A. Family

A theoretically rich but controversial research tradition finds the origin of delinquency, affiliation with delinquent groups, and other personal and social disorders primarily in the defects of family relationships, parental character, and early childhood rearing (Rutter and Giller 1983). Very little research has been done on the relation between family variables and participation in delinquent gangs.

Vigil (1988, p. 3) states that gang members in southern California generally are "raised in poorer homes, disproportionate mother-centered family situations with more siblings and problematic impoverished economic pressures (unemployment and welfare). . . . In large part, [there are] early childhood indications of deviant activities (e.g., running away from home, petty shoplifting, and street fighting stem from such conditions)." He argues that the process of becoming a gang member occurs through an accumulation of parental physical or emotional neglect to abuse from older street children, punitive educational incidents, and poor role models.

Disruption or disorganization of the family may somehow lead youths to seek compensatory values in gang membership (Sherif and Sherif 1965, 1975). Research observers and gang members have indicated that the gang in many ways is like a family. The gang can be very appealing to immigrant or newcomer youths in urban areas who are cut off culturally and socially as well as economically from their families. The gang leader often adopts a paternal, or even a maternal, role—somewhat passive but controlling, also providing guidance, warmth, and affection (New York City Youth Board 1960).

Defects of family structure and relationship have not, however, been related directly to gang membership. For example, not all male offspring of the same family will join a gang or even the same gang (Horowitz 1983). Why one brother joins and another does not is not clear. Equal numbers of nongang lower-class boys came from the same family structure as gang boys (Tennyson 1967; see also Shaw and McKay 1931). Gang and nongang delinquents do not differ on such characteristics as broken homes, having parents with criminal histories, level of intelligence, or the highest school grade achieved (Friedman, Mann, and Friedman 1975). The educational level of the parents of gang members is not especially low (Cartwright and Howard 1966; Klein 1968).

In a recent cohort study of sixth through eighth graders in four inner-city schools in Chicago, Spergel and Curry (1988) found that the absence of a father was a fairly strong predictor of arrests for Hispanic youth, but it was a weak predictor of arrests for black youth. Further, and more important, family structure did not enter a second series of regression equations to explain gang-related activities. Instead, the presence of a gang-member sibling or parent in the home was the best predictor of gang activity, particularly for Hispanic youth (Spergel and Curry 1988).

There seems to be a consensus that other variables interact with family variables to produce a gang-problem youth (Rutter and Giller 1983). Thrasher (1936) saw the lack of adequate parental or family supervision as contributing to the likelihood that a youth would become a gang member in a poor disorganized community. Based on a series of recent studies, Reiss's (1988) essay concludes that "it is the territorial concentration of young males who lack firm controls of parental authority that leads them into a peer-control system that supports co-offending and simplifies the search for accomplices."

Thus, the defects of family relationships or pressures (Joe and Robinson 1980) may not lead to gang membership except where gangs are developing or already exist. For the nondelinquent, less gang-oriented boy, "satisfying experiences in the family as a normative reference group could overcome the effect of the gang as a delinquent reference group" (Stanfield 1966, p. 412; see also Haskell 1960).

Miller (1976b) suggests that the family and the gang may play complementary socialization roles for gang members, teaching them different survival skills. Sager (1988) sees the gang as complementary to the family in the lower-class Mexican-American barrio culture in Los Angeles; the women perform dominant roles in the home and the men perform their warrior roles on the street.

Gang members do not appear to be particularly rebellious or hostile toward family members. Indeed a good deal of warmth, closeness, and affection may exist. Yet the family, school, and gang exist in distinctive and parallel social and cultural subsystems. There may be little inter-penetration or interdependency among them. Even in the two- or three-generation gang family, there may be little explicit support or encouragement for gang membership, but a functional relationship may still exist culturally and economically. The gang youth does occasionally make a contribution of funds to the household.

B. School

Considerable attention has been paid to delinquency in the school (Toby 1983; Elliott, Huizinga, and Ageton 1985; and Gottfredson and Gottfredson 1985). There has, however, been little examination of the relation of gang problems to schools. Thrasher (1936), for example, paid scant attention to gangs in schools. Albert Cohen (1955) noted that delinquent subcultures were often in opposition to the norms of the school's middle-class culture. Hargreaves (1967) and Rutter et al. (1979) have described delinquent groups and subcultures in public schools in Great Britain that developed not so much in opposition to the school's system or norms and values but as alternatives to them.

More recent concern with gangs and schools arose in the mid-1970s. National surveys, however, scarcely addressed group-related delin-quency in or around the school or differentiated between delinquent group and gang-related problems (National Institute of Education 1978; Gottfredson and Gottfredson 1985). The few studies that specifically address the school and gang problem are based often on nonrandom informant, nonsystematic, and subjective data sources. Statistics are usually not provided or are open to question. Issues of reliability, validity, and, especially, consistency of operational definitions abound.

In six large cities, informants reported "the presence of identified gangs operating in the schools, stabbings, beatings, and other kinds of assaults on teachers"; the schools in Philadelphia are "citadels of fear" with "gang fighting in the halls" (Miller 1975, p. 46). In Chicago, 50 percent of public school students believe that "identifiable gangs are operating in and around the majority of schools, both elementary and secondary." One in ten students reports that street-gang members make them afraid when they are in school, have either attacked or threatened them, and have solicited them for membership, although mainly when they are not at school. Gangs are present in all twenty districts of the Chicago school system (Chicago Board of Education 1981, pp. 182–84, 189).

Kyle (1984) reports that 45 percent of the males and 22 percent of the females in two public high schools in probably the most gang-ridden community of Chicago were asked to join gangs in or around the school. The major reason for dropping out of school "was fear of gangs;" 25 percent of the students interviewed stated that they dropped out because of gangs. Kyle (1984, p. 10) also claims that "the authority within the schools ultimately belonged to the gangs rather than the school administrators."

A report on the Evanston, Illinois, school system provides a somewhat similar picture. Ninety-one percent of the high school students "personally know one or more students who are gang members" and "almost half (47 percent) of the students describe the gang problem as a big problem" (Rosenbaum and Grant 1983, p. 16). In an evaluation of alternate education programs in fifty schools around the country in 1982, 13 percent of males and 5.2 percent of females reported they had been involved in a gang fight (Gottfredson, Gottfredson, and Cook 1983).

Ley (1975) observes that the majority of school transfers in Philadelphia's inner-city schools, particularly at the high school level, were related to the student's fear of gangs or to the desire and need of high school officials to move students either to protect them or to get rid of key "gang bangers." Two law-enforcement officers from Los Angeles claim that "student opportunity transfers and busing programs" served to "spread gang violence" into the immediate area of the school as well as back to the original neighborhoods and expressed the hope that "these programs will not be prolonged any longer than is necessary" (Jackson and McBride 1985, p. 28).

The school-related gang problem appears different in character from the street-level gang problem. It is generally less serious and involves younger youths. Self-report and police arrest data appear to tap different dimensions of the gang problem. The Chicago Board of Education study reports that younger students twelve or thirteen years of age are as likely as students eighteen years or older to be solicited for gang membership (1981, pp. 184–87). However, a substantial majority of youths arrested for gang-related crimes are over fourteen years of age (Spergel 1986). Teachers and principals perceive gangs to be considerably less of a problem in and around schools than do students (Chicago Board of Education 1981, p. 189).

Police data generally indicate a more limited school gang problem than do other reports. Chicago Police Department statistics show that 10–11 percent of reported gang incidents in 1985 and 1986 occurred on school property. Only 3.3 percent of the reported gang incidents took place on public high school property in 1985. Chicago public school discipline reports for the same period show that only 2 percent of discipline code violations were gang related but that gang incidents were disproportionately serious: 12 percent of weapons violations, 26 percent of robberies, and 20 percent of aggravated batteries (Spergel 1985).

Participant-observation studies over three decades consistently indicate that gang members are typically behind in their studies or are school dropouts (Klein 1968). All of the forty-seven gang "founders" interviewed in Milwaukee had dropped out or been kicked out of school; most had been suspended (Hagedorn, Macon, and Moore 1986). School is regarded as alien ground by many gang members, and they seek to leave as quickly as possible (Horowitz 1983). The school is a place where gang members' weaknesses and inadequacies are made public (New York City Youth Board 1960). In one recent study, 80 percent of gang members were high school dropouts (Reddick 1987). In another study, less than a third of gang members graduated from high school or later returned for a general equivalency diploma (Hagedorn 1988). Some gang members do not devalue school and do not necessarily criticize gang members or others for doing well (Short and Strodtbeck 1965; Horowitz 1983); most gang members do not believe that formal public school education has anything to offer them: "In an environment where education is meaningless, the gang-barrio fulfills the young man's needs. . . . It is not the school where the 'American' teachers tell him about a world in which he has no real part . . . but in the neighborhood gang is the stuff of living as he knows it" (Pineda 1974, p. 15).

Gang researchers have observed that gang behavior may result as much from school defects as from problems and pressures at home (Short and Strodtbeck 1965; Joe and Robinson 1978). School variables are apparently highly predictive of later criminal adaptations and careers of delinquent group or gang youths (Gold and Mattick 1974; Sarnecki 1986).

C. Politics

Youth gangs have often been linked to urban political systems in times of rapid change and social turmoil. Gangs in some cities, particularly Chicago, and in some contexts, notably prisons, have provided a means of communication between elites and alienated low-income populations. The short-term costs of using gangs in this way are relatively low in terms of provisions of funds and additional status. The long-term costs are higher since the gang is legitimized, its organizational strength increased, and its opportunities for illegal behavior may be enhanced.

In the middle of the nineteenth century, according to one analyst, "gangs were the medium through which the grassroots and City Hall communicated. Politicians relied on the gangs for contact and stability, while residents used the gangs to acquire and distribute services and jobs. The gang imposed a social conscience on local businessmen by policing the neighborhoods and periodically sacking the homes, hotels, warehouses, and factories of the rich, instantly redistributing scarce goods to the needy. From the 1850s through the dismemberment of the Tweed Ring in the 1870s, New York's political machine was largely run from below" (Stark 1981, p. 441).

At times of social and political crisis or urban disorganization, the gang is more fully recognized as an instrument of power and influence. A symbiotic relationship between urban politicians and gangs has been observed in low-income communities with highly fluid, weak, or fragmented political systems.

Of Chicago in the first third of this century, Thrasher (1936) observed: "the political boss . . . provides uniforms, camping funds, children's picnics to 'get him in good' with the parents and friends of the gang boys. . . . To repay the politician for putting gang members on official pay-rolls, and providing subsidies, protections, and immunities . . . the gang often splits . . . the proceeds of its illegal activities, controls for him the votes of its members . . . and performs for him various types of work at the polls, such as slugging, intimidation . . . vandalism (tearing down signs, etc.), ballot-fixing, repeating, stealing ballot boxes" (pp. 452, 477).

Kornblum (1974, p. 166) observed the continuity of this pattern in Chicago in the early 1970s. "A second group of neighborhood influentials which joined the opposing tenth ward faction was a small group of superannuated Mexican street fighters. Men with nicknames, such as 'The Rat' and 'The Hawk,' and with reputations in the Mexican precincts to match . . . were in ward politics. . . . When a campaign becomes heated . . . a challenging faction may see fit to call upon its 'heavies' for various strategies of intimidation, including the systematic removal of the opposition's street signs and lamp posters."

Use of gang members was evident in recent elections in Chicago. The primary elections of 1986 in the 26th Ward, containing mainly newcomer, low-income Puerto Ricans, involved fierce competition between Hispanic Alderman Torres, supported by the established Democratic machine, and his challenger, Gutierrez, supported by Mayor Harold Washington, who was attempting to consolidate his newly gained power. Both candidates used gang members to perform a variety of tasks—getting the vote out, hanging election posters, persuading or "intimidating" opposition voters. Members of one gang were mainly involved in support of one candidate, and members of the opposing gang supported the other. One candidate's coordinator of precinct captains was the former leader of a major Hispanic gang renowned for its violence and drug-dealing activity.

Participation of gangs in urban community affairs took different forms during the turbulent 1960s. Gangs were not an essential component or precipitant of urban riots or civil-rights-related disorders but were peripheral and opportunistic participants (Knopf 1969; Skolnick 1969). Gangs are ordinarily not committed to social or political causes or ideology (however, see Anti-Defamation League 1986, 1987). Gangs were, nevertheless, enlisted in Chicago and elsewhere during the riot period to "cool" and control local residents. They were used by the police as an auxiliary force to maintain order; sometimes they were organized into youth patrols with identifying hard hats and arm bands to patrol riot-torn streets. Some gangs protected storekeepers against riot damage for a fee.

Gangs in the 1960s were also solicited by frightened government departments, foundations, social agencies, and community organizations to participate, as partners or recipients of funds, in a variety of community development and social service projects. Gangs were viewed as one of the few viable organizations that could stabilize the disordered ghettoes. That gangs represented criminal interests and contained disoriented and incapable members was usually overlooked or misunderstood.

Gangs were sometimes asked to participate in campaigns and support political candidates. Gang members themselves ran for political office, including alderman and model cities representatives in Chicago. Major controversies arose among politicians, community organizations, and units of government over such gang involvements (see Spergel 1969, 1972; Spergel et al. 1969; Poston 1971; Short 1976). The participation of gangs in community and political affairs subsided in the 1970s.

Gangs continue to serve the interests of a variety of organizations and officials concerned with urban problems. The media, law-enforcement agencies, youth-serving organizations, and even local political adminis-trations use the gang problem as a means to mount campaigns or inter-vention programs. Such efforts benefit youth agencies, criminal justice and community organizations, and political administrations in a variety of ways, but there is little evidence of their effectiveness in controlling gang problems.

Law-enforcement agencies are particularly prone to cite gang activi-ties as a rationale for increased manpower, specialized equipment, and the organization of gang units and special task forces to attract public support and additional tax dollars. The police have also tended to politicize the gang problem, using it to protect "police turf" and philos-ophy and to attack or gain dominance over other competing organiza-tions, such as probation departments, youth agencies, and community organizations. The "fight" against gangs is usually "won," at least ini-tially, by the law-enforcement agency (see Miller, Baum, and McNeil 1968; Sherman 1970).

D. Organized Crime

Some case studies (Spergel 1964; Ianni 1974) and theoretical specula-tions (Cloward and Ohlin 1960) portray certain youth gangs as stepping stones to roles in adult organized crime. Although a significant number of gang youths become adult criminals, it is unclear what proportion move into organized crime. Much depends on how "organized crime" is defined. A narrow definition is offered by the President's Commission on Organized Crime (1985, p. 181): "Groups that engage in a variety of criminal activities are organized crime when they have the capacity to corrupt governments." Ianni's (1974, pp. 14–15) broader definition is "any gang or group of criminals organized formally or informally to extort money, shoplift, steal automobiles or rob banks is part of orga-nized crime regardless of its size or whether it operates locally or na-tionally." If burglary, selling of weapons, and drug selling are added, most youth gangs or gang segments would be considered to be engaged in organized crime.

Thrasher (1936, p. 409) noted more than fifty years ago that there is "no hard and fast dividing line between predatory gang boys and criminal groups of younger and older adults. They merge into each other by imperceptible gradations, and the latter have their real explanations for the most part in the former. Many delinquent gangs contain both adolescents and adults." Scholars in the 1950s and 1960s probably exaggerated the distinctiveness of youth-gang subcultures in different types of lower-class neighborhoods (Cloward and Ohlin 1960; but see Short and Strodtbeck 1965) and the differential likelihood that members of different kinds of gangs would graduate to roles in organized crime.

Youth gangs and adult criminal subcultures have probably become far more integrated with each other in the 1970s and 1980s than they were in the 1950s and 1960s with the increased entry of newer minority groups into organized crime, greater competition among nascent criminal organizations, the relative increase in older youth and adults in street gangs, and the expanded street-level drug markets.

Gangs, drugs, and violence are related, but in diverse ways. The increase of gang violence and homicides in some black communities on the West Coast, and elsewhere, has been attributed to competition over drug markets. By contrast, the reduction of gang violence in certain black inner-city communities in Chicago has been attributed in part to control and domination of the drug market by black gangs. The decline in the traditional gang problem in still other cities, such as New York and Detroit, may be attributed to increased opportunities for drug trafficking and the ready transfer of street-gang knowledge and skills to street-level drug distribution.

The development of motorcycle gangs and especially prison gangs with close ties to street gangs has further weakened the distinction between violent gangs and criminal enterprises. Motorcycle gangs may share characteristics similar to those of street gangs. They seek to control and protect territory and illegal markets. They "will resort to bloody violence if the threats and acts of intimidation fail" (Daley 1985, p. 2).

Planning and organization characterize at least some of the actions of street gangs, or their subgroups, particularly those engaged in drug trafficking. The penetration of gangs into property ownership under questionable circumstances and into slum management appears to have occurred in Chicago (Pleines 1987). Members of one street gang have recently been convicted of conspiracy to acquire and sell illegal weapons and to commit terrorist acts for Libya (Sly 1987a, 1987b).

Ianni (1974) suggests a close relation between youth gangs and organized adult crime. In New York City, he reports, "Black and Hispanic crime activists follow the street 'rep' of youngsters just as carefully as the Italians did and use the same process of gradual involvement to draw youngsters into the networks" (1974, p. 124). The youth gang and the prison are the two major institutions that prepare youth for participation in criminal networks.

Ianni predicted the creation of "what is now a scattered and loosely organized pattern of emerging black control in organized crime into a Black Mafia" and in the future an Hispanic Mafia (1974, p. 11). Youth gangs and organized crime may serve social functions of integrating deprived minority groups into the larger American culture, in effect serving as early and middle stages in America's complex social mobility system (Ianni 1974, p. 15; see also Bell 1953).

Gangs are undergoing, it has been said, an evolution from "fighting and relatively disorganized criminality to the level of organized criminal activity with adult participation . . . the transition from 'protecting' a street corner to the utilization of the gang as a 'power base' to control narcotics flow on those same street corners should not be an unexpected one" (Sampson 1984, pp. 7–8). However, it is possible to exaggerate the "organized" character of gangs. It remains fragmentary and ad hoc even as gang members move "up" to street-level drug trafficking, as a rule.

My own recent observations of gangs in a lower-class Puerto Rican community in Chicago suggest that a variety of pressures and opportunities exist for youths in violent gangs to participate sporadically in organized criminal endeavors. Gang youths fourteen to fifteen years of age may engage part-time in drug peddling, often to augment family income. One gang leader led and encouraged younger gang members in violent intergang rivalries and shootings while simultaneously engaging in burglary, possession of stolen goods, and selling cocaine. In another instance, a local drug dealer employed a gang leader on a "contract" of $4,000 to kill a rival drug dealer.

Gangs and drug dealers have developed symbiotic relations in some inner-city slum neighborhoods where drug selling is rampant. Gang members provide protection for drug dealers and in return are paid well for running errands and performing other favors. Antagonisms between drug dealing and youth-gang membership may no longer be as serious as reported in the earlier literature; youth gangs may no longer chase dealers out of the neighborhood (New York City Youth Board 1960; Spergel 1964; see also Moore 1978).

There is some recent evidence, furthermore, that the youth gang/

drug symbiosis has progressed. Gang/drug trafficking integration may not be confined to inner-city or ghetto areas and to low-income residents. Taylor (1988, p. 27) speaks of a small group of "organized corporate gang members" thirteen to nineteen years of age. Some attend school regularly, and a few may do better than average academic work. He estimates that 30 percent come from middle-class and 2 percent from upper-class homes. The preponderant majority, 80 percent, said they did not use drugs. But all said their main objective in joining gangs was money. Their primary criminal operation was drug sales.

There is recent but spotty evidence that Asian youth gangs are more directly linked to organized crime than are black or Hispanic youth gangs. Chin states that "the emergence of Chinese street gangs is closely related to the Tongs . . . when members dropped out of schools and began to hang around street corners in the community, Tong leaders hired them to run errands for gamblers and to protect the gambling places from outsiders and the police" (1989, pp. 83–84). Furthermore, he observes the socialization sequence as follows: "In 1964, the first foreign-born Chinese gang known as the Wah Ching (Youth of China) was organized by young immigrants to protect themselves from American-born Chinese. . . . A year later, when the immigration laws were changed, the Wah Ching rapidly evolved into a powerful gang by recruiting members from the influx of new arrivals. . . . Later, Wah Ching members became the soldiers of the Hip Sing Tong. The gang converted itself from an ordinary street gang into the youth branch of the well-established adult organization" (1989, pp. 87–88).

A police official in California indicates that the Bamboo gang from Taipei "invited some of our young street gang members in and they organized and established [a local faction of] the Bamboo gang. . . . They remained in our city at that time laying out an organizational structure, areas of responsibility for all the crimes and in effect took control over certain types of racketeer activities in our city and in the surrounding cities" (President's Commission on Organized Crime 1985, p. 188).

A police official in the Miami Police Department recently reported that black and Hispanic street-gang leaders from Chicago and New York recently arrived to hold a convention and "have a good time." Relations between youth gangs in New York, Ohio, Florida, Illinois, and elsewhere were cemented. Discussions centered on drug distribution and increased contact with main suppliers, avoiding middle-level dealers to maximize profits (Wade 1987).

Johnson et al. (1990) suggests that New York City youth gangs have replaced existing basic institutions no longer able to perform legitimate socialization functions and are channeling youth into roles in a "criminal underclass economy": "The power of the crew lies in being highly structured at a time when other structures, once taken for granted (schools, family, traditional work), are either weak or transient. The crew recruits naturally aggressive youngsters, channels their energy into productive money-making work, accepts them into a group and provides a foundation where loyalty and honesty are rewarded."

One may speculate that a certain rough sequence of stages develops in the relation of law-violating youth groups, youth gangs, and criminal organizations. Deviant youths in lower-class communities often find their way into law-violating youth groups or cliques that may develop into youth gangs under conditions of population change, intense poverty, community disorganization, and social isolation. In due course, youth gangs may splinter and dissolve or lose their violent character when criminal opportunities, such as drug trafficking, and adult criminal organizational controls are imposed. If such controls are partial, the levels of individual violence may rise as gang violence decreases. Criminal market conditions then facilitate the development of law-violating youth groups and cliques as recruitment pools and distribution networks in preparation for the next sequence.

E. Prisons

Prison and street gangs are interrelated. In most states, prison gangs are outgrowths of street gangs, but there is some evidence that gangs formed in prison may also immigrate to the streets. The prison gang has been defined as a "close-knit and disruptive group of inmates organized around common affiliation for the purpose of mutual caretaking, solidarity, and profit-making criminal activity" (C. Camp and G. Camp 1988, p. 71). Of thirty-three state correctional systems reporting the presence of gangs, twenty-one indicated counterpart organizations in the streets of cities within the same states (G. Camp and C. Camp 1985). The leaders of the inmate gangs are usually individuals who held high reputation and influence on the streets.

The prison gangs of the 1970s may not be quite like the prison gangs of an earlier period. The earlier tradition of accommodation between inmate culture and prison administration appears no longer to be functioning well. Many of the prison gangs exist not as a response to the prison but to the streets. The power of prison gangs in recent decades appears to result both from urban social and economic breakdown and from the breakdown of the prison control system (Jacobs 1977).

Gang problems on Chicago's streets increased in the 1960s during a period of rapid social change and political instability. Mass jailing of gang leaders and members followed. The Chicago gangs gained a foothold in the Illinois prisons in the early 1970s. Some observers attribute contemporary gang problems in the Illinois prisons to a mistaken approach in the 1970s when certain prison administrators acknowledged the gangs as organizations and tried to work with them to maintain inmate control. Leaders were expected to keep order and in return were rewarded with special privileges and prestige. The result was "increased gang power and control as well as gang rivalries and violence" (C. Camp and G. Camp 1988, pp. 57–58).

The rise of prison gangs and disorders in the Washington State prisons has been attributed to the development of "the drug culture, civil disobedience as a result of the Vietnam War, black nationalism and the civil rights movement, increasing prison numbers, changes in political power, changes in the state corrections system, and rehabilitative prison reforms. . . . Unprecedented latitude was given to the prisoner population . . . organizations occupied physical space that was off limits to staff" (C. Camp and G. Camp 1988, pp. 59–60).

When prison officials recognize, legitimize, and collaborate formally with gangs, the result may be a short-term improvement in housekeeping routines but a long-term struggle among staff, administration, and gang leaders for power (G. Camp and C. Camp 1985). As on the street, the gang can serve as a residual source of quasi control and stability but with negative consequences for legitimate order and the long-term social adaptation of individual gang members.

The criminal activities of gangs in prison have a distinctive character. Money, drugs, and property represent important symbols of the gang's ability to control and exercise influence. The sense of ganghood is reflected in macho images, tattoos, special attire (G. Camp and C. Camp 1985), official titles, and sometimes even religious symbolism. The activities of prison gangs include "extortion, intimidation, drugs, gambling, strong-arm robbery and homosexual prostitution. . . . Violence has centered around enforcement of threats, discipline of members, and gang rivalry over turf. Gangs infiltrate strategic job assignments, bribe weak officers, and abuse visitation, programs, and commissaries to gain privileges, money and drugs" (C. Camp and G. Camp 1988, p. 57).

The special problems that confront prison administrators and staff include intimidation of weaker inmates; extortion that results from strong-arming; requests for protective custody; violence associated with gang activity; occasional conflicts between gangs (usually racial) that create disturbance; and contracted inmate murders (G. Camp and C. Camp 1985, pp. 46–55; see also Smith 1987). Discipline problems are far more severe among gang members than nongang members. Jacobs (1977) observes that disciplinary tickets were considerably higher for gang members, whether in segregated cells or not. Most depredations of gangs are not generally directed against prison officials but are related to "taking care of gang business."

Intergang conflict has assumed serious proportions both in prisons and in jails for many individuals not yet sentenced. According to the Los Angeles County Sheriff's Department (1985, p. 7), "In 1984 CRIPS were responsible for 25 percent of all robberies and 54 percent of felonious assaults reported in the Men's Central Jail. In just the first six months of 1985, the CRIPS and Bloods were responsible for 40 percent of the robberies and 61 percent of all felony assault cases there." A special unit of the Los Angeles County Sheriff's Department gang squad was assigned to duty within the jail.

VII.   Organized Responses to Gangs

There have been four basic strategies for dealing with youth gangs: local community organization or neighborhood mobilization; youth outreach or street gang work; social and economic opportunities provision; and gang suppression and incarceration. A possible fifth strategy, organizational development, sometimes accompanies the primary strategies. These developments include police gang units, specialized gang probation services, and hard-core gang crisis intervention programs. The strategies are sometimes intermixed. This discussion focuses primarily on youth work. No other strategy has been systematically assessed. Despite their popularity, we have no systematic evidence on suppression approaches.

Klein (1971) has described and analyzed traditional youth work programs. He attributes their continuing failure to a variety of program defects. There is confusion over goal priorities. Programs are usually not clear whether the central goal is control of gang fighting, treatment of individual problems, providing access to opportunities, value change, or prevention of delinquency (see also Spergel 1966). Gang programs tend to be atheoretical or "blandly eclectic" and produce "inconsistency, random or uncoordinated programming and uncertainty," making it difficult to determine what approach has been employed and indeed what constitutes success. Agencies and their workers seem to find values in activities for their own sake or for moral and fiscal accounting purposes—with little or no relation to delinquency, gang control, or prevention (Klein 1971, p. 53). This state of inadequate or "disorganized" program intervention has produced "extreme flexibility with respect to client targets, intervention techniques and theoretical" positions; extreme reliance on generalized counseling techniques and group programming with emphasis on club meetings, sports, dances, and camping trips. Klein suggests that the continued use of these approaches that consist mainly of value transformation, attitude change, or worker-client identification, despite repeated evaluations "which prove them worthless is enigmatic and suggests that a major function of gang control and prevention programs continues to be to sustain rather than solve the problem" (1971, p. 150).

Others have asserted the positive value of street-work approaches, generally without supporting data. For example, Cloward and Ohlin (1960) referred to two "successful" street-work projects—the New York City Youth Board Project and the Roxbury Project in Massachusetts: *The advent of the street-gang worker symbolized the end of social rejection and the beginning of social accommodation*" (Cloward and Ohlin 1960, p. 176). They also observed that "a successful street-gang program . . . is one in which detached workers can create channels to legitimate opportunity; where such channels cannot be opened up, the gang will temporize with violence only as long as a street worker maintains liaison with them" (1960, p. 177). In fact, the New York City Youth Board Project, the largest in the country and which endured for at least a dozen years, was never evaluated. Despite initial claims for the Roxbury Project's success, Miller (1962) in his full assessment concluded that delinquency was not reduced.

Short and Strodtbeck (1965, p. 197), observing YMCA detached workers, speculated that the presence of workers "makes less frequent the need for status maintaining aggression by [gang] leaders . . . the gang also recognizes its obligation to the worker as a *quid pro quo* for services performed by the worker and the additional status within the gang world that accrues to a gang by virtue of their having a worker." No data are provided to support these claims. Later, somewhat contradictorily, they note, "Whatever the effectiveness of the detached worker . . . it seems to arise from his monitoring of the flow of events, rather than his effectiveness in changing personality or values of gang boys" (1965, p. 270). The quid pro quo notion was tested a few years later in terms of the idea of "tightness" of worker/youth-gang member relationship, with negative results (Gold and Mattick 1974).

The Roxbury street-work project, in the late 1950s and early 1960s, included a comprehensive set of intervention components—community organization, family casework, detached work with gangs, organized group work, recreation, and job referral. An evaluation, using comparison groups and a variety of data sources, indicated no reductions in immoral, law-violating behavior or in court appearances; the project's impact was determined to be negligible (Miller 1962).

The Chicago Youth Development Project of the Chicago Boys' Club, conducted between 1960 and 1966, was based on the same assumptions as the New York City Youth Board (1960), Roxbury (Miller 1962), and Chicago YMCA detached worker (Short and Strodtbeck 1965) projects. The project emphasized "aggressive street work and community organization" and worked with groups rather than with individuals. Results indicated that the target areas continued to account for "more than" or "at least their share" of delinquency (Gold and Mattick 1974, p. 257) and failed to support a key expectation that an intensive worker-youth relationship ("tightness") was positively related to effective outcome. Rather, those youths who said they were closest to their workers were most often in trouble with the police (p. 189). Recreational programs were concluded to "accomplish little." A bright spot was that the project seemed significantly to raise educational aspirations of youths; there was measurable reduction in delinquency among those who were helped with their school adjustment (pp. 205, 265). Overall, the evaluators had a negative and pessimistic view: "Despite the successful efforts of the staff in finding jobs, returning school dropouts and intervening in formal legal processes, the youth unemployment rate remained at about the same level. The school drop-out rate increased slightly and the arrests of youngsters in the CYDP areas increased over time, with a lesser proportion of them being disposed of as station adjustments. . . . On balance, and in the final analysis, the 'experimental' population resident in the action areas of the CYDP seemed to be slightly worse off than the 'control' population resident in a similar area selected for comparative purposes" (Mattick 1984, pp. 296–97).

Yablonsky's (1962) project in the Morningside Heights area of New York City was established about the same time to control delinquency and gang activities; it was not formally evaluated. But Yablonsky's (1962, p. 53) observations are consistent with the findings of the analysts of other projects: "to direct the gang's energies into constructive channels such as baseball did not seem necessarily to change the Balkans and their patterns . . . working with them . . . to play baseball resulted mainly in bringing some additional 'baseball players' into the gang."

The Wincroft Youth Project in the United Kingdom also used an outreach approach; a variety of group and casework services were supplied by a large volunteer staff (Smith, Farrant, and Marchant 1972). While there was no overall reduction in delinquency rates, the younger youths fourteen and under with low maladjustment scores, who had not been convicted before, appeared to do best, possibly contrary to findings of some other projects (Smith, Farrant, and Marchant 1972).

The Los Angeles Group Guidance Project, a four-year detached worker effort under the auspices of the Los Angeles County Probation Department between 1961 and 1965, was similar to the Roxbury Project and emphasized group programming, including use of "parent clubs." A "transformational approach," that is, change of gang member values, attitudes, and perceptions through counseling and group activities was the key strategy. Klein (1968, pp. 291–92) concluded that the "project was clearly associated with a significant increase in delinquency among gang members." The gangs most intensively served did worst, and the delinquency increase was greatest at the lower age levels. He attributed much of the rise in delinquency to an increase in programming, especially group activities that may have increased gang cohesion and the commitment of younger youths, especially to delinquent patterns (Klein 1968).

Klein (1971) conducted a follow-up project to test the idea that a reduction in gang cohesion by reducing group programming and providing alternative individualized services would reduce delinquency. The project lasted eighteen months with a six-month follow-up period. He found that the overall amount of gang delinquency was reduced, but the delinquency rate of individual gang members remained unchanged. The size of the gang was reduced by completely stopping the entry of new members. Group cohesion was partially reduced. Klein viewed his project as promising but concluded that cohesion reduction was not sufficiently achieved, and therefore the hypothesis was not adequately tested (1971, pp. 301–7).

Other analysts have endorsed the strategy of attacking gang cohesion as a means to control and prevent gang delinquency. Yablonsky, for example, notes that the street worker can sometimes unintentionally provide services that give "a formerly amorphous collectivity structure and purpose," thereby increasing cohesion and delinquency (1962, p. 290). Lo, a Hong Kong social worker and researcher, recently suggested (1986) that gang subgroups should be kept apart and worked with as independent systems, especially avoiding communication and cooperation between younger and older members. "Some older gangsters . . . likely to grow out of delinquency" should be "accelerated" out of the gang, and "fringe gangsters, isolated members, 'scape-goats,' outcasts, and new members weaned away" (1986, pp. 94–97).

Group-work and value-transformation approaches, nevertheless, have persisted. The California Youth Authority mounted a three-year gang violence reduction project in the late 1970s, which was evaluated through 1981 and again for a follow-up three-year period, 1982–84 (Torres 1985). The project negotiated antagonisms between gangs to resolve feuds, provided positive group activities, particularly sports and recreation, and employed gang consultants, who were generally influential members of the gangs (Torres 1980). More recently, emphasis has shifted to prevention of youngsters joining gangs and to community improvement activities (Torres 1985, p. 1).

The reported results from the California Youth Authority project have been positive but also ambiguous and controversial. Claimed reductions in gang homicides, for example, may result from a decision to exclude from the analysis offenders and victims whose gang affiliations were unclear (Torres 1985, p. 8). There is also some dispute as to whether the declining trend of gang violent incidents began prior to the start of the project. The use of violent gang leaders as workers and the nature of their performance have been continuing sources of controversy (Berstein 1980).

The extreme case of use of the gang structure itself to prevent and control gang crime, especially violence, was the Youth Manpower Project of the Woodlawn Organization in Chicago, conducted for one year, 1967–68. The highly controversial million-dollar project was conceived by the Community Action Program of the U.S. Office of Economic Opportunity and was developed by a militant grass-roots organization in conflict with Mayor Daley's office. Its goals were manpower development, including job training and referral for jobs, reduction of gang violence, and reduction of the risk of riots. The project was staffed in part by leaders of two major gangs, the East Side Disciples and the Blackstone Rangers. Each gang was to control and staff two training centers. The professional supervising staff of four was too small to deal with both a gang staff of approximately thirty young adults and approximately 600 program participant youths sixteen to nineteen years and older.

The project stirred great community and political controversy. The police, local and national legislators, community agencies, and the news media took sides in praising or condemning the project. The program was shut down. Key gang members were charged and successfully prosecuted for fraud by the U.S. Attorney's office. The available aggregate outcome data indicated that there was a decline in crime generally in the community during the project period but a rise in aggravated battery and gang homicides. There was no evidence of abatement of gang conflict or success in job training or placement (Spergel et al. 1969; Spergel 1972). The two major gangs served by the project survive and thrive twenty years later—more violent, criminal, and notorious than ever.

Gang-staffed community development projects in the late 1960s and early 1970s were part of a national grass-roots movement. Especially noteworthy programs were established in New York, Philadelphia, Los Angeles, and Chicago. Gang leaders or ex-convicts with gang background were involved in social agency programs, manpower development, housing rehabilitation, and even community planning and economic development. An attempt was also made to develop a national association of youth gang organizations called Youth Organizations United (Poston 1971). No systematic evaluation or comparative analysis of these programs exists. A variety of anecdotal reports indicates that sooner or later all of them foundered. The programs were not conceptually well developed; they were poorly administered, and malfeasance occurred (Poston 1971). Kahn and Zinn (1978, pp. 59–63) report that ex-convict gang members took over some of the programs. "Gangs, especially Mexican Mafia, have infiltrated drug treatment and other social programs, [and] committed bank robberies in Los Angeles, starting in the early 1970s."

G. Camp and C. Camp (1985) describe a government-funded project in 1976 that relied heavily on gang structure to carry out a service and community development program. A key objective was to help ex-convicts—mainly gang members—"to readjust to living in society." Funds were apparently misappropriated for vehicles used in gang homicides and in the purchase of heroin before the project was finally investigated and shut down (1985, p. 98). In these projects, it should be noted that traditional youth-work programming had shifted in focus from juveniles to older adolescents and young adults.

Interest and faith in generalized outreach and coordinated social services for gang youth did not die easily. Just prior to the prototype Crisis Intervention Network program in Philadelphia, a series of outreach social service efforts was attempted. Youths, many of them from gangs, were recruited from the streets and enrolled or referred to counseling, educational, and employment programs. The premise of one of these programs in Philadelphia was that adequate delivery of services would be sufficient to curtail violent gang disruption by providing alternative incentives and activities (Royster 1974). Evaluators concluded, however, that such highly individualized service referral programs were "not effective." Gang homicides rose. Services to youth did not improve. Failure of the program was laid to "poor management techniques, lack of visibility in the community, a lack of ability on the part of workers to deliver services" (Royster 1974, pp. 4–17).

Unique to the Crisis Intervention Network program, as it evolved in Philadelphia, was the integration of a probation unit into the street work program to provide control or supervision services to older influential gang members. Street workers and probation officers worked hand in hand. A variety of mothers' groups and grass-roots organizations were also closely involved in crisis control, community education, and mediation activities. While a formal evaluation has not been conducted, police data suggested a substantial continuing reduction in gang incidents and especially gang homicides since 1974 (Needle and Stapleton 1983, p. 81). Some questions remain, however, whether the decline may have begun prior to the initiation of the program. The adequacy of gang-incident reporting by the Philadelphia police since 1973–74 has also been questioned. A significant decline of the gang problem in Philadelphia in the past decade or more also seems to be correlated with other community organization activities.

A unique program in Philadelphia coexisting with the Crisis Intervention Network has been UMOJA, a resident and nonresident program for gang and other delinquent youth that creates "a sanctuary, a sheltered environment." The program requires adherence to strict house rules and a signed contract. Individual counseling, assistance with educational development, job development, and help with personal problems are provided to each youth. The program is comprehensive and addresses health and recreational needs. The basic and unique aspect of UMOJA is its fostering of a "sense of togetherness and group unity imparting the values inherent in African culture" (Fattah 1987).

Earlier, UMOJA was successful in its employment of a gang-mediation or gang-summit strategy, particularly as it mobilized and involved all sectors of the community. "UMOJA . . . called for a summit meeting on gang matters . . . 75 percent of the gangs responded. Over 500 members . . . were in attendance, along with social workers, ministers, police, teachers, and other interested persons. The meeting produced a 60-day truce in which no one died from gang warfare" (Fattah 1987, p. 39). The summit was preceded by visits to gang members in prison throughout the state "to solicit their support." "No gang war posters became the symbol of a city-wide campaign in which state and city authorities as well as businesses participated. Continued peace meetings were held in schools, police stations, and campsites throughout the year 1974. Young people apparently responded massively and positively" (Fattah 1988).

While these anecdotal and news media reports indicate a high degree of success in this comprehensive program, no systematic evaluation of UMOJA is yet available. A replication was under way in Wilmington, Delaware, through the Juvenile Education Awareness Program.

Gang "summits" or mediation meetings continue to be tried on a more limited basis in a variety of contexts with mixed results. Sometimes they appear to succeed for a brief period. One knowledgeable law-enforcement gang expert states, "From time to time, these 'accords' have averted intergang turmoil, but there hasn't been a peace treaty to date that can prohibit the disorder that breaks out when a gang leader summons his 'boys' to retaliate against any foe who offends him, or dishonors the gang" (Collins 1979, p. 64). Further, many gang analysts and practitioners subscribe to Haskell and Yablonsky's (1982, p. 457) statement that "violent gangs should not be treated by any official community program as a 'legitimate' societal structure." Giving such credence to an illegitimate structure feeds gang leader megalomania and legitimizes the possibility of further violence.

Whether the activities of the Crisis Intervention Network, the efforts of other community organizations or agencies, special police task forces, or indeed alternate criminal opportunities, especially drug trafficking, were primarily responsible for the reduction in gang violence in Philadelphia remains unclear. A major decline in gang activity reportedly occurred in New York City at about the same time without benefit of special crisis intervention programs or community efforts.

Support for a crisis intervention approach with strong deterrent and community involvement characteristics arises from a recent brief experiment in Humboldt Park, an extremely violent gang-ridden community of Chicago. Ecological and individual level analyses indicated that the program exercised significant control of violent gang activity in comparison with three other similar parts of the city but had little effect on nongang crime. The effectiveness of the program appeared more evident for juveniles than young adults (Spergel 1986). Other contemporary crisis intervention programs in Los Angeles and Chicago have apparently not fared as well as the early Philadelphia program, in part possibly because they de-emphasized or even replaced the combined deterrence, community involvement, and crisis intervention strategy with the older generalized social services gang prevention, value transformation, or group work model (see Klein and Maxson 1989).

A recent street-work program in San Diego that emphasized counseling and job referral and worked through existing gang structures seemed to be successful. Gang-related felonies decreased by 39 percent in the target area over two one-year periods. However, such crimes were also reduced by 38 percent in the control area. Furthermore, it should be noted that while the street-work program was in operation, the probation department and the district attorney's office were concentrating on gang crime. It is not clear what the separate effects of the detached worker program were in comparison to the effects of law enforcement. The gang problem appeared to abate in San Diego in the early 1980s (Pennell 1983). However, the gang and drug problem again grew more serious in the middle and late 1980s, and stronger deterrent approaches are now in progress in this city.

With broadening concern about youth-gang problems in many parts of the country, there remains a strong focus on group and individual counseling with younger youth, coupled with stronger emphasis by law enforcement, probation, and parole agencies on older youths. This may reflect an evolving division of labor in which service agencies deal with younger peripheral gang youths and the established control agencies deal with the older core gang members. This is clearly apparent in the current strategies of the Los Angeles and Chicago crisis intervention programs. The effectiveness of such division of labor remains to be demonstrated.

Gottfredson (1987) recently reviewed the results of a series of experiments on peer group or counseling approaches in schools and community agencies and concluded that they lend "no support to any claim of benefit of treatment, with the possible exception that the treatment may enhance internal control for elementary school students. For the high school students, the effects appear predominantly harmful." He concluded that "it may be useful to avoid delinquent peer interaction entirely rather than to attempt to modify its nature" (Gottfredson 1987, p. 710). Community-based peer group experiences seem to be somewhat successful when small group activities integrate a limited number of delinquent or predelinquent youth into small groups dominated by conventional youth and guided by conventional youth leaders (Feldman, Caplinger, and Wodarski 1983).

Individual counseling approaches with gang youths, where evaluated, have also produced poor results. The individual gang member seems to be more strongly influenced in what he does, rather than in what he says in individual counseling sessions, by gang norms and gang pressures (Short and Strodtbeck 1965). Caplan (1968, pp. 84–85) reported that "over time individual subjects repeatedly demonstrate a tendency to *nearly* succeed in adopting final change behaviors advocated by the treatment plan . . . remotivation remains a major hurdle to overcome in reorienting the activities of urban [gang] youth."

In sum, youth-work programs, whether agency based, street work, or in some cases crisis intervention, continue to emphasize traditional approaches that have served often to worsen the youth-gang problem. There are, however, some glimmers of hope when comprehensive approaches have been tried. Multiple-agency service approaches, including value transformation, deterrent, and supervisory strategies, and closely integrated with community involvement and targeted on younger gang youth, may be promising.

I know of no analysis or evaluation of a primary deterrent strategy, that is, a police suppression or incarceration approach to gang delinquency or crime. Police sweeps and sentence "enhancements" for gang offenders are being tried in California, with no evidence yet of a reduction of gang violence. A process evaluation was conducted of the vertical prosecution or "hard-core gang prosecution" program of the Los Angeles County District Attorney's office. Under vertical prosecution, one prosecutor, rather than a shifting array of prosecutors, handles a case from its inception until its disposition.

An evaluation of the Los Angeles County vertical prosecution unit found an increase in conviction rates to 95 percent compared to a preprogram rate of 71 percent and compared to a rate of 78 percent for contemporaneous nonvertical prosecutions. There was a substantial increase in trial conviction and incarceration rates (Dahmann 1983). Comparable achievements have been described in Cook County (Daley 1985). Bruce Coplen, supervisor of the gang unit, Los Angeles City Attorney's Office, claims a 33 percent reduction in gang crime in the Cadillac Corning neighborhood after aggressive use of nuisance-abatement laws, compared with other areas of Los Angeles (Coplen 1988). This claim has been disputed, and there has been no comparable reduction of gang crime through use of the procedure elsewhere in Los Angeles. Also, it should be noted that a relatively small number of gang offenders are subjected to vertical prosecution. While over 71,000 gang members were arrested in California counties with a prosecution unit in fiscal year 1986/87, only 546 defendants were vertically prosecuted. The large majority of gang arrestees were probably accused of minor offenses (Office of Criminal Justice Planning 1987, pp. 17–18).

Some school systems are experimenting with programs for elementary grade students on the dangers of gang activity. "The Alternatives to Gang Membership" curriculum of the City of Paramount, Los Angeles County, provides comic books, posters, and discussion opportunities for students and sponsors neighborhood meetings led by bilingual leaders. Informal counseling of individual youth who appear to be at special risk is also carried out. The fifth-grade antigang curriculum introduced in the Paramount Unified School District in 1982 emphasized constructive youth activities to be carried out in the neighborhood.

At least fifteen other cities in California have developed school gang diversion programs modelled after the Paramount plan. For example, the Santa Ana Council recently approved a school antigang program "aimed at students in fourth, fifth, or sixth grades. Students will receive weekly one-hour lessons on gangs intended to counteract the 'glamorizing' they may be offered by older students already in gangs" (Schwartz 1988).

Few evaluations of school antigang programs have been conducted, and the results thus far are ambiguous, mainly because of the incompleteness or inadequacy of the research. The findings of Paramount's "Alternatives to Gang Membership" program, based on questionnaire responses, are that attitudes of elementary and middle school children about gangs can be changed in a positive direction after exposure to the curriculum. The program is not directed primarily to current gang members but to marginal or peripheral younger youth. Where the program has been offered, according to one set of news accounts, the number of active gang members has dropped from 1,000 to 200 since 1981. According to other reports, there has been an increase in gang cases known to the Paramount police from 286 in 1986 to 396 in 1987 (Schwartz 1988; Donovan 1988).

A variety of prevention, early intervention, limited job placement, aftercare, collaborative agency, comprehensive community, vertical probation, and integrated suppression approaches across criminal justice units are also currently being tried, with little prospect of evaluation or research. However, the Office of Juvenile Justice and Delinquency Prevention, U.S. Justice Department, and the Administration for Children, Youth, and Families, Office of Human Development Services, U.S. Department of Health and Human Services, have recently initiated research and development and drug-juvenile gang intervention programs, respectively, which may provide further insight into the nature of the youth-gang problem and how effectively to cope with it.

VIII.   Conclusions and Policy Implications

The youth-gang problem has increased in scope and severity in recent years. Youth gangs are reported to exist in areas where they did not exist, and, in many places, their behavior is more serious and noticeable than before. Violence and criminal activity, especially relating to drug trafficking, has escalated.

Increasing numbers of youths and young adults in certain communities have developed alternate social, cultural, and economic subsystems to meet common human needs in an increasingly complex urban society. Gang systems or subsocieties have become increasingly costly and difficult to modify or eliminate.

Interactions between poverty and social disorganization seem to be conducive to the most troubling forms of youth-gang structure and activity. These general conditions may be activated through the presence of weak social institutions, such as family and school, and by the inadequacy of training and legitimate job opportunities. It is not entirely clear why certain cities, low-income communities, and social contexts suffer from youth-gang problems while others do not. It is possible that other, better forms of social control, whether formal or informal, are present or that alternative illegitimate opportunity systems are now available in these areas and social contexts. Social disorganization is indicated by the development of social situations where social controls are inadequate. The failure of subunits of a system to be adequately integrated in terms of norms and relationships, whether at family, school, prison, or neighborhood level, appears to be distinctively conducive to youth-gang problems in poverty sectors or neighborhoods. The single most important antecedent factor to social disorganization appears to be substantial population movement and change, especially the immigration of low-income, minority, or ethnic or cultural groups to an area.

At this stage of the development of approaches to control and reduction of the gang problem, recommended policies may be briefly summarized as follows.

Definition. Efforts should be made both to recognize the gang problem where it exists and to avoid excessive labeling. Delinquent youth groups should be defined as "gangs" when they maintain a high profile, and engage in serious violence and crime, and when their primary reason for existence is symbolic or communal rather than economic gain. Drug trafficking or criminal gain organizations per se should not ordinarily be considered youth gangs. The definition of the "gang incident" should be based on gang function, motivation, or particular circumstances, not gang membership alone; otherwise there are few limits to what is classified as gang related. A gang incident therefore should be any illegal act that arises out of gang motivation or gang-related circumstances. This is not to deny that nongang motivated crimes of gang youths should be closely monitored and documented, but they need to be distinguished in order to more accurately assess the scope of the problem and also to avoid development of a "gang-fighting industry."

Targeting Gang Youth. Youths who give clear indication of gang involvement should be the primary targets of early intervention and comprehensive gang-control programs. A relatively small number of such youths probably should be targeted for special intensive, remedial, and supervisory attention. The tendency to identify at-risk youths without clear criteria of potential gang membership should be avoided. Preventive programs should be directed primarily at changing social, economic, and organizational circumstances, particularly in large low-income and disorganized communities that are conducive to gang formation.

Comprehensive Approach. The importance of community disorganization and lack of opportunities should guide the development of strategies to deal with the gang problem, especially in chronic gang-problem cities.

A special coordinative body or even a local authority, perhaps with special statutory powers, comprising public and voluntary agencies and community organizations, should be established to integrate efforts by police, prosecutors, judges, correction officials, parole, and probation, with support from schools, key voluntary agencies, businesses, and local community groups. A more informal collaborative strategy may suffice in emerging gang problem communities and cities.

Leadership of such a comprehensive community effort, particularly in a chronic gang problem city or community, should probably be in an official agency with a tradition of rehabilitation, community education and involvement, and offender supervision, possibly a probation, parole, or law-enforcement agency. A strategy of social control, including suppression, social support, community mobilization, and social opportunities, should guide the development of program activities and the roles of various personnel. The strategy should be directed at both core and fringe gang members.

The police department should expand its gang unit/juvenile division structures to incorporate sophisticated intelligence, community prevention, social support (including counseling, social and vocational referrals), community development, and criminal justice coordination strategies. Functions of both deterrence of gang behavior and social reintegration of gang offenders into the community should be carried out. A community policing strategy is required.

Schools, social agencies, and community groups should give first priority to juveniles and adolescents and second priority to older adolescent and young-adult gang members in collaboration with law-enforcement and other criminal justice agencies in gang-program development. An authoritative as well as community support character should be integrated into the various social, educational, and vocational programs that are developed, preferably on a long-term basis.

Special training and job-opportunity programs should be made available to older adolescent and adult gang members likely to leave the gang under structured and supervised conditions to the extent possible within a normalized business and community-development framework. Criteria for the selection of older youth with likely prospects or at "good risk" of leaving the gang will have to be determined. These new training and job-development structures should be closely connected to or integrated into the justice system.

Early Intervention Approach.   Ideas of both personal and community disorganization should guide the development of strategies to deal with the emergence of the gang problem in certain schools, neighborhoods, correctional institutions, and other contexts.

Ideally, a special local educational administrative unit, in collaboration with law enforcement, courts, social agencies, and community groups, should take responsibility for the development of programs directed to social education and social control of youths, especially those between ten and fifteen years, in the middle grades who are beginning to take on gang roles and are already engaged in law-violating behaviors.

Special efforts must be developed to improve the academic performance of targeted youths. This should include not only tutorial assistance and remediation but also outreach parent educational counseling and teacher education focused on the special needs, supports, and controls required for these youths.

All youths in middle grades in gang neighborhoods should, nevertheless, be provided with some instruction on how to avoid gang membership and how to develop conflict resolution skills. Teachers, with the assistance of law-enforcement personnel, should take special responsibility for social education.

Elementary and middle schools at risk in high-gang-crime neighborhoods should be responsible for the development of school-community advisory groups and crisis-intervention programs to control the influence of older youths in gangs on middle school youths, to protect nongang youths in the pursuit of an effective education, and to mobilize local school-parent-community groups to control and reduce the gang problem.

The notions of social control, social and economic opportunities, and institution building should underlie policies for dealing with youth-gang problems. Social control minimally includes two interrelated components, *coercive* controls that use or employ legal force and *persuasive* controls exercised by social development agents to encourage individual self-regulation and self-actualization (Mayer 1983; Dahrendorf 1985). The intertwining elements of social support and opportunity and close supervision should guide the reconstruction of existing institutions and the formulation of new arrangements to forestall the need for and development of youth gangs. However, a community or institution level approach to the problem cannot succeed without adequate central government provision of resources in support of appropriate social and criminal justice policies.

REFERENCES

Allen, Robert. 1981. "Discussion: The Youth's Experience." In *Youth Crime and Urban Policy*, edited by Robert L. Woodson. Washington, D.C.: American Enterprise Institute for Public Policy Research.

Anti-Defamation League. 1986. "Extremism Targets the Prisons." A special report. New York: Anti-Defamation League of B'nai B'rith, Civil Rights Division.

———. 1987. " 'Shaved' for Battle: Skinheads Target America's Youth." A special report. New York: Anti-Defamation League of B'nai B'rith, Civil Rights Division.

Arlacchi, Pino. 1986. *Mafia Business*. London: Verso.

Asbury, Herbert. 1971. *Gangs of New York: An Informal History of the Underworld*. New York: Putnam. (Originally published 1927. New York: Knopf.)

Baca, Chris. 1988. "Juvenile Gangs in Albuquerque." Coordinating council meeting, Office of Juvenile Justice and Delinquency Prevention, Washington, D.C., June.

Baker, Bob. 1988a. "Gang Murder Rates Get Worse." *Los Angeles Times* (April 10).

———. 1988b. "Tough Boss Shows Gang Members New Way of Life." *Los Angeles Times* (April 15).

Beavers, Gerald. 1988. Personal communication. National Youth Gang Suppression and Intervention Project. School of Social Service Administration, University of Chicago, September.

Bell, Daniel. 1953. "Crime as an American Way of Life." *Antioch Review* 13:131–54.

Bernstein, Dan. 1980. "East L.A.'s Gang Project." *Corrections Magazine* 6:36–42.

Bernstein, Saul. 1964. *Youth on the Streets: Work with Alienated Youth Groups*. New York: Association Press.

Berntsen, Karen. 1979. "A Copenhagen Youth Gang: A Descriptive Analysis." In *New Paths in Criminology*, edited by Sarnoff A. Mednick, S. Giora Shoham, and Barbara Phillips. Lexington, Mass.: Lexington Books.

Bloch, H. A., and A. Niederhoffer. 1958. *The Gang*. New York: Philosophical Library.

Block, Carolyn B. 1985. *Lethal Violence in Chicago over Seventeen Years: Homicides Known to the Police, 1965–1981*. Chicago: Illinois Criminal Justice Information Authority, Statistical Analysis Center.

Bobrowski, Lawrence J. 1988. "Collecting, Organizing and Reporting Street Gang Crime." Special Functions Group, Chicago Police Department, Chicago. Mimeographed.

Bowker, Lee H., Helen Shimota Gross, and Malcolm W. Klein. 1980. "Female Participation in Delinquent Gang Activity." *Adolescence* 15:509–19.

Breen, Lawrence, and Martin M. Allen. 1983. "Gang Behavior: Psychological and Law Enforcement Implications." *FBI Law Enforcement Bulletin* 52(2): 19–24.

Brown, Waln K. 1977. "Black Female Gangs in Philadelphia." *International Journal of Offender Therapy and Comparative Criminology* 21(3):221–28.

California Council on Criminal Justice. 1986. *State Task Force on Youth Gang Violence*. Sacramento: California Council on Criminal Justice.

Caltabriano, Michael L. 1981. "National Prison Gang Study." Unpublished report to the Federal Bureau of Prisons, August. Quoted in *Prison Gangs: Their Extent, Nature and Impact on Prisons*, edited by George M. Camp and Camille Graham Camp. Washington, D.C.: U.S. Government Printing Office, July 1985.

Camp, George M., and Camille Graham Camp. 1985. *Prison Gangs: Their Extent, Nature and Impact on Prisons*. Washington, D.C.: U.S. Government Printing Office.

Camp, Camille Graham, and George M. Camp. 1988. *Management Strategies for Combatting Prison Gang Violence*. South Salem, N.Y.: Criminal Justice Institute.

Campbell, Anne. 1984*a*. "Girls' Talk: The Social Representation of Aggression by Female Gang Members." *Criminal Justice and Behavior* 1:139–56.

———. 1984*b*. *The Girls in the Gang*. Oxford: Blackwell.

Caplan, Nathan S. 1968. "Treatment Intervention and Reciprocal Interaction Effects." *Journal of Social Issues* 24:63–88.

Cartwright, Desmond S., and Kenneth I. Howard. 1966. "Multivariate Analysis of Gang Delinquency: I. Ecological Influence." *Multivariate Behavioral Research* 1(3):321–37.

Cartwright, Desmond S., Kenneth I. Howard, and Nicholas A. Reuterman. 1970. "Multivariate Analysis of Gang Delinquency: II. Structural and Dynamic Properties of Gangs." *Multivariate Behavioral Research* 5(3):303–23.

Cartwright, Desmond S., Barbara Tomson, and Hershey Schwartz. 1975. *Gang Delinquency*. Monterey, Calif.: Brooks/Cole.

Chein, I., D. L. Gerard, R. S. Lee, and E. Rosenfeld. 1964. *The Road to H: Narcotics, Delinquency, and Social Policy*. New York: Basic.

Chicago Board of Education. 1981. "The Chicago Safe School Study." A report to the General Superintendent of Schools, Chicago.

Chin, Ko-Lin. 1989. "Triad Subculture and Criminality: A Study of Triads, Tongs, and Chinese Gangs." New York City Criminal Justice Agency, New York. Unpublished.

Cloward, Richard A., and Lloyd E. Ohlin. 1960. *Delinquency and Opportunity: A Theory of Delinquent Gangs*. Glencoe, Ill.: Free Press.

Cohen, Albert K. 1955. *Delinquent Boys: The Culture of the Gang*. Glencoe, Ill.: Free Press.

Cohen, Albert K., and James F. Short, Jr. 1958. "Research in Delinquent Subcultures." *Journal of Social Issues* 14(3):20–37.

Cohen, Bernard. 1969*a*. "The Delinquency of Gangs and Spontaneous Groups." In *Delinquency: Selected Studies*, edited by Thorsten Sellin and Marvin E. Wolfgang. New York: Wiley.

———. 1969*b*. "Internecine Conflict: The Offender." In *Delinquency: Selected Studies*, edited by Thorsten Sellin and Marvin E. Wolfgang. New York: Wiley.

Cohen, Stanley. 1972. *Folk Devils and Moral Panics*. London: MacGibbon & Kee.

Collins, H. Craig. 1979. *Street Gangs: Profiles for Police.* New York: New York City Police Department.

Commission de Police du Québec. 1980. *Motorcycle Gangs in Quebec.* Québec: Ministère des Communications.

Coplen, Bruce R. 1988. "Interview." National Youth Gang Suppression and Intervention Project. School of Social Service Administration, University of Chicago.

Coplon, Jeff. 1988. "Skinhead Nation." *Rolling Stone* 540:54–62, 65, 94.

Curry, G. David, and Irving A. Spergel. 1988. "Gang Homicide, Delinquency and Community." *Criminology* 26:381–405.

Dahmann, Judith S. 1983. *An Evaluation of Operation Hardcore: A Prosecutorial Response to Violent Gang Criminality.* Alexandria, Va.: Mitre Corp.

Dahrendorf, Rolf. 1985. "Law and Order." *Hamlyn Lectures.* London: Stevens.

Daley, Richard M. 1985. *Gang Prosecutions Unit.* Chicago: Cook County State's Attorney's Office.

Davidson, John L. 1987. "Juvenile Gang Drug Program." Grant Proposal to Office of Criminal Justice Planning, Sacramento, California, September.

Davis, Roger H. 1982*a*. "Outlaw Motorcyclists: A Problem for Police (Part 1)." *FBI Law Enforcement Bulletin* 51(10):12–17.

———. 1982*b*. "Outlaw Motorcyclists: A Problem for Police (Part 2)." *FBI Law Enforcement Bulletin* 51(11):16–22.

Deukmejian, George. 1981. *Report on Youth Gang Violence in California.* Sacramento: State of California, Department of Justice.

DeVos, George A., Hiroshi Wagatasuma, William Caudill, and Keiichi Mizushima. 1973. *Socialization for Achievement: Essays on the Cultural Psychology of the Japanese.* Berkeley: University of California Press.

Dinitz, Simon, and C. Ronald Huff. 1988. *The Figgie Report. Part VI: The Resources of Crime: The Criminal Perspective.* Richmond, Va.: Figgie International.

Dolan, Edward F., Jr., and Shan Finney. 1984. *Youth Gangs.* New York: Julian Messner.

Donovan, John. 1988. "An Introduction to Street Gangs." A paper prepared for Senator John Garamendi's Office, Sacramento, California, August.

Downes, David M. 1966. *The Delinquent Solution.* New York: Free Press.

Drug Enforcement Administration. 1988. *Crack Cocaine Availability and Trafficking in the United States.* Washington, D.C.: U.S. Department of Justice, Drug Enforcement Administration, Cocaine Investigation Sector.

Duran, Miguel. 1987. "Specialized Gang Supervision Program Progress Report." Los Angeles County Probation Department, Los Angeles.

Elliott, Delbert S., David Huizinga, and Suzanne S. Ageton. 1985. *Explaining Delinquency and Drug Use.* Beverly Hills, Calif.: Sage.

Erickson, Maynard L., and Gary F. Jensen. 1977. " 'Delinquency Is Still Group Behavior!': Toward Revitalizing the Group Premise in the Sociology of Deviance." *Journal of Criminal Law and Criminology* 68:262–73.

Fagan, Jeffrey. 1988. "The Social Organization of Drug Use and Drug Dealing among Urban Gangs." John Jay College of Criminal Justice, New York. Mimeographed.

Fagan, Jeffrey, Elizabeth Piper, and Melinda Moore. 1986. "Violent Delinquents and Urban Youths." *Criminology* 24:439–71.

Farrington, David P., Leonard Berkowitz, and Donald J. West. 1982. "Differences between Individual and Group Fights." *British Journal of Social Psychology* 21:323–33.

Fattah, David. 1987. "The House of UMOJA as a Case Study for Social Change." *Annals of the American Academy of Political and Social Science* 494 (November):37–41.

Fattah, Sister Falaka. 1988. "Youth and Violence: The Current Crisis." Written statement. The Select Committee on Children, Youth and Families, U.S. House of Representatives, Washington, D.C. Mimeographed.

Federal Register. 1987. "Juvenile Gang Suppression and Intervention Program." 52(133):26254–59.

Feldman, Ronald A., Timothy E. Caplinger, and John S. Wodarski. 1983. *The St. Louis Conundrum: The Effective Treatment of Anti-social Youths.* Englewood Cliffs, N.J.: Prentice-Hall.

Frazier, Michael. 1988. "Statement about Gangs in Phoenix, Arizona." Coordinating Council Meeting. Office of Juvenile Justice and Delinquency Prevention, Washington, D.C., June.

Friedman, C. Jack, Frederica Mann, and Howard Adelman. 1976. "Juvenile Street Gangs: The Victimization of Youth." *Adolescence* 11(44):527–33.

Friedman, C. Jack, Frederica Mann, and Alfred S. Friedman. 1975. "A Profile of Juvenile Street Gang Members." *Adolescence* 10(40):563–607.

Galea, John. 1982. "Youth Gangs of New York." In *Aggression and Violence*, edited by Peter Marsh and Anne Campbell. New York: St. Martin's.

———. 1988. Personal communication with author, September 22.

———. 1989. "Gang Activity in New York City." *Youth Gang Intelligence Unit 1988 Annual Report.* New York: New York Police Department.

Genelin, Michael. 1989. *Los Angeles Street Gangs.* Report and recommendations of the countywide Criminal Justice Coordination Committee. Los Angeles: Inter-agency Gang Task Force.

Gerrard, Nathan L. 1964. "The Core Member of the Gang." *British Journal of Criminology* 4:361–71.

Giordano, Peggy C. 1978. "Girls, Guys and Gangs: The Changing Social Context of Female Delinquency." *Journal of Criminal Law and Criminology* 69:126–32.

Gold, Martin. 1987. "Social Ecology." In *Handbook of Juvenile Delinquency*, edited by Herbert C. Quay. New York: Wiley.

Gold, Martin, and Hans W. Mattick. 1974. *Experiment in the Streets: The Chicago Youth Development Project.* Ann Arbor: University of Michigan, Institute for Social Research.

Gordon, Robert A. 1967. "Social Levels, Social Disability, and Gang Interaction." *American Journal of Sociology* 1(73):42–62.

Gott, Ray. 1988. "Statement." Coordinating Council Meeting. Office of Juvenile Justice and Delinquency Prevention, U.S. Department of Justice, Washington, D.C., June.

Gottfredson, Gary D. 1987. "Peer Group Interventions to Reduce the Risk of

Delinquent Behavior: A Selective Review and A New Evaluation." *Criminology* 25:671–714.

Gottfredson, Gary D., and Denise C. Gottfredson. 1985. *Victimization in Schools*. New York: Plenum.

Gottfredson, Gary, Denise Gottfredson, and Michael S. Cook, eds. 1983. *School Action Effectiveness Study*. Second interim report, pt. 1. Baltimore: Johns Hopkins University.

Hagedorn, John. 1988. *People and Folks: Gangs, Crime and the Underclass in a Rust Belt City*. Chicago: Lake View Press.

Hagedorn, John, Perry Macon, and Joan Moore. 1986. "Final Report, Milwaukee Gang Research Project." Urban Research Center, University of Wisconsin—Milwaukee, December.

Hargreaves, David H. 1967. *Social Relations in a Secondary School*. New York: Routledge & Kegan Paul.

Hargrove, Sergeant James. 1981. "Discussion: The Youths' Experiences." In *Youth Crime and Urban Policy*, edited by Robert L. Woodson. Washington, D.C.: American Enterprise Institute for Public Policy Research.

Haskell, Martin R. 1960. "Toward a Reference Group Theory of Juvenile Delinquency." *Social Problems* 8:219–30.

Haskell, Martin R., and Lewis Yablonsky. 1982. *Juvenile Delinquency*, 3d ed. Boston: Houghton Mifflin.

Hayes, Ronald. 1983. Testimony before U.S. Senate Subcommittee on Juvenile Justice on Gang Violence and Control. Committee on the Judiciary, 98th Congress, 1st Session.

Hinshaw, Dwayne. 1988. Personal communication. National Youth Gang Suppression and Intervention Project. School of Social Service Administration, University of Chicago, Chicago.

Hollopeter, Clayton. 1988. Personal communication. National Youth Gang Suppression and Intervention Project. School of Social Service Administration, University of Chicago, Chicago.

Horowitz, Ruth. 1983. *Honor and the American Dream*. New Brunswick, N.J.: Rutgers University Press.

Howenstein, G. Albert, Jr. 1988. "From the Executive Director." *Newsletter* 3(2):1. Sacramento, Calif.: Office of Criminal Justice Planning.

Huff, C. Ronald. 1988. "Conference Summary." Ohio Conference on Youth Gangs and the Urban Under Class, Ohio State University, Columbus, May 25.

Hyman, Irwin A. 1984. Testimony before the Subcommittee on Elementary, Secondary, and Vocational Education of the Committee on Education and Labor, U.S. House of Representatives.

Ianni, Francis A. J. 1974. *Black Mafia*. New York: Simon & Schuster.

Jackson, Robert K., and Wesley D. McBride. 1985. *Understanding Street Gangs*. Costa Mesa, Calif.: Custom Publishing.

Jacobs, James B. 1974. "Street Gangs behind Bars." *Social Problems* 24:395–409.

———. 1977. *Stateville: The Penitentiary in Mass Society*. Chicago: University of Chicago Press.

Jansyn, Leon R., Jr. 1966. "Solidarity and Delinquency in a Street Corner Group." *American Sociological Review* 31(5):600–614.

Joe, Delbert, and Norman Robinson. 1978. "Chinese Youth Gangs: An Investigation of Their Origins and Activities in Vancouver Schools." Paper presented at the annual conference of the American Educational Research Association, Toronto, March.

———. 1980. "Chinatown's Immigrant Gangs." *Criminology* 18:337–45.

Johnson, Bruce D., Terry Williams, Kojo Dei, and Harry Sanabria. 1990. "Drug Abuse in the Inner City: Impact on Hard Drug Users and the Community." In *Drugs and Crime*, edited by Michael Tonry and James Q. Wilson. Vol. 13 of *Crime and Justice: A Review of Research*, edited by Michael Tonry and Norval Morris. Chicago: University of Chicago Press (forthcoming).

Johnstone, John W. C. 1981. "Youth Gangs and Black Suburbs." *Pacific Sociological Review* 24(3):355–75.

Kahn, Brian, and R. Neil Zinn. 1978. *Prison Gangs in the Community: A Briefing Document for the Board of Corrections*. Sacramento, Calif.: Department of Corrections.

Klein, Malcolm W. 1968. *From Association to Guilt: The Group Guidance Project in Juvenile Gang Intervention*. Los Angeles: University of Southern California, Youth Studies Center, and the Los Angeles County Probation Department.

———. 1969. "Violence in American Juvenile Gangs." In *Crimes of Violence*, vol. 13, edited by Donald J. Mulvihill, Melvin M. Tumin, and Lynn A. Curtis. U.S. National Commission on the Causes and Prevention of Violence, Task Force on Individual Acts of Violence. Washington, D.C.: U.S. Government Printing Office.

———. 1971. *Street Gangs and Street Workers*. Englewood Cliffs, N.J.: Prentice-Hall.

———. 1989. Personal communication with author, March 22.

Klein, Malcolm W., and Lois Y. Crawford. 1967. "Groups, Gangs, and Cohesiveness." *Journal of Research in Crime and Delinquency* 4(1):63–75.

Klein, Malcolm W., and Cheryl L. Maxson. 1989. "Street Gang Violence." In *Violent Crime, Violent Criminals*, edited by Neil Weiner and Marvin E. Wolfgang. Newbury Park, Calif.: Sage.

Klein, Malcolm W., Cheryl L. Maxson, and Lea C. Cunningham. 1988. "Gang Involvement in Cocaine 'Rock' Trafficking." Project summary/final report, Center for Research on Crime and Social Control, Social Science Research Institute, University of Southern California, Los Angeles, May.

Klein, Malcolm W., Cheryl L. Maxson, and Margaret A. Gordon. 1987. "Police Response to Street Gang Violence: Improving the Investigative Process." Center for Research on Crime and Social Control, Social Science Research Institute, University of Southern California, Los Angeles.

Klein, Malcolm W., and Barbara G. Myerhoff, eds. 1967. *Juvenile Gangs in Context: Theory, Research, and Action*. Englewood Cliffs, N.J.: Prentice-Hall.

Knapp, Elaine S. 1988. "Kids, Gangs and Drugs." In *Embattled Youth*, edited by Council of State Governments. Lexington, Ky.: Council of State Governments.

Knopf, Terry Ann. 1969. *Youth Patrols: An Experiment in Community Participation*. Waltham, Mass.: Brandeis University, Lemberg Center for the Study of Violence.

Kobrin, Solomon. 1951. "The Conflict of Values in Delinquency Areas." *American Sociological Review* 16(1):653–61.

Kornblum, William S. 1974. *The Blue Collar Community*. Chicago: University of Chicago Press.

Kornhauser, Ruth R. 1978. *Social Sources of Delinquency*. Chicago: University of Chicago Press.

Kowski, Kim. 1988. "Cities Use Variety of Strategies to Wage War on Violence." *Los Angeles Herald* (May 13).

Krisberg, Barry. 1974. "Gang Youth and Hustling: The Psychology of Survival." *Issues in Criminology* 8(1):115–31.

Kyle, Charles L. 1984. *"Los Precios": The Magnitude of and Reasons for the Hispanic Dropout Problem: A Case Study of Two Chicago Public Schools*. Ph.D. dissertation, Sociology Department, Northwestern University.

Ley, David. 1975. "The Street Gang in Its Milieu." In *The Social Economy of Cities*, edited by Gary Gappert and Harold M. Rose. Beverly Hills, Calif.: Sage.

Lo, T. Wing. 1986. *Outreaching Social Work in Focus*. Hong Kong: Caritas.

Lockwood, Bill. 1988. "Parole Services Branch." Gang Information Unit, Department of the Youth Authority, Sacramento, California. Mimeographed.

Los Angeles City News Service. 1988. "Police Chief Urges Declaration of National Drug Emergency" (April 20).

Los Angeles County Probation Department. 1988. "Gang Community Reclamation Project." Application submitted to Office of Juvenile Justice and Delinquency Prevention, U.S. Department of Justice, Washington, D.C.

Los Angeles County Sheriff's Department. 1985. "Testimony." California State Task Force on Youth Gang Violence, Los Angeles.

McBride, Wesley D. 1988. "Street Gangs—Specialized Law Enforcement Problem—a Law Enforcement Perspective and Response." Los Angeles County Sheriff's Department, Los Angeles.

McGahey, Richard M. 1986. "Economic Conditions, Neighborhood Organization, and Urban Crime." In *Communities and Crime*, edited by Albert J. Reiss, Jr., and Michael Tonry. Vol. 8 of *Crime and Justice: A Review of Research*, edited by Michael Tonry and Norval Morris. Chicago: University of Chicago Press.

Mattick, Hans W. 1984. "The Chicago Youth Development Project." In *The Pursuit of Criminal Justice*, edited by Gordon Hawkins and Franklin E. Zimring. Chicago: University of Chicago Press.

Maxson, Cheryl L., Margaret A. Gordon, and Malcolm W. Klein. 1985. "Differences between Gang and Nongang Homicides." *Criminology* 23:209–22.

Mayer, John A. 1983. "Notes towards a Working Definition of Social Control in Historical Analysis." In *Social Control and the State*, edited by Stanley Cohen and Andrew Scull. New York: St. Martin's.

Metropolitan Court Judges' Committee. 1988. "Drugs—the American Family in Crisis: A Judicial Response." National Council of Juvenile and Family Court Judges, University of Nevada, Reno.

Miller, Walter B. 1958. "Lower Class Culture as a Generating Milieu of Gang Delinquency." *Journal of Social Issues* 14(3):5–19.

————. 1962. "The Impact of a 'Total-Community' Delinquency Control Project." *Social Problems* 10(2):168–91.

————. 1975. *Violence by Youth Gangs and Youth Gangs as a Crime Problem in Major American Cities.* National Institute for Juvenile Justice and Delinquency Prevention, Office of Juvenile Justice and Delinquency Prevention, U.S. Justice Department. Washington, D.C.: U.S. Government Printing Office.

————. 1976a. "Violent Crimes in City Gangs." In *Juvenile Delinquency*, 3d ed., edited by Rose Giallombardo. New York: Wiley.

————. 1976b. "Youth Gangs in the Urban Crisis Era." In *Delinquency, Crime and Society*, edited by James F. Short, Jr. Chicago: University of Chicago Press.

————. 1977. *Conceptions, Definitions, and Images of Youth Gangs.* Cambridge, Mass.: Harvard Law School, Center for Criminal Justice.

————. 1980. "Gangs, Groups, and Serious Youth Crime." In *Critical Issues in Juvenile Delinquency*, edited by David Schichor and Delos H. Kelly. Lexington, Mass.: D. C. Heath.

————. 1982. "Crime by Youth Gangs and Groups in the United States." A report prepared for the National Institute of Juvenile Justice and Delinquency Prevention of the U.S. Department of Justice, Washington, D.C., February (draft).

Miller, Walter B., Rainer C. Baum, and Rosetta McNeil. 1968. "Delinquency Prevention and Organizational Relations." In *Controlling Delinquents*, edited by Stanton Wheeler. New York: Wiley.

Ministry of Justice. 1984a. "White Paper on Crime, 1983." Foreign Press Center, Tokyo.

————. 1984b. "Annual Report on Crime." Foreign Press Center, Tokyo.

Moore, Joan W. 1978. *Homeboys.* Philadelphia: Temple University Press.

————. 1988. "Gangs and the Underclass: A Comparative Perspective." Introduction. In *People and Folks: Gangs, Crime and the Underclass in a Rust Belt City*, by John Hagedorn. Chicago: Lake View Press.

Moore, Joan W., Diego Vigil, and Robert Garcia. 1983. "Residence and Territoriality in Chicano Gangs." *Social Problems* 31(2):182–94.

Morash, Merry. 1983. "Gangs, Groups, and Delinquency." *British Journal of Criminology* 23(4):309–35.

Morgan, W. P. 1960. *Triad Societies in Hong Kong.* Hong Kong: Government Press.

Muehlbauer, Gene, and Laura Dodder. 1983. *The Losers: Gang Delinquency in an American Suburb.* New York: Praeger.

Myerhoff, Howard L., and Barbara G. Myerhoff. 1976. "Field Observations of Middle Class 'Gangs.' " In *Juvenile Delinquency*, 3d ed., edited by R. Giallombardo. New York: Wiley.

National Advisory Committee on Criminal Justice Standards and Goals. 1976. *Report of the Task Force on Juvenile Justice and Delinquency Prevention.* Washington, D.C.: U.S. Government Printing Office.

National Institute of Education. 1978. *Violent Schools, Safe Schools: The Safe School Study Report to the Congress*, vol. 1. Washington, D.C.: U.S. Government Printing Office.

Needle, Jerome A., and William V. Stapleton. 1983. *Police Handling of Youth Gangs*. Washington, D.C.: U.S. Department of Justice, Office of Juvenile Justice and Delinquency Prevention, National Institute for Juvenile Justice and Delinquency Prevention.

New York City Youth Board. 1960. *Reaching the Fighting Gang*. New York: New York City Youth Board.

New York State Assembly, Subcommittee on the Family Court. 1974a. "The Resurgence of Youth Gangs in New York City." Study report no. 1. New York, July. Albany: New York State Assembly.

———. 1974b. "Armies of the Streets: A Report on the Structure, Membership and Activities of Youth Gangs in the City of New York." Study report no. 2. New York, October. Albany: New York State Assembly.

Nidorf, Barry J. 1988. *Gang Alternative and Prevention Program*. Program Policy and Procedure Handbook. Los Angeles: County of Los Angeles Probation Department.

O'Connell, Richard J. 1988. "L.A. Gangs: Setting Up Shop All over the U.S." *Crime Control Digest* 22(48):1, 7–9.

Office of Criminal Justice Planning. 1987. "California Gang Violence Suppression Program: Program Guidelines." Office of Criminal Justice Planning, Sacramento, California.

Oschlies, W. 1979. *Juvenile Delinquency in Eastern Europe: Interpretations, Dynamics, Facts*. Cologne: Boehlau Verlag.

Overend, William. 1988. "New LAPD Tally May Cut Gang Killing Score." *Los Angeles Times* (October 20).

Patrick, James. 1973. *A Glasgow Gang Observed*. London: Eyre Methuen.

Pearson, Geoffrey. 1983. *Hooligan: A History of Reportable Fears*. New York: Schocken.

Pennell, Susan. 1983. *San Diego Street Youth Program: Final Evaluation*. San Diego: Association of Governments.

Philadelphia Police Department, Preventive Patrol Unit. 1987. *Policy and Procedure*, vol. 1. Philadelphia: Philadelphia Police Department, Juvenile Aid Division.

Philibosian, Robert H. 1983. Testimony before U.S. Senate Subcommittee on Juvenile Justice on Gang Violence and Control. Committee on the Judiciary, 98th Congress, 1st Session.

———. 1989. *State Task Force on Gangs and Drugs*. Sacramento: California Council on Criminal Justice.

Pineda, Charles, Jr. 1974. "Chicano Gang—Barrios in East Los Angeles—Maravilla." California Youth Authority, Sacramento, California.

Pitchess, Peter J. 1979. "Street Gangs." Youth Services Bureau, Los Angeles County Sheriff's Department, Los Angeles County, May.

Pleines, Edward. 1987. Personal communication with author, Chicago, December 15.

Poston, Richard W. 1971. *The Gang and the Establishment*. New York: Harper & Row.

President's Commission on Law Enforcement and Administration of Justice.

1967. *The Challenge of Crime in a Free Society.* Washington, D.C.: U.S. Government Printing Office.

President's Commission on Organized Crime. 1985. *Organized Crime of Asian Origin.* Washington, D.C.: U.S. Government Printing Office.

Puffer, J. Adams. 1912. *The Boy and His Gang.* Boston: Houghton Mifflin.

Quicker, John C. 1983. *Homegirls.* San Pedro, Calif.: International Universities Press.

Rand, Alice. 1987. "Transitional Life Events and Desistance from Delinquency and Crime." In *From Boy to Man, from Delinquency to Crime,* edited by Marvin E. Wolfgang, Terence P. Thornberry, and Robert M. Figlio. Chicago: University of Chicago Press.

Reddick, Alonzo J. 1987. "Issue Paper: Youth Gangs in Florida." Committee on Youth, Florida House of Representatives.

Reiss, Albert J., Jr. 1988. "Co-offending and Criminal Careers." In *Crime and Justice: A Review of Research,* vol. 10, edited by Michael Tonry and Norval Morris. Chicago: University of Chicago Press.

Robin, Gerald D. 1967. "Gang Member Delinquency in Philadelphia." In *Juvenile Gangs in Context: Theory, Research, and Action,* edited by Malcolm W. Klein and Barbara G. Myerhoff. Englewood Cliffs, N.J.: Prentice-Hall.

Roper, Clinton. 1988. Personal communication with author, December 12.

Rosenbaum, Dennis P., and Jane A. Grant. 1983. "Gangs and Youth Problems in Evanston: Research Findings and Policy Options." Center for Urban Affairs and Policy Research, Northwestern University.

Royster, Eugene. 1974. "Final Report: Philadelphia Evaluation of the Youth Development Program." Institute for Policy Analysis and Program Evaluation, Lincoln University, Philadelphia.

Rutter, Michael, and Henri Giller. 1983. *Juvenile Delinquency: Trends and Perspectives.* New York: Guilford Press.

Rutter, Michael, Barbara Maugham, Peter Mortimore, Janet Ouston, and Alan Smith. 1979. *Fifteen Thousand Hours.* Cambridge, Mass.: Harvard University Press.

Sager, Mike. 1988. "Death in Venice." *Rolling Stone* 535:64–72, 114–116.

Sampson, Edwin H., III. 1984. "Final Report of the Grand Jury." Circuit Court of the Eleventh Judicial Circuit of Florida in and for the County of Dade.

Sampson, Robert J. 1986. "Effects of Socioeconomic Context on Official Reaction to Juvenile Delinquency." *American Sociological Review* 51:876–85.

San Diego Association of Governments. 1982. *Juvenile Violence and Gang-related Crime.* San Diego, Calif.: Association of State Governments.

Sarnecki, Jerzy. 1986. *Delinquent Networks.* Report no. 1986:1. Stockholm: Research Division, National Swedish Council for Crime Prevention.

Savitz, Leonard D., Lawrence Rosen, and Michael Lalli. 1980. "Delinquency and Gang Membership as Related to Victimization." *Victimology* 5(2–4):152–60.

Schumacher, Michael. 1989. "Youth Gang Drug Prevention Program Grant Application." Santa Ana, Calif.: Orange County Probation Department.

Schwartz, Bob. 1988. "Santa Ana OKs School Anti-gang Pilot Project." *Los Angeles Times* (March 8).

Scott, Peter. 1956. "Gangs and Delinquent Groups in London." *British Journal of Delinquency* 7(1):4–60.

Shaw, Clifford R., and Henry D. McKay. 1931. "Social Factors in Juvenile Delinquency." In *Report on the Causes of Crime*, vol. 6, edited by George W. Wickersham. National Commission on Law Observance and Enforcement. Washington, D. C.: U.S. Government Printing Office.

———. 1943. *Juvenile Delinquency and Urban Areas*. Chicago: University of Chicago Press.

Sherif, Muzafer, and Carolyn W. Sherif. 1965. "The Adolescent in His Group in Its Setting: II. Research Procedures and Findings." In *Problems of Youth: Transition to Adulthood in a Changing World*, edited by Muzafer Sherif and Carolyn W. Sherif. Chicago: Aldine.

Sherman, Lawrence W. 1970. "Youth Workers, Police and the Gangs: Chicago, 1956–1970." Masters thesis, Division of Social Sciences, University of Chicago.

Short, James F., Jr. 1963. Introduction to *The Gang: A Study of One Thousand Three Hundred and Thirteen Gangs in Chicago*, rev. ed., by Frederic M. Thrasher. Chicago: University of Chicago Press.

———. 1976. "Gangs, Politics, and the Social Order." In *Delinquency, Crime and Society*, edited by James F. Short, Jr. Chicago: University of Chicago Press.

Short, James F., Jr., and Fred L. Strodtbeck. 1965. *Group Process and Gang Delinquency*. Chicago: University of Chicago Press.

Silbert, Jeffrey M., Leon Cristiano, and Gina Nunez-Cuenca. 1988. "Juvenile Gang Information and Coordination Project." A draft of a proposal prepared for the Dade-Miami Criminal Justice Council, Juvenile Justice Committee by the Department of Justice Assistance, Dade County, Florida.

Skolnick, Jerome H. 1969. *The Politics of Protest*. Washington, D.C.: U.S. National Commission on the Causes and Prevention of Violence.

Skolnick, Jerome H., with Theodore Correl, Elizabeth Narrio, and Roger Rabb. 1988. "The Social Structure of Street Drug Dealing." University of California at Berkeley, Center for the Study of Law and Society, Berkeley.

Sly, Liz. 1987a. "Rukns Sought Terrorist Work, U.S. Says." *Chicago Tribune* (October 15).

———. 1987b. "Fort, Rukn Followers Convicted of Conspiracy." *Chicago Tribune* (November 25).

Smith, Cyril S., M. R. Farrant, and H. J. Marchant. 1972. *The Wincroft Youth Project*. London: Tavistock.

Smith, Wes. 1987. "4 Guards are Injured at Pontiac." *Chicago Tribune* (September 17).

Specht, Walter. 1988. "Personal communication." Fachhochschule für Socialwesen. Esslingen, West Germany, February.

Spergel, Irving A. 1964. *Slumtown, Racketville, Haulburg*. Chicago: University of Chicago Press.

———. 1966. *Street Gang Work: Theory and Practice*. Reading, Mass.: Addison-Wesley.

———. 1969. *Problem Solving: The Delinquency Example*. Chicago: University of Chicago Press.

———. 1972. "Community Action Research as a Political Process." In *Community Organization: Studies in Constraint*, edited by Irving A. Spergel. Beverly Hills, Calif.: Sage.

———. 1983. *Violent Gangs in Chicago: Segmentation and Integration*. Chicago: University of Chicago, School of Social Service Administration.

———. 1984. "Violent Gangs in Chicago: In Search of Social Policy." *Social Service Review* 58(2):199–226.

———. 1985. *Youth Gang Activity and the Chicago Public Schools*. Chicago: University of Chicago, School of Social Service Administration.

———. 1986. "The Violent Gang in Chicago: A Local Community Approach." *Social Service Review* 60:94–131.

Spergel, Irving A., and G. David Curry. 1988. "Socialization to Gangs: Preliminary Baseline Report." School of Social Service Administration, University of Chicago, Chicago.

Spergel, Irving A., G. David Curry, Ruth Ross, and Ronald Chance, eds. 1989. "Survey." National Youth Gang Suppression and Intervention Project. Chicago: School of Social Service Administration, University of Chicago.

Spergel, Irving A., C. Turner, J. Pleas, and P. Brown. 1969. *Youth Manpower: What Happened in Woodlawn*. Chicago: University of Chicago, School of Social Service Administration.

Stafford, Mark. 1984. "Gang Delinquency." In *Major Forms of Crime*, edited by Robert F. Meier. Beverly Hills, Calif.: Sage.

Stanfield, Robert E. 1966. "The Interaction of Family Variables and Gang Variables in the Aetiology of Delinquency." *Social Problems* 13(4):411–17.

Stark, Evan. 1981. "Gangs and Progress: The Contribution of Delinquency to Progressive Reform." In *Crime and Capitalism: Readings in Marxist Criminology*, edited by David F. Greenberg. New York: Mayfield.

Suttles, Gerald D. 1968. *The Social Order of the Slum*. Chicago: University of Chicago Press.

Taylor, Carl S. 1988. "Youth Gangs Organize for Power, Money." *School Safety* (Spring), pp. 26–27.

Tennyson, Ray A. 1967. "Family Structure and Delinquent Behavior." In *Juvenile Gangs in Context: Theory, Research, and Action*, edited by M. W. Klein and B. G. Meyerhoff. Englewood Cliffs, N.J.: Prentice-Hall.

Testa, Mark. 1988. Personal communication with author. University of Chicago, School of Social Service Administration, August.

Thomas, William I., and Florian Znaniecki. 1918. *The Polish Peasant in Europe and America*. Chicago: University of Chicago Press.

Thrasher, Frederic M. 1936. *The Gang*, 2d ed. Chicago: University of Chicago Press.

Toby, J. 1983. "Violence in School." In *Crime and Justice: An Annual Review of Research*, vol. 4, edited by Michael Tonry and Norval Morris. Chicago: University of Chicago Press.

Torres, Dorothy M. 1980. *Gang Violence Reduction Project Evaluation Report*. Sacramento: California Youth Authority.

———. 1985. "Gang Violence Reduction Project Update." California Department of the Youth Authority Program Research and Review Division, Sacramento, California. Mimeographed.

Tracy, Paul E. 1982. "Gang Membership and Violent Offenders: Preliminary Results from the 1958 Cohort Study." Center for Studies in Criminology and Criminal Law, University of Pennsylvania, Philadelphia.

———. 1987. "Subcultural Delinquency: A Comparison of the Incidence and Severity of Gang and Nongang Member Offenses." College of Criminal Justice, Northeastern University, Boston.

Utne, M. K., and L. J. McIntyre. 1982. *Violent Juvenile Offenders on Probation in Cook County*. Public Affairs Research Practicum. Chicago: University of Chicago Press.

Valdivia, Steve E. 1988. "Community Youth Gang Services—Report." Prepared for the Coordinating Council Meeting, Office of Juvenile Justice and Delinquency Prevention, U.S. Department of Justice, Washington, D.C., by the Community Youth Gang Service Project, Los Angeles, California, June.

Vigil, James Diego. 1983. "Chicano Gangs: One Response to Mexican Urban Adaptation in the Los Angeles Area." *Urban Anthropology* 12(11):45–75.

———. 1988. "Street Socialization, Locura Behavior, and Violence among Chicano Gang Members." In *Violence and Homicide in Hispanic Communities*, edited by Jess Kraus and Armando Morales. Washington, D.C.: National Institute of Mental Health.

Wade, Barbara. 1987. Personal communication with author, Miami Police Department, July 17.

Washington, Erwin. 1988. "Despite Violence Official Response to Drug Connection Was Slow." *Los Angeles Daily News* (April 24).

Whyte, William F. 1943. *Street Corner Society*. Chicago: University of Chicago Press.

Wolfgang, Marvin E., Robert M. Figlio, and Thorsten Sellin. 1972. *Delinquency in a Birth Cohort*. Chicago: University of Chicago Press.

Yablonsky, Lewis. 1962. *The Violent Gang*. New York: Macmillan.

Zimring, Franklin E. 1981. "Kids, Groups, and Crime: Some Implications of a Well-known Secret." *Journal of Criminal Law and Criminology* 72(3):867–85.

Robert Barr and Ken Pease

Crime Placement, Displacement, and Deflection

ABSTRACT

Patterns of crime should be seen as the outcome of crime-control policies and the distribution of opportunities. Such crime-control policies are often argued to have the limited effect of displacing crime, that is, substituting new crimes for prevented crimes. Displacement alone is an inadequate concept; a better formulation centers on the deflection of crime from a target. Some patterns of deflected crime can be regarded as "benign" displacement, while others are considered "malign." Thus conceived, deflection can be used as a policy tool to achieve a more "desirable" pattern of crime. It is already so used, inter alia, by insurance companies with a commercial motive. Better information systems are required to show displacement or deflection, and to assist in monitoring the distribution of crime through space and time. Patterns of criminal activity and victimization can be conceptualized as an outcome of conscious and unconscious decisions by the public, politicians, and the police. These patterns are not immutable, and alternative policies, incorporating an understanding of crime deflection, could lead to new, more equitable, patterns of victimization.

Crime patterns take the form they do because of a combination of circumstances: offender motivation, the absence of legitimate routes to personal satisfaction, the availability of vulnerable targets, the degree of preparation and investment required to commit different crimes, and

Robert Barr is lecturer in geography, University of Manchester, and Ken Pease is clinical associate professor in the Department of Psychiatry, University of Saskatchewan, and consultant criminologist, Correctional Service of Canada. We are grateful to Mike Hough for his analysis of the British Crime Survey and to Mike Chatterton and Dave Forrester for their helpful suggestions.

277

the perceived consequences of crime commission. These are the headings under which lie the common explanatory variables of criminology. Acting together, the factors yield a pattern of offending that shifts in response to changes in any or all of them.

This essay examines "displacement," the usually unintended effect of crime-control programs, by which efforts to prevent one kind of crime sometimes lead would-be offenders to commit a different kind of crime or the same kind of crime at a different time or place. Many evaluations of crime-control innovations conclude, or suggest, that displacement has reduced or eliminated apparent crime-reduction effects of the innovation. Thus, displacement is generally seen as a frustrating side effect. Displacement can, however, be seen as a predictable effect of specific policies and, accordingly, as a manipulative tool of crime control.

Here is how this essay is organized. Section I elaborates on the concept of displacement. It is suggested that the term "deflection" better characterizes the situation in which a specific target is protected from victimization. The pessimism induced by the extreme assumption, that all crime is displaced by "preventive" action, is discussed. Section II develops an argument that, while total displacement can never be discounted, the real question of interest is how displacement could be used purposefully to create an "optimal" distribution of crime and offers illustrations from the literature of "benign" and "malign" forms of displacement. Section III describes speculative accounts of how displacement may be expected to occur, outlines criteria by which some kinds of displacement might be regarded as preferable to others, examines current differences in levels of victimization at the aggregate and individual levels, and discusses problems in the measurement of victimization. Section IV presents a conceptual model of possible distributions of crime, proposes a form of measurement for the inequality of crime victimization, and presents criteria according to which displacement/deflection should be measured. Section V elaborates the conclusion which lies at the center of this essay, that crime displacement/deflection should be conceived as a tool of crime-control policy rather than as an unwanted constraint on crime-prevention program success.

I. Prevention, Displacement, or Deflection

When a target of criminal opportunity is blocked, the would-be offender does something else. This alternative may lie within the law. If it does, the result is typically known as "crime abatement" or "desistance." If it lies outside the law, the result is known as "crime displacement." Thus, an individual's shift in intention from burglary to check fraud is defined as crime displacement. Shifting from burglary to mowing the lawn is an example of crime abatement.

Hakim and Rengert (1981), following and modifying Reppetto (1976), identify five types of crime displacement: *temporal*—doing the intended crime at a different time; *spatial*—doing the intended crime to the intended type of target in another place; *tactical*—doing the intended crime using a different method; *target*—doing the intended type of crime to a different type of target; *crime type* or *functional*—doing a different type of crime from that intended.

These types of displacement are, in principle, measurable by changes in victimization experience and offender self-report. A sixth type of displacement, never described as such in the literature, is substitution or *perpetrator displacement*. Here, a crime opportunity is so compelling that different offenders are always available to commit the crime. The most obvious example of this type of displacement is international drug trafficking. Remarkably high profits appear to produce an inexhaustible supply of willing couriers. The crime is displaced from offender to offender but is committed repeatedly.

Since each of the types of displacement covers many possible courses of action, the ways in which crime displacement can occur are indeed varied. While an appreciation of crime displacement seems central to understanding crime patterns generally, it has been brought into play as an explanatory device almost exclusively when crime prevention is under discussion. Its invocation has served to limit the attractiveness of crime prevention measures. Cornish and Clarke (1986, p. 3) refer to the assumption of total displacement as inducing a "paralyzing extreme-case pessimism." Heal and Laycock (1986, p. 123) opine that "there is little point in the policy-maker investing resources and effort into situational [crime] prevention if by doing so he merely shuffles crime from one area to the next but never reduces it. For this reason, the possibility of displacing crime by preventive intervention is a crucial issue for the policy-maker." Svensson (1986, p. 122) concludes a review of crime prevention in Sweden by emphasizing that "in particular, we need to ensure that situational prevention does not merely displace offending in time or space." Heal and Laycock (1988, p. 239) note that "the argument most frequently levelled against prevention, particularly 'situational' prevention, is that it will displace crime from one setting to the next, or from one type of crime to another. If this is indeed the case, the limits to prevention are considerable." Trasler (1986) takes the view that we are a long way from understanding patterns of crime switching in ways that would facilitate the assessment of crime displacement. Cornish and Clarke (1986, p. 2) write, "Tentative and anecdotal though much of the evidence for displacement undoubtedly is, the concept . . . alerts the policy-maker to the possibility that a range of unanticipated consequences may attend novel (or ill-considered) crime-control policies."

Experience in mounting crime-prevention initiatives shows that skepticism about their worth is often and frustratingly based on the presumption of total displacement. Since there is no such thing as free crime prevention, the presumption of total displacement, with its associated cost considerations, will usually triumph over the wish to prevent a particular crime in a particular place. Most galling is the frequency with which extreme-case pessimists are to be found among police officers whose confidence about the crime-reduction effects of patrolling choices has failed to be justified by research. For the extreme-case pessimist, installing better locks on a type of car merely displaces theft to other types of cars. Increasing controls on the availability of one category of firearm increases the use of other kinds of weapons in crime.

We should add that although we have often heard police officers expound extreme-case pessimism, it is difficult to imagine such an argument ever being used as a reason for not responding to the concerns of community leaders. Neither can we envisage a politician standing before a group of voters and denying money for a crime-prevention initiative on the grounds that the crime would simply go somewhere else to happen. Personal lobbying and political influence are to be counted among the factors making for a particular crime pattern.

Displacement, then, is discussed as a limit on the efficacy of crime prevention. In the gloom that attends such discussion, it is too readily forgotten that for a crime to be displaced, it must first be unplaced; in other words, that a crime at a particular place and time must have been prevented. The word "deflected" gives a better sense of the achievement at the heart of the process. It also has the advatage of presuming nothing about the extent to which crime goes somewhere else to happen.

Extreme-case pessimism is, with some difficulty, an arguable position. However, as an argument against crime prevention programs, it reflects an excessively narrow view of displacement. It focuses only on changes as requiring explanation, and a restricted set of changes at that—those that are introduced with an explicit crime-prevention purpose. The basic error made about crime displacement is to conceive of it as an explanation of change but not of the status quo. It is almost as though a snapshot of crime represented a state of nature with which people tamper by the introduction of crime-prevention initiatives. The premise stated earlier is that any pattern of crime can be thought of as the distribution of people and places from which crime has not been displaced. The observed pattern is a temporary product of a particular set of physical and social arrangements. Crime patterns at any time are frozen displacement patterns. Displacement is but another placement. Bennett and Wright (1984, p. 264) comment, "In a sense, the offender is continually being displaced from one potential target to another until he finds a suitable opportunity to burgle."

The distribution of crime can be likened to that of iron filings held in a magnetic field. Change the field and the filings are rearranged. As magnets create a force field, so do policy and practice create a crime pattern. As we choose a field by positioning magnets, so do we "choose" a crime pattern by selecting particular policies and practices. This is well illustrated by Cook (1983) in his discussion of the complexities that attend apparently simple changes in law and practice. For instance, increases in enforcement directed toward suppliers, middlemen, or consumers of stolen goods or drugs will produce corresponding or compensatory changes in the other actors in the chain. Increase drug price, and habit-feeding property crime will probably increase. When enforcement of taxation becomes more stringent, embezzlement may substitute for tax fraud. Someone forgets to switch off a bedroom light, and a burglary is moved down the street.

The appropriate response to the complexity of determination of crime patterns should not be supine acceptance that the distribution of crime should be what we observe it to be; this is precisely what happens when discussions of crime displacement are restricted to the negative evaluation of crime-prevention initiatives. We must not be content with the notion that crime, like economic well-being, is the product of a hidden hand with whose movements we interfere at our peril. Rather, we should ask ourselves what kinds of crimes, perpetrated against whom, would we most like to prevent? Such a question does not admit of a sensible, unqualified answer. Most answers would be conditional on assumptions about displacement patterns. A daytime burglary should be prevented or displaced so long as the displacement was not to armed robbery or to burglary at night. Rape prevention or displacement would be desirable as long as it did not become murder. Displacement to other crimes would be regarded with relative equanimity. Prevention of armed robbery at the cost of an increase in tax or welfare fraud may come into this category. Displacement from domestic to nondomestic burglary may also be regarded as something short of a disaster.

In one sense, a crime displaced is a crime prevented. A chosen target is, through displacement, protected from crime. Crime displacement or deflection is one of the consequences—welcomed, tolerated, and suffered in varying extents—of any change in our way of life. Certain forms of consequence will be regarded as unacceptable and the choice reconsidered. Absent those consequences, the choice will be vindicated. Seeing displacement in these terms limits the scope of relevant measurement and makes that measurement possible.

The story (which, lacking freedom-of-information legislation, we should regard as apocryphal) is told of a Western European Minister of the Interior, who was briefed by a senior civil servant about the phenomenon of displacement. He was advised that preventing a major crime in one place might merely move it somewhere else. His reply was, "Try to displace it as far as the border." The notion that some displacement is good is implicit in many practical crime-related contexts. For instance, companies preyed on by their employees through sophisticated computer techniques are alleged to be reluctant to prosecute (Scholberg and Parker 1983). While this reluctance may be put down to the fear of being made to look foolish, another component could be the preferability of allowing the predator to go to work with a competitor that might result in even larger losses to the host company.

Less speculatively, the insurance industry is explicitly concerned to displace hazardous business to other insurers. In the aggregate, the insurance industry is concerned to shift such business out of the insured segment of the market altogether. Roger Litton is the director of an insurance brokerage who took time out from his work to complete a doctorate in criminology. His thesis detailed the relation between crime prevention and insurance practice (Litton 1986, 1990). His probably unique combination of expertise makes his discussion of displacement worthy of close attention. He writes, "Individual insurers attempt to create displacement by shifting losses from properties which they insure by stipulating requirements for crime-prevention devices. . . . If all insurers are taking similar action, then criminals will find easier pickings among those risks which are not insured. . . . If displacement can be shown—or presumed—to occur it would be rational for [insurers] to encourage such displacement even if the total volume of crime were not to be thereby diminished" (Litton 1986, pp. 256–57). Litton could have gone further to state that, for the insurer, from a perspective of narrow economic self-interest, displacement is actually preferable to crime prevention because a high level of crime is helpful in justifying commensurately high premiums and adding plausibility to advertising that argues the need for insurance protection to be bought.

A further displacement sought by insurers is the movement from large to small losses. "Insurers are concerned with making an overall profit, and therefore large potential losses are of more importance to them than small ones. They will thus be more concerned to prevent the large loss than the small loss and will direct their priorities accordingly. . . . To the other parties, however, whether police or victim, a crime is a crime is a crime. Thus the unit of accounting for insurers is the pound sterling, dollar, or whatever, whereas for the police the unit of accounting is the crime" (Pease and Litton 1984, p. 191).

There is some evidence that rates of crime do track insurance or other attention to some sectors of the market. For example, in the United Kingdom during the 1970s, insurance attention to the protection of commercial risks was closely followed by an increase in losses due to domestic burglary (see Litton 1986, 1990).

II. The Link between Crime Displacement and Crime Prevention

Cornish and Clarke (1986, pp. 2–3) discern the conceptual roots of displacement in drive theories of motivation, "which depict behavior as being largely governed by the necessity of reducing tensions created by an organism's internal needs." Crime-control strategies concentrating on target protection "could expect little real success, since they would merely influence the mode of expression of the offender's internal drives or predispositions without in any way tackling the underlying conflict or frustration which continued to energize and motivate offending." Dissatisfaction with the implication that crime control can be achieved only through changing hearts and minds led Ronald V. Clarke and Derek B. Cornish (1985) to the development of situational crime prevention and, through that, to a rational-choice perspective on offending.

A first step in the move away from drive theories of criminality was to demonstrate that a form of behavior, for which motivation can be presumed to be high, can nonetheless be prevented. To that end, much time has been spent over the last decade demonstrating that the aggregate rate of suicide falls when one convenient means of taking one's life (e.g., toxic gas) is denied (see Clarke and Mayhew 1988). This is a powerful demonstration that displacement is not total in circumstances where it would be plausible to regard total displacement as likely. Killing oneself is a major decision. Burglary (say) is less so. If the decision to kill oneself is reversed by the nonavailability of toxic gas, then the decision to commit burglaries should be even less robust in the face of obstacles.

The gas suicide story is indeed a powerful argument by analogy, but it is only an argument by analogy and will therefore not be compelling to the extreme-case pessimist. The analogy is imperfect in that the would-be suicide wants to be dead. The would-be burglar probably does not want to commit burglaries as an end but only as a means to being richer. The suicide event is the end of the road. If someone chooses to commit suicide, and follows through, a death results. If there is no such choice, there is no such death. If someone chooses to commit a burglary, and follows through, the event is a burglary. If no such choice is made, there still may be a crime. In short, for suicide studies, there is no alternative end state of relevance. In crime displacement there is. A prevented burglary in a house in Kansas City can change into a burglary of a house in another area, a burglary of a factory or an office, theft from a shop, drug sales, or check fraud, to name but a few. If some burglars choose each of these options, the displacement will be invisible since the crimes will merge into the background variation in the rates of these offenses. Crime displacement can never be conclusively shown not to have occurred in the way that suicide displacement can.

It is important to assert early that we do believe there to have been many instances of crime-prevention programs in which displacement has not been total. However, we believe that the important problem is not whether crime displacement is total but how displacement or deflection can be used to achieve a spread of crime that can be regarded as equitable. For this purpose, it is often helpful to argue as if the extreme-case pessimist were right because he can never be conclusively proven wrong.

A. *Illustrations of Benign Displacement*

Our major thrust is the recasting of the concept of crime displacement. While it has been thought of as an obstacle to crime prevention, it should rather be considered as a tool with which to work toward distributive justice. Therefore, rather than review the literature on crime displacement, we will use some of that literature to point out that, in some cases, even with a presumption of total displacement, an argument could be made that the redistribution of crime achieved is socially desirable. An apology should be recorded here for the preponderance of U.K. research cited. This is because of a combination of availability and confidence. As will become clear, displacement aspirations and plans are bound to rely substantially on local patterns and priorities.

The acknowledgment that displacement can be benign is not original, having been anticipated by Brantingham (1986). Toward the end of a chapter on trends in crime prevention, she notes, "Displacement is always a possibility, and while the displacement of crime through a planning intervention has target-specific value, it has no overall value unless it takes the form of displacement from more serious forms of criminal behavior to a less serious form" (1986, p. 111). However, Brantingham does not pursue the implications of the argument. She does not specify the kinds of displacement that should be examined in different prevention contexts. Nor does she consider the possibility that displacement to crimes of the same seriousness inflicted at other times and places may still represent a net social gain.

1. *Gun Control.* The issue of displacement is central to the bitter argument about the merits of gun control legislation. In essence, the question is whether murderous intent is translated into murder using whatever weapon comes to hand (total tactical displacement) or whether the weapon facilitates greater harm than would have been inflicted in its absence. Morris and Hawkins (1970, pp. 71, 84) entertainingly dismiss the former argument as follows: "Particularly from . . . 'sportsmen,' we must never tolerate the argument that if the murderer lacked a gun, he would kill in some other way. If they believe that, they should, on the grounds of sportsmanship, throw away their guns and club the deer to death, knife the bears, and poison the ducks." This aptly provides a reductio ad absurdum of the argument as it applies to hunting but has proven less conclusive in relation to violent crime.

As recently as 1983, Philip Cook decided that he could reach no conclusions on the effects of gun law and enforcement policy on rates of violent crime, preferring to speak of a "shopping list" of the research that would enable conclusions to be reached. A similarly circumspect review is that of Bordua (1986). In response to the tactical displacement arguments about gun control introduced by Wright, Rossi, and Daly (1983), Zimring and Hawkins (1987, p. 17) can respond only with circumstantial evidence about the greater effective lethality of intent: "A greater percentage of knife attacks than of gun attacks resulted in wounds to vital areas of the body—such as the head, neck, chest, abdomen and back—where wounds were likely to be fatal. Also, many more knife attacks resulted in multiple wounds, suggesting that those who used the knife in those attacks had no great desire to spare the victim's life."

The obvious riposte from gun control opponents would be that a process of danger compensation is operating; a change in the level of danger inherent in the equipment leads to a compensatory change in behavior to maintain the same degree of threat to life (see Cook 1986). Accordingly, sublethal intent is consistent with a greater degree of knife damage than gun damage and is accurately reflected in weapon use.

The nearest thing to a conclusive analysis appeared, perhaps strangely, early in the debate. Zimring (1972) presented data that strongly showed that the likelihood of death in a violent encounter was directly related to the lethality of the instrument of violence even when the context was controlled for. In domestic assaults, for example, fists deal death less often than knives, which do so less than small guns, and so on through the ballistic ratings of firearms. Further suggestive evidence favoring the view that weapon potential is a factor in harm inflicted comes from the repeated references in witness accounts of mass slayings that, at least for part of the time, the shooting is said to be indiscriminate. Indiscriminate use of a weapon relies on the potency of that weapon for its impact.

We thus have a situation surrounding gun control where the evidence suggests that harm inflicted does depend, to some extent, on the nature of the weapon used. However, let us assume that harm inflicted does quite precisely reflect harm intended, so that efforts to reduce criminal violence by gun control policies would be thwarted by tactical displacement. There is, nonetheless, an argument to be made that gun control would have benign effects. Zimring and Hawkins (1987, p. 60) note, "A survey of all U.S. adults in 1978 . . . found that four percent of the respondents had been involved in a handgun accident, half of them resulting in a personal injury. Ten percent reported that a family member had been involved in such an accident, and fifteen percent reported a similar experience for a close personal friend." They also note 900 deaths in which firearms were accidentally used in the home in the United States in 1978. Whereas crime displacement makes sense, accident displacement does not. It is difficult to contend that if you do not have a gun to play with, you might kill yourself with a pool cue.

One could develop the argument. If you want to harm someone and have to work harder to do so, superior strength is a great advantage; so the option is not available to the unarmed puny predator. Further, the time taken to achieve the same end will be greater, giving more opportunity (in public confrontation) for help to arrive. Here, then, is an instance where total displacement, if it occurs, is nonetheless more likely than not to be benign in its consequences.

2. *Car Security.*   In a pioneering study, Mayhew and her colleagues (1976) examined the effect of legislation requiring the installation of steering column locks in new cars. Their introduction did seem to displace crime to older cars, which were not fitted with such locks. "A main finding of the present study is that although steering column locks have substantially reduced the risk of cars fitted with them being illegally driven away, they seem also to have the effect of redirecting thieves to cars without them" (Mayhew et al. 1976, p. 17).

The study found that the total number of cars taken was virtually identical, with only the proportion of new and old cars differing. Although there was no preventive effect, was the change without value? It was not. Three outcomes of a car theft are possible. First, the car is not returned, or is returned so damaged that it is written off by the insurance company. In this case, the values involved after the introduction of the legislation are smaller than they would have been had new cars been taken. Second, the car is returned with some damage. In this case, the values are also self-limiting because of the lower ceiling at which older cars are written off. Third, the car is returned undamaged. For this category, there is no greater loss than if the car were new (perhaps less because the scope for insurance fraud by attributing previously incurred damage to theft will be smaller).

While somewhat money-oriented and unsentimental, the approach taken suggests that total target displacement of the kind achieved is not necessarily worthless.

3. *Domestic Burglary Prevention.*   Allatt (1984) showed that an area of public housing that had undergone a major program of "target hard-

ening" exhibited a reduction in domestic burglary. However, she considered the extent of displacement to other property crimes within the area and to burglary in an adjacent area. The increase in other crimes within the target area and in burglary in the comparison area led her to conclude that there was a "total saving of 29 crimes" (Allatt 1984, p. 110). She acknowledges, however, that she did not measure crimes other than domestic burglary in the comparison area; the numbers are such that the twenty-nine crimes claimed to have been saved could easily have been deflected into other forms of crime. Allatt's study is unusual in the scope it allows for extreme-case pessimism.

Other studies typically measure displacement that is partial and often slight. Forrester, Chatterton, and Pease (1988), studying a run-down area similar to that investigated by Allatt, found that a package of target hardening and social measures yielded a 60 percent reduction in domestic burglary. Measuring property crime throughout the rest of the police subdivision in which the area was situated showed a degree of displacement that could account for no more than one-quarter of the reduction. This is a typical finding of burglary-prevention programs on both sides of the Atlantic (see, e.g., Wilson 1978; Gabor 1981; Bennett and Wright 1984; Laycock 1985).

However, as noted earlier, none of these studies will persuade the extreme-case pessimist. Nor is it necessary that they should. The important question is, assuming total displacement, Could the distribution of crime be regarded as preferable after the implementation of crime-prevention programs? In the cases of the Allatt (1984) and Forrester, Chatterton, and Pease (1988) studies, if even distribution of crime is to be desired, the answer must be "yes." The estates (large, public housing areas) were chosen for their high rates of burglary victimization. In the latter study, one in four households was victimized in a given year. In both, the high rate of victimization was one of the reasons for the choice of the area in the first place. As long as there was no evidence of malign displacement elsewhere, the programs were, on a particular view of optimal crime distribution, entirely defensible. Insofar as crime fear is reduced in burglary-prevention programs (the data on the point are mixed), a net social advantage may be gained.

4. *Police Patrol.* A variety of experimental studies have now been carried out on the effects of police patrol. In brief, little if any change in rates of crime has been reported (Kelling et al. 1974; Kelling, Wycoff, and Pate 1980; Police Foundation 1981; Kelling 1988). At best, then, we may assume total spatial or temporal displacement inside an area as

a result of patrol differences within the range studied. It is, of course, possible that there was no effect. In either event, what does stand out from the research is that citizens noticed the changed patrolling, and that, more often than not, they became less concerned about crime problems. This was not a universal effect. For instance, Kelling et al. (1974) showed that commercial interests became, in some respects, more concerned. Nonetheless, total crime displacement with a reduction in crime concern and no serious consequential costs may yield a net gain.

B. Malign Displacement

Malign displacement occurs when crime changes in ways that are deemed to be socially undesirable. The question of what constitutes undesirable change is itself contentious and is addressed later. Instances here are restricted to cases where, if displacement were total in the ways described, then, intuitively, things have gone from bad to worse. In fact, within the limits of our search, it has proved impossible to locate a well-designed study which persuasively identifies malign displacement. This is because the kinds of crimes that are measured to estimate displacement are typically similar in seriousness to those prevented. To identify malign displacement, one needs to identify crimes committed that are more serious than those prevented. The examples of possible malign displacement instanced below are, therefore, inconclusive.

Letkemann (1973, p. 89) relies on criminal informants' accounts of displacement. "The development of night depositories coincided with complex burglar alarm systems. . . . My informants agreed that these technical developments have left only the most skilled criminals operating as safe-crackers. Alarm systems and the credit card systems have discouraged the burglary of major business establishments; banks, for example, are seldom burglarized today. For this reason, say my informants, the burglary of business establishments has given way to armed robbery."

Brantingham and Brantingham (1984) suggest, without stated evidence and in passing, a possible displacement from pharmacy burglaries to pharmacy robberies as nighttime security of restricted drugs is increased. A similar possibility is presented by Laycock (1984). She showed that after pharmacies had been "hardened," they showed much lower rates of burglaries in which controlled drugs were taken. Two percent of protected pharmacies suffered such a crime compared with

14 percent of unprotected premises during 1981. At least a proportion of these burglaries could have been displaced to become robberies of pharmacies; although, based on the available figures of recorded robberies, robbery could have accounted for, and thereby offset, perhaps 10 percent of the reduction. Since robberies were not disproportionately experienced in hardened pharmacies, as might have been anticipated, this estimate could be overstated. Thefts of drugs from doctors' cars and hospitals and offices over the same period increased so that total displacement (combining all three categories of diverted crime) is possible; this makes the highly implausible assumption of a stable number of drug users over the period. Whether the pattern constitutes malign displacement depends on one's view of the relative seriousness of burglary, robbery, and theft from cars. Taking robbery as exceptionally serious, the Laycock (1984) study could arguably represent an instance of malign displacement.

Ekblom (1987a) shows that target hardening can reduce robberies on sub post offices (shops franchised to offer a restricted range of postal services). Unfortunately, there was a parallel increase in raids on vans delivering to sub post offices so that it was impossible to demonstrate that displaced robberies had not occurred. Further, on questions of displacement beyond the post office, Ekblom (p. 21) argues that the issue turns on "the extent to which robbers fit the stereotype of the determined professional who . . . will ruthlessly seek out other targets if baulked in his choice." In brief, Ekblom's study allows the interpretation of total spatial displacement. The desirability of this change turns on the dangers presented to members of the public by robberies inside as opposed to outside shops. The change is arguably malign.

Ekblom's study is a good example of the advantage held by the extreme-case pessimist. Although it demonstrated a specific crime reduction, it was unable to indicate the range of targets of possibly displaced crime. It was eventually reduced to arguments about criminal stereotypes. At this point, the extreme-case pessimist would have won the argument.

In another study, Chaiken, Lawless, and Stevenson (1974) report that a police crackdown on subway robberies in New York City was associated with an increase in street robberies, providing another possible instance of malign displacement. In England, the Home Office (1986) noted generally a movement to robbery of cash in transit, when places that keep money are hardened.

Taken together, these studies show the diversity of research on displacement, both benign and malign. They also indicate some of the difficulties with demonstrating whether crime displacement has occurred. Some writers go beyond the attempt to measure or infer displacement and generate sophisticated accounts of how displacement may occur, and we turn to them next.

C. Directions of Displacement

Brantingham and Brantingham (1984) present a classification of burglar types and the patterns of crime displacement to which they will be prone. They argue, "We do not yet know enough to make firm statements about what will happen when a crime-prevention program is introduced, but we can logically deduce some patterns that may hold by looking at characteristics of burglars" (1984, p. 84). The features of burglars that they take to be relevant are time commitment to burglary (full- or part-time), age, commitment to burglary as an economic activity, and orientation (or otherwise) toward specific goods. For instance, adult burglars with low commitment are seen to have only a low level of likelihood to displace their crimes. Adults with high commitment are taken to have moderate potential for geographic displacement and for displacement to other nonconfrontational crimes. All groups but one are taken to have a low potential for displacement to confrontational crimes. The exceptional group is full-time goods-oriented burglars, who are said to have a high potential for displacement to confrontational crimes. With the exception of this group, all the groups have very incomplete potential for displacement to other nonconfrontational crimes.

Taking the Brantingham classification to be correct and confrontational crime to be more serious than burglary, even under extreme-case pessimism, then displacement would not be malign unless a large proportion of burglars were goods-oriented adult full-timers and the possibilities for displacement to other nonconfrontational crimes were in short supply. In all other sets of circumstances, displacement would be neutral or benign.

Heal and Laycock (1986) speculate on the motivational factors that are presumed to lead to a high or low level of displacement. Consistent with Brantingham and Brantingham (1984), they argue that "displacement is more likely to take place where the individual's motivation is sufficiently high to drive him on even when his initial target of criminal activity is well-defended" (1986, p. 124). The missing element in this formulation is the nature of the motivation. Few people, surely, have ever had the motivation to commit any crime just because it is a crime. The motivation is more specific than that and is likely to restrict the range of alternative targets of displaced crime. In 1988, the same writers refined their position to the following: "Displacement is more likely to occur following a preventive intervention when: 1) the offender's personal motivation or drive is strong; 2) when many alternative targets are available or perceived to be available; 3) where those designing preventive measures fail to take account of the potential for action and counter action; and 4) where low vulnerability targets are in close proximity to highly vulnerable targets" (Heal and Laycock 1988, p. 240).

Clarke (1978, p. 73) likewise takes the view that "the extent to which displacement should be anticipated depends upon the intentionality or purposiveness of the behavior. In the case of young children playing unsupervised, it is perhaps fair to say that the vulnerability of targets itself generates much of the behavior which tends to its destruction. Reducing opportunities for damage in those places where young children play is, therefore, likely to result in reductions in vandalism."

In two recent important works (Cornish and Clarke 1988a, b), the tendency to displace is considered in terms of the constellation of opportunities, costs, and benefits that attend the potential criminal act. These are referred to as the "choice-structuring properties" of situations and have been worked through in more detail with respect to gambling and suicide. The gambler, for instance, moves to places where his prior behavior can most easily be generalized. The dimensions along which this generalization takes place include amount per play, elapsed time before payment, probability of winning on an individual bet, payout ratio, degree of personal participation, role of luck, and masculine image of the game. Desistance occurs when available games do not fall within the area that he is prepared to generalize. Tolerance for difference is perhaps an individual characteristic.

The possible similarities with crime make the notion of choice-structuring properties a seductive one. Cornish and Clarke make the point that crime is too wide a category to be useful in this context. They cite Tremblay (1986) as one starting point for the identification of choice-structuring properties. Tremblay studied credit card fraud and noted the potential for displacement between credit card and check guarantee fraud and the functional relation between the components of crime that contribute to the fraud cluster (like wallet theft and opening accounts under a false name).

Criminal behavior that transcends choice-structuring behavior (i.e., versatility) is characteristic of those people with the worst criminal careers (Farrington 1987). Displacement potential may be greatest when the offenders committing a particular type of crime are the most versatile. This link may allow cross-fertilization between studies of criminal careers and applications in crime prevention. Work on choice-structuring properties of criminal contexts is, in short, clearly an important complement to crime-prevention endeavors.

In summary, insights into the ways in which displacement is likely to occur have been thoughtful and ingenious. Nonetheless, no research on crime prevention has convincingly shown that total displacement does not occur. Nor can this be shown. If, in truth, displacement is complete, some displaced crime will probably fall outside the areas and types of crime being studied or be so dispersed as to be masked by background variation. In such an event, the optimist would speculate about why the unmeasured areas or types of crime probably escaped displaced crime, while the pessimist would speculate about why they probably did not. No research study, however massive, is likely to resolve the issue. The wider the scope of the study in terms of types of crime and places, the thinner the patina of displaced crime could be spread across them; thus disappearing into the realm of measurement error. Even if the degree of displacement were demonstrated in a particular context, problems of generalizability would arise.

III. Choosing Crime

All individuals or groups may be presumed to have preferences about crime displacement. We would rather that our own friends or families were not victimized and care more about this than we do about the victimization of others. We fetch our own children home from school, and only exceptionally escort those of strangers. We install locks and alarms in our own houses, and not in houses belonging to other people. We care little about displacement effects in so doing. When did we last take a door lock off on the grounds that it would decrease victimization elsewhere? Much of the recent thrust of crime-prevention thinking in, to name but a few Western countries, France, Canada, the United States, and the United Kingdom has focused on the role of the community in preventing crime (Hope and Shaw 1988). The extension of self-interested action from the individual to the community level is the common factor in these enterprises. Are there any principles that could apply to choices of crime-prevention measures even if displacement were total?

One of the things we can be sure of is that there is widespread social consensus on the relative seriousness of crimes. This is clear from national victimization surveys in both the United States and the United Kingdom (Wolfgang et al. 1985; Pease 1988). Certain crimes (terrorism, murder, rape, and violent and sexual offenses toward children) are uniformly toward the top of the scale. How should we address issues of displacement from such offenses? Assuming total displacement, for the most serious crimes, these can only be to crimes of an equal level or a lower level of seriousness since the offenses being displaced are the most serious that could be committed. Because displacement could not increase seriousness, and because attention should be given to limiting all opportunities to commit the most heinous crimes, we would argue that considerations of displacement are irrelevant (and would be considered distasteful) when dealing with the most serious crimes.

The picture is more complex for less serious offenses. In brief, our contention is that displacement makes a crime-prevention initiative undesirable when the substituted crimes are as serious or more serious than the displaced crimes, and there is no other reason why crimes in the place originally victimized should be deflected from their target. If there are other reasons why crimes should be deflected, only displacement to crimes that are more serious should serve to cast doubt on the crime-prevention initiative. The perhaps startling implication of this formulation is that the displacement effect should not be sought in similar crimes, but in crimes of similar or greater seriousness—often in crimes of greater seriousness only.

What would constitute legitimate social reasons for acknowledging the success of a crime-prevention initiative that merely deflected crimes of equal seriousness to other times and places? The discussion of this issue must start with a brief examination of extant patterns of crime victimization.

A. Inequality of Victimization by Time and Place

The traditional geographic approach to the study of crime has been to map the places where offenses take place and, to a lesser extent, to map offenders' and victims' homes. The statistical analysis of crime proceeds by aggregating events spatially or temporally. The aim of such analysis is to relate the incidence of crime to crime vulnerability, whether in terms of the physical environment or of areas of vulnerable populations. Once aggregated, such statistics are compared to area characteristics, and "ecological" inferences are drawn (Herbert 1982).

A consistent theme throughout criminology has been that crime is concentrated in particular areas. Felson (1983) gives precedence in the field of crime ecology to Colquohoun (1796) by virtue of the latter's quasi-statistical study of a crime wave in London in the late eighteenth century. Better known is Guerry's (1833) study in France, which mapped convictions for property and violent crimes by area. The twentieth-century tradition of such study is often associated with the pioneering work of Clifford Shaw and his colleagues in Chicago (see Shaw et al. 1929).

Urban-rural differences have consistently been shown in such studies. Enormous differences exist within city areas, with "zones of transition" and "interstitial areas" being terms used to characterize those inner-city areas with high rates of crime. The terms are used to represent the transitory nature of populations there and the areas' intermediate position between the central business district and more stable residential areas. Uneven distribution appears to be a characteristic of crime, however small the geographical unit chosen. Ramsay (1982, p. 23) notes that "this is well recognized by police forces, which have traditionally divided up their areas of responsibility into different beats of varying dimensions. Similarly, manpower is concentrated more in some places or beats than other, quieter spots."

Classification of housing types (associated with area "type") yields massive differences in rates of residential crime (Hough and Mayhew 1985; Hope and Hough 1988). Even within a city-center area, settings for crime are not distributed evenly. In two English cities, it was found that 15 percent of all public houses (pubs) accounted for 42 percent of all disorder associated with licensed premises (Ramsay 1986). In a study of burglary of schools, "some 38 schools (64 percent) had less than five burglaries between 1977 and 1978 including 11 schools (19 percent) which had no burglaries at all. In contrast, 19 percent had 10 or more burglaries each during this two year period. The most victimized school had 24 burglaries" (Hope 1982, p. 8).

Differences between areas in rates of crime do seem to hold up in victimization surveys down to the smallest analyzable level. For instance, Sparks, Genn, and Dodd (1977) showed differences in level of victimization in three areas of London. Kinsey (1984) did the same in Merseyside. Jones, McLean, and Young (1986) showed similar differences within a single London borough (Islington).

In the United States, analyses of official (Uniform Crime Reports) and victimization (National Crime Survey) data show that family structure, mobility, and opportunity factors had their strongest effect on personal criminal victimization rates in a specific area. Poverty and income inequality were found to be related to official rates of property crime. Property (but not violent) crime rates were positively associated with the percentage of divorced and black people in an area (Sampson 1985). Hakim et al. (1979) and Hakim and Rengert (1981) identify crime spillover between adjacent areas in response to changes in police expenditure, thus suggesting (but not conclusively demonstrating) crime deflection across administrative boundaries.

In their review, Brantingham and Brantingham (1981, p. 10) conclude that "spatial variance in crime remains a fundamental fact requiring explanation." Although somewhat less studied, as it is across space so it is across time, even for short periods. Some evidence exists for offenses of public disorder, where incidents cluster around midnight and late afternoon/early evening (Ramsay 1982).

Time distribution of burglaries is similarly nonrandom by time of day or by day of the week (Scarr 1973; Maguire 1982; Rengert and Wasilchick 1985; Forrester, Chatterton, and Pease 1988; Nee and Taylor 1988), with times of low occupancy consistently overrepresented. Rengert and Wasilchick (1985) structure their analysis of burglaries around the dimension of time and the movements of burglars over time. The type of property taken also varies by day, with cash being taken proportionately more often in midweek (Forrester, Chatterton, and Pease 1988) and luxury goods on weekends. Studies in the United States and Canada have shown that residential burglaries also vary with the phase of the moon (Purpura 1979; Polvi et al. 1989). Offenses of theft from shops (Ekblom 1987b) also cluster around particular times of the working day. Murders and other serious offenses of violence are found to be concentrated around particular times (Walmsley 1986). In short, when it has been possible to identify offense time, that time is scarcely ever distributed evenly across the range of the possible. The only exception of which we are aware is the distribution of the times of rape in Minneapolis (Sherman 1989).

Although the distribution of crimes in both space and time is scarcely ever found to be random, caution is required when working with aggregate data. Spatially, it is often difficult to identify meaningful entities to which data may be aggregated. As a result, arbitrary statistical or administrative boundaries are used. This leads to the possible misinterpretation of figures, as it becomes impossible to discern whether crimes are highly clustered in a small part of the unit of analysis or spread more evenly across it. Further, highly clustered crimes may disappear, statistically, if clusters fall on administrative boundaries so that crimes within the cluster are shared between more than one statistical zone. For both of these reasons, it is more likely that real clusters will be missed than that imaginary ones will be invented. Also because the clusters in victimization surveys can be noticed, however small the unit of analysis, one can be confident of the reality of crime clustering. As for the time dimension, many geographers have recognized that the character of a location and its relationship with other locations varies over time (Lynch 1972; Parkes and Thrift 1980).

B. Individual Differences in Crime Victimization

Some people are victimized more than others. Sparks, Genn, and Dodd (1977) were the first researchers in the United Kingdom seriously to address the issue. National crime surveys, wherever conducted since 1977, have confirmed the same patterns of victimization by age, sex, and social status (Gottfredson 1984). Pease (1988), in a reanalysis of British Crime Survey data, also showed that those groups that suffer most crime are also those that suffer the most serious crime, as rated by victims. It has been demonstrated that the incidence of second or subsequent burglary victimizations is well in excess of the statistically expected rate (Forrester, Chatterton, and Pease 1988). Canadian research has shown that this is especially marked during the month immediately after a burglary, when the observed rate of a second victimization is some twelve times the rate that would be expected if the burglaries were to be regarded as independent events (Polvi, Looman, and Pease 1989). Some automobile models are especially likely to be stolen (Burrows, Ekblom, and Heal 1979). Some shops are especially vulnerable to shop theft (Ekblom 1986). Women vary by age and marital status in their chances of receiving obscene telephone calls (Pease 1985).

Table 1 summarizes data about inequality in victimization gleaned from the British Crime Surveys of 1982 and 1984. It depicts the observed and, assuming a natural random distribution, the expected numbers of people victimized twice or three times in a given type of crime. The observed rate of multiple victimization is several times higher than would be expected for each type of crime. Of course, these differences could be a function of area inhabited, age, and lifestyle (see Gottfredson 1984). Thissen and Wainer (1983) report a preliminary technical study, using National Crime Survey data, setting out to model the probability of becoming a crime victim. Their data show nonindependence of vic-

TABLE 1

Rates of Multiple Victimization:
British Crime Surveys, 1982 and 1984

| Offense | N | No. of Victimizations | | | |
| | | 2 | | 3 | |
		Observed	Expected	Observed	Expected
Domestic burglary with loss	21,073	50	8	10	0
Theft from person	21,883	31	4	6	0
Violence	21,834	91	14	43	0
Theft of motor vehicle	15,789	56	12	7	0
Theft from motor vehicle	15,722	270	138	80	7
Criminal damage to motor vehicle	15,634	466	256	156	17
Theft of pedal cycle	9,545	34	10	4	1

SOURCE.—Hough and Mayhew (1983, 1985).
NOTE.—Unweighted data.

timization experience across crime categories. Sparks (1981) distinguishes five possible reasons for disproportionate multiple victimization. They are:

1. *Precipitation.* "A victim who precipitates an offender action does or says something that works on the emotions or passions of the offender to such an extent that he makes the offender act as he does" (p. 772).

2. *Vulnerability.* "Some people . . . are less than normally capable of preventing crimes against themselves. . . . Thus, the very young and the elderly are physically less able to resist violent attack, as are some adult females. The mentally defective, immigrants, and the uneducated or inexperienced are especially vulnerable to deception and fraud" (p. 773).

3. *Opportunity.* This is "of course a logically necessary condition for crime" (p. 774). People with a car, a boat, and a checkbook provide opportunities for car theft, boat theft, and check fraud.

4. *Attractiveness.* "Plainly some targets are more attractive than others from a criminal's point of view. Thus, persons who look affluent are better prospects for robbery than persons who look impoverished;

expensive houses full of durable consumer goods are more attractive to a burglar than tenements in a slum. . . . Some varieties of attractiveness cannot logically be concealed. How do you make a Lamborghini look less like a Lamborghini, for example, by letting it get very dirty or painting it a hideous shade of chartreuse?" (p. 775).

5. *Impunity.* "Some persons are selected as victims precisely because they are believed to have limited access to the usual machinery of social control. Thus, homosexuals are said to be frequent victims of blackmail and extortion because they are thought to be reluctant to notify the police. Similarly criminals, ex-criminals, neighborhood paranoiacs, and members of minority groups may be chosen as victims because they are thought to be unable or unwilling to call the police" (pp. 775–76).

Whatever their origin, there is a case for looking at policy options for the multiple victim. If there is a choice to be made for priorities in crime deflection, there is a case for prior victimization to confer such priority.

C. Measuring Inequality in Victimization

We have contended that the appropriate principle for examination is not whether complete crime displacement occurs, but, if we were to make an explicit policy that accepted the inevitability of a certain level of crime, how we would choose to have crime distributed across time, place, and victims. Such apparently intolerable policy decisions are already taken by certain police forces. For example, a point-scoring system is used to assess the solvability of crimes, and only those offenses that exceed a certain threshold have manpower allotted to them by certain English forces (Leppard 1989). If part of the force's jurisdiction comprises a difficult-to-police area where public cooperation is poor, it would, under this scheme, have fewer, if any, resources deployed within it. Such effectively unpoliced "no-go" areas are reputed to exist in British cities. The police have, in effect, decided that these are areas where a higher-than-average level of criminal activity should be allowed to continue. This decision implies a knowledge of the present distribution of crime.

Ekblom (1988) discusses strategies for the collection and analysis of data on reported crime. In his diagram (see fig. 1), the analysis and interpretation of data lead naturally to devising and implementing preventive strategies. Our approach can provide a rationale for breaking out of the reactive cycle that such a process often implies and could lead

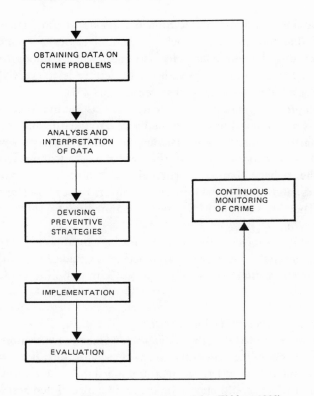

FIG. 1.—The preventive process (after Ekblom 1988)

to a proactive approach. The probabilities of particular crimes taking place in particular locations at particular times would be known on the basis of previous experience. In addition, an explicit policy would exist that would concede that the reduction of crime levels to zero was unlikely to be achieved and that would establish acceptable levels for particular crimes in particular areas. Such policies are implicit in most policing, but in our view an explicit philosophical and technical framework is required to understand the extent to which such policies are adopted and to formulate future policy.

The emergence of powerful desktop microcomputers, with the capacity to store data bases of several million characters and with good graphics facilities for the presentation of data in the form of statistical diagrams or maps, has revolutionized the possibilities for the collection and analysis of crime data. For example, the arrival of "desktop-mapping" programs that are designed for use with standard microbased data-base software has made automated crime analysis at precinct level routinely possible.

The geographical aspects of such analysis, however, are unsophisticated. Crimes are located by the computer on a base map that is analogous to the pin map on the wall. The main advantage of the computerized system is the possibility of selecting types of crime or time periods and replotting the points on the map. This ability can reveal spatial or temporal patterns that were not anticipated. However, it is more usual to shade areas of the map, corresponding to some operational unit, such as a beat or a precinct. Different levels of shading correspond to aggregated crime levels over some fixed period of time.

Typically the data for such a system are kept in a simple computer data-base file including coded data for offense characteristics such as nature of offense (crime category); location of offense (both site details, e.g., car park or stairway, and locational details, such as the intersection of Fifth Avenue and Thirty-second Street, may be recorded); timing (time, date, day of the week); method (modus operandi); target (e.g., person, car, property); victim (age, sex, home address, etc.); circumstances (lighting, crowding, potential intervenors); success (attempted or completed); cost (amount, to whom); offender (age, sex, home address, etc.); and find location (location where goods or vehicle have been found) (after Ekblom 1988).

Within that selected list of variables, there are a number of geographical references. In addition to the location of the crime, the home locations of both victim and offender and the location where the goods, vehicle, or even body were found may be recorded. These characteristics of the individual crime must be assigned some spatial framework in order to allow us to analyze the geography that underlies the observed patterns of crime and to explore whether spatial and temporal displacements are taking place.

Such a structure was suggested by Berry (1964) who proposed a geographic data matrix. This three-dimensional matrix comprised rows, each of which represents a distinct "place"; columns, which contain attributes of that place; and slices, which reflect the passage of time (fig. 2). Each individual cell within this matrix would contain a single geographic "fact," or item of data. Berry proceeded to use this matrix to demonstrate the range of methods geographers use to analyze spatial relations. Purely descriptive traditional studies concentrated on a limited time period, during which all other characteristics of a place were considered to remain constant and so were limited to a number of

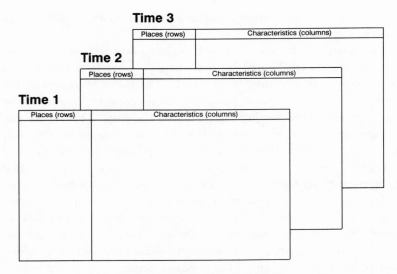

FIG. 2.—The geographic data matrix (after Berry 1964)

adjacent rows in the matrix. In crime-pattern analysis this might correspond to a weekly summary of reported crime by city precinct. Each row in the matrix would correspond to a precinct, each column a crime type, and each cell entry the number of occurrences of the crime in the time period. The principal object of interest here is the geographical reporting unit, the beat, block, or precinct. Repeated returns or crimes over time, in this form, provide the third dimension of time. Such an approach is essentially descriptive rather than analytical and serves mainly to compare one area with another.

The matrix lends itself also to systematic studies. Such studies concern a limited time span but concentrate on a small number of columns (characteristics of place). In the case of crime, a single crime type would be the focus of attention, and its prevalence in each place would constitute one of the columns. This would be treated as the dependent variable. Additional columns would contain further characteristics of the places that might help to explain variation in the prevalence of the given crime. These independent variables might be any characteristics, such as the nature and vulnerability of the population or the physical nature of the places, that could predispose them to the occurrence of that particular crime. Such an analysis lends itself to "ecological" explanations of crime. Where a series of explanatory variables are found to vary with the incidence of a particular crime type, it can be concluded that those variables *may* account for that type of crime. Such explanations have to be treated with caution, however, as they include no evidence for the relation being a causal one, and it is possible to commit an "ecological fallacy" by attributing a relation that exists at an areal level to individuals. For example, a correlation between the proportion of the population of a set of areas who are members of ethnic minorities and the mugging rates does not tell us whether members of those minorities are the perpetrators, the victims, or even the innocent bystanders in an area where mugging is prevalent.

One avenue of geographical analysis proposed by Berry (1964) worth exploring is the impact that events at one place and time could have on other places later. This approach has been important in such fields as the study of the spread of innovations and other information (Hagerstrand 1952) and in epidemiology where the diffusion of infectious diseases has been investigated (Haggett, Cliff, and Frey 1977). It is equally appropriate to use for looking at movements in criminal activity as long as it is consistent with our liberalized view of the displacement issue.

A problem with Berry's matrix is that place is undefined. As a result, any arbitrary spatial unit for which data are collected is considered to be a place, and it is assumed that the definition of these entities is independent of the phenomenon under study. This will never be the case for official criminal statistics (but could be for victimization data) because statistics will be collected by police districts or other spatial units, making it difficult to discriminate between the characteristics of the "place" and the actions of the police force.

Ideally, for our purposes, an information system would be required that would allow the vulnerability of different people and environment groupings to be plotted. A common device is that of a surface that can be presented as a contour map. One can think of such a surface for all crime or for particular types of crime. Locations with a high number of reported crimes appear as high points. If action were successfully directed at such a high spot, it would be reduced in height. Myopic crime control would look only at high spots. More balanced crime control would consider the surface as a whole. An implausible ideal would be to pull the plug and reduce the surface uniformly to zero. If that is not feasible (as it never is), the question is raised, Which is more desirable, a surface with a few high peaks of vulnerability surrounded by low foothills of relatively safe environments or a plateau of relatively uniform vulnerability?

IV. A Conceptual Model for the Distribution of Crime

Figure 3 represents a way of thinking about crime inequality and the response to it in the form of a triangle. The apex of the triangle represents the ideal state of no crime (uniform surface at zero). The base of the triangle represents the conflict between two possible aims if only the distribution, but not the extent, of crime could be controlled (i.e., total displacement). The left corner represents the socially equitable state of equal exposure to crime victimization (the plateau), in which each citizen is equally likely to become a victim of any type of crime. The right corner represents the "crime-fuse situation" (the high peaks and low foothills). This last term is the only one that is not self-explanatory, although the concept underlying it will be from the discussion of the surface. The term is used as an analogy to an electrical circuit, in which a deliberately weak point, the fuse, is included so that a power surge will have quite minor consequences. Similarly, one can choose to concentrate the crime in particular areas, limiting the number of areas that have to be controlled and making an obvious starting point for inquiries once an event has occurred.

If a state of no crime is the goal, measures are taken against the crime whenever and wherever it occurs independently of victim or location. This objective is the naive crime-prevention goal of political rhetoric. It is, however, difficult to think of an instance where, in practice, all cases of an offense type are attacked with equal enthusiasm.

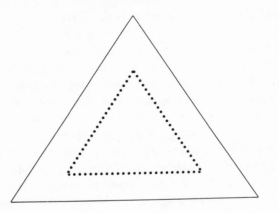

FIG. 3.—Schematic representation of crime inequality

If equal "access" to victimization is taken to be the aim, enforcement emphasis is concentrated on those areas or victim groups suffering disproportionately. In its pure form, this approach would not concern itself with the lightly victimized. In practice, effort would be concentrated on the inner cities and on young males.

Fuses are contentious, but they are practiced. If crime is concentrated in particular areas or at particular times, it is easier to control and to clear and possibly less upsetting to those who know which times and places to avoid. Entrapment is consistent with fuse thinking, even where no offenders are caught. A fuse philosophy would tacitly accept the existence of a place where, for instance, prostitution is rife on the basis that, while women living in such places are subject to much sexual harrassment, the net effect is preferable to what it would be if all women had equal exposure to this kind of victimization. Both men and women at least know the places to avoid. Fuse thinking would not seek to deny licenses to drink from unruly pubs on the grounds that you know where to look for suspected people, while people in other pubs take their ease in relative peace and quiet.

Within the larger triangle is included another with dotted lines. This can be thought of as the realistically achievable range of crime states. Actions may be taken to move crime toward or away from the "fuse" or equal opportunity states. Movement toward equal opportunity would consist in offering protections toward the most highly victimized individuals, times, or places. Movement toward fuses would involve offering protections to those who have not yet been victimized. Movement toward no crime would involve the removal of opportunities irrespective of prior victimization experience.

In fact it would be better to think of the picture as a pyramid. Each section of the pyramid represents one type of crime, but movement of the type of crime currently under consideration would affect the state of affairs for other types of crime. For instance, reduction of domestic burglary would likely involve an increase in criminal damage, if only to the extent reflecting the unsuccessful attempt to force entry.

A massive range of social and physical factors moves victimization experience toward fuse situations. With respect to individual victims, Sparks (1981) lists five factors which we mentioned earlier. Supplementing these are economic factors. Those who can afford to move to areas of low victimization turn those who remain into fuses. Women who can afford private transport thereby make those who cannot into fuses. The whole pattern of crime is a result of forces that pull toward either the fuse or the equal exposure position. In essence, when we direct policy toward preventing an observed distribution of crime, we are not interfering with a state of nature but are instead injecting policy choices into a situation where the pattern is already determined.

While the fact of unequal victimization is a commonplace of criminology research, its measurement has not been seriously undertaken in any general way; still less have its implications for crime-prevention strategy been considered. This is not true of social geography where the measurement of inequalities between areas is commonplace in order to help devise compensatory policies.

Two measures are generally used. The first is the location quotient, an index measuring the over- or underrepresentation of some phenomenon in each of a number of areas. Perhaps the easiest way to understand the location quotient is to think of it as the number by which the rate of crimes in a particular area would have to be divided in order to bring it to the overall average crime rate for the region being studied. For example, if the national annual rate for auto theft is one in a hundred, a town where one car in fifty was stolen every year would have a location quotient of two. That means the chance of having your car stolen in that town is twice the national average. Or, put another way, the auto theft rate in that town would have to be halved in order to bring it to the national average.

Mathematically the quotient is very easy to calculate:

$$Q = \frac{Xi/Yi}{X/Y},$$

where, for example,

Q = location quotient;
Xi = total number of households burgled in area i;
X = total number of households burgled in all areas under consideration;
Yi = total number of households in area i; and
Y = total number of households in all areas under consideration.

The location quotient is calculated for each area and varies between zero (no burglaries in that area), less than one (a lower than average proportion of burglaries in that area), and through one (exactly the expected number of burglaries if they are equally distributed). Values greater than one reflect an overrepresentation of burglary in the area.

The location quotient allows us to assess the vulnerability of individual areas to a particular crime and is potentially useful in the plotting of our vulnerability surface independently of the absolute number of victims. This is of interest if we are concerned with policies for the adjustment of these vulnerabilities as it relates the propensity of a particular social environment to generate an excess, or to enjoy an underrepresentation, of a particular crime.

However, if we wish to try to calibrate our triangle using empirical data, a summary measure or index is needed that will place each type of crime on the equal distribution–fuse axis. The Gini coefficient is an index of concentration that measures the degree to which a distribution deviates from being equal. It is calculated using the following formula:

$$G = \frac{1}{2} \sum_{i=1}^{N} \frac{100 \, Xi}{X} - \frac{100 \, Yi}{Y},$$

where, for example,

G = Gini coefficient;
N = total number of areas;
Xi = total number of households burgled in area i;
X = total number of households burgled in all areas under consideration;
Yi = total number of housholds in area i; and
Y = total number of households in all areas under consideration.

A Gini coefficient value of zero corresponds to perfect equality of distribution, a value of 100 perfect inequality (all of that crime type concentrated in one region). Values between zero and 100 measure the degree of concentration of a crime.

The vertical axis of our conceptual triangle can be calibrated by a measure of the prevalence of a given crime. This is calculated as the number of actual victims of a given crime type divided by the number of potential victims of that crime type.

Crime statistics for small areas suffer from serious inconsistencies, as discussed above. Ideally an information system could be devised that would enable us to complete a small subset of the Berry geographic matrix for crime. However, such systems do not yet exist. Large-scale victimization surveys do exist; one such survey is the British Crime Survey, which was carried out in 1982 and 1984 (Hough and Mayhew

1983, 1985). This is a large sample survey that has accumulated, over those two years, some 22,000 responses from members of the general public. The sample is spatially stratified and adjusted for the actual populations living in different types of areas. Although geographical areas are not identified, two variables give us a reasonable surrogate for different types of neighborhood in the British context. These are residential pattern (whether a household lives in owner-occupied, public-sector rented, or privately rented accommodation) and area type, which separates rural, suburban, urban, and inner-city environments.

In Britain, residence patterns are a very strong social-status indicator. The public housing system, run by local government (authorities are known as councils reflecting their elected status, hence such housing is known as council housing), though declining in size still accounts for some 35 percent of British households. Potential council tenants are subjected to stringent needs tests, and council housing is generally perceived to be low-income and low-status housing. The present government in Britain has, since 1979, encouraged a rapid run down of the local authority sector by giving tenants a right to buy their rented properties at a substantial discount. The effect of this has been to remove much of the more desirable public rented housing from local authority control, leaving the larger, less popular housing estates in public hands. In urban areas, large concentrations of council property are associated with areas of low income, unskilled workers, high unemployment, and low car ownership. In the British preoccupation with class, knowing whether a person owns their house, albeit with a large mortgage, is the first, and possibly the most vital clue to their social position. As a result, housing areas are increasingly segregated by status, with council housing and some privately rented property occupying the bottom rungs of the ladder.

The classic Burgess and Park (see Burgess 1927) model of city structure, which differentiates the central business district from the transitional inner-city zone through the zone of workers' housing to the better-off suburban and commuter areas, remains a useful descriptive tool for British cities. Cities are socially differentiated, and, with the exception of London's West End, social status generally increases with distance from the center. Thus the inner city, urban, suburban, rural classification used in the British Crime Survey offers another useful correlate for the types and the social status of neighborhoods in which the victims live. The combination of these two variables, residential pattern and position on the urban-rural continuum, accounts for much of the social variability that one would expect to find between different places.

It is possible to calculate location quotients, Gini coefficients, and prevalence rates from the crime surveys, and such an analysis gives a useful insight into the potential for, and the possible effects of, distributing crimes more equally, or, conversely, concentrating them in a small number of fuse areas.

We have calculated an overall propensity rate and a Gini coefficient for each of thirty-nine types of crime, dividing crimes against the person from crimes against property. A remarkable result of this analysis is that there is a relatively high correlation between prevalence and concentration for both types of crime. When concentration is plotted against prevalence, a negative J-shaped distribution is obtained in the case of both personal and property crimes. For crimes against property, the correlation coefficient between prevalence and concentration is $-.48$, rising to $-.74$ when a logarithmic transformation is applied to the prevalence scores. (This has the effect of straightening out the J-shaped curve.) A higher correlation between prevalence and concentration is found for crimes against the person, $-.67$ and $-.95$, respectively. If both categories of crime are amalgamated, the correlations are $-.55$ and $-.85$, respectively.

How can we interpret these findings? First we must assure ourselves of the nature of the relation. Prevalence is clearly the independent variable, as it would be a tortuous argument to say that the concentration of crime (a pattern that emerges only after the crimes are committed) accounts for the frequency with which crimes are committed. The second question we need to ask is whether these observations are simply a statement of an obvious relation between prevalence and concentration. At the extremes, the observed relationship is self-evident. The very rare crime will inevitably appear concentrated because it is committed insufficiently frequently to be distributed equally through space, while a universal crime will inevitably appear to be equally distributed because every possible victim or perpetrator will be involved. For example, if Fort Knox were to be broken into, the crime would inevitably appear to be totally concentrated because the opportunity to perpetrate that crime exists in only one place, and a successful robbery would probably be a unique event. If, on the other hand, one were to take the opposite extreme, and probably unfair, proposition that nobody fills in a tax return honestly, then tax evasion would have a prevalence of 100 percent and would be completely evenly distributed.

However, between those extremes, once the prevalence rate exceeds some threshold, crimes are free to be concentrated or distributed more equally; yet the relations still hold. Over 90 percent of the variation in concentration of crimes against the person is explained by the log of the prevalence. Rare and usually more serious crime is concentrated in a small number of areas—our fuses standing above a plateau of less serious, more evenly distributed crimes. Bearing in mind that this analysis is based on a victim survey and crimes are attributed to the home area of the victim rather than the location where the crime was committed, it appears plausible that many of the recorded crimes against the person resulted from a victim venturing into a hostile environment. This hypothesis is supported by an examination of the distribution of crimes against property. In this case, many crimes against fixed property, such as houses, are concentrated, while the plateau is of crimes related to motor vehicles and other movable property. It appears that the issue in both of these cases is not the displacement of criminal activity to more likely target areas but the very reverse. Victims make themselves vulnerable by venturing from their relatively safe home environments into areas where they become highly vulnerable to crimes against their person or their property.

The consistent pattern that emerges from our analysis is the existence of highly criminalized fuse areas. These usually run-down inner-city areas contain a highly victimized population and present a dangerous environment to the stranger. The "flight from the cities" and the increasing wariness of visitors leads to a displacement of crime toward the local, already highly victimized, population. The standard response to the public outcry about the state of affairs in such areas is often to increase police activity substantially, usually temporarily.

To summarize, we have been at pains to specify how geographic information systems have the capacity to measure crime distribution in ways that succinctly identify the extent and nature of inequality in crime victimization. They thus provide the basis for the understanding and measurement of what constitutes benign and malign displacement in spatial terms. The value position that we take is that crime victimization should not exacerbate inequalities of other origin. On that basis, other things being equal, crime deflection that makes for a more equal spread of victimization is benign. Taken together with earlier conclusions, we would articulate a prescription for the proper measurement of displacement/deflection which incorporates the following elements. For the most serious crimes, deflection is not an issue. It can never be a reason for failing to try to prevent such crimes. For crime-prevention attempts generally, malign displacement would be measured as an increase in offending of equal or greater seriousness against more highly victimized groups or areas. It would, however, be measured only as offenses of greater seriousness outside these areas. In other words, displacement of crime of the same level of seriousness is malign only if it serves to exacerbate inequalities in victimization. It is benign if it serves to equalize them.

Such a formulation would serve to make the assessment of displacement/deflection distinctly different from that currently encountered. However, in its simple form set out above, it will generate anomalies. For instance, since young males are a heavily victimized group, it would take displacement to be benign which transfers crime from young male victims to old female victims, although the impact of victimization is very much greater in the latter group. A more sophisticated version of the approach, in effect a simple extension of it, would involve the measurement of inequality in victimization weighted by its anticipated seriousness. The elements in the assessment of deflection set out above would be unaffected, merely being based on a more sophisticated variant of the notion of victimization.

V. Conclusions

Displacement has been addressed in much of the literature as the degree of successful search for alternative criminal opportunities by individuals thwarted in their pursuit of one type of crime or victim. Our argument is that displacement, which we prefer to call deflection to draw attention to the initially prevented crime, can be seen in a much broader framework where the distribution of crimes and their victims is the end result of a series of choices taken by society as a whole. The prevalent choice of allowing both crime and its victims to become spatially concentrated is not the only choice available. Actions can be taken that will displace crime not only temporally, spatially, and tactically, and to new targets or types of crime as suggested at the beginning of this essay, but also from those currently likely to commit crimes to other potential criminals. Thus conceived, displacement/deflection becomes an issue less concerned with how crime can be prevented than one of how we are prepared to see crime distributed across space and different groups in society, although we are by no means of the opinion that all deflected crime occurs somewhere else. Once it has been accepted that present patterns of crime can be viewed as a response to the distribution of criminal opportunities and that all such opportunities cannot be eliminated, we must decide whether to continue to share the burden of victimization unequally as at present, or more equally where an acceptable degree of risk is borne by the whole population.

Explicit policies of crime redistribution are clearly difficult for politicians to promote publicly. They address the fears and prejudices of the individual voter who is more likely to be concerned that his risk of being a victim is being increased than with any concept of social equity. Even if that increase is a marginal one, leaving his probability of becoming a victim very low, the individual can imagine only one of two possibilities: he is safe or a crime is committed against him. He is unlikely to be impressed by the aggregate patterns on which our approach is based. For the politician, the Holy Grail of prevention by apprehending criminals and hardening targets is, therefore, taken as the organizing principle for most crime-control programs because it is most likely to appeal to the individual voter's self-interest. If the displacing or deflecting effect of most such actions were to be recognized by politicians whose social conscience extended beyond their own constituencies, a different type of policy might emerge.

Both in Britain and in the United States, cities bear witness to a long-standing preference for relatively extreme versions of the fuse philosophy. Deprived inner-city areas suffer from a very high degree of criminal activity of most types. Such activity can be tolerated by the rest of society for a variety of reasons. It is easy to blame the plight of unsuccessful members of society, both as perpetrators and victims of crime, on their own shortcomings. The problem is localized in an alien culture, and the rest of society feels safer as a result. The police are seen as a valiant army fighting against insuperable odds. Their role in society is enhanced because of their undoubted heroism, while their relative lack of success is excusable because of the size of the task. By contrast, those living outside the fuse areas feel safe and usually are safe.

Let us assume that unlimited resources were made available to apply the whole spectrum of remedies favored by politicians of right or left to the fuse areas. Such remedies might include routine deterrent sentences, massively increasing policing, or martial law, the effective organization of protection for property and individuals through to wealth creation and income-enhancement programs to offer potential criminals an alternative way of life. Even after such a program, would a consensus be arrived at that the elimination of highly criminalized fuse areas was a desirable solution to the worst excesses of the crime problem? The elimination of fuse areas is only likely to prove attractive if two conditions are satisfied; the fuse areas must be perceived to impinge on personal quality of life or civic pride, and it must be presumed by most citizens that the elimination of fuse areas would not materially detract from their own quality of life. For instance, areas of active drug dealing may be seen to attract your own children and may cause the inconvenience of avoiding fuse areas while traveling on foot. So long as you do not believe that people will be dealing on *your* street if moved on, elimination of the fuse may be favored. We contend that the circumstances under which both conditions are satisfied are likely to be rare and may be limited to drug-related crime and prostitution. With these exceptions, we believe that society may have a vested interest in containing most activity within a limited geographical, temporal, and opportunity space. Most attempts to alter the opportunity surface would threaten that interest.

Crime displacement or deflection is an idea that is valuable not only for the planning of specific short-term strategies, but because it illuminates the choices that have been made which lead to the present pattern of crime. Alternative choices exist, but the will to exercise them probably does not.

REFERENCES

Allatt, Patricia. 1984. "Residential Security: Containment and Displacement of Burglary." *Howard Journal of Criminal Justice* 23:99–116.

Bennett, Trevor, and Richard Wright. 1984. *Burglars on Burglary: Prevention and the Offender.* Aldershot: Gower.

Berry, Brian J. L. 1964. "Approaches to Regional Analysis: A Synthesis." *Annals of the Association of American Geographers* 54:114–36.

Bordua, David J. 1986. "Firearms Ownership and Violent Crime: A Comparison of Illinois Counties." In *The Social Ecology of Crime*, edited by James M. Byrne and Robert J. Sampson. New York: Springer-Verlag.

Brantingham, Patricia L. 1986. "Trends in Canadian Crime Prevention." In *Situational Crime Prevention: From Theory into Practice*, edited by Kevin Heal and Gloria K. Laycock. London: H.M. Stationery Office.

Brantingham, Patricia L., and Paul J. Brantingham. 1984. "Burglary Mobility and Crime Prevention Planning." In *Coping with Burglary*, edited by Ronald V. Clarke and Tim J. Hope. Lancaster: Kluwer-Nijhoff.

Brantingham, Paul J., and Patricia L. Brantingham, eds. 1981. *Environmental Criminology*. Beverly Hills, Calif.: Sage.

Burgess, Edward W. 1927. "The Determination of Gradients in the Growth of the City." Research paper. Chicago: University of Chicago, Department of Geography.

Burrows, John, Paul Ekblom, and Kevin Heal. 1979. *Crime Prevention and the Police*. Home Office Research Study no. 55. London: H.M. Stationery Office.

Chaiken, Jan M., M. W. Lawless, and K. A. Stevenson. 1974. *Impact of Police Activity on Crime: Robberies on the New York City Subway System*. Report no. R-1424-NYC. Santa Monica, Calif.: Rand.

Clarke, Ronald V. 1978. *Tackling Vandalism*. Home Office Research Study no. 47. London: H.M. Stationery Office.

Clarke, Ronald V., and Derek B. Cornish. 1985. "Modeling Offenders' Decisions: A Framework for Policy and Research." In *Crime and Justice: An Annual Review of Research*, vol. 6, edited by Michael Tonry and Norval Morris. Chicago: University of Chicago Press.

Clarke, Ronald V., and Patricia M. Mayhew. 1988. "The British Gas Suicide Story and Its Criminological Implications." In *Crime and Justice: A Review of Research*, vol. 10, edited by Michael Tonry and Norval Morris. Chicago: University of Chicago Press.

Colquohoun, Patrick. 1796. *A Treatise on the Police of the Metropolis, Containing a Detail of the Various Crimes and Misdemeanours by Which Publick and Private Property Are, at Present, Injured and Endangered; and Suggesting Remedies for Their Prevention*. London: Mawman.

Cook, Philip J. 1983. "The Influence of Gun Availability on Violent Crime Patterns." In *Crime and Justice: An Annual Review of Research*, vol. 4, edited by Michael Tonry and Norval Morris. Chicago: University of Chicago Press.

———. 1986. "Criminal Incapacitation Effects Considered in an Adaptive Choice Framework." In *The Reasoning Criminal*, edited by Derek B. Cornish and Ronald V. Clarke. New York: Springer-Verlag.

Cornish, Derek B., and Ronald V. Clarke, eds. 1986. *The Reasoning Criminal*. New York: Springer-Verlag.

Cornish, Derek B., and Ronald V. Clarke. 1988a. "Understanding Crime-Displacement: An Application of Rational Choice Theory." *Criminology* 7:933–47.

———. 1988b. "Crime Specialization, Crime Displacement and Rational Choice Theory." In *Criminal Behavior and the Justice System: Psychological Perspectives*, edited by H. Wegener, F. Losel, and J. Haisch. New York: Springer-Verlag.

Ekblom, Paul. 1986. *The Prevention of Shop Theft*. Home Office Crime Prevention Unit Paper no. 5. London: H.M. Stationery Office.

————. 1987*a*. *Preventing Robberies at Sub-Post Offices*. Home Office Crime Prevention Unit Paper no. 9. London: H.M. Stationery Office.

————. 1987*b*. Personal communication, March 4.

————. 1988. *Getting the Best out of Crime Analysis*. Home Office Crime Prevention Unit Paper no. 10. London: H.M. Stationery Office.

Farrington, David P. 1987. "Predicting Individual Crime Rates." In *Prediction and Classification: Criminal Justice Decision Making*, edited by Don M. Gottfredson and Michael Tonry. Vol. 9 of *Crime and Justice: A Review of Research*, edited by Michael Tonry and Norval Morris. Chicago: University of Chicago Press.

Felson, Michael. 1983. "Ecology of Crime." In *Encyclopedia of Crime and Justice*, vol. 2, edited by S. H. Kadish. New York: Free Press.

Forrester, David H., Michael R. Chatterton, and Ken Pease. 1988. *The Kirkholt Burglary Prevention Demonstration Project*. Home Office Crime Prevention Unit Paper no. 13. London: H.M. Stationery Office.

Gabor, Tomas. 1981. "The Crime Displacement Hypothesis: An Empirical Examination." *Crime and Delinquency* 27:390–404.

Gottfredson, Michael. 1984. *Victims of Crime: The Dimensions of Risk*. Home Office Research Study no. 81. London: H.M. Stationery Office.

Guerry, Andre M. 1833. *Essai sur la statistique morale de la France: precede d'un rapport a l'Academie des Sciences par MM. Lacroix, Silvestre et Girard*. Paris: Crochard.

Hagerstrand, Torsten. 1952. "The Propagation of Innovation Waves." *Lund Studies in Geography, B, Human Geography* 4:3–19.

Haggett, Peter, Andrew D. Cliff, and Allan Frey. 1977. *Locational Analysis in Human Geography*. 2d ed. London: Edward Arnold.

Hakim, Simon, and George F. Rengert. 1981. *Crime Spillover*. Beverly Hills, Calif.: Sage.

Hakim, Simon, A. Ovadia, E. Sagi, and J. Weinblatt. 1979. "Interjurisdictional Spillover of Crime and Police Expenditures." *Land Economics* 55:200–212.

Heal, Kevin, and Gloria K. Laycock. 1986. *Situational Crime Prevention: From Theory into Practice*. London: H.M. Stationery Office.

————. 1988. "The Development of Crime Prevention: Issues and Limitations." In *Communities and Crime Reduction*, edited by Tim Hope and Margaret Shaw. London: H.M. Stationery Office.

Herbert, David. 1982. *The Geography of Urban Crime*. Harlow: Longman.

Home Office. 1986. *Report of the Standing Conference Working Group on Commercial Robbery*. London: H.M. Stationery Office.

Hope, Tim. 1982. *Burglary in Schools: The Prospects for Prevention*. Home Office Research and Planning Unit Paper no. 11. London: H.M. Stationery Office.

Hope, Tim, and Michael Hough. 1988. "Crime and Incivilities: Data from the Second British Crime Survey." In *Communities and Crime Reduction*, edited by Tim Hope and Margaret Shaw. London: H.M. Stationery Office.

Hope, Tim, and Margaret Shaw, eds. 1988. *Communities and Crime Reduction*. London: H.M. Stationery Office.

Hough, Michael, and Patricia Mayhew. 1983. *British Crime Survey: First Report*. Home Office Research Study no. 76. London: H.M. Stationery Office.
———. 1985. *Taking Account of Crime*. Home Office Research Study no. 85. London: H.M. Stationery Office.
Jones, Trevor, Brian McLean, and Jock Young. 1986. *The Islington Crime Survey*. London: Tavistock.
Kelling, George L. 1988. *What Works—Research and the Police*. Washington, D.C.: National Institute of Justice.
Kelling, George L., Tony Pate, Duane Dieckman, and Charles E. Brown. 1974. *The Kansas City Preventive Patrol Experiment: A Summary Report*. Washington, D.C.: Police Foundation.
Kelling, George L., Mary Ann Wycoff, and Tony Pate. 1980. "Policing: A Research Agenda for Rational Policy Making." In *The Effectiveness of Policing*, edited by Ronald V. Clarke and J. Michael Hough. Farnborough: Gower.
Kinsey, Richard. 1984. *Merseyside Crime Survey First Report*. Liverpool: Merseyside City Council.
Laycock, Gloria K. 1984. *Reducing Burglary: A Study of Chemists' Shops*. Home Office Crime Prevention Unit Paper no. 1. London: H.M. Stationery Office.
———. 1985. "Property Marking: A Deterrent to Domestic Burglary." Home Office Crime Prevention Unit Paper no. 3. London: H.M. Stationery Office.
Leppard, David. 1989. "A Screen That Shields Thieves." *Sunday Times* (February 5, London, N.W. edition).
Letkemann, Peter. 1973. *Crime as Work*. Englewood Cliffs, N.J.: Prentice Hall.
Litton, Roger A. 1986. "Crime Prevention and Insurance." Ph.D. dissertation. Open University, Milton Keynes, Buckinghamshire, England.
———. 1990. *Crime, Crime Prevention, and Insurance*. Farnborough: Gower (forthcoming).
Lynch, Kevin. 1972. *What Time Is This Place?* Cambridge, Mass.: MIT Press.
Maguire, Michael. 1982. *Burglary in a Dwelling*. London: Heinemann.
Mayhew, Patricia, Ronald V. Clarke, Andrew Sturman, and J. Michael Hough. 1976. *Crime as Opportunity*. Home Office Research Study no. 34. London: H.M. Stationery Office.
Morris, Norval, and Gordon Hawkins. 1970. *The Honest Politician's Guide to Crime Control*. Chicago: University of Chicago Press.
Nee, Claire, and Maxwell Taylor. 1988. "Residential Burglary in the Republic of Ireland: A Situational Perspective." *Howard Journal of Criminal Justice* 27:80–95.
Parkes, David N., and Nigel J. Thrift. 1980. *Times, Spaces, and Places*. New York: Wiley.
Pease, Ken. 1985. "Obscene Telephone Calls to Women in England and Wales." *Howard Journal of Criminal Justice* 24:275–81.
———. 1988. *Judgements of Crime Seriousness: Evidence from the 1984 British Crime Survey*. Home Office Research and Planning Unit Paper no. 44. London: H.M. Stationery Office.

Pease, Ken, and Roger A. Litton. 1984. "Crime Prevention: Practice and Motivation." In *Psychology and Law*, edited by D. J. Muller, D. E. Blackman, and A. J. Chapman. New York: Wiley.

Police Foundation. 1981. *The Newark Foot Patrol Experiment*. Washington, D.C.: Police Foundation.

Polvi, Natalie, T. Looman, C. Humphries, and Ken Pease. 1989. "Repeat Break and Enter Victimisation: Time Course and Crime Prevention Opportunity." *Journal of Police Science and Administration* (forthcoming).

Polvi, Natalie, T. Looman, and Ken Pease. 1989. "Beware the Moonlit Sabbath." University of Saskatchewan, Department of Psychiatry, Saskatchewan, mimeographed.

Purpura, Philip P. 1979. "Police Activity and the Full Moon." *Journal of Police Science and Administration* 7:350–53.

Ramsay, Malcolm. 1982. *City-Centre Crime: The Scope for Situational Prevention*. Home Office Research and Planning Unit Paper no. 10. London: H.M. Stationery Office.

———. 1986. "Preventing Disorder." In *Situational Crime Prevention: From Theory into Practice*, edited by Kevin Heal and Gloria K. Laycock. London: H.M. Stationery Office.

Rengert, George, and John Wasilchick. 1985. *Suburban Burglary: A Time and a Place for Everything*. Springfield: Thomas.

Reppetto, Thomas A. 1976. "Crime Prevention and the Displacement Phenomenon." *Crime and Delinquency* 22:166–77.

Sampson, Robert J. 1985. "Neighborhood and Crime: The Structural Determinants of Personal Victimization." *Journal of Research in Crime and Delinquency* 22:7–40.

Scarr, H. A. 1973. *Patterns of Burglary*. Washington, D.C.: National Institute of Law Enforcement and Criminal Justice.

Scholberg, Stein, and Donn B. Parker. 1983. "Computer Crime." In *Encyclopedia of Crime and Justice*, vol. 1, edited by Sanford H. Kadish. New York: Free Press.

Shaw, Clifford R., H. D. McKay, F. M. Zorbaugh, and L. S. Cottrell. 1929. *Delinquency Areas*. Chicago: University of Chicago Press.

Sherman, Lawrence. 1989. Personal communication, March 7.

Sparks, Richard F. 1981. "Multiple Victimization, Evidence, Theory and Future Research." *Journal of Criminal Law and Criminology* 72:762–78.

Sparks, Richard F., Hazel Genn, and David Dodd. 1977. *Surveying Victims*. Chichester: Wiley.

Svensson, Bo. 1986. "Welfare and Criminality in Sweden." In *Situational Crime Prevention: From Theory into Practice*, edited by Kevin Heal and Gloria K. Laycock. London: H.M. Stationery Office.

Thissen, David, and Howard Wainer. 1983. "Toward the Measurement and Prediction of Victim Proneness." *Journal of Research in Crime and Delinquency* 20:243–61.

Trasler, Gordon. 1986. "Situational Crime Control and Rational Choice: A Critique." In *Situational Crime Prevention: From Theory into Practice*, edited by Kevin Heal and Gloria K. Laycock. London: H.M. Stationery Office.

Tremblay, Pierre. 1986. "Designing Crime." *British Journal of Criminology* 26:234–53.

Walmsley, Roy. 1986. *Personal Violence*. Home Office Research Study no. 89. London: H.M. Stationery Office.

Wilson, Sheena. 1978. "Vandalism and 'Defensible Space' on London Housing Estates." In *Tackling Vandalism*, edited by Ronald V. Clarke. Home Office Research Study no. 47. London: H.M. Stationery Office.

Wolfgang, Marvin E., Robert M. Figlio, Paul E. Tracy, and Simon I. Singer. 1985. *The National Survey of Crime Severity*. Washington, D.C.: U.S. Department of Justice.

Wright, James D., P. H. Rossi, and K. Daly. 1983. *Under the Gun: Weapons, Crime, and Violence in America*. New York: Aldine.

Zimring, Franklin E. 1972. "The Medium is the Message: Firearm Caliber as a Determinant of Death from Assault." *Journal of Legal Studies* 1:97–123.

Zimring, Franklin E., and Gordon Hawkins. 1987. *The Citizen's Guide to Gun Control*. New York: Macmillan.

A. *Keith Bottomley*

Parole in Transition: A Comparative Study of Origins, Developments, and Prospects for the 1990s

ABSTRACT

The main elements of modern parole can be traced back to a variety of sources, including "good-time" laws, tickets-of-leave, executive pardons, and compulsory aftercare. Parole developed at different times and in response to different pressures in the United States, Canada, and England and Wales. In the 1970s, the whole penal edifice of rehabilitation, indeterminate sentencing, and parole came under attack for its alleged ineffectiveness, uncontrolled discretion, and denial of due process. In the United States, many states abolished parole and introduced determinate sentencing; others developed parole or sentencing guidelines. In England, the pressures of prison crowding led to a rapid expansion of parole release, but at some cost to its original principles and to the independence of the parole board. Canada sought a new focus for parole decisions and introduced mandatory supervision for prisoners denied parole. In all three countries, the roles and purposes of parole release and postrelease supervision remain in controversy.

On both sides of the Atlantic, traditional parole systems began to come under severe attack in the mid-1970s, in sharp contrast with the optimistic expansionist era of the 1950s and 1960s, and before the decline and fall of penological faith in the "rehabilitative ideal." The antiparole

A. Keith Bottomley is professor of criminology, University of Hull, England, and director of its Centre for Criminology and Criminal Justice. I am grateful to William Fittall, Keith Hawkins, Ken Pease, Michael Tonry, Ben Van den Assem, and Leslie Wilkins for materials and thoughts on parole in the United States and Canada.

bandwagon gathered momentum toward the end of the 1980s, when major legislative changes or official governmental inquiries[1] suggested the end of parole as we have known it. This essay attempts to disentangle some of the factors underlying this recent retreat from parole and to consider the rear-guard actions that have been taken to preserve some of parole's traditional functions within the criminal justice and correctional process.

My primary interest and experience derive from involvement with the English parole system during the last two decades, both as a researcher (Bottomley 1973, 1984*a*, 1984*b*) and as a former member of the parole board for England and Wales.[2] For the purposes of this essay, I also draw on my more limited knowledge of North American penal policy to outline similarities and contrasts with the parole systems of the United States and Canada, despite the potential problems of misunderstanding or misinterpretation, in the hope that a comparative approach might enhance the value of the analysis.[3]

Here is how this essay is organized. Section I charts the origins and precursors of parole in the three jurisdictions, in order to explain some of their emergent features. Section II examines the main challenges leveled against the theory and practice of parole in the 1970s and the responses to those challenges. Section III looks ahead to possible options and prospects for parole in the 1990s.

I. Origins and Emergent Features of Parole in Three Jurisdictions

In order to understand the complexities of contemporary parole systems, it is necessary to begin by investigating the origins and precursors of parole in the United States, Canada, and England and Wales. This should serve to undermine any naive assumption that "parole" is a universal concept that is identical in meaning and in practice wherever it is to be found. In fact, parole was introduced and labeled as such by each country at a specific stage in its penal history in response to

---

[1] In particular, the prospective abolition of federal parole and the establishment of the U.S. Sentencing Commission in 1984; the government's Parole System Review (Chairman: Lord Carlisle) in England, 1987–88; and the report of the Canadian Sentencing Commission (1987).

[2] Throughout this essay "English" refers to the jurisdiction of England and Wales, which is separate from those of Scotland and Northern Ireland.

[3] The discussion of Canadian parole focuses on the federal system, although I recognize that there are certain differences in the application of parole rules and procedures at the provincial and federal levels.

specific pressures and needs, and with purposes that could and did change in line with the penal and political contexts in which they operated. The search for the origins of parole, like any consideration of its future, suggests that it can most usefully be viewed not as a unitary process that can be tightly defined in theoretical or pragmatic terms but as a rather amorphous group of functions in the correctional process. Thus, in charting the origins and development of parole in any particular country, we must first consider, as far as possible, the main reasons for its introduction at a particular point, noting any changes of function with the passage of time; second, we must investigate the links, if any, between the newly introduced parole system and existing penal powers and procedures. There probably can never be any definitive statement of what parole is or should be that stands over and above specific historical and contemporary examples.

Most parole systems include three basic elements: discretionary early release from custody; supervision of prisoners so released; and recall to custody (or revocation) of parolees in breach of conditions of release. Although there are many differences of detail in the procedures for parole supervision and revocation, and also differences of emphasis in the objectives of supervision, the main differences between parole systems are in the principles and practice of early-release decisions. Table 1 outlines the main dimensions, albeit in an oversimplified format.

The following brief sketches of the emergence and development of parole in the three countries indicate the extent to which parole was introduced to meet similar needs, how far it replaced or was grafted onto existing penal mechanisms, or whether it filled gaps in the range of functions that an early-release scheme providing supervision of prisoners in the community might fulfill.

A. United States

The origin of parole in the United States has traditionally been associated with the emergence of indeterminate sentencing toward the end of the nineteenth century and, more specifically, with the 1869 New York State legislation that established Elmira Reformatory for young offenders, opened in 1876. Its superintendent, Zebulon Brockway, introduced a system for the supervised release of selected young prisoners, whose time in custody was dependent on their response to training and their behavior in the institution. In fact, Michigan may deserve the credit for first passing legislation, in the 1850s and 1860s, that provided for the early release of prisoners by formalizing the gov-

TABLE 1

Purposes, Roles, and Principles of Early Release

Grounds for Early Release	Role of Parole Authority	Penal Principle (or Pragmatism)
A. Sentence length/condition:		
1. Mitigation, or conditional remission of part of sentence	Clemency	Humanitarianism
2. Reduction of sentence disparity	Resentencing	Justice (and fairness)
B. Institutional management:		
3. Earned reward for program participation	Reward	Rehabilitation
4. Incentive for good behavior	Discipline	Institutional control
5. Regulation of prison crowding	Population control	Systems management (and humanitarianism)
C. Rehabilitation and crime control:		
6. Recognition of changed attitudes or behavior	Treatment, risk reduction	Rehabilitation (and public protection)
7. Ensuring supervised release from custody	Control, aftercare	Public protection (and rehabilitation)

ernor's power to grant conditional pardons (Zalman 1977, p. 55). Wherever the true credit lies for this initiative, both indeterminate sentencing and parole (for adults as well as young offenders) spread rapidly to many other states. By 1900, as many as twenty states had introduced parole statutes, and ten years later some form of parole system was in operation in thirty-two states (including twenty-one with indeterminate sentencing laws), and the U.S. Congress had introduced parole for federal prisoners. By 1922, forty-four states, Hawaii, and the federal government had parole systems, and thirty-seven states had indeterminate sentencing (Lindsey 1925). By 1930, every American state had established a parole board (Rothman 1980). The combination of indeterminate sentencing and parole release existed in every American state and in the federal system until 1975, when Maine abolished its parole board, and parole release remains in place in a majority of American states at this writing.

Although some early commentators saw the rise of the indeterminate sentence as a rejection of retributive and deterrent theories of punishment and justified it "solely on the ground of the protection of society by confining the criminal until by reformation he shall be judged fit to be released" (Lindsey 1925, p. 23), indeterminacy was often favored because of its potential to incapacitate incorrigible and dangerous prisoners (Zalman 1977, p. 77). By the end of the 1920s, a consensus seemed to have emerged that whatever may have been the initial reasons for the introduction of parole, its rehabilitative aspects had quickly taken second place in many states, where it was "a tool, used by the institutions, to make better prisoners rather than better residents of the community" (Lane 1933, p. 92); parole had outrun its reformatory objectives (Lindsey 1925).

That less than one-third of those states that adopted parole early included supervision requirements in their statutes also raised questions about the seriousness with which "parole-as-rehabilitation" was taken (Lindsey 1925, p. 81). In any case, supervision often required only the dispatch of a monthly report, signed by a best friend or employer (McKelvey 1968, p. 216; Messinger et al. 1985, p. 88). This conventional interpretation of the early development of parole in the United States as a reform gone wrong, and as the contamination of high ideals by the practical constraints of prison management, needs reexamining in the light of a broader appreciation of the nineteenth-century penal context.

Parole is often portrayed as a successor to the "ticket-of-leave" system that was originally developed by Britain in its Australian penal settlements. This was a conditional pardon that allowed convicts freedom to work for themselves within the settlement, instead of being dependent on government support. No supervision was initially attached to tickets-of-leave in Australia, although they could be suspended or withdrawn on the most trivial grounds. The emergence of parole was influenced by the work of Captain Alexander Maconochie, who was appointed commandant of Norfolk Island in 1840, and Sir Walter Crofton, who became the Director of the Irish Prison System in 1854. Crofton's system of graded progression through a program of education and training appealed to American reformers keen to establish reformatories for young offenders in the 1860s, but there was less enthusiasm for the tightly controlled supervision and reporting of his ticket-of-leave system (Killinger and Cromwell 1974, pp. 412–14). With these reservations about surveillance, it is perhaps not too surprising that supervision was not seen as an essential component of many of the parole schemes that mushroomed across America at the end of the nineteenth century. However, American parole systems did, if only tacitly, assume one of the very earliest functions of tickets-of-leave in England, which was to reduce the pressure of numbers in penal custody by granting conditional release to those awaiting transportation in overcrowded hulks and convict prisons (Hawkins 1971, p. 25).

There are two other aspects of early correctional practice that deserve attention in attempting to explain how and why parole was adopted and developed in late-nineteenth-century America: good-time laws, and the exercise of executive clemency by the use of governors' pardons. Before parole was introduced, the main ways in which a prisoner might expect mitigation of the sentence of the court were either by the operation of good-time laws, allowing a limited period of remission or time off for good conduct, or by appealing successfully to the clemency of the governor to grant a pardon.

New York State was the first to introduce good-time legislation in 1817, permitting a reduction of up to 25 percent in the time served by those sentenced to five years or more, on the grounds of good behavior, and with appropriate savings for release. Although this law may have remained a dead letter, other states soon followed, so that between 1817 and 1876 twenty-nine states and the federal government passed similar good-time laws (Parisi and Zillo 1983; Allen et al. 1985). Although the primary aim of such legislation was to give prison officials some control over inmates' behavior, it also served as a safety valve for relieving prison overcrowding and to enhance the rehabilitative prospects of inmates (Parisi and Zillo 1983, p. 230).

As invariably happens with remission schemes, what started out as a reward to be earned by good behavior gradually lost its rehabilitative and disciplinary effect by being automatically granted. Jacobs (1982) has shown how, as a bureaucratic matter, prisoners are routinely credited with maximum allowable good time on entry into imprisonment; thus, as a practical matter, good time is seldom "earned" and can generally be lost only by the affirmative act of prison administrators. This may explain why parole quickly assumed both disciplinary and rehabilitative functions, although from 1876 on parole and good-time schemes coexisted in most states.

The good-time laws were not able on their own to cope with the institutional problems and crowded prisons of nineteenth-century America. As a result, state governors began to grant *pardons* to large numbers of inmates in order to control the size of prison populations, with this pardoning power occasionally being delegated to prison wardens (Serrill 1977, p. 5; Allen et al. 1985, p. 26). In the early decades of the twentieth century, up to one-half of those released from some prisons were discharged by pardons (McKelvey 1968, p. 18). By the middle of the century, this practice still flourished and served to undermine not only internal prison discipline but also the sentencing authority of the courts; prisoners, too, were often opposed to the arbitrariness of a system where "luck, religious 'mush,' or outside 'pull' seemed to determine one's fate" (McKelvey 1968, p. 45).

A recent study of the foundations of parole in California showed how the introduction of parole there was intended as a direct substitute for the executive clemency of the governor's pardons and to counter the disparity caused by pardons and good-time laws (Berk et al. 1983; Messinger et al. 1985). Although only about 200 prisoners (out of at least 4,500 eligibles) applied for parole in California during the first ten years after its introduction in 1893, the number of clemency applications to the governor dropped substantially, so that only 2 percent of releases in 1894–1901 were by clemency, compared with 13 percent in 1865–80 (Messinger et al. 1985, pp. 85–91). As the prison population began to increase again between 1900 and 1906, causing considerable overcrowding, measures were introduced to extend parole eligibility to all prisoners after twelve months of imprisonment, so that "parole was changing from a special privilege for which exceptional prisoners might apply to a standard mode of release from prison, routinely considered upon completion of a minimum term of confinement" (Messinger et al. 1985, p. 97). What had started as a partial alternative to executive clemency, and then came to be used as a mechanism for controlling prison growth, gradually developed a distinctively rehabilitative rationale, incorporating the promise of help and assistance as well as surveillance.

The dynamics and sequence of parole development in California may have been atypical, with many other states beginning with rehabilitative ideals for parole, which had then to be compromised in the face of the need to maintain internal prison discipline and to control the size of prison populations. For whatever reasons, by the mid-1930s, parole and indeterminate sentencing had swept through the country (Serrill 1977).

Figures for 1936 indicate that, in six states, over 90 percent of released prisoners were paroled, and in a further eleven states, the proportion released on parole was over 75 percent (U.S. Department of Justice 1939, p. 122); nevertheless, the population of sentenced prisoners in state and federal institutions increased between 1925 and 1939 at an annual average rate of 5 percent, almost doubling from 92,000 in 1925 to 180,000 in 1939 (Bureau of Justice Statistics 1986). So far, the only other period in this century to match this rate of increase was when the national prison population more than doubled from 241,000 in 1975 to 627,000 in 1988 (Bureau of Justice Statistics 1989).

Although, as is discussed below, parole came under attack much later as a symbol of the "rehabilitative ideal" in penal policy, it is doubtful whether it ever really operated consistently in the United States either in principle or in practice according to the true canons of the rehabilitative model. From that point of view, it was a straw man that never realized the ideals of its more fervent advocates but reacted to the more pressing demands of an ever-increasing prison population and the wider issues of social control (Cavender 1982).

B. England and Wales

Although the ticket-of-leave system originated under English authority in Australia, it was not until April 1, 1968, that the first prisoners were released on parole license in England and Wales. Before considering the more immediate political and penological context of the 1960s, in which parole emerged rather belatedly in Britain, it is worth looking briefly at the role of the ticket-of-leave system in this country and some other precursors of parole.

Early in the seventeenth century, the English Privy Council authorized the granting of reprieves and stays of execution to those convicted of serious crimes who were fit enough to be transported and employed in government service overseas. Initially these royal pardons had no conditions attached to them, but due to abuse by convicts returning prematurely to England from the American colonies, it was found necessary to attach conditions. Here we have the forerunner of the later, more developed, ticket-of-leave system whose existence may have helped to postpone the introduction of a more formal parole system in England.

The beauty of transportation, as far as the English public and penal administrators were concerned, was that it promised to provide almost as permanent a solution to the problem of "criminals in our midst" as the system of capital punishment that it partially replaced. With or without a ticket-of-leave system, once they were transported overseas, relatively few convicts returned to their native shore to put the local communities at risk, especially when penal settlements were on the other side of the world (Ekirch 1987; Hughes 1987). The conditional release arrangements for convicts in Van Diemen's Land or Norfolk Island were only of academic interest to the general population at home. This changed dramatically in 1853, however, when the Penal Servitude Act partly abolished transportation and replaced it with terms of penal servitude to be served in English convict prisons, followed (from 1857) by a ticket-of-leave stage of release on license (Radzinowicz and Hood 1986). An ostensible reason for this arrangement was to satisfy the expectations of transportees (possibly numbering up to 8,000) then serving their sentences in government prisons, but less altruistic concerns also influenced this decision: "This was not gratuitous philanthropy on the part of the government. The virtual cessation of transportation meant that the prospect of remission, to which convicts could look forward, disappeared with the result that prison discipline was threatened by men whose hopes of early release were suddenly shattered. . . . Thus was the ticket-of-leave system introduced in England—largely at the behest of [the Director of Convict Prisons] who was himself motivated by the need to maintain prison discipline" (Bartrip 1981, p. 154).

Once these ticket-of-leave men began to be released onto the streets of English towns and villages, a public outcry arose against them, with an ensuing "moral panic" fueled by an outbreak of garroting in London. This resulted in tougher prison discipline and increased police surveillance of ticket-of-leave men, who now had to earn remission of up to one-third of their sentence lengths (Davis 1980; Bartrip 1981). During the 1860s, about 80 percent of all those discharged from convict prisons were on ticket-of-leave; prison authorities had to be informed of their place of residence, and the released prisoner had to report to the police within three days of arrival. Failure to report was an offense, and the police could rearrest without warrant anyone suspected of committing an offense or in breach of license (Bartrip 1981, p. 170). This revised system proved difficult to enforce (see Radzinowicz and Hood 1986, pp. 246–61) but, perhaps fortuitously, it was accompanied by a general decline in the recorded crime rate for the rest of the nineteenth century, and a drop in the total prison population from over 30,000 in the 1870s to 17,000 by 1900.

In the first decade of the twentieth century, a number of penal measures were introduced that also may have contributed to the postponement of any consideration of a parole system as such, although they provided partial models and structures on which parole in Britain would ultimately be able to build. The probation service was created in

1907, to supervise offenders in the community on probation orders imposed by the courts, with conditions and supervision requirements whose breach could result in return to court to be resentenced for the original offense. A new custodial sentence of Borstal Detention was introduced for young adult offenders, aged sixteen to twenty-one years, by the Prevention of Crime Act of 1908. This sentence included an element of indeterminacy, with release being determined by institutional staff within a minimum of six months for males (three months for females) and a maximum of three years—or a judicially fixed lower maximum—followed by a period of supervision on license.

Borstal was based on broadly reformative principles, expressed in terms of "instruction and discipline," and intended for those of "criminal habits and tendencies" or who associated with "persons of bad character." Judges remained selective in whom they sentenced to Borstal even in its "golden age," between the two World Wars (Hood 1965). However, by the early 1960s, Borstal had become the only medium-term custodial sentence for that age group (within reduced limits of six months to two years), and the actual time served tended to be determined as much by the constraints of numbers in custody as by response to training.

Also included in the 1908 Prevention of Crime Act was provision for preventive detention, a new form of custody intended for serious habitual offenders from whom the public was deemed to need protection and who could now be given a preventive sentence in addition to that of penal servitude. Release from preventive detention at the discretion of an advisory board resulted in a period of "positive" license to the Central Association for the Aid of Discharged Convicts (later, from 1949, the Central After-Care Association)—a system that was viewed favorably by a subsequent chairman of the English Prison Commission in comparison with the "negative" police license following penal servitude (Ruggles-Brise 1921, pp. 54–55).

During the early years of the new century, there was an unexpected rise in the prison population, which increased by almost 25 percent from 17,435 in 1900 to 21,423 in 1905. In response to growing concern, expressed by the Prison Commission and the Home Office, the government response was equally dramatic. By a series of initiatives, set in train in 1910–11 by Winston Churchill, then the home secretary, the prison population was halved to a level of 10,000–12,000 at which it remained for more than thirty years (Rutherford 1986, pp. 123–31), defusing any pressure there might otherwise have been for introducing an early-release scheme for the shorter-term prisoners mainly affected by these changes, and despite a steady increase in the recorded crime rate, especially during the 1930s, when it increased by about 7 percent each year.

Despite the social and economic upheaval created by World War II, there was no overall increase in the recorded crime rate in England and Wales for the first ten years following cessation of hostilities in 1945. The situation began to change in the mid-1950s when crime started to rise at a constant and alarming rate of 10 percent a year. This rate of increase continued into the 1960s and provided the setting within which the idea of a parole system for Britain was first officially discussed in political and penal reform circles.

The report of a Labour Party Study Group, headed by Lord Longford, *Crime—a Challenge to Us All*, was published in 1964, shortly before the general election of that same year that brought the Labour party into office. In response to "the gross overcrowding of our prisons today," the study group stated: "We doubt the value of keeping men in prison after they have learned their lesson; at this point the cost of continuing to keep them in prison is no longer justified" (Labour Party Study Group 1964, p. 43). It recommended that the home secretary appoint a parole board, with powers to release a prisoner under supervision after serving at least a quarter of the sentence similar to the powers vested in the prison department to release Borstal trainees.

This attracted very little attention at the time, but when the new Labour government in December 1965 published its white paper, *The Adult Offender*, it gave prominence to the proposal for release on parole license, with the following rationale:

Prisoners whose character and record render them suitable for this purpose should be released from prison earlier than they are at present. Prisoners who do not of necessity have to be detained for the protection of the public are in some cases more likely to be made into decent citizens if, before completing the whole of their sentence, they are released under supervision with a liability to recall if they do not behave. . . . What is proposed is that a prisoner's date of release should be largely dependent upon his response to training and his likely behaviour on release. A considerable number of long-term prisoners reach a recognizable peak in their training at which they may respond to generous treatment, but *after* which, if kept in prison, they may go downhill. To give such prisoners the opportunity of supervised freedom at the right moment may be decisive in securing their return to decent citizenship. [Home Office 1965, paras. 4–5]

It was recognized that imprisonment "progressively unfits" prisoners for release, and that new ways were necessary to ease the transition back to freedom in the community. Not only would the new system offer "the strongest incentive to reform," but it would "incidentally go some way to relieve the existing overcrowding in prisons" (Home Office 1965, para. 8). Thus, from the start, a distinctive characteristic of the English parole system was the way in which an essentially rehabilitative element was grafted onto a well-established, tariff-based system of determinate sentencing.

Although there were some significant changes in the proposed machinery of the parole system during the passage through Parliament of the subsequent 1967 Criminal Justice Bill, the underlying rehabilitative principle remained largely unchallenged (Morgan 1983). The original proposal was for informal local committees at each prison to advise the home secretary, but the government eventually agreed to the establishment of an independent parole board to make recommendations to the home secretary who would be unable to release on parole anyone not recommended by the board but could veto any of its favorable recommendations.

Another important theme in understanding the background to the introduction of parole in England was the relationship between parole and the extension of compulsory aftercare supervision. "Aid-on-discharge" to prisoners had been available on a voluntary basis, provided by charitable aid societies, since early in the nineteenth century. From early in the twentieth century, certain categories of prisoners were required to have compulsory aftercare (i.e., supervision on license), as distinct from the largely unsupervised penal servitude license or ticket-of-leave. This began with those sentenced to Borstal detention and preventive detention (1907–8) and was later extended to corrective trainees, young prisoners (aged seventeen to twenty-one years), and those given detention-center orders. Supervision was initially provided by members of the voluntary Central (aftercare) and Borstal Associations but later became the responsibility of the Probation and Aftercare Service.

A report of the Government's Advisory Council on the Treatment of Offenders, *The After-Care and Supervision of Discharged Prisoners* (Home Office 1958), had recommended that there should be a phased extension of compulsory aftercare to several additional categories of prisoners, in the belief that it was a necessary complement to prison training for "those prisoners who are in special need of guidance and help on release and are likely to be diverted thereby from further crime" (Home Office 1958, para. 40). Legislation for the recommended extension of aftercare was included in the 1961 Criminal Justice Act but never implemented due to the resource implications for the probation service in undertaking the supervision of 5,000–6,000 extra discharged prisoners. Support for parole in some quarters, therefore, came from those who saw it as achieving some of the aftercare objectives of the 1958 Advisory Council report. Initial estimates of the number of prisoners likely to be released on parole were 800–900 a year, which would mean no more than about 600 extra licensees for the probation service to supervise at any one time. That these would turn out to be gross underestimates could not have been foreseen at the time.

Although royal pardons, executive clemency, and tickets-of-leave had operated in England several centuries earlier, the final gestation and birth of this most recent of parole systems took place over a relatively short span of three years. Despite having a relatively independent national parole board, to which local review committees in each prison made recommendations, the English system was recognized from the start as being basically administrative and bureaucratic, rather than judicial. The main characteristics of the "administrative model" of parole included rehabilitative objectives, complementing prison "treatment," and based on information not available to the sentencing court; close links with institutional management, allowing it to be used for encouraging good behavior and regulating overcrowding (see Home Office 1981, para. 28); early release as an act of "grace," not a prisoner's "right"; principles and criteria for decision making not clearly enunciated; lack of due process, including no personal hearing, and no reasons given for decisions; and parole license as a contract, an integral part of the custodial sentence, although served at liberty in the community (adapted from Barnard 1976). Of course, no system conforms perfectly to a single model. There were some quasi-judicial elements in the origins of the English parole system (Howard League for Penal Reform 1981, pp. 3–6), as there continued to be in its operation. Particular tension was created by a basically bureaucratic system operating with an individualistic approach to decision making, so that "consistency of treatment of a limited kind becomes an objective, albeit contradictory to the correctional ideal of individualized diagnosis and treatment by experts" (Barnard 1980, pp. 46–47; see also Home Office 1981, para. 66).

An ideological commitment toward the rehabilitative potential of parole was a primary motivation behind the Labour government's support for parole (Morgan 1983). Yet even before the proposals reached the statute book, the impending prison population crisis must have loomed large for politicians, Home Office officials, and prison managers alike. The convenient way in which parole supervision would meet the identified need for the extension of aftercare for discharged prisoners tended to deflect consideration of the conflict this might generate in parole-release decisions, although the parole board was quick to see the problems this raised: "Parole has two aspects, early release and compulsory supervision. By statute the two must go together, but in practice the cases that most need supervision are not necessarily the ones that the Board would feel able to recommend for early release. . . . This means that on occasion . . . the Board finds itself reluctantly forced to choose between recommending at least some period of parole or allowing a sentence to terminate in the ordinary course and the offender to emerge from prison without any form of control" (Home Office 1970, para. 117).

The fundamental dilemmas of the English parole system as it entered the 1970s were highlighted in a perceptive review by Roger Hood, which summarized the problems—whether acknowledged or not— inherent in all parole systems and identified the key issues that were to dominate the debates of the next two decades: "The major tensions are between the use of parole as a reward and its use as a means of ensuring after-care; between the emphasis on reconsidering the prisoner in the light of the circumstances prevailing at the date of his review and in the light of the original offense and the court's intention in imposing the sentence; between protecting the public by not releasing men before their normal date and protection by ensuring that they are released under supervision and with some practical aid" (Hood 1974, p. 2).

C. Canada

I have suggested, so far, that the link between the ticket-of-leave system and the origins of parole in the United States has been overemphasized, and that the ticket-of-leave system in nineteenth-century England probably helped to divert attention from the need for a distinct parole system. In contrast, when considering the origins of parole in Canada, the ticket-of-leave, both as a concept and a practical reality, was directly linked to the eventual creation of the National Parole Board in 1958. Furthermore, it could be argued that the system of early release established in Canada by the Ticket-of-Leave Act of 1899, and its development during the following sixty years, was in practice quite similar (except in the name) to the parole systems established in many parts of the United States at the end of the nineteenth century and the beginning of the twentieth century. For many commentators, the 1899 Act *was* the first Canadian Parole Act (Miller 1965), and the terms in which Canadian Prime Minister Laurier introduced the 1899 bill were strikingly similar to sections of the government white paper, *The Adult Offender*, which introduced parole into Britain (Home Office 1965). He divided prisoners into two classes, the "dangerous" or "hopeless" ones who need to be confined for public protection, and those "who are the victims of accidents rather than of criminal instincts, whom prison can only make worse but for whom conditional release is designed to give them a chance to redeem their characters" (quoted in Mandel 1975, p. 527). The Act made all sentences indeterminate, within maxima to be set by the court. The governor general of Canada could grant conditional release to any person serving a term of imprisonment, with no statutory limits on eligibility (Miller 1965, p. 324).

The term "clemency" was frequently applied to the Ticket-of-Leave Act of 1899, and it featured prominently in the debates that led to its eventual abolition by the Parole Act of 1958. Superficially, there might appear to be some parallels with the governors' pardons in the United States during the nineteenth century, but the system of early release and supervision established by the Canadian Ticket-of-Leave Act was so different from the frequently abused pardoning powers of state governors that such a comparison has little merit.

The 1899 Act introduced a system of supervised freedom that soon developed into something far removed from the licensed freedom enjoyed by convicts in Australia in New South Wales or Van Diemen's Land, or the surveillance and harassment suffered by ticket-of-leave men on the streets of London in the 1860s. Initially, supervision was not easy in such a large and sparsely populated country as Canada, so "parolees" were relied on to report monthly to the local police. It was not long, however, before it was recognized that closer guidance was necessary, and voluntary organizations such as the Salvation Army Prison Gates section took up this challenge to develop its aftercare work with prisoners, with one of its officers taking up the post as first dominion parole officer in 1905 (Miller 1965, p. 330). The job of this officer, who became part of a section of the Department of Justice later known as the Remission Service, was to visit penal institutions to interview inmates and assess their release plans, although other staff of the Remission Service investigated the cases of those applying for ticket-of-leave and made recommendations to the minister. The importance of assistance to prisoners on release was recognized by the report of the Archambaut Commission in 1938, and the link between ticket-of-leave and aftercare grew much stronger in the postwar period, as an increasing number of voluntary societies took an interest in helping discharged prisoners.

At the same time as the work of the Remission Service was developing in the early decades of this century, indeterminate sentencing was introduced in British Columbia and Ontario for young offenders sent to certain borstal-type institutions, and parole boards were established in those two provinces with jurisdiction to grant early release on supervised parole to suitable inmates who had fulfilled their minimum sentences (Miller 1965, p. 335). These provisions relating to indeterminate sentences in British Columbia and Ontario were repealed in 1977, following the virtual abolition of indeterminate sentences in Canada (except for "dangerous offender" legislation) after the recommendations of the Ouimet Committee report (1969).

The work of the Remission Service expanded further in 1957, with four new regional offices to organize and coordinate supervision of prisoners deemed to be on parole. Miller commented on these developments: "Except for short sentences or cases presenting strongly compassionate features, the Service had ceased to look on tickets of leave as primarily exercises of clemency. *In keeping with the original intent of the legislators, tickets of leave were thought of more as authentic parole releases.* Consistent with this concept, the Service accepted the responsibility of following the progress of each individual parolee through the supervisors it had appointed" (Miller 1965, p. 332, emphasis added).

The eventual transition from the ticket-of-leave system to the creation of the National Parole Board stemmed mainly from the publication, in 1956, of the report of the Fauteux Committee appointed to inquire into the work of the Remission Service. Fauteux sought to clarify, once and for all, the distinction between clemency and parole: "There has been in Canada a tendency to confuse two completely different ideas in the field of corrections. One is parole. The other is clemency. . . . Clemency has very little, if anything to do with reformation or rehabilitation. . . . In a well designed system of corrections there should be few occasions for its use" (Fauteux report 1956, p. 51, quoted in Zalman 1975, p. 534). Parole, conversely, "is a well-recognized procedure which is designed to be a logical step in the reformation and rehabilitation of a person who has been convicted of an offense and as a result is undergoing imprisonment" (Fauteux report 1956, p. 51). It was envisaged by the Fauteux Committee as a way of releasing virtually all prisoners under conditional supervision (Jobson 1972, p. 268). The new parole authority for Canada should be a "quasi-judicial body rather than, as is presently the case, a Minister of the Crown acting in an exclusively administrative capacity," to ensure that no undue external or internal pressures influence it (Miller 1965, p. 334).

The Parole Act of 1958 came into force on February 15, 1959. Section 8(a) said simply that the board may grant parole if it considers that "the inmate has derived the maximum benefit from imprisonment and that the reform and rehabilitation of the inmate will be aided by the grant of parole." A later addition to this section, in 1969, authorized the board to take into consideration "whether release would constitute an undue risk to society."

It appeared that the Canadian experience of the previous sixty years had reinforced the need to sever release decisions from the notion of clemency and to stress, above all, the concept of the rehabilitative value of early release and supervised aftercare. The First Annual Report of the National Parole Board stated that "the purpose of parole is to aid in the reformation and rehabilitation of the offender having due regard, of course, for the protection of the public" (p. 3). Similarly, the Ouimet report (1969, p. 330) described parole as "a treatment-oriented correctional measure, not a sentence-correcting method," which determines the portion of the sentence that is to be spent in the community and the kind of control and supervision that will be needed.

A special feature of the Canadian parole system was the way it chose to handle the issues of remission and compulsory aftercare by the introduction, in 1970, of "mandatory supervision." The Fauteux report (1956) questioned the effectiveness of traditional remission or good-time systems in the promotion of good institutional behavior, particularly as by that time inmates were automatically granted remission on reception into custody, which could then only be forfeited by misbehavior. As those who gained early release through remission had not, therefore, necessarily been reformed, the Fauteux Committee recommended a statutory period of parole supervision in the community for all persons released, corresponding to the time earned by way of remission (Solicitor General Canada 1981*a*, p. 6; Ross and Barker 1986, p. 10). However, no such provision was incorporated in the 1958 Parole Act. Between 1959 and 1968, the proportion of applicants granted parole varied from 29 percent (1963) to 49 percent (1968), and initially around 40 percent of all those eligible failed even to apply for parole, so that only about a quarter of all releases from federal prisons received parole; "to some extent, therefore, the legislation of mandatory release arose in response to this refusal to apply for parole" (Jobson 1972, p. 275; Hugessen report 1973; see also Mandel 1975, pp. 505–6).

In 1961 two forms of remission had been established: "statutory remission," which was credited on admission and equal to one-quarter of the sentence, and "earned remission," to be gained by good behavior, up to a total maximum of one-third of the sentence. Prisoners released under either kind of remission were without supervision, whereas those selected for parole were required to serve the balance of their full sentence under supervision in the community or in the penitentiary until further parole or discharge if they were returned for parole violation or a new offense (Solicitor General Canada 1981*a*, p. 8). This inequity undoubtedly contributed to support for the introduction of mandatory supervision, recommended by the Ouimet report (1969), which expressed concern that the most dangerous offenders were being released without any of the controls or benefits of supervision accorded to the better-risk parolees.

After an unsuccessful experiment with minimum parole, under which those denied parole could opt for one month's reduction for each year of their sentences, to be followed by supervision for the expiration of the full term, mandatory supervision (MS) was brought into force on August 1, 1970, by an amendment to section 15 of the Parole Act. It applied to those released from prison without parole and with more than sixty days' remission. They were offered the same degree of control and assistance as parolees. The official objectives of the program were: "(1) to reduce reoffending . . . by providing some degree of control and/or assistance; (2) to be humane (by assisting offenders with anxieties, practical problems involved in leaving prison); (3) to increase the rate at which inmates apply for parole; (4) to reassure the public that virtually all penitentiary releases are supervised; and (5) to assist the police to know the whereabouts and movements of MS releases" (Solicitor General Canada 1981*b*, pp. 9–11). Mandatory supervision was therefore presented as a program with rehabilitative, incapacitative, and deterrent aims, which would complement the recently introduced parole system. I consider below how successful it was in achieving its objectives and enhancing the value and credibility of parole itself.

II. Parole under Attack: Challenges and Responses in the Late Twentieth Century

Despite the different emphases in the history of parole in the three countries, rehabilitation featured prominently in each at one time or another, albeit sometimes more as a theoretical ideal than as a practical reality in the experience of prisoners. Not surprisingly, therefore, when the whole notion of the rehabilitative ideal began to be challenged, parole and indeterminate sentencing were inevitable targets.

A. Some Fundamental Challenges in the 1970s

The early 1970s witnessed attacks on rehabilitation from all sides following the seminal writings of Francis Allen (1959, 1964; e.g., Irwin 1970; American Friends Service Committee 1971; Frankel 1973; Fogel 1975; Twentieth Century Fund Task Force 1976; von Hirsch 1976; Bottomley 1980).

There is neither space nor need to rehearse in detail the arguments of all these important contributions to the penal climate of the mid-1970s. They focused on four main issues: the ineffectiveness of prison and parole treatment; uncontrolled discretion and sentencing disparities; denial of justice and due process; and crime and political convergences.

1. *Ineffectiveness of Prison and Parole "Treatment."* Lipton, Martinson, and Wilks (1975) never actually said that "nothing works" regarding the rehabilitative effects of penal measures, but that is how their work was interpreted. This claim, though subsequently challenged, nevertheless had very damaging effects on the rehabilitative underpinnings of parole. The so-called peak theory, suggesting that it is possible for parole boards to identify the optimal point in prisoners' sentences when they might "respond to generous treatment" (Home Office 1965, para. 5) was seen to be untenable. The signs for parole were ominous (Kastenmeier and Eglit 1973).

The evidence on the effects of parole supervision on reoffending is mixed but is certainly not as uniformly bleak as the "nothing works" perspective suggests. The few evaluation studies of parole supervision that had been carried out in the 1950s and 1960s offered little evidence of its effectiveness in reducing reoffending, and several studies in the 1970s seemed to confirm that, having controlled for differences between parolees and nonparolees, parole had, at best, only a *delaying* effect on reoffending (Waller 1974; Nuttall et al. 1977). However, a recent Home Office revalidation study using the Reconviction Prediction Score (RPS) found that the reconviction rates of those given parole were significantly better for a two-year period than those not paroled (Ward 1987, p. 7), although this could indicate that other factors (not in the RPS) were taken into account by the local review committees and parole board or, alternatively, the action of granting parole may itself reduce (either by changes of attitude or by supervision) the risk of reconviction (Ward 1987, p. 7). There is similar evidence of reduced reconviction rates for those paroled from sentences of over four years (Home Office 1979, pp. 75–76; Home Office 1981, para. 39).

The evidence from parole-effectiveness studies in the United States provides ammunition for both supporters and detractors of the value of parole supervision (see Lerner 1977; Sacks and Logan 1979; Gottfredson, Mitchell-Herzfeld, and Flanagan 1982; Abadinsky 1987, chap. 12).

It would seem unwise to dismiss out of hand the claim that parole release might have some positive effects on those to whom it is granted—certainly during the period of supervision, if not beyond. To disentangle the particular aspects of parolee status that might be responsible for these effects is very much more challenging—whether it is indeed rehabilitation via "aid and assistance," surveillance, deterrence (to avoid recall), or "all in the mind" must remain an open question.

2. *Uncontrolled Discretion and Sentencing Disparities.* A second pervasive theme and major target in critiques of rehabilitation and the "medical model" of corrections was the discretionary power in the hands of decision makers. This led directly to attacks on the exercise of discretion, and consequent disparities, in sentencing and parole decisions (American Friends Service Committee 1971; Frankel 1973; Zalman 1977). At the heart of the attack on the discretionary power of parole boards was not only the essential arbitrariness of many of their decisions but also a general lack of concern to articulate the principles and criteria underlying them (e.g., Davis 1969). At times, parole authorities appeared to take pride in the indecipherability of their work (Frankel 1973, p. 48). Even when parole authorities did have explicit criteria and principles, this did not necessarily resolve the problem, as they never really have clarified the process by which decisions to grant or deny parole were made or indicated what precise weighting was given to each factor (Schmidt 1977, p. 21).

The only consolation for some observers of parole and sentencing was that this discretionary power enabled parole boards to fulfill a sentence equalization function, thereby *reducing* disparities caused by unbridled sentencing authorities. However, this raises the controversial question of the alleged resentencing function of executive authorities such as parole boards, which is addressed in the final section of this essay.

3. *Denial of Justice and Due Process.* The lack of explicit criteria for parole decisions, combined with the possibility that time served in prison might be extended because of a general lack of response, created a degree of uncertainty and sense of injustice that made the pains of parole for many inmates more difficult to cope with than the better-known pains of imprisonment (Mandel 1975). These complaints raised two sets of concerns. The first was the absence from Canada, England and Wales, and most United States parole jurisdictions of established, published standards for release decisions. The consequent unpredictability of release decisions fostered enormous uncertainties among prisoners and left open the appearance and, no doubt, too often the reality of decisions that were inconsistent and arbitrary. The second concern was procedural and emphasized the absence from parole of due process requisites such as the right to a hearing, to know the nature of complaints against one, and to be informed of the reasons for adverse decisions.

A system of early release that was created, in part at least, to mitigate the harshness of long terms of imprisonment, had come to be viewed by many prisoners in the early 1970s as a primary pain of the prison experience: "replacing hope and accompanying disillusionment is a sense of injustice of new proportions" (Irwin 1970, p. 54). In California, half of the inmates' demands that preceded the February 1968 demonstrations focused on the parole practices of the Adult Authority and parole issues featured in many prison disturbances and prisoners' rights charters from Attica onward, reflecting a deeply felt grievance among many prisoners (Kastenmeier and Eglit 1973, p. 487). If, despite all the uncertainty and arbitrariness of its procedures and outcomes, parole was to be retained, reformers urged that explicit criteria and principles should be laid down and publicized to all those concerned, with an early "time-fix" to minimize the potential for manipulation and institutional control (e.g., von Hirsch and Hanrahan 1979). In the United States particularly, civil rights litigators persuaded the courts that fundamental precepts of due process required that prisoners be accorded a right to a personal hearing before the board, and that reasons be given for denial of parole. In many American jurisdictions, prisoners were afforded the opportunity to initiate an administrative appeal from an adverse parole-release decision.

4. *Crime and Political Convergences.*   In the early 1970s, it seemed, thus, as if the rehabilitative ideal was without any friends to rally to its defense. A curious consensus seemed to be emerging that spanned the social and political spectrum, with elements of the "anti-rehabilitative" case appealing to radicals, liberals, and conservatives alike (Blumstein 1984, p. 130; Allen et al. 1985, p. 165). Once it was realized that rehabilitative measures seldom changed offenders' behavior, the debate moved from a quasi-scientific to a quasi-philosophical phase with emphasis on concepts of justice and just deserts.

In those American states where the political convergence for reform of sentencing and parole was most pronounced, parole typically was radically altered. In some states, parole release and parole supervision were abandoned. In others, parole release was abandoned but parole supervision was retained for some or all released prisoners. In still other states, parole guidelines were established.

The way in which parole systems were targeted for demolition, together with the rest of the rehabilitative superstructure, was understandable but perhaps misconceived. The diversity and ambivalence that characterizes the history of parole systems shows the variety of functions that have been deliberately or incidentally fulfilled by parole over many decades, as it has molded itself, or been molded, to suit a variety of ideological and pragmatic concerns. Instead of unthinkingly sweeping up parole into the broader rehabilitative net, a more sensible strategy would have been to consider whether there were some of its functions that needed to be preserved or expanded. Those states that abandoned parole release, for example, were left with no politically feasible, systematic way to reduce prison crowding by means of well-considered selective advances of release dates. Similarly, the parole boards' ability to even out grosser disparities in judicially declared prison sentences disappeared.

B. *Retreat and Reassessment into the 1980s*

Each jurisdiction responded differently to the challenges facing parole in the 1970s. The direct criticisms were rather more muted in England and Canada than in the United States. The official reactions were correspondingly less dramatic. This is explicable partly by the very different political, legal, and cultural traditions of each country and partly by the different "natural histories" of parole in each jurisdiction, varying in length from 100 to fewer than ten years.

1. *United States: Controlling Sentencing.*   The most direct response in the United States was to abolish parole. This drastic step was taken first by Maine in 1975. By 1984, at least eleven other states and the federal system had also formally abolished parole;[4] there were, however, already signs of a countermovement as, for example, in Colorado, which reinstated parole in 1985 after having adopted determinate sentencing and removed the parole board's power to set prisoner release dates in 1979 (Krauth 1987). The abolition of parole meant different things in different states. Three other states followed Maine's example in abolishing postrelease supervision: Connecticut, Washington, and Florida. As a result, in Maine and Connecticut, some judges began passing split sentences, sometimes in Maine called "judicial parole," with a prison term being followed by probation (Krajick 1983, p. 31). The supervision element of parole was retained by the majority of "abolitionist" states, with release dates determined by good-time laws permitting reductions of up to one-half of the sentence (e.g., Indiana, Illinois). In at least five states the equivalent of a parole board was retained to set conditions for mandatory supervision and to revoke violators (Krauth 1987, pp. 53–54).

The abolition of parole-release procedures was usually accompanied by the introduction of some form of determinate-sentencing legislation. Some states allowed considerable judicial discretion in determining the time to be served in prison. In Maine, very broad ranges of sentence were provided for four general classes of offense (with statutory maxima only), within which the judge selected a single term as the flat sentence to be served by the inmate. Illinois provided sentencing ranges for seven classes of offense, with extensions permitted for aggravating circumstances. In other abolitionist states the discretion allowed to judges was very narrow, so that the presumptive sentence specified by law largely determined the actual time served. California was the best-known example of a state that set out detailed sentencing criteria in statutory forms. Indiana, alternatively, adopted the mechanics of presumptive sentencing with ten categories of crime but with mitigating and aggravating provisions that were not binding on the court (Lagoy,

[4] California, Colorado, Indiana, Illinois, Minnesota, Connecticut, North Carolina, Washington, Florida, New Mexico, and Idaho.

Hussey, and Kramer 1978). Finally, in Idaho, a unique "hybrid" scheme was adopted that permitted judges to impose *either* fixed terms (with no parole eligibility) *or* indeterminate sentences with the parole board setting release dates (National Institute of Corrections 1985). In contrast, Georgia, Tennessee, and Texas expanded early release or parole, and provided additional resources for field supervision. Thirteen states developed accelerated release programs for certain categories of offender during periods of prison crowding, although in some cases the overcrowding levels have not yet triggered the programs (National Institute of Corrections 1985, p. 7).

Alternative provision for the management and control of prison population numbers was particularly important in states without parole-release schemes, reflecting the crucial role that they had played in this respect—whether officially acknowledged or not. Since 1976, Maine has had to open four new prisons to handle the overflow population from county jails (Tilton 1987, p. 60). In Michigan the Emergency Overcrowding Act required that when prisons are over their official capacity for thirty days, all parole eligibility dates are moved forward by ninety days (Bureau of Justice Statistics 1983).

The net effect of these changes was that the proportion of prison releases by discretionary parole dropped from 72 percent in 1977 to 40.6 percent in 1987, with a corresponding increase in mandatory supervised release from 6 percent (1977) to 31 percent (1987) (Bureau of Justice Statistics 1988). In both 1977 and 1987, 16 percent of discharges from prison were unconditional releases by expiration of sentence.

The reduced capacities of parole boards to control prison population numbers by use of early-release authority was a contributing factor in the dramatic increase in the sentenced prisoner population which, after a period of relatively slow growth in the previous two decades—an 18 percent increase from 166,000 (1950) to 196,000 (1970)—increased by 160 percent between 1975 (241,000) and 1988 (627,000) (see table 2).

The varied responses of the states that chose *not* to abolish early release on parole included the development of parole guidelines, sentencing guidelines (with or without sentencing commissions), and the extension of mandatory or similar determinate-sentence legislation. In 1979 alone, eighteen states introduced mandatory sentences for selected crimes, with most other states already having such provisions (Cavender 1982, p. 60). By 1983, almost all states had mandatory prison sentences for one or more categories of offense (Bureau of Justice Statistics

TABLE 2

Sentenced Prisoners in State and U.S. Federal Institutions and Release Method, 1975–88

Year	Total Sentenced Prisoner Population (N)	Total Releases from Prison (N)	Method of Prison Release			
			Discretionary Parole (%)	Mandatory Supervised Release (%)	Expiration of Term (%)	Other (%)
1975	240,593	106,742	68.3	5.1	19.1	7.5
1976	262,833	106,928	68.9	5.8	19.2	6.0
1977	278,141*	115,213	71.9	5.9	16.1	6.1
	285,456*					
1978	294,396	119,796	70.4	5.8	17.0	6.8
1979	301,470	128,954	60.2	16.9	16.3	6.7
1980	329,821	136,968	57.4	19.5	14.9	8.2
1981	369,930	142,489	54.6	21.4	13.9	10.1
1982	413,806	157,144	51.9	24.4	14.4	9.3
1983	437,248	191,237	48.1	26.9	16.1	8.9
1984	464,567	191,499	46.0	28.7	16.3	9.0
1985	502,507	203,895	43.2	30.8	16.9	9.1
1986	545,133	230,672	43.2	31.1	14.8	10.8
1987	581,609	270,506	40.6	31.2	16.2	12.0
1988	627,402	N.A.	N.A.	N.A.	N.A.	N.A.

SOURCE.—Bureau of Justice Statistics (1986, 1987, 1988). Figures in col. 2 for 1980–87 are taken from Bureau of Justice Statistics (1987). Column 2 figure for 1988 is from Bureau of Justice Statistics (1989). All other figures for 1986 and 1987 are from Bureau of Justice Statistics (1988).

NOTE.—N.A. = not available.

* Before 1977, only prisoners in the custody of state and federal correctional systems were counted; after 1977, all prisoners under state and federal jurisdiction were counted. Both figures are given to facilitate comparison.

1983). Such laws inevitably restricted the term-setting function of parole boards (where these were retained) but could coexist with a variety of sentencing structures, whether determinate, presumptive, or indeterminate (Allen et al. 1985, pp. 109–11).

Parole guidelines were first adopted by the U.S. Board of Parole (as it was then called) in 1974, following research by the National Parole Institutes and the Research Center of the National Council on Crime and Delinquency. Essentially, the guidelines were based on a "rationalization of the Board's past practice," in which rehabilitation did not emerge as a factor in parole-release determination, but which could best be reflected in a decision matrix based on the two dimensions of offense seriousness and a "salient factor score" indicating the risk of reoffending (Gottfredson et al. 1975; O'Donnell, Curtis, and Churgin 1977; Gottfredson, Wilkins, and Hoffman 1978). Within the next ten years, at least fifteen jurisdictions followed the example of the federal system and introduced explicit parole guidelines (Bureau of Justice Statistics 1983), which went a long way toward meeting the criticisms of uncontrolled discretion, disparities in time served, and lack of explicit criteria and stated reasons for grant or denial of parole. At the same time, however, their very success raises the fundamental question whether the parole board is the most appropriate authority for determining the time to be served (Alschuler 1980).

An evaluation by Arthur D. Little, Inc. of parole guidelines in four jurisdictions (Federal, Minnesota, Oregon, and Washington) showed that they could be adapted to various correctional philosophies, including just deserts, deterrence, rehabilitation, and incapacitation. They achieved many of the objectives for which they were set up, providing clear standards for decision making, early time setting, representation, and provision of reasons for denial or "outside-guidelines" decisions (Burke and Lees 1981). Analysis of the effect of guidelines on sentencing disparities in the federal system and Minnesota found "measurable reduction in disparity of the time served among similarly situated offenders" (Burke and Lees 1981, p. 70), and this has been confirmed by other studies (Gottfredson 1979; Blumstein et al. 1983, p. 438).

However, guidelines are only as good as the concept of parole on which they are based, and they can take as many forms as there are functions of parole. They can be constructed on either a prescriptive or a descriptive model, with the central risk-assessment factors being used either as predictive tools or measures of culpability. Despite their many real achievements, they are not necessarily the panacea for all the ills of parole, which, with or without guidelines, must still justify for itself a legitimate role in a criminal justice system that is moving toward greater determinacy and certainty of sanction (Burke and Lees 1981, p. 95).

Four of the jurisdictions that experimented with parole guidelines eventually abolished parole while, in a few other cases, they were combined with sentencing guidelines. Minnesota, Washington, and the federal system have discontinued their parole guidelines systems in favor of presumptive sentencing guidelines (Tonry 1988). The development of sentencing guidelines and the associated establishment of sentencing commissions probably represented the most significant response in the United States to the 1970s critiques of rehabilitation, disparity, and unprincipled time setting. The ultimate fate of parole may well depend on the success, or otherwise, of the U.S. Sentencing Commission, established in November 1984, as, in Canada, its future will depend on the response to the report of the Canadian Sentencing Commission (1987), which recommended establishment of a permanent sentencing commission and adoption of sentencing guidelines in Canada (for an instructive comparison of the United States and Canadian federal initiatives, see von Hirsch 1988).

A review of the impact of guidelines on sentencing patterns in the three states that first established presumptive sentencing guidelines showed that "sentencing severity appears to have increased in Minnesota and Pennsylvania and to have decreased in Washington" (Tonry 1988, p. 306). This is likely to be a major factor in assessing the success of the guidelines devised by the U.S. Sentencing Commission, whose complex and controversial development (past, present, and future) needs an outsider bolder than I am to fathom or predict. The enactment of the Comprehensive Crime Control Act of 1984 marked the end of a long struggle toward the reform of federal sentencing and parole by establishing the U.S. Sentencing Commission and phasing out the U.S. Parole Commission. Many looked to it as the beginning of a new phase in federal criminal justice; others saw it as an ill-conceived end to a progressive chapter of penal history in which parole played a major role. There would certainly have been little sense in retaining two parallel commissions, both exercising decision-making responsibility over the time to be served in prison, based on a similar set of factors that were known at the time of sentence—a sure recipe for conflict, inefficiency, or both. The main criticisms of the U.S. Sentencing Commission include its lack of clear objectives, priorities, or sentencing rationale; its failure to approach the task of guideline construction in a consistent or scientific way, according to a truly prescriptive or accurately descriptive model; and a culpable neglect of the likely effect of its recommended sentencing scale on the size of the prison population. Andrew von Hirsch, an outspoken critic of the commission's work, observes, "According to the Commission's belated projections, applications of the guidelines will lead to a huge increase in prison population. Even under a so-called 'low growth' scenario, the federal prison population would more than double within the next decade, from its present 42,000 to nearly 100,000 in 1997. . . . The Commission offered no recommendation on how the federal correctional system should deal with a doubling in population" (von Hirsch 1988, p. 6).

By contrast, it has been argued that the effects of the sentencing provisions of the federal guidelines per se will be relatively modest compared to those of the mandatory sentences required by anti-drug-abuse legislation and the career offender provisions of the 1984 Comprehensive Crime Control Act (Block and Rhodes 1987).

The precise effects of the abolition of parole in the federal system must remain to be seen. Are there any hints of what to expect from the experience of the states that have abolished parole during the last decade or so? Unfortunately, as we have seen, no single pattern of sentencing replaced parole authorities, and a variety of ways were adopted for coping with the non-time-fixing functions of parole. Nonetheless, in the majority of abolitionist states, provisions were retained or extended for setting conditions for postrelease supervision; allowing good-time remission (of up to 58 percent) for good behavior or instituting emergency overcrowding provisions when the level of prison populations reached certain specified limits above maximum capacity. Measures in the last two categories were either in anticipation or as a direct result of increases in prison populations following parole abolition and the move to a more determinate sentencing structure (similar measures in response to prison crowding were also undertaken in states that did not abolish parole release).

The evidence for the effect of parole abolition on sentence lengths is mixed and is virtually impossible to separate from other simultaneous influences. The experience of California indicated an increase in prison commitments following the introduction of determinate sentencing, including longer sentences for some of the more serious offenses, balanced by shorter sentences for others. However, the increase in prison population was a continuation of a preexisting trend and could not be attributed definitely to the abolition of parole and indeterminacy (Brewer, Beckett, and Holt 1981; Berk et al. 1983; Tonry 1988, p. 319). Nationwide statistics show an unprecedented rate of increase in the period 1975–88 (see table 2), which was likely to be due in part, at least, to the abolition of parole in almost a quarter of all states. This does not augur well for the next decade, when the U.S. Parole Commission will have been phased out, and when public concern about the crime problem is likely to continue apace.

2. *England and Wales: Pragmatism and Politics.*   The parole system in England and Wales began very cautiously, indeed, on April 1, 1968, with only 8.5 percent of the 4,764 prisoners eligible on that day being recommended for release on license. Eligibility was initially restricted to those who had served at least twelve months in prison, or one-third of their sentences, whichever was the longer. In the first nine months (April–December 1968) 1,157 prisoners were recommended for parole, or less than 11 percent of those eligible. Initially, officials in the Home Office Parole Unit screened out from the parole board those cases they judged unsuitable, notwithstanding favorable recommendations by local review committees (LRCs) in each holding prison. However, the board took the view that this unduly limited its independent role and persuaded the secretary of state to drop this restrictive practice as of June 1968 (Home Office 1969, paras. 30–31; see Howard League 1981; Morgan 1983).

Under the positive leadership of Lord Hunt, its first chairman (1968–73), the parole board quickly gained in confidence, so that by 1972 almost one-third of all eligible cases considered by LRCs were finally released on parole. Fifteen years later, following a number of legislative and procedural changes that extended parole eligibility and relaxed the criteria for release, almost six out of ten (or 14,000 out of 24,000 eligible) prisoners were recommended for parole in 1987 (see table 3). Significantly, this rapid expansion of parole in England and Wales during its first twenty years took place at a time when the prison population increased by 50 percent from 32,461 (1968) to 48,962 (1987), and the recorded crime volume increased by over 200 percent from 1,289,090 (1968) to 3,892,200 (1987).

Although an ideological commitment to the notion of rehabilitation and the treatment model played an important part in the introduction of parole in Britain, it was never regarded, in theory or in practice, as an exclusive principle. Consequently, the official *Review of Parole in England and Wales* (1981) was able to state, "The 'peak of treatment' was

TABLE 3

Summary of Decisions Made in Determinate Sentence Cases in Selected Years 1969–87, England and Wales

	1969	1972	1975	1978	1981	1984	1987
Average Daily Prison Population	34,667	38,328	39,820	41,796	43,311	43,295	48,962
a. Total eligible for parole	7,264	9,644	10,154	10,829	10,243	19,592	24,432
b. Declined consideration	490	710	699	646	623	521	654
c. Recommended for parole by local review committees	2,189	3,410	3,894	5,160	5,063	12,080	15,199
(% of cases considered)	(32.2)	(38.2)	(41.2)	(50.7)	(52.6)	(62.3)	(63.9)
d. LRC recommendations for parole accepted, without further reference	...	...	923	1,622	1,916	8,446	10,482
(% of LRC recommendations)			(23.7)	(31.4)	(37.8)	(69.9)	(69.0)
e. Referred to parole board	2,562	4,450	4,662	5,303	5,058	5,884	7,508
	(373)*	(1,040)*	(1,691)*	(1,765)*	(1,908)*	(2,250)*	(2,791)*
f. Recommended for parole by parole board	1,835	2,926	3,106	3,193	3,363	3,463	3,524
	(164)*	(275)*	(581)*	(406)*	(638)*	(609)*	(405)*
(% of cases referred to PB)	(71.2)	(65.8)	(66.6)	(60.2)	(66.5)	(58.9)	(46.9)
g. Total recommended for parole: d + f	1,835	2,926	4,029	4,815	5,279	11,909	14,006
h. % of those considered by local review committees	27.1	32.7	42.6	47.3	54.9	62.4	58.9
i. % of total eligible	25.2	30.3	39.7	44.5	51.5	60.8	57.3

SOURCES.—The parole statistics are abstracted from the relevant annual reports of the Parole Board for England and Wales (Home Office 1970–).
NOTE.—LRC = local review committee; PB = parole board.
* Cases within the categories concerned which were considered by the local review committees to be unsuitable for parole.

never, as some have supposed, the sole criterion for the grant of parole. . . . Consequently criticisms of the scheme on the ground that its reliance on the peak of treatment theory is unsound are now no longer even partially in point" (Home Office 1981, para. 4). The parole board had quickly become aware of the significance of the compulsory-supervision element in parole, and the dilemmas this could pose in release decisions that had to balance the needs of the offender against the risk to the community. Confusion about what were meant to be the main objectives and principles of the parole system stemmed from the failure of the initial legislation, the 1967 Criminal Justice Act, to spell out primary aims and the subsequent reluctance of the Home Office and the parole board to formulate principles or criteria. Throughout the early 1970s, the annual reports of the parole board simply reiterated that each case should be determined on its own merits in the light of the factors mentioned in the white paper, *The Adult Offender* (Home Office 1965), and the statements by government ministers in the debates of the 1967 Criminal Justice Bill (see Home Office 1970, para. 52).

Only in 1975 were official guidelines and criteria for parole selection drawn up as part of an initiative by the home secretary, Roy Jenkins, to extend the use of parole. The new guidelines were intended to achieve this "without loss of public confidence in the scheme." In a written answer to Parliament, on August 4, 1975, the home secretary emphasized that "the grant of parole should not expose the public to serious danger during a period when a prisoner would otherwise be serving his sentence in prison" but that, even in cases of serious crime, parole need not be ruled out if there were good reason to believe a prisoner would avoid such crime in the future; in the other or more numerous cases, where there was little likelihood of a serious crime being committed on parole, there was a good case for its being granted "and earlier rather than later" (Home Office 1976, para. 4).

The criteria listed six groups of factors affecting parole decisions: the nature of the offense, criminal history, prison behavior and response to treatment, medical treatment, home circumstances and employment prospects, and cooperation with parole supervision. The parole board then set out guidelines for the assessment of suitability for release, indicating how the various factors should be weighted against one another. It was clear that the assessment of the risk of reoffending was intended to be the overriding principle in parole decision making (Bottomley 1984*a*). What also clearly emerged from the guidelines statement was the importance attached to the element of compulsory supervision by the probation service, particularly for those prisoners with moderate or long records of nonmajor crime who are unlikely to accept aftercare voluntarily after release, but for whom "parole with its attendant compulsory supervision may be the only hope left (however slender it may be) of removing them from the vicious circle" (Home Office 1976, app. 4, para. 29).

The new guidelines, combined with an extension of the classes of prisoner to be dealt with by section 35 of the 1972 Criminal Justice Act without further reference to the parole board (see below), appeared to provide the necessary impetus, as the proportion of those eligible who were paroled increased from one-third to over one-half in the early 1980s. To what extent the decisions of local review committees and the parole board closely followed the guidelines is difficult to know as it has not been systematically monitored. It seems likely that many earlier habits of decision making continued, with the LRCs and parole board tending to operate on an individualized "each case on its merits" basis within a broad framework of relevant factors but without clear overriding decision rules. Experience of the paroling process suggests that even after the 1975 initiative, with its endorsement of the primacy of the criterion of risk assessment, factors were taken into account that were not entirely compatible with the spirit of the new guidelines but reflected considerations of just deserts, deterrence, public opinion, and so on (Bottomley 1984a). For example, "seriousness of the offense" might be used to delay or deny parole to a prisoner without necessarily being linked to future risk but simply on the basis that he had not yet been adequately punished for the crime (see also Hawkins 1983). Other evidence of the inclination of paroling authorities to reinforce the impact of the sentencing decision was their reluctance sometimes to grant early release on license to offenders whose sentences had been primarily intended to be deterrent and for whom supervision on release was unnecessary or impossible—such as overseas "visitors" involved in drug smuggling or, nearer to home, local government officials or police officers convicted of corrupt practices. Finally, elements of fairness and just deserts also came into the reckoning when considering those who misbehaved in prison, as "the grant of parole to a badly behaved prisoner would affect the morale of both staff and prisoners: the staff because they would see it as an encouragement to bad behavior, and the prisoners because they would see it as unjust to those who behave well but do not get parole" (Home Office 1976, app. 4, para. 9). Anomalies of this kind meant that parole decisions continued to be somewhat unpredictable. They did not always fall strictly within the new guidelines but added to the general sense of confusion and injustice experienced by good-risk prisoners denied parole.

This sense of injustice was compounded by the continued official insistence throughout the 1970s and 1980s that the English parole system was not based on a judicial concept but was essentially "an administrative modification, at the discretion of the Home Secretary, of the manner in which the sentence set by the court is served" (Home Office 1974, para. 4), so that "to graft some aspects of judicial process onto a basically administrative system might prove a short lived compromise" (Home Office 1981, para. 67). Parole remained a privilege to be earned, not a right to be automatically granted. Prisoners in England and Wales have never been allowed a personal hearing before the parole board or the LRC, but have to be satisfied with an interview with a member of the LRC (prior to the meeting), which is meant to help them present their case for early release. Similarly, despite pressure from many quarters, prisoners are not given reasons for denial of parole—partly, it has been claimed, because some factors are outside the prisoner's control to alter and partly because different factors may have influenced the members of the particular panel of the LRC or parole board, and a yet different panel may consider their next application (see Home Office 1981, paras. 72–81). Furthermore, to add to the complication, a prisoner's application may be turned down at any one of three stages—LRC, parole board, or home secretary—each of which has little direct knowledge of the reasoning of the others. None of these arguments has proved to be persuasive to those who have advocated greater due process in the parole system and have regarded the giving of reasons and personal hearings as basic requirements of "natural justice." The additional argument that reasoned decisions would inevitably result in prisoners and their legal representatives having recourse to the courts on appeal would, for them, be a desirable consequence of, rather than an argument against, the change. Yet the parole board and Home Office have appeared adamant: "Whilst this in principle may or may not be undesirable, it would be a significant step towards changing the concept of parole from a privilege to a right and by this token a major departure from the scheme intended by Parliament" (Home Office 1981, para. 80).

The potential for serious disparities in the English parole system is enhanced not only by the initial lack of formal guidelines but also by the three-tier structure of decision making, under which all cases are first considered by local review committees in each prison; their favorable recommendations are submitted to the national parole board, based in London; it, in turn, makes recommendations to the home secretary. There was early evidence that LRCs in different prisons were recommending varying proportions of those eligible (Home Office 1970, pp. 44–46), and although this was to be expected in view of the different types of inmates held in each prison, research revealed considerable variation among prisons dealing with similar classes of offenders (Nuttall et al. 1977). In order to even out some of these discrepancies, a procedure was implemented toward the end of 1969, by which prisoners turned down by LRCs but with low reconviction prediction scores were referred for consideration to the parole board (Home Office 1981, par. 23). Thus in 1970, 996 cases of prisoners considered unsuitable for parole by the LRCs were referred to the parole board, mainly on the basis of their low predicted reconviction scores or on other grounds for such referral, for example, where their criminal associates were being considered by the board. Table 3 shows that an increasing number of LRC "unsuitables" were referred to the parole board for a second opinion, reaching almost 2,000 by 1981 and continuing to rise during the 1980s. Between 25 and 30 percent of these cases were recommended for release by the parole board.

Conversely, in arguably one of the most important developments of the English parole system during this period, provision was made (by section 35 of the 1972 Criminal Justice Act) for certain classes of cases recommended by local review committees as suitable for parole to be accepted by the Home Office *without further reference to the parole board*. After a cautious start, the classes of cases to be covered by this bypass provision were extended in 1974 and again in January 1976 (as part of the "Jenkins initiative"), so that they included all cases with sentences of four years or less, except where the offense involved sex, violence, arson, or drug trafficking, and the sentence was over two years. In 1973, the number of such section 35 recommendations was 813; within five years the number had doubled, and by the early 1980s, around 2,000 cases a year were being released under this procedure, constituting almost 40 percent of all those released on parole. Among the reasons for the introduction of the section 35 procedure were that it would permit the parole board to concentrate on the more serious cases; it was also, no doubt, intended to increase the number granted parole, but the claim that "this devolutionary measure . . . is an indication of the large measure of agreement between the decisions of the committees and the

Board" (Home Office 1973, para. 25) did not really address the continuing problems of disparities between LRCs. When a major change in parole eligibility was introduced in July 1984, reducing the threshold from a minimum of twelve to six months served and, at a stroke, doubling the number of prisoners eligible for parole consideration, the retention of this procedure meant that in 1985 over 11,000 prisoners were released without further reference to the parole board, representing more than three-quarters of all cases recommended for parole in that year. The introduction, in August 1987, of half remission (in place of one-third) for prisoners serving sentences of twelve months or less, slightly reduced the number of prisoners to be considered by LRCs, but still more than 10,000 prisoners were released without further reference, or 75 percent of the total recommended (see table 3).

The trends that gathered pace during the 1970s, increasing administrative control by the Home Office and devolving decision making from the parole board to the local review committees (Morgan 1983), were given extra impetus not only by the massive expansion of parole eligibility with the introduction of the six-month eligibility rule but also by another very controversial change announced by the home secretary at that time, Leon Brittan (in November 1983), that, in effect, removed certain classes of serious offender (those sentenced to more than five years for offenses of violence or drug trafficking) from consideration for release on parole, save in exceptional circumstances (Home Office 1984; Bottomley 1984b). A former member of the parole board commented, "It can be argued that such a class definition negates the intention of the 1967 statute, which was concerned to make provision for individual offenders. Whether that be the case or not, some offenders will now be refused parole not on grounds of desert or risk but of offense category" (McCabe 1985, p. 489). A senior member of the parole board resigned in protest, and the legitimacy of the home secretary's actions was challenged in the Appeals Courts where it was eventually upheld by five Law Lords (Findlay v. Secretary of State [1984] 3 All ER 801).

One factor that has probably affected the development of the English parole system more than anything else is the pressure created by a continual and apparently inexorable growth in the prison population, which reached levels in the late 1980s that were inconceivable just ten or fifteen years ago. While recognizing that every parole system fulfills a key role in the management and control of prison populations, the special significance of this factor in the British context cannot be overstated. The political response to this penal crisis provided one of the clearest examples of the *penological pragmatism* that Anthony Bottoms identified as one of the major themes of contemporary British penal policy, with its "heavy preoccupation with the urgent practical problems of the moment" and "no clear or coherent philosophical or other theoretical basis" (Bottoms 1980, p. 4).

However genuine, if rather naive, may have been the motives of the original proponents of parole in the 1960s, when 700–800 prisoners were expected to be released on license each year, the potential scope of a completely different kind of system was quickly grasped by politicians, penal reformers, and prison-department officials, as the prison population continued to rise despite all the legislative attempts to control it. Local review committees were given new powers to recommend certain short-sentence prisoners for parole without reference to the parole board, the official criteria were relaxed in order to parole more prisoners (and earlier in their sentence), and the twelve-month minimum qualifying period was halved in 1984, with the effect that, in the mid-1980s, about twice as many prisoners were serving part of their sentence on supervision in the community at any one time than was the case five years before.

Perhaps the clearest symptom of what would have been a pragmatic transformation of parole in England and Wales was an abortive proposal of the 1981 Home Office review that all prisoners under sentences of fewer than three years be automatically released after a third of the sentence had been served, placed under the supervision of a probation officer until the two-thirds point, and then be free of all further restrictions. This was admittedly *not* applying "parole in its present form" to those serving shorter sentences, as no selection was involved, but extending "the central idea of parole," that is, release under supervision (Home Office 1981, para. 55).

Among the arguments put forward in support of the proposed new system was that it would strengthen the remainder of the parole scheme by enabling it to concentrate on the more serious cases (even though it would increase the burden of supervision on the probation service), but the main reason for the proposal was that it would reduce the prison population by up to 7,000 (Home Office 1981, para. 60). Despite the obvious attraction of its projected "prison-reducing" effect to government, prison management, and penal reform groups, this radical set of proposals was opposed by the judiciary with such vehemence (albeit largely behind the scenes in the corridors of power) that it was not proceeded with. Judges apparently felt that, to release all prisoners with sentences of up to three years after they had served just one-third of their sentences in custody (with one further third on supervision in the community), would make a mockery of the meaning of judicially imposed sentences, so that the courts might react by inflating their sentences to ensure a certain minimum period in custody.

A few years later, following the major impact of the reduction of the minimum qualifying period to six months (in July 1984) and the introduction of 50 percent remission for those serving twelve months or less (in August 1987), it was again judicial dissatisfaction that was a significant influence on the government's decision to institute, under Lord Carlisle of Bucklow, the first independent review of the English parole system in its twenty-year history. The Carlisle Committee's report was published in 1988.

Many judges had been particularly concerned at the way the high parole rate (75–80 percent) for those serving sentences less than two years had changed the nature of parole from a privilege (to be conferred selectively) to a virtual entitlement and, second, at the effect of the six-month minimum qualifying period (MQP) in rendering sentencing differentials nugatory (Carlisle Committee 1988, para. 36). There had, of course, always been similar consequences for sentencing differentials when the MQP was twelve months as well as anomalies due to the counting of time served in custody before conviction toward the one-third eligibility period but not toward the flat-rate MQP. But the impact was less apparent because of the smaller numbers involved and the generally lower parole rate of longer-sentence prisoners. Other causes of concern voiced by many of those involved in the parole decision-making process were the inadequate time and information for decisions on shorter-sentence cases and, at the other end of the scale, the charade of going through the motions of reviewing prisoners sentenced to over five years for offenses involving violence, sex, or drugs, who were subject to the restricted policy announced by the Home Secretary in November 1983.

The approach of the Carlisle Committee to these and other issues was bold and logical. Its central principle was the need to restore meaning to the full sentence imposed by the court, in order to reassure the judiciary (and the public) that control of the basic character of custodial measures was firmly in the hands of the courts. The committee was not persuaded by arguments for wiping out part of the total sentence by generous remission simply because a prisoner had kept out of serious trouble while in custody. Thus its main recommendations were that remission should be abolished, to be replaced by a power for governors and boards of visitors to impose "extra days to be served," and that no prisoner should be released before having served at least 50 percent of the sentence imposed by the court. In the case of prisoners sentenced to four years or less, conditional release at 50 percent (plus any extra days for misconduct) should be mandatory, with all those sentenced to twelve months or more subject to supervision up to the three-quarters point of their sentences. Those sentenced to over four years would be eligible for discretionary release on parole after having served 50 percent and, in any case, released no later than the two-thirds point (plus any extra days for misconduct), with all being subject to supervision up to the three-quarters point. All prisoners would be at risk after release until the end of the full sentence and, in the event of further offenses during that period, liable to be recalled to prison to serve the remaining time in custody. The restricted release policy for certain categories of prisoners serving sentences of over five years should be abolished, as it was "flawed in principle and harmful in practice" (Carlisle Committee 1988, para. 190). The parole decision (for those sentenced to over four years) should be based solely on "an evaluation of the risk to the public of the person committing a further serious offense at a time when he would otherwise be in prison" (Carlisle Committee 1988, paras. 321, 244), with questions of deterrence and punishment for the court alone to determine at the time of sentence.

Much of the secrecy surrounding the parole decision-making process in England and Wales should be removed, with all the reports prepared for the parole board disclosed to the inmate except in highly exceptional cases, and the board required to give inmates meaningful reasons for refusing to grant parole (Carlisle Committee 1988, paras. 331–36, 354–57). Inmates should receive help in submitting their written representations from local voluntary parole counselors in each prison and by being permitted to hire lawyers to assist them in preparing their cases. A minority of the committee believed that prisoners should have the right of a personal hearing before the board, but the majority were in favor of cases being reviewed on the basis of reports and written representations alone. Finally, among the many important recommendations of the Carlisle Committee, it urged that the home secretary cease to be responsible for (or have any power of veto over) individual parole decisions, and that the parole board should assume full executive powers in all parole cases (except those of life-sentence prisoners that were outside the committee's terms of reference) (Carlisle Committee 1988, paras. 309–13).

Estimates of the effect of this total package of recommendations on prison population numbers were that the new scheme was, at worst, likely to be broadly neutral but, at best, if sentencing tariffs were to be reduced (because of judicial confidence in the proposed real-time sentencing measures), could bring about a reduction of 10 to 15 percent (Carlisle Committee 1988, paras. 432–34). Although sentencing was also strictly outside its terms of reference, the committee recommended that the implementation of its proposals should be accompanied by a thorough reassessment of present sentencing levels in a determined attempt to reduce tariffs, and that, if such reductions were not forthcoming, a "root and branch review of sentencing law and practice, and its interaction with early release mechanisms" was called for (Carlisle Committee 1988, paras. 295–98).

The initial response to the Carlisle report by the government was cautious, in view of its political and practical implications, particularly in relation to the constitutional status of the parole board, its likely impact on the size of the prison population, and possible ramifications of the disclosure of parole reports to prisoners. Disappointment about its lack of guaranteed impact on the numbers in prison was also felt by several penal reform and professional groups. The report certainly challenged a number of the cherished principles and practical achievements of the parole system over the previous two decades, and its proposals went further than many expected in the direction of real-time sentencing, by restoring meaning to the full sentence during which prisoners would remain at risk of recall for further offenses. It reasserted the value of a period of supervision after release from custody for all but the very shortest-sentence prisoners, which would thereby resolve a central dilemma for parole authorities in having to choose between early release with supervision and later release (on grounds of risk) but without supervision. Whether the new principles and careful arguments of the Carlisle report will prevail over political sensibilities and penal pragmatism remains to be seen.

3. *Canada: In Search of a Purpose for Parole.* The introduction of mandatory supervision (MS) by the Canadian legislature in 1970 was intended to solve one of the perennial dilemmas of parole, that denial of parole means denial of the help or control of compulsory supervision. The main effect of MS was not an increase in the number applying for

and being granted parole but a large swing away from parole and toward MS as the commonest form of release from custody. From 1973 onward, only between one-quarter and one-third of prisoners were released on parole, with up to two-thirds released on mandatory supervision (Solicitor General Canada 1981*a*). This suggests that some rethinking was needed about the respective roles and procedures of the various forms of conditional release in Canada. Throughout the 1970s and early 1980s, hardly a year passed without the publication of an official report that directly or indirectly addressed this issue.

A trenchant article by Michael Mandel (1975) set the contours for the debate. He challenged the assumptions that parole resulted in substantial economic savings for the penal system, and that it significantly reduced the average time served in custody. From the humanitarian point of view, inmates typically suffered more from the "pains of parole"—the "anxiety, fear, loss of dignity, excessively limited freedom, uncertainty of one's future"—than they benefited from its supposed advantages, in terms of early release and assistance on resettlement (Mandel 1975, pp. 520–26). In his view, there were very few grounds, if any, to justify retaining "parole's juggernaut" which continues "to roll mindlessly over time, money, prisoners and public alike" (Mandel 1975, p. 541).

Several common themes emerged from the deliberations of the various Canadian task forces and committees in the 1970s that mirrored the concerns in Britain and the United States during this period. There was a particular focus on the criteria and objectives of parole and on the extension of due process (see Jobson 1972).

The Hugessen report (1973) criticized the existing criteria for parole release for being too vague and unclear, so that "neither inmates nor members of the board are able to articulate with any certainty or precision what positive and negative factors enter into the parole decision" (Hugessen report 1973, para. 32). In place of the three general considerations set out in the amended Parole Act's Section 10(1), Hugessen recommended the adoption of more extended provisions based largely on the American Law Institute's (1962) *Model Penal Code*, where the onus was on those wishing to *deny* parole on specified grounds. The approach of the Goldenberg Committee, which reported in 1974, was rather different. In its view, parole was not to be regarded as sentence amelioration, clemency, proof of rehabilitation, a reward, a right, or a prison management function, but "the parole system's basic purpose is the protection of all members of society from seriously harmful and dangerous conduct" (Goldenberg report 1974, p. 37; National Parole Board 1987a, p. 85). It should be seen as an aid to social control of offenders or "custody without bars" and for the longer-term process of social reintegration.

Both reports recommended changes in the organizational structure of the parole system, with a greater degree of regionalization or (in Hugessen's case) a two-tier structure of local and regional boards, in the hope that these changes would not only improve the efficiency of the system but also reduce the degree of disparity within each region and across Canada (Hugessen report 1973, p. 55).

There was an increased concern in Canada throughout the 1970s with due process and the need to develop procedural safeguards for those in the criminal justice and parole process. The Hugessen report recommended that "every parole decision, at whatever level, should be preceded by a hearing at which the inmate is present," which provides "the opportunity to the decision-makers to communicate their reasons to the inmate and, to the extent possible, obtain his acceptance of it" (Hugessen report 1973, p. 34). Reasons should be set down in writing, with a copy given to the prisoner. Goldenberg similarly advocated the right to a personal parole hearing with written notice, reasons for the decisions, and so on (Goldenberg report 1974). In sharp contrast to the resistance such ideas and proposals aroused in England, Hugessen firmly believed in the need for a radical conceptual shift, so that "parole boards be viewed and recognized by the legislation as quasi-judicial bodies" (Hugessen report 1973, p. 36). Most of these recommendations for additional procedural safeguards were put into effect in the next few years, so that federal inmates were provided with a parole hearing if they so wished, oral and written reasons were given in all cases of parole denial, and similar rights of due process were provided for those whose parole or mandatory supervision was suspended (National Parole Board 1987a, pp. 87–88).

Canada was not free from the problems of crime and law-and-order politics that beset the United States and England in the 1970s. Following a number of disturbances at major penal institutions, it was clear that the apparent arbitrariness in parole and revocation decisions was an unsettling factor in the prisons. Problems in the prisons were symptomatic of an increased public concern about problems of crime on the streets, which led to calls for a clampdown on crime and a more effective criminal justice system to ensure greater public protection. The introduction of MS in 1970 reflected these growing concerns, and the so-called peace and security legislation of 1976 increased the minimum parole eligibility period for those convicted of homicide (following the abolition of capital punishment), with new indeterminate sentencing powers introduced in 1977 for all dangerous offenders, including sexual offenders.

The 1980s opened with the publication of the *Solicitor General's Study of Conditional Release* (Solicitor General Canada 1981*a*). Several of the themes of the preceding decade were rehearsed but not resolved. Existing criteria for early release were criticized for being too vague or inappropriate and beyond assessment, leading to disparities and raising problems of accountability and evaluation (see Law Reform Commission of Canada 1977). The working group did not feel able to recommend which objectives full parole should adopt but gave a clear message to the National Parole Board that it "must resolve questions of objectives which are before it, and must provide more specific criteria in law to guide its decisions and provide notice of its policies" (Solicitor General Canada 1981*a*, p. 64). The working group commended the idea of rewriting the statute to reflect reasons for denial rather than granting full parole, but opinion within the group was divided on MS and remission schemes.

Mandatory supervision was resented by offenders, who felt that earned remission should not have to be spent subject to compulsory supervision; it was unpopular with the police, who had to arrest MS violators, and added considerably to the burden of supervision and paperwork carried by probation officers, with around 2,000 persons on MS at any one time. However, removing compulsory supervision from some of the worst offenders could cause serious public alarm (Solicitor General Canada 1981*a*, pp. 90–92).

In view of the important issues of effectiveness, fairness, and public concern raised by MS, a special committee on mandatory supervision had been set up and reported later in the same year (Solicitor General Canada 1981*b*). It argued that the MS program was sound in principle and provided substantial benefits over the pre-1970 situation in terms of the reintegration and control of released offenders and of public reassurance. Statistics showed that, throughout the mid-1970s, six out of ten MS cases completed supervision successfully, without revocation either for a new offense or a technical violation, which compared quite favorably with the figures for full parole (66–70 percent success); although the average supervision period was shorter for MS cases than parolees, the selection process resulted in more "poor-risk" cases being released on MS (Solicitor General Canada 1981*b*; Harman and Hann 1986, chap. 5). Most of the new offenses committed by those on MS were property offenses, and the committee felt that public concern about violence by released inmates was out of proportion to its incidence. It concluded that the impact of abolishing MS for the 2,500 persons so released each year would be "costly and of little ultimate benefit" (Solicitor General Canada 1981*b*, p. 47). The committee recommended greater attention to identifying the high-risk, dangerous MS cases for more structured release programs and more intensive supervision; if such cases were revoked on MS, they would not be eligible for re-release, thus giving all offenders "one chance to prove themselves on the street and have the opportunity for access to some assistance in reestablishing themselves" (Solicitor General Canada 1981*b*, p. 58). Amending legislation, incorporating these recommendations, was passed in July 1986, together with the so-called gating provisions authorizing the National Parole Board to keep in custody certain dangerous or violent offenders for the whole duration of the sentence, without either parole or earned remission.

Most critics agreed that the official criteria being used by the National Parole Board (NPB) were inadequate, allowing too much discretion and failing to indicate the clear purposes and objectives of parole. In the light of these criticisms, and aware of the developing guidelines movement in the United States, the board set up its own parole guidelines project in 1975. This group proposed that the National Parole Board adopt a standardized set of presumptive parole guidelines, in which the assessment of risk would be the central consideration in parole release decisions (Nuffield 1982, p. 60).

Subsequently, a series of research studies was carried out in the Ministry of the Solicitor General, in consultation with the National Parole Board, focusing on risk assessment and parole decision making (see Harman and Hann 1986). In November 1986, the board adopted its first mission statement, which asserted that "the NPB has as its primary objective the protection of society." Assessing the risk of further crimes by the offender after release thereby became its major focus. The board later stated that a major corporate objective for 1987–88 was "the development of decision-making policies which will provide the framework for exercising, without unduly restricting, discretion" (National Parole Board 1987*a*, p. 104). Furthermore, the board's chairman emphasized that, in applying the criteria set out in section 10 of the Parole Act, "the perceived risk is the critical issue in the decision-making process" (National Parole Board 1987*b*, p. 9). Finally, in February 1988, the *National Parole Board Pre-Release Decision Policies* document was published, intended "to render the criteria and process for NPB decisions more open and understandable." The policies were based on three key assumptions. First, risk to society is the fundamental consideration in any conditional release decision; second, the limits on the freedom of the offender in the community must be limited to those that are necessary and reasonable for the protection of society and for facilitating the safe reintegration of the offender; and third, supervised release increases the likelihood of reintegration and contributes to the long-term protection of society (National Parole Board 1988, p. 4). Whether these policies and assumptions provide sufficient justification for retaining parole release alongside mandatory supervision and remission schemes was a question addressed in the major inquiry into the future of sentencing in Canada by the Canadian Sentencing Commission (1987). Having reviewed many of the familiar arguments against parole, the commission concluded that "there did not seem to be any positive benefits of discretionary parole release which could possibly justify its continued existence within the integrated set of reforms advocated by this Commission. . . . The length of time an offender will spend in custody should be fixed, as much as possible, at the time of sentencing" (Canadian Sentencing Commission 1987, p. 244). It therefore recommended the abolition of full parole (except in cases of life imprisonment) for three reasons: because parole systems in operation conflict with the principle of proportionality in punishment, because discretionary release introduces a great deal of uncertainty into the sentencing process, and because parole release transfers sentencing decisions from the judge to the parole board (Canadian Sentencing Commission 1987, p. 244).

The Canadian Sentencing Commission did, however, recommend the retention of a form of earned remission, partly on the grounds that "if remission is abolished, harsher measures will have to be systematically used to ensure prison discipline, . . . making prisons an even more punitive environment than they already are" (1987, p. 247), and partly because the commission estimated that the abolition of all forms of early release would result in at least doubling the prison population. A system of earned remission was therefore proposed in which credits awarded for good behavior could reduce by up to one-quarter the custodial portion of the sentence. The mandatory supervision of those released during the period of remission should be abolished "unless the judge, upon imposing a sentence of incarceration, specifies that the offender should be released on conditions" (Canadian Sentencing Commission 1987, p. 251)—which may be modified, or even deleted, by the releasing authority under certain circumstances. The needs of offenders for some assistance on release from custody were recognized by recommendations that the provision of voluntary assistance programs prior to release should be available to all inmates, and that all should be eligible for day release or "day parole" programs after serving two-thirds of their sentences unless remission has been withheld (Canadian Sentencing Commission 1987, pp. 255–56).

There was a persuasive logic and coherence to this set of proposals from the Canadian Sentencing Commission. However, it was not persuasive enough to convince the solicitor general or the members of a parliamentary committee of the merits of its proposals. In August 1988, the Daubney Committee's report recommended that "conditional release in its various forms be retained and improved upon," as it believed that "public protection will be enhanced by preparing inmates for release into the society while they are still incarcerated and then providing them with the requisite degree of supervision and assistance once they are released into the community" (Daubney Committee 1988, pp. 187–88). Although the committee believed that the time served in prison should, in many cases, correspond more closely to the length of the sentence than it did currently, it did not support the initial proposal of the solicitor general (June 15, 1988) that parole eligibility should generally be increased from one-third to one-half of the sentence but broadly endorsed his revised notion (August 1988) of applying the later eligibility date to inmates convicted of violent offenses—who cause the greatest public concern and do, in fact, already often serve 50 percent or more of their sentences. The committee also accepted the solicitor general's proposal that earned remission should be abolished and inmates statutorily released, under appropriate conditions and supervision, for the final one-third or twelve months (whichever is shorter) of their sentence.

These recommendations represented something of a setback for those campaigning to abolish discretionary early release in Canada. They seem likely to make only slight progress toward achieving a greater degree of real-time sentencing and proportionality (in time served) between offenders. Although risk to society has been officially recognized as the primary criterion for conditional release decisions, it is not clear that public fears will be entirely assuaged.

III. Prospects for Parole in the 1990s

This comparative survey of the origins and development of parole in three jurisdictions has confirmed the complexity of the task facing those who wish to understand the way in which penal policies and practice emerge and change. There may be little consensus on what lessons, if any, can be learned from the past history of parole to inform policy or predictions for the final decade of this century. Whatever else may be said, it is clear that parole has survived (or emerged late in the day) with a chameleon-like capacity to adapt to changing social, political, and penal environments. Whether, in the process, it has lost its distinct identity is a moot point. Perhaps the time has come to disentangle and discard traditional terminology, at the same time disentangling the multiplicity of functions subsumed by parole over the years. Consideration of the possible justifications for its retention, abolition, or change may result in its nominal disappearance but the preservation of many of its important functions: "Parole is dead—long live parole!" Certain themes and competing pressures within parole and criminal justice systems can be identified as the basis for speculation on what the future may hold. Key elements around which this continuing debate seems likely to revolve are, first, time-fixing and the control of sentences and, second, community protection and accountability.

A. *Time-Fixing and the Control of Sentences*

At the heart of any debate about the future of parole lies the question posed by Norval Morris: "Why should the judicial sentencing discretion be shared at all with the parole board?" (Morris 1974, p. 47). A common response has been that a parole board provides a more appropriate (and, by implication, enlightened) forum for deciding on the length and conditions of sentences of imprisonment, especially where there is a general lack of confidence in the sentencing practice of the judiciary. Furthermore, parole board decisions may, in principle, be less subject to disparity than court decisions because of the respective size and nature of the networks within which they operate. The development of parole guidelines may also help to reduce disparities, although their very success highlights the pertinence of the original question about the justification for any executive modification of or interference with the judicially imposed sentence. If there is a future for parole, it seems that it will increasingly be within the context of a predominantly determinate sentencing structure—as has always been the case in Britain (except for the rather special case of life sentences)—into which it necessarily imports an element of indeterminacy. So the question could be rephrased as, What principled grounds are there for varying a determinate into an indeterminate sentence? Or, alternatively, Why should a fixed sentence of custody not "mean what it says"?

To answer such questions requires a reexamination of the fundamentals of sentencing, with its mixed objectives of retribution, deterrence, incapacitation, rehabilitation, and so on. Parole can be (and has been) viewed as a way of lessening or confirming the retributive and deterrent aspects of custodial sentences, although in origin, as we have seen, it was more often associated with the rehabilitative concept of imprisonment. This latter justification for early release has now been largely discredited on theoretical, empirical, and ethical grounds. The movement toward just deserts in sentencing, and the reaffirmation of tariff-based penal measures, has weighted the balance of sentencing firmly on the side of the courts and the judiciary. To the extent that the combined effect (even if unintentional) of conditional early release and remission, or good-time provisions, undermines the retributive and deterrent impact of a custodial sentence, it is becoming increasingly necessary to justify this de facto executive resentencing, either in terms of changed circumstances and new information that was not known to the judge at the time of sentence or by urging the claims of alternative sentencing objectives in place of the discredited rehabilitative justification for parole.

Thus the trends that appear to be gaining ground are, first, toward real-time sentencing and the restoration of meaning to the judicially imposed sentences (see Carlisle Committee 1988) and, second, toward the reaffirmation of the primacy of risk assessment in conditional-release decisions. The first trend is likely to be associated with the replacement of discretionary early release on parole by mandatory or automatic release at a rather later stage in the sentence than is now normal for many prisoners, together with a questioning of generous "discounts" on custodial sentences for good behavior in prison. The second trend should ensure a greater clarity of purpose for all those concerned with the conditional early-release schemes that may survive but, if combined with an extension of real-time sentencing, it may result in an ironic reversal of the functions of parole in which selected prisoners come to be denied the early release that is automatic for others on the grounds that they pose too great a risk to the community.

A residual parole system of this sort might become indistinguishable in practice from a system of preventive detention based on a principle of incapacitation.

B. Community Protection and Accountability

There seems little doubt that the perceived need and media-fueled demand for the community to be protected from criminals at large in its midst will continue to influence, if not largely dictate, the shape of parole developments in the 1990s as it has done during the 1980s. In this respect, the clock has turned full circle back to the nineteenth century, when there was a public outcry in London against the wave of muggings and street crime allegedly committed by the ticket-of-leave men, paroled from sentences of penal servitude. The late twentieth century is witnessing similar public concern about violence on the streets and widespread fear of the apparently ever-increasing lawlessness—in the face of which it seems neither sensible nor fair to indulge in the large-scale early release of convicted criminals. Public opinion is increasingly in tune with the judiciary in supporting retributive and deterrent sentences that "mean what they say" and in opposition to any substantial reductions of sentence by the executive on grounds that appear irrelevant to their fears.

To the extent that custodial sentences may be partly commuted, the general public would look for continued assurance of protection via the mandatory supervision and surveillance of released prisoners until the expiration of their sentences. Consequently, the supervision which, for advocates of the rehabilitative theory of parole, was primarily justified as aid and assistance for the resettlement of offenders would come to be seen as a simple transfer of control from prison into the community (custody without bars). Supervisors would not, of course, be precluded from offering help and support, but the essential raison d'etre would be an extension of control. The public would also, no doubt, be further reassured by the knowledge that all discretionary decisions to grant early release to selected prisoners would focus on the risk of reoffending, which could, in certain circumstances, lead to the *denial* of a normal release date and still be followed by mandatory supervision and control.

In a very real sense, therefore, prison and parole systems are gradually being given back to the community and becoming more responsive to public pressures—whether or not this is considered a good thing. There are two counteracting factors that are still liable to impede the gathering momentum toward community control of this sort. The judiciary, in their independence, may diverge from public opinion in the application of the sentencing tariff, so that the length of real-time prison sentences becomes out of line with general expectations and wishes. In this respect, the development of guidelines and sentencing commissions offers a potential mechanism for the monitoring and control of sentencing standards to bring them more in tune with public opinion.

The other factor is the extent to which strategic management problems of prison overcrowding and discipline can be dealt with separately from systems of conditional release. Mechanisms for maintaining prison discipline, in the shape of good-time laws and remission, existed long before parole came onto the scene, and they have continued or been expanded in the American states that abolished parole early-release schemes. Indications that prison disciplinary offenses in California increased following parole abolition in 1976 were probably explicable in terms of the effects of overcrowding rather than of parole changes per se (Nacci, Teitelbaum, and Prather 1977; Hawkins 1980, p. 52). The granting of presumptive parole dates by the U.S. Parole Commission early in the sentence did not appear to have any effect on discipline, suggesting that "implementation of a presumptive parole date plan can eliminate the uncertainty associated with traditional parole practice without adversely affecting disciplinary behavior" (Stone-Meierhoefer and Hoffman 1982, p. 289). Although undoubtedly parole adds to the perceived power of prison staff over release dates, there is little evidence that, at that level at least, ordinary remission is less successful (Mandel 1975, pp. 532–33).

So the clear message that emerges is that parole is an inappropriate and unnecessary mechanism for maintaining prison discipline, whether tacitly or overtly, and tends to create additional problems in this very sensitive area.

Similarly, parole developments in the past have often been directly linked to the pressure of numbers in the prison system, from the tickets-of-leave onward. Whatever value it may have as a safety valve, which marginally eases the living conditions for prisoners, this need not be its primary objective but is a secondary bonus at most. The more parole is used for and relied on as essentially a prison population-control mechanism, the less likely it is to adhere to any overriding principles of policy or practice; rather it will be debased for administrative convenience. Systems should be able to be controlled by the normal processes of management and planning, with provision made for emergency-release powers—echoing again the earliest precursors of parole in the powers of executive clemency and royal pardons. In order to retain their respect and credibility, parole and conditional-release schemes of the future need to distance themselves from possible management "contamination" or allegations of being influenced by essentially secondary institutional or political considerations. To that end, there is great value in establishing or enhancing the operational and constitutional independence of parole authorities, so that they are no longer subservient or open to manipulation by either prison management or their political puppet masters.

What we see, then, in trying to forecast the future direction of parole, is the likelihood of a diminishing role for many of the functions that played an important part in its origins and development and a reassertion of the need to take account of the wider public interest and community concerns at a time of increasing crime rates and fear of crime. It is possible that this groundswell of popular feeling might lead to the disappearance of parole as we have known it and its replacement by a system of preventive detention for dangerous offenders. The extent to which jurisdictions may go down this road lies mainly in the hands of politicians, whose assessment of the climate of public and judicial opinion, as well as their own self-interest in retaining control over the ultimate decisions on which and how many prisoners to release, will be crucial.

Finally, alongside the predicted "democratization" of early release, there may be a role for criminologists in developing more accurate ways of assessing the risk posed by prisoners released under different conditions and at different stages of their sentence and in evaluating the effects of statutory supervision—whether from a control or an assistance perspective. We might thus, at best, envisage parole systems of greater fairness and accountability for prisoners, with an increased professional input for the assessment and management of risk, and a depoliticization of operational responsibility within prison systems that can manage to control themselves.

REFERENCES

Abadinsky, Howard. 1987. *Probation and Parole: Theory and Practice.* 3d ed. Englewood Cliffs, N.J.: Prentice-Hall.
Allen, Francis A. 1959. "Criminal Justice, Legal Values and the Rehabilitative Ideal." *Journal of Criminal Law, Criminology, and Police Science* 50:226–32.

————. 1964. *The Borderland of Criminal Justice: Essays in Law and Criminology.* Chicago: University of Chicago Press.

Allen, H. E., C. W. Eskridge, E. J. Latessa, and G. F. Vito. 1985. *Probation and Parole in America.* New York: Free Press.

Alschuler, Albert W. 1980. "Sentencing Reform and Parole Release Guidelines." *University of Colorado Law Review* 51:237–45.

American Friends Service Committee. 1971. *Struggle for Justice.* New York: Hill & Wang.

American Law Institute. 1962. *Model Penal Code.* Proposed Official Draft. Philadelphia: American Law Institute.

Barnard, Elizabeth. 1976. "Parole Decision-making in Britain." *International Journal of Criminology and Penology* 4:145–59.

————. 1980. "The Context of the British Parole System." *Probation Journal* 27:44–51.

Bartrip, Peter W. J. 1981. "Public Opinion and Law Enforcement: The Ticket-of-Leave Scares in Mid-Victorian Britain." In *Policing and Punishment in Nineteenth-Century Britain,* edited by V. Bailey. London: Croom Helm.

Berk, Richard A., Sheldon L. Messinger, David Rauma, and John E. Berecochea. 1983. "Prisons as Self-regulatory Systems: A Comparison of Historical Patterns in California for Male and Female Offenders." *Law and Society Review* 17:547–86.

Block, Michael K., and William M. Rhodes. 1987. *The Impact of the Federal Sentencing Guidelines.* Washington, D.C.: National Institute of Justice.

Blumstein, Alfred. 1984. "Sentencing Reforms: Impacts and Implications." *Judicature* 68:129–39.

Blumstein, Alfred, Jacqueline Cohen, Susan E. Martin, and Michael Tonry, eds. 1983. *Research on Sentencing: The Search for Reform,* vol. 2. Washington, D.C.: National Academy Press.

Bottomley, A. Keith. 1973. "Parole Decisions in a Long-Term Closed Prison." *British Journal of Criminology* 13:26–40.

————. 1980. "The 'Justice Model' in America and Britain: Development and Analysis." In *The Coming Penal Crisis,* edited by A. E. Bottoms and R. H. Preston. Edinburgh: Scottish Academic Press.

————. 1984a. "Dilemmas of Parole in a Penal Crisis." *Howard Journal of Criminal Justice* 23:24–40.

————. 1984b. "Questioning Parole: Whose Discretion? What Principles?" *Prison Service Journal* 56(October):21–24.

Bottoms, Anthony E. 1980. "An Introduction to 'The Coming Crisis.' " In *The Coming Penal Crisis,* edited by A. E. Bottoms and R. H. Preston. Edinburgh: Scottish Academic Press.

Brewer, David, Gerald E. Beckett, and Norman Holt. 1981. "Determinate Sentencing in California: The First Year's Experience." *Journal of Research in Crime and Delinquency* 18:200–231.

Bureau of Justice Statistics. 1983. "Setting Prison Terms." Washington, D.C.: U.S. Department of Justice.

————. 1986. "State and Federal Prisoners, 1925–85." Washington, D.C.: U.S. Department of Justice.

———. 1987. "Prisoners in 1986." Washington, D.C.: U.S. Department of Justice.

———. 1988. "Probation and Parole 1987." Washington, D.C.: U.S. Department of Justice.

———. 1989. "Prisoners in 1988." Washington, D.C.: U.S. Department of Justice.

Burke, Peggy B., and Joan F. Lees. 1981. *Parole Guidelines in Four Jurisdictions: A Comparative Analysis*. Washington, D.C.: National Institute of Corrections.

Canadian Sentencing Commission. 1987. *Sentencing Reform: A Canadian Approach*. Ottawa: Canadian Government Publishing Centre.

Carlisle Committee. 1988. *The Parole System in England and Wales*. Report of the Review Committee. London: H.M. Stationery Office.

Cavender, Gray. 1982. *Parole: A Critical Analysis*. New York: Kennikat.

Daubney Committee. 1988. *Taking Responsibility*. Report of the Standing Committee on Justice and Solicitor General on Its Review of Sentencing, Conditional Release, and Related Aspects of Corrections. Ottawa: Queen's Printer.

Davis, Jennifer. 1980. "The London Garotting Panic of 1862: A Moral Panic and the Creation of a Criminal Class in Mid-Victorian England." In *Crime and the Law: The Social History of Crime in Western Europe since 1500*, edited by V. A. C. Gattrell, B. Lenman, and G. Parker. London: Europa.

Davis, Kenneth Culp. 1969. *Discretionary Justice: A Preliminary Inquiry*. Baton Rouge: Louisiana State University Press.

Ekirch, A. Roger. 1987. *Bound for America: The Transportation of British Convicts to the Colonies, 1718–75*. Oxford: Clarendon.

Fauteux report: *Report of a Committee to Inquire into the Principles and Procedures Followed in the Remission Service of the Department of Justice of Canada*. 1956. Ottawa: Queen's Printer.

Fogel, David. 1975. *"... We Are the Living Proof..."*: The Justice Model for Corrections*. Cincinnati: Anderson.

Frankel, Marvin E. 1973. *Criminal Sentences: Law without Order*. New York: Hill & Wang.

Goldenberg report: *Parole in Canada: Report of the Standing Committee on Legal and Constitutional Affairs*. 1974. Ottawa: Queen's Printer.

Gottfredson, Don M., Peter B. Hoffman, M. H. Sigler, and Leslie T. Wilkins. 1975. "Making Paroling Policy Explicit." *Crime and Delinquency* 21:34–44.

Gottfredson, Don M., Leslie T. Wilkins, and Peter B. Hoffman. 1978. *Guidelines for Parole and Sentencing*. Lexington, Mass.: Lexington.

Gottfredson, Michael R. 1979. "Parole Guidelines and the Reduction of Sentencing Disparity: A Preliminary Study." *Journal of Research in Crime and Delinquency* 16:218–31.

Gottfredson, Michael R., S. D. Mitchell-Herzfeld, and T. J. Flanagan. 1982. "Another Look at the Effectiveness of Parole Supervision." *Journal of Research in Crime and Delinquency* 19:277–98.

Harman, William G., and Robert G. Hann. 1986. *Release Risk Assessment: An Historical Descriptive Analysis*. Ottawa: Solicitor General Canada.

Hawkins, Keith O. 1971. *Parole Selection: The American Experience.* Ph.D. dissertation, Cambridge University, Faculty of Law.

————. 1980. "On Fixing Time: Reflections on Recent American Attempts to Control Discretion in Sentencing and Parole." Paper presented to Howard League seminar series "The Future of Parole." Oxford: Centre for Sociolegal Studies. Mimeographed.

————. 1983. "Assessing Evil: Decision Behaviour and Parole Board Justice." *British Journal of Criminology* 23:101–27.

Home Office. 1958. *The After-Care and Supervision of Discharged Prisoners.* Report of the Advisory Council on the Treatment of Offenders. London: H.M. Stationery Office.

————. 1965. *The Adult Offender.* Cmnd. 2852. London: H.M. Stationery Office.

————. 1969. *Report of the Parole Board for 1968.* London: H.M. Stationery Office.

————. 1970. *Report of the Parole Board for 1969.* London: H.M. Stationery Office.

————. 1973. *Report of the Parole Board for 1972.* London: H.M. Stationery Office.

————. 1974. *Report of the Parole Board, 1973.* London: H.M. Stationery Office.

————. 1976. *Report of the Parole Board, 1975.* London: H.M. Stationery Office.

————. 1979. *Prison Statistics England and Wales 1978.* Cmnd. 7626. London: H.M. Stationery Office.

————. 1981. *Review of Parole in England and Wales.* London: H.M. Stationery Office.

————. 1984. *Report of the Parole Board, 1983.* London: H.M. Stationery Office.

Hood, Roger G. 1965. *Borstal Reassessed.* London: Heinemann.

————. 1974. "Some Fundamental Dilemmas of the English Parole System and a Suggestion for an Alternative Structure." In *Parole: Its Implications for the Criminal Justice and Penal Systems,* edited by D. A. Thomas. Cambridge University, Cambridge Institute of Criminology.

Howard League for Penal Reform: *Freedom on Licence: The Development of Parole and Proposals for Reform.* 1981. Sunbury: Quartermaine House.

Hugessen report: *Report of the Task Force on the Release of Inmates.* 1973. Ottawa: Information Canada.

Hughes, Robert. 1987. *The Fatal Shore: A History of the Transportation of Convicts to Australia, 1787–1868.* London: Collins Harvill.

Irwin, John. 1970. *The Felon.* Englewood Cliffs, N.J.: Prentice-Hall.

Jacobs, James B. 1982. "Sentencing by Prison Personnel: Good Time." *UCLA Law Review* 30:217–70.

Jobson, Keith. 1972. "Fair Procedure in Parole." *University of Toronto Law Journal* 22:267–303.

Kastenmeier, Robert W., and Howard C. Eglit. 1973. "Parole Release Decision-making: Rehabilitation, Expertise and the Demise of Mythology." *American University Law Review* 22:477–525.

Killinger, G. G., and P. F. Cromwell, eds. 1974. *Corrections in the Community: Alternatives to Imprisonment.* Selected readings. St. Paul, Minn.: West.

Krajick, Kevin. 1983. "Abolishing Parole: An Idea Whose Time Has Passed." *Corrections Magazine* (June), pp. 32–40.

Krauth, Barbara. 1987. "Parole: Controversial Component of the Criminal Justice System." In *Observations on Parole: A Collection of Readings from Western Europe, Canada, and the United States,* edited by E. E. Rhine and R. W. Jackson. Boulder, Colo.: National Institute of Corrections.

Labour Party Study Group. 1964. *Crime—A Challenge to Us All.* London: Labour Party.

Lagoy, Stephen P., F. A. Hussey, and J. H. Kramer. 1978. "A Comparative Assessment of Determinate Sentencing in the Four Pioneer States." *Crime and Delinquency* 24:385–400.

Lane, Winthrop D. 1933. "A New Day Opens for Parole." *Journal of Criminal Law, Criminology and Police Science* 24:88–108.

Law Reform Commission of Canada. 1977. *The Parole Process: A Study of the National Parole Board.* Ottawa: Ministry of Supply and Services.

Lerner, Mark J. 1977. "The Effectiveness of a Definite Sentence Parole Program." *Criminology* 15:211–24.

Lindsey, Edward. 1925. "Historical Sketch of the Indeterminate Sentence and the Parole System." *Journal of American Institute of Criminal Law and Criminology* 16:9–126.

Lipton, David, Robert Martinson, and Judith Wilks. 1975. *The Effectiveness of Correctional Treatment.* New York: Praeger.

McCabe, Sarah. 1985. "The Powers and Purposes of the Parole Board." *Criminal Law Review* 1985:489–99.

McKelvey, Blake. 1968. *American Prisons: A Study in American History prior to 1915.* Montclair, N.J.: Patterson Smith. (Originally published 1936. Chicago: University of Chicago Press.)

Mandel, Michael. 1975. "Rethinking Parole." *Osgoode Hall Law Journal* 13:501–46.

Messinger, Sheldon L., John E. Berecochea, David Rauma, and Richard Berk. 1985. "The Foundations of Parole in California." *Law and Society Review* 19:69–106

Miller, Frank P. 1965. "Parole." In *Crime and Its Treatment in Canada,* edited by W. T. McGrath. Toronto: Macmillan.

Morgan, Neil. 1983. "The Shaping of Parole in England and Wales." *Criminal Law Review* 1983:137–51.

Morris, Norval. 1974. *The Future of Imprisonment.* Chicago: University of Chicago Press.

Nacci, Peter L., Hugh E. Teitelbaum, and Jerry Prather. 1977. "Population Density and Inmate Misconduct Rates in the Federal Prison System." *Federal Probation* 41(2):26–31.

National Institute of Corrections. 1985. *Parole in the United States, 1985.* Boulder, Colo.: National Institute of Corrections.

National Parole Board. 1987a. *Briefing Book for Members of the Standing Committee on Justice and Solicitor General.* Ottawa: National Parole Board.

———. 1987b. *Chairman's Presentation to the Standing Committee on Justice and Solicitor General.* Ottawa: National Parole Board.

———. 1988. *National Parole Board Pre-release Decision Policies.* Ottawa: Ministry of Supply and Services.

Nuffield, Joan. 1982. *Parole Decision-making in Canada: Research towards Decision Guidelines.* Ottawa: Ministry of Supply and Services.

Nuttall, Christopher P., et al. 1977. *Parole in England and Wales.* Home Office Research Study no. 38. London: H.M. Stationery Office.

O'Donnell, Pierce, Dennis E. Curtis, and Michael J. Churgin. 1977. *Toward a Just and Effective Sentencing System: Agenda for Legislative Reform.* New York: Praeger.

Ouimet report: *Report of Committee on Corrections.* 1969. Ottawa: Queen's Printer.

Parisi, Nicolette, and Joseph A. Zillo. 1983. "Good Time: The Forgotten Issue." *Crime and Delinquency* 29:228–37.

Radzinowicz, L., and R. Hood. 1986. *A History of English Criminal Law and Its Administration from 1750.* Vol. 5, *The Emergence of Penal Policy.* London: Stevens & Sons.

Ross, R. R., and T. G. Barker. 1986. *Incentives and Disincentives: A Review of Prison Remission Systems.* Ottawa: Solicitor General Canada.

Rothman, David J. 1980. *Conscience and Convenience: The Asylum and Its Alternatives in Progressive America.* Boston: Little, Brown.

Ruggles-Brise, Sir Evelyn. 1921. *The English Prison System.* London: Macmillan.

Rutherford, Andrew. 1986. *Prisons and the Process of Justice.* 2d ed. Oxford: Oxford University Press.

Sacks, Howard R., and Charles H. Logan. 1979. *Does Parole Make a Difference?* West Hartford, Conn.: University of Connecticut School of Law Press.

Schmidt, Janet. 1977. *Demystifying Parole.* Lexington, Mass.: Lexington.

Serrill, Michael S. 1977. "Determinate Sentencing: The History, the Theory, the Debate." *Corrections Magazine* 3(September):3–13.

Solicitor General Canada. 1981*a*. *Solicitor General's Study of Conditional Release.* Ottawa: Minister of Supply and Services.

———. 1981*b*. *Mandatory Supervision.* Ottawa: Ministry of Supply and Services.

Stone-Meierhoefer, Barbara, and Peter B. Hoffman. 1982. "The Effects of Presumptive Parole Dates on Institutional Behavior: A Preliminary Assessment." *Journal of Criminal Justice* 10:283–97.

Tilton, Peter J. 1987. "The Status of Parole in Maine." In *Observations on Parole: A Collection of Readings from Western Europe, Canada, and the United States,* edited by E. E. Rhine and R. W. Jackson. Boulder, Colo.: National Institute of Corrections.

Tonry, Michael. 1988. "Structuring Sentencing." In *Crime and Justice: A Review of Research,* vol. 10, edited by Michael Tonry and Norval Morris. Chicago: University of Chicago Press.

Twentieth Century Fund Task Force on Criminal Sentencing. 1976. *Fair and Certain Punishment.* New York: McGraw-Hill.

U.S. Department of Justice. 1939. *The Attorney General's Survey of Release Procedures.* Vol. 4, *Parole.* Washington, D.C.: U.S. Government Printing Office.

von Hirsch, Andrew. 1976. *Doing Justice: The Choice of Punishments*. New York: Hill & Wang.

————. 1988. *Federal Sentencing Guidelines: The United States and Canadian Schemes Compared*. New York: New York University School of Law, Center for Research in Crime and Justice.

von Hirsch, Andrew, and Kathleen J. Hanrahan. 1979. *The Question of Parole: Retention, Reform or Abolition*. Cambridge, Mass.: Ballinger.

Waller, Irvin. 1974. *Men Released from Prison*. Toronto: University of Toronto Press.

Ward, Denis. 1987. *The Validity of the Reconviction Prediction Score*. Home Office Research Study no. 94. London: H.M. Stationery Office.

Zalman, Marvin. 1977. "The Rise and Fall of the Indeterminate Sentence." *Wayne State Law Review* 24:45–94, 856–937.

Rolf Loeber and Marc Le Blanc

Toward a Developmental Criminology

ABSTRACT

The study of criminality will benefit from a developmental perspective that employs analyses of within-subject changes. A review of the evidence shows continuity in offending between adolescence and adulthood and continuity between prepubertal conduct problems and later offending. Three developmental processes of offending include activation, aggravation, and desistance. A variety of documentation indicates that developmental sequences can be identified for conduct problems, substance use, and delinquency. Quantitative and qualitative changes occur in the course of offending. Understanding developmental processes provides valuable insights into formulating strategies for longitudinal studies that can help to discriminate better between correlates and causes of crime. Examining developmental processes as youngsters grow older, such as increases in physical strength and motor skills, the emergence of personality traits, sexual maturation, and greater opportunities for crime commission, provides important contextual information for studies of offending. Developmental theories have direct implications for the prevention of offending and treatment of offenders.

The application of developmental perspectives to the study of offending is likely to advance current understanding of offending's causes and courses. A number of practical and tactical decisions by researchers in

Rolf Loeber is associate professor at the University of Pittsburgh, School of Medicine, Western Psychiatric Institute and Clinic. Marc Le Blanc is professor at the University of Montreal, School of Psycho-education. The authors are grateful for critical advice from Jane Costello, Marcel Fréchette, Magda Stouthamer-Loeber, Celia Nourse Eatman, and members of the Working Group on Onset of the Program on Human Development and Criminal Behavior. Preparation of the essay was supported by grants from the Office of Juvenile Justice and Delinquency Prevention, the National Institute of Mental Health, and the Ministry of the Solicitor-General of Canada. Special thanks to Jean Cottage for preparation of the references.

traditional criminology have limited what can be learned. For example, researchers have often studied delinquents' course of offending as indicated by official records, as though the onset of "real" delinquency occurs with the first arrest (see, e.g., Blumstein et al. 1986). Working only with official records, however, precludes considering whether, unbeknownst to the police, juveniles have been engaging in serious delinquent behaviors for a number of years. Similarly, the preference of many researchers to examine differences among *groups* of offenders has led to a neglect of study of changes in *individuals'* offending over time. As a result, we know very little about changes in individuals' rates of offending and how rates of offending wax and wane over the life cycle. Along that same line, it remains to be seen to what extent individuals' offense mix and degree of seriousness of delinquency develop over time in an orderly and predictable manner.

Work on the putative causes of crime likewise has been hindered by researchers' focus on other matters. Cross-sectional research has not required criminologists to specify whether correlates were different from causes. Similarly, they rarely addressed the question whether causes were invariant during the life cycle, or whether different constellations of causes operated for offenders who started delinquency at an early age compared with those starting later in life (e.g., Hirschi and Gottfredson 1987). Another question, inherently foreign to cross-sectional research, is which causal factors often occur *only* in close temporal proximity to the delinquent acts and which factors operate over long periods of time. Also unexamined is the extent to which causes operate singly or jointly in a temporal sequence unfolding over a period of years.

All of these neglected areas of inquiry share a common component; they originate from a developmental perspective on both offending and its causes. In elaborating on, and illustrating, developmental approaches in this essay, we depart from the criminological and sociological tradition of studying *between-group* differences among socioeconomic strata or ethnic groups in their degree of participation and frequency of offending (see review by Blumstein et al. [1986]). We employ, instead, a complementary approach, focusing on *within-individual* changes in offending over time, in which comparisons are made between individuals' offending at one time and that at other times. An important feature of this approach is that individuals serve as their own controls.

In the interest of conciseness, we use the term "developmental criminology" to refer to temporal within-individual changes in offending. Developmental criminology is the study, first, of the development and dynamics of problem behaviors and offending with age; this approach is largely descriptive and concerns the processes of behavioral development. The second focus of developmental criminology is the identification of explanatory or causal factors that predate, or co-occur with, the behavioral development and have an impact on its course. These two foci make it possible to shed light on the causes of individuals' initiation into offending, how their offense pattern may become more frequent and more serious over time, and how it may cease. Such inquiry also may attempt to explain individual differences among offenders in these respects.

A developmental perspective can be especially fruitful in periods of greatest behavior change, particularly in the juvenile years when there also are many changes in youngsters' social environment (McCall 1977). Major transitions in the life cycle, such as shifts in youngsters' relationships from parents to peers, the transition from school to work, and transitions from peers of the same sex to peers of the opposite sex, are of particular interest. In these periods, offending may usefully be examined against the backdrop of other life changes, such as the development of personality and physical maturation.

Another goal of developmental criminology is to increase the options for differentiating between correlates or risk factors and causal factors. To achieve this goal, developmental criminology uses as a principal tool longitudinal studies with repeated measurements. In order to ascertain the potential status of causal factors, it is necessary to consider a variety of questions, such as, Which factors are correlated with offending? Which correlates predate and predict later delinquency, and do so independently from third factors? Which discrete life events predict a change in offending? Which predictors (which may vary in frequency or duration) covary with within-individual changes over time in offending? and, Which sequences of predictors best explain increments in behavioral deviance? These are merely quasi-experimental procedures but constitute a necessary preliminary screening of potential causal factors. Where possible, a final and more superior test of the causal status of risk factors is the experimental manipulation of the antecedent factors (Hirschi and Selvin 1967; Loeber and Stouthamer-Loeber 1986).

Although developmental approaches to the study of criminology have been proposed in the past, they have not been embraced; the developmental perspective has been much more accepted in psychology

(Lerner 1986). The nonrandomness of changes in individuals' behavior during the life cycle is reflected in the orthogenetic principle that development exists when a system changes from being organized in a very general, undifferentiated way to having differentiated parts that are organized into an integrated hierarchy (Werner 1957; Kaplan 1983). From that perspective, can we not conceptualize offending as a behavior that initially is generalized and unspecific and which becomes more and more patterned over time? If this were the case, it would be worthwhile to test whether three principles derived from developmental psychology also apply to the study of crime: namely, whether the course of offending is predictable, hierarchical, and orderly.

Developmental criminology is not proposed here as a panacea for resolving all basic questions in criminology, but as a perspective that will give important new insights into the study of offending and its causes. As Zubin (1972) has pointed out, various scientific models have been formulated to explain psychopathology, including ecological, learning, hereditary, biochemical, and neurophysiological models; each of these can contribute to the explanation of offending. This essay focuses on the developmental approach and, among others, addresses the following questions: (1) Does individuals' offending develop in a sequential and orderly manner? (2) Are there qualitative and quantitative differences in offense patterns during the onset, maintenance, and termination of delinquency? (3) Which causal factors are responsible for some but not other youngsters progressing to serious delinquent outcomes? (4) Why is it that, even within a group of individuals who reach the same serious outcomes over time, some do so within a shorter time span and at an earlier age than others? (5) Which factors cause some individuals, after progressing to some degree in conduct problems and delinquency, to reach a plateau and desist from progressing to more serious levels? (6) Which factors cause some individuals, after progressing to a serious pattern of delinquency, to desist from these behaviors later?

This essay examines these questions and is organized in the following manner. Section I specifies developmental concepts that may serve to operationalize changes in offending over time. Section II examines evidence about the continuity of offending from the juvenile to the adult years and about the continuity between conduct problems and delinquency. Section III then describes the core features of three processes that take place during the course of offending: activation (or initiation), aggravation, and desistance. Empirical data are presented for each process to show current findings and illustrate how knowledge may be advanced in future studies. Section IV illustrates how qualitative and quantitative changes in offending can be assessed and how individuals' positions on developmental changes can be operationalized. Section V examines analytical strategies for distinguishing correlates from causes. Section VI places findings within the context of other developmental processes that take place during the course of offending. Section VII sets out conclusions and recommendations. We attempt to cover a broad gamut of factors that may affect developmental aspects of offending; owing in part to lack of space, we touch only lightly on biological and genetic factors.

I. Developmental Descriptors of Offending

Core concepts of offending are seldom adequately specified or given quantified meaning in the criminological literature. Most specifications refer to static aspects of offending, such as participation in offending, frequency of offending, and seriousness of offenses, rather than to developmental features of offending. Many concepts are unidirectional and limited in scope; for example, escalation is used to refer to the movement toward more serious offending, but writers rarely refer to de-escalation, the reverse. The concept of "specialization" is sometimes used in contrast to generalized or "cafeteria style" offending (Klein 1984), but researchers rarely offer a comprehensive approach that represents the entire continuum.

In this section we examine concepts commonly used in criminology and others that might usefully be imported from developmental psychology. To avoid conceptual difficulties, some criminologists have suggested better integrated and more consistent conceptualizations. For instance, Blumstein et al. (1986) proposed use of "individual offending" over delinquency. This generic concept has the advantage of describing the subject of study while avoiding the ambiguities of legal and moral meaning that the term delinquency often carries. Following this example of conceptual clarification, we present generic concepts of offending, then we define its temporal boundaries and follow by presenting dynamic concepts that reflect developmental changes over time. All of the proposed terminology is set out in table 1.

A. Generic Concepts

The distinction between prevalence and incidence was made early in criminology (e.g., Quételet 1842). More recently, Blumstein et al.

TABLE 1
Summary of the Core Concepts

Generic Concepts	Boundary Concepts	Dynamic Concepts
Participation	Age at onset	Activation:
Lambda	Age at termination	Acceleration
Crime mix	Duration	Diversification
Seriousness	Transfer/crime switching	Stabilization
Variety		Aggravation:
		Developmental sequence
		Escalation
		Desistance:
		Deceleration
		De-escalation
		Reaching a ceiling
		Specialization

(1986) reviewed these concepts and suggested new terms for eliminating former ambiguities. They proposed that prevalence be replaced by *current* or *cumulative participation* in crime and suggested that the terms *annual* and *cumulative frequency* (also called *lambda*) replace incidence, to refer to the number of crimes committed by an individual within a given time period.

According to Pinatel (1963), these two generic measures may be complemented by ascertaining the content of offending, that is, by establishing the combination of crimes committed by an individual; Blumstein et al. (1986) refer to this as the *crime mix*. The content of offending may also be differentiated in terms of the number of individuals for each different level of *seriousness* involved. A final concept refers to diversity or *variety* of types of offenses, the number of categories of crimes accumulated (see Hindelang, Hirschi, and Weis 1981; Loeber 1982).

B. Boundary Concepts

The preceding five distinctive indices (participation, frequency, variety, seriousness, and crime mix) are generic terms in that they apply to offending as a whole and in that the indices synthesize all the offenses committed by an individual. Other indices represent the temporal boundaries of offending (Le Blanc and Fréchette 1989). Some of these markers go back to the work of the Gluecks (Glueck and Glueck 1930, 1937, 1943), such as the idea of *age at onset* (the age at which an individual commits his or her first crime) and the *age at termination*. Other boundary concepts have more recently been refined, such as *duration* (the interval between the first and the last crime), within which Blumstein and his collaborators (Blumstein, Cohen, and Hsieh 1982; Blumstein et al. 1986) make a distinction between partial, total, and residual duration.[1] Still other concepts were either created or revised by longitudinal studies (Wolfgang, Figlio, and Sellin 1972; Shannon 1978; Wolfgang, Thornberry, and Figlio 1987), such as the transition from juvenile delinquency to adult criminality or the transfer from one type of criminal activity to another, which Blumstein et al. (1986) define as *crime switching*. All boundary concepts concern continuity in offending and may be viewed in two ways. The first is quantitative, where the data are the age at the time of the first offense, the duration of offending, and the age at the time of the last offense. The second is qualitative; the data consist of the transfer from one type of criminal activity to another over at least two moments in time. This transfer can be assessed in two ways: through transition matrices that show crime switching—that is, the changes in crime mix over time—or through the transfer of offending from juvenile delinquency, before the age of eighteen, to adult criminality, beginning from the age of eighteen.

C. Dynamic Concepts

Longitudinal studies have furnished data on the relations among several of the generic and boundary concepts of offending. These concepts are now standard in criminology, but the developmental perspective is usually underdeveloped. Syntheses, however (Loeber 1982, 1988*a*; Blumstein et al. 1986), have led to clarification of the conceptualization of certain dynamic processes and to the construction of models of offending. All of this work, as shown by Le Blanc and Fréchette (1989), is semi-intuitive because it is not based on a well-thought-out procedure for reconstructing the natural dynamics of the course of offending.

Duncan (1984) proposed such a procedure: a list of fundamental elements is compiled, then the variables are defined according to the combinations of these basic elements. By way of analogy, Le Blanc and Fréchette (1989) proposed to combine two or more generic and boundary concepts of offending in order to delimit processes that influence the course of offending. By applying this procedure, they distinguish

[1] When examining career duration it is possible to distinguish between criminal career duration (including the active and passive career; the latter includes time spent in prison) and the duration of the precriminal career, i.e., the time between onset of pervasive conduct problems and the onset of official delinquency.

among three basic processes of *activation*, *aggravation*, and *desistance*, each of which is given operational meaning by distinct concepts (see table 1).

Activation refers to the way the development of criminal activities, once begun, is stimulated and the way its continuity, frequency, and diversity is assured. They distinguish among three subprocesses of activation, namely, *acceleration* (increased frequency of offending over time—the combination of onset and frequency), *stabilization* (increased continuity over time—the combination of onset and duration), and *diversification* (the propensity for individuals to become involved in more diverse criminal activities—the combination of onset and variety).

The second process, *aggravation*, refers to the existence of a *developmental sequence* of diverse forms of delinquent activities that *escalate* or increase in seriousness over time (the combination of the concepts of seriousness and crime switching). Individuals can progress or regress within this developmental sequence.

The third process, *desistance*, concerns a slowing down in the frequency of offending (*deceleration*), a reduction in its variety (*specialization*), and a reduction in its seriousness (*de-escalation*). The relevant boundary concept for all these subprocesses is the *age at termination*.

Finally, several other terms help to describe and summarize the course of offending from its onset to termination. The term *developmental trajectory* is reserved for a description of systematic developmental changes in offending involving one or more of the processes of activation, aggravation, and desistance (and may cover also the realms of conduct problems and substance use). The understanding is that researchers may need to distinguish between multiple, rather than single, trajectories that reflect different *dynamic career types* (Huizinga 1979). Offenders may travel a segment of the trajectory, which is indicated by the term *path*. Since sequences in offending are hierarchical rather than embryonic, individuals often may start at the same stage but differ in the number of stages they move through subsequently.

D. Limitations of Past Methods

Boundary and dynamic concepts are far from new in criminology and have been the focus of research on within-individual changes in offending. Studies, however, have been controversial, and the findings far from optimal for three reasons: a too-high reliance on representative population samples, the study of official rather than self-reported delinquency, and an overdose of transition matrix technology.

Cernkovich, Giordano, and Pugh (1985) concluded that samples of convicted delinquents, who are virtually absent from representative samples, are essential for the advancement of knowledge in criminology. Le Blanc and Fréchette (1989) compared the level of delinquency in a representative population sample and a sample of wards of the court and concluded that the two types of samples provide unique and complementary information about offending. A representative sample has the advantage of establishing whether findings extend to the entire population, offers the opportunity to study the transition between conduct problems and offending, and makes it possible to study factors leading to activation in offending. By contrast, a delinquent sample has the advantage of a higher base rate of otherwise rare offenses, the study of processes that lead to aggravation in offending, and the examination of whether causes found in representative samples also apply to delinquent samples.

Much criminological research relies on official records. Unfortunately, official records are far from ideal for studying individuals' development in offending. The official records usually are a dim reflection of the "true" range of offenses committed because many of the crimes are not reported to the police or solved by them, independent from the age of the perpetrators (Farrington 1989c). Even when the perpetrator is found, this may not lead to official processing because of the many possibilities for diversion that are available in most justice systems. Le Blanc and Fréchette (1989) showed that developmental mechanisms of offending could not be specified clearly from official data but could be inferred more clearly from self-reports of delinquent acts. Official records are especially weak for studies of escalation or specialization: the justice system, with its selection biases, tends to uncover only the most serious incidents of the criminal career (Gottfredson and Gottfredson 1980). All types of crime, however, either official or self-reported, reflect a similar underlying construct, but this probably applies more to the former than to the latter (Farrington 1989c).

In addition to these methodological difficulties, the methods of analysis in most of the past studies, especially when based on factor analysis or transition matrices of delinquent behaviors, may reveal more about the interrelation of offenses than about within-individual changes in offending. Factor analysis tends to lump together offenders, who may be heterogeneous in several developmental features, such as their propensity to commit serious or trivial crimes and whether they start offending early or late.

Transition matrices, by contrast, are excellent for the study of crime switching. Transition matrices are cross-tabulations of offenses committed during one time period against offenses committed during a subsequent period. But, with their limit of two points in time, transition matrices open only a very narrow window on the entire criminal career over the life span of an individual. Cohen's (1986) and Le Blanc and Fréchette's (1989) reviews have identified various difficulties and limitations of this mode of analysis. Even if successive transition matrices are constructed and chains are tested with the Markovian analysis introduced in criminology by Wolfgang, Figlio, and Sellin (1972), the studies usually are inconclusive. The array of offenses often is either too large or too restrictive, while the use of official data impedes the understanding of the total course of offending. Moreover, this method lumps together offenders indiscriminately at different stages of their delinquent careers and, for that reason, confuses individual changes with developmental sequences in offending.

II. Continuity

There are several reasons why the study of the continuity of antisocial behavior is useful. First, such studies elucidate the degree of individuals' continuity in antisocial acts and demonstrate that continuity is much higher for some individuals than for others. Second, such studies help to establish the extent to which continuity between conduct problems and offending reflects the continuity of a more general deviance (Sroufe 1979, p. 834). Third, such studies may aid in the identification of early markers that distinguish between those whose deviance is more persistent and those whose deviance is occasional and temporary.

A. Continuity in Offending

Continuity often is measured by means of the correlation between measures taken at two moments in time. A major disadvantage, however, is that correlations are inadequate for within-individual analyses as they do not reveal what proportion of individuals scoring high or low at one time also score high or low at a later time (McCall 1977). Two-by-two tables, or more complex contingency tables, are more appropriate in that respect. Since existing prediction indices for two-by-two tables had major limitations, Loeber and Dishion (1983) proposed the predictive index called "relative improvement over chance," or RIOC (see the Appendix for an exposition of RIOC). Its advantages are that it summarizes the valid positives and valid negatives in two-by-two prediction tables and corrects the outcome for chance and for discrepancies between base rate and selection ratio, which are very common in these studies. The index varies from zero to 100 for predictors that are better than chance. Relative improvement over chance makes it possible to compare data from very different studies and to aggregate results so that the conclusions reached are more generalizable than is possible through single studies.[2]

Relevant longitudinal studies linking juvenile to adult male offending have been summarized by Loeber and Stouthamer-Loeber (1987) and are shown in table 2. The results, based on delinquency by age sixteen to eighteen and evidence of criminality by age twenty-four to forty, show RIOCs that ranged from 30.4 to 45.5 for three samples of mostly white males (Polk 1975; Osborn and West 1978; McCord 1979). An RIOC of 60.0 was found in Wolfgang's (1977) Philadelphia study, which consisted of white and black males.

Formulated in percentages of delinquent juveniles who were rearrested or convicted as adults, there were 62.0 percent and 51.3 percent in the Polk (1975) and the McCord (1979) studies, respectively, 71.1 percent in the Osborn and West (1978) study, and 39.2 percent in the Wolfgang (1977) study. There are large differences in the continuity of offending from the juvenile to the adult years depending on whether known delinquent or representative samples of juveniles are studied. For example, Le Blanc and Fréchette (1989) report on the continuity of offending among wards of the court and a representative sample of boys. Among the latter group, 37.9 percent of the delinquents were also arrested as adults, compared with twice as many (75.2 percent) of the wards of the court. Shannon's (1988) data, however, show an increase, cohort by cohort, in the continuity of offending from juvenile to adult delinquency from 20 percent in the 1942 cohort, 26 percent in the 1949 cohort, and 32 percent in the 1955 cohort. Across studies, about three to seven out of each ten juvenile offenders continued to offend, and were caught at least once during adulthood. Thus, studies from a variety of countries, using different arrest standards, different attrition rates for follow-up, and different age groups studied, all demonstrated a degree of continuity between juvenile and adult offending. Not only is there a continuity in prevalence, but the probability of adult offending increases as the severity of juvenile delinquency rises, as shown by Kempf (1988) with the data of the Philadelphia birth cohort study.

[2] Confidence intervals for RIOC can be found in Copas and Loeber (1990).

TABLE 2

Delinquency as a Predictor of Male Recidivism

Study	Predictor	Criterion	Prediction Interval (Age)	RIOC*
Le Blanc (1980)	Average and high delinquency (self-report)	Ditto	14–16 to 16–18	41.2
Le Blanc (1980)	High delinquency (self-report)	Ditto	14–16 to 16–18	34.5
Osborn and West (1978)	Delinquency (self-report)	Reconviction	14–16 to 19–23	30.4
Polk (1975)	Delinquent	Adult criminal record	15–16 to 28	45.5
McCord (1979)	Juvenile delinquent	Adult conviction for serious crimes	5–17 to 18–40	35.4
Wolfgang (1977)	Offense before age 18	Rearrest	<18 to 18–20	60.0
Osborn and West (1978)	Prior convictions	Reconviction	8–18 to 19–23	32.0
Elliott, Dunford, and Huizinga (1983)	Composite self-report index	Career offender (self-report)	11–17 to 15–22	33.6
Robins and Ratcliff (1979)	Arrest before age 15	Adult crime	–18 to –48	36.5

SOURCE.—Loeber and Stouthamer-Loeber (1987).
* RIOC = relative improvement over chance.

The question can be raised as to what proportion of adult offenders purportedly experienced an onset of offending in adulthood rather than earlier in life, judging from official records. In the Polk (1975) and McCord (1979) studies, 59.2 percent and 54.8 percent of the adult offenders had not been arrested or convicted during the juvenile years. This percentage, however, was much lower in the Wolfgang (1977), the Osborn and West (1978), and the Le Blanc and Fréchette (1989) studies (24.4 percent, 39.3 percent, and 15 percent, respectively).

The preceding findings should be accepted with caution since the studies have a number of limitations. First, they are based on official records of delinquency both as a predictor and as an outcome. Reliance on these records inevitably omits the calculation of continuity of delinquency for those whose offending began either early in life, or later, but was not detected by the police or the court. Second, offense continuity does not necessarily mean continuity of convictions since some studies are based on police contact only, rather than on findings of guilt. Third, the absence of studies on official reports of offending in females is glaring; consequently, there is little known about their continuity of offending.

There are several studies that have examined the continuity of self-reported delinquency. In most studies, the interval between the administration of the self-report measures was two years, took place during adolescence or early adulthood, and produced RIOCs in the thirties and low forties (Elliott, Dunford, and Huizinga 1983; Fréchette and Le Blanc 1987; for details, see Loeber and Stouthamer-Loeber [1987]). Only the Osborn and West (1978) study covered a longer interval, leading to a RIOC of 30.4 (Loeber and Stouthamer-Loeber 1987). Thus, prediction was only moderately strong when self-reports were used. It is unclear whether these results were influenced by the inclusion of minor offenses in the self-report measures or by the fact that some studies followed up individuals in a period characterized by a reduced participation rate in offending.

B. Continuity between Conduct Problems and Delinquency

One of the main tenets of developmental criminology is that conduct problems often predate and predict involvement in delinquency. Child developmental studies offer a firm consensus that particular conduct problems—aggression, lying, truancy, stealing, and general problem behavior—are predictive of later delinquency, as are early educational problems. Most of these studies have been summarized by Loeber and Stouthamer-Loeber (1987) and have been summarized in table 3,[3] which shows that each behavior is predictive of general delinquency (whether the child was arrested), serious delinquency (a felony arrest), and recidivism. The number of studies on which this meta-analysis was based, however, was sometimes small, and studies on girls are again underrepresented. The predictive power of various conduct problems varies as is evident from the median RIOC column, with drug use, stealing, and aggression ranking highest in that order.

[3] The median value for aggression is 32.9 in this table instead of the 45.3 in the original source, due to a computational error.

TABLE 3

Summary of Youth Behaviors as Predictors of Later Delinquency

Predictor	Sex	General Delinquency			Serious Delinquency			Recidivism		
		Number of studies	Median RIOC*	Range	Number of studies	Median RIOC*	Range	Number of studies	Median RIOC*	Range
Aggression	M	5	32.9	16.4–51.4	...	...	...	3	38.3	28.1–38.5
	M+F	3	25.2	17.0–30.3	...	...	...	...	...	...
Drug use	M	2	53.0	27.0–79.0	...	...	...	1	41.6	...
Truancy	M	4	25.5	20.4–26.3	2	46.5	27.8–65.1	...	...	...
Lying	M	2	22.4	22.0–22.7	...	...	...	1	31.0	...
Stealing	M	2	37.4	17.1–57.8	1	37.5	...	1	60.6	...
General problem behavior	M	12	26.6	4.0–64.2	3	66.3	9.1–91.8	3	52.5	26.0–89.0
	F	1	82.9	...	...	...	...	...	...	...
	M+F	2	41.3	32.3–50.2	...	...	...	...	...	...
Educational achievement	M	11	22.9	11.1–46.1	...	...	...	1	42.9	...
Prediction scales	M	3	64.4	27.8–78.0	...	...	...	1	87.0	...
Delinquency	M	...	...	...	...	...	...	8	38.3	30.4–81.3
	M+F	...	...	...	...	...	...	2	35.1	33.6–36.5

SOURCE.—Loeber and Stouthamer-Loeber (1987).

NOTE.—M = male; F = female.

* RIOC = relative improvement over chance.

Not shown in table 3 is the period covered by the predictions in each study (see Loeber and Stouthamer-Loeber [1987] for details). Briefly, the majority of studies examined conduct problems in late childhood or early adolescence. There is a scarcity of studies that have pushed back the prediction of offending using predictors measured in early to middle childhood (see fig. 4 in Loeber and Dishion [1983] and a recent analysis of the Cambridge self-reported and official data by Farrington [1989a]). Therefore, conclusions about the duration of the continuity of conduct problems and their relation to offending are necessarily restricted. In the domain of aggressive behavior, however, it has been shown recently that there is a high level of continuity between troublesome behavior in late childhood and violent delinquency during adolescence and adulthood (Farrington 1989a) and between parental reports of aggression from one generation to the next (Huesmann et al. 1984).

In the realm of conduct problems, too, there are large individual differences in the frequency, seriousness, variety, and duration of these problems. Not surprisingly, the continuity is highest for individuals whose early problem behavior was either highly frequent, high in variety, occurred at an early age, or was observed in multiple rather than in single settings (Loeber 1982). More extreme cases, such as children referred to child guidance clinics for their problem behavior, show the highest continuity. Robins (1978) concluded that, in retrospect, *virtually all* of those children who as adults were diagnosed as sociopaths had been antisocial as children. Studies on two other samples of black men and Vietnam veterans led to the same conclusion, that "antisocial personality rarely or never arose *de novo* in adulthood" (Robins 1978, p. 617; see also Zeitlin 1986). Viewed retrospectively, most chronic offenders were highly aggressive when young (Justice, Justice, and Kraft 1974; Loeber and Stouthamer-Loeber 1987). The other important point made by Robins (1978) was that, for those who become antisocial adults, deviant behavior patterns accelerated from childhood to adulthood in terms of the frequency, variety, and seriousness of the offenses committed.

C. Summary

Continuity of individuals' offending into adulthood characterizes a segment of the juvenile delinquent population; likewise, a proportion of conduct problem children become offenders later. However, about half of the at-risk children do not reach the serious outcomes of chronic offender, sociopath, or drug abuser. Studies illustrate that the onset of offending is spread from late childhood to adulthood, again reflecting large individual differences in the continuity and duration of deviant careers (Farrington 1983; Wilson and Herrnstein 1985). In that context, many, but not all, of those who are deviant in adulthood experienced an onset of deviant behavior during childhood.

Against the backdrop of continuity, studies also show large within-individual changes in offending, a point understressed by Gottfredson and Hirschi (1987). We believe that study of these changes will reveal developmental sequences of offending and that such knowledge will help researchers to establish individuals' positions within the sequences.

III. Developmental Processes of Offending

In Section I, in setting out a vocabulary for describing and understanding developmental sequences, we discussed three dynamic concepts to characterize delinquent processes that influence the course of offending. These were *activation*, *aggravation*, and *desistance*. In this section, we use these concepts to address a series of central questions about offending processes. Which systematic changes can be observed in individual offending through the life span? Which quantitative changes, such as increases or decreases in the number of crimes along the criminal career, are common to all delinquents? Which qualitative changes can be discerned, such as variations in the crime mix and the seriousness of the offenses? Are there any mechanisms or laws that govern the course of criminal activity? These developmental questions will guide our analysis of the literature on the course of offending and our formulation of the processes of activation, aggravation, and desistance, which make up that course.

A. Activation

Activation refers to the process by which the development of criminal activities is initiated and stimulated. Most criminologists have focused on adolescence as a time when many youngsters initiate their delinquent careers. Although this co-occurs with an acceleration of participation in delinquency (Farrington 1983; Kandel 1988), this focus ignores the finding that early onset of offending is not uncommon (Loeber 1987a), is predictive of frequent, persisting, varied, and serious offenses in males, and may result from causal factors that differ from those associated with later onset of delinquency.

One of the reasons criminologists have focused more on adolescence than on earlier ages is their reliance on official records, which rarely document the age at onset for delinquency prior to age twelve and more generally around age fifteen (Snyder 1988). In contrast, self-reports of delinquency often reveal that delinquent acts occur earlier than that. For example, table 4 shows retrospective data collected by Belson (1975) on a London sample of boys, which suggest incremental steps in the age at onset of theft with less serious forms of theft—such as theft at home—occurring earliest (mean age 10.0), and more serious forms of theft—such as vehicle theft—occurring later (mean age 14.2). Theft, however, often occurs against a backdrop of other problem behaviors. Robins (1985), in a large retrospective study, also shown in table 4, found that the average age at onset for theft took place at about age ten for males and females, and a number of other problem behaviors—such as running away and truancy—for half of the sample first occurred prior to age twelve. The results for girls show a slight trend for a later age at onset in truancy than for boys. These findings should be accepted with caution since subjects' recall was after many years. Shorter recall, however, in the Fréchette and Le Blanc (1987) study on male adolescents from Montreal also shows the average age at onset for minor larceny, shoplifting, and vandalism to be before the age of twelve. The emphasis here on early onset does not serve to diminish the importance of later onset, a point to which we return.[4]

The focus on the average or median age at onset for a particular behavior conceals the different implications that early onset has for the subsequent course of the behavior than does later onset. For example, age at first arrest often occurs much earlier for those who later become chronic offenders than for those who become nonchronic offenders. Farrington (1988), in the Cambridge Study in Delinquent Development, found that those chronic offenders with six or more convictions were on average 13.8 years old at their first conviction, compared with 16.2 for nonchronic offenders. All of the eventual chronic offenders experienced their first conviction by age fifteen. These findings are much in line with those reported by Le Blanc and Fréchette (1989), who found that chronic offenders in a representative population sample

---

[4] It should be kept in mind, however, that average age at onset in the Belson (1975) study, and to a lesser extent in the other studies, is a function of the age at which subjects were interviewed. In fact, average age at onset is positively related to the age at interview, with reports of earlier average age at onset occurring when subjects are interviewed at a young age, while later average onsets are more apparent when individuals are interviewed at a higher age.

TABLE 4

The Average or Median Age at Onset for Conduct Problems and Delinquency

London Boys*	Mean	Adults in St. Louis Area†	Median M	Median F	Montreal Male Delinquents‡	Median	St. Louis Male Blacks§	Median
					Minor larceny	8.3		
		School discipline problem	9.0	9.8				
		Fighting	9.4	10.0				
		Lying	9.9	9.6				
Theft from relatives	10.0	Stealing	10.0	9.7				
Shoplifting	10.0				Shoplifting	11.3		
Theft by trespass	10.8	Truancy	11.0	12.0				
Theft from school	11.1	Vandalism	11.2	10.7	Vandalism	11.7		
Theft from peers	11.4	Runaway	11.6	12.3			School absence	7.3
Theft by threatening others	12.0				Running away	13.0	Drinking	13.1
					Alcohol use	13.1		
					Vagrancy	13.5		
					Petty theft	13.6		

	Drugs				
Breaking and entering	12.1				
Motor vehicle theft	14.2				
		12.7	13.1	Drug use	13.6	Marijuana use	15.7

	Age		
Drug use	13.6	Marijuana use	15.7
Burglary	14.2		
Personal larceny	14.8		
Motor vehicle theft	15.2		
Public mischief	15.6		
		Amphetamine use	15.8
		Barbiturate use	16.5
Aggravated theft	16.6		
Personal attack	16.8		
Sexual offense	17.0		
		Opiate use	17.1
Drug trafficking	17.2		
Fraud	19.8		
Homicide	19.9		

* SOURCE.—Belson (1975).
† SOURCE.—Robins (1985).
‡ SOURCE.—Fréchette and Le Blanc (1987).
§ SOURCE.—Robins and Wish (1977).
NOTE.—M = male, F = female.

were on average 13.9 years old at first conviction, compared with 15.3 for the nonchronics. Boys in a delinquent sample were likewise precocious by about one year, that is, the average ages of first conviction for the chronic and nonchronic offenders were 13.2 and 14.0, respectively. Perhaps significantly, when onset was based on self-reports in the delinquent sample, this was 10.3 for the chronics, compared with 11.4 for the nonchronics.

One useful way to look at the emergence of several offense types or types of problem behavior is to identify the distribution of ages at onset. Such a distribution can help to contrast different groups of offenders or antisocial youths. For example, Reitsma-Street, Offord, and Finch (1985) compared antisocial youngsters and their brothers and found that, on the average, antisocial youngsters experienced ages at onset for several problem behaviors two years earlier than their brothers. This implies that age at onset for one problem behavior is correlated with the age at onset for other problem behaviors (see, e.g., Bohman et al. 1982, for substance abuse and offending). Thus highly antisocial individuals experience an early onset of each of a series of successive problem behaviors, and each of these onsets occurs significantly earlier compared with those for less seriously antisocial individuals (see also Offord et al. 1979). It is, therefore, likely that early onset is a marker for later deviancy processes; this assumption is supported by research findings reviewed below.

1. *Early Age at Onset as a Marker for Future Deviancy.* A large number of studies have found that the age at onset of several deviant behaviors is predictive of later delinquency, sociopathy, and substance abuse (e.g., Glueck and Glueck 1940; Robins 1966; Shannon 1978; Brunswick and Boyle 1979; Robins and Ratcliff 1980; Kandel 1982; Loeber 1982; Robins and Przybeck 1985). The predictive relation is not limited to predicting the presence or absence of a delinquent record; rather, age at onset reflects *activation*, that is, the process by which offending after its onset becomes frequent, stable, and more varied over time. Activation is composed of three separate, but closely interrelated, subprocesses: acceleration, stabilization, and diversification. *Acceleration* refers to increases in the frequency of offending and deviant behavior in general (see, e.g., White 1988). *Stabilization* more directly refers to the way in which offending becomes persistent, resulting in its longevity. *Diversification* refers to the way offending becomes more heterogeneous and generalized. An early age at onset of offending, at least in males, predicts each of the three components of the activation process— acceleration, stabilization, and diversification.

Fréchette and Le Blanc (1979) were the first to describe the relation between early onset and the rate of self-reported offending, while Loeber (1982) noted the relation between early onset and the rate of officially recorded crime, based on reports by Farrington (1982a) and Hamparian et al. (1978). Several other studies have demonstrated that males with an early age of first arrest or conviction tend to commit crimes at a much higher rate than those with a later age at onset (Farrington 1983; Block and Van der Werff 1987; Wikström 1987; Loeber and Snyder 1988). Using American and English data, Cohen (1986) and Farrington (1983) found, respectively, that those arrested or convicted by age thirteen subsequently averaged about *two or three* times higher rates of crime per year compared with those whose onset was later, although this was not found by Loeber and Snyder (1988).[5] The findings are not simply the result of younger offenders having a longer period of risk compared with those with a later onset. The larger volume of crime over the years, however, implies that those with an early onset are more at risk for becoming chronic offenders than are those with a later age at onset (Mannheim and Wilkins 1955; Glueck and Glueck 1968; Farrington 1983; Hamparian et al. 1985; Loeber and Snyder 1988). In addition, early onset is also predictive of a longer duration of offending (Le Blanc and Fréchette 1989).

Tolan (1987), in an important study, asked fifteen- to eighteen-year-olds to indicate when after age nine they first had committed "minor, less serious delinquent acts of theft, vandalism, status offenses, and drug and alcohol use" (p. 51), including being questioned by the police. An early onset group (prior to age twelve) was then compared with a later onset group. At the time of the study, the frequency of self-reported delinquency (on a fifty-nine-item scale) in the past year was, on the average, about three-and-a-half times higher for the early group than for the late onset group. Along that line, Fréchette and Le Blanc's (1987) follow-up of boys in Montreal found that the annual rate of self-reported offending was about twice as high for those who started their delinquency prior to ages twelve to thirteen compared with those who started later. Overall, the difference between the two groups was maintained over the two-year follow-up but increased for certain age groups.

How far back in time do the behavior problems originate, and is there a group of individuals whose problem behavior dates back to the

[5] One American study (Snyder 1988) failed to find that age of first arrest predicted the rate of later offending, but this was possibly due to the fact that analyses concerned official delinquency and included active and nonactive offenders.

preschool period? Several studies have shown large individual differences in youngsters' onset of behavior problems or their first referral to child health clinics for behavior problems (Robins 1966; Stewart et al. 1981; Loeber and Baicker-McKee 1989). Similarly, parental reports and clinical records of the age at onset of problem behavior in seriously disruptive youngsters (such as conduct disorder or hyperactivity) often make mention of an onset before the preschool years (Stewart et al. 1966; Lewis, Shanok, and Pincus 1981; Taylor et al. 1986). One of these studies (Loeber, Stouthamer-Loeber, and Green 1989) divided boys into two groups depending on whether the caretaker recalled that the child had been "easy" to deal with or not between the ages of one and five. Subjects were fourth-, seventh-, and tenth-grade boys, who were followed up after five years. Arrest records showed that those who had been troublesome before age six had a two-times higher rate of contact with the police compared with those with a later age at onset of problem behavior. Results from the youngsters' self-reported delinquency were of the same magnitude. Although the study may have suffered from a recall bias, its findings are concordant with the results from other studies, all showing that early onset of problem behaviors is associated with a higher rate of offending compared with later onset.

Early age at onset is predictive also of diversification in offending. Mills and Noyes (1984) observed that subjects' retrospective reports of their age of first drug use was significantly correlated with the variety of different drugs used at the time of the assessment (see also White 1988). Similarly, the aforementioned study by Tolan (1987) found that early onset offenders averaged 3.16 types of offenses (out of a maximum of five) compared with 2.28 (for later onset offenders) for a recall period of one year. The difference increased if a longer time interval was taken into account, and it was on the order of seven to one for hidden delinquency and seven to three for official delinquency (Le Blanc and Fréchette 1989).[6]

---

[6] Since seriousness of offending is highly correlated with frequency, and early onset with frequency, it comes as no surprise that early onset is also highly correlated with seriousness (Le Blanc and Fréchette 1989). Using official records of delinquency, Shannon (1978) found that those who start early commit more serious crimes later on (see also Snyder 1988). Other studies, however, report contradictory results (Cohen 1986). Turning to self-reported delinquency, again Tolan's (1987) study is illuminating since it shows that, when seriousness was classified on five different, ascending levels, the early onset offenders averaged 3.64 on the most serious crimes committed compared to an average of 2.96 for the late onset offenders. The rate of more serious felonies was more than eight times higher for the early onset group compared with the later onset group.

2. *Summary.*   Data from a variety of studies thus indicate that age at onset of deviant behavior is predictive of the frequency, variety, and duration of offending. Many chronic offenders tend to have experienced an early onset of problem behavior and delinquency. It should be kept in mind, however, that many early problem behaviors in children, predictive of later delinquency, take place during a period characterized by age-normative problem behavior. At this stage, predictive accuracy is not sufficiently high to discriminate between those youngsters who will outgrow age-normative problem behavior and those who will not.

Early onset in conduct problems or delinquency appears more predictive of later offending for males than for females (Block and Van der Werff 1987; Loeber and Snyder 1988; Loeber 1988*a*). Wikström (1987, p. 50) reported that "for young ages at onset female persisters [in offending] are less persistent than the male persisters, while for the late ages at onset, female persisters are more persistent than the male persisters."[7] Studies in the field of substance abuse, however, indicate that early age at onset of substance use is predictive of continued high use in both sexes (Jessor, Donovan, and Widmer 1980; Fleming, Kellam, and Brown 1982; Robins and Przybeck 1985).[8]

Only a minority of the late-onset male offenders become high-rate offenders. These late onset offenders have been poorly studied but are of importance, nevertheless, for the study of later serious forms of delinquency. For example, Robins and Ratcliff (1980) documented that "the violent criminal [with few offenses] was 'more normal' as a child than the property offender" (p. 258), suggesting a late onset of problem behavior. This agrees with findings reported by Hamparian et al. (1978) that youths arrested for homicide and armed robbery tended to start their official careers in midadolescence rather than earlier. Likewise, Vera et al. (1980) found that those offenders charged with a violent (or nonviolent) sexual offense typically had a criminal record that did *not* begin prior to age fifteen (see also McCord 1980). Only one follow-up study of clinic-referred children documented that those arrested for violent acts in adulthood had been aggressive when young,

---

[7] The only known exception is reported by Tracy, Wolfgang, and Figlio (1985), who found that although age at onset was not related to the mean number of offenses in females, those who began at ages ten through twelve "had the highest mean number of offenses" (p. 14).

[8] White, Johnson, and Garrison (1985) reported that among twelve-year-olds (either male or female), those who used alcohol were more likely to engage in delinquent behavior than those who abstained. This may imply that, for either sex, the use of alcohol enhances the likelihood of delinquency involvement by that age.

which for some was the only recorded early antisocial behavior (Zeitlin 1986).

B. Aggravation of Offending

After activation, the second process in the course of offending is called *aggravation*. Its main feature is escalation in offending, which has been the subject of numerous controversies in the criminological literature. Blumstein et al. (1986, p. 84) defined escalation as "the tendency for offenders to move to more serious offense types as offending continues." Le Blanc and Fréchette (1989, p. 102), however, defined escalation from a developmental perspective as "a sequence of diverse forms of delinquent activities that go from minor infractions to the most serious crimes against the person as the subject increases in age."

The study of the individual development of offending requires that a sequence of behavior be demonstrated before we can begin measuring developmental changes in offending. This view has long been accepted in psychology; it refers, following Wohlwill (1973), first, to the particular sequence of behaviors and, second, to an individual's progress along that sequence. In criminology the two issues have been indirectly addressed for some time. Below, we first review available data and show that there are developmental sequences in conduct problems, substance use, and offending. We then demonstrate that these sequences can be combined into developmental trajectories and that it is more likely that there are multiple trajectories rather than a single trajectory.

1. *Developmental Sequences: Methods of Analysis.* In the 1940s the question of the existence of a developmental sequence in offending was studied by examining variations in offending patterns over time. Glueck and Glueck (1940) compared adult and juvenile offense patterns and found that property offenses were more common for juveniles and violent offenses more common for adults. The findings have been replicated subsequently in several countries (McCord and McCord 1959; Wolfgang, Figlio, and Sellin 1972; Moitra 1981; Cohen 1986; Wikström 1987; Wolfgang, Thornberry, and Figlio 1987; Le Blanc and Fréchette 1989). These analyses were crude but suggested a sequence of two stages in official offending from property to violent offenses. The findings did not receive much attention; instead, researchers turned to other means of identifying sequences in offending.

With the advent of cross-sectional data on self-reported delinquency, two techniques were successively used, Guttman scalogram analysis (Guttman 1944) and factor or cluster analysis. In the 1950s, Nye and

Short (1957) attempted to construct a unidimensional scale of delinquency for which they used the Guttman scalogram technique, consisting of an increasing scale of delinquency seriousness. In such a scale, an individual reporting positive on rare or infrequent behaviors should also report positive on the more common items. This type of scale was replicated but rapidly discarded because it could not be used with a large pool of items and was criticized for its inadequate methodology (see Leik and Matthews 1968; Robinson 1973; Hindelang, Hirschi, and Weis 1981).

In the 1960s and the 1970s, statistical clustering techniques were used to divide heterogeneous collections of delinquent acts into homogeneous subsets (see Hindelang, Hirschi, and Weis [1981] for a review of these attempts with self-reported delinquency, and Cohen [1986] for a review of equivalent studies with official delinquency). The results were mixed, but certain types of offense were common to most studies (such as thefts, drugs, and aggression).

Statistical clustering techniques also were used to address escalation and specialization (see Klein 1984; Cohen 1986). Specialization studies produced contradictory results, which raised much controversy; this was due in part to three types of defects. First, the statistical techniques were inappropriate because they optimized the exclusiveness of behavior patterns and neglected the possibility that response generalizability and specialization may coexist (Loeber and Waller 1988). Second, specialization and escalation often cannot be inferred from these studies because the concepts refer to repeated successive offenses or to increased seriousness and because most studies were cross-sectional rather than longitudinal. How can the direction of within-individual change be described with data at only one moment in time? The study of changes in individual offending naturally requires at least two data points if a developmental sequence is to be identified. Third, we referred earlier to the limitations of transition matrices for the identification of developmental sequences. Transition matrices have been inappropriately used for uncovering developmental sequences in offending, especially if we are concerned with all of the offenses committed by individuals, rather than by two adjacent crimes only.

Below we provide evidence that shows there is an orderly, hierarchical ordering of behaviors in the respective realms of conduct problems, substance use, and delinquency and that these behaviors do not occur randomly over time.

2. *Developmental Sequences in Conduct Problems.* Patterson (1982),

Loeber (1985a), and Farrington (1986) have provided theoretical and empirical support for the hypothesis that child conduct problems often constitute stepping stones toward delinquency, with trivial antisocial acts preceding serious acts. Kagan (1971) spoke of heterotypic continuity, in which phenotypically different behaviors manifest themselves at different points in the life cycle. Loeber (1990) and Loeber and Baicker-McKee (1989) similarly proposed a model of antisocial development in which different manifestations of antisocial behavior succeed and predict one another from childhood. Within this framework, continuity implies that, for example, conduct problems may be followed by delinquent acts and later by other forms of maladaptation such as alcoholism, drug abuse, or mental health problems. Thus, against the backdrop of continuity, various manifestations of antisocial or delinquent behaviors may remain stable or may replace each other over time.

Recent decades have produced an impressive body of research findings showing that disruptive behavior in youngsters can manifest itself very differently at different ages and that each manifestation tends to predict the next *and* later manifestations. The evidence has been reviewed by Loeber and Baicker-McKee (1989), showing, for example, that boys' oppositional behavior in the preschool years predicts conduct problems later, as well as juvenile delinquency, substance use, and adult criminality.

Loeber (1985a, 1988a), in reviewing the literature, concluded that there are probably three types of qualitative changes in conduct problems over time: an increasing seriousness of problem behavior, a shift from problem behavior at home to other social environments, and a developmental sequence from overt (fighting and threatening) to covert conduct problems (truancy, vandalism, stealing, and alcohol and drug use).[9] Findings on an overall sequence of conduct problems, however, are unsatisfactory because data usually were cross-sectional (e.g., Patterson 1982); when longitudinal data were available, the follow-up period usually was only a few years, repeated measurements were rare, and analyses have been rather simplistic. Nevertheless, the existence of a hierarchical, heterotypic sequence of conduct problems seems plausible.

3. *Developmental Sequences in Substance Use.* There is a consensus

[9] Additionally, there probably is a developmental sequence from the victimization of familiar individuals (relatives, friends) to unfamiliar individuals.

that substance use evolves over time according to an orderly developmental sequence; this is evident from panel studies (Kandel 1978, 1980; Brennan, Elliott, and Knowles 1981; Newcomb 1988; White 1988), retrospective studies (Robins and Wish 1977; Glassner and Loughlin 1987; Carpenter et al. 1988), and cross-sectional studies in a variety of countries (Adler and Kandel 1981; Le Blanc and Tremblay 1987). The four common developmental stages are initial beer and wine use; use of cigarettes, hard liquor, or both; marijuana use; and consumption of other illicit drugs. This sequence can probably be refined since Jessor, Donovan, and Widmer (1980) have shown that problem drinking follows marijuana use. Moreover, Le Blanc and Tremblay (1987) have established that the selling of drugs precedes the use of hard drugs.

The basic sequence holds for adolescents and even for young adults (Yamaguchi and Kandel 1984). Moreover, substances used earlier in the sequence tend to be retained rather than replaced by other substances (see Jessor, Donovan, and Widmer 1980; Mills and Noyes 1984). The sequence of substance use fits better a *hierarchical* rather than an *embryonic* model because only some individuals go through the full developmental sequence.

4. *Developmental Sequences in Offending.* In the 1960s, cross-sectional research on self-reported delinquency was on the verge of addressing the question of a developmental sequence in offending but, for reasons explained below, these studies were put aside. Slocum and Stone (1963) discussed "offense sequences" and "consistent patterns of misbehavior." Dentler and Monroe (1961) proposed a cumulative theft scale, and Arnold (1965) constructed three cumulative scales of theft, vandalism, and attacks against persons. When only cross-sectional rather than longitudinal data were available, the question of developmental sequences could not be pursued other than by means of retrospective reports.

Even when longitudinal data became available, analyses concentrated on crime switching rather than on developmental sequences (Wolfgang, Figlio, and Sellin 1972). In addition, reports from the Youth in Transition Project (Bachman, O'Malley, and Johnston 1978) and the National Youth Survey (Elliott, Huizinga, and Ageton 1985), although longitudinal and valuable in many respects, have not been fully exploited for the identification of stages in offending. The Cambridge Study in Delinquent Development addressed that question slightly, demonstrating that self-reported theft predicted engagement in burglaries in later years (Farrington 1973). Sellin and Wolfgang

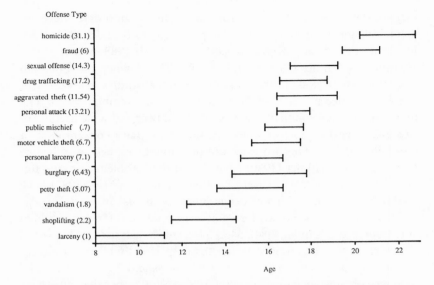

Fig. 1.—Median age of onset and duration of offense types (with average seriousness rating) in a sample of delinquent boys. Source.—Le Blanc and Fréchette (1989).

(1964) earlier invented a method for scaling the seriousness of offenses, which was applied to various age groups demonstrating that seriousness increased with age in the Philadelphia cohort (Wolfgang, Figlio, and Sellin 1972; Wolfgang, Thornberry, and Figlio 1987).

Fréchette and Le Blanc (1979) were among the first to address developmental sequences in offending in a more comprehensive manner. Using data from a three-panel, self-reported delinquency study, in which male delinquents were followed up to age twenty-five, they constructed a graph showing median ages at onset of various types of offense committed from late childhood to adulthood (fig. 1). The abscissa represents the average seriousness score for each category of crime, based on Wolfgang's method of scaling seriousness (Wolfgang et al. 1985). Offense types seem to be ordered in a specific way according to their starting age, seriousness, and duration.[10] This ordering can be summarized in an orderly sequence of five developmental stages, which were labeled in the following order: *emergence, exploration, explosion, conflagration,* and *outburst* (Le Blanc and Fréchette 1989). On the aver-

[10] See Cline (1980), Farrington (1983), Wilson and Herrnstein (1985), and Wikström (1987) for similar ordering of ages at onset of first arrest or conviction for different types of crime.

age, the first stage, emergence, takes place usually between the ages of eight and ten, when offending is homogeneous and benign and almost always expressed in the form of petty larceny. The next stage of exploration, generally between the ages of ten and twelve, is marked by a diversification and an aggravation of offenses, usually shoplifting and vandalism. Later on, at about age thirteen, there is a substantial increase in the variety and seriousness of offending, and four new types of crime develop: common theft, public mischief, burglary, and personal larceny. This is the explosion stage, with burglary constituting the major component of this escalation. Following, around the age of fifteen, the variety and seriousness of offending increases further and, at the same time, is complemented by four more types of crime—drug trafficking, motor vehicle theft, armed robbery, and personal attack; this is the stage of conflagration. The fifth stage, outburst, occurs during adulthood only and consists of a transition toward astute (e.g., fraud) or more violent (homicide) forms of offending.

This demonstration of the sequence of offending was based solely on the median values of the age at onset and duration of different types of crime, ranked by seriousness. They also used Guttman scaling to test their observations and concluded that the developmental sequence of offense types should not be conceived of as a particular ordering of all offenses but, rather, as the sequence of three specific categories of delinquency. The first category is composed of shoplifting and vandalism between the ages of eleven and fourteen; this is followed by four other types of theft between the ages of fourteen and seventeen (common theft, burglary, personal larceny, automobile theft), while the more serious categories of crime (personal attack, armed robbery, drug trafficking, sex-related crimes) occur between the ages of sixteen and nineteen.[11]

Even though Le Blanc and Fréchette's (1989) analysis of the developmental sequence of offending was comprehensive, it lacked statistical sophistication, while the retrospective nature of the data in each of its three waves set limits on the validity of the findings. Segments of the observed developmental sequence, however, have been replicated by Loeber (1988a) in his reanalysis of Belson's (1975) data. The offender classification based on the self-reported delinquency in the National

---

[11] These analyses do not refer to the variance of each stage; this implies that some offenders begin their delinquent careers earlier and progress at a higher velocity than others during the age range indicated here.

Youth Survey (Dunford, Elliott, and Huizinga 1983) is also relevant. These longitudinal findings may be interpreted as a six-step sequence of patterned offending (status offenses, minor thefts, vandalism, aggression, selling and use of drugs, major thefts). More recent analyses of this longitudinal data set confirmed a developmental sequence from minor delinquency to Index offenses (Elliott, Huizinga, and Menard 1989).

In addition, Le Blanc, Côté, and Loeber (1988) systematically examined sequences in offending through self-reported delinquency in a representative sample of adolescents, who were studied over an interval of two years. Eleven one-step sequences from less serious to more serious offense types were uncovered. Since several one-step sequences had several elements in common, Le Blanc, Côté, and Loeber (1988) hypothesized several multiple-step sequences: minor thefts to aggression to major thefts, minor thefts to vandalism to major thefts, status offenses to minor thefts to major thefts, and status offenses to vandalism to major thefts. Last, one four-step sequence was hypothesized: status offenses to minor thefts to aggression to major thefts.

Moreover, the findings indicated four one-step de-escalation sequences: minor or major thefts to status offenses, vandalism to minor thefts, and aggression to vandalism. Le Blanc, Côté, and Loeber (1988), based on different one-step sequences with common elements, hypothesized one four-step de-escalation sequence from aggression to vandalism to minor thefts to status offenses.

The last sequence was the reverse of one of the escalation sequences. The results can be summarized as follows: major thefts and aggression were outcomes or end states in that they did not cluster with any other types of offenses; adolescents were either escalating to these types of offenses or de-escalating from them. As to theft, two sequences introduced the adolescents to drug use and were supported by a movement back and forth between status offenses and minor thefts; eight sequences led directly or indirectly to major thefts, and one sequence was a withdrawal from this more serious type of offense.

Le Blanc, Côté, and Loeber (1988) concluded that the pattern of offending in the delinquent sample could be characterized in the following ways: it was primarily stable and versatile, in that it was a combination of the most serious types of offenses. The escalation sequences were toward three most serious types of offenses, the selling and use of drugs, major thefts, and aggression, as compared with major thefts and aggression only in the adolescent sample. Using the same sample, but taking into account offending from onset to the end of the twenties and the five developmental stages described earlier, Le Blanc and Fréchette (1989) showed that the most frequently occurring sequences were exploration to explosion, and exploration to explosion and conflagration.

Finally, studies of patterns of official offenses have also supported the conclusion of a progression from less to more serious offenses (Smith, Smith, and Noma 1984; Snyder 1988; Le Blanc and Fréchette 1989). For example, Smith, Smith, and Noma (1984) relied on the official careers of incarcerated juveniles aged thirteen to eighteen and uncovered three sequences: from status offenses to auto theft, from burglary to serious crimes against persons, and from any type of crime to drug offenses. Most of these results and the aforementioned sequences fit the various trajectories proposed by Loeber (1988a) and are discussed below in some detail.

In summary, a number of studies document developmental sequences in offending. Some studies have revealed developmental sequences from one specific type of offense to another, while other studies have shown developmental sequences between different stages of offending in which each stage may consist of different offense categories. One criterion for establishing a stage model is that transitions *between* stages follow a relatively orderly sequence, but transitions *within* a stage can occur less systematically. The results give us reason to think that it is more likely that a developmental rather than a random model of offending will eventually prevail. The evidence, however, is far from complete and requires replication.

5. *Trajectories.*   There is a need to integrate the findings concerning conduct problems, substance use, and offending and to show how developmental sequences in each are part of an overarching developmental sequence in antisocial behavior. Trajectories are defined as developmental sequences—of activation, aggravation, and desistance—that span more than one developmental period of individuals' lives, such as childhood, adolescence, and adulthood. Trajectories, for that reason, incorporate information from more than one realm of deviance, combining the temporal ordering, for example, of conduct problems with delinquency and conduct problems with substance use. Trajectories may also include developmental sequences of age-normative behaviors (such as sexual acts), health-threatening behaviors (such as suicide), and other forms of maladjustment (such as depression).

Normative trajectories have been demonstrated for the life cycle of men. Hogan (1978) established an ordering of social life events from completing schooling to obtaining a full-time job and forming a family. He discussed cohort effects concerning the disruptive effects of military service and higher education for cohorts born after 1937 in the United States. The ability of men to order their life course events in a normative fashion fosters a successful reaching of adulthood according to Hogan. Such trajectories are also well known in psychology, for example, the stages of intellectual and moral development of Piaget (1932) and the stages of personal development of Erickson (1959).

One of the advantages of the formulation of developmental trajectories is the reintroduction of individual differences into the developmental perspective. A number of researchers have maintained that, although individuals may progress in antisocial and delinquent behavior in many different ways, their diverse behavior patterns reflect a single underlying antisocial tendency (Robins 1966; Jessor and Jessor 1977; Snyder, Dishion, and Patterson 1986; Hirschi and Gottfredson 1987; Osgood et al. 1988). Another view, however, would maintain that, because antisocial outcomes in adulthood are not uniform (e.g., chronic delinquents display undifferentiated delinquency; white-collar criminals are more specialized; others are noncriminal substance abusers), the outcomes reflect different underlying antisocial tendencies expressed in distinctly different developmental trajectories (Loeber 1985a, 1988a).

In 1985, Loeber proposed a dual-track theory of antisocial behaviors based on a review of the literature; he recently extended the tracks to three developmental trajectories (Loeber 1985a, 1988a), an *aggressive/versatile trajectory*, a *nonaggressive trajectory*, and an *exclusive substance use* trajectory. The aggressive/versatile trajectory includes individuals whose early aggressive behaviors are complemented by nonaggressive antisocial behaviors during childhood and by violent, property, and drug offenses later in adolescence. The nonaggressive trajectory includes individuals who display primarily concealing, nonaggressive acts, usually without aggression; development over time is expressed through increased seriousness and frequency of nonaggressive antisocial behaviors. Finally, the exclusive substance use trajectory includes individuals who show neither appreciable antisocial behaviors during childhood nor serious offenses during adolescence; they are characterized by a developmental sequence in substance use from adolescence. Empirical evidence for these trajectories remains sketchy since they have been inferred from findings of longitudinal and cross-sectional studies (Loeber 1988a).

6. *Summary.* We have argued the need for making a clear distinction between a developmental sequence of offenses and individuals' developmental changes in offending; demonstration of the existence of the former is a necessary condition for the study of the latter. Little is known about developmental changes in individual offending over more than two moments in time, and very little about the existence of a developmental sequence of offenses. A developmental sequence for substance use has been well replicated. A developmental sequence remains a good hypothesis in the domain of conduct problems. Existing data on substance use and on offending support the hypothesis that developmental changes occur in a hierarchic rather than embryonic sequence. Most offenders start at the same level, but not every offender progresses through all the levels of the developmental sequence in offending. Moreover, all observed sequences have in common that trivial antisocial behaviors precede more serious behaviors. Finally, there are probably a number of developmental trajectories that overarch several domains. For example, Elliott, Huizinga, and Menard (1989) found, throughout adolescence and youth, a developmental progression from delinquency to polydrug use to mental health problems, with many individuals stopping permanently at each of these stages. As we show in Section VI, developmental sequences in conduct problems, substance use, and offending partly co-occur with developments in other domains of functioning, such as physical maturation and the formation of personality.

C. Desistance from Offending

The last and least-studied process, desistance, is a subject whose importance is recognized by some criminologists (Cormier et al. 1959; Cusson and Pinsonneault 1986; Farrington, Ohlin, and Wilson 1986; Mulvey and LaRosa 1986). "Desistance" refers to the processes that lead to the cessation of crime, either entirely or in part. Contrary to activation and aggravation, which concern the building up of offending, the process of desistance concerns its decline.

Recent reviews have concluded that relatively little is known about desistance (Blumstein et al. 1986). In the Le Blanc and Fréchette (1989) study, which included a follow-up to age twenty-five, the median age of last official crime was virtually identical for the representative sample

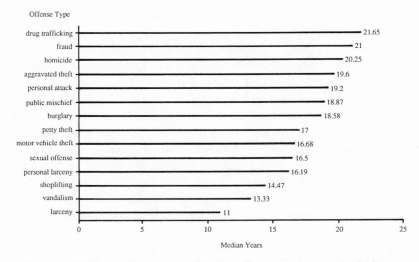

FIG. 2.—Median age of termination of various offense types in a sample of delinquent boys. Source.—Le Blanc and Fréchette (1989).

of adolescents and for the sample of delinquents (19.8 and 19.9 years old, respectively); it is not surprising, however, that the standard deviation was larger among the latter group. Figure 2 shows the median ages of termination for different self-reported offenses in their delinquent sample. Four periods of desistance can be identified. First, larceny, vandalism, and shoplifting are often desisted from by age thirteen. Second, another group of delinquent acts are often desisted from around age sixteen, including personal larceny, sex offenses, motor vehicle theft, and petty theft. Third, another period of desistance occurs around age eighteen to nineteen, when burglary, public mischief, personal attack, and aggravated theft are terminated. Last, the most serious offenses are terminated in the period from age twenty on: homicide, fraud, and drug trafficking. This examination of the median age at desistance shows that offense types with an early onset were desisted from earlier on, while those with a later onset were terminated later. The most serious offenses ceased at the most advanced age, while the least serious delinquent acts were desisted from at an earlier age. This shift in the crime mix over time, however, produced a forward thrust in more serious forms of crime.

The findings on the ages at termination in this study inevitably are a product of a cut-off at age twenty-five and may very well be different in samples with a longer follow-up. Hare, McPherson, and Forth (1988), for example, in their comparison of psychopaths and nonpsychopaths, showed that the former group continued to be arrested at a high rate well into their forties. Likewise, Blumstein, Cohen, and Hsieh (1982) documented from official records that between ages twenty and thirty desistance rates are rather high, fairly low between ages thirty and forty-two, and from forty-two to sixty are high again. In addition, it should be noted here that desistance is particularly high in adolescence for those whose first arrest was later rather than early (Barnett and Lofaso 1985). Elliott, Huizinga, and Menard (1989), in their representative sample of the U.S. adolescent population, showed that desistance rates (called by them "net suspension rates") were higher than initiation rates for self-reported delinquency.

Since high frequency of offending is highly correlated with the variety of offending (Le Blanc and Fréchette 1989; Loeber 1988a), one would expect that full desistance from delinquency or sociopathy is least likely to occur for those individuals who earlier in life had a high variety of conduct problems (Robins 1966; Dunford, Elliott, and Huizinga 1983). Thus, it may be concluded that desistance is inversely related to progression (Loeber 1988a).

Le Blanc and Fréchette (1989) proposed that the process of desistance is composed of four subprocesses: *deceleration*, which refers to a reduction in frequency prior to terminating offending; *de-escalation*, the return to a less serious form of delinquency; *reaching a ceiling*, which refers to a delinquent remaining at or below a particular level of seriousness in offending without further escalating to more serious acts, and *specialization*, which refers to desistance from a versatile pattern of criminal activity to a more homogeneous pattern. It seems clear that study of the mechanism of desistance must focus exclusively on persons whose delinquency has been recurrent; one cannot speak of desistance for the occasional delinquent. Moreover, true desistance has occurred only if there is continued cessation of delinquency, rather than temporary pauses in offending. We now briefly discuss each of the four subprocesses of desistance.

1. *Deceleration.* Deceleration, a reduction in frequency prior to termination of offending, may occur in three ways: the aging out of the criminal career in midlife, early desistance from offending in adolescence, and desistance from specific offense types in the middle of a delinquent career.

First, the rate of offending tends to decrease with age and signals the end of the criminal career by a general slowing down of delinquent activity; for many active offenders, this takes place in their thirties, but for others, in their forties or fifties (Blumstein et al. 1986). This slowing down in frequency usually is accompanied by a reduction in the diversification of crime and the reaching of a ceiling in the seriousness of offenses. Little is known about the actual decline in frequency other than from official arrest records; self-reports of the decline of offending are very scarce.

The second mode of deceleration concerns a decline in the frequency of offending observed when adolescents cease certain types of delinquent activities. Le Blanc and Fréchette (1989) have shown that when this decline occurs in hidden delinquency generally it is on the order of two to one, while it is less in official delinquency.

The third mode of deceleration concerns desistance from particular types of offenses simultaneously with a diversification into other offense types (see figs. 1 and 2). We have already mentioned Le Blanc and Fréchette's (1989) findings that, when individuals progressed to more serious crime, they dropped minor infractions such as petty larceny and shoplifting. It is not clear whether this form of desistance is the result of a progression toward increased value of theft, as observed by Langan and Farrington (1983), when the yield of shoplifting is too small to satisfy the offender's needs. Some research indicates that the financial needs of offenders increased from the juvenile years to adulthood (Petersilia, Greenwood, and Lavin 1978).

2. *De-escalation.*   De-escalation, a decrease in the level of seriousness over time, has been studied much less than escalation, either when occurring naturally or occurring as a result of an intervention program. Le Blanc, Côté, and Loeber (1988) found several one-step de-escalation sequences in adolescence, such as from minor or major thefts to status offenses, from vandalism to minor thefts, and from aggression to vandalism. In addition, the authors hypothesized one longer sequence from aggression to vandalism to minor thefts to status offenses. Along that line, partial desistance usually took place by shedding the behavior that was only one step removed from another, earlier behavior, but preserving the latter.

Two studies have addressed de-escalation in offending during adulthood. Robins (1966) recomputed the desistance in the Glueck and Glueck (1943) study and found that 45 percent of the cases fitted a "pattern of diminishing from major to minor crimes, with only . . . (16%) going on to reform completely" (p. 112). In her own study of individuals formerly seen in a child guidance clinic, Robins (1966) observed that 50 percent of the offenders in middle adulthood had decreased in the seriousness of their offenses, with the sociopaths being the most intractable. In all, however, the preceding studies have revealed very little about the process of de-escalation, particularly the sequence by which offense seriousness decreases over time.

3. *Ceiling Effects.* Another form of desistance concerns the phenomenon in which offenders may reach a plateau or ceiling in offense seriousness. Although not directly observable, for some offenders a ceiling may extend to petty theft, but individuals may never proceed to more serious forms of theft. Desistance that occurs through ceiling effects, then, involves the absence of further escalation, although escalation is still theoretically possible and opportunities for escalation are available. In some extreme cases of ceiling effects, the most serious forms of delinquency may have emerged over time, thus exhausting virtually all possible forms of crime typical for a particular culture. Le Blanc and Fréchette (1989) showed that 61 percent of the subjects of their delinquent sample reached their maximum level of seriousness in offending during adolescence even if they continued offending after age eighteen. Culmination was also associated with a large decrease in frequency even if offending was ongoing.

4. *Specialization.* Specialization has often been inferred from cross-sectional studies; however, such studies can merely show the degree of variety of crimes committed by offenders, with some engaging in a cafeteria style of offending (sampling many types of crime) and others displaying one or only a few categories of offenses (Klein 1984). Blumstein et al. (1986, p. 81) defined specialization as "the tendency to repeat the same offense type on successive arrests." In this case, specialization refers to a narrowing down of the crime mix over time, which we consider to be the essential component of a dynamic definition of specialization.

Taking into consideration the orthogenetic principle of behavior development, that behaviors tend to become more and more organized and interdependent over time, we expect that an individual's initial diffuse offending will become more patterned over time, with the shedding of certain types of crime in favor of those categories of crime that have the highest payoff and, perhaps, the lowest degree of apprehension by the police. Along the same line, we would expect a gradual narrowing of the repertoire of offense types, particularly in offenders who persist over time. This is in contrast with the early part of delinquent careers, where diversification of offending is much more typical.

We expect that the specialization process is more common from middle to late adolescence into adulthood.

It is important to note that the dynamic of specialization cannot be inferred from group data on offenders but from within-individual changes in offending over time. Data on these within-individual changes may be garnered from autobiographical and biographical accounts of offenders' lives and also from empirical analyses of offense careers from young adulthood onward (e.g., Cormier et al. 1959). Blumstein et al. (1986) documented specialization from official delinquency records in adulthood; similarly, Farrington, Snyder, and Finnegan (1988) documented changes in specialization over the delinquent career and produced an algorithm to express the degree of specialization on the specialization-generalization dimension.

Wikström (1987) approached the question of specialization in a new way. He calculated the proportion of crimes belonging to a particular category of crime; if two-thirds were of a specific type, then the criminal activity of an offender was considered specialized. Also, in order to exclude occasional delinquents who are necessarily specialized, he calculated the degree of specialization only for subjects who had committed three or more crimes. According to his data on arrests of offenders born in Stockholm in 1953, 27 percent of the delinquents who had committed at least three infractions before their midtwenties were specialists, particularly in theft. Likewise, Le Blanc and Fréchette's (1989) sample of adolescents in Montreal showed that 38 percent were specialists. The difference between the two studies probably occurs because the infractions in Stockholm were those known to the police, whereas in Montreal the infractions had led to convictions. In comparison, only 14 percent of the wards of the courts in Montreal had specialized.

5. *Summary*. The dearth of studies on deceleration, de-escalation, reaching a ceiling, and specialization contributes to speculation about their nature. One such speculation is that the subprocesses probably co-occur and are intertwined in some manner. Second, each process may have distinct characteristics depending on the degree of initial aggravation in offending. For instance, it seems plausible that sequences in desistance from low-level offending are quantitatively and qualitatively different from those following high-level offending. Third, sequences in desistance may differ depending on whether they take place during adolescence or adulthood.

The search for such differences, however, should not deny the possibility that certain general principles apply to all desistance at whatever points in the delinquent career. For example, desistance appears inversely related to progression in offending, while sequences in desistance may mirror sequences in progression. Moreover, the orthogenetic principle implies that behaviors may therefore decrease in their likelihood for desistance. In other words, we see a direct relation between the sequence of different acts that are involved in the commission of crime, progressions in their development, and their likelihood for desistance. Finally, desistance is embedded in other developmental contexts, such as a decrease in physical strength and fitness with age.

IV. The Course of Offending

If the hypothesis of an invariant sequence in offending is accepted, the second question can be addressed: how can the individual's changes in offending in the form of activation, aggravation, and desistance best be expressed and understood? To answer that question, we distinguish between *quantitative* and *qualitative* changes (Lerner 1986) and adapt some propositions from Wohlwill (1973).

A. Quantitative Changes

Even though criminology has not rigorously explored the identification of a developmental sequence of offenses, many studies show quantitative changes in the course of offending (see reviews by Cohen [1986] and Loeber [1988a]). The changes can be assessed in at least three ways. First, the proportion of individuals who move from one stage to another on a developmental sequence of offenses can be measured. Second, the quantitative changes can be evaluated in terms of their direction—the proportion of individuals' progress or regress. And, finally, individuals' rate of change, or their velocity, can be measured, including the speed of their behavior change, the time interval between their occupying successive stages of offending, and the timing of the changes. Table 5 presents a summary of operationalizations for quantifying individuals' quantitative (and qualitative) changes in offending.

1. *The degree of change.*   The simplest measure of degree of change is to contrast the proportion of subjects who changed their offense mix with those who did not change. Studies on crime switching in delinquent samples, using transition matrices to analyze official records, indicate that more subjects changed offense patterns than remained stable (see Cohen 1986; Le Blanc and Fréchette 1989). This has been confirmed in recent studies (Kempf 1987; Farrington et al. 1988).

TABLE 5

Summary of Operationalizations to Measure Individuals' Changes in Offending

A. Quantitative Changes		
Degree	Direction	Velocity
Percent of subjects who are stable or change	Percent of subjects who progress or regress	Changes in subjects' lambda

B. Qualitative Changes		
Conservation	Synchrony	Paths
Innovation rate Retention rate	Probability (behavior *b* given behavior *a*)	Percent of subjects who follow developmental sequence

For substance use, Kandel and Faust (1975) reported that 36 percent of their sample of high schoolers changed their pattern of use within half a year, as compared with 40 percent of their sample of graduate seniors. The authors concluded that continuity rather than change was the modal behavior. They also showed that the level of change varied with the level of initial use (frequency), the recency of use (over the last thirty days), and the nature of the initial drug use. Frequent and recent users tended not to maintain their pattern of use; this was especially true if their initial drug use was illicit.

Concerning the degree of developmental change in self-reported offending, all studies agree that there is more change than stability (Farrington 1973; Chaiken and Chaiken 1982; Dunford, Elliott, and Huizinga 1983; Le Blanc, Côté, and Loeber 1988; Le Blanc and Fréchette 1989). Researchers arrived at this conclusion whether they were studying a representative sample of the general population, a population of lower-class children, or samples of convicted or incarcerated delinquents. From the Farrington data (1973), it can be calculated that 63 percent of his London subjects changed over a two-year period. Le Blanc, Côté, and Loeber (1988) demonstrated that 68 percent of their sample of Montreal adolescents changed their level of delinquency, progressing to a more serious category of crime over a two-year period or regressing to a less serious level of delinquency. Dunford, Elliott, and Huizinga (1983) showed, with the five waves of the National Youth Survey, that the probability of moving to another delinquency status (there were four categories of offending, based on frequency and seriousness) was higher than the probability of staying in the same category of offending (an average probability of .66 for mobility vs. .33 for stability). This was evident for three of their four classes of offending but did not apply to their least serious category of nondelinquency, which included abstinents and occasional delinquents (less than three nonserious offenses). For this category, the probability was higher for stability than for mobility. Without knowing the exact overall probability of mobility, as compared to stability in this study, it is difficult to draw conclusions confidently. Interestingly, the probability of mobility decreased with the variety of offending. This observation was true in the Farrington study (1973), where he distinguished four frequency levels of self-reported delinquency. The probability of mobility tended to decrease with the level of variety, going from .76 to .86, to .60, to .29. If seriousness is included in the measure of delinquency, as in the Dunford, Elliott, and Huizinga (1983) study, the same tendency is observed (.69 for exploratory delinquency, .66 for patterned nonserious delinquency, and .56 for patterned serious delinquency). In the Le Blanc, Côté, and Loeber (1988) study of a representative sample, 68 percent of cases were mobile compared with only 48 percent in their sample of convicted delinquents. The figures from the Chaiken and Chaiken (1982) study on incarcerated offenders, as calculated by Loeber (1988a), were even lower.

2. *The direction of change.*   The degree of developmental change in offending is important, but what about its direction? In criminology, researchers have focused more on individuals' progressing and have neglected the opposite, individuals' regressing in offending (the Blumstein et al. [1986] review is illustrative of this tendency).

Findings from studies using transition matrices between types of official categories of delinquency, arranged in an increasing order of seriousness, indicate that more individuals regress than progress (see the review by Cohen [1986]). Three self-reported studies on representative samples, however, have looked at the direction of the changes in offending, but they produced divergent results (Farrington 1973; Dunford, Elliott, and Huizinga 1983; Le Blanc, Côté, and Loeber 1988).

Dunford, Elliott, and Huizinga (1983) reported that the probabilities of desisting from one of the delinquency statuses were higher than the probabilities of progressing to these same statuses, that is, from exploratory delinquency to nondelinquency (.47 compared to .10), from patterned nonserious delinquency to exploratory delinquency (.26 compared to .17), and from patterned serious delinquency to patterned nonserious delinquency (.26 compared to .10). Individuals' regression would then be more common than individuals' progression.[12] In the Le Blanc, Côté, and Loeber (1988) study, the proportion of individuals regressing and progressing was about the same, with 31 percent of the subjects de-escalating and 32 percent escalating. In the Farrington (1973) study, the percentage of individuals' regressing was one-fourth the percentage of those progressing (12 percent vs. 51 percent). The surprisingly high levels of regression in the first two studies can probably be explained by the representative nature of the samples with a large proportion of occasional or situational offenders. In contrast, the Farrington (1973) sample was drawn from a low-income area which is known to produce a higher rate of chronic offenders.

We conceptualize the course of chronic offending as an inverted U-shaped curve, with offending progressing in seriousness, reaching a ceiling, and then regressing. Analysis of self-reported delinquency on a sample of known delinquents over the period from onset to the third decade of life supports that view (Le Blanc and Fréchette 1989). Smith, Smith, and Noma (1984) looked at the official career lines of chronic offenders and found that a high proportion of them *failed* in one of their three forms of progressive careers. Notwithstanding these studies, research findings on the direction of change in offending are inconclusive because studies focused more on individuals' progression than regression.

For drug use, the results of the Kandel and Faust (1975) study were different from the above studies. Overall, with one exception, more individuals progressed than regressed. Only in the case of the "other drug" category (cocaine, heroin, and so on) did more individuals regress than progress. These results can be explained by three factors: the time interval between waves was six months rather than two years, as in most of the above studies, while the age distribution of the sample was older. Also, it should be noted that school dropouts were not systematically included in this study, which took place in 1971 when drug use was on the increase.

3. *The Velocity of Changes.* Velocity refers to the growth rate of offending, particularly changes in the rate of offending per unit of time,

---

[12] This result may explain why the studies on crime switching are so inconclusive; see Cohen (1986), which focused almost exclusively on escalation in changes from one crime type to the next, instead of considering the whole criminal career.

as expressed by changes in *lambda*. Changes in the rate of offending were first addressed by Wolfgang, Figlio, and Sellin (1972) in terms of the length of the time interval between offenses, from the first to the second, from the second to the third, and so on. They concluded that as the number of offenses increases, the time interval tends to decrease (later confirmed by Wolfgang, Thornberry, and Figlio 1987). Results from the Dangerous Offender Project showed also that a high velocity of offending was indicative of increased seriousness of delinquency over time (Hamparian et al. 1978) and that the velocity of early arrests was relatively slow but sped up rapidly during the first phase of the delinquent career (Miller, Dinitz, and Conrad 1982). The latter results have been replicated by Loeber and Snyder (1988) in a more general delinquent sample, where the rate of official offending accelerated especially in late childhood and early adolescence. Le Blanc and Fréchette (1989) reported similar findings by using self-reported delinquency.

Relatively little is known about changes in the rate of offending in later periods. Some evidence suggests that lambda is relatively stable over time (Gottfredson and Hirschi 1986; Blumstein, Cohen, and Farrington 1988). However, these average figures could very well conceal different trends for different categories of offenders. For example, Hare and Jutai (1983) showed that the rate of criminal charges for male psychopaths was still *increasing* by age thirty-six, while those for non-psychopaths began to *decline*.

If we take as a focal point a developmental sequence in offending, the criminological literature is not informative about the different rhythms of individuals' moving from one stage to another. Along with the expected differential velocities, we may also find many different kinds of rhythms: a slow start followed by an acceleration; a fast start followed by a slow down; and many other possibilities. Another important factor to consider is the length of the time during which an individual's offending remains stable within a particular stage.

B. *Qualitative Changes*

Qualitative changes in individuals' offending refer to changes in the crime mix, relations between offenses, and paths through segments of developmental sequences. In reference to the content of behaviors, Wohlwill (1973) called for an analysis of *conservation* and *synchrony*, while Loeber (1988a) referred to *innovation* and *retention*. The conservation concept assesses individuals' retention of certain offense types while moving to a new stage in offending (retention) or the addition of new types of offenses to the existing crime mix (innovation). The concept of synchrony examines the probability that individuals will make the transition on a developmental sequence from one stage to an adjacent stage within a given time period. Finally, paths are defined as segments of a developmental sequence that individuals have followed over a period of time. The operationalizations for the qualitative aspects of offending have been summarized in table 5.

Several studies (reviewed by Cohen [1986]) indicated that the crime mix changes over time and that certain categories of crime are discarded by offenders, while other crimes are introduced and added to the existing crime mix. Cohen's (1986) review of official delinquency indicates that the adolescent crime mix typically is different from the adult crime mix, with violent acts being less prominent. Longitudinal self-report studies, such as Le Blanc and Fréchette (1989), show that the crime mix is very different in the first part of adolescence than in the second half or in adulthood and that certain types of offenses are discarded or introduced with age. The literature on onset and termination supported the possibility that qualitative developmental changes occur within the delinquent career.

1. *Conservation.*   This term refers to retention and innovation, each of which conserves offending. Retention occurs when offenders persist in the commission of offenses of a lower stage in seriousness, while moving to a higher stage in seriousness. In contrast, innovation has been defined as the progression to a higher stage of offending without retaining offenses that were characteristic of the earlier stage.

Robins (1980) was the first to address the question of conservation in the development of antisocial behavior; she concluded that accretion of different antisocial behaviors is more common than the succession of one antisocial behavior by another. Typically, progression to more advanced or serious antisocial behaviors does not lead to the replacement of previous problem behaviors but, rather, builds on them. Retention dominates individuals' progression in offending. The area of substance use is an example, where individuals who have progressed to drinking hard liquor do not necessarily stop drinking beer and wine (Kandel and Faust 1975); likewise, those who have progressed to cocaine use have been shown to continue marijuana and legal substance use (White 1988). This phenomenon is also typical of individuals' progression in conduct problems and delinquency. Individuals who manifest serious antisocial acts (stealing, vandalism, or fire setting) usually also manifest less serious conduct problems also (arguing, swearing, and lying) (Cernkovich, Giordano, and Pugh 1985; Loeber 1985a). Figure 1 on the developmental sequence of offenses, presented earlier, clearly illustrates how the phenomenon of retention operates. For example, when juveniles begin to burglarize, they continue to commit petty theft. Retention seems to integrate the immediately preceding stage of behavior with the next stage rather than to integrate stages that occurred earlier. Figure 1 shows that when juveniles progress to robbery or attacks on persons, they usually have ceased performing offenses such as shoplifting, which is characteristic of earlier stages.[13]

Le Blanc, Côté, and Loeber (1988), in the study of a representative sample mentioned earlier, showed that 49 percent of the juveniles displayed retention (21 percent in the direction of progression and 28 percent in the direction of regression), which was much higher than the 13 percent showing innovation (11 percent progression and 2 percent regression). In the delinquent sample, the proportion of innovation and retention were both 4 percent (3.7 percent progression and .3 percent regression).

Although the findings are sketchy, we expect that offense conservation more often consists of retention than of innovation. This is probably affected by the very low base rate of most serious offenses. In substance use, the same situation should occur if hard drugs are considered; we know that the probability of individuals' progression to other illicit drugs from marijuana is much lower than the probability of their progression to marijuana from hard liquor (see Kandel 1980). Research must not only appreciate the relative weight of retention and innovation but should also consider the content of the crime mix in the process of conservation.

2. *Synchrony.* The term "synchrony" refers to the probability that individuals will make the transition on a developmental sequence from one stage or behavior to an adjacent stage or behavior. We propose that the transition probabilities are synchronous in that they are higher for the transition to an adjacent stage or behavior than to a nonadjacent stage or behavior. This has been confirmed for substance use. Kandel and Faust (1975) showed, for example, that the probability of moving from marijuana to other illicit drugs is higher than the probability of moving directly from hard liquor or cigarette use to other illicit drugs;

---

[13] See Robins and Wish (1977) for other evidence of selective desistance. Figure 2 in the present essay also illustrates that innovation can be of two kinds: the introduction of a new kind of offense within a stage; or movement to a higher stage of seriousness.

they even concluded that changes in each of the time intervals mostly involved only adjacent categories of substance use. Likewise, Brennan, Elliott, and Knowles (1981), using data from the National Youth Survey, confirmed that predictions over time are substantially higher for the transitions between adjacent steps in an offense sequence compared with nonadjacent steps. Le Blanc and Fréchette (1989) showed that only a small proportion of delinquent subjects (16 percent) deviated from the synchronous model by jumping over one or more stages or starting at a higher level and then de-escalating.

3. *Paths.* Individuals may progress or regress on developmental sequences, but they rarely move through an entire sequence or trajectory. In order to indicate this difference, we reserve the term *path* to describe segments that individuals travel along a developmental sequence or trajectory. Longitudinal data can show us which paths individuals travel over time or, rather, the measurement points they occupy along the path, to be more exact, and the extent to which the traveled paths correspond with the hypothesized developmental sequence or with a segment within the sequence. Paths can be quantified by the calculation of the percentage of individuals whose behavioral development fits the postulated sequence or trajectories.

Earlier in this essay, we presented the five-stage developmental sequence identified by Le Blanc and Fréchette (1989): emergence, exploration, explosion, conflagration, and outburst. They showed that, up to age twenty-five, 92 percent of their convicted delinquent sample moved through that developmental sequence: 31 percent covered one stage only (they went from a less serious to the next more serious level of offending), 43 percent covered two stages, 25 percent covered three stages, while 3 percent went through all five stages in offending.

4. *Summary.* The question of individuals' changes in offending becomes pertinent once a developmental sequence has been established. Quantitative changes may be assessed in terms of individuals' degree, direction, and velocity of change. We are suggesting that qualitative changes can be evaluated in terms of individuals' conservation, that is, retention and innovation of offenses, and paths they move along. We have pointed out two principles of developmental change in individual offending, that is, synchrony (changes on a developmental sequence are more likely to occur to adjacent rather than to nonadjacent stages) and hierarchy (the majority of individuals will start at the same level, but not all will go through every stage of a developmental sequence).

We have thus far highlighted only a limited number of representations of developmental change; there are several other methods for expressing quantitative and qualitative changes in behavior that occur in the course of development. For these, the reader is referred to other sources (Wohlwill 1973; Hinde and Bateson 1984; Magnusson 1988).

V. Correlates and Causes

A logical next step is to translate the developmental perspective into the theory domain and to incorporate it into empirical studies in order to distinguish better between correlates and causes of offending. In this section, we first evaluate the extent to which the developmental perspective has penetrated into criminological theories. Then we outline six ways to elucidate causal factors and review empirical results pertinent to that purpose. Finally, we discuss the importance of the duration and timing of causal factors.

A. Are There Developmental Theories in Criminology?

Most criminological theories are not developmental in nature, and, when they carry some developmental potential, they have not always been interpreted in that way. An exception is labeling theory, and particularly Lemert's (1951) theory of primary and secondary deviance. Briefly, Lemert's theory states that when an individual is labeled deviant because of some antisocial behavior, the label is a primary cause for other behaviors to emerge as part of a deviancy amplification process. Differential association theory (Sutherland and Cressey 1960) also can be interpreted in a developmental manner because its authors' central thesis is that criminal behavior is learned over time. Strain and cultural deviance theories have not been translated in a developmental way but imply some temporal aspects of offending. For example, Cohen's (1955) theory stated that the contrast between working-class socialization and middle-class values of success leads first to failure in school, then to low self-esteem, then to school dropout and association with delinquent peers, then to a reaction formation and, finally, to a delinquent status. Control theory, as formulated by Hirschi (1969), probably would not be interpreted in a developmental manner by its author, but attachment and commitment are clearly bonds that are formed progressively through interaction with others and society, rather than de novo psychosocial states. The developmental aspects of control theory have recently been captured in a social development model of offending and substance use (Catalano and Hawkins 1986; Hawkins et al. 1986). This model, which includes aspects of strain theory, social learning, and differential association, seeks to explain the origins of bonding through several social and opportunistic variables. It explicitly refers to distinct developmental phases in children's lives and aims at connecting certain influences and behaviors characteristic of one phase to those of another phase. In the same vein, Kaplan (1983) proposed a theory that integrates concepts from strain, differential association, labeling, and self-concept theories and proposed an integrative explanation of onset and continuation of delinquent behavior.

The time is ripe to further Hawkins et al.'s (1986) and Kaplan's (1983) efforts and to reinterpret basic criminological theories from a developmental perspective. Ferdinand (1987) proposed that cultural deviance theory should be tested with longitudinal data and that control theory should be verified with cross-sectional data because the first explains initiation into offending while the second explains its maintenance. Tests of models using these two categories of theories (Agnew 1985; Liska and Reed 1985) have demonstrated delayed effects and reciprocal or more proximal effects for cultural deviance variables. The recent fashion for integrative models (Elliott, Huizinga, and Ageton 1985) and theories (Albany Conference 1987) has done little to enhance our knowledge of the ordering of causal factors, aside from confirming that delinquency is the most powerful predictor of future delinquency. This integrative movement has not been developmental because these models and theories failed to emphasize processes over time or temporal ordering and changes in causal factors with age. Some new criminological models, however, are clearly developmental because they do propose a specific time ordering of causal factors (West 1982; Farrington 1986b; Hawkins et al. 1986; Fréchette and Le Blanc 1987; Le Blanc 1987; Thornberry 1987; Le Blanc, Ouimet, and Tremblay 1988). Still, the ordering of factors often merely refers to certain classes of factors as operating at specific age periods while other factors are active at other ages, rather than being based on distinct developmental processes. For example, Thornberry (1987) proposed an interactional theory that links dynamic concepts to the person's position in the social structure; he advocated that control, learning, and delinquency are reciprocally related over the person's life cycle and may be conceptualized developmentally with different variable contents and structures in various age periods and phases of life; for instance, commitment may be conceptualized as commitment to school during adolescence and commitment to work during young adulthood.

In our view, theorists in criminology generally have not explored all of the developmental implications or exploited all of the potential strengths of their theories. Only very recently have they initiated theories that include a more comprehensive developmental perspective. In the next section, we discuss the current empirical underpinnings of correlates and causes of offending that have resulted from this reorientation.

B. Correlates and Causes of Offending

In cross-sectional studies, it is impossible to disentangle correlations from causes because the variables are measured at the same time, and temporal priority cannot be established. In that sense, longitudinal studies have obvious advantages as argued by Farrington (1989c). Longitudinal data are required to establish causes because they are obtained through a quasi-experimental before-and-after design that offers the highest internal validity after the randomized experiment. It is the second-best way to control for extraneous influences as demonstrated by Cook and Campbell (1979). Farrington (1989c) stated, however, that it does not imply that longitudinal surveys are necessary because longitudinal data can be obtained retrospectively in cross-sectional surveys, but he also argued that because of the methodological difficulties associated with retrospective data, longitudinal surveys should be preferred.

Le Blanc (1989) argued, however, that empirical criminology has not advanced much by longitudinal studies because researchers did not make full use of the potentials of the longitudinal design. With a few exceptions, they often did not distinguish between correlates and causes or, at least, establish the temporal order of events. Labouvie (1986) evaluated in the same way the impact of longitudinal research in psychopathology.

A major argument in Gottfredson and Hirschi's (1987) critique of the need for longitudinal studies is that findings on correlates of crime, based on longitudinal surveys, merely confirm those from cross-sectional surveys, rather than shedding light on new correlates (Blumstein et al. 1986; Farrington et al. 1986). We find this argument impossible to refute: Farrington et al.'s (1986) and Blumstein et al.'s (1986) reviews of findings from longitudinal studies do not present any information on correlates that was not already known from concurrent studies.

What is necessary, however, is to distinguish better between those factors that are causal as well. For that reason, we review six analysis methods that resulted in insights about the correlates and causes of offending: (1) correlation, particularly the concomitant change approach and cross-lagged analysis; (2) prediction; (3) the analysis of life events; (4) the analysis of sequential covariation; (5) the stepping-stones approach; and (6) experimental manipulation.

1. *Correlation.* Some potential causal variables may occur in such close proximity to offending that, for all practical purposes, it is impossible to measure which comes first; moreover, they may have reciprocal influences on each other (Thornberry 1987). The analysis of *concomitant change* is aimed at addressing this situation and allows an examination of the parallel evolution of delinquency (or problem behaviors) and personal and social explanatory factors. Jessor and Jessor (1977) analyzed concomitant change in a descriptive manner, while Le Blanc et al. (1980) used a bivariate statistical approach. The Jessors, in their report on their four-wave panel study of high school and college youth, concluded that changes in the areas of personality, perceived context, and deviant behavior were consonant and that the magnitude of the changes appeared to be greater in the earlier part of adolescence than later. The evolution was as follows: in personality, there was a decline in value on achievement, an increase in intolerance for deviance and religiosity, and an increase in value on independence and social criticism; concerning the environment, there was a decline in parental control and an increase in friends' support and friends' approval for problem behavior; finally, in behavior, there was an increase in problem drinking, sexual experience, general deviance, and drug use and a decline in conventional behaviors, such as church attendance.

The Le Blanc et al. (1980) study used a different strategy of analysis on a representative sample of adolescents and a sample of convicted youth; each sample was studied over two waves. In an initial phase the researchers described the changes on behavioral, personality, bond, and constraint variables using Davis's (1963) measure of turnover (the proportion of individuals whose behavior between measurement waves can affect the distribution of the phenomenon over time). In a second phase, on each of these variables, they constructed four classes of changes: increase, decrease, stability at a low level, and stability at a high level. These change variables were cross-classified with the same measure of change in delinquency. The main conclusions from this study were similar for the adolescent and the delinquent samples and confirmed Jessor and Jessor's (1977) findings. Overall, Le Blanc et al. (1980) concluded that for conventional adolescents the following factors were associated with their low probability of offending: an improvement in the attachment to an intimate person, a firmer commitment to school, and a more realistic view of persons in positions of authority. Among the convicted youth, the regulatory effects seem to come more from outside than from the natural milieu; delinquency diminished under the influence of meaningful adults and with an involvement in work; these positive experiences were the main sources of a new psychological maturity.

The second correlational approach, *cross-lagged* analysis, refers to studies that use two waves of panel data in which the temporal ordering of variables is specified at two moments in time (Kaplan and Robbins 1983; Agnew 1984; Elliott, Huizinga, and Ageton 1985). When self-reported delinquency is introduced as the independent variable at time 1, it is very common that the most important predictor of later delinquency is prior delinquency. When it comes to the content of the causal variables, Agnew (1984) and Elliott, Huizinga, and Ageton (1985) agreed that social control variables were not very efficient in explaining subsequent self-reported delinquency. Elliott, Huizinga, and Ageton (1985) showed that bonding to delinquent friends was the most important factor as compared with conventional bonding, social disorganization, and strain variables. These results also applied to substance use. In tests of the model, both concurrent and prospective factors were included so that the causal status of delinquent friends remains to be elucidated (Loeber 1987*b*).

Two studies have made full use of the two waves by analyzing all of the independent and dependent variables in a cross-lagged model (Liska and Reed 1985; Le Blanc, Ouimet, and Tremblay 1988). The findings converged and demonstrated that the reciprocal effects at each time of measurement were stronger than the lag effects. Liska and Reed (1985) clearly showed that parental attachment affected delinquency, which in turn determined school attachment; this variable had a reciprocal effect on parental attachment. Concerning substance use, there are many longitudinal models with at least two data waves (e.g., Huba and Bentler 1982; Stein, Newcomb, and Bentler 1987), which are of interest to criminologists but are not reviewed here due to space limitations.

Both the concomitant change and the cross-lagged correlational studies have several disadvantages for causal analysis. The study of concomitant change may support the covariation between offending and its explanatory variables, but it usually fails to inform about the temporal order between the two variables. Studies using the cross-lagged approach have the advantage of informing us about the sequence of events. The cross-lagged studies, however, do not distinguish between behaviors that emerged from those that persisted over time and offer only a very limited time perspective on the causes of offending over two moments in time only (with an interval usually of one or two years) (Rogosa 1980).

2. *Prediction*.   Prediction, as an analysis strategy, often spans much longer intervals; contrary to the preceding approaches, prediction tables can tell us the proportion of individuals who changed position or remained stable over time.

Researchers using prediction data are interested in establishing that an independent variable precedes and predicts offending or a change in the level of offending. As mentioned in the introduction, an important commonly held assumption of earlier criminological investigations is that causes and correlates of offending are similar in different segments of the delinquency career. Therefore, researchers have rarely highlighted differential predictors of activation, aggravation, or desistance from offending. This is inconsistent with known shifts in social influences that youngsters experience in the first two decades of their lives, with, for example, parents initially being the prime socializing agents and peers often later becoming the predominant influence (LaGrange and White 1985; Farrington and Hawkins 1988).

a) Predictors of Activation.   Several studies have systematically distinguished predictors of early versus late onset of offending. For example, Kolvin et al. (1988) followed up a birth cohort of 847 boys and girls to age thirty-three. Data for the males showed that nearly a third (29.9 percent) of those who had been exposed to marital instability during the preschool years were first convicted before age fifteen, compared with 13.8 percent who were first convicted at age fifteen or older. Likewise, 28.4 percent of those boys who experienced parental illness during the preschool years were first convicted before age fifteen, compared with 6.9 percent who were first convicted at age fifteen or older.[14] Remarkably, another preschool study was able to predict to some degree later delinquency on the basis of data collected when youngsters were two years old (Werner and Smith 1977), even though data on the age at onset of offending were not reported.

A second set of longitudinal studies examined the effect of the clini-

[14] The following variables did not distinguish between early and late conviction but significantly distinguished between convicted and nonconvicted boys irrespective of age: poor physical or domestic care of children or home, social dependency, overcrowding, and poor mothering.

cal syndrome of attention deficit with hyperactivity and impulsivity (called "HIA" here) on the age at onset of offending. The impetus behind this research rested on a large number of studies with findings that HIA (or its components) is associated with an aggravation of conduct problems and later delinquency. For example, Offord et al. (1979) were among the first to draw attention to the fact that some delinquent juveniles scored higher on hyperactivity than others. They found that hyperactive delinquents were on the average 10.8 years old when the youngsters, according to their caretakers, first displayed four different antisocial symptoms. In comparison, the average age was 12.5 for nonhyperactive delinquents. Other research also confirms that hyperactives develop a larger number of behavioral problems and that these behaviors tend to be more serious (Minde et al. 1971; Weiss et al. 1971; McGee, Williams, and Silva 1984). Studies of youngsters who score high on aggression and hyperactivity early in life show that they are particularly vulnerable to delinquency (Loney, Kramer, and Milich 1982; Magnusson 1988; Loeber 1988b), compared with those who score high on hyperactivity only or on aggression only.

It would follow, since hyperactivity (and its associated features of impulsivity and attention problems) is linked with early onset of offending, that those with an onset of delinquency in adulthood would be much less likely to have been hyperactive as children. This was one of the questions addressed by Farrington, Loeber, and Van Kammen (1989) in a reanalysis of the data on the Cambridge Study in Delinquent Development. Inner-city boys from London were divided at ages eight to ten on the basis of the child's behavior and information from teachers, peers, and parents into four groups: those scoring high on HIA only, those scoring high on conduct problems (CP) only, those scoring high on CP and HIA, and those scoring high on neither. Using follow-up data to the age of twenty-five, the results showed that HIA predicted the number of convictions independently of CP and that the reverse was also true. Attention deficit with hyperactivity and impulsivity was a better predictor of early conviction (before the age of fourteen) than was CP. In addition, relatively few (8 percent) of the HIA-only subjects were first convicted in early adulthood, compared with 25 percent and 32 percent of those scoring high on CP, or on CP and HIA, respectively. These findings lend strong support to the notion that hyperactivity and its associated handicaps are particularly implicated in an early age at onset of crime and rarely so in a later age at onset, at least as measured through official records of conviction (see

Loeber, Brinthaupt, and Green 1989.[15] Because most of the above research on hyperactivity concerned boys, it remains to be seen whether the results also apply to girls.

Turning to drug use, Kandel, Kessler, and Margulies (1978) used multivariate techniques to show that parental influence best explained individuals' initiation into other illicit drugs (40 percent of the explained variance), followed by peer influence (33 percent), while for marijuana use peer influence dominated (48 percent), followed by beliefs and values (26 percent), and, finally, for the initiation of use of hard liquor, prior behaviors dominated (41 percent), followed by peer influence (34 percent) (see also Kandel and Andrews 1987). Robins and Przybeck (1985) examined predictors of the age at onset of drug use in three age periods. They found that school discipline problems, stealing, vandalism, and truancy much better predicted onset of drug use prior to age fifteen than afterward (ages eighteen to twenty-four). Likewise, Smith and Fogg (1978, 1979) showed that lack of obedience correlated more highly with early age at onset of drug use in males and females than with late age at onset of use.

Turning to social influences relevant for early onset, recent analyses of the Cambridge Study in Delinquent Development have demonstrated that in two-parent families, lack of involvement of the father with the boy in leisure activities was particularly associated with early conviction between ages ten and thirteen (Farrington and Hawkins 1988). Mannheim and Wilkins (1955), in their study of Borstal boys, found that broken homes were not associated with age at first recorded crime, but that delinquency in the parent was. The latter finding, however, was not replicated by Farrington and Hawkins (1988), who found that parental criminality was associated with late, rather than early, conviction of the child. Finally, Wikström (1987) reported on Project Metropolitan in Stockholm and found that the age at onset of offending varied with parents' social class: the median age for youngsters with lower-class parents was sixteen, compared with seventeen for

[15] Although hyperactivity, impulsivity, and attention problems are associated with early onset of delinquent acts, it should be stressed that a proportion of high HIA youngsters *without* appreciable conduct problems later became delinquent also (Loeber and Baicker-McKee 1989). Although little is known about the developmental course of delinquent acts for this group, we assume that these youngsters adopted delinquent ways of life in adolescence or, perhaps, eluded detection by the police. Similarly, Maughan, Gray, and Rutter (1985) found that nonconduct problem youngsters with reading problems at age ten, often associated with HIA, still were at risk to be arrested by age nineteen.

those with working-class or lower-middle-class parents and eighteen for upper-middle-class parents.

Few studies have systematically explored predictors of antisocial behavior in late adolescence, which itself is associated with delinquency. An exception is, again, the Cambridge Study, which showed that antisocial tendency at age eighteen (mostly covert delinquent and rule-breaking acts, but without prior convictions) was best predicted by teacher rating of aggression at ages twelve to thirteen and high self-reported delinquency and aggression at ages fourteen and sixteen, but it was *not* predicted by conduct problems at age eight to nine or troublesomeness at school at ages eight to eleven (West and Farrington 1977, p. 150).

In summary, the available evidence indicates that a set of predictors applies to early compared with late onset of offending. Few studies, however, have examined systematically which factors uniquely predict activation and its subprocesses of acceleration, stabilization, and diversification.

b) Predictors of aggravation.   Loeber and Stouthamer-Loeber's (1987) review of prediction studies pointed out that many predictors of delinquency status (e.g., whether the individual has ever been arrested or convicted) also predict recidivism. Very few studies, however, have examined predictors of escalation in offending. An exception is Wadsworth (1979), who scaled juvenile delinquent acts according to the seriousness of offenses committed by members of a birth cohort who were studied until age twenty-one; for example, he found that boys' physical maturity at age fifteen was predictive of the seriousness of offending, but only in the case of boys from a low socioeconomic class, with those experiencing physical infantile, or early, puberty advancing to the most serious and violent level of offenses. More indirect evidence of predictors of aggravation can be found in Fréchette and Le Blanc's (1987) study showing that social factors better predicted occasional offending in a representative sample, while personality factors better predicted offending in a chronic delinquent sample. In the latter case, the variance explained by personality factors was 35 percent, while it was 7 percent in the former case.

Recent studies have looked at aggravation in terms of frequency and crime switching. Tontodonato (1988) and Tolan and Lorion (1988) concurred in showing that early onset was by far the best predictor of more frequent and serious delinquency. Tontodonato (1988) studied the rate changes in delinquent arrest transitions and concluded that race was relatively important in explaining the transitions among injury and theft arrests but that socioeconomic status and co-offending were rarely significant. Tolan and Lorion (1988), using a larger set of variables and self-reported delinquency, showed that, second only to age at onset of offending, family systemic/interactional characteristics were the most helpful for predicting subsequent frequency, while individual and school factors, family demographics, and social status had virtually no explanatory power on a subsequent high frequency of delinquency.

c) *Predictors of desistance.*   Most known predictors of desistance appear to be the reverse of risk factors predicting offending (Loeber and Stouthamer-Loeber 1987). Thus, since marital conflict is a strong predictor of offending, the lower the degree of marital conflict, the lower the likelihood of offending by offspring. Along that line, Farrington and Hawkins (1988) found that the father's participation in the boy's leisure activity at age eleven was associated with desistance from crime between ages twenty-one and thirty-two.

There is an obvious need to identify "unique" predictors of desistance, which are not simply the opposite of predictors of activation or aggravation. One possibly unique set of predictors has been identified so far: emotional problems, anxiety, or neurotic problems all predict the absence or reduced likelihood of later offending (see evidence summarized by Loeber and Stouthamer-Loeber [1987]).

In summary, whereas the prediction data have been more available for the prediction of the activation of offending than for its aggravation or desistance, the causal status of the risk factors still remains to be established. Rarely have prediction studies systematically controlled for third factors. Finally, although much emphasis has been placed on unique predictors for activation and aggravation, many predictors apply to both and may reflect long-acting, stable deviance causal factors. Probably another way to look at that question might be to study resilient individuals, as did Werner and Smith (1982), or subjects from vulnerable backgrounds, as did Farrington et al. (1989). Identification of the protective factors that may be operating could help to rule out some causal factors pertaining to activation, aggravation, or desistance.

3. *Analysis of Life Events.*   The life events approach is concerned with the impact of specific salient and discrete life events on subsequent offending: events such as leaving school, entering the labor force, going into the armed forces, and getting married have been considered. Over the last two decades, several longitudinal studies have addressed the influences of life events on within-individual changes in offending and

substance use. These studies must be distinguished from the studies that are correlational (correlating employment and crime, for example) or comparative (comparing the level of delinquency of married and nonmarried individuals).

The following propositions derive from these studies: (1) young men commit fewer criminal acts and become less deviant after marriage (West 1982; Rand 1987), especially if they marry someone who is not socially deviant (Bachman, O'Malley, and Johnston 1978; Newcomb and Bentler 1987), but they become more delinquent after cohabitation (Rand 1987); (2) parenthood has negligible impact on subsequent offending (Rand 1987); (3) young men who move out of the city are less criminal in their new environment (West 1982); (4) going into the armed forces has no impact on the offending of whites, but it decreases the subsequent criminal activity of nonwhites, especially if they receive job training in the armed forces (Rand 1987); going into the armed forces is followed by an increase in the use of tolerated substances and a decrease in restricted substances (Newcomb and Bentler 1987); (5) getting caught for the first time increases subsequent offending (Farrington 1977), but a reconviction does not have such an amplification effect (Farrington, Osborn, and West 1978); harsher penalties increase offending (Wolfgang, Figlio, and Sellin 1972) and the rate of violent crime (Miller, Dinitz, and Conrad 1982); novice, never arrested offenders are more likely to terminate their criminal careers while experienced offenders are more likely to reduce future rates of offending (Smith and Gartin 1989); (6) dropping out of school does not increase the level of delinquency, as determined by official records (Elliott 1966; Farrington et al. 1986; Rand 1987) or self-reported behaviors (Bachman, Green, and Wirtanen 1971; Pronovost and Le Blanc 1980); it leads to a decrease in offending if it is followed by an entry into the job market (Elliott and Voss 1974; Pronovost and Le Blanc 1980); Thornberry, Moore, and Christenson (1985), however, have shown that it increases the likelihood of criminality between the ages of twenty-one and twenty-four; (7) unemployment increases delinquency, especially if it happens in the second half of adolescence (Farrington et al. 1986); unemployment and crime are reciprocally related; unemployment has a direct effect on crime, while crime has a delayed effect on unemployment (Thornberry and Christenson 1984).

The results show that some life events may have important and influential effects on offending, not only in terms of presence or absence but also in their order (Hogan 1978). Nevertheless, there is a scarcity of replications with different subject populations, while the impact of third variables seldom has been controlled. The life-events analysis, however, constitutes an important approach to the study of the causes of offending because a change in the independent variable can be timed very precisely and its impact gauged from a comparison between prior and subsequent offending. This timing is more difficult with most psychosocial factors.

4. *Analysis of Sequential Covariation.* The analysis of sequential covariation differs from the previously discussed concomitant change and life-events analyses. In concomitant change analysis, covariation between the independent variable and the dependent variable may be observed, but the temporal relation may remain obscure. In the life-event analysis, an event may trigger a change in offending, but because the event is of a discrete nature, it is not possible for its duration or its offset to be directly linked to a change in offending. Making that linkage is the core feature of sequential covariation. We distinguish between two types of sequential covariation: the first is concerned with the *frequency* of the independent variable; the second is concerned with the *duration* of that variable.

As to frequency, we can speak of sequential covariation when increases *and* decreases in the frequency of an independent variable are associated with increases *and* decreases in offending, respectively. For example, if marital strife is related to juvenile delinquency, we may find that the onset of severe marital strife would precede juvenile offending; its increased frequency would be related to a higher frequency of offending; and the offset of marital strife would be followed by a decrease or cessation in offending. We have been unable to unearth studies in criminology documenting sequential covariation between independent and dependent variables. Loeber and Stouthamer-Loeber (1986) reviewed studies showing covariation between child-conduct problems and parent behaviors.

Duration is the central feature in the second type of sequential covariation. Some youngsters may be exposed to a short duration of the independent variable, and others to a longer duration. The basic idea, borrowed from epidemiology, is that the longer the exposure to a noxious influence, the more likely the offending. The increased likelihood may be shown by either the probability that offending will begin or the probability that individuals advance to more serious forms of delinquency the longer their exposure to the noxious stimulus or setting. In an important study by Cohen and Brook (1987), the authors followed up children over a period of eight years. They demonstrated that the duration of familial handicaps was associated with the later onset or aggravation of juvenile conduct problems. More particularly, worsening forms of child rearing were associated with increased prevalence of conduct disorder. These findings lend some support to the notion that extended rather than brief exposure to risk factors facilitates deviant child behavior and that examining the duration of exposure is one of the techniques that may help to distinguish between correlates and causes.

5. *The Stepping-Stone Approach.* All of the preceding modes of analysis have assumed a relatively straightforward relation between an independent and dependent variable. The developmental approach to criminology, however, assumes that there are a multitude of such one-to-one causal relations, that formerly dependent variables may become independent variables over time, that causality is best represented by a developmental network of causal factors or by a series of stepping stones representing the factors, and that such networks can extend over long time periods.

Given that the base rate of chronic offenders and substance abusers in representative populations is low, Robins, Davis, and Wish (1977) suggested that a way out of the dilemma of studying low base-rate events is to decompose these events into a series of stages or stepping stones and to calculate the transition rates from one stage to the other. These aspects are incorporated in the stepping-stone model, which allows the identification of factors that are uniquely associated with particular developmental processes of offending and allows specification of the sequence and duration of potential causal factors along the developmental time line.

In the stepping-stone approach, identification of the time ordering of factors is fundamental; factors from different age periods are used and their predictive ability on a distal outcome is assessed. When applying this technique in its simplest form, a number of risk factors are combined and their joint predictive efficiency is assessed in forecasting later delinquency. Kolvin and colleagues (1988), in the aforementioned study on a British birth cohort, included measurements of various forms of deprivation experienced by the children during their first five years of life: marital disruption, parental illness, poor physical or domestic care, social dependency, overcrowding, and poor quality mothering. Figure 3 shows the mean number of convictions for the multiply-deprived group (at least three deprivation factors), the de-

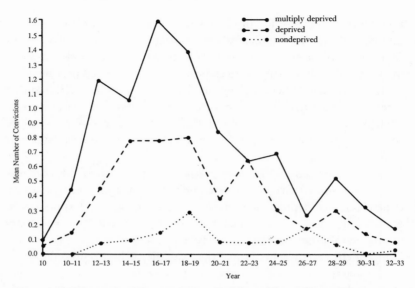

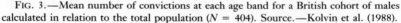

FIG. 3.—Mean number of convictions at each age band for a British cohort of males calculated in relation to the total population (N = 404). Source.—Kolvin et al. (1988).

prived group (at least one factor), and the nondeprived group. It reveals that, with one exception, boys in the multiply-deprived group received the highest number of convictions in each age period (except ages twenty-two and twenty-three and twenty-six to twenty-seven), the singly-deprived group had an intermediate level of convictions, and the nondeprived group the lowest level. The results illustrate three points. First, there appears to be a dose-response relation between the degree of deprivation and subsequent rates of offending. Second, the relation is not fleeting or restricted to the juvenile years but is maintained from age ten through thirty-three.[16] Third, although multiple-risk factors were incorporated in the calculation of deprivation levels, the study does not reveal the sequence of occurrence of the risk factors within the preschool period.

[16] The findings parallel those reported by Wadsworth (1979) and Werner and Smith (1977). Kolvin et al. (1988) also found that the average age at first court appearance for the multiply-deprived group was 16.7, compared with 18.2 for the deprived group and 19.4 for the nondeprived group. Thus, the multiply-deprived group was, on the average, brought to court more than two years younger than the nondeprived group. This implies that the multiply-deprived group was criminally active in the adolescent years, which are usually characterized by a high rate of offending compared with early adulthood. Not surprisingly, 24.5 percent of the multiply-deprived boys became chronic offenders (six or more convictions), compared with 14.6 percent of the deprived boys and 3.0 percent of the nondeprived boys.

A more sophisticated stepping-stone model was developed by Farrington (1986) (which we will consider at some length because he has developed the approach more fully than anyone else), using a range of factors measured during childhood, adolescence, and young adulthood to predict official criminality up to age twenty-four. The results, shown in figure 4, are twofold. First, he demonstrated a stepwise continuity in antisocial behavior: troublesomeness and daring behavior at ages eight to ten predicted convictions at ages ten to thirteen; the latter predicted convictions at ages fourteen to sixteen, which predicted convictions at ages seventeen to twenty, which, in turn, predicted convictions at twenty-one to twenty-four. Convictions at ages ten to thirteen also predicted self-reported delinquency at age fourteen; the latter, and convictions at ages fourteen to sixteen, predicted antisocial tendency at age eighteen. All these predictions held when a number of other factors were taken into account.

Second, Farrington (1986) identified four factors during late childhood (economic deprivation, family criminality, parental mishandling, and school failure) that were significantly associated with troublesome or daring behavior at age eight to ten. All of these factors independently predicted conviction in the juvenile years (until the seventeenth birthday). Turning to convictions in the young adult years (age eighteen to the twentieth birthday), these were best predicted by two former predictors, family criminality (measured at age ten) and economic deprivation (age fourteen), as well as two new predictors, truancy (age twelve to fourteen) and delinquent friends (age fourteen). Economic deprivation (age fourteen) continued to be a predictor of adult offending (age twenty to twenty-five), together with two new predictors, unstable job record (age eighteen) and antiestablishment attitude (age eighteen). Thus, some predictors exerted nearly constant influence on antisocial behavior throughout the age range under investigation (family criminality and economic deprivation), while some predictors were particularly relevant for the early part of the career (parental mishandling and school failure); other predictors were more important for offending in young adulthood (truancy, delinquent friends) or for offending in adulthood (unstable job record, antiestablishment attitude). What is more significant is that these predictors of delinquency and crime are also virtually the same for frequent offending (Farrington 1987), adolescent aggression, and adult violence (Farrington 1989b), suggesting that all these measures of delinquency are referring to a general antisocial tendency.

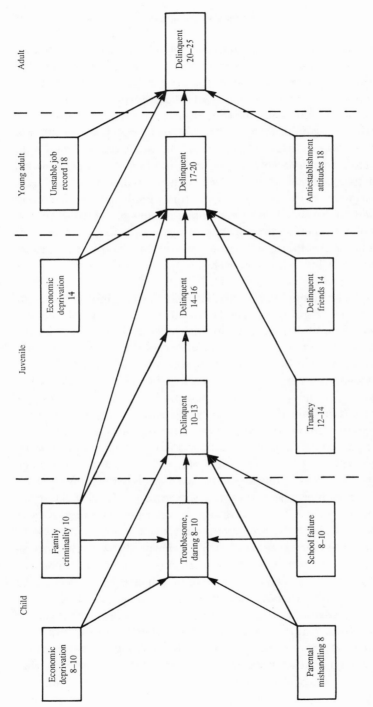

Fig. 4.—Stepping-stone model of the temporal sequence of causal influences on the course of conduct problems and delinquency in the Cambridge Study in Delinquent Development. Source.—Farrington (1986).

The stepping-stone approach to the study of causes of offending, as compared with the other techniques discussed, offers a wider perspective on the entire sequence of the causes of individual offending. Some limitations in the Farrington (1986) study are that the number and variety of variables used were rather small at each phase of life and that most of them were of a structural nature (economic deprivation, parental criminality, work record, etc.); in addition, psychosocial variables, which traditionally have been the basis for criminological theories, were relatively underrepresented in Farrington's (1986) model.

The effectiveness of the stepping-stone approach to causality can be increased by means of the following modifications. First, prediction of onset of offending is needed within a given period rather than lumping together in a given time period those whose delinquency is ongoing and those who started law breaking. Second, measurement of the cumulative impact of risk factors occurring in prior phases, either in terms of their frequency and number or in terms of individuals' length of exposure to them, is required; this would allow us to examine a possible dose-response relation between the risk factors and offending. Third, examination of sleeper effects is necessary (Kagan and Moss 1962) where the effect of an independent variable tends to emerge over time rather than being present instantaneously or at equal strength along the developmental time line. Fourth, examination of both short-term and long-term causal factors should be undertaken.

6. *Experimental Manipulation.* In comparison with the preceding techniques, experimental manipulation is the most powerful strategy for distinguishing between correlates and causes of crime. Its crucial feature is the random assignment of a sufficiently large number of subjects to experimental and control conditions; this should randomize potential causal factors other than those that are manipulated in the course of the intervention. Thus, the power of manipulation or intervention in randomized experiments rests on establishing control over an independent variable or set of variables and then demonstrating that the introduction of the variable or variables is followed by a reduction in outcome in the experimental but not in the control group. Certain categories of variables do not lend themselves to manipulation, particularly most discrete events. However, when variables can fluctuate over time, and when it is ethically permissible for them to change, they constitute a powerful tool for discriminating between correlates and causes.

According to Schwartz, Flamant, and Lelouch (1980),[17] experimental manipulations can serve two basic purposes: first, they can show that a particular intervention or preventive strategy works (called a *pragmatic clinical trial*), and, second, they can demonstrate that causal control can be established in a small segment of the causal network (called an *explanatory trial*). The first category of experimental manipulation has as a direct goal the amelioration of existing problem behavior or its prevention. Ideally, subjects should be representative of the population at risk. Usually, the large number of variables manipulated during an intervention give only a hint of the causal status of each.

The second form of experimental manipulation, explanatory trial, may serve to compensate for the imprecise nature of pragmatic trials. Explanatory trials focus on the proximal link between a potential cause and an intermediate rather than an ultimate outcome. For instance, the intervention may concentrate on showing that certain forms of teacher training improve classroom attendance (which, in turn, is thought to be associated with delinquent activities). Unlike pragmatic clinical trials, exploratory trials require relatively homogeneous groups of subjects. In the example, the subjects would be those at risk for truancy, rather than all of those attending the class.

Lack of space does not allow us to review studies on explanatory trials, although it seems clear that they would provide the building blocks for pragmatic interventions. For studies on pragmatic interventions in delinquency, the reader is referred to several reviews (Farrington 1982*b*; Kazdin 1985; Loeber 1985*b*). Among the most successful early interventions, the Perry Preschool Project is the one best known among criminologists (Berrueta-Clement et al. 1984). It provided concentrated Head Start training to disadvantaged preschoolers and demonstrated a lower rate of delinquency in adulthood for the experimental group compared with the control group, over nearly two decades. Even though the focus was on the acquisition of cognitive skills by the youngsters, unlike Kolvin et al.'s (1988) study, which focused on early deprivation in the preschool period, both studies share an important emphasis on early conditions that could have been alleviated. That is not to say that factors emerging after the preschool period are unimportant. In fact, they provide opportunities for multiple entry points for intervention at several intermediate steps (see Loeber [1990] for exam-

---

[17] We are grateful to Dr. Richard Tremblay for drawing our attention to this source.

ples). Another notable example of pragmatic intervention was under-taken by Feldman, Caplinger, and Wodarski (1984), in which delin-quent youngsters were assigned either to an all delinquent peer group or to a prosocial peer group; the latter had a significantly better treat-ment outcome.

C. The Nature of Causes

Whether particular strategies for determining causality can be used depends, in part, on the nature of independent variables, among which three categories can be distinguished: unchanging variables, discrete variables, and variable states. In criminology, unchanging variables are sometimes referred to as structural variables (such as socioeconomic status or sex) but may also include parental criminality and race. The task is to examine which of the unchanging factors are long-acting, stable causal factors that may predict both activation *and* aggravation, not only of offending, but also of manifestations of other antisocial behavior occurring prior to, or subsequent to, offending. This implies that, even though an unchanging variable may constitute a long-term causal factor, its impact may not have to emerge instantly; rather, it may emerge gradually over time and then stabilize.

In criminology, discrete variables and variable states are sometimes labeled "change variables." Discrete variables concern changes in a state (e.g., from being in school to being in the work force, from being not married to being married) or the occurrence of a life event such as moving to another city. Usually, the impact of discrete variables on the course of offending can be gauged by a subsequent change in activa-tion, aggravation, or desistance in offending. A discrete variable, how-ever, is limited in its variability; its impact on offending is immediate and cannot affect more than one process at the time; as a consequence it can have an impact on either activation, aggravation, or desistance.

Last, variable states concern variables that may vary over time in terms of their frequency. In contrast to discrete variables, a change in a variable state can be related to positive and negative changes in offend-ing, thus explaining activation, aggravation, and desistance. Discrete variables and variable states often occur in proximity to a change in offending.

Each type of variable has different options for causal analyses, as is illustrated in table 6. Unchanging variables can be correlated with delinquency, serve as predictors, be incorporated in stepping-stone

TABLE 6

The Relationship between Type of Independent Variable and Strategies to Establish Causality in Developmental Studies

Type of Independent Variable	Causal Strategies					
	Correlation	Prediction	Life Event Analysis	Sequential Covariation	Stepping Stones	Experimental Manipulation
Unchangeable variable (e.g., sex, race)	Yes*	Yes*	No	No	Yes*	No
Discrete life event (e.g., death of parent, etc.)	Yes*	Yes*	Yes*	No	Yes*	No
Variable state (e.g., marital conflict, peer influences)	Yes*	Yes*	N/A	Yes*	Yes*	Some

NOTE.—N/A = not applicable.
* Control is desirable for third variables.

models, or be controlled for.[18] The causal strategies for analysis of life events, sequential covariation, and experimental manipulation, however, do not apply to unchanging variables; therefore, the options are limited for establishing their causal status.

As to discrete variables, when the point of transition falls outside the period in which offending takes place, these variables merely become background factors like race or sex. The restrictions on causal analyses discussed above also apply here. When the transition from one state to another, however, takes place closer to the offense history, these variables can be more directly incorporated into developmental models. Event history analyses are a potential tool for this purpose (Allison 1985). Causal strategies include all those that applied to unchanging factors and do not include sequential covariation and experimental manipulation. It should be kept in mind, however, that the effect of unchanging variables, such as life events, may rest on other consequences that flow from the events; for instance, death of a father may be followed by poverty in the family and reduced supervision of the children.

Turning to variable states, the options for causal analyses increase even further. Aside from the causal strategies applicable to discrete variables, options now include sequential covariation and, in certain instances, experimental manipulation, depending on feasibility and ethical considerations.

Thus, our ability to narrow down causality of offending and distinguish it from noncausal correlates depends in part on the nature of the independent variable. Central, in the quest for causality, are variables that can either change naturally over time or can be made to vary by means of a systematic experimental manipulation. Also important, however, are stable factors with long-term effects. Their causal status is more difficult to assess; criteria, however, are that a stable causal factor correlates with different manifestations of antisocial behavior over time (such as conduct problems and offending); correlates with offending at different age periods; correlates positively both with individuals' activation and aggravation in offending and negatively with desistance; and a

[18] As Hirschi and Selvin (1967) have argued rightly, these variables must be statistically controlled for or partialed out in analyses. We would add that this is especially necessary for within-individual analyses, where the invariant nature of these variables cannot be linked readily to changes in offending over time. In this instance, invariant factors should be examined in between-group analyses, where groups of offenders are distinguished on the basis of some developmental characteristic, such as early versus late onset.

final, more conventional, criterion is that the level of offending by those
with the stable factor is significantly different from the offending by
those without that factor.

It seems plausible that stable causal factors are of importance for the
explanation of the continuity of antisocial behavior over time. As has
been pointed out by Hewitt et al. (1988), two mechanisms may be
responsible for the continuity in youngsters' behavior. One mechanism
is based on a "common genetic or environmental disposition"; the other
is "that earlier influences are transmitted from occasion to occasion . . .
as a consequence of learning" (p. 134). One possible way to distinguish
between the two mechanisms is to examine test-retest correlations and
variance, each of which would increase over time. Another method is to
examine the degree to which relations between putative causal factors
persist at time n when the effect at times $n - 1$, $n - 2$, and so forth, is
partialed out.

D. The Timing of Causes

Studies in offending seldom refer to the possibility that the timing of
causes may be important and that individuals may be more vulnerable
to specific causes in certain life phases but not in others. Criminologists
often fail to acknowledge that causes of deviant behavior do not operate
equally strongly along the time line but interact with children's susceptibility or vulnerability. Developmental psychology refers to this life-
phase vulnerability as "sensitive periods" in youngsters' development,
in which susceptibility to causal influences is enhanced, compared with
other periods (Bateson and Hinde 1987). Thus, causes would have a
more powerful effect during a sensitive period than at other times in the
child's life. For instance, it is likely that the preschool period especially
is the period in which children's attachment to adults is established.
This is evident from studies comparing youngsters who experienced
disruptions in the continuity of child care (adoption, exposure to many
different caretakers, and marital breakdown) with those who did not
experience such disruptions (Werner and Smith 1977; Wadsworth
1979; Cadoret and Cain 1980; Behar and Stewart 1984; MacDonald
1985; Kolvin et al. 1988).

A final example of the sensitive period concept concerns the development of the central nervous system in children, which from gestation to
about age six is particularly vulnerable to neurotoxins, such as lead.
Research findings show that exposure to even very small amounts may

produce nonclinical degrees of handicaps in intelligence and impulsivity, which may eventually result in poor academic performance and behavior problems (e.g., Needleman and Bellinger 1981; Yule et al. 1981; and Bellinger et al. 1984).

E. Summary

In this section, we have attempted to demonstrate three points. First, few criminological theories have made optimal use of the developmental perspective. Second, too few empirical studies have tried to sequence causal factors in relation to individual offending; even those studies that have attempted to accomplish this task have been hampered by methodological difficulties. Third, the nature of independent variables influences the options for making causal inferences, with those variables which can vary over time being most optimal. We have also drawn a distinction between causal factors that are long-acting and stable and those that occur proximally and are changeable. Not all causal influences appear equally potent at all life phases of children, and much remains to be learned about sensitive periods in which causal potency is enhanced.

Overall, the study of the correlates of individual offending is very well advanced; it may even have reached a ceiling in cross-sectional studies. But the study of the causes of individual offending is only just beginning. We have outlined some ways to optimize causal inferences from longitudinal studies. We would warn readers, though, to guard against simplifying causal effects by conceiving them unidirectionally, that is, so that only independent factors have a causal impact on dependent factors. It is important to remember that independent and dependent factors may have reciprocal effects. Much work remains to be done before it will be possible to distinguish among the many putative causes of crime. Criminologists and therapists involved in interventions to reduce delinquency rarely distinguish between various durations of causal factors. We come back to this in Section VII, the conclusion.

VI. Some Developmental Contexts

Findings on offense activation, aggravation, and desistance must be viewed against the backdrop of other developmental processes, which occur simultaneously with changes in offending behavior. In this section, we briefly discuss contexts such as changes in physical strength, motor and other skills, personality development, sexual development, and opportunities for crime. Where possible, we focus especially on how these contexts may be associated with offense activation and desistance and how they may mediate changes in offending.

A. *Physical Strength, Motor and Other Skills*

Some forms of rule- or lawbreaking, such as truancy or minor theft, involve virtually no physical strength or motor skills. Many other types of offenses, however, require all or some of the following: physical strength, motor control and dexterity, and planning skills. We hypothesize that skills that facilitate offending usually develop over time through practice and increased maturation, allowing for better motor control, specifically as related to finger movements. For example, the picking of locks involves finger control which, presumably, few four year olds have, but it is within the scope of most adolescents. Moreover, it seems likely that the skills involved in planning offenses, such as staking out the location, developing a new identity, provision of a disguise, planning escape routes, and rehearsing the crime, are used by offenders increasingly from the juvenile years to adulthood (Petersilia, Greenwood, and Lavin 1978).

1. *Development.*   Physical strength increases dramatically during adolescence. Figures for male adolescents, for example, show an increase in the pulling and pushing force they can exert with their arms; this increases, on average, by a factor of three from early to late adolescence (Tanner 1972). Their increased strength not only enables them to force open doors or windows that they formerly could not budge, but their bodies also can become a more lethal weapon because the impact of blows carries so much more force and weight. This may explain in part why there is likely to be a progression from aggression to violence, judging from the fact that 80 percent to 90 percent of violent criminals have been highly aggressive in early adolescence (Magnusson 1984; Loeber and Stouthamer-Loeber 1987, reinterpreting Farrington [1973]). Such physical changes may also explain why some researchers have observed an increase in the sophistication of crime with age (Petersilia, Greenwood, and Lavin 1978) and an increase in impulsive violence (Le Blanc and Fréchette 1989).

2. *Desistance.*   Once physical strength has reached a peak in late adolescence, it takes several decades before this strength wanes. The decrease in the prevalence of violent offenses after the second and third decade of life (Miller, Dinitz, and Conrad 1982) may be related to a decline in physical strength. Likewise, as physical fitness decreases

with age, it may explain shifts from breaking and entering to less physically taxing crimes such as fraud (Le Blanc and Fréchette 1989).

We hypothesize that desistance from offenses involving skills is less likely than from offenses that require no skills. We propose that, once individuals have acquired the skill of, for example, cracking safes, that skill will basically stay in their repertoire of potential behaviors, even if the behavior itself is not displayed for many years. Thus, desistance may refer in this instance to the cessation of the overt behavior but not to the loss of the skill that is a prerequisite for the behavior. Two conclusions follow: full desistance is *more* likely in the formative stages of skill acquisition, when the skill for crime commission has not yet been perfected; and full desistance is *less* likely when repeated, successful practice has occurred, allowing the behavior to become ingrained in the person's behavioral repertoire.

B. Personality

We take the position that personality is composed of several traits and that traits refer to stable behavior patterns and cognitions that characterize and distinguish individuals. Delinquent acts are likely not only to correlate with a number of personality traits (Megargee and Bohn 1979; Wilson and Herrnstein 1985; Fréchette and Le Blanc 1987) but are functionally related to particular traits. For example, delinquency has been associated with extroversion (Eysenck 1977; Rushton and Chrisjohn 1981), psychopathic deviance (Hathaway and Monachesi 1953), and criminal personality (Yochelson and Samenow 1976).

Robins (1978) concluded that antisocial personality rarely emerges de novo in adulthood but, rather, develops from childhood onward. Although evidence on the development and continuity of psychopathic traits is scarce, some support is provided by Hathaway and Monachesi (1953), who found that ninth-grade public school students with more than one delinquent record scored significantly differently on the Minnesota Multiphasic Personality Inventory (MMPI) than students with no delinquent record. Their personality pattern (high on personality traits of "psychopathic deviate," "schizophrenia," and "hypomania") is remarkably similar to the profile shown by adult repeat offenders.

Even on a concurrent level, it is likely that certain legitimate behaviors and cognitions characteristic of personality traits may facilitate offending or aid its concealment afterwards. For example, a pattern of dominating male chauvinistic behavior may precipitate and facilitate the offense of wife abuse; the same dominating behavior may be expressed in subsequent threats to the wife to hinder her in seeking help, thereby aiding the offender in the concealment of his offense. Thus, certain traits are relevant for offending when they include behaviors and cognitions that occur in sequence with offending and, therefore, may be functionally auxiliary to delinquency. The behaviors and cognitions, characteristic of a particular personality type, occur within chains of behaviors that include offenses; it is thought that the practice of these chains increases the likelihood of the repetition of the chains over time and strengthens the interdependence of the behaviors (Patterson 1982).

Personality traits, considered within this context, are important since individual differences in personality traits may emerge alongside or precede activation in offending; personality traits may persist simultaneously with partial or full desistance from offending; and the presence of certain personality features appears uniquely associated with desistance from offending.

1. *Development.* Here we consider activation of offending within the context of the development of personality traits or, more simply, within the context of the development of networks of nonillegal behaviors and cognitions which facilitate offending. For example, in a careful follow-up of male and female students from junior to senior high school, Block (1971) found continuity in undercontrolled acts, simultaneously with an increase in sexual interest and a decrease in dependence. Between senior high school and adulthood, the subjects accentuated their individual differences through, for example, direct expression of hostile feelings and through self-defensiveness (during a time period when violent crimes are most prevalent, although these were not measured in this study). Hathaway and Monachesi (1957) showed that many boys, prior to their first officially recorded delinquent act, already scored higher on these traits than nondelinquent boys, with the difference being exacerbated when boys scored high on more than one of the traits. A closer examination, however, of the discriminating items of the MMPI showed that many refer to misbehavior and others, to impulsive, careless acts. It is not clear, however, to what extent the MMPI adds to the prediction of offending above what already is known about nonillegal conduct problems and the hyperactivity/impulsivity syndrome (see, e.g., Farrington, Biron, and Le Blanc 1982). These and other difficulties with personality scales, when applied to the study of delinquency, have been highlighted by Rutter and Giller (1983).

The personality traits that encourage initiation of offending may not be the same as those that support its aggravation. For example, Fréchette and Le Blanc (1987) have shown, in their study of the development of the personalities of the delinquents in their sample, that psychotism, a scale from the Eysenck inventory, was the best predictor of the initiation of delinquency, while interpersonal skills, as measured by the Kelly REP test, had the highest explanatory power for the continuation of delinquency.

2. *Desistance.*   Several studies have examined, either directly or indirectly, the extent to which personality traits supportive of delinquency persist when offending ceases. Osborn and West (1980, p. 111), in the Cambridge Study, found that recidivists with no subsequent convictions "retained some traits typical of delinquents most notably their relative high scores on the scale of 'antisociality.'" Charland (1985), who investigated self-reported offending by wards of the Montreal courts from middle to late adolescence, distinguished between three groups of desisters, depending on their initial frequency level of offending, and contrasted these with those who did not desist. A large variety of personality measures was administered, resulting in the finding that desisting offenders whose delinquency was initially the most frequent continued to display the most profound personality deficits even when offending had ceased. Among these deficits were difficulties with interpersonal relations and a tendency to remain undersocialized.

It is important to consider whether there is any particular personality trait that is associated with desistance. Charland (1985), in the aforementioned study, found that the *only* personality variable that systematically covaried with the likelihood of desistance was anxiety. This finding agrees with, first, studies showing that the most serious offenders and psychopaths suffer from a lack of normal anxiety (Robins 1966; Hare 1986) and, second, findings that the presence of anxiety earlier in life *negatively* predicts delinquency and *positively* predicts success in treatment (summarized by Loeber and Stouthamer-Loeber [1987]), while increases in anxiety are associated with subsequent desistance (Cormier et al. 1959; Cusson and Pinsonnealt 1986; Mulvey and LaRosa 1986).

C. Sexual Behavior and Maturation

Sexual behaviors are related to offending in two broad ways: their onset is associated with the onset and frequency of delinquency; a more direct link occurs when sexual behavior violates a criminal law. Findings from a number of studies agree that early onset of sexual activity is associated with higher frequency of offending (Elliott and Morse 1985; Rowe et al. 1989). Likewise, early age at menarche (with its attendant hormonal changes) has been linked to earlier offending. Magnusson (1988) grouped Swedish girls into four categories of age at menarche, with the youngest being those reaching the onset of menarche prior to age eleven. Self-reports of delinquency and reports of norm violation were collected at age fourteen-and-one-half. For all behaviors, onset of menarche prior to age eleven was associated with a higher percent of the girls committing crimes or norm breaking than for those with a later onset of menarche. For example, 14.6 percent of the early group reported pilfering from a shop, compared with about 5 percent for those with an onset between ages eleven and thirteen, and 1.8 percent with an onset over the age of thirteen. These findings do not necessarily mean that early onset of menarche is criminogenic in and of itself; rather, it is likely that the effect is mediated through older peers. Magnusson (1988) found that about two-thirds of the early-maturing girls sought out, or were sought out by, older friends, compared with 39 percent of the later maturing girls. The association with older friends was linked particularly to norm violation for the early-maturing group and less so for the later group.

A similar situation may exist for boys since their level of testosterone is increased by a factor of ten to twenty as compared to a factor of two for girls as reported by Udry (1988). He also shows that biological variables (hormones) are more important than sociological variables (social control variables) in explaining adolescent sexuality; it also has been established that juvenile deviance is influenced by biological factors (Rowe and Osgoode 1984; Udry, n.d.).

Turning to the development of sexually deviant behaviors with age-inappropriate partners, Quinsey (1986, p. 167) concluded that "there is little known about the development of normal [and deviant] sexual age preferences despite the well documented interest children have in sexual activities." He hypothesized several, not mutually exclusive, scenarios of the development of sexual preference in males: "[i] A preference for adult females exists from birth or from a very early age; [ii] this preference for adults develops slowly over the course of childhood; [iii] there is a preference for same-age female peers that shifts upward with age; and [iv] there is an initial preference for same-age peers and older females but the interest in younger females is progressively inhibited" (Quinsey 1986, p. 167). Unfortunately, knowledge of these and other scenarios is handicapped by a lack of empirical studies. Retrospective reports have documented that erotic gender preferences have already appeared before puberty (e.g., Bell, Weinberg, and Hammersmith 1981). It is possible that developmental timing of sexual experiencing may play a role in sexual offenses. For instance, Robins and Ratcliff (1980) found a trend for those *without* early sexual experience (prior to age fifteen) to be more frequently involved in rape.

D. Opportunities

The type and frequency of opportunities for crime vary as individuals grow older. The following categories of opportunities have been documented for adolescents: part-time work (Greenberger and Steinberg 1986), activities increasingly taking place at night along with the mobility offered by cars, and more activities taking place outside the purview of responsible adults and away from the immediate neighborhood in which the youngster lives (Petersilia, Greenwood, and Lavin 1978; Felson and Gottfredson 1984).

1. *Development.* Opportunities probably play a significant role in activation and aggravation processes. For example, monitoring by parents of children's whereabouts, choice of friends, and activities, tends to decrease as the child grows older (Loeber and Stouthamer-Loeber 1986), thereby increasing opportunities for mischief. Such opportunities are likely to be a major influence in molding the expression of crime. For instance, sexual contacts with minors may result directly from the opportunity to baby-sit, while fraud may be facilitated by the opportunity to be in charge of a petty cash fund. It should be recognized, however, that, although certain opportunities present themselves more often to some individuals than to others, there are large differences among individuals in their propensity to explore their environment, to seek out risk-taking situations, and to recognize opportunities for lawbreaking. Rowe, Rodgers, and Meseck-Bushey (1987) have recently proposed an epidemic model to explain the spread of sexual activity among adolescents; they divided youngsters into those who are "affected" (sexually active) and those who are "susceptible" (not yet sexually active). The model also rests on the proliferation of opportunities, in which affected adolescents introduce sex to susceptible adolescents. Such a model may be applied to the spread of delinquency as well, with affected peers introducing susceptible youngsters to crime (see also Reiss 1988).

2. *Desistance.* Opportunities are an equally important factor for ob-

served desistance from offending. Clearly, a portion of naturally occurring desistance takes place when former opportunities for crime are no longer available and when opportunities for satisfying needs in legitimate ways become available, particularly as adolescents or young adults enter the labor force. Thus, although desistance may be observed for a period of time in some former offenders, the litmus test for desistance is whether it continues in the presence of opportunities for crime. This essential distinction is rooted in our conviction that deviant behaviors may become dormant, but that this does not necessarily mean that they have been desisted from fully (Barnett, Blumstein, and Farrington 1987).

E. Summary

This brief survey merely illustrates developmental contexts for offending, such as changes in physical strength, motor skills, personality traits, sexual behavior, and opportunities. Each of these contexts is insufficient in itself to explain offense activation, aggravation, or desistance; however, in conjunction with other causal processes, they each may mediate deviant outcomes. The conceptualization presented here attempts to explain why certain offending patterns, once established, are so highly persisting and to present some certain and possible explanations for desistance when it occurs. Activation may be more likely when physical strength increases, together with motor control and other skills that facilitate offending; auxiliary behaviors and cognitions, often perceived as traits, probably are in place prior to offending; hormonal changes occur; and there is a higher frequency of opportunities for crime commission.

Desistance may be less likely when behaviors are dependent on the acquisition of skills for the commission of crimes, behaviors are embedded in a wider personality development—as in the case of aggressive traits—or when behaviors are part of a chain of other behaviors and opportunities for crime are scarce.

This brief summary cannot do justice to other developmental contexts—such as the development of intelligence (Morash 1983; Pelletier 1988), the development of psychoneurological functioning (Moffitt, in this volume), the internalization of moral standards (Hirschi and Hindelang 1977; Wilson and Herrnstein 1985), and hormonal and other physiological changes (Udry 1988, n.d.)—that take place during the growing-up years. This list also should include the nature of the social milieu, the urban environment (see Gabrielli and Mednick 1984), and, particularly, the inner city. Shannon's (1988) recent book provides a clear illustration of its impact on the initiation and the development of offending. In addition, there are genetic factors that may influence the course of offending, which we will touch on in the next section.

VII. Conclusion

This essay set out to demonstrate the advantages of adopting a developmental view of offending and of focusing on the study of within-individual changes in offending over time. We have proposed that these changes, especially when measured by means of self-reported delinquency, do not occur randomly but, rather, are predictable, hierarchical, and orderly. The first aim of a developmental criminology, therefore, is to document such systematic effects, especially within periods of increased change in offending, either after onset or during desistance. The second aim is to identify explicative or causal factors predating developmental change and influencing its course. We see the latter aim as being crucial in bringing about improvements in our ability to discriminate better between correlates and causes of crime. A third aim is to challenge several assumptions, listed in the introduction to this essay, that are common in criminological thinking and that, in our opinion, have impeded the advancement of knowledge.

Developmental criminology quantifies dynamic concepts for capturing important ingredients of change and stability. It distinguishes between continuity and stability and, therefore, recognizes that manifestations of deviancy in the course of offenders' lives may change, while the underlying propensity for deviancy probably remains stable. It considers the course of offending in other developmental contexts, such as life transitions and developmental covariates, which may mediate the developmental course of offending. It aims at generating new knowledge about the etiology and precursors of offending, which may be relevant for much-needed improvements in future prevention and intervention programs. Developmental criminology poses new questions and, therefore, encourages innovation in analytic methods that may help to describe and explain longitudinal changes in individuals' offending.

Within the context of developmental research, we have stressed the importance of first identifying developmental sequences before attempting to locate individuals' positions on a developmental continuum. We first described what we see as the three primary developmental processes of offending: activation, aggravation, and desistance.

With regard to activation, we distinguished among three subprocesses of acceleration, stabilization, and diversification and provided evidence for each. In particular, we highlighted the important effect of early onset of offending in males as facilitating these subprocesses. This is not to say that late onset is any less important; fragmentary evidence points to late-onset offenders displaying a different crime mix from early onset offenders, and a proportion of these crimes are of a serious nature.

The central characteristic of the process of aggravation is escalation in the seriousness of antisocial behavior. Most past research in this area probably obscured rather than clarified developmental sequences in offending. The evidence, however, clearly indicates that substance use, for example, develops along an orderly, hierarchical sequence. The evidence for developmental sequences in the area of conduct problems is less complete but points to similar developmental paradigms. Increasingly, studies are documenting developmental sequences in offending from trivial to more serious forms of crime. The evidence is more available for male offending compared with female offending due to a scarcity of studies for the latter. Developmental sequences in each of the three areas—conduct problems, substance use, and offending—can be productively combined into developmental trajectories that span from childhood to adulthood. Evidence indicates that probably more than one trajectory can be discerned, with each trajectory leading to distinctly different antisocial outcomes in adulthood.

The third process, desistance, includes four subprocesses: deceleration, de-escalation, reaching a ceiling, and specialization. Evidence for each subprocess was reviewed, but this review is limited inherently due to a scarcity of studies on desistance in general.

We considered the processes of activation, aggravation, and desistance and demonstrated that they do not occur merely as a function of individuals' chronological age. One reason for this is that each of the processes may take place over a wide age span with, for example, activation for some occurring in late childhood and for others in late adolescence; similarly, for some individuals, desistance may take place in adolescence, but for others much later. Another reason for these processes not being merely a function of age is that age is not an effective explanatory variable without reference to causal processes. We agree with Wohlwill (1973) that it is more important to search for variables that determine or mediate the variation of behavior with age.

After having identified developmental sequences, it is possible to quantify individuals' positions within a sequence. For that purpose, we have distinguished between individuals' qualitative and quantitative changes in offending. Included in the qualitative category is the proportion of individuals who move from one stage to another, the direction of their change, and the velocity of change. Included in the quantitative category is the conservation and synchrony of offenses over time. Finally, we have defined paths as that portion of a developmental trajectory that individuals travel within a given time period. We pointed out several principles of individuals' moving along a developmental path: a person's movement along a path is more likely to be to a developmentally adjacent than to a developmentally nonadjacent behavior; individuals' likelihood of desistance appears to be inversely related to progression.

Longitudinal studies usually have not taken full advantage of studying both developmental sequences and individuals' positions within these sequences. It is, therefore, not surprising that there is a scarcity of references to developmental aspects of offending in most criminological theories. We believe that this situation has been aggravated by the failure of researchers to optimize the inherent possibilities for analyses of causation, which may aid in distinguishing better between correlates and causes. For this reason, we have reviewed and contrasted six strategies for determining causality: correlation, prediction, the analysis of life events, sequential covariation, the stepping-stone approach, and experimental manipulation. The results of these approaches depend on how well findings hold when third factors are partialled out (see, e.g., O'Donnell and Clayton 1982). It is also recognized that not all causal influences fit recursive models but that reciprocal models of crime causation need to be tested as well. Lastly, even when cause is statistically inferred from the relation between one variable and another, the causal mechanism remains to be explained (O'Donnell and Clayton 1982).

We have shown here that independent variables that can change offer more options for causal analyses than those that are unchanging. We also have made a distinction between long-lasting, stable causal factors that may predict both activation and aggravation in offending and proximal, changeable causal factors that may be more relevant for the explanation of participation rather than for aggravation in offending.

Moreover, we argued that, because some factors are better predictors of early onset of offending than of late onset, while other factors are associated with desistance, there probably are distinct causes for each process of offending. We also have demonstrated that activation and desistance may occur against the backdrop of other developmental contexts, such as changes in physical strength, motor and other skills; personality development; sexual development; and opportunities for crime. The extent to which each of these phenomena mediate or cause offending remains unclear.

A. Genetic Influences

Because of space limitations, we have not discussed in detail evidence for the effects of genetic disposition on changes in offending over time. There are, however, several themes that suggest that familial (and probably inherited) factors influence not only whether individuals become delinquent but also the course of offending. For instance, there are abundant research findings from other fields of psychopathology that early age at onset in one family member is associated with early age at onset in other family members (Meyer and Eaves 1989), and this may also apply to offending. For example, early onset of criminality or alcoholism in fathers predicted these behaviors in the child, even when the child was adopted away. It also is possible that sex-specific links operate here (Sigvardsson et al. 1982). In the area of alcohol use, for example, Heath and Martin (1989) in their study of Australian twins found that early, versus late, onset of alcohol use was more associated with inherited factors in females than in males. Twin studies offer the additional advantage of helping to distinguish between two types of causes for continuity of behavior through common genetic or environmental factors or through transmission from occasion to occasion as in the case of learning (Hewitt et al. 1988). We come back to this important distinction when discussing interventions. These genetic links are found not only in psychopathology and substance abuse but also in aggression (Huesmann et al. 1984), delinquency (West 1982; Rowe and Osgood 1984), and parenting breakdown (Quinton and Rutter 1988).

B. Theories of Offending

Along with a renewed interest in theoretical criminology (see Meier 1985; Albany Conference 1987; Weis 1987) have come a few statements supporting a developmental explanation of offending. This orientation is of such importance that it must be emphasized and pursued with vigor. We can no longer be satisfied with a myopic view of the causes of individual offending, rooted in a specific moment in time, all of which are assumed to be invariant with developmental stages; rather, there is a need to adopt a system view in which numerous factors operate and interact along the developmental time line. The level of youngsters' attachment to school during adolescence, for example, cannot be viewed as a sui generis reality; it has emerged progressively through the influences of numerous structural and psychosocial influences in a context of specific antecedent factors (Hawkins et al. 1986). More complete theories will emerge in criminology, not only through the integrative theoretical movement but also from the current theoretical dead-end through the consideration of the developmental perspective.

C. Future Longitudinal Studies

In North America a new generation of longitudinal studies is building momentum; although still in their infancy, they have a potential for advancing our knowledge of individuals' offending and are likely to exploit the advantages offered by the longitudinal design for distinguishing correlates from causes of crime. In the area of causation, these studies are enabling us to formulate and to answer fundamental questions. What is the time ordering of putative causal factors? Do certain factors operate primarily and specifically during the perinatal period or infancy and others during childhood, adolescence, or young adulthood? Is it possible to distinguish stage-specific causal factors from other factors that may be stable and long-lasting, influencing activation and aggravation throughout the delinquency career? And, are some factors primarily associated with the activation and aggravation of offending, while other factors are mainly associated with desistance?

D. Prevention and Intervention

We have presented many possible explanations for full desistance being more common once offending has been activated and when personality, physical strength, and, probably also, intellect have matured. Researchers who have worked for decades with juvenile repeat offenders are convinced that some degree of desistance can be brought about through intensive efforts by adults in controlled environments, such as group homes supervised by trained surrogate parents or by specially trained foster parents (Hawkins et al. 1985; Wolf, Braukmann, and Ramp 1987). Once released into their old environment, however, relapse in offending and other problem behaviors is very common. Wolf, Braukmann, and Ramp (1987) write of the chronic nature of the "social disability" displayed by these youngsters, a disability that requires long-term containment and care.

It is not surprising in this context that calls for preventive intervention have been sounded more frequently in recent years. As has been pointed out by Lorion (1982), knowledge of the etiology of offending is essential for the development of preventive programs since the modification of etiological factors is the backbone of prevention. Advocates of early intervention have proposed that there are at least two viable strategies: postponing the onset of the age-inappropriate behavior, as in the case of early alcohol use or teenage pregnancy (e.g., Jessor 1982), and eliminating early problem behaviors (labeled "stepping stones" or "gateway behaviors"), which occur early in a developmental sequence in order to arrest the activation of other, subsequent antisocial behaviors (O'Donnell and Clayton 1982; Voeltz and Evans 1982).

The postponement strategy assumes that there is a period of vulnerability to activation and that, once youngsters pass that period, activation is either less likely to occur or will take place more benignly and in accordance with age norms (as in the case of alcohol use). The second assumption of the postponement strategy is that postponement leads to a higher likelihood of youngsters' completion of age-normative milestones, such as the finishing of high school.

In contrast, the stepping-stone/gateway approach assumes that the prevention of learning of one behavior impedes the acquisition of behaviors that typically occur later in the developmental sequence. Thus, "intervention to prevent expression of the behavior at one age would have directly transmitted benefits at later ages" (Hewitt 1988, p. 36).

The rationales for postponement or early intervention can be challenged. What if successive onsets are determined by a common underlying cause that is stable over time and has long-term rather than short-term effects? For example, Robins and Wish (1977) studied black youngsters' developmental sequences in antisocial behavior and examined whether one act was "either a necessary or a sufficient cause of the second" (p. 466). A necessary cause was inferred "if the second act almost never occurs unless preceded by the first . . . ; [while] a sufficient cause [can be inferred] if the first act is almost invariably followed by the second." The authors found only three sequences out of seventy-eight comparisons that fulfilled these criteria, which hardly produced evidence that one behavior was "causing" another. Instead, it is more plausible that a common underlying tendency of antisocial behavior could explain the findings, although the authors did not address this. As has been pointed out by Hewitt (1988, p. 36), if this were the case, "intervening to prevent the expression of behavior . . . at one age would not confer subsequent benefits *in the absence of continued intervention.*" Along that line, Kazdin (1987) and Wolf, Braukmann, and Ramp (1987) have drawn attention to the need for continued administration of treatment of antisocial youngsters.

Given our imperfect state of knowledge of stable and variable causes of crime, conclusions about optimal types of intervention are inherently premature. We see, however, promise in the approaches offered by developmental criminology, for addressing these issues, and ultimately lending support to particular types of preventive or rehabilitative interventions, within both the mental health arena and the criminal justice system.

APPENDIX

The Characteristics of RIOC

As mentioned in the text, RIOC corrects for chance and maximum levels within a 2 × 2 table. This is illustrated in figure A1, which gives an example of data. In this case, there are 100 subjects, of whom thirty have characteristic *B* and sixty have characteristic *A*. Figure A1 gives the observed values, the expected values (in parentheses), and the maximum values (in square brackets). For example, in cell *a* (the valid positives), the observed value is twenty-five, but the expected value by chance is eighteen. The latter is calculated by $(a + d) \times (a + b/t)$. Cell *a* has a maximum value in that it can never contain more than thirty subjects because of the difference between the base rate, $(a + d)/t$, and the selection ratio, $(a + b)/t$. As a consequence, the maximum table in this case contains zero subjects in cell *d* and forty subjects in cell *c*. This means that, under this condition, the maximum valid positives (*a*) and the valid negatives (*c*) is seventy. In other words, thirty of the subjects can *never* be correctly identified in this table. The larger the difference between the selection ratio and the base rate, the higher the proportion of subjects that fall in this unidentifiable category.

The formula for RIOC is

$$\text{RIOC} = \frac{\text{total correct} - \text{chance correct}}{\text{maximum correct} - \text{chance correct}} \times 100.$$

Using the parameters shown in figure A1, this is computed in the following way:

$$\text{RIOC} = \frac{(a + c) - \dfrac{(a + d) \times (a + b)}{t} + \dfrac{(b + c) \times (d + c)}{t}}{\max (a + c) - \dfrac{(a + d) \times (a + b)}{t} + \dfrac{(b + c) \times (d + c)}{t}} \times 100.$$

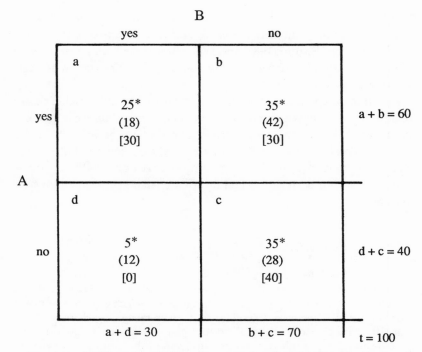

FIG. A1.—An illustration of observed, expected, and maximum values in a 2 × 2 table: the observed value is superscripted by an asterisk; numbers in parentheses are the expected value; and numbers in square brackets are the maximum value. Source.— Loeber and Stouthamer-Loeber (1986), p. 133, app. B.

A simplified formula can be found in Farrington and Loeber (1989), while significance tests and confidence levels can be found in Copas and Loeber (1990).

This Appendix is taken from Loeber and Stouthamer-Loeber (1986), p. 132, app. B.

REFERENCES

Adler, I., and D. B. Kandel. 1981. "Cross-cultural Perspectives on Developmental Stages in Adolescent Drug Use." *Journal of Studies on Alcohol* 42:701–15.

Agnew, R. 1985. "Social Control Theory and Delinquency: A Longitudinal Test." *Criminology* 23:47–61.

Albany Conference. 1987. *Theoretical Integration in the Study of Deviance and Crime: Problems and Prospects.* Albany: State University of New York at Albany, Department of Sociology.

Allison, P. D. 1985. *Event History Analysis: Regression for Longitudinal Event Data.* Beverly Hills, Calif.: Sage.

Arnold, W. R. 1965. "Continuities in Research: Scaling Delinquent Behavior." *Social Problems* 13:59–66.

Bachman, J. G., S. Green, and I. D. Wirtanen. 1971. *Youth in Transition: Dropping Out, Problems or Symptom.* Ann Arbor, Mich.: Institute for Social Research.

Bachman, J. G., P. M. O'Malley, and J. Johnston. 1978. *Youth in Transition: Adolescence to Adulthood. Change and Stability in the Lives of Young Men.* Ann Arbor, Mich.: Institute for Social Research.

Barnett, A., A. Blumstein, and D. P. Farrington. 1987. "Probabilistic Models of Youthful Criminal Careers." *Criminology* 25:83–108.

Barnett, A., and A. J. Lofaso. 1985. "Selective Incapacitation and the Philadelphia Cohort Data." *Journal of Quantitative Criminology* 1:3–36.

Bateson, P., and R. A. Hinde. 1987. "Developmental Changes in Sensitivity to Experience." In *Sensitive Periods in Development: Interdisciplinary Perspectives,* edited by M. H. Bornstein. Hillsdale, N.J.: Erlbaum.

Behar, D., and M. A. Stewart. 1984. "Aggressive Conduct Disorder: The Influence of Social Class, Sex and Age on the Clinical Picture." *Journal of Child Psychology and Psychiatry* 25:119–24.

Bell, A. P., M. S. Weinberg, and S. K. Hammersmith. 1981. *Sexual Preference: Its Development in Men and Women.* Bloomington: Indiana University Press.

Bellinger, D. B., H. L. Needleman, R. Bromfield, and M. Mintz. 1984. "A Follow-up Study of the Academic Attainment and Classroom Behavior of Children with Elevated Dentine Lead Levels." *Biological and Heavy Metal Research* 6:207–33.

Belson, W. A., ed. 1975. *Juvenile Theft: The Causal Factors.* London: Harper & Row.

Berrueta-Clement, J. R., L. J. Schweinhart, W. S. Barnett, A. S. Epstein, and D. P. Weikart. 1984. *Changed Lives: The Effects of the Perry Preschool Program on Youths through Age 19.* Ypsilanti, Mich.: High Scope.

Block, C. R., and C. Van der Werff. 1987. "Career Criminals in the Netherlands." Paper presented at the meeting of the American Society of Criminology, Montreal, November.

Block, J. 1971. *Lives through Time.* Berkeley, Calif.: Bancroft.

Blumstein, A., J. Cohen, and D. P. Farrington. 1988. "Criminal Career Research: Its Value for Criminology." *Criminology* 26:1–36.

Blumstein, A., J. Cohen, and P. Hsieh. 1982. *The Duration of Adult Criminal Careers.* Final report submitted to National Institute of Justice. School of Urban and Public Affairs, Carnegie-Mellon University, Pittsburgh.

Blumstein, A., J. Cohen, J. A. Roth, and C. A. Visher, eds. 1986. *Criminal Careers and "Career Criminals."* Washington, D.C.: National Academy Press.

Bohman, M., C. R. Cloninger, S. Sigvardsson, and A. L. Von Knorring. 1982. "Predisposition to Petty Criminality in Swedish Adoptees. 1. Genetic and Environmental Heterogeneity." *Archives of General Psychiatry* 39:1233–41.

Brennan, T., D. S. Elliott, and B. A. Knowles. 1981. *Patterns of Multiple Drug Use: A Descriptive Analysis of Static Types and Change Patterns, 1976–78. A Report of the National Youth Survey.* Project report no. 15. Boulder, Colo.: Behavioral Research Institute.

Brunswick, A. F., and J. M. Boyle. 1979. "Patterns of Drug Involvement: Developmental and Secular Influences on Age at Initiation." *Youth and Society* 11:139–62.

Cadoret, R. J., and C. Cain. 1980. "Sex Differences in Predictors of Antisocial Behavior in Adoptees." *Archives of General Psychiatry* 37:1171–75.

Carpenter, C., B. Glassner, B. D. Johnson, and J. Loughlin. 1988. *Kids, Drugs, and Crime.* Lexington, Mass.: Lexington.

Catalano, R. F., and J. D. Hawkins. 1986. "The Social Development Model: A Theory of Antisocial Behavior." Paper presented at the Safeco lecture on "Crime and Delinquency," School of Social Work, University of Washington, Seattle.

Cernkovich, S. A., P. C. Giordano, and M. D. Pugh. 1985. "Chronic Offenders: The Missing Cases in Self-reported Delinquency Research." *Journal of Criminal Law and Criminology* 76:705–32.

Chaiken, J., and M. R. Chaiken. 1982. *Varieties of Criminal Behavior.* Santa Monica, Calif.: Rand.

Charland, R. 1985. "La resorption de la délinquence a l'adolescence." Dissertation, University of Montreal, School of Criminology.

Cline, H. F. 1980. "Criminal Behavior over the Life Span." In *Constancy and Change in Human Development,* edited by O. G. Brim and J. Kagan. Cambridge, Mass.: Harvard University Press.

Cohen, A. K. 1955. *Delinquent Boys: The Subculture of the Gang.* Glencoe: Free Press.

Cohen, J. 1986. "Research on Criminal Careers: Individual Frequency Rates and Offense Seriousness." In *Criminal Careers and "Career Criminals",* vol. 1, edited by A. Blumstein, J. Cohen, J. A. Roth, and C. A. Visher. Washington, D.C.: National Academy Press.

Cohen, P., and J. Brook. 1987. "Family Factors Related to the Persistence of Psychopathology in Childhood and Adolescence." *Psychiatry* 50:332–45.

Cook, T. D., and D. T. Campbell. 1979. *Quasi-experimentation.* Chicago: Rand McNally.

Copas, J. B., and R. Loeber. 1990. "Relative Improvement over Chance (RIOC) for 2 × 2 Tables." *British Journal of Mathematical and Statistical Psychology* (forthcoming).

Cormier, B. M., M. Kennedy, J. Sangowicz, and M. Trottier. 1959. "The Natural History of Criminality and Some Tentative Hypotheses on Its Abatement." *Canadian Journal of Corrections* 1:35–49.

Cusson, M., and P. Pinsonneault. 1986. "The Decision to Give Up Crime." In *The Reasoning Criminal,* edited by D. K. Cornish and R. V. Clarke. New York: Springer-Verlag.

Davis, J. A. 1963. *Panel Analysis: Techniques and Concepts in the Interpretation of*

Repeated Measurements. Chicago: University of Chicago, National Opinion Research Center.

Dentler, R. A., and L. J. Monroe. 1961. "Social Correlates of Early Adolescent Theft." *American Sociological Review* 26:733–43.

Duncan, O. D. 1984. *Notes on Social Measurement: Historical and Critical.* New York: Russell Sage Foundation.

Dunford, F. W., D. S. Elliott, and D. Huizinga. 1983. *Characteristics of Career Offending: Testing Four Hypotheses.* Project report no. 2, submitted to the National Institute of Justice. Boulder, Colo.: Behavioral Research Institute.

Elliott, D. S. 1966. "Delinquency, School Attendance and Dropout." *Social Problems* 13:307–16.

Elliott, D. S., F. W. Dunford, and D. Huizinga. 1983. "The Identification and Prediction of Career Offenders Utilizing Self-reported and Official Data." Unpublished manuscript, Institute of Behavioral Research, University of Colorado, Boulder.

Elliott, D. S., D. Huizinga, and S. S. Ageton. 1985. *Explaining Delinquency and Drug Use.* Beverly Hills, Calif.: Sage.

Elliott, D., S. D. Huizinga, and S. Menard. 1989. *Multiple Problem Youth: Delinquency, Substance Use and Mental Health Problems.* New York: Springer-Verlag.

Elliott, D. S., and B. J. Morse. 1985. "Delinquency and Sexual Activity." Paper presented at the National Institute on Drug Abuse conference on "Drug Abuse and Adolescent Sexual Activity, Pregnancy and Parenting," Bethesda, Md.

Elliott, D. S., and H. L. Voss. 1974. *Delinquency and Dropout.* Lexington, Mass.: Heath.

Erickson, E. 1959. "Identity and the Life Cycle." *Psychological Issues* 1:1–71.

Eysenck, H. J. 1977. *Crime and Personality.* 3d ed. London: Granada.

Farrington, D. P. 1973. "Self-Reports of Deviant Behavior: Predictive and Stable?" *Journal of Criminal Law and Criminology* 64:99–110.

———. 1977. "The Effects of Public Labeling." *British Journal of Criminology* 17:112–25.

———. 1982a. Personal communication with author. Institute of Criminology, University of Cambridge.

———. 1982b. "Randomized Experiments on Crime and Justice." In *Crime and Justice: An Annual Review of Research,* vol. 4, edited by M. Tonry and N. Morris. Chicago: University of Chicago Press.

———. 1983. "Offending from 10 to 25 Years of Age." In *Prospective Studies of Crime and Delinquency,* edited by K. T. Van Dusen and S. A. Mednick. Boston: Kluwer-Nijhoff.

———. 1986. "Stepping-Stones to Adult Criminal Careers." In *Development of Antisocial and Prosocial Behavior,* edited by D. Olweus, J. Block, and M. R. Yarrow. New York: Academic Press.

———. 1987. "Early Precursors of Frequent Offending." In *From Children to Citizens.* Vol. 3 of *Families, Schools and Delinquency Prevention,* edited by J. Q. Wilson and G. C. Loury. New York: Springer-Verlag.

————. 1988. Unpublished data. Institute of Criminology, University of Cambridge.

————. 1989a. "Childhood Aggression and Adult Violence: Early Precursors and Later Life Outcomes." In *The Development and Treatment of Childhood Aggression*, edited by K. H. Rubin and D. Pepler. Hillsdale, N.J.: Erlbaum.

————. 1989b. "Early Predictors of Adolescent Aggression and Adult Violence." *Violence and Victims* 4(2):79–100.

————. 1989c. "Studying Changes within Individuals: The Causes of Offending." In *The Power of Longitudinal Data*, edited by M. Rutter. Cambridge: Cambridge University Press.

Farrington, D. P., L. Biron, and M. Le Blanc. 1982. "Personality and Delinquency in London and Montreal." In *Abnormal Offenders, Delinquency, and the Criminal Justice System*, edited by J. Gunn and D. P. Farrington. New York: Wiley.

Farrington, D. P., L. Gallagher, L. Morley, R. J. St. Ledger, and D. J. West. 1986. "Unemployment, School Leaving, and Crime." *British Journal of Criminology* 26:335–56.

————. 1988. "A 24-Year Follow-up of Men from Vulnerable Backgrounds." In *The Abandonment of Delinquent Behavior*, edited by R. L. Jenkins and W. K. Brown. New York: Praeger.

Farrington, D. P., and J. D. Hawkins. 1988. "Prediction of Participation, Early Onset, and Later Persistence in Officially Recorded Offending: The Relevance of Social Development Model Constructs." Unpublished manuscript, School of Social Work, University of Washington, Seattle.

Farrington, D. P., and R. Loeber. 1989. "RIOC and Phi as Measures of Predictive Efficiency and Strength of Association in 2 × 2 Tables." *Journal of Quantitative Criminology* 5:201–13.

Farrington, D. P., R. Loeber, and W. B. Van Kammen. 1989. "Longterm Criminal Outcomes of Hyperactivity-Impulsivity-Attention-Deficit and Conduct Problems in Childhood." In *Straight and Devious Pathways to Adulthood*, edited by L. N. Robins and M. R. Rutter. New York: Cambridge University Press.

Farrington, D. P., L. E. Ohlin, and J. Q. Wilson. 1986. *Understanding and Controlling Crime: Toward a New Research Strategy*. New York: Springer-Verlag.

Farrington, D. P., S. G. Osborn, and D. J. West. 1978. "The Persistence of Labeling Effects." *British Journal of Criminology* 18:277–84.

Farrington, D. P., H. S. Snyder, and T. A. Finnegan. 1988. "Specialization in Juvenile Court Careers." *Criminology* 26:461–88.

Feldman, R. A., T. E. Caplinger, and J. S. Wodarski. 1984. *The St. Louis Conundrum*. Englewood Cliffs, N.J.: Prentice-Hall.

Felson, M., and M. Gottfredson. 1984. "Social Indicators of Adolescent Activities near Peers and Parents." *Journal of Marriage and the Family* 46:709–14.

Ferdinand, T. N. 1987. "The Methods of Delinquency Theory." *Criminology* 25:841–63.

Fleming, J. P., S. G. Kellam, and C. H. Brown. 1982. "Early Predictors of

Age at First Use of Alcohol, Marijuana, and Cigarettes." *Drug and Alcohol Dependence* 9:285–303.

Fréchette, M., and M. Le Blanc. 1979. "La délinquance cachée à l'adolescence." Unpublished manuscript, Groupe de la Recherche sur l'Inadaptation Juvènile, University of Montreal, Quebec.

———. 1987. *Délinquances et délinquants*. Chicoutimi, Quebec: Gaetan Morin.

Gabrielli, W. F., and S. A. Mednick. 1984. "Urban Environment, Genetics, and Crime." *Criminology* 22:645–52.

Glassner, B., and J. Loughlin. 1987. *Drugs in Adolescent Worlds*. London: Macmillan.

Glueck, S., and E. Glueck. 1930. *Five Hundred Criminal Careers*. New York: Knopf.

———. 1937. *Later Criminal Careers*. New York: Commonwealth Fund.

———. 1940. *Juvenile Delinquents Grown Up*. New York: Commonwealth Fund.

———. 1943. *Criminal Careers in Retrospect*. New York: Commonwealth Fund.

———. 1968. *Delinquents and Nondelinquents in Perspective*. Cambridge, Mass.: Harvard University Press.

Gottfredson, D. M., and T. Hirschi. 1987. "The Methodological Adequacy of Longitudinal Research on Crime." *Criminology* 25:581–614.

Gottfredson, M. R., and D. M. Gottfredson. 1980. *Decision-making in Criminal Justice: Toward the Rational Exercise of Discretion*. Cambridge, Mass.: Ballinger.

Gottfredson, M. R., and T. Hirschi. 1986. "The True Value of Lambda Appears to be Zero: An Essay on Career Criminals, Criminal Careers, Selective Incapacitation, Cohort Studies, and Related Topics." *Criminology* 24:113–34.

Greenberger, E., and L. Steinberg. 1986. *When Teenagers Work: The Psychological and Social Costs of Adolescent Employment*. New York: Basic.

Guttman, J. 1944. "Cognitive Morality and Cheating Behavior in Religious and Secular School Children." *Journal of Educational Research* 77:249–54.

Hamparian, D. M., J. M. Davis, J. M. Jacobson, and R. E. McGraw. 1985. "The Young Criminal Years of the Violent Few." Report prepared for National Institute of Juvenile Justice and Delinquency Prevention, U.S. Department of Justice, Washington, D.C.

Hamparian, D. M., R. Schuster, S. Dinitz, and J. P. Conrad. 1978. *The Violent Few—a Study of Dangerous Juvenile Offenders*. Lexington, Mass.: Heath.

Hare, R. D. 1986. "Twenty Years of Experience with the Cleckley Psychopath." In *Unmasking the Psychopath*, edited by W. H. Reid, D. Dorr, J. I. Walker, and J. W. Bonner. New York: Norton.

Hare, R. D., and J. W. Jutai. 1983. "Criminal History of the Male Psychopath: Some Preliminary Data." In *Prospective Studies of Crime and Delinquency*, edited by K. T. Van Dusen and S. A. Mednick. Boston: Kluwer-Nijhoff.

Hare, R. D., L. M. McPherson, and A. E. Forth. 1988. "Male Psychopaths and Their Criminal Careers." *Journal of Consulting and Clinical Psychology* 56:710–14.

Hathaway, S. R., and E. D. Monachesi. 1953. *Analyzing and Predicting Juvenile Delinquency with the MMPI*. Minneapolis: University of Minnesota Press.

————. 1957. "The Personalities of Predelinquent Boys." *Journal of Criminal Law, Criminology and Police Science* 48:149–63.

Hawkins, J. D., D. M. Lishner, R. F. Catalano, and M. O. Howard. 1986. "Childhood Predictors of Adolescent Substance Abuse: Toward an Empirically Grounded Theory." *Journal of Children in Contemporary Society* 8:11–40.

Hawkins, R. P., P. Meadowcroft, B. A. Trout, and W. C. Luster. 1985. "Foster Family-based Treatment." *Journal of Clinical and Child Psychology* 14:220–28.

Heath, A. C., and N. G. Martin. 1989. "Teenage Alcohol Use in the Australian Twin Register: Genetic and Social Determinants of Starting to Drink." *Alcohol and Clinical Experimental Research* (forthcoming).

Hewitt, J. K. 1988. "Adolescent Behavioral Development: Twin Study." Research proposal to the National Institute of Mental Health, Washington, D.C., submitted by the Medical College of Virginia, Richmond.

Hewitt, J. K., L. J. Eaves, M. C. Neale, and J. M. Meyer. 1988. "Resolving Causes of Developmental Continuity or 'Tracking.' I. Longitudinal Twin Studies during Growth." *Behavior Genetics* 18:133–51.

Hinde, R. A., and P. Bateson. 1984. "Discontinuities versus Continuities in Behavioral Development and the Neglect of Process." *International Journal of Behavioral Development* 7:129–43.

Hindelang, M. J., T. Hirschi, and J. G. Weis. 1981. *Measuring Delinquency.* Beverly Hills, Calif.: Sage.

Hirschi, T. 1969. *Causes of Delinquency.* Berkeley: University of California Press.

Hirschi, T., and M. Gottfredson. 1987. "Causes of White-Collar Crime." *Criminology* 25:949–74.

Hirschi, T., and M. J. Hindelang. 1977. "Intelligence and Delinquency: A Revisionist Review." *American Sociological Review* 42:571–87.

Hirschi, T., and H. C. Selvin. 1967. *Delinquency Research: An Appraisal of Analytic Methods.* New York: Free Press.

Hogan, D. P. 1978. "The Variable Order of Events in the Life Course." *American Sociological Review* 43:573–86.

Huba, G. J., and P. M. Bentler. 1982. "A Developmental Theory of Drug Use: Derivation and Assessment of a Causal Modeling Approach." In *Life-Span Development and Behavior*, vol. 4, edited by P. B. Baltes and O. G. Brim, Jr. New York: Academic Press.

Huesmann, L. R., L. D. Eron, M. M. Lefkowitz, and L. O. Walder. 1984. "Stability of Aggression over Time and Generation." *Developmental Psychology* 20:1120–34.

Huizinga, D. 1979. "Dynamic Typologies." Paper presented at the tenth annual meeting of the Classification Society, Gainesville, Fla., April.

Jessor, R. 1982. "Critical Issues in Research on Adolescent Health Promotion." In *Promoting Adolescent Health*, edited by A. C. Peterson and C. Perry. New York: Academic Press.

Jessor, R., J. E. Donovan, and K. Widmer. 1980. "Psychosocial Factors in Adolescent Alcohol and Drug Use: The 1978 National Sample Study, and the 1974–78 Panel Study." Unpublished manuscript, Institute of Behavioral Science, University of Colorado, Boulder.

Jessor, R., and S. L. Jessor. 1977. *Problem Behavior and Psycho-social Development.* New York: Academic Press.

Justice, B., R. Justice, and I. A. Kraft. 1974. "Early Warning Signs of Violence: Is a Triad Enough?" *American Journal of Psychiatry* 131:457–59.

Kagan, J. 1971. *Change and Continuity in Infancy.* New York: Wiley.

Kagan, J., and H. A. Moss. 1962. *Birth to Maturity.* New York: Wiley.

Kandel, D. B. 1978. "Convergence in Prospective Longitudinal Surveys of Drug Use in Normal Populations." In *Longitudinal Research on Drug Use,* edited by D. B. Kandel. New York: Wiley.

———. 1980. "Developmental Stages in Adolescent Drug Involvement." In *Theories on Drug Abuse: Selected Contemporary Perspectives,* edited by D. J. Lettieri, M. Sayers, and H. W. Pearson. Rockville, Md.: National Institute on Drug Abuse.

———. 1982. "Epidemiological and Psychosocial Perspectives on Adolescent Drug Use." *Journal of the American Academy of Child Psychiatry* 21:328–47.

———. 1988. "Age of Onset into Drugs and Sexual Behavior." Unpublished manuscript. Columbia University, School of Public Health, New York.

Kandel, D. B., and K. Andrews. 1987. "Processes of Adolescent Socialization by Parents and Peers." *International Journal of the Addictions* 22:319–42.

Kandel, D. B., and R. Faust. 1975. "Sequence and Stages in Patterns of Adolescent Drug Use." *Archives in General Psychiatry* 32:923–32.

Kandel, D. B., R. C. Kessler, and R. Z. Margulies. 1978. "Antecedents of Adolescent Initiation into Stages of Drug Use." *Journal of Youth and Adolescence* 7:13–14.

Kaplan, H. B. 1983. *Patterns of Juvenile Delinquency.* Beverly Hills, Calif.: Sage.

Kaplan, H. B., and C. Robbins. 1983. "Testing a General Theory of Deviant Behavior in Longitudinal Perspective." In *Prospective Studies of Crime and Delinquency,* edited by K. Van Dusen and S. A. Mednick. Boston: Kluwer-Nijhoff.

Kazdin, A. E. 1985. *Treatment of Antisocial Behavior in Children and Adolescents.* Homewood, Ill.: Dorsey Press.

———. 1987. "Treatment of Antisocial Behavior in Children: Current Status and Future Directions." *Psychological Bulletin* 102:187–203.

Kempf, K. L. 1987. "Specialization and the Criminal Career." *Criminology* 25:399–420.

———. 1988. "Crime Severity and Criminal Career Progressions." *Journal of Criminal Law and Criminology* 79:524–40.

Klein, M. W. 1984. "Offense Specialization and Versatility among Juveniles." *British Journal of Criminology* 24:185–94.

Kolvin, I., F. J. W. Miller, M. Fletting, and P. A. Kolvin. 1988. "Social and Parenting Factors Affecting Criminal-offense Rates: Findings from the Newcastle Thousand Family Study." *British Journal of Psychiatry* 152:80–90.

Labouvie, E. W. 1986. "Methodological Issues in the Prediction of Psychopathology: A Life-Span Perspective." In *Life-Span Research on the Pre-*

diction of Psychopathology, edited by L. Erlenmeyer-Kimling and N. E. Miller. Hillsdale, N.J.: Erlbaum.

LaGrange, R. L., and H. R. White. 1985. "Age Differences in Delinquency: A Test of Theory." *Criminology* 23:19–46.

Langan, P. A., and D. P. Farrington. 1983. "Two-Track or One-Track Justice? Some Evidence from an English Longitudinal Survey." *Journal of Criminal Law and Criminology* 74:519–46.

Le Blanc, M. 1980. "Développement psycho-social et evolution de la délinquance au cours de l'adolescence." Unpublished manuscript. University of Montreal, Groupe de la Recherche sur l'Inadaptation Juvènile, Montreal, Quebec.

———. 1987. "The Effectiveness of the Reeducation of Juveniles—Boscoville: A Classic Case." Unpublished manuscript. Centre International de Criminologie Comparée, Montreal, Quebec.

———. 1988. Unpublished data. University of Montreal, Department of Psycho-education, Quebec.

———. 1989. "Designing a Self-reported Instrument for the Study of the Development of Offending from Childhood to Adulthood: Issues and Problems." In *Cross-national Research in Self-reported Crime and Delinquency*, edited by M. W. Klein. Boston: Kluwer-Nijhoff.

Le Blanc, M., R. Charland, G. Côté, and L. Provonost. 1980. *Développement psycho-social et evolution de la délinquance au cours de l'adolescence: Recherche, structure, et dynamique du comportement delinquent*. Vol. 3 of the final report. Montreal: University of Montreal, Groupe de Recherche sur l'Inadaptation Juvènile, Quebec.

Le Blanc, M., G. Côté, and R. Loeber. 1988. "Temporal Paths in Delinquency: Stability, Regression and Progression Analyzed with Panel Data from an Adolescent and a Delinquent Male Sample." Unpublished manuscript. University of Montreal, Centre International de Criminologie, Quebec.

Le Blanc, M., and M. Fréchette. 1989. *Male Criminality Activity from Childhood through Youth: Multilevel and Developmental Perspectives*. New York: Springer-Verlag.

Le Blanc, M., M. Ouimet, and R. E. Tremblay. 1988. "An Integrative Control Theory of Delinquent Behavior." *Psychiatry* 53:164–76.

Le Blanc, M., and R. Tremblay. 1987. "Drogues illicites et activités delictueuses chez les adolescents de Montreal: Epidemiologie et esquisse d'une politique sociale." *Psychotropes* 3:57–72.

Leik, R. K., and M. Matthews. 1968. "A Scale for Developmental Processes." *American Sociological Review* 33:62–75.

Lemert, E. M. 1951. *Social Pathology*. New York: McGraw-Hill.

Lerner, R. M. 1986. *Concepts and Theories of Human Development*. New York: Random House.

Lewis, D. O., S. S. Shanok, and J. H. Pincus. 1981. "Juvenile Male Sexual Assaulters: Psychiatric, Neurological, Psycho-educational, and Abuse Factors." In *Vulnerabilities to Delinquency*, edited by D. O. Lewis. New York: SP Medical & Scientific Books.

Liska, A., and M. Reed. 1985. "Ties to Conventional Institutions and Delinquency: Estimating Reciprocal Effects." *American Sociological Review* 50:547–60.

Loeber, R. 1982. "The Stability of Antisocial and Delinquent Child Behavior: A Review." *Child Development* 53:1431–46.

———. 1985*a*. "Patterns and Development of Antisocial Child Behavior." In *Annals of Child Development*, vol. 2, edited by G. J. Whitehurst. Greenwich, Conn.: JAI.

———. 1985*b*. "Experimental Studies to Reduce Antisocial and Delinquent Child Behavior: Implications for Future Programs and Optimal Times for Intervention." In *Proceedings of the ADAMHA/OJJDP Research Conference on Juvenile Offenders with Serious Drug, Alcohol and Mental Health Problems.* Washington, D.C.: U.S. Government Printing Office.

———. 1987*a*. "The Prevalence, Correlates, and Continuity of Serious Conduct Problems in Elementary School Children." *Criminology* 25:615–42.

———. 1987*b*. "Explaining Delinquency and Drug Use." Book review. *Aggressive Behavior* 13:97–98.

———. 1988*a*. "The Natural Histories of Juvenile Conduct Problems, Substance Use and Delinquency: Evidence for Developmental Progressions." In *Advances in Clinical Psychology*, vol. 11, edited by B. B. Lahey and A. E. Kazdin. New York: Plenum.

———. 1988*b*. "Behavioral Precursors and Accelerators of Delinquency." In *Explaining Crime*, edited by W. Buikhuisen and S. A. Mednick. London: Brill.

———. 1990. "Development and Risk Factors of Juvenile Antisocial Behavior and Delinquency." *Clinical Psychology Review* (forthcoming).

Loeber, R., and C. Baicker-McKee. 1989. "The Changing Manifestations of Disruptive/Antisocial Behavior from Childhood to Early Adulthood: Evolution or Tautology?" Unpublished manuscript. University of Pittsburgh, Pittsburgh, Penn.

Loeber, R., V. Brinthaupt, and S. M. Green. 1989. "Attention Deficits, Impulsivity and Hyperactivity with or without Conduct Problems: Relationships to Delinquency and Unique Contextual Factors." In *Behavior Disorders of Adolescence: Research, Intervention and Policy in Clinical and School Settings*, edited by R. J. MacMahon and R. D. Peters. New York: Plenum.

Loeber, R., and T. J. Dishion. 1983. "Early Predictors of Male Delinquency: A Review." *Psychological Bulletin* 94:68–99.

Loeber, R., and H. Snyder. 1988. "Age at First Arrest and Rate of Offending: Findings on the Constancy and Change of Lambda." Unpublished manuscript. University of Pittsburgh, Pittsburgh, Penn.

Loeber, R., and M. Stouthamer-Loeber. 1986. "Family Factors as Correlates and Predictors of Juvenile Conduct Problems and Delinquency." In *Crime and Justice: An Annual Review of Research*, vol. 7, edited by M. Tonry and N. Morris. Chicago: University of Chicago Press.

———. 1987. "Prediction." In *Handbook of Juvenile Delinquency*, edited by H. C. Quay. New York: Wiley.

Loeber, R., M. Stouthamer-Loeber, and S. Green. 1989. "Age at Onset of

Problem Behavior in Boys, and Later Disruptive and Delinquent Behaviors." In *Criminal Behaviour and Mental Health* (forthcoming).

Loeber, R., and D. Waller. 1988. "Artifacts in Delinquency Specialization and Generalization Studies." *British Journal of Criminology* 28:461–77.

Loney, J., J. Kramer, and R. S. Milich. 1982. "The Hyperactive Child Grows Up: Predictors of Symptoms, Delinquency, and Achievement at Followup." In *Psycho-social Aspects of Drug Treatment for Hyperactivity*, edited by K. D. Gadow and J. Loney. Boulder, Colo.: Westview.

Lorion, R. P. 1982. "Methodological Criteria for Prevention Research." Paper presented at the Prevention Research Seminar to the Center for Studies of Prevention, National Institute of Mental Health, Rockville, Md., July.

McCall, R. B. 1977. "Challenges to a Science of Developmental Psychology." *Child Development* 48:333–44.

McCord, J. 1979. "Some Child-rearing Antecedents of Criminal Behavior in Adult Men." *Journal of Personality and Social Psychology* 9:1477–86.

———. 1980. "Patterns of Deviance." In *Human Functioning in Longitudinal Perspective*, edited by S. B. Sells, R. Crandall, M. Roff, J. S. Strauss, and W. Pollin. Baltimore: Williams & Wilkins.

McCord, W., and J. McCord. 1959. *Origins of Crime*. New York: Columbia University Press.

MacDonald, K. 1985. "Early Experience, Relative Plasticity, and Social Development." *Developmental Review* 5:99–121.

McGee, R., S. Williams, and P. A. Silva. 1984. "Behavioral and Developmental Characteristics of Aggressive, Hyperactive and Aggressive-Hyperactive Boys." *Journal of the American Academy of Child Psychiatry* 23:270–79.

Magnusson, D. 1984. "Early Conduct and Biological Factors in the Developmental Background of Adult Delinquency." Paper presented at Henry Tajfel Memorial Lecture, Oxford University, September.

———. 1988. *Individual Development from an Interactional Perspective: A Longitudinal Study*. Hillsdale, N.J.: Erlbaum.

Mannheim, H., and L. T. Wilkins. 1955. *Prediction Methods in Relation to Borstal Training*. London: H.M. Stationery Office.

Maugham, B., G. Gray, and M. Rutter. 1985. "Reading Retardation and Antisocial Behavior: A Follow-up into Employment." *Journal of Child Psychology and Psychiatry and Allied Disciplines* 26:741–58.

Megargee, E. I., and M. J. Bohn. 1979. *Classifying Criminal Offenders*. Beverly Hills, Calif.: Sage.

Meier, R. F. 1985. *Theoretical Methods in Criminology*. Beverly Hills, Calif.: Sage.

Meyer, J. M., and L. J. Eaves. 1989. "Estimating Genetic Parameters of Survival Distributions: A Multifactorial Model." *Genetic Epidemiology* (forthcoming).

Miller, S. J., S. Dinitz, and J. P. Conrad. 1982. *Careers of the Violent*. Lexington, Mass.: Lexington.

Mills, C. J., and H. L. Noyes. 1984. "Patterns and Correlates of Initial and Subsequent Drug Use among Adolescents." *Journal of Consulting and Clinical Psychology* 52:231–43.

Minde, K., D. Lewin, G. Weiss, H. Lavigueur, V. Douglas, and E. Sykes.

1971. "The Hyperactive Child in Elementary School: A 5-Year Controlled Follow-up." *Exceptional Children* 38:215–21.

Moffitt, Terrie E. In this volume. "The Neuropsychology of Juvenile Delinquency: A Critical Review."

Moitra, S. D. 1981. "Analysis of Sentencing Policies Considering Crime Switching Patterns and Imprisonment Constraints." Unpublished Ph.D. dissertation, Carnegie-Mellon University, School of Urban and Public Affairs.

Morash, M. 1983. "An Explanation of Juvenile Delinquency: The Integration of Moral Reasoning Theory and Sociological Knowledge." In *Personality Theory, Moral Development and Criminal Behavior*, edited by W. S. Laufer and J. M. Day. Lexington, Mass.: Lexington.

Mulvey, E. P., and J. F. LaRosa. 1986. "Delinquency Cessation and Adolescent Development: Preliminary Data." *American Journal of Orthopsychiatry* 56:212–24.

Needleman, H. L., and D. C. Bellinger. 1981. "The Epidemiology of Low-Level Lead Exposure in Childhood." *Journal of the American Academy of Child Psychiatry* 20:496–512.

Newcomb, M. D. 1988. *Drug Use in the Workplace*. Dover, Mass.: Auburn House.

Newcomb, M. D., and P. M. Bentler. 1987. "Changes in Drug Use from High School to Young Adulthood: Effects of Living Arrangement and Current Life Pursuit." *Journal of Applied Developmental Psychology* 8:221–46.

Nye, F. I., and J. F. Short. 1957. "Scaling Delinquent Behavior." *American Sociological Review* 22:326–31.

O'Donnell, J. A., and R. R. Clayton. 1982. "The Stepping-Stone Hypothesis—Marijuana, Heroin, and Causality." *Chemical Dependencies: Behavioral and Biomedical Issues* 4:229–41.

Offord, D. R., K. Sullivan, N. Allen, and N. Abrams. 1979. "Delinquency and Hyperactivity." *Journal of Nervous and Mental Disorders* 167:734–41.

Osborn, S. G., and D. J. West. 1978. "The Effectiveness of Various Predictors of Criminal Careers." *Journal of Adolescence* 1:101–17.

———. 1980. "Do Young Delinquents Really Reform?" *Journal of Adolescence* 3:99–114.

Osgood, D. W., L. D. Johnston, P. M. O'Malley, and J. G. Bachman. 1988. "The Generality of Deviance in Late Adolescence and Early Adulthood." *American Sociological Review* 53:81–93.

Patterson, G. R. 1982. *Coercive Family Interactions*. Eugene, Oreg.: Castalia Press.

Pelletier, D. 1988. "Intelligence et délinquance." Unpublished manuscript. University of Montreal, School of Criminology, Quebec.

Petersilia, J., P. W. Greenwood, and M. Lavin. 1978. *Criminal Careers of Habitual Felons*. Santa Monica, Calif.: Rand.

Piaget, J. 1932. *The Moral Judgment of the Child*. New York: Harcourt-Brace.

Pinatel, J. 1963. *Traité de Criminologie*. Paris: Dalloz.

Polk, K. 1975. "Schools and the Delinquency Experience." *Criminal Justice and Behavior* 2:315–38.

Pronovost, L., and M. Le Blanc. 1980. "Transition statutaire et délinquance." *Revue Canadienne de Criminologie* 22:288–97.

Quételet, A. 1842. *A Treatise on Man and the Development of His Faculties*. Edinburgh: William & Robert Chambers.

Quinsey, V. L. 1986. "Men Who Have Sex with Children." In *Law and Mental Health: International Perspectives*, edited by D. N. Weisstub. New York: Pergamon.

Quinton, D., and M. Rutter. 1988. *Parenting Breakdown: The Making and Breaking of Inter-generational Links*. Studies in Deprivation and Disadvantage 14. Aldershot: Avebury.

Rand, A. 1987. "Transitional Life Events and Desistance from Delinquency and Crime." In *From Boy to Man, from Delinquency to Crime*, edited by M. E. Wolfgang, T. P. Thornberry, and R. M. Figlio. Chicago: University of Chicago Press.

Reiss, A. J., Jr. 1988. "Co-offending Influences on Criminal Careers." In *Crime and Justice: A Review of Research*, vol. 10, edited by M. Tonry and N. Morris. Chicago: University of Chicago Press.

Reitsma-Street, M., D. Offord, and T. Finch. 1985. "Pairs of Same-sexed Siblings Discordant for Anti-social Behaviour." *British Journal of Psychiatry* 146:415–23.

Robins, L. 1966. *Deviant Children Grow Up: A Sociological and Psychiatric Study of Sociopathic Personality*. Baltimore: Williams & Wilkins.

———. 1978. "Sturdy Childhood Predictors of Adult Antisocial Behavior: Replication from Longitudinal Studies." *Psychological Medicine* 8:611–22.

———. 1980. "Epidemiology of Adolescent Drug Use and Abuse." In *Psychopathology of Children and Youth*, edited by E. F. Purcell. New York: Josiah Macy, Jr., Foundation.

———. 1985. "Epidemiology of Antisocial Personality." In *Psychiatry*, vol. 3, edited by J. O. Cavenar. Philadelphia: Lippincott.

Robins, L. N., D. H. Davis, and E. Wish. 1977. "Detecting Predictors of Rare Events: Demographic, Family and Personal Deviance as Predictors of Stages in the Progression toward Narcotic Addiction." In *Origins and Course of Psychopathology: Methods of Longitudinal Research*, edited by J. Strauss, H. Babigian, and M. Roff. New York: Plenum.

Robins, L. N., and T. R. Przybeck. 1985. "Age of Onset of Drug Use as a Factor in Drug and Other Disorders." *National Institute of Drug Abuse Research Monograph Series* 56:178–92.

Robins, L. N., and K. S. Ratcliff. 1979. "Risk Factors in the Continuation of Childhood Antisocial Behavior into Adulthood." *International Journal of Mental Health* 7:96–118.

———. 1980. "Childhood Conduct Disorders and Later Arrest." In *The Social Consequences of Psychiatric Illnesses*, edited by L. N. Robins, P. J. Clayton, and J. K. Wing. New York: Brunner/Mazel.

Robins, L. N., and E. Wish. 1977. "Childhood Deviance as a Developmental Process: A Study of 223 Urban Black Men from Birth to 18." *Social Forces* 56:448–73.

Robinson, J. P. 1973. "Toward a more Appropriate Use of Guttman Scaling." *Public Opinion Quarterly* 37:260–67.

Rogosa, D. 1980. "A Critique of Cross-lagged Correlation." *Psychological Bulletin* 88:245–58.

Rowe, D. C., and D. W. Osgood. 1984. "Heredity and Sociological Theories of Delinquency." *American Sociological Review* 49:526–40.

Rowe, D. C., J. L. Rodgers, and S. Meseck-Bushey. 1987. "An 'Epidemic' Model of Sexual Intercourse Prevalence among Black and White Adolescents." Unpublished manuscript. University of Arizona, Tucson.

Rowe, D. C., J. L. Rodgers, S. Meseck-Bushey, and C. St. John. 1989. "Sexual Behavior and Nonsexual Deviance: A Sibling Study of Their Relationship." *Developmental Psychology* 35:61–69.

Rushton, J. P., and R. D. Chrisjohn. 1981. "Extroversion, Neuroticism, Psychoticism and Self-reported Delinquency: Evidence from Eight Separate Samples." *Personality and Individual Differences* 2:11–20.

Rutter, M., and H. Giller. 1983. *Juvenile Delinquency: Trends and Perspectives.* Harmondsworth: Penguin.

Schwartz, D., R. Flamant, and J. Lelouch. 1980. *Clinical Trials.* London: Academic Press.

Sellin, T. J., and M. Wolfgang. 1964. *The Measurement of Delinquency.* London: Wiley.

Shannon, L. W. 1978. "A Cohort Study of the Relationship of Adult Criminal Careers to Juvenile Careers." Paper presented at the International Symposium on Selected Criminological Topics, University of Stockholm, Sweden, August.

———. 1988. *Criminal Career Continuity: Its Social Context.* New York: Human Science Press.

Sigvardsson, S., R. Cloninger, M. Bohman, and A-L. Von Knorring. 1982. "Predisposition to Petty Criminality in Swedish Adoptees." *Archives of General Psychiatry* 39:1248–53.

Slocum, W. L., and C. L. Stone. 1963. "Family Culture Patterns and Delinquent Type Behavior." *Marriage and Family Living* 25:202–8.

Smith, D. A., and P. R. Gartin. 1989. "Specifying Specific Deterrence: The Influence of Arrest on Future Criminal Activity." *American Sociological Review* 54:94–105.

Smith, D. E., W. R. Smith, and E. Noma. 1984. "Delinquent Career-Lines: A Conceptual Link between Theory and Juvenile Offenses." *Sociological Quarterly* 25:155–72.

Smith, G. M., and C. P. Fogg. 1978. "Psychological Predictors of Early Use, Late Use, and Non-use of Marijuana among Teenage Students." In *Longitudinal Research on Drug Use,* edited by D. B. Kandel. New York: Wiley.

———. 1979. "Psychological Antecedents of Teenage Drug Use." In *Research in Community and Mental Health,* vol. 1, edited by R. G. Simmons. Greenwich, Conn.: JAI.

Snyder, H. N. 1988. *Court Careers of Juvenile Offenders.* Washington, D.C.: U.S. Department of Justice, Office of Juvenile Justice and Delinquency Prevention.

Snyder J., T. J. Dishion, and G. R. Patterson. 1986. "Determinants and Consequences of Association with Deviant Peers during Preadolescence and Adolescence." *Journal of Early Adolescence* 6:29–43.

Sroufe, L. A. 1979. "The Coherence of Individual Development." *American Psychologist* 34:834–41.

Stein, J. A., M. D. Newcomb, and P. M. Bentler. 1987. "Stability and Change in Personality: A Longitudinal Study from Early Adolescence to Young Adulthood." *Journal of Research in Personality* 20:276–91.

Stewart, M., C. Cummings, S. Singer, and C. S. DeBlois. 1981. "The Overlap between Hyperactive and Unsocialized Aggressive Children." *Journal of Child Psychology and Psychiatry* 22:35–45.

Stewart, M., F. N. Pitts, A. G. Craig, and W. Dieruf. 1966. "The Hyperactive Child Syndrome." *American Journal of Orthopsychiatry* 36:861–67.

Sutherland, E. H., and D. R. Cressey. 1960. *Principles of Criminology*. 6th ed. Chicago: Lippincott.

Tanner, J. M. 1972. "Sequence, Tempo, and Individual Variation in Growth and Development of Boys and Girls Aged Twelve to Sixteen." In *12 to 16: Early Adolescence*, edited by J. Kagan and R. Coles. New York: Norton.

Taylor, E., B. Everitt, R. Thorley, R. Schachar, M. Rutter, and M. Wiselberg. 1986. "Conduct Disorder and Hyperactivity: II: A Cluster Analytic Approach to the Identification of a Behavioural Syndrome." *British Journal of Psychiatry* 149:768–77.

Thornberry, T. 1987. "Toward an Interactional Theory of Delinquency." *Criminology* 25:863–92.

Thornberry, T., and R. L. Christenson. 1984. "Juvenile Justice Decisionmaking as a Longitudinal Process." *Social Forces* 63:433–45.

Thornberry, T., M. Moore, and R. L. Christenson. 1985. "The Effect of Dropping Out of High School on Subsequent Criminal Behavior." *Criminology* 23:3–18.

Tolan, P. H. 1987. "Implications of Age of Onset for Delinquency Risk." *Journal of Abnormal Child Psychology* 15:47–65.

Tolan, P. H., and R. P. Lorion. 1988. "Multivariate Approaches to the Identification of Delinquency Proneness in Adolescent Males." *American Journal of Community Psychology* 16:547–64.

Tontodonato, P. 1988. "Explaining Rate Changes in Delinquent Arrest Transitions Using Event History Analysis." *Criminology* 26:439–59.

Tracy, P. E., M. E. Wolfgang, and R. M. Figlio. 1985. *Delinquency in Two Birth Cohorts*. Executive summary. Office of Juvenile Justice and Delinquency Prevention, U.S. Department of Justice, Washington, D.C.

Udry, J. R. 1988. "Biological Predispositions and Social Control in Adolescent Sexual Behavior." *American Sociological Review* 53:709–22.

———. n.d. "Biosocial Models of Adolescent Problem Behavior." Unpublished manuscript. University of North Carolina, Chapel Hill.

Vera, H., G. W. Barnard, C. W. Holtzer, and M. I. Vera. 1980. "Violence and Sexuality: Three Types of Defendants." *Criminal Justice and Behavior* 7:243–55.

Voeltz, L. M., and I. M. Evans. 1982. "The Assessment of Behavioral Interrelationships in Child Behavior Therapy." *Behavioral Assessment* 4:131–65.

Wadsworth, M. 1979. *Roots of Delinquency: Infancy, Adolescence and Crime*. Oxford: Martin Robertson.

Weis, J. G., ed. 1987. Special issue on theory. *Criminology*, vol. 25, no. 4.

Weiss, G., K. Minde, J. S. Werry, V. I. Douglas, and E. Nemeth. 1971. "Studies on the Hyperactive Child, VII: Five-Year Follow-up." *Archives of General Psychiatry* 24:409–14.

Werner, E. E., and R. S. Smith. 1977. *Kauai's Children Come of Age*. Honolulu: University of Hawaii Press.

———. 1982. *Vulnerable but not Invincible*. New York: McGraw-Hill.

Werner, H. 1957. "The Concept of Development from a Comparative and Organismic Point of View." In *The Concept of Development*, edited by D. B. Harris. Minneapolis: University of Minnesota Press.

West, D. J. 1982. *Delinquency: Its Roots, Careers, and Prospects*. London: Heinemann.

West, D. J., and D. P. Farrington. 1977. *The Delinquent Way of Life*. London: Heinemann.

White, H. R. 1988. "Longitudinal Patterns of Cocaine Use among Adolescents." *American Journal of Drug and Alcohol Abuse* 14:1–16.

White, H. R., V. Johnson, and C. G. Garrison. 1985. "The Drug-Crime Nexus among Adolescents and Their Peers." *Deviant Behavior* 6:183–205.

Wikström, P.-O. 1987. *Patterns of Crime in a Birth Cohort: Age, Sex and Class Differences*. Project Metropolitan; a longitudinal study of a Stockholm cohort, no. 24. Stockholm: University of Stockholm, Department of Sociology.

Wilson, J. Q., and R. J. Herrnstein. 1985. *Crime and Human Nature*. New York: Simon & Schuster.

Wohlwill, J. F. 1973. *The Study of Behavioral Development*. New York: Academic Press.

Wolf, M. M., C. J. Braukmann, and K. A. Ramp. 1987. "Serious Delinquent Behavior May Be Part of a Significantly Handicapping Condition: Cures and Supportive Environments." *Journal of Applied Behavior Analysis* 20:347–59.

Wolfgang, M. E. 1977. "From Boy to Man—from Delinquency to Crime." Paper presented at the national symposium on "The Serious Juvenile Offender," Minneapolis, Minn., September.

Wolfgang, M. E., R. M. Figlio, and T. Sellin. 1972. *Delinquency in a Birth Cohort*. Chicago: University of Chicago Press.

Wolfgang, M. E., R. M. Figlio, P. E. Tracy, and S. I. Singer. 1985. *The National Survey of Crime Severity*. Washington, D.C.: U.S. Government Printing Office.

Wolfgang, M., T. Thornberry, and R. M. Figlio. 1987. *From Boy to Man, from Delinquency to Crime*. Chicago: University of Chicago Press.

Yamaguchi, K., and D. B. Kandel. 1984. "Patterns of Drug Use from Adolescence to Young Adulthood: II. Sequences of Progression." *American Journal of Public Health* 74:668–72.

Yochelson, S., and S. E. Samenow. 1976. *The Criminal Personality. Vol. 1: A Profile for Change*. New York: Jason Arenson.

Yule, W., R. Lansdown, I. Millar, and M. Urbanowicz. 1981. "The Relationship between Blood Lead Concentrations, Intelligence, and Attainment in a School Population: A Pilot Study." *Developmental Medicine and Child Neurology* 23:567–76.

Zeitlin, H. 1986. *The Natural History of Psychiatric Disorder in Children*. Oxford: Oxford University Press.

Zubin, J. 1972. "Scientific Models for Psychopathology in the 1970s." *Seminars in Psychiatry* 4:283–96.